Hypothesis A/Hypothesis B

Current Studies in Linguistics
Samuel Jay Keyser, general editor

A complete list of books published in the Current Studies in Linguistics series appears at the back of this book.

Hypothesis A/Hypothesis B

Linguistic Explorations in Honor of David M. Perlmutter

Donna B. Gerdts, John C. Moore, and Maria Polinsky, editors

The MIT Press
Cambridge, Massachusetts
London, England

© 2010 Massachusetts Institute of Technology

All rights reserved. No part of this book may be reproduced in any form by any electronic or mechanical means (including photocopying, recording, or information storage and retrieval) without permission in writing from the publisher.

For information about special quantity discounts, please e-mail special_sales@mitpress.mit.edu

This book was set in Times New Roman and Syntax on 3B2 by Asco Typesetters, Hong Kong. Printed and bound in the United States of America.

Library of Congress Cataloging-in-Publication Data

Hypothesis A-Hypothesis B : linguistic explorations in honor of David M. Perlmutter / Donna B. Gerdts, John C. Moore, and Maria Polinsky, editors.
    p. cm. — (Current studies in linguistics ; 49)
Includes bibliographical references and index.
ISBN 978-0-262-13487-3 (hardcover : alk. paper) — ISBN 978-0-262-63356-7 (pbk. : alk. paper)
1. Linguistics. I. Perlmutter, David M. II. Gerdts, Donna B. III. Moore, John C., 1955– IV. Polinsky, Maria.
P125.H87   2010
410—dc22
                                                                                  2009013168

10 9 8 7 6 5 4 3 2 1

Contents

Contributors ix
Preface xiii
My Path in Linguistics xvii
David M. Perlmutter

1 **Depictives and Serialization in Tzotzil** 1
  Judith Aissen

2 **Prolegomenon to Any Future Typology of Impersonal Sentences** 19
  Leonard H. Babby

3 **Romanian as a Two-Gender Language** 41
  Nicoleta Bateman and Maria Polinsky

4 **1-handed PERSONs and ASL Morphology** 79
  J. Albert Bickford

5 **Six Arguments for *Wh*-Movement in Chamorro** 91
  Sandra Chung

6 **On the Existence (and Distribution) of Sentential Subjects** 111
  William D. Davies and Stanley Dubinsky

7 **Syntax and Semantics of Polish Emotion Verbs: A Corpus Study** 129
  Katarzyna Dziwirek

8 **Term Relations and Relational Hierarchies** 151
  Patrick Farrell

9	Constraints on Verb Stem Stacking in Southern Tiwa 173 Donald G. Frantz	
10	Three Doubling Constructions in Halkomelem 183 Donna B. Gerdts	
11	Origins of Differential Unaccusative/Unergative Case Marking: Implications for Innateness 203 Alice C. Harris	
12	Underlying and Surface Grammatical Relations in Greek *consider* Sentences 221 Brian D. Joseph	
13	French Inchoatives and the Unaccusativity Hypothesis 229 Géraldine Legendre and Paul Smolensky	
14	On the Analytic Expression of Predicates in Meskwaki 247 Philip S. LeSourd	
15	Unpassives of Unaccusatives 275 Joan Maling	
16	Semantic and Syntactic Subcategorization in Seri: Recipients and Addressees 293 Stephen A. Marlett	
17	Impersonals in Irish and Beyond 323 James McCloskey	
18	Does Spatial Make It Special? On the Grammar of Pointing Signs in American Sign Language 345 Richard P. Meier and Diane Lillo-Martin	
19	Object-Controlled Restructuring in Spanish 361 John Moore	
20	Against All Expectations: Encoding Subjects and Objects in a New Language 383 Carol A. Padden, Irit Meir, Wendy Sandler, and Mark Aronoff	
21	Clitic Placement in Romance: A Phase-Theoretic Approach 401 Eduardo P. Raposo	

22   Missing Obliques: Some Anomalies in Ojibwe Syntax   427
     Richard A. Rhodes

23   Modeling the Mapping from "Conceptual Structure" to Syntax   457
     Annie Zaenen

     Publications of David M. Perlmutter   475
     Author Index   481
     Subject Index   487

Contributors

Judith Aissen
Department of Linguistics, University of California, Santa Cruz

Mark Aronoff
Department of Linguistics, Stony Brook University

Leonard H. Babby
Department of Slavic Languages and Literatures, Princeton University

Nicoleta Bateman
Liberal Studies Department, California State University, San Marcos

J. Albert Bickford
SIL International; Department of Linguistics, University of North Dakota

Sandra Chung
Department of Linguistics, University of California, Santa Cruz

William D. Davies
Department of Linguistics, University of Iowa

Stanley Dubinsky
Linguistics Program, Department of English, University of South Carolina

Katarzyna Dziwirek
Polish and Slavic Languages and Literatures, University of Washington

Patrick Farrell
Department of Linguistics, University of California, Davis

Donald G. Frantz
Department of Native American Studies, University of Lethbridge

Donna B. Gerdts
Department of Linguistics, Simon Fraser University

Alice C. Harris
Department of Linguistics, Stony Brook University; Centre for Advanced Study, Oslo

Brian D. Joseph
Department of Linguistics, The Ohio State University

Géraldine Legendre
Cognitive Science Department, Johns Hopkins University

Philip S. LeSourd
Department of Anthropology, Indiana University

Diane Lillo-Martin
Department of Linguistics, University of Connecticut

Joan Maling
Language and Linguistics Program, Brandeis University

Stephen A. Marlett
SIL International; Department of Linguistics, University of North Dakota

James McCloskey
Department of Linguistics, University of California, Santa Cruz

Richard P. Meier
Department of Linguistics, University of Texas at Austin

Irit Meir
Departments of Hebrew Language and Communication Disorders, University of Haifa

John Moore
Department of Linguistics, University of California, San Diego

Carol A. Padden
Department of Communication, University of California, San Diego

Maria Polinsky
Department of Linguistics, Harvard University

Eduardo P. Raposo
Department of Spanish and Portuguese, University of California, Santa Barbara

Richard A. Rhodes
Department of Linguistics, University of California, Berkeley

Wendy Sandler
Department of English Language and Literature, University of Haifa

Paul Smolensky
Cognitive Science Department, Johns Hopkins University

Annie Zaenen
Palo Alto Research Center

Preface

This collection of linguistic studies is a Festschrift to honor David M. Perlmutter, Professor Emeritus, University of California, San Diego. He was born October 28, 1938, in New York City. His father, Victor M. Perlmutter, was an artist and educator; his mother, Fruma Shapiro Perlmutter, was a teacher and social worker. They moved frequently during his childhood, so he lived in many different parts of the United States, graduating from Rich Township High School, Park Forest, Illinois, in 1955. He entered Harvard College and graduated magna cum laude in 1959. His honors thesis in Social Relations, "Commitment to Norms and Social Control: The American Shakers," was supervised by famed sociologist and "communitarian" Robert N. Bellah. He entered the MIT graduate program in linguistics in 1964, earning his PhD in 1968 with his dissertation *Deep and Surface Structure Constraints in Syntax*. He held professorships at Brandeis University (1967–1970), MIT (1970–1977), and the University of California, San Diego (1977–2005), as well as at the Université de Paris VIII (fall 1972) and the Richard Turner Professorship in the Humanities at the University of Rochester (1993–1994). He also taught at the Scandinavian Summer School of Linguistics (Säby, Sweden, 1970; Gentofte, Denmark, 1971), Brown University (spring 1974 and 1975), UCLA (fall 1984), and at Summer Linguistic Institutes of the Linguistic Society of America (University of Massachusetts 1974, UCLA 1983, Stanford 1987 (Edward Sapir Professor), and UC Santa Cruz 1991). He has received much recognition for his scholarship. His fellowships include a John Simon Guggenheim Memorial Foundation Fellowship in 1977–1978, the I. W. Killam Fellowship at the University of British Columbia in 1980–1981, a Fellowship at the Center for Advanced Study in the Behavioral Sciences, Stanford, California, in 1987–1988, and the University of California President's Fellowship in the Humanities in 1990–1991. He has had NSF grants and visiting research positions at the University of Tokyo in 1973 and the Max Planck Institute in Leipzig, Germany, in 1999. He served as president of the Linguistic Society of America in 2000. Since retiring from UCSD in 2005, he continues to do linguistic research and has begun work on a book for a general audience about the importance of sign languages for understanding the origin of languages.

Anyone who has studied linguistics in the last half century has been affected by the work of David Perlmutter. He is probably best known for founding Relational Grammar (RG) with Paul Postal, but in fact he is one of the most versatile linguists around. And though he has made contributions in a number of areas of linguistics, including theoretical morphology and sign language phonology, his most significant contribution has been through his teaching and his mentoring. He is quite simply the best teacher many of us have had the pleasure to learn from, and he has provided for us a superior model that we have emulated in our own teaching. Moreover, through his mentoring he has taught us much about formulating and investigating linguistic hypotheses, showing us firsthand how to work through the syntactic analysis of a large-scale problem and how to ask the right questions to lead to a suitable solution.

The authors of these twenty-three papers, who are his colleagues, his students, and his students' students, keenly feel that Professor Perlmutter has had a direct and lasting influence on their careers and thus are eager to express their appreciation by dedicating the enclosed chapters to him. The topics covered in these chapters are all ones on which Professor Perlmutter has published influential work. Among the topics addressed are grammatical relations and their mapping (Farrell, Gerdts, Marlett, Rhodes, and Zaenen); unaccusatives, passives, impersonals, and their ilk (Babby, Harris, Legendre and Smolensky, Maling, and McCloskey); issues in complex verbs, complex clauses, and *wh*-constructions (Aissen, Chung, Davies and Dubinsky, Frantz, Joseph, LeSourd, and Moore); and the nature of sign languages (Bickford, Meier and Lillo-Martin, and Padden et al.).

One noteworthy aspect of Professor Perlmutter's research is the fact that he has published detailed analyses of a variety of languages as well as more broad-based crosslinguistic comparisons. This book honors his commitment to the study of the world's languages. Nine of the chapters deal with topics in Indo-European languages: English (Davies and Dubinsky), French (Legendre and Smolensky), Greek (Joseph), Irish (McCloskey), Polish (Dziwirek), Portuguese (Raposo), Romanian (Bateman and Polinsky), Russian (Babby), and Spanish (Moore). Three chapters deal with sign languages (Bickford, Meier and Lillo-Martin, and Padden et al.). Six chapters, all based on original fieldwork, deal with languages of the Americas: Halkomelem (Gerdts), Ojibwe (Rhodes), Meskwaki (LeSourd), Seri (Marlett), Southern Tiwa (Frantz), and Tzotzil (Aissen). One chapter is on the Austronesian language Chamorro (Chung), one is on Bantu languages (Zaenen), and three are crosslinguistic (Farrell, Harris, and Maling).

We would like to express our appreciation to the many people who helped make this book possible. First, we thank our colleagues who took on the crucial task of anonymously reviewing contributions. Their comments greatly improved the quality of the book. Our appreciation goes to MIT Press editors Tom Stone and Ada Brunstein for shepherding this through to completion. Thanks to Zoey Peterson, who served as editorial assistant for the project. Generous funding for the production and editing of the book came from the University Publication Fund, Simon Fraser University; the Department of Linguistics, University of California, San Diego; and the Center for Research in Language at UCSD.

Last, of course, we would like to thank David Perlmutter. The authors, reviewers, and many other scholars, more than we were able to accommodate in this book, send their best regards. Preparing a Festschrift in honor of a scholar who is still actively engaged in the field affords two great pleasures. First is the satisfaction of knowing that he will have the opportunity to read and comment on the contributions. Second is having a chance to interview him about his life and work, though it rapidly became clear that the best person to write about him is David himself, not only because he has great insight into the history of linguistics, but also because he is a great storyteller. Thus, we are delighted to have him participate by writing the brief survey of his career as teacher and scholar with which the book begins.

David Perlmutter, 2006. Photo by Michelle Parent.

My Path in Linguistics

David M. Perlmutter

How I Came to Linguistics

I came to linguistics through languages.

I was aware of languages from earliest childhood. About six of my first eight years were spent in immigrant communities in New York and Philadelphia where the main languages were English and Yiddish. My parents were native speakers of both English and Yiddish, were fluent in Hebrew, knew some German, and my mother, French. I learned to bridge the language barrier with my paternal grandparents, who didn't speak English, though my grandmother spoke Yiddish, Polish, and German. My maternal grandfather was fluent in Yiddish, English, and Hebrew and knew German. He was principal of a Jewish school in Philadelphia where I began to learn Yiddish and Hebrew. I still remember how severely he bawled me out when I was six or seven because I responded in English when one of his friends spoke to me in Yiddish. "You must *always*," he insisted, "answer in the language in which you are spoken to!"

For several years I lived in his home in Philadelphia, where I met Yiddish writers, poets, and educators. In the New York home of my paternal grandfather, who was active in the Yiddish theater, I met Yiddish actors, playwrights, and theater people. Both grandfathers wrote and published books in Yiddish. At home we spoke English, but it was clear to me that Yiddish was the language of culture.

Those early years made me comfortable with languages and taught me that being multilingual is natural. I studied Latin, French, and Spanish in high school, German and Russian in college. Later, in my early years as a linguist, I broadened my crosslinguistic perspective by acquiring a working knowledge of Portuguese, Dutch, Italian, Romanian, Serbo-Croatian, and Macedonian. I became proficient in Slovenian doing fieldwork in Slovenia and studied Japanese before spending part of a sabbatical year in Japan.

In my college years at Harvard I pursued a broad liberal arts education and did a social science major that combined sociology, anthropology, and psychology. I never took a linguistics course. Looking for a summer job in 1957, I could find nothing but selling door to door. I realized that people would hire me only for those jobs they don't want to do themselves or for those they can't do themselves. Lacking a marketable skill, I was in the first category. To be in the second, I needed to acquire a marketable skill to support myself until I found a career.

Just a few months later, on October 4, 1957, the first Soviet Sputnik went up. There was a strong current of opinion that the United States had been surpassed technologically by the Soviet Union. I figured there would now be a demand for Russian, which very few Americans spoke. Knowing I was good at learning languages, I decided to learn Russian and make it my marketable skill. The next summer I enrolled in a private Russian course, and in my senior year a friend and I took an advanced Russian course and agreed to speak only Russian to each other outside of class.

With Khrushchev in power, the first cultural exchange agreement between the United States and the Soviet Union provided for an American exhibition in Moscow and a Soviet exhibition in New York in the summer of 1959. I was interviewed in Washington in both Russian and English and was chosen to be a "guide" at the American exhibition in Moscow. I worked at the IBM exhibit, where an early computer was on display. Most of my time was spent talking with Soviet visitors who had never met a foreigner before and whose only source of information about the United States had been the Soviet media—a fascinating encounter of minds from two different worlds. It was an unforgettable experience.

Speaking and hearing Russian all day in Moscow did wonders for my Russian. As planned, after returning to the United States I used Russian to support myself. From 1960 to 1965 I taught Russian at MIT, where I was the founder and live-in faculty adviser of a Russian-speaking dormitory, and at defense research and development labs in the Boston area. I was escort-interpreter for the Moiseyev Dance Company of Moscow on their American tour in 1961. I translated a monograph from Russian into English.

During this period I was in graduate school at Harvard twice—first in Sociology and Far Eastern Languages (I studied Mandarin Chinese) and later in Economics. However, I was not cut out for either field and withdrew after a year.

My interest in linguistics was stimulated by working with Alex Lipson, my first Russian teacher, on improving the teaching of Russian by using the insights of Jakobson's (1948) analysis of the Russian verb. The first analysis (as far as I know) to posit abstract underlying forms distinct from any surface realization, it strongly influenced Morris Halle and, through him, the development of generative phonology. Instead of the infinitive, we gave students Jakobson's underlying forms as lexical entries and taught them how to derive the inflected verb forms from them. Most forms that were irregular with the infinitive as lexical entry could be derived from Jakobson's stems by a few simple rules.

Curious about linguistics, I sat in on classes: Jakobson at Harvard, Chomsky at MIT, and classes in the Romance and Slavic departments at Harvard. I got to know some of the graduate students in linguistics at MIT, but I resisted going into linguistics because it didn't seem important; I didn't see how it could improve people's lives. Eventually, however, I came to the realization that this was the wrong criterion. Knowing that I liked languages and was good at them, I thought I might be suited for linguistics.

Student Days at MIT

I entered the graduate program at MIT in 1964, when it was the center of considerable intellectual ferment. Noam Chomsky had given a plenary address at the International Congress of Linguists in Cambridge two years earlier. His increasing fame was attracting the attention of linguists and scholars in other fields, some of whom were spending their sabbaticals at MIT to learn about what was going on. Others, already in Cambridge, were attending linguistics classes, seminars, and talks.

The graduate program in linguistics, begun in 1961, tended to attract students with an iconoclastic bent at a time when students who wanted to play it safe saw the upstart program at MIT as a risky bet. They went to Cornell to study with Hockett, to Yale to study with Bloch, to Berkeley to study Amerindian linguistics, or to other programs that promised a more secure career. A visiting linguist who was sitting in on classes remarked: "These MIT students are certainly learning something. I'm not sure what it is, but it isn't linguistics." He wondered how they would ever get jobs. He was speaking of people like Tom Bever, Paul Kiparsky, Yuki Kuroda, Terry Langendoen, Jim McCawley, Barbara Hall Partee, Haj Ross, Arnold Zwicky, and others who went on to distinguished careers. Younger linguists today may not realize how radical generative grammar seemed to linguists at that time. My fellow students the next few years included Steve Anderson, Joan Bresnan, Janet Dean Fodor, Jim Harris, Ray Jackendoff, Richard Kayne, and others. I could always find someone to talk linguistics with in Building 20, where we students shared offices.

The excitement was palpable and contagious. Generative grammar was "hot" and MIT was *the* place to do it. The pervasive feeling was that previous theories were now irrelevant; the course that dealt with them was nicknamed "bad guys." There was a new theory to be built and everyone wanted to be part of the "Chomskyan revolution."

Exciting as this atmosphere was, it was also intimidating. What made MIT linguistics intellectually vibrant made it far from ideal for a beginner to learn the ropes. There wasn't a curriculum that taught students how to do linguistics. Most of our classes consisted of a professor talking about the results of his own research, but not about how he arrived at them. Chomsky's classes were dominated by questions from advanced students, PhDs, and visiting scholars. Much of the discussion was over my head. I took the courses, passed the general exams in my second year, and looked forward to doing my own research.

The next summer I had a job at the System Development Corporation in Santa Monica, California, where I could work on any topic I chose. I worked hard but didn't get any real results. Indeed, at that point I didn't even know what a real result would have been. I realized I hadn't learned how to do linguistic research. I had to do something to get on track.

Returning to Cambridge that fall, to make sure I learned what I had missed the first time around, I sat in on the first-year syntax courses taught by the newly hired Haj Ross at MIT and George Lakoff at Harvard. I volunteered to help students who were having difficulties in those courses, which solidified my knowledge.

I also had started analyzing syntactic data on my own, although I did not yet have a well-defined topic. One day Haj Ross, always willing to hear what I was doing, casually told me that my work was getting better: "At least now you're constructing arguments." Bingo! It was an epiphany. Constructing arguments! So that's what it's about! No one had ever made that explicit to me before. That day I vowed that if I ever got a job teaching linguistics, I would make it crystal clear from the outset that it's about making the alternatives explicit and constructing arguments. The idea for Hypothesis A and Hypothesis B was born that day.

The research that led to my dissertation progressed quickly after that. Although Chomsky, my dissertation adviser, had suggested to me a topic dealing with English, I was more interested in working with data from several languages. What initially seemed like separate topics coalesced into a plan for a coherent dissertation and I began to write.

Those who had thought the MIT grad program was a risky bet had been wrong: by the end of my third year I had opportunities for tenure-track teaching positions and postdocs. I accepted a position at Brandeis University so that I could stay in the Boston area and continue to participate in the intellectual life at MIT. In 1967–1968 I gave my first LSA talk and was invited to my first conference, but most of the year was consumed with teaching at Brandeis (and activities to end the Vietnam War). The following summer I finished my dissertation.

Developing an Approach to Linguistics

I have tried to emphasize four things in my work in linguistics: explicit arguments for one hypothesis over others, extending the range of languages and phenomena for which linguistic theory is to be held accountable, making explicit the ways languages differ and the ways they are alike, and explanation in linguistics. All four were already present in my 1968 doctoral dissertation (Perlmutter 1971), especially in the chapter arguing for surface structure constraints on the order of clitic pronouns in Spanish and French (Perlmutter 1970b).

In writing that chapter, I was teaching myself how to do linguistics. I was learning how to construct alternative hypotheses and test their predictions against additional data. I discovered that the question of how such a surface structure constraint is to be formulated covered a range of issues, each statable as a separate hypothesis on which evidence could be brought to bear.

The idea of a surface structure constraint on clitic order first occurred to me as an alternative to Wayles Browne's (1968) transformational analysis of Serbo-Croatian clitics. I switched from Serbo-Croatian to Spanish when I realized that the spurious *se* rule of Spanish could be used to make a stronger argument: no set of transformations could account for clitic order in Spanish. I was learning how to exploit language-particular peculiarities to construct arguments that could not be made for other languages.

With a few exceptions, work in generative grammar at that time made claims about universal grammar based on English alone. Ross's (1967, 1986) dissertation was a major breakthrough, using data from many languages to show that his constraints, originally proposed for English, held in other languages as well. My thesis took a different tack, using language-particular phenomena of Spanish, French, and Serbo-Croatian to argue for theoretical conclusions that could not be based on English.

The surface structure constraints I proposed perform a filtering function: sentences that do not satisfy them are filtered out as ungrammatical. Conceiving of them in this way led to a discovery: certain semantically well-formed potential sentences of Spanish and French have no grammatical realization because they don't satisfy the constraints.

This chapter also attempted explanation: why are clitic pronouns subject to such a constraint and why does it have the properties it does? I proposed that universally clitic sequences are subject to surface structure constraints stated in the notation I used, spelling out what these claims predict for additional data in Spanish, French, and other languages. This was the standard generative way of positing something universal from which language-particular facts would follow. It also owes much to Chomsky and Halle's (1968) work on English stress, where predictions were also extracted from proposed universal notation.

A basic goal of linguistics, prominent in my work in Relational Grammar (discussed below), is to make explicit the ways languages differ. The last chapter of my thesis proposed that three ostensibly unrelated differences between two classes of languages could be unified by means of a single surface constraint shared by some languages but not others. It may have been the first attempt to do syntactic typology in generative grammar, ultimately leading to the pro-drop parameter (Jaeggli and Safir 1989, among others) in the Principles-and-Parameters approach. It made testable predictions that were subsequently falsified.

Explanation internal to one language came to the fore in Perlmutter and Orešnik 1973a, 1973b, on Slovenian and in Perlmutter and Moore 2002 on Russian, which seek to solve language-particular puzzles. In Slovenian, why are masculine singular headless NPs that should be accusative in the genitive case? In Russian, finite clauses can be personal or impersonal; why can't infinitival clauses be impersonal? These language-particular facts are shown to follow from others; they are explained without reference to anything universal.

More generally, any hypothesis that makes multiple correct predictions explains the data it predicts. An illustration comes from Spanish, where clitic objects of a verb generally appear on that verb. Why can they also appear on some higher verbs but not others? The answer proposed in Aissen and Perlmutter 1976b, 1983d, is that certain higher verbs form a single clause with their complements (Clause Reduction or Clause Union). Consequently, complement objects behave like objects of the united clause not only for clitic placement, but also for Reflexive Passive, Object Raising, Clause Union in causatives, and Passive with certain verbs. The Clause Reduction hypothesis explains all these phenomena.

Teaching

The goal of teaching, as I see it, is to enable students to experience the thrill of making a discovery, and to experience it again and again. Everything else follows from this. I can think of nothing more likely to awaken a student's intellectual interest than making a discovery, nothing better able to give a student the experience of intellectual depth than making a whole series of discoveries, each going deeper than the one before. In each case, the discovery is an event internal to the student. A teacher cannot do that for a student or ensure that it will happen. All a teacher can do is set up the conditions that make it possible.

To make a discovery, students need to be able to see generalizations in data. They need to learn how to formulate an explicit hypothesis that captures those generalizations and discern the predictions it makes. They must learn the reasons for rejecting one hypothesis in favor of another. By solving problems they acquire these skills and learn how to do linguistics.

Solving problems is not just learning basic skills or preparation for more advanced work. Students can make discoveries even within the restricted world of a homework problem. After staring at the data in a problem and going up many blind alleys, when they finally see what is going on, they can experience the thrill of discovery.

Teaching undergraduates at Brandeis University, starting in 1967, I began to write problems that required students to see generalizations in syntactic data, develop arguments for one hypothesis over others, and learn how to formulate and test hypotheses. When I began teaching at MIT in 1970, I made the intensive introductory graduate course in syntax a problem-centered course, revising the problems again and again. Sequenced by and large along the lines discussed in Perlmutter 1974b, the problems brought students ever closer to what they would face in their own research. Some of the more challenging problems required creative solutions that made anomalies in the data fall into place.

A key element in fostering discovery is interactive teaching. In class we discussed students' solutions to the homework problems, focusing on the predictions made by different solutions and the reasons for rejecting one in favor of another. I rarely gave answers. My role was to guide the students in solving problems and in making explicit the predictions and consequences of their solutions. I sometimes introduced new data (perhaps from a language unknown to them) or posed novel problems, challenging them to figure out what was going on and account for it. They were both participants and observers as discoveries unfolded in class.

Most of the problems in introductory syntax classes at both the graduate and undergraduate levels focused on constructing a grammar of English. As new data came to light, we continually revised what had already been posited. What have to be clear are the underlying assumptions, the data already accounted for, and the devices used to account for it. When the generalizations they find in new data force them to change what had previously been posited, students experience discovery.

I have enjoyed working with stellar TAs over the years. One of them, Scott Soames, volunteered to help me write and revise problems; this collaboration resulted in *Syntactic Argumentation and the Structure of English*. Another, Jorge Hankamer, adopted and improved these teaching methods in the linguistics program at the University of California, Santa Cruz. I developed them further at the University of California, San Diego. Graduate students taught with these methods have developed them further in their own teaching.

Beyond discovery within the restricted world of a problem set or course, graduate students can experience the thrill of discovering something new to the field. This requires knowledge of the field, of current theoretical debates, and of the data and arguments previously brought to bear on them. Teaching graduate students has given me the opportunity to train future linguists and to share in their discoveries. It has made me familiar with the many languages my students have worked on, enriching my knowledge of the variety of linguistic structures. In these relationships students and I have contributed to each other's discoveries and have made joint discoveries. This is where teaching and research merge into a single gratifying enterprise.

My Work in Relational Grammar in Its Intellectual Context

Virtually no one who has thought seriously about language and its structure has been able to avoid using the terms "subject" and "object." This is a remarkable fact—that perceptive and knowledgeable observers have been willing to talk about "subjects" and "objects" in very disparate languages and feel reasonably confident that they knew what they were talking about. It is all the more remarkable, then, that in the intellectual traditions represented by the frameworks of "Government and Binding," "Principles and Parameters," and the "Minimalist Program," the notions play no (recognized) role at all. That tradition has always insisted that talk of "subjects" and "objects" is either illicit or casual, and that reference to such terms is to be cashed out in terms of more primitive notions (phrase-structural measures of prominence, featural properties of heads, the theory of A-movement, and so on).

That is how McCloskey (2001, 157) characterizes the contrast between grammarians' use of grammatical relations and their status in the Chomskyan tradition, which Relational Grammar (RG) challenged by making grammatical relations primitive notions of linguistic theory.

RG is a theory of clause structure. It claims that grammatical relations are needed to describe and analyze clause structure in individual languages, to characterize the class of clause structures that occur crosslinguistically, and to formulate universals of clause structure. RG thus has little to say about long-distance dependencies, anaphora, tense and aspect systems, information structure, and other aspects of linguistic structure, except insofar as they are sensitive to clause structure and grammatical relations.

The origins of RG go back to 1972, when Paul Postal and I hypothesized that the NP-movement rules of transformational grammar (TG) obscured an important distinction. TG's Passive transformation, for example, moved the postverbal NP to preverbal position, the preverbal NP to postverbal position, added the preposition *by*, and changed verbal morphology. We hypothesized that the essence of Passive is making the object a subject, the other changes being side effects. Similarly, Raising creates subjects or objects and TOUGH-Movement creates subjects, their other effects being side effects. The key distinction obscured by TG's NP-movement rules, we concluded, was that Passive, Raising, and TOUGH-Movement create subjects or objects, while Question Movement and Relativization affect NPs' linear position but not their grammatical relations. Crucially, where the former rules moved NPs to preverbal position, it was because this is the usual position of subjects in English.

In TG, passivization was different in each language. Transformations moved NPs to different positions in different languages and added language-particular material such as prepositions, postpositions, or case and/or verbal morphology, obscuring what we claimed is common to passivization crosslinguistically. Characterizing passivization universally as promotion of a direct object to subject captures the crosslinguistic generalization (Perlmutter and Postal 1974, 1977/1983g; Postal 1986a).

As research proceeded on a variety of languages, it became apparent that clause-level constructions drawn from a small set reappear in genetically unrelated and typologically diverse languages, despite differences in word order, morphology, and other features. This set consists of advancements to direct and indirect object and to subject, demotions to direct or indirect object (added later), ascensions (such as Raising), Clause Union (the merger of two clauses), and expletive constructions. This typology provides an account of the ways languages are alike in clause structure and of the ways they differ: in whether or not they have passivization, indirect-object advancement to direct object, and so on for each construction in the typology, and in the language-particular conditions on each. Viewing clause structures in relational terms reduces what had appeared to be wide variation to a small set of constructions and provides a basis for typology independent of Greenberg's (1963) basic word-order typology (SOV, SVO, etc.). It also brings out crosslinguistic regularities statable as laws of grammar.

Postal and I presented these ideas, with proposed universal laws of grammar and analyses of data from diverse languages, in our course at the LSA Summer Linguistic Institute at the University of Massachusetts in 1974. Later work led to a shift from the derivational approach to grammar inherited from TG to one where each construction has a distinct representation as a relational network. Instead of rules changing one representation to another, a language's clause structure could now be viewed as a set of constructions drawn from a small universally available set.

These discoveries put new tools at linguists' disposal that facilitate research on diverse languages. Studying a new language begins with identifying which of the set of crosslinguistically attested basic clausal constructions are present and determining whether that language provides evidence for expanding that set.

In this my research and teaching came together. In addition to my work on languages I am familiar with, I worked with students on a wide range of languages, including Albanian, American Sign Language, Cebuano (Austronesian, Philippines), Chamorro (Austronesian, Marianas Islands), Choctaw (Muskogean, Oklahoma and Mississippi), French, Georgian, Greek, Halkomelem (Salish, British Columbia), Ilocano (Austronesian, Philippines), Italian, Japanese, K'ekchi (Mayan, Guatemala), Kinyarwanda (Bantu, Rwanda), Polish, Portuguese, Seri (Hokan, northwestern Mexico), and Spanish. Each language offered a new opportunity to learn about the ways languages differ and the ways they are alike. Together with work by colleagues and their students on other languages, these languages contributed to RG's typology of basic clausal constructions (see Dubinsky and Rosen 1987).

For me, being able to learn about and work on such a collection of languages was thrilling. When I began to get away from generative grammar's emphasis on English by using data from a few European languages in my doctoral dissertation, I never dreamed that in my lifetime it would be possible to figure out *anything* about such a wide range of languages.

The tools provided by RG facilitated analyses with wide crosslinguistic applicability, of which I will mention just two from my own work.

The first argues against the widespread assumption that a nominative NP with which the verb agrees is necessarily the subject. I argued that in Italian such NPs are subjects when in preverbal subject position but not when postverbal (Perlmutter 1983b). What had been assumed to be freedom of word order is really a systematic contrast between personal clauses, in which these NPs are subjects, and impersonal clauses (with a phonologically null expletive subject), in which they are not. This result can be extended, mutatis mutandis, to many other languages.

The second is the Unaccusative Hypothesis, developed in joint work with Postal (Perlmutter and Postal 1984c, 1984d), which claims that there are two kinds of intransitive clauses: unaccusative clauses have an initial direct object rather than subject, while unergatives have an initial subject. The argument for it in Perlmutter 1978 and Perlmutter and Postal 1984c, 1984d, was based on the prediction it makes together with the 1-Advancement Exclusiveness Law or 1AEX: impersonal and pseudopassives of unaccusative clauses will universally be ill-formed. Supporting data was given from Dutch, Turkish, English, and Welsh. Thus, the Unaccusative Hypothesis is a hypothesis about syntactic representations. Together with syntactic principles, it predicts universal gaps in the set of well-formed passives. Maling (chapter 15, this volume) argues that putative passives of unaccusatives, claimed to counterexemplify this prediction, are not passives and therefore not counterexamples.

Different kinds of evidence for the Unaccusative Hypothesis have been found in a wide range of languages, including Albanian (Hubbard 1985), Basque (Levin 1983; Mejías-Bikandi 1990), Choctaw (Davies 1986), English (Levin and Rappaport-Hovav 1995), French (Olié 1984; Legendre 1989; Legendre and Smolensky, chapter 13, this volume; Postal 1989, 1990), Georgian and other Caucasian languages (Harris 1982, 1985; chapter 11, this volume), Germanic (Perlmutter 1978; Abraham 1986; Grewendorf 1989; Haider 1985; Levin 1988; Steinbach 2003; Zaenen 1993), Halkomelem (Gerdts 1984, 1988, 1991), Irish (McCloskey 1984, 1996; chapter 17, this volume), Italian (Perlmutter 1980, 1983b, 1989; Belletti 1988; Belletti and Rizzi 1981; Burzio 1986; Rosen 1982, 1984, 1988) and Romance (La Fauci 1988), Russian (Pesetsky 1981; Schoorlemmer 2003), Turkish (Knecht 1986; Özkaragöz 1980, 1986), and Tzotzil (Aissen 1987), among many other works and languages.

In Perlmutter 1978 three forms of the Unaccusative Hypothesis are distinguished. Under the strongest, which reflects the Universal Alignment Hypothesis (discussed below), initial unergativity versus unaccusativity is universally predictable from semantic roles. However, subsequent research has shown that this version of the hypothesis cannot be maintained (Perlmutter 1982a, 297–298; Rosen 1984).

The Unaccusative Hypothesis has given rise to a literature too large to do it justice here. A fundamental issue concerns the division of labor between syntax and lexical semantics (Rosen 1984; Van Valin 1990; Levin and Rappaport-Hovav 1995; Alexiadou, Anagnostopoulou, and Everaert 2003; among many others). The key issue is whether the relevant phenomena can be accounted for in semantic terms without syntactic representation of unaccusativity. For some phenomena attributed to unaccusativity in some languages this has been shown to be the case. On the other hand, there are languages where lexical subcategorization for subjects or objects is needed, at least in some cases, because the unergative-unaccusative contrast is not always predictable from semantic notions. Most importantly, there are languages where syntactic representation of unaccusativity (whether predictable from semantic notions or not) captures generalizations uniting transitive and intransitive clauses.

Early on I focused on Italian as providing evidence for syntactic representation of unaccusativity. The partitive clitic *ne*, the participial absolute construction, and the use of past participles as adjectives show unaccusative nominals behaving like direct objects of transitive clauses and contrasting with the subjects of both transitive and unergative clauses. The syntactic representation of unaccusatives is also crucial to solving a language-particular puzzle of Italian: what do unaccusative clauses have in common with clauses with a reflexive clitic such that both have the auxiliary *essere* instead of *avere*? I presented these results at a colloquium at Harvard in May 1978 and in other talks, with publication coming later (Perlmutter 1980, 1983b, 1989; Rosen 1982, 1984, 1988).

In Choctaw (Davies 1986), another language that provides evidence for syntactic representation of unaccusativity, unaccusative NPs that are arguably surface subjects behave like direct objects with respect to two types of agreement, switch reference, and interclausal reflexives. Exceptions to semantic predictability further support syntactic representation.

RG developed three kinds of explanation. First, explanation is achieved by universals. For example, the Stratal Uniqueness Law explains why promotions to subject or object and demotions to direct or indirect object do not result in clauses with two surface subjects or direct or indirect objects, as well as limitations on the class of Clause Union constructions (Gibson and Raposo 1986). Second, crosslinguistically applicable hypotheses such as the Unaccusative Hypothesis explain data in a variety of languages. Third, data in individual languages can be explained as instantiations of constructions drawn from the small set of basic clausal constructions: advancements, demotions, ascensions, Clause Union, and expletive constructions, themselves constrained by universal laws.

Many RG ideas, incorporated into other frameworks, have outlived RG itself. The key distinction that launched RG—that between TG's movement rules that create subjects or objects and those that do not—is fundamental to current frameworks, albeit in different form. The distinction between clause structure and non-clause-level phenomena in RG corresponds, mutatis mutandis, to the distinction between A-movement and Ā-movement in frameworks in the Chomskyan tradition and that between lexicon and syntax in LFG and HPSG.

The success of grammatical relations in bringing out crosslinguistic commonalities in clause structure led to the adoption of devices with similar effects in other frameworks, including LFG, which gives grammatical relations an analogous role, and devices in the frameworks in the Chomskyan tradition, starting with Government-Binding Theory, which achieve many of the same effects. Consequently, there has been a dramatic increase in the number of languages brought to bear on theoretical issues in multiple frameworks.

Widely accepted RG ideas such as the Unaccusative Hypothesis and Clause Union (Perlmutter and Postal 1974; Aissen and Perlmutter 1976b/1983d; Fauconnier 1983; Gibson and Raposo 1986; Davies and Rosen 1988; Moore, chapter 19, this volume) have been incorporated into other frameworks, mutatis mutandis, as have some universals proposed in RG such as a counterpart of the Stratal Uniqueness Law (Perlmutter and Postal 1974, 1977/1983g, 1983f) in LFG and the effect of the Final 1 Law (Perlmutter and Postal 1974, 1983f) in Chomsky's (1982) Extended Projection Principle. Baker (1988) develops a theory to account for the effects of the 1AEX (Perlmutter and Postal 1984c, 1984d; see also Marantz 1984 and Baker, Johnson, and Roberts 1989).

Analyses of individual languages developed in RG have been translated into other frameworks as well. For example, Burzio (1986) develops the unaccusative analysis of Italian in Government-Binding Theory, and RG analyses of Chamorro, Chichewa, Indonesian, Kinyarwanda, Southern Tiwa, and Tzotzil provide much of the foundation for Baker's (1988) theory of incorporation.

At the heart of RG are the three hierarchical "term relations" (subject, direct object, and indirect object) to which nominals can advance, demote, or ascend. Nominals bearing each of them in a given language have a variety of thematic roles. In contrast, the nominals bearing a given oblique relation (instrument, locative, etc.) all have the same thematic role.

The Universal Alignment Hypothesis or UAH (Perlmutter and Postal 1974, 1984c) claimed that the relation borne by each nominal in a clause's initial stratum is universally predictable from the clause's semantics. Adopted by Baker (1988, 1997), mutatis mutandis, as the Uniformity of Theta Assignment Hypothesis (UTAH), the UAH has since proven wrong (Rosen 1984; Farrell 1994; Newmeyer 2001; among others).

In some cases the UAH alone was used to motivate multistratal analyses, initially a natural carryover from derivational TG. The emergence of monostratal syntactic theories raised the issue of whether there is evidence for multistratal representations independent of the UAH. My own work presents evidence from Russian reflexives (Perlmutter 1978b, 1980, 1982a, 1984a), the Unaccusative Hypothesis and auxiliary selection in Italian (see the references above), nominals that behave like subjects in some ways and indirect objects in others in Russian, Italian, and other languages (Perlmutter 1978b, 1979/1984b), and switch reference in Seri (Farrell, Marlett, and Perlmutter 1991c), among others. Other such phenomena for which monostratal and multistratal theories make different predictions are found throughout the RG literature, but there have been few attempts to account for them in monostratal theories. One exception is Farrell (chapter 8, this volume), who proposes a novel term relation for Italian I-nominals, analyzed in Perlmutter 1979/1984b as initial subjects demoted to indirect object.

The expansion of the set of languages under intense syntactic study has challenged RG's claim that there are exactly three universal term relations. Postal (1990) proposed two more. Gerdts (1992, 1999) proposed a bistratal theory with a stratum representing morphologically licensed argument positions (MAPs) that function essentially as term relations. Based on a survey of typologically diverse languages, she concluded that languages with two, three, and four MAPs are all attested. Farrell (chapter 8, this volume) proposes a monostratal theory in which language-particular rules map semantic roles onto hierarchical term relations whose number and identity vary crosslinguistically. Marlett (chapter 16, this volume) captures both regularities and exceptions in the ways thematic roles are aligned with grammatical relations in Seri. These proposals and those of Gerdts (chapter 10), Rhodes (chapter 22), and Zaenen (chapter 23) in this volume capture language-internal generalizations and cross-linguistic contrasts that have emerged from research on a wide range of languages. To the extent that they are successfu, they add to the evidence against the UAH, with which they are incompatible.

Syntactic theory has moved in new directions since the development of RG. Grammatical relations liberated syntax from dependence on language-particular features such as constituent order and brought out commonalities and differences in the clause structures of genetically and typologically diverse languages. This led to an explosion in the number and variety of languages cited in theoretical discussions of syntax. RG has made a signal contribution to the transformation of syntactic theory from a field dominated by studies of English to the field comfortable with crosslinguistic data that we know today.

The Role of Sign Language

Sign languages pose a direct challenge for the basic question of linguistics: in what ways do natural languages differ and in what ways are they all alike? No linguistic theory can answer this question without offering an account of how sign languages differ from spoken languages. The obvious differences are that sign languages are articulated not in the vocal tract, but with the hands, face, and body, and are perceived not auditorily but visually. The question for linguistic theory concerns the extent to which these differences make their grammars different from those of spoken languages. Is there a general blueprint that all languages follow, regardless of modality, or does the modality affect the form of language in significant ways?

Important as this question is, what led me to work on American Sign Language (ASL) was not a research agenda but my teaching. I had directed work on ASL syntax by Judy Kegl at MIT, but I had no direct experience with ASL until I was at UC San Diego, where Carol Padden, a native signer, asked me to be her dissertation adviser. I found ASL hard to deal with. When I directed student work on spoken languages, however exotic, data in written form enabled me to see what was going on. Not so with ASL. With no way to write the signs down, I had difficulty recognizing and remembering them. I found the data hard to grasp. Padden was sometimes unaware of any difference between forms that looked different to me. In other cases her examples depended on a contrast I had failed to notice. I often couldn't tell whether a sign that differed slightly from one I had seen before was an optional variant, had a somewhat different meaning or grammatical function, or was an entirely different sign. To get enough of a working knowledge of ASL to understand what Padden was telling me, I took an ASL course at a community college. This enabled me to direct her thesis, but initially I had no intention of working on ASL myself. The leap from spoken language to sign was daunting.

But I had seen enough to pique my interest. I thought it would not be surprising if ASL has a syntax like spoken languages, but sign phonology raises deeper issues because key theoretical constructs of phonology have been assumed to reflect properties of speech. If there is evidence for them in ASL, it would show that there are phonological principles that transcend the difference in modality—potentially an interesting discovery. This drew me to ASL phonology rather than syntax.

Remembering that after one semester of French, Spanish, and other languages I had some idea of what was a possible word in each language, I wondered to what extent my semester of ASL had given me similar intuitions about possible signs of ASL. I began to look for patterns and regularities in the vocabulary I had acquired. I was excited by what I found. I wrote notes to myself, which I shared with Padden. We began to work together.

Our paper (Padden and Perlmutter 1987), my first on ASL, had two key results. First, incorporating earlier work on ASL, we showed that there are rules of derivational morphology and phonology that interact to produce a welter of similar but different forms like those that had bewildered me. Some result from derivational morphology, which typically alters a sign's movement rather than adding prefixes or suffixes, some from phonology, some from both. It was all regular and systematic. Second, we showed that rules of derivational morphology feed each other and the phonology, but crucially, outputs of the phonology must be prevented from undergoing rules of derivational morphology. With derivational morphology in the lexicon and a postlexical phonological component, no constraint is needed to account for this; it follows from the architecture of grammars. This is evidence that ASL grammar has a postlexical phonological component. In having derivational morphology,

References

References to works in the list of my publications at the end of this book are not repeated here. To find "Moore and Perlmutter 2000b," for example, look for "2000b" in that list.

Unpublished items *are* listed here. Hence "Perlmutter and Postal 1974" and "Perlmutter 1978b" are listed here, while "Perlmutter 1978" is in the list of publications at the end of the book.

Abraham, Werner. 1986. Unaccusatives in German. *Groninger Arbeiten zur germanistischen Linguistik* 28:1–72.

Aissen, Judith. 1987. *Tzotzil clause structure*. Dordrecht: Reidel.

Alexiadou, Artemis, Elena Anagnostopoulou, and Martin Everaert, eds. 2003. *The unaccusativity puzzle: Explorations of the syntax-lexicon interface*. New York: Oxford University Press.

Baker, Mark. 1988. *Incorporation: A theory of grammatical function changing*. Chicago: University of Chicago Press.

Baker, Mark. 1997. Thematic roles and syntactic structure. In Liliane Haegeman, ed., *Elements of grammar: Handbook of generative syntax*, 73–137. Dordrecht: Kluwer.

Baker, Mark, Kyle Johnson, and Ian Roberts. 1989. Passive arguments raised. *Linguistic Inquiry* 20:219–251.

Belletti, Adriana. 1988. The case of unaccusatives. *Linguistic Inquiry* 19:1–34.

Belletti, Adriana, and Luigi Rizzi. 1981. The syntax of "ne": Some theoretical implications. *Linguistic Review* 1:117–154.

Browne, Wayles. 1968. Srpskohrvatske enklitike i teorija transformacione gramatike [Serbo-Croatian enclitics and the theory of transformational grammar]. *Zbornik Matice Srpske za filologiju i lingvistiku* 11:25–29.

Burzio, Luigi. 1986. *Italian syntax: A government-binding approach*. Dordrecht: Reidel.

Chomsky, Noam. 1982. *Some concepts and consequences of the theory of government and binding*. Cambridge, MA: MIT Press.

Chomsky, Noam, and Morris Halle. 1968. *The sound pattern of English*. New York: Harper and Row.

Dante Alighieri. 1305. *De vulgari eloquentia* [On the eloquence of the vernacular]. Unfinished manuscript. First published Paris, 1577. Prepared for publication by Jacopo Corbinelli. English translation in Steven Botterill, ed., *Dante, De vulgari eloquentia*, Cambridge Medieval Classics 5. New York: Cambridge University Press, 1996.

Davies, William D. 1986. *Choctaw verb agreement and universal grammar*. Dordrecht: Reidel.

Davies, William D., and Carol G. Rosen. 1988. Unions as multi-predicate clauses. *Language* 64:52–88.

Dubinsky, Stanley, and Carol Rosen. 1987. *A bibliography on Relational Grammar through May 1987 with selected titles on Lexical Functional Grammar*. Bloomington: Indiana University Linguistics Club.

Farrell, Patrick. 1994. *Thematic relations and Relational Grammar*. New York: Garland.

Fauconnier, Gilles. 1983. Generalized Union. *Communication and Cognition* 16:3–37.

I am lucky to have found in linguistics a field that excites me and to have been able to make contributions to linguistic theory and to the understanding of individual languages. As I look at the list of my publications, I see that many are attempts to solve a puzzle.

Language-particular puzzles in Italian, Russian, Slovenian, and Spanish have been mentioned above. The biggest crosslinguistic puzzle concerns the ways languages differ. Do rules that reference the notion "subject" target the same set of NPs crosslinguistically (Perlmutter 1982a; Farrell, Marlett, and Perlmutter 1991c)? Why do some dative NPs behave like subjects in certain respects (but not others) in Russian, Italian, and other languages (Perlmutter 1978b, 1979c/1984b, 1982a; Moore and Perlmutter 2000b)? Crosslinguistically, plural inflection tends to occur outside derivational affixation. Why, then, can diminutive suffixes appear outside plural inflection in Yiddish (Perlmutter 1988a)? Is there evidence for the syllable in a mora-counting language like Japanese (Perlmutter 1991b) and a sign language like ASL (Perlmutter 1992c, 1993)? Of course, my solutions to these puzzles and others have had varying degrees of success in withstanding the test of time.

Looking back, I see that my research has been driven by my desire to experience the thrill of discovery by solving puzzles like these and discovering the consequences of the solutions for linguistic theory. My teaching has been driven by my zest for enabling others to experience the thrill of discovery for themselves.

When I came up for tenure at MIT in my midthirties, Provost Walter Rosenblith asked me what I would be doing for the next thirty years or more. I told him that the main focus of my research would continue to be increasing the range of languages for which linguistic theory is to be held accountable. That statement turned out to be a better predictor of my future research interests than I could possibly have foreseen at the time. I have learned and discovered more about a wider variety of spoken languages than I would ever have thought possible. I have also made the leap to sign language. All this has taken me beyond my wildest dreams.

Notes

I am indebted to Judith Aissen, Mark Aronoff, Eric Bakovic, Bill Davies, Patrick Farrell, Brian Joseph, Joan Maling, Rachel Mayberry, John Moore, Donna Jo Napoli, Carol Padden, Barbara Partee, Masha Polinsky, Paul Postal, Haj Ross, John Spertus, and Tom Wasow for helpful comments on earlier versions of this essay. I am solely responsible for errors and shortcomings.

Most of the cited works authored by me alone or with coauthors are included in the list of my publications at the end of this book and therefore are not repeated in the references at the end of this essay, where only unpublished works of mine are listed. Since this essay focuses on my life and work, I have not attempted to cite all relevant works by other authors.

from English has had a profound and salutary effect on the Deaf community. Deaf people began to think of themselves as a linguistic and cultural minority in the larger society, with a new pride in their language, culture, and traditions (Padden and Humphries 1988, 2005). It stimulated a literary culture (stories, theater, and poetry) in ASL, rooted in their vibrant storytelling tradition.

Undergraduates generally find ASL and Deaf people's lives more interesting than most of linguistic theory. I viewed this as an opportunity to address my department's chronic problem of low enrollments. Taking advantage of a state law requiring undergraduates to take a course dealing with some aspect of the cultural diversity of the United States, I introduced a lower-division course (mostly freshmen and sophomores) called "Sign Language and Its Culture" to satisfy this requirement. It ran on two parallel tracks: one compared ASL with English and other spoken languages to bring out what is essential to human language, while the other dealt with Deaf history and culture, including literature in ASL (primarily poetry), which drew on what the students had learned about Deaf people's language and history.

The key to giving students the feeling of discovery was figuring out what they assumed about language in general, about sign language, and about Deaf people. This enabled me to introduce material that shattered their assumptions. Their most common reaction ("I had no idea of any of this!") told me they had experienced discovery. They spread the word to their friends. Despite its reputation for being difficult, the course grew until it attracted 350–400 students each time it was offered. Most were content to satisfy the requirement and move on, but a significant number went on to take other linguistics courses and some majored or minored in linguistics.

Excitement

When undergraduates ask me whether they should go to graduate school in linguistics, I have a standard answer. I tell them that many more PhDs are awarded in linguistics than the job market can absorb. I explain the difference between a job and a career: Charles Ives and Benjamin Lee Whorf, for example, made their living in the insurance business; in their spare time Ives wrote music and Whorf did linguistics. Then I ask: "How much do you like doing linguistics? If you had to get some other job to support yourself, would you do linguistics in your spare time? If so, by all means go to grad school in linguistics. If not, what's the point?" This gives students a realistic view of their prospects. And even if they get a job in linguistics, there will be so many demands on their time that they will end up doing it in their spare time.

My question is meant to identify those students whose interest in doing linguistics is strong enough to make them productive linguists. If there is a domain of data or an area of linguistics that truly excites them, they will make discoveries and survive in the field.

phonology, and the same kinds of interactions between them, ASL is just like spoken languages!

A key issue for phonological theory is the extent to which the different means of articulation of signed and spoken languages affect their phonology. I was especially intrigued by the question of whether signing is organized into syllables as speech is. Are syllables a property of language or only of speech? What is essential to syllable structure and how could I recognize it if it exists in sign? I immersed myself in this puzzle for a long time.

In spoken languages, phonological segments are organized into syllables, with relative sonority peaks as syllable nuclei, the less sonorous adjacent segments serving as onsets and codas. I argued that ASL has two segment types that differ in sonority, as vowels and consonants do, and that relative sonority peaks are syllable nuclei, as in spoken languages. This was supported by distributional arguments for syllable structure: secondary movement (finger wiggling is one type) or a change from one handshape to another can occur on syllable nuclei but not on syllable margins (onsets or codas) (Perlmutter 1992c, 1993). This is evidence that phonological constructs such as sonority and the contrast between syllable nuclei and margins are properties of language, not speech.

I was intrigued by sign language poetry as a novel test of the hypothesis that any natural language can serve as the vehicle of poetry (Dante 1305). Analyzing an ASL poem in detail (Perlmutter 2008), I found clear evidence for both the line and the hemistich—not obvious in poetry published as performance on videotape or DVD in a language whose metrical system, if any, is unknown. I examined the way the poet exploits both visual and manual aspects of sign to achieve poetic effects, but limits himself to what is allowed by ASL grammar, which he tweaks in limited but interesting ways. I also explored the extent to which signed and spoken languages offer different resources to their poets and sought to explain why any natural language can serve as the vehicle of poetry.

Through my interest in ASL, I have come into contact with Deaf people, their community, and their culture. Some of what I encountered connected with earlier experiences. Discussions about whether ASL has all the properties of a "real" language brought me back to my childhood, when I had heard similar discussions about Yiddish: is it really a language or just a *zhargon* 'jargon'? Sign language also brought me back to my twenties, when I had resisted going into linguistics because I did not see how it could improve people's lives. Sign language research, beginning with Stokoe's (1960) pioneering monograph that launched the field, has done just that. Before researchers started to study ASL, even Deaf people who used it daily and knew they could express themselves fully in sign were unaware it was a language. They tended to interpret any differences they noticed between sign and English as evidence that sign was ungrammatical English. The discovery that ASL is a language distinct

Gerdts, Donna B. 1984. A relational analysis of Halkomelem causals. In Eung-Do Cook and Donna B. Gerdts, eds., *Syntax and semantics 16: The syntax of Native American languages*, 169–204. San Diego: Academic Press.

Gerdts, Donna B. 1988. *Object and absolutive in Halkomelem Salish*. New York: Garland.

Gerdts, Donna B. 1991. Unaccusative mismatches in Halkomelem Salish. *International Journal of American Linguistics* 57:230–250.

Gerdts, Donna B. 1992. Morphologically mediated relational profiles. In *Proceedings of the Annual Meeting of the Berkeley Linguistics Society* 18:322–337. University of California, Berkeley.

Gerdts, Donna B. 1999. Mapping possessors: Parameterizing the external possession construction. In Doris L. Payne and Immanuel Barshi, eds., *External Possession*. Typological Studies in Language 39. Philadelphia: John Benjamins.

Gibson, Jeanne, and Eduardo Raposo. 1986. Clause Union, the Stratal Uniqueness Law, and the chômeur relation. *Natural Language and Linguistic Theory* 4:295–331.

Greenberg, Joseph H. 1963. Some universals of grammar with particular reference to the order of meaningful elements. In Joseph H. Greenberg, ed., *Universals of language*, 58–90. Cambridge, MA: MIT Press. Reprinted in Keith Denning and Suzanne Kemmer, eds., *On language: Selected writings of Joseph H. Greenberg*, 40–70. Stanford, CA: Stanford University Press, 1990.

Grewendorf, Günther. 1989. *Ergativity in German*. Dordrecht: Foris.

Haider, Hubert. 1985. Über *sein* und nicht *sein*: Zur Grammatik des Pronomens *sich* [On *to be* and not *to be*: On the grammar of the pronoun *sich*]. In Werner Abraham, ed., *Erklärende Syntax des Deutschen*, 223–254. Tübingen: Narr.

Harris, Alice. 1982. Georgian and the Unaccusative Hypothesis. *Language* 58:290–306.

Harris, Alice. 1985. *Syntax and semantics 18. Diachronic syntax: The Kartvelian case*. San Diego: Academic Press.

Hubbard, Philip. 1985. *The syntax of the Albanian verb complex*. New York: Garland.

Jaeggli, Osvaldo, and Kenneth J. Safir. 1989. *The null subject parameter*. Dordrecht: Kluwer.

Jakobson, Roman. 1948. Russian conjugation. *Slavic Word* 2:119–129. Reprinted in Linda R. Waugh and Morris Halle, eds., *Russian and Slavic grammar: Studies 1931–1981*, 15–26. Berlin: Mouton.

Knecht, Laura. 1986. *Subject and object in Turkish*. Unpublished doctoral dissertation, Harvard University.

La Fauci, Nunzio. 1988. *Oggetti e soggetti nella formazione della morfosintassi romanza* [Objects and subjects in the formation of Romance morphosyntax]. Pisa: Giardini editori e stampatori.

Legendre, Géraldine. 1989. Unaccusativity in French. *Lingua* 79:95–164.

Levin, Beth. 1983. Unaccusative verbs in Basque. *NELS* 13:129–144.

Levin, Beth, and Malka Rappaport Hovav. 1995. *Unaccusativity: At the syntax-lexical semantics interface*. Cambridge, MA: MIT Press.

Levin, Lori. 1988. *Operations on lexical forms: Unaccusative rules in Germanic*. New York: Garland.

Marantz, Alec. 1984. *On the nature of grammatical relations*. Cambridge, MA: MIT Press.

McCloskey, James. 1984. Raising, subcategorization, and selection in modern Irish. *Natural Language and Linguistic Theory* 1:441–487.

McCloskey, James. 1996. Subjects and subject positions in Irish. In Robert Borsley and Ian Roberts, eds., *The syntax of the Celtic languages: A comparative perspective*, 241–283. Cambridge: Cambridge University Press.

McCloskey, James. 2001. On the distribution of subject properties in Irish. In William D. Davies and Stanley Dubinsky, eds., *Objects and other subjects: Grammatical functions, functional categories, and configurationality*, 157–192. Dordrecht: Kluwer.

Mejías-Bikandi, Errapel. 1990. Clause union and case marking in Basque. In Katarzyna Dziwirek, Patrick Farrell, and Errapel Mejías-Bikandi, eds., *Grammatical relations: A cross-theoretical perspective*, 263–277. Stanford, CA: Center for the Study of Language and Information.

Newmeyer, Frederick J. 2001. Grammatical functions, thematic roles, and phrase structure. In William D. Davies and Stanley Dubinsky, eds., *Objects and other subjects: Grammatical functions, functional categories, and configurationality*, 53–75. Dordrecht: Kluwer.

Olié, Annie. 1984. L'Hypothèse de l'inaccusatif en français [The Unaccusative Hypothesis in French]. *Lingvisticae Investigationes* 8:363–401.

Özkaragöz, Inci. 1980. Evidence from Turkish for the Unaccusative Hypothesis. *Proceedings of the Sixth Annual Meeting of the Berkeley Linguistics Society*, 411–422. University of California, Berkeley.

Özkaragöz, Inci. 1986. *The relational structure of Turkish syntax*. Unpublished doctoral dissertation, University of California at San Diego.

Padden, Carol, and Tom Humphries. 1988. *Deaf in America: Voices from a culture*. Cambridge, MA: Harvard University Press.

Padden, Carol, and Tom Humphries. 2005. *Inside Deaf culture*. Cambridge, MA: Harvard University Press.

Perlmutter, David M. 1978b. Evidence for inversion in Russian, Japanese, and Kannada. Unpublished paper, MIT.

Perlmutter, David M., and Paul M. Postal. 1974. Lectures on Relational Grammar. Summer Linguistic Institute of the Linguistic Society of America, University of Massachusetts, Amherst.

Pesetsky, David. 1981. *Paths and categories*. Unpublished doctoral dissertation, MIT.

Postal, Paul M. 1986a. *Studies of passive clauses*. Albany: State University of New York Press.

Postal, Paul M. 1986b. Why Irish raising is not anomalous. *Natural Language and Linguistic Theory* 4:333–356.

Postal, Paul M. 1989. *Masked inversion in French*. Chicago: University of Chicago Press.

Postal, Paul M. 1990. French indirect object demotion. In Paul M. Postal and Brian D. Joseph, eds., *Studies in Relational Grammar* 3. Chicago: University of Chicago Press.

Rosen, Carol G. 1982. The Unaccusative Hypothesis and the "inherent clitic" phenomenon in Italian. *Papers from the Eighteenth Annual Meeting of the Chicago Linguistic Society* 18:530–541. Chicago: University of Chicago.

Rosen, Carol G. 1984. The interface between semantic roles and initial grammatical relations. In Perlmutter and Rosen 1984, 38–77.

Rosen, Carol G. 1988. *The relational structure of reflexive clauses: Evidence from Italian*. New York: Garland.

Rosen, Carol G. 1990. Italian evidence for multi-predicate clauses. In Katarzyna Dziwirek, Patrick Farrell, and Errapel Mejías-Bikandi, eds., *Grammatical relations: A cross-theoretical perspective*, 415–444. Stanford, CA: Center for the Study of Language and Information.

Ross, John Robert. 1967. *Constraints on variables in syntax*. Unpublished doctoral dissertation, MIT.

Ross, John Robert. 1986. *Infinite syntax!* Norwood, NJ: ABLEX.

Schoorlemmer, Maike. 2003. Syntactic unaccusativity in Russian. In Artemis Alexiadou, Elena Anagnostopoulou, and Martin Everaert, eds., *The unaccusativity puzzle: Explorations of the syntax-lexicon interface*, 207–242. New York: Oxford University Press.

Steinbach, Markus. 2003. Unaccusatives and anticausatives in German. In Artemis Alexiadou, Elena Anagnostopoulou, and Martin Everaert, eds., *The unaccusativity puzzle: Explorations of the syntax-lexicon interface*, 181–206. New York: Oxford University Press.

Stokoe, William C., Jr. 1960. Sign language structure: An outline of the visual communication system of the American deaf. *Studies in Linguistics* 8.

Van Valin, Robert D., Jr. 1990. Semantic parameters of split intransitivity. *Language*, 66:221–260.

Zaenen, Annie. 1993. Unaccusativity in Dutch: Integrating syntax and lexical semantics. In James Pustejovsky, ed., *Semantics and the lexicon*, 129–161. Dordrecht: Kluwer.

1 Depictives and Serialization in Tzotzil

Judith Aissen

1.1 Serial Directionals

Within the class of serial-verb constructions is a subtype that Schiller (1990) terms *serialized directionals.* Serialized directionals involve a transitive verb that denotes direct contact between an external and internal argument and an intransitive verb of directed motion that applies to the internal argument (i.e., there is "sharing" of the internal argument in serialized directionals). Examples from three unrelated languages are shown in (1):

(1) a. Em i karim diwai i kam.   Tok Pisin
       he   carry wood come
       'He brought the wood.' (Foley and Olson 1985, 48)
   b. Koat yɔɔk mhoup nɔɔk phteah.   Khmer
       PRO take food   come house
       'He brought the food home.' (Schiller 1990, 44)
   c. Kɔkú sɔ̀   àsɔ́ yì àxì.   Fon
       Koku take crab go market
       'Koku take a crab to the market.' (Lefebvre 1991, 39)

These examples meet the criteria for serial-verb constructions (SVCs) (see especially Aikhenvald 2006). Each contains two verbs, either of which could function independently as the predicate of its own clause, and depicts what is conceived as a single event. The overall argument structure corresponds to that of a single clause (one internal and one external argument), and features of tense, aspect, polarity, and modality have a single value.

Examples like (1a–c) raise the question of how to accommodate two verbal predicates within a single clause. Developments in the conception of phrase structure within the principles-and-parameters model and the Minimalist Program provide a way of thinking about the structure of serialized directionals (and serialized causatives, more generally) that assigns them structures that are very like those of simple transitive clauses. In current theorizing, even simple transitives involve two verbal

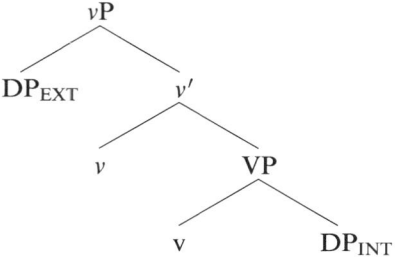

Figure 1.1

heads, a higher one (*v* = "little v") and a lower one (V). Each head introduces one nominal argument into the clause. In this structure, *v* is an abstract head associated with causation. It introduces the external argument (DP_{EXT}), the initiator of the causative event, in its specifier position, and an internal argument (VP) in its complement position. The VP complement denotes the caused event and introduces the internal argument, DP_{INT}. In simple transitives, the usual assumption is that V raises to *v*, yielding a single surface verb. In independent clauses, *v*P is dominated by further functional projections associated with the categories of tense, polarity, and modality.

As Lefebvre (1991) observes, the clausal architecture in figure 1.1 provides the basis for an analysis of serial causatives if we accept one assumption, namely, that both verbal heads may be overtly instantiated by lexical material (see also McIntyre 2004). If this is granted, then the analysis accommodates in a simple way the fact that SVCs involve two verbal predicates within a single clause.

Serialized directional constructions are fairly widely attested in the world's languages, and have been documented especially in Niger-Congo languages (Fon, Ijo, Yoruba), in Austro-Asiatic (Khmer, Thai), and in a number of creoles, both English- and French-based (Tok Pisin in Papua New Guinea; Sranan, Saramaccan, and Haitian Creole in the Caribbean).

Although Mayan languages are not generally serializing, some dialects of Tzotzil have a construction (2a,b) that closely resembles directional serialization.[1]

(2) a. S-kuch-oj   la bat taj antz   ta xch'en   une. OCK 401[2]
       A3-carry-PF CL go DET woman to his.cave ENCS
       'That woman was carried off to his cave.'
    b. Ja'=te s-lap-oj   la lok' ti   tzekil une. OCK 49
       then   A3-wear-PF CL exit DET skirt   ENC
       'He left wearing the skirt.'

This construction displays most of the features associated with directional serialization in other languages: two lexical predicates in a single clause (e.g., *xkuchoj* and *bat* in (2a)), either of which could function independently as the primary predicate of a simple clause. The first is a transitive verb of direct contact; the second is an intransitive verb of directed motion, with the expected sharing of the internal argument. The construction allows only a single value for aspect, mood, and polarity, there is no clause boundary between the two predicates, and it depicts what is conceived as a single event.

At the same time, the Tzotzil construction has properties that are unexpected under figure 1.1. Under that structure, Aspect would command both verbal projections and would be expected to surface on the higher (first) verb, henceforth *v1*. However, in fact, it is the lower (second) verb (*v2*) that carries aspect marking for the entire clause. v1 is identical to the transitive perfect (formed with the suffix -*oj*). In this construction, however, v1 is not interpreted as a perfect. Rather, the aspect of v2 extends over the entire clause, suggesting that v1 is dependent or nonfinite. Under most definitions, dependent status of either verb would exclude the construction from the class of SVCs.

As we will see, the particular properties of the Tzotzil construction suggest a syntactic analysis in terms of depictive secondary predication. Secondary predication has in common with serialization the presence of multiple predicates within a single clause, and thereby provides another way to package a complex event involving caused and accompanied motion within the confines of single clause. I return to the depictive analysis in section 1.5.1, but will refer to the construction exemplified by (2a,b) as a *causative of directed motion (CDM)*, a term that implies no particular syntactic analysis.

1.2 Tzotzil

1.2.1 Surface Features

Typological features of Tzotzil relevant here include the fact that it is a verb-initial language, has head marking, and is morphologically ergative.

In pragmatically unmarked contexts, both subject and object occur postverbally in Tzotzil, with fronting operations always associated with some pragmatic or semantic force (Aissen 1992). Although transitive clauses with two overt postverbal arguments are infrequent, the unmarked order is VOS, as in the text examples (3a,b).

(3) a. I-s-pet   lok'-el   antz   ti   t'ul-e.   OCK 47
       CP-A3-hug exit-DIR woman DET rabbit-ENC
       'The rabbit carried the woman out.'
    b. I-s-k'opon   pale   ti   vinik-e.   OCK 80
       CP-A3-address priest DET man-ENC
       'The man spoke to the priest.'

Tzotzil has an ergative agreement system, with one set of markers indexing subjects of transitive clauses, and a distinct set indexing subjects of intransitives and objects of transitives. The two sets, called Set A and Set B by Mayanists, correspond then to ergative and absolutive markers. While the transitive subject in (4a) is indexed by A3 (*s-*), the intransitive subject in (4b) is indexed by B1 (*-i-*). The same prefix indexes the object in (4a). There is no overt index for third-person absolutives—that is, no overt B3 marker. I assume that none exists, and that it is the absence of any Set B marker that indicates that the absolutive is third person (4c).

(4) a. Ch-i-s-maj.
 ICP-B1-A3-hit
 'She/he hits me.'
 b. Ch-i-bat.
 ICP-B1-go
 'I'm going.'
 c. Ch-bat.
 ICP-go
 'She/he/it's going'

The verbs of (3a,b) are in completive aspect, while those of (4a–c) are incompletive. Incompletive aspect (= *imperfective*) can be interpreted as habitual or as denoting a durative event set in the past, present, or future. Completive aspect (= *perfective*) denotes a bounded event, usually set in the past.

There are also several stative forms of the verb, derived by suffixes that index the transitivity status of the stem. Transitive statives, which are relevant to the discussion of CDM, are formed with the suffix *-oj* and may function as primary predicate expressing *perfect aspect*:

(5) S-kuch-oj-on.
 A3-carry-PF-B1SG
 'She/he has carried me.'

1.2.2 Phrase Structure

In line with the earlier discussion, I assume that transitive clauses in Tzotzil have the structure shown in figure 1.2, but with a right-hand specifier for *v*P, thereby deriving VOS order directly, and not by movement.[3] V raises to v_{TRANS} in the course of the derivation, yielding a single surface verb. Unergative intransitives have the same structure, but with a distinct functional verb v_{INTRANS} and without an internal argument. In unaccusative intransitives, I assume that VP is immediately dominated by AspP, though nothing crucial hinges on this.

Two assumptions about Case licensing are relevant to what follows. The first is that v_{TRANS} licenses (abstract) Ergative case on the external argument that it intro-

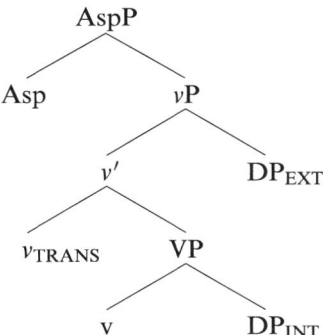

Figure 1.2

duces (reflected by Set A agreement). The other is that the v_{INTRANS} differs sharply from v_{TRANS} in having no Case-licensing capacity. Instead subjects of intransitive clauses are, I assume, Case-licensed as Nominative by the closest c-commanding Aspect (reflected in Tzotzil by Set B).[4]

1.3 Tzotzil "Causative of Directed Motion"

The Tzotzil CDM shares many of the core properties of directional serialization in other languages. Semantically, it expresses directed motion that is the direct result of an atelic activity. Examples (2a,b) denote complex events involving atelic activities (carrying, wearing) that cause movement along a path (going, leaving). While each example denotes a complex event, the two components of meaning that compose it are cleanly partitioned between the two predicates, with the atelic activity denoted by the transitive participle v1 (*skuchoj, slapoj*), and the resulting movement by the finite v2 (*bat, lok'*). The CDM in Tzotzil is restricted further to complex events in which *both* agent and patient travel along the directed path. When a man carries a woman off (to some place), as in (2a), both the man and the woman move away from the deictic point of reference. Likewise, if a man wears a skirt out of some place, both the man and the skirt leave that place.

These restrictions determine the range of verbs in the Tzotzil CDM. The first verb, v1, is limited to atelic activity verbs of the type Levin (1993) calls "causation of accompanied motion." Verbs attested in corpus material include *kuch* 'carry', *lap* 'wear', *net'* 'push', *ik'* 'take', *ich'* 'take', *mak* 'drive', and *kil* 'drag'. As in English, these verbs "do not lexicalize a particular direction of motion. Instead they differ from each other in meaning with respect to the manner/means of motion" (Levin 1993, 136). In English, the direction of motion must be overtly specified in a prepositional phrase (p. 136), but in the Tzotzil CDM, direction is specified by a (closed) set of intransitive verbs of motion that function as v2. This set is larger than that of serialized directionals of most other languages. In addition to *go* and *come*, attested verbs include *arrive*, *return*, *exit*, and *enter*, as well as the absence-of-motion verb, *remain*.[5] Together, the atelic activity verb plus the verb of motion yield meanings like *carry x in (carry x, x enter)*, and *chase x away (chase x, x go)*. See the further examples in (6).[6]

(6) a. S-kuch-oj i-'och ti stem une. OCK 85
    A3-carry-PF CP-enter DET his.bed ENCS
    'His bed was carried in by him.'
   b. S-net'-oj i-bat ta=j-mek. OCK 117
    A3-chase-PF CP-go very.much
    'He was chased a long way.'

1.4 A Proposal for the "Causative of Directed Motion"

The proposal for Tzotzil CDM is shown in figure 1.3. The structure in figure 1.3 involves two layers of verbal projection, an inner projection (VP) headed by the intransitive verb of motion *lok'* 'exited, left' and an outer projection (*v*P_TRANS), which hosts the transitive participle *slapoj* 'wearing'. What is peculiar in this structure is that the two verbal projections are separated by Aspect. Hence, though the heads that make up this structure (V, Asp, *v*_TRANS) are exactly those associated with basic transitive clauses in Tzotzil (as well as serialized directionals, under some conceptions), they are composed in an order that is quite different. In figure 1.3, the func-

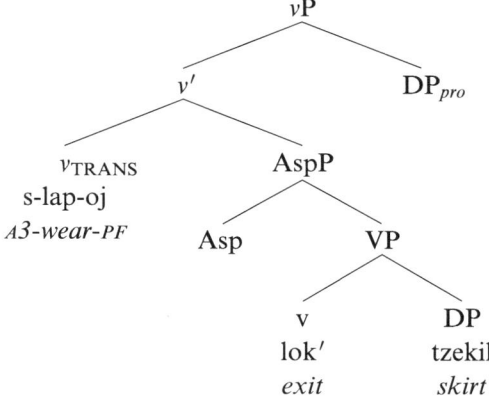

'he wore the skirt out (of the house)'

Figure 1.3

tional *v* head that introduces the external argument commands a constituent (AspP) that itself constitutes a complete, finite intransitive clause. I suggest in section 1.5.1 that figure 1.3 reflects the syntactic composition involved in depictive secondary predication.

The following sections show how the structure in figure 1.3 accounts for the order of elements in the CDM (section 1.4.1), agreement, and the related issue of Case (sections 1.4.2 and 1.4.3). Evidence that it is the internal argument that is shared between the two predicates is presented in section 1.4.2, and section 1.4.4 discusses how that sharing is expressed in the analysis represented by figure 1.3.

1.4.1 Word Order

The structure in figure 1.3 positions the external argument in a right-hand specifier, where it would follow the internal argument. This is the normal position for the external argument, because Tzotzil is a VOS language. I have only one text example of the CDM in which both arguments are overt; the order is as predicted.

(7) Ja' te s-lap-oj [i-kom tzekil] li vinik-e. OCK 49
       v1   v2   O   S
    then A3-wear-PF CP-stay skirt DET man-ENC
    'The man was left wearing the skirt [sic].'

This is also the standard order in elicitation contexts.

1.4.2 The Inner Clause

Figure 1.3 posits what amounts to a full, finite intransitive clause, embedded beneath the projection of v_{TRANS}. Under this structure, the internal argument should be theta-marked by the intransitive verb, and Case-licensed within AspP.

A key claim of figure 1.3 is that the inner verb introduces the internal argument of the entire clause—that is, that in (2a) the argument introduced by *bat* 'go' is *taj antz* 'that woman', and likewise that in (2b) the argument introduced by *lok'* 'exit' is *ti tzekile* 'the skirt'. Showing this is a little tricky. Since the construction always denotes 'accompanied motion', it follows that in situations described by the CDM, the participants corresponding to both the internal and the external argument travel along the path denoted by the verb of directed motion. If a man wears a skirt out of the house, then both the man and the skirt leave the house. Thus, in *the man wore the skirt out of the house* and *the man left the house, wearing the skirt* have truth conditions that are hard to distinguish (see the translation of (2b) and note 2).

However, with certain verbs of motion, it is possible to tease apart this issue. The most useful verb for this purpose is *sut* 'return'. Like English *return*, *sut* is associated not only with the assertion that an entity arrives at a particular location, but also with a presupposition that the same entity was at that location earlier. In the intransitive,

I returned to my father's house, it is understood that I arrived at my father's house, and also that I had been there at some point in the past. Both the assertion and the presupposition are associated with the subject, the only argument of intransitive *return*. In the transitive *we returned the girl to her father's house*, both we and the girl most likely arrived at her father's house, but the presupposition applies only to the girl: we need never have been at the father's house in order to return the girl there, but she must have been there earlier. This suggests a way to show that the inner verb of motion licenses the internal argument of the clause.

Consider (8), bracketed per the analysis in figure 1.3:[7]

(8)   [S-kuch-oj   [i-sut   s-nuti'] ti   vinik-e]
      v1   v2
     A3-carry-PF CP-return A3-bag DET man-ENC
     'The man carried his bag back.'

With this bracketing, the presupposition associated with *return* should apply to the bag. It must have been at the (implicit) location earlier. Consider a scenario then in which a man goes to the market, buys a bag there, and carries it home. Since it is highly unlikely that the bag was ever at the man's house before he bought it, (8) should be inappropriate (in this context). In fact, speakers are quite secure in judging that (8) does not describe this scenario. Example (8) would be appropriate, though, in a scenario in which a man brings a bag of fruit to his girlfriend's house as an offering to her parents—as is traditionally required when a man asks permission to marry a woman—but is rejected. He then returns home carrying the bag. In this case, the presupposition that the bag was at the man's house before being carried home is quite plausible.

Furthermore, if in this construction, the internal argument is introduced into the structure by the inner verb v2, then v2 should be limited to unaccusatives, since only an unaccusative intransitive introduces an internal argument into the clause. We have already seen that the inner verb is restricted in the corpus to intransitive verbs of motion. As in many other languages, these are unaccusative in Tzotzil.[8]

In fact, although they do not occur in the corpus material, it is possible to elicit other (noncanonical, i.e., nonmotion) verbs in the position of the inner verb:[9]

(9)   v1   v2   DP   DP
    a. S-kuch-oj [i-vok' p'in] ti   antz-e.
       A3-carry-PF CP-break pot DET woman-ENC
       'The pot broke, while the woman was carrying it.'
       v1   v2   DP
    b. S-kuch-oj [i-cham yol]   *pro*].
       A3-carry-PF CP-die her.child
       'Her child died, while she [the mother] carried him.'

In both (9a,b), v2 is unaccusative; other verbs elicited in this context include intransitive change-of-state verbs like *k'as* 'break', *k'unib* 'soften', *jat* 'tear'. Interestingly, both (9a,b) lack the causative meaning present in canonical instances of the CDM: (9a) does not imply that the woman broke the pot, nor does (9b) imply that the woman killed the child, or even that her carrying the child killed him. They imply only temporal overlap, as suggested by the translations. I take this to mean that the structure in figure 1.3 does not encode causation per se, though it is canonically used in Tzotzil to express causation. This is important because it means we can ask whether unergatives can instantiate the inner verb. It turns out that they cannot. Example (10a), which is trying to mean 'they chased (the sheep), the sheep fled', is simply impossible apparently because *flee* is unergative, not unaccusative.

(10)   v1   v2   DP
    a. *S-nutz'oj   [i-jatav chij].
       A3-chase-PF CP-flee sheep
       ('The sheep fled, while they were being chased.')
    b. *S-kuch-oj   [i-k'el-van   skrem].
       A3-carry-PF CP-watch-AP his.son
       ('His son was watching [people], while being carried (by his father).')
    c. *S-kuch-oj   [i-k'evujin].
       A3-carry-PF CP-sing
       ('He sang, while he was being carried.')

It appears then that the CDM contains exactly one external argument and one internal argument, with the internal argument introduced by the inner V.

Turning now to agreement, since the CDM includes a full, finite inner clause, its sole argument should be Case-licensed as Nominative, and indexed on the intransitive verb through Set B affixes. In most of the examples considered so far, the internal argument has been third person, yielding no audible agreement on the inner verb regardless of the person of the external argument (recall that there is no Set B third-person marker). In (11), for example, the inner verb cannot carry a Set B marker; audible agreement on v2 results in ungrammaticality (11b).

(11)   v1   v2   DP
    a. J-kuch-oj   [i-bat j-nuti'].
       A1-carry-PF CP-go A1-bag
       'I carried my bag away (lit., *I-carried my bag-went*).'
          v1   v2   DP
    b. *J-kuch-oj   [l-i-bat   j-nuti'].
       A1-carry-PF CP-B1-go A1-bag

Key examples are ones in which the internal argument is first or second person; when it is, the inner verb should agree with it. This is correct—example (12), a text example, is particularly clear on this point:

(12) As I was standing there a man came up to me...
    v1   v2
    y-ik'-oj   [l-i-bat   *pro* ta sna] (Laughlin 1980, 38)
    A3-take-PF CP-B1-go 1SG to his.house
    'He took me to his house (lit., *he-took I-went to his house*).'

Agreement with the first-person internal argument is registered on v2, the finite verb. The example in (13) makes the same point.

        v1   v2
(13) S-net'-oj   ch-i-k'ot   batel. (Laughlin 1975, 251)
    A3-push-PF ICP-B1-arrive REP
    'I was pushed down again and again [sic].'

Evidence from agreement in (12, 13) also suggests that the internal argument is not a syntactic argument of the outer verb at any point, as per the structure in figure 1.3. If it were, it would presumably be indexed on the higher verb via Set B markers. However, examples (12) and (13) show that there is no Set B agreement on the higher verb (the forms with such agreement would be *y-ik'-oj-on* A3-TAKE-PF-B1SG and *s-net'-oj-on* A3-PUSH-PF-B1SG). The conclusion that v_{TRANS} plays no role in syntactically licensing the internal argument is consistent with the assumption that it is syntactically licensed in the inner clause.

1.4.3 Licensing the External Argument

Turning now to the external argument, like the external argument in any transitive clause, it requires Case licensing. Since v_{TRANS} prominently figures in the structure proposed in figure 1.3, that node should syntactically license the external argument. All evidence suggests that is correct. V1, the transitive participle, always bears Set A agreement in this construction, with its form varying according to the person of the external argument. The example in (12), for example, shows agreement with a third-person ergative (A3), while (11a) shows agreement with a first-person ergative (A1). The absence of Set A agreement on the transitive participles in (11a) or (12) would result in complete ungrammaticality.

1.4.4 Argument Sharing

Like serialized directionals, the CDM in Tzotzil involves argument sharing, for the internal argument of the overall clause is interpreted both as the sole argument of the inner verb and as the internal argument of the outer verb. In the analysis developed up to this point, however, the internal argument is formally related only to the inner verb. It is semantically selected (theta-marked) by that verb and syntactically licensed in situ. The issue for this analysis, then, is how it accounts for the semantic relation of the internal argument to the higher verb.

I suggest that though the internal argument is neither syntactically licensed by the outer verb nor merged into the structure to satisfy its (semantic) selectional requirements, it identifies the internal argument of that verb. One way this could be achieved is through a relation like *Linking* (i.e., Predication), proposed by Winkler (1997) for depictive secondary predication. Linking establishes a connection between an unsaturated predicate and a DP merged earlier in the structure to satisfy the selectional requirements of a distinct predicate. As a result of Linking, the unsaturated position is filled.[10]

Some evidence for this comes from the morphosyntax of depictives in Tzotzil. Tzotzil lacks secondary predication of the resultative type, but has a highly productive system of depictive secondary predication. Depictives come from all nonfinite predicative categories in Tzotzil, and are rigidly fixed to the left of the primary predicate. The primary predicate may be transitive (14a) or intransitive (14b,c); statistically, depictives occur most frequently with intransitive verbs of motion (14c).

(14) a. Vayem(-on)   l-i-y-ikta.
       asleep(-B1SG) CP-B1-A3-leave
       'She/he left me asleep.'
   b. Vinik(-ot)   x-a-k'opoj.
       man(-B2SG) NT-B2-speak
       'You speak (like) a man.'
   c. Kil-bil   ch-bat ta nab. OCK 368
       drag-PSV.PRT ICP-go to river
       'He was dragged off to the river.'

I assume that depictives left-adjoin to AspP, accounting for their position immediately to the left of the inflected verb. Let us assume that Linking, as characterized above, is responsible for identifying the argument of the depictive. What is relevant here is that while the primary predicate in (14a–c) obligatorily agrees with its argument(s),[11] the depictive *may* agree with the argument to which it is linked, but need not (and usually does not). In other words, agreement under Linking is optional.

The same is true of the outer verb in the Tzotzil CDM, which may *optionally* agree with the internal argument.

```
              v1                  v2
(15) a. S-kuch-oj (-on)    l-i-bat    li   jmakbeetik-e.
        A3-carry-PF-B1SG   CP-B1-go   DET  highwaymen-ENC
        'The highwaymen carried me away.'
     b. S-kuch-oj (-on)    l-i-sut       tal  li   viniketik-e.
        A3-carry-PF-B1SG   CP-B1-return  DIR  DET  men-ENC
        'The men carried me back here.'
```

If the relation between the internal argument and the higher verb in the CDM is one of Linking, then the patterns of (14) and (15) fall together. In this view, the two instances of Set B morphology in (15a,b) reflect two modes of agreement. Agreement on the inner verb is obligatory, and reflects syntactic (Case) licensing of the internal argument by Asp(ect); agreement on the outer verb is optional, and reflects a semantic relation (e.g., Linking) that holds between the outer verb and the internal argument.[12]

1.5 The Markedness of the Tzotzil CDM

The structure in figure 1.3 provides an account of some of the key formal properties of the Tzotzil CDM—in particular, its word order and the inflection of each verb. The success of this analysis depends on the idea that internal and external arguments are introduced into clauses by distinct heads and that the two heads may be separated by other heads (here, Aspect). Assuming this is correct, the low position of Aspect is, nonetheless, unusual and presumably marked.

That the CDM is indeed marked is suggested by the fact that (to my knowledge) no other Mayan language has such a structure. Even in Tzotzil, the CDM is not robust. While speakers of the dialect in Zinacantán are familiar with the construction and use it, it is unknown to at least some speakers of the neighboring Chamulan dialect. And even in Zinacantec Tzotzil, the CDM is never spontaneously volunteered and as soon as the syntax gets complex, speakers fall back on less marked constructions. In view of this, one must wonder how the CDM has arisen and what function it serves for speakers. I address these two questions in closing.

1.5.1 Serialization and Depictives

An explanation for why aspect is marked on the *inner* verb (v2) in the CDM—that is, for the arrangement of heads in figure 1.3—may be found in the syntax of depictive secondary predication (see section 1.4.4, including (14a–c)). The CDM resembles secondary depictive predication, and may be an instance or an extension of that construction.

Depictives are fixed to the immediate left of the primary (aspect-bearing) predicate, (16a,b). The transitive participle in the CDM occurs in the same position, (17).

(16) *Depictive secondary predication*
 a. Vay-em(-on)   l-i-y-ikta.
    sleep-PF(-B1SG) CP-B1-A3-leave
    'She/he left me asleep.'
 b. Vinik(-ot)   x-a-k'opoj.
    man(-B2SG) NT-B2-speak
    'You speak (like) a man.'

(17) CDM
    S-kuch-oj(-on)   l-i-bat   li   jmakbeetik-e.
    A3-carry-PF-B1SG CP-B1-go DET highwaymen-ENC
    'The highwaymen carried me away.'

I assumed earlier that depictives are adjoined to AspP, and assume the same for v1 in the CDM.

In both constructions, there is argument sharing between the two predicates and the agreement patterns are the same. The aspect-bearing verb obligatorily agrees with the shared argument; the other predicate shows only optional agreement.

The simplest possibility is that the CDM simply *is* depictive secondary predication where the secondary predicate happens to be a (transitive) participle. This makes sense from a paradigmatic perspective since then *every* type of nonfinite predicate would be attested in depictive function. This approach faces a significant challenge, however, which is how a depictive, which is ordinarily a clausal adjunct, adjoined above AspP, comes to function as an integral part of the clausal spine, projecting its own structure (v′, vP) higher (see figure 1.3).

One way to understand this might be in terms of argument saturation. While other (i.e., intransitive) depictives saturate their argument structure through Linking, transitive depictives do not. The internal argument is identified through Linking (section 1.4.4), but the external argument is left free. Hence, a transitive depictive remains unsaturated until its external argument is merged into the structure. It is the need, then, to saturate the depictive through merger of an external argument that motivates projection of v_{TRANS}, the head that introduces the external argument into the structure and Case-licenses it.

In this view, the CDM is a special case of depictive syntax in Tzotzil. However, it is the very properties that set it apart from canonical depictive syntax—in particular, the fact that it *augments* the valence of the clause—that align it closely with directional serialization (more generally, with causative serialization).

1.5.2 The Function of the CDM in Tzotzil

As noted earlier, speakers generally prefer a different construction for the expression of directed motion, one that involves a *directional* (see (3a) for an example). Directionals are based on the same class of intransitive verbs of motion that figure in the CDM. Derived by the suffix *-el*, they follow the main verb and often express notions translated by particles in English (e.g., *up, down, in, out, by, away*) (see Haviland 1991, 1993).[13]

Asked to translate from Spanish to Tzotzil, speakers will always offer a directional construction over the CDM, and whenever the syntax gets complex, speakers will revert to the directional construction, preferring it to the CDM. Since the CDM does occur, however, there must be conditions under which it is favored over the directional construction, though these conditions are difficult to replicate in an elicitation context.

Looking at a corpus containing twenty-six textual examples of the CDM, one feature that stands out is the high discourse prominence of the internal argument. It is striking that of the twenty-six textual examples, sixteen involve an *inanimate* internal argument that is highly salient. In six instances, it is a magical object (e.g., a magic ring, a magic staff); in two examples, it is a ritual object (e.g., a bed that must be carried around a house three times for curing purposes); and in eight more it is highly topical. That is, it plays an important role in the narrative and is mentioned repeatedly (e.g., a skirt, worn by a man).

The question then is why the CDM provides a suitable vehicle for presenting a highly salient internal argument. Here a proposal due to Winkler seems promising. Winkler (1997, 391) suggests that Linking (Predication), which is central to her analysis of depictives, is associated with topic status and with an "aboutness" interpretation. This seems exactly right for the internal argument in the CDM, and is reflected in the way that Laughlin (1977) translates many of the corpus examples of CDM clauses. A substantial number (about half) were translated as passives (see notes 2 and 6).

The status of the internal argument in the *directional construction* is quite different. Haviland (1991) shows that directionals associate a trajectory with an event, not an individual argument.[14] Hence, the internal argument does not enter into a predication relation, and the construction itself therefore carries no association with topicality for the internal argument.

1.6 Conclusion

Tzotzil CDMs are like simple transitive clauses in their argument structure, in the fact that they involve a single value for aspect and polarity, and in their depiction of a single, complex event. These parallels are due in part to the fact that the two structures involve the same inventory of heads, Asp, v, V. However, the principles that compose these heads are different. In canonical transitive clauses, general principles arrange these heads in the order Asp $> v >$ V ($>=$ c-command). But the principles of composition that operate in the CDM probably come instead from the domain of depictive secondary predication and result in the order $v >$ Asp $>$ V.

The serial character of clauses with transitive depictives arises from the fact that transitive depictives, but not intransitive ones, augment the valence of the clause. This yields a tighter link between the two predicates and is probably responsible for the fact that the construction is, to some degree, grammaticized. Transitive depictives are found only with unaccusative intransitive verbs of motion, and are themselves drawn only from verbs of direct contact. The result is that clauses with transitive depictives are restricted to expressing caused and accompanied motion, thereby largely coinciding with the domain of serialized directionals in other languages. It is an interesting question why transitive depictives in Tzotzil are restricted in this particular way. The answer is perhaps related to the idea that scenes involving *directly caused motion*—exactly as in the Tzotzil CDM—are basic or prototypical (Slobin 1985), hence are more likely to be expressed by a "construction" than less prototypical scenes. As Goldberg (1995, 42) notes, "Events encoded by constructions are in some sense basic to human experience."

Notes

Earlier versions of this work were presented at WAIL (Santa Barbara, 2004), to the Syntax Group at UCSC (2005), and at the VIII Encuentro Internacional de Lingüística en el Noroeste (2004). I am grateful to those audiences for their questions, comments, and suggestions. I am also indebted to two speakers of Zinacantec Tzotzil, with whom I have worked over a long period on the material discussed here, Chep Hernantis Kontzares and Manvel Peres. I would like to especially thank Sandy Chung, Florence Woo, John Moore, and an anonymous reviewer for their comments on earlier drafts, as well as John Haviland, Lourdes de Léon, Beth Levin, Jim McCloskey, and Roberto Zavala for discussions of this material at various points. Finally, I am pleased to dedicate this chapter to David Perlmutter, who first sparked my interest in syntax.

1. Abbreviations used in glosses include A1,3 = Set A 1st, 3rd person; AP = antipassive; B1,2 = Set B 1st, 2nd person; CL = clitic; CP = completive; DET = determiner; DIR = directional; ENC(S) = enclitic(s); EXT = external; ICP = incompletive; INT = internal; INTRANS = intransitive; NT = neutral aspect; OCK = Laughlin 1977; PF = perfect; PRO = pronoun; PSV.PRT = passive participle; REP = repetitive; SG = singular; TRANS = transitive.

2. Both (2a) and (2b) are from Laughlin 1977, a text collection cited here as OCK. I have retained Laughlin's translations. On the passive translation of (2a), see section 1.5.2; on the translation of (2b), see the discussion in section 1.4.2.

3. Chung (2006) discusses some of the problems facing a movement analysis of VOS in Tzotzil.

4. I assume that the internal argument in a transitive clause—which is also indexed via Set B markers—is likewise nominative.

5. These verbs belong to a closed set of about twelve intransitive verbs of motion that figure in several distinctive constructions (Haviland 1991, 1993). Members of the set that are not attested in serial function in corpus material can be elicited. It appears then that all members are possible in the CDM.

6. Note that Laughlin 1977 translates both (6a,b) by English passives. See section 1.5.2.

7. Tzotzil examples with no source indicated are from my own fieldnotes.

8. For example, each verb of directed motion derives a morphological causative. These verbs also function like unaccusatives with respect to phenomena that distinguish unaccusatives and unergatives—for instance, the possibility of extracting the possessor from the subject (Aissen 1996).

9. Whether one would want to say these examples are grammatical is not clear to me. However, the speakers I consulted were able and willing to work with these examples and say what they meant. Crucially, they sharply distinguished examples like those in (9) from those in (10).

10. Alternatively, the internal argument of the outer verb might be identified through pragmatic inference (McIntyre 2004).

11. But recall that there is no visible agreement morphology in the case of third-person Nominative/Absolutive.

12. Various issues remain to be addressed here if Linking is a viable solution. One is that the locality condition that Winkler imposes on Linking (mutual m-command) is not satisfied in the structure I am assuming (figure 1.3). I leave open here the appropriate locality condition for Linking in Tzotzil depictives and the CDM.

13. I do not consider verb + directional, as in (3), to be an instance of serialization because the directional generally cannot function independently as a predicate. Further, the directional need not take an individual as its argument, but may be construed as applying to the event denoted by the main verb (for discussion, see Haviland 1991, 1993).

14. Thanks to John Haviland for discussion of this point.

References

Aikhenvald, Alexandra. 2006. Serial verb constructions in typological perspective. In A. Aikhenvald and R. M. W. Dixon, eds., *Serial verb constructions: A cross-linguistic typology*. Oxford: Oxford University Press.

Aissen, Judith. 1992. Topic and focus in Mayan. *Language* 63:43–80.

Aissen, Judith. 1996. Pied piping, abstract agreement, and functional projections in Tzotzil. *Natural Language & Linguistic Theory* 14:447–491.

Chung, Sandra. 2006. Properties of VOS languages. In M. Everaert and H. v. Riemsdijk, eds., *The Blackwell companion to syntax (Syncom)*, 685–720. Malden, MA: Blackwell.

Foley, William, and Mike Olson. 1985. Clausehood and verb serialization. In J. Nichols and A. Woodbury, eds., *Grammar inside and outside the clause*. Cambridge: Cambridge University Press.

Goldberg, Adele. 1995. *Constructions.* Chicago: University of Chicago Press.

Haviland, John. 1991. *The grammaticalization of motion (and time) in Tzotzil.* Working Paper No. 2. Nijmegen: Cognitive Anthropology Research Group, Max-Planck Institute for Psycholinguistics.

Haviland, John. 1993. The syntax of Tzotzil auxiliaries and directionals: The grammaticalization of "motion." In *Proceedings of the Nineteenth Annual Meeting of the Berkeley Linguistics Society.* Berkeley: Berkeley Linguistics Society.

Laughlin, Robert. 1975. *The great Tzotzil dictionary of San Lorenzo Zinacantán.* Washington, DC: Smithsonian Institution Press.

Laughlin, Robert. 1977. *Of cabbages and kings.* Washington, DC: Smithsonian Institution Press.

Laughlin, Robert. 1980. *Of shoes and ships and sealing wax.* Washington, DC: Smithsonian Institution Press.

Lefebvre, Claire. 1991. *Take* serial verb constructions in Fon. In C. Lefebvre, ed., *Serial verbs: Grammatical, comparative and cognitive approaches,* 37–78. Amsterdam: John Benjamins.

Levin, Beth. 1993. *English verb classes and alternations.* Chicago: University of Chicago Press.

McIntyre, Andrew. 2004. Event paths, conflation, argument structure, and VP shells. *Linguistics* 42:523–571.

Schiller, Eric. 1990. On the definition and distribution of serial verb constructions. In B. Joseph and A. Zwicky, eds., *When verbs collide: Ohio State Mini-Conference on Serial Verbs,* 34–64. Columbus: Department of Linguistics, OSU.

Slobin, Dan. 1985. Cross-linguistic evidence for the language-making capacity. In D. Slobin, ed., *A crosslinguistic study of language acquisition.* Hillsdale, NJ: Erlbaum.

Winkler, Susanne. 1997. *Focus and secondary predication.* Studies in Generative Grammar 43. Berlin: Mouton de Gruyter.

2 Prolegomenon to Any Future Typology of Impersonal Sentences

Leonard H. Babby

2.1 Introduction

I dedicate this chapter to David Perlmutter, a pioneer in the formal analysis of impersonal sentences.[1] Its purpose is not to present a new typology of Russian impersonal sentences (I-S), but rather to lay the groundwork for such a project by proposing explicit definitions, eliminating from consideration certain types of sentences that appear to be impersonal but are not, and by proposing a *principium divisiones* on which to base an "explanatory typology." This typology is intended to be a classification of I-Ss that reflects the kinds of information that Russian speakers must have when deciding whether to use an impersonal or "personal" sentence, and whether such a choice is licensed by a given predicator V (cf. the *adversity* I-S in (1b) and its personal counterpart in (1a)); see Perlmutter 1983. How does a Russian speaker know whether an impersonal syntactic projection of a given V is obligatory, optional, or impossible?[2]

(1) a. Peredatočnyj remen' otrezal učeniku palec.
Drive belt.NOM.M cut-off.M student.DAT.M finger.ACC
'The drive belt cut off a student's finger.'
b. Učeniku otrezalo palec (peredatočnym remnem).
student.DAT.M cut-off.N finger.ACC (drive belt.INST)
'The student's finger got cut off by the drive belt.'

My hypothesis is that impersonal morphosyntax is canonically determined by V's argument structure (A-S) and the semantic properties of the verb class it belongs to. We will see that I-Ss that appear to be lexically unconstrained turn out on closer inspection to be either lexically constrained or personal. I will therefore be arguing that a classification of I-Ss should be based on a typology of the A-Ss that project I-Ss and that all Russian I-Ss are more or less lexically determined—that is, there is no evidence for lexically unconstrained impersonal constructions.

In the theory I am assuming (Babby 2009), A-S is represented as a two-tiered, four-positioned *diathesis*, each of whose positions maps onto a homologous syntactic position in V's Extended Lexical Projection: [xP nP$_{i.NOM}$ [x′ [V-x] [VP⟨i⟩ nP$_{j.ACC}$ [v′ t$_v$ nP$_k$]]]], where xP is VP's first functional projection and the subject nP$_i$ in spec-xP is the projection of V's external argument; x is typically an affix in Russian. A fundamental distinction is made between the diatheses of lexically impersonal Vs (e.g., *Stemnelo* 'It got dark') and impersonalized Vs; the latter are derived by diathesis-based operations from Vs with external arguments. I use the term *impersonal* to denote a V whose syntactic projection has no external theta role.

The class that V belongs to plays a crucial role in licensing impersonalization—for example, we see in section 2.9 that the personal Vs that head adversity I-Ss like (1b) belong to a well-defined semantic class. Existential sentences are headed by basic or derived unaccusative Vs, which is relevant since negated existential sentences like (2b) are mistakenly classified as impersonal (see section 2.6).[3]

(2) a. V lesu **rastut griby**.
   in forest grow.PL mushrooms.NOM.PL
   'There are mushrooms growing in the forest.'
  b. V lesu **ne raslo gribov**.
   in forest NEG grew.SG.N mushrooms.GEN.PL
   'There were no mushrooms growing in the forest.'

Impersonal Vs are lexically impersonal: their basic diathesis has no external argument and thus obligatorily projects an I-S (see section 2.7). Impersonalization is an affix-driven operation on a personal V's diathesis that eliminates its external argument.

Argument is defined as an s-selected theta role and the c-selected categorial head (typically **N**) it is linked to in V's diathesis. The *external argument* is V's external theta role **i** (canonically an agent) linked to its external categorial head **N**, which is represented as {i ^ N}$_1$.[4] Unaltered {i ^ N}$_1$ maps onto the nominative subject NP of a personal sentence: {i ^ N}$_1$ ⇒ [vP NP$_{i.NOM}$ v′]. Impersonalization can be represented as {i ^ N}$_1$ > {- ^ -}$_1$. While a null expletive may be introduced syntactically (see Perlmutter and Moore 2002), expletives are syntactic "place fillers" and as such have no theta role and are not projected from V's diathesis; their introduction is a purely syntactic operation analogous to *do*-support in English.

2.2 Argument Structure and Its Syntactic Projection

An analysis of I-Ss is as good as the definition of subject it is based on. My approach to subject is multidimensional (see Williams 2003), encompassing several primitive types of subject: (i) *morphological subject* (nominative case plus verbal agreement); (ii) *theta subject* (the phrase assigned V's **i**); (iii) *syntactic subject* (expletives are syntactic but not theta subjects; see Rothstein 1985, 2001).[5] *Subject* is thus a bundle of primitive subject types, just as the phoneme is a bundle of distinctive features. This definition captures the intuition that a given NP can be more or less subjectlike and that more than one NP in a clause can have "subject properties" (see Keenan 1976). Most important: a sentence is impersonal iff the main V *has no theta subject*.

My typology of I-Ss presupposes an explicit theory of the internal organization of V's diathesis, how it is altered by affix-driven rules, and how it projects to syntactic structure. The diathesis' two-tiered architecture encodes the number of V's arguments (zero to three arguments). The arguments' right-to-left order in the diathesis determines the order in which they merge to form binary-branching syntactic constituent structure: $[_{vP}\ NP_i + [_{vP}\ NP_j + [_{V'}\ V + NP_k]]]$ ("+" = merge). The diathesis thus encodes that first oblique NP_k merges with V to form V′, V′ then merges with the direct object NP_j to form VP, and so on. This means that the diathesis' 2 × 4 architecture in (3a) encodes the arguments' bottom-to-top merger, their grammatical relations, the binary-branching syntactic structures they project, and, indirectly, their structural case realizations; quirky case is represented as a c-selection property of V in its lower tier.

Implicit in this conception of A-S is the hypothesis that Vs have *external c-selection*, which plays a crucial role in the derivation of I-Ss. If there were no external subcategorization, we could not distinguish between inherently impersonal transitive Vs like *tošnit'* 'to experience nausea', optional impersonal Vs like *korčit'* 'to writhe', and unaccusative Vs (see section 2.7).

The diathesis of the ditransitive V in (3a) encodes the right-to-left order of syntactic merger that determines the diathesis-to-syntax projection rules in (3b). The sentence's syntactic structure in (3c) is projected from (3a) via (3b): first (b.i), then (b.ii), and finally (b.iii). "Small v" is the finite suffix; i, j, and k represent theta roles.

(3) a. $\{\{i \wedge N\}_1\ \{j \wedge N\}_2\ \{k \wedge N\}_3\ \{-\wedge V\}_4\}$
 b. i. $\{k \wedge N\}_3 + V \Rightarrow [V\ NP_{k.oblique/PP}]_{V'}$
  ii. $\{j \wedge N\}_2 + V' \Rightarrow [_{VP}\ NP_{j.ACC}\ V']$
  iii. $\{i \wedge N\}_1 + VP \Rightarrow [_{vP}\ NP_{i.NOM}\ [_{v'}\ v\ VP]]$
 c.
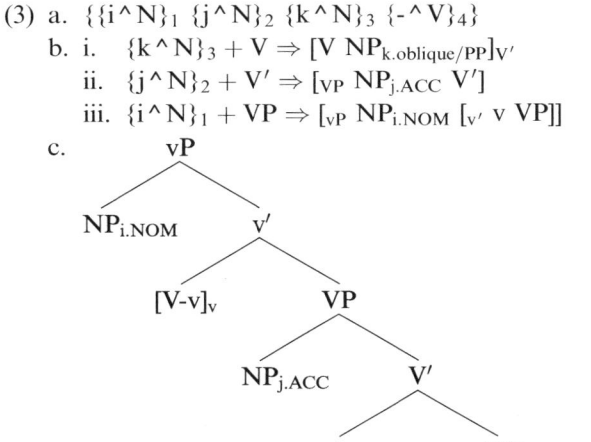

2.3 Faux-Impersonal Sentences in Russian

It is often difficult to determine whether common Russian sentences are impersonal or merely have nonnominative subjects, which lack agreement features. Not having a nominative morphological subject does not automatically entail that the sentence is impersonal: if a Russian sentence has an external theta role, initial or derived, it is "personal." The following are examples of "faux-impersonal" sentences. Consider (4), which would have to be classified as impersonal if subject were defined exclusively in terms of nominative case and agreement. (*-o* is the "absence-of-agreement" suffix.)

(4) a. Emu   imelo   smysl   zanimat'sja muzykoj.
     him.DAT.M made.N sense.ACC.M to-study   music.INST.F
     'It made sense for him to study music.'

   b. Emu ne imelo smysla   zanimat'sja muzykoj.
      him NEG made sense.GEN to-study   music
      'It didn't make sense for him to study music.'

   c. Emu$_{DAT}$ imelo$_{N.SG}$ smysl$_{ACC.M}$ [t$_N$ zanimat'sja muzykoj]
      (for)him   made   sense   to-study   music

   d. Vas   emu   ubivat' smysla   ne bylo.
      you:ACC him:DAT to-kill sense:GEN NEG was:N
      'It made no sense for him to (try to) kill you.'

But (4) is not impersonal: (i) *smysl* is the direct object of *imeet* and genitive under negation, as in (4b); (ii) *imeet* does not assign dative case; (iii) Russian infinitive clauses have dative subjects (see Babby 1998); (iv) *emu$_{DAT}$* is the left-displaced subject of the infinitive clause; (v) since infinitive clauses have no inherent agreement features, the finite verb cannot agree with them when they are subject, and the same nonagreement suffix *-o* is used here as in impersonal sentences; (vi) the infinitive clause (*emu zanimat'sja muzykoj*) is the theta and syntactic subject of (4); (vii) (4) is thus not impersonal.

(5b) is a personal sentence with no *morphological* nominative subject and no verbal agreement: its theta subject NP is enclosed in square brackets.

(5) S''edeno bylo mnogo sladkogo, i noč'ju.
    'Lots of candy was eaten and at night.'

   a. u odnogo iz bliznecov **zabolel**   [zub]$_{NP.NOM}$
      at one   of twins   began-to-hurt.M   tooth.NOM.M
      'One of the twins got a toothache.'

   b. u oboix bliznecov **zabolelo**   [po zubu]$_{NP.NOM}$
      at both twins   began-to-hurt.N   per tooth.DAT
      'Each of the twins got a toothache (one tooth per twin began to hurt).'

(6) a. Iz   každoj mašiny **vyšli**   [**po pare**]$_{NP}$.
   from each   car   emerged$_{PL}$ per pair.DAT.SG
   'Two people ((lit.) a couple) got out of each car.'
   b. [$_{NP_i.NOM}$ Okolo trex samoletov$_{GEN}$] tol'ko i ždut$_{PL}$ pojavlenija podlodki.
   'About three planes are just waiting for the sub's appearance.'

(7) a. Oni ubeždeny, [$_{CP}$ čto [$_{PP}$ o bytovyx meločax] najdetsja [$_{CP}$ komu$_{DAT}$ [$_{infP}$ t$_N$ pobespokoit'sja t$_{PP}$]]].
   'They are sure that someone will be found to worry about (take care of) the minor details.'
   b. Bol'še vsego ix$_{ACC}$ volnovalo$_N$ [$_{CP}$ počemu ja ne rabotaju].
   '(It) worried them more than anything [$_{CP}$ why I was not working].'
   c. [$_{CP}$Kakoj$_{PRED-INST}$ [budet obščaja tema$_{NOM}$ razgovora$_{GEN}$]] zavisit ot Anny$_{GEN}$.
   '(It) depends on Anna what the general theme of our conversation will be.'
   d. i. Emu$_{DAT}$ predstojalo$_N$ [$_{infP}$ t$_N$ rešit' očen' složnuju problemu$_{ACC}$].
   'He was-going-to-have [to-solve a very complex problem].'
   ii. Emu$_{DAT}$ predstojala$_F$ [$_{NP.NOM}$ interesnaja poezdka$_{NOM.F}$].
   'He was-going-to-have [an interesting trip].'

Zub in (5a) is the morphological, syntactic, and theta subject of *zabolel*; the prepositional quantifier *po* 'each, per' in (5b) assigns quirky dative case to the NP's head *zubu*, but [*po zubu*]$_{NP.NOM}$ is nevertheless the syntactic and theta subject of (5b), just as *zub* is in (5a); see Babby 1985.[6] The plural agreement in (6a) leaves no doubt that *po pare* is the theta subject.[7] The sentences in (7) have CP or infinitive clause theta subjects and are thus not impersonal.[8]

2.4 The Semantics of Impersonal Sentences

This section is concerned with the following question: Do all types of I-Ss in Russian share a common "impersonal meaning"? Russian is important for a theory of I-Ss because it has many more kinds of I-Ss than the familiar Romance and Germanic languages. For example, the I-S in (8) cannot be translated into English by (9); (10) is an additional example.

(8) (Anna sidela za stolom. Rabota šla ploxo, potomu čto v dome naxodilsja postoronij čelovek.) Nakonec—**zadvigalos', zašlepalo** bosymi nogami, **zažurčalo** dušem. (V. Tokareva)

(9) '(Anna was sitting at her desk. Her work wasn't going well because there was a stranger in the house.) *Finally **it moved**, **it began-to-shuffle** with bare feet, **it began to gurgle** with the shower.'[9]

(10) **Gudnulo** xriplo, **poexalo**, **dernulo**, poexalo.
    tooted hoarsely started moving jerked started-moving
    'There was a hoarse tooting sound, (I felt the train) lurch, jerk, lurch.'[10]

The boldface Vs in (8) and (10) are basic personal Vs and normally have nominative subjects; they are being "used impersonally" in (8) and (10), where they have no theta subject and V-*o* denotes nonagreement. These sentences suggest that impersonalization is related to *thetic* semantics (see Kuroda 1972; Babby 1980): the event denoted by V is dissociated from its subject and its semantics shifts from predication to a *thetic judgment*, which focuses narrowly on the perception of the event itself. It is clear from (8) and (10) that impersonalization in Russian is canonically accompanied by the introduction of a human "perceptor" at the level of lexicosemantic structure (see Zubizarreta 1987; Chierchia 1995), which can be realized as a dative adjunct (see (35)). More specifically, the function of impersonalized *zadvigalos'* 'began-to-move', whose lexical semantics does not involve an auditory component, is to assert that Anna perceived sounds of someone or something moving. The closest we can get to conveying this meaning in English is to translate *zadvigalos'* in (8) as '(Finally) there were sounds of someone/something moving (perceived by Anna).'

This type of impersonalization is productive in Russian: any V that denotes an event that can be experienced (heard, seen, felt, etc.) can normally be impersonalized; see the impersonalized adjectives in (11). It is the introduction of a human perceptor/experiencer that explains why it is so common for impersonalized verbs to denote symptoms of pain, illness, physical discomfort, and so on, as in (12).

(11) a. Komnata   dušnaja / ogromnaja.
       room.NOM.F stuffy.F / huge.F (= an inherent property of the room)
       'The room is stuffy / huge.'
   b. V komnate   dušno / *ogromno.
       in room.LOC.F stuffy.N / huge.N
       'People are experiencing the room as stuffy (*huge) on this occasion.'
   c. V komnate   nam   bylo   dušno.
       in room.LOC.F us.DAT was.N stuffy.N (*nam* = adjunct perceptor)
       'It was (too) stuffy for-us in the room.'

(12) a. **Davilo**   grud',   **sžimalo**   viski.
       pressed.N chest.ACC squeezed.N temples.ACC
       '(He) felt a pressing in (his) chest (and) a squeezing in (his) temples.'
   b. Emu   **žglo**$_N$ glaza.
       him:DAT.M burned:N eyes:ACC.PL
       'His eyes were burning.'
   c. **Polomilo**$_N$ pojasnicu$_{ACC.F}$, no skoro bol'$_{NOM.F}$ prošla$_F$.
       '(He) felt pain in the small of his back, but soon the-pain passed.'

d. Voda_{NOM.F} okazalas' takoj xolodnoj, čto **zalomilo**_N zuby_{ACC.PL}.
'The water turned-out (to-be) so cold that (it) made (his) teeth ache.'

If the personal verb is transitive or unergative, impersonalization typically entails deagentification, which makes it possible to construe the event as "unagentive"— that is, as an assertion that the potentially human-controlled event denoted by V is not under human control. This entails a perceptor—a human experiencer, witness, or victim of the out-of-control event—that is either understood (see (12a) and (12c)) or realized overtly, as in (12b) and (13).

(13) a. Emu   **otorvalo**   ruku.
       him.DAT.M tore-off.N arm.ACC.F
       'His arm got torn off.'
    b. V tot mig   emu   **obožglo** šeju.
       at that moment him.DAT.M burned.N neck.ACC.F
       'At that instant he felt his neck burning.'

2.5 Epiphenomenal Impersonals

This section is devoted to a type of I-S that does not have the thetic semantics discussed in section 2.4. The *impersonal passives* in (14) are characterized as epiphenomenal because impersonalization here is the automatic result of passivizing an unergative V, which explains why they do not have impersonal semantics: when an unergative V passivizes, there is no internal argument in its diathesis to *advance* and be projected as subject. Since impersonal passives typically have an understood unspecified human agent they are closer in meaning to Russian *indefinite personal* sentences like (15),[11] which are not impersonal despite the fact that they cannot have an overt subject (note the verb's obligatory *plural* agreement morphology): their $\{i \wedge N\}_1$ is realized as a null pronoun denoting an unidentified human agent (see Mel'čuk 1974, 343).[12]

(14) a. Saat on iki-de tiyatro-dan **çık-ıl-dı**. (Turkish)
       '(lit.) Emerging-was-being-done from the-theatre at 12.' (*çıkmak* 'emerge')
    b. Sonntags **wird** nicht **gearbeitet**. (German)
       'One does not work on Sundays.'

(15) a. Dlja otmetki mesta, gde   vy končili čitat', **upotrebljajut**
       for marking place where you finished to-read use:3.PL
       zakladku.
       bookmark:ACC.F.SG
       'To mark the place where you finished reading one uses a bookmark.'

b. On podal znak$_{ACC}$ oficiantu$_{DAT}$, čtoby **prinesli**$_{3.PL}$ sčet$_{ACC}$.
   he gave sign   to-waiter   C   bring   check
   'He signaled the waiter to bring the check ((lit.) that someone bring the check).'

When a transitive verb passivizes (see (16b)), its direct internal argument $\{j \wedge N\}_2$ externalizes (diathetic 2-to-1 advancement) and projects as the nominative subject. Since unergative Vs have no $\{j \wedge N\}_2$, there is no internal argument to advance to V's dethematized external position, and the resulting passive sentence is impersonal by default, as schematically represented in (16a).

(16) a. *Impersonal passive*
        $\{i \wedge N\}_1 \ldots \{-\wedge V\}_4 > \{-\wedge -\}_1 \ldots \{i \wedge [V - af_{pass}]\}_4$
     b. *Personal passive*
        $\{i \wedge N\}_1 \{j \wedge N\}_2 \ldots \{-\wedge V\}_4 > \{j \wedge N\}_1 \ldots \{i \wedge [V - af_{pass}]\}_4$

2.6 Negated Existential Sentences

Negated existential sentences (NES) like (2b) and (17b) are classified in traditional grammar as impersonal: impersonalization here is assumed to be the secondary effect of negating an affirmative existential sentence (AES), which is personal, as in (17a). Russian AESs have canonical [Locative-adjunct+verb$_{intr}$+subject NP$_{NOM}$] word order and no expletive; the obligatorily postposed nominative subject agrees with the verb. When an AES is negated, (i) the nominative subject is obligatorily assigned genitive case; (ii) verbal agreement becomes impossible and V assumes the nonagreement *-o* form, as in (17b); and (iii) NESs do not have the fixed word of AESs (see Babby 1980 for an explanation). Additional examples are given in (18): the *-sja/-s'* suffix tells us that the Vs in (17) and (18) are derived unaccusatives.

(17) a. [$_{ADV}$ V universitete] **čitalis'**$_{PL}$ kursy$_{NOM.PL.M}$ [$_{PP}$ po ètim disciplinam].
        'There were courses being-given at the university on these subjects.'
     b. [$_{ADV}$ V universitete] **ne čitalos'**$_{N.SG}$ kursov$_{GEN.PL.M}$ [$_{PP}$ po ètim disciplinam].
        'There were no courses being given at the university on these subjects.'

(18) a. [$_{NP}$ Nikakix opytov$_{GEN.PL}$ s bombami] **ne delalos'**$_{N.SG}$.
        'There were no experiments with bombs being-done.'
     b. Anna obnaružila, [$_{CP}$ čto **ne zapisalos'**$_{N.SG}$ [$_{NP}$ ni slova$_{GEN.SG}$]].
        'Anna discovered that not a single word had-been-recorded.'
     c. [$_{ADV}$ V to vremja] [$_{NP}$ nikakix inyx versij$_{GEN.PL}$] **ne vydvigalos'**$_{N.SG}$.
        'At that time there were no other explanations proposed.'

It is routinely assumed that the nominative *subject* in AESs becomes a genitive *object* in the corresponding NES and, therefore, that NESs are impersonal (see Galkina-Fedoruk 1958). The putative impersonalization of NESs is thus viewed as the automatic consequence of negating AESs. While this scenario meets our citeria for epiphenomenal impersonalization, there is virtually no crosslinguistic evidence to support the hypothesis that the introduction of negation can alter a sentence's syntactic relations. We thus need to determine whether the NP_{GEN} in NESs is an object or a genitive subject. In the latter case, NESs have a genitive theta subject and are thus not impersonal.[13]

Consider the following two properties of ESs: (i) ESs are headed by unaccusative Vs, whose argument is initially internal (i.e., $\{j \wedge N\}_2$ where j = 'theme'); (ii) the basic word order of ESs is crosslinguistically V-S, which means that subject in NESs falls within the scope of negation and is thus assigned the genitive of negation in Russian, just as direct objects are. But this fact does not solve our problem: if the genitive NP_j in (17)–(18) remains VP-*internal* when genitive, NESs lack theta subjects and are indeed epiphenomenal impersonals. But if $NP_{j.GEN}$ in NESs is VP-*external*—that is, occupy the same position as the postposed nominative subject in the corresponding AESs (right-adjoined to VP; see McCloskey 1997)—then it is a "genitive subject" and NESs are personal. For example, *gribov* in (2b) would be the genitive theta subject (but not the morphological or syntactic subject) rather than the genitive object of a negated unaccusative verb.

The following facts favor the hypothesis that NESs have genitive subjects: *-sja* affixed to a transitive V *detransitivizes* it, creating a derived unaccusative-V. This means that *kursov* in (17b) cannot be occupying the VP-internal object position and, therefore, (17b) is a personal sentence with a postposed genitive theta subject in the same syntactic position as the postposed nominative subject in the corresponding AES. The only difference is that the postposed subject NP is assigned genitive of negation, which precludes verbal agreement. If negation does not alter grammatical relations and NESs have genitive theta subjects, they are not I-Ss. Note that *partitive genitive* theta subjects in affirmative nonexistential sentences are common in Russian (see Babby 1980).

Sentences like (19) demonstrate that the subject of a negated unergative V can be assigned genitive if it is in the scope of emphatic negation (whose left edge is marked by *ni* or *i* 'even'); see Kozinskij 1983, 21. This provides additional evidence that argument NPs assigned the structural genitive case in Russian do not all occupy the VP-internal, direct object position.

(19) U nas togda [NP i trex   gostej]   ne obedalo.
     at us then   even three.GEN guests.GEN NEG were-dining.N.SG
     'We didn't even have three guests dining with us then.'

2.7 Impersonal Verbs and Impersonal Sentences

We turn now to *impersonal verbs*, which are the lexical extremity of our diathesis-based typology; they are lexical verbs whose projected impersonal syntax is entirely encoded in their diatheses; they cannot be used personally. For example, *tošnit'* 'to experience nausea' has the following criterial properties: (i) it does not select an external theta role or an external categorial argument—its $\{-\wedge-\}_1$ external argument is specified in its *initial* diathesis in (20a); (ii) it is thus always affixed with the nonargeement suffix; (iii) it is transitive; the O-V word order in (20b) is neutral.[14]

(20) a. $\{-\wedge-\}_1$ $\{j\wedge N\}_2$ ... $\{-\wedge\text{tošni-}\}_4$
 b. **Ee tošnilo ot zapaxa tabaka**.
   her.ACC nauseated.N.SG from smell of-tobacco.GEN
   'She felt nauseated from the smell of tobacco.'
 c. *Ona$_{\text{NOM.F}}$ tošnilas'$_{\text{F}}$ ot zapaxa tabaka.
   'She became-nauseated from the smell of tobacco.'
 d. *Ee$_{\text{ACC}}$ tošnil$_{\text{M}}$ zapax$_{\text{NOM.M}}$ tabaka.
   'The smell of tobacco nauseated her.'

The external argument $\{-\wedge-\}_1$ in (20a) encodes the information that $\{j\wedge N\}_2$ cannot externalize (i.e., $\{j\wedge N\}_2 > \{j\wedge N\}_1$) and project as subject. It must remain in situ in *tošnit'*'s diathesis and project to syntax as its direct object (*ee* in (20b)): $\{\{-\wedge-\}_1$ $\{j\wedge N\}_2 ...\} \Rightarrow [_{vP}\ [_{v'}\ [_{VP}\ NP_{j.ACC}\ [_{v'}\ ...\ ]]]]$. This is because $\{-\wedge-\}_1$ does not provide the diathesis-level analogue of a "landing site" for externalization (cf. *korčit'* below). Thus the speaker has no options: the sentence that *tošnit'* heads must be impersonal.

The diathesis-based representation of A-S neatly captures the crucial difference between transitive impersonal verbs like *tošnit'* and basic unaccusative Vs, which have *identical theta tiers*: $\{-_1\ j_2\ -_3\ -_4\}$. Unlike *tošnit'*, unaccusative Vs project personal syntax despite the fact that, like *tošnit'*, they do not select an external theta role and have an initial $\{j\wedge N\}_2$. To see how this works, let us first compare the formal differences of *tošnit'* and *korčit'* 'to writhe', which also have the identical set of theta roles, but, as (21) shows, *korčit'* has a radically different morphosyntactic realization. Since the morphosyntactic differences between *tošnit'* and *korčit'* are entirely unpredictable in terms of their lexical semantics and theta roles, these differences must be encoded in the categorial tier of the verbs' diatheses. Compare (20) to (21): the internal $\{j\wedge N\}_2$ argument of *korčit'*, but not *tošnit'*, can *optionally* externalize and project as the nominative subject, as in (21c).

(21) a. **Ee korčilo ot boli**. (= (20b))
   her.ACC writhed.N.SG from pain
   'She was writhing in pain.'

b. *Ee$_{ACC}$ korčila$_F$ bol'$_{NOM.F.}$ (= (20d))
     'Pain made her writhe.'
  c. Ona$_{NOM.F}$ **korčilas'**$_F$ **ot boli**. (cf. *(20c))
     'She was writhing in pain.'

These differences are captured in terms of the diathetic representations in (22), where the external categorial selection of the three V-types differs.

(22) a. *Tošnit'*
       $\{-\wedge-\}_1$ $\{j\wedge N\}_2$ ... $\{-\wedge V\}_4$
   b. *Korčit'*
       $\{-\wedge(N)\}_1$ $\{j\wedge N\}_2$ ... $\{-\wedge V\}_4$
   c. *Unaccusative*
       $\{-\wedge N\}_1$ $\{j\wedge-\}_2$ ... $\{-\wedge V\}_4$

The diathesis in (22a) encodes the information that *tošnit'* has no external position to project, which predicts that $\{j\wedge N\}_2$ cannot become subject. *Korčit'* too has no external theta role, but it has an optional external **N**, which, if selected, provides a diathetic "landing site" for $\{j\wedge N\}_2$ to advance to and project as subject. *Korčit'sja* is a derived unaccusative V: when *-sja* is affixed to transitive Vs, it deletes N_2, which requires **j** in derived $\{j\wedge-\}_2$ to externalize (relink to $\{-\wedge N\}_1$). That is, $\{\{-\wedge N\}_1 \{j\wedge N\}_2 \ldots \{-\wedge V\}_4\} > \{\{-\wedge N\}_1 \{j\wedge-\}_2 \ldots \{-\wedge V\text{-sja}\}\}_4 > \{\{j\wedge N\}_1 \{-\wedge-\}_2 \ldots \{-\wedge V\text{-sja}\}_4$. If the optional external **N** in (22b) is not selected, *korčit'* projects the same impersonal morphosyntax as *tošnit'*. The obligatory unlinked external **N** in the diathesis of basic unaccusative verbs in (22c) requires that **j** advance to initial $\{-\wedge N\}_1$, and $\{j\wedge N\}_1$ projects as the sentence's subject (see section 2.6). The parenthesis notation in (22b) thus tells us that *korčit'*-type Vs project either I-Ss or personal unaccusative sentences. Our formalism correctly predicts a fourth type of verb, whose initial diathesis is (23a): **j** must relink to $\{-\wedge N\}_1$ since unlinked N_1 in Russian does not project to syntax. But this means that this class of verbs must always be affixed with *-sja* (or *-en-*), which delete N_2, freeing **j** to link to initial $\{-\wedge N\}_1$. For example, see *atrofirovat'sja* (*atrofirovat'*) 'to atrophy' in (23b).

(23) a. $\{-\wedge N\}_1$ $\{j\wedge N\}_2$ ... $\{-\wedge V\}_4$
   b. Ruka u nego atrofirovalas' (atrofirovana).
      arm at him atrophied   (has atrophied)
      'His arm atrophied (has atrophied).'

2.7.1 Other Types of Impersonal Vs in Russian

There are thousands of personal verbs in Russian that have idiomatic impersonal uses, which must be entered in each V's lexical entry as a separate diathesis; see (24), whose derivation is identical to that of *korčit'* (the basic meaning of *zatjanut'* is 'to tighten').

(24) a. Ranu_ACC.F zatjanulo_N.
      'The-wound healed (a scab formed).'
    b. Rana_NOM.F zatjanulas'_F.
      'The-wound healed (a scab formed).'

(25) a. Bol'nogo_ACC.M proneslo_N.
      'The-patient had diarrhea.' (*pronesti* 'carry through')
    b. Tormoza_ACC.PL zaelo / zaklinilo_N.SG.
      'The-brakes jammed.' (*zaest'* 'devour', *zaklinit'* 'to-wedge')
    c. Ej   vsegda vezet.
      her.DAT always is-lucky
      'She is always lucky.' (*vezti* 'to convey, drive')

2.8 Infinitive Impersonal Sentences

In section 2.7 we saw the *lexical* end of the I-S typology. In this section we look at infinitival impersonals, which appear to be at the opposite, lexically unconstrained end of the spectrum: no aspect of this type of sentence needs to be encoded in V's diathesis. There are two types of infinitive sentences in Russian, the modal-infinitive sentences in (26) and existential-infinitive sentences; we will be concerned here only with the former.[15]

(26) a. Emu   ne rešit'   ètoj zadači.
      him.DAT.M NEG to-decide this problem.GEN
      'He won't be able to solve this problem.'
    b. Emu   bylo ne rešit'   ètoj zadači.
      him.DAT.M was.N NEG to-decide this problem.GEN
      'He was not able to solve this problem.'
    c. Vremja   ne ostanovit'.
      time:ACC NEG to-stop
      'One cannot stop time.'
    d. Teper' nam_DAT platit' ego dolgi_ACC.
      now   us   to-pay his debts
      'Now we have to pay his debts.'
    e. (Generala ona uvidela izdaleka.) Lico_ACC v temnote bylo_N ne različit'.
      '(She saw the general from afar.) It wasn't possible to see his face in the dark.'
    f. i. [_PP Ot vsex nas] prestupniku   bylo ne ujti.
              from all of-us criminal:DAT.M was:N NEG to-escape
              'The-criminal wasn't able to-escape from all of us.'
       ii. *[_PP Ot vsex nas] prestupnik_NOM.M byl_M ne ujti.

Since infinitive clauses in Russian have dative theta subjects (see Babby 1998; Perlmutter and Moore 2002) and modal-infinitive sentences do not have *thetic* semantics, we need to explore the possibility that sentences like (26) are personal sentences with dative subjects. More specifically, assuming that *emu* is the displaced dative subject of the infinitive *rešit'* in (26a), the question is whether *emu* becomes the derived dative subject of the matrix clause (see (26f)). If it does, modal infinitives are not impersonal. There are two related possibilities: if *emu* is moved by scrambling or the need to satisfy T's EPP requirement, it does not become the matrix theta subject and modal-infinitive sentences are impersonal.

There is, however, a problem with the scrambling/EPP analysis. Given that infinitives are not inherently modal, it does not account for the *deontic modal meaning* of the sentences in (26). That fact suggests another analysis: the modal meaning in (26) is a function of the modal projection mP, whose head m(odal) is either null or overt (e.g., m is lexicalized by uninflected *nel'zja* 'it-is-impossible', *nado* 'have to', the modal enclitic *by*, etc.) and takes an infinitive clause complement. If mP has its own dative subject, for which there is some evidence[16] (see Babby 1998, 2009, chap. 4), modal-infinitive sentences are personal—that is, they have dative theta subjects, which bind the infinitive clause's PRO$_{DAT}$ subject. This means that the overt dative NPs in (26) are m's subject in spec-mP and, therefore, there are no lexically unconstrained I-Ss in Russian. This is not an unwelcome outcome given that the principal meaning of sentences like (26) is *modal* rather than the impersonal *thetic* semantics identified in section 2.4. This analysis is also viable if it can be demonstrated that the uninflected null and overt modal predicators like *nel'zja*, *nado*, and *by* in Russian are formally modal auxiliaries, which "inherit" the external argument of its complement, making it their own external argument (cf. the inflected modal auxiliaries *dolžen* 'must', *moč* 'able') (see Williams's 1994 account of auxiliary-verb external-argument inheritance). I leave this task to future research.

2.9 Adversity Impersonal Sentences

The adversity impersonal (A-I) is a highly productive type of Russian I-S. See the examples in (1) and (27)–(32), as well as Babby 1994 and 1996.

(27) a. Menja na mgnoven'e **oslepila molnija**.
me:ACC for a moment blinded:F lightning:NOM.F
b. Menja na mgnoven'e **oslepilo molniej**. (A-I)
me:ACC for a moment blinded:N lightning:INST.F
'Lightning blinded me for a moment.'

(28) a. Palec **priščemilo** dver'ju. (A-I)
finger:ACC.M jammed:N door.INST.F
'(His) finger got jammed in the door.'

b. On **priščemil** sebe palec dver'ju.
he.NOM.M jammed.M himself.DAT finger.ACC door.INST
'He jammed his finger in the door.'

(29) Vorota priotkryli i my očutilis' vnutri, no vual' moej.
gates:ACC opened:PL and we found-ourselves inside but veil:ACC of my
šljapy zaščemili i menja **potaščilo** nazad.
hat caught:PL and me:ACC dragged:N back
'(Unidentified agent) opened the-gates and we found-ourselves inside, but they (the gates) snagged the-veil of my hat and I got-dragged back.'

(30) a. (On popal pod gruzovik$_M$ i) ego$_{ACC.M}$ **ubilo**$_N$ nasmert'.
'(He fell under a truck and) he got killed dead.'
b. Pod utro byla$_F$ groza$_{NOM.F}$ i **slomalo**$_N$ (?slomala$_F$) derevo$_{ACC.N}$ v sadu.
'Toward morning there was a storm and a tree in the garden got smashed.'

I will focus on the formal and semantic restrictions on the personal verbs used in A-Is, which are the polar opposite of I-Ss headed by impersonal verbs like *tošnit'*.

The verbs used in A-Is do not have to stipulate this fact in their diatheses since it can be inferred from other, independent properties: there is nothing idiomatic about A-Is (see section 2.7). The head of an A-I must be a transitive verb denoting a real-world "physical" event that can be controlled by a human agent, but can also occur without the involvement of a human agent—for example, *povalit'* 'knock down', *unesti* 'carry away', *ubit'* 'kill', *ranit'* 'wound', *oprokinut'* 'knock over', *pridavit'* 'crush', *zasypat'* 'cover (with)', *trjasti* 'shake'. A-Is cannot be headed by verbs denoting mental and other exclusively human activities (*emu* in (31a) is the dative adjunct human perceptor discussed in section 2.4; the 3rd-PL verbal suffix in (31c) ensures that it is construed as having a human agent). See (15):

(31) a. Emu otrezalo nogu.
him.DAT.M severed.N leg.ACC.F
'His leg was severed (not by a human agent).'
b. *Emu amputirovalo nogu.
'He got his leg amputated off.'
c. U nego amputirovali nogu.
'His leg was amputated.'

The agent optionality of A-Is is encoded by the optionality of V's agent **i** role in the diathesis of potential A-I personal verbs: $\{(i) \wedge N\}_1$. Elimination of V's external **N** is associated with affixation of the nonagreement suffix -*o*; see Babby 1994, 1996.

The A-I is a specialized construction whose function is to assert that a potentially agent-controlled event is not controlled (i.e., deagentified), which can be construed as denoting a "natural event" (*Komnatu*$_{ACC.F}$ *zalilo*$_N$ *svetom*$_{INST.M}$ 'Light flooded/filled the room'), but is typically construed as an event that is out of control and therefore dangerous vis-à-vis humans. The Russian verbal paradigm thus has the specialized unspecified/unspecifiable human-agentive construction in (32a), the specialized unagentive construction (A-I) in (33b), and the agent-neutral construction in (32c).

(32) a. Nedaleko ot berega **perevernuli**$_{PL}$ lodku$_{ACC.F.SG}$.
'Not far from shore (someone/people) turned a boat over.'
b. Nedaleko ot berega lodku$_{ACC.F.SG}$ **perevernulo**$_{N.SG}$.
'Not far from shore a boat overturned/capsized.'
c. Nedaleko ot berega lodka$_{NOM.F.SG}$ **perevernulas'**$_{F.SG}$.
'Not far from shore a boat turned over.'

2.10 Impersonal Uses of -sja and -en- in Russian

While Russian does not have a productive impersonal passive (see section 2.5), it has a family of lexically restricted constructions that qualify as impersonal passives. (33) demonstrates that labile[17] verbs of communication license impersonal passives: (i) the distribution of -*sja* (with imperfective verbs) and -*en*- (with perfective verbs) conforms to the passive pattern; (ii) accusative direct objects are not possible; and (iii) the external argument (agent) is dethematized (but normally not realized as a *by*-phrase).[18]

(33) a. Ob   ètom   vo vsex učebnikax   **napisano**.
about this.LOC in all textbooks.LOC.M.PL written.N.SG
'This has been written about in all the textbooks.'
b. V pesne **rasskazyvalos'** o   razbojnike.
in song told   about robber
'(lit.) In the song was told about a robber = The song was about a robber.'
c. On dejstvoval, kak bylo **obgovoreno**.
'He acted as had-been discussed.'
d. V letopisi **ukazyvaetsja** na to, čto...
'(It) is pointed out in the chronicle that...'
e. Gde **govoritsja** o pagode.
'Where does it talk about the weather / where is the weather discussed?'

The sentences in (34) appear to be epiphenomenal impersonal passives of ditransitive verbs with the neutral word order: V-NP$_{DAT}$-infinitive-clause. NP$_{DAT}$, which controls the infinitive clause's null subject, is V's quirky-case direct object ({j ^ N$_{DAT}$}$_2$) and thus cannot be replaced by nominative case under passivization, as in (34c) (cf. (26f)). Since passivization's primary function is to dethematize V's external argument, not to promote its direct object to subject (see (33)), we are faced with a familiar problem. Is the dative direct object in "active" (34a) the dative subject or object in the corresponding passive sentence in (34b) (i.e., $\{j \wedge N_{DAT}\}_1$), or is (34b) an impersonal passive (i.e., $\{j \wedge N_{DAT}\}_2$ remains the direct object)? Subject-sensitive diagnostics indicate that the dative direct object does not become the dative theta subject $\{j \wedge N_{DAT}\}_1$ under passivization and sentences like (34b) are epiphenomenal I-Ss. The dative object moves to the main clause's left edge to check its EPP feature in (34b), which does not make it the theta or morphological subject.

(34) a. Pozvoljali **emu** [PRO$_i$ ryt'sja v biblioteke]. (active)
allowed.PL him.DAT to-dig in library
'(Unspecified person(s)) allowed him to-root-around in the library.'
b. **Emu** pozvoljalos' / bylo pozvoleno ryt'sja v biblioteke. (passive)
him.DAT.M was-allowed.N to-dig in library
'He was allowed to-root-around in the library.'
c. *On pozvoljalsja / byl pozvolen ryt'sja v biblioteke.
he.NOM.M was-allowed.M to dig in the library.'
d. **Mne**$_{DAT}$ poručeno / zapreščeno / razrešalos' / rekomendovalos' èto obsuždat'.
'I was ordered / forbidden / allowed / recommended to discuss this.'
e. **Mne**$_{DAT}$ predpisano (rukovodstvom$_{INST}$) [èto s vami obsuždat'].
'I ((lit.) me) was ordered (by the administration) [to discuss this with you].'

The productive impersonal construction illustrated in (35) is formed from intransitive and labile verbs that denote human-specific activities: -*sja* dethematizes V's external **i** and the nonagreement -*o* suffix is responsible for the deletion of its unlinked external N_1: $\{i \wedge N\}_1 + $-sja$ > ($- $\wedge N\}_1 + $-o$ > \{$- $\wedge$ -$\}_1$. According to Šeljakin 1993, 253, this construction denotes an event that proceeds without the active will of a (human) subject, and almost any human-specific intransitive verb can be affixed with -*sja* in the derivation of sentences with this meaning. It is usually negated: *Emu*$_{DAT}$ *ne xodilos'* 'He didn't feel like walking' (*xodit'* 'walk'), *ne guljalos'* (*guljat'* 'stroll'), *ne spitsja* (*spat'* 'sleep'), *ne igraetsja* (*igrat'* 'play'), and so on. The animate/human dative here is the adjunct "perceptor," introduced as a result of impersonalization to denote the experiencer (affected human) (see section 2.4; Trofimov 1957, 148), which is completely consonant with the thetic meaning of Russian impersonal sentences.[19]

(35) a. Emu ne **stojalos'** (ne **ležalos'** v posteli).
'He didn't feel like standing (lying in bed).' (*stojat'* 'stand', *ležat'* 'lie')
b. (Nikita vzjal v ruki kusok xleba, xotel otkusit', no ne mog.) Ne **kusalos'** i ne **glotalos'**. (*kusat'* 'bite', *glotat'* 'swallow') (Tokareva)
'(Nikita took a piece of bread and wanted to take a bite but couldn't.) He couldn't chew or swallow.'

c. Nikita zanimaetsja tem, o čem (emu) vsegda **mečtalos'**.
'Nikita is doing what he always dreamed about.' (*mečtat'* 'to dream')
d. Ej_DAT ne **tancuetsja**.
'She doesn't feel like dancing.'
e. V mae ne **siditsja** doma.
'One doesn't feel like sitting home in May.' (*sidet'* 'sit')
f. Mne_DAT **dremletsja**.
'I feel sleepy.' (*dremat'* 'to nap')

The sentences in (36) are impersonal, but not passive (-*sja* is not used to passivize perfective verbs); they are formed from basic transitive verbs. Since in this type of I-S both the external and the direct internal arguments are both eliminated from V's diathesis, I assume that the Vs used in this construction are labile: their optional internal argument is not selected and affixes -*sja* and -*o* work in tandem just as in (35), eliminating V's external argument. Its semantic function is quintessentially thetic, focusing narrowly on the event denoted by V, which entails dissociation of both arguments in V's diathesis; adjunct human perceptors are not as common as in (35) (see *u nee* 'at her' in (36c) and *u nego* in (36d)).

(36) a. (My vygnali stado na baxčú, gde s dovoennoj pory) ne **paxalos'** i ne **sejalos'**.
'(We drove the herd onto a field where since before the war) there had been no plowing or sowing done.' (*paxat'* 'to plow,' *sejat'* 'to sow') (A. Leonov)
b. Sam ne veril, kogda **napisalos'**. (Trusinovskaja)
'I didn't believe (it) myself when it (the play) got-written_N.'
c. (Ona pytalas' **ob"edinit'** ètix dvux v odnu kompaniju, no) **u nee ne ob"edinilos'**. (*ob"edinit'* 'to unite') (Tokareva)
'(She tried to unite these two (people) into a couple (= get them together)), but it didn't work out ((lit.) at her uniting did not occur).'
d. V golove **zakružilos'**. V živote u nego **sžalos'**.
'(His) head began to spin (in-head began-to-spin). His stomach tightened ((lit.) in his stomach there was contracting).'

2.11 The USO Construction

The highly productive type of colloquial I-S in (37) is important because it appears initially to challenge my main hypothesis that the typology of I-Ss should be based on predicate argument structure.[20]

(37) a. U nego   s   nej   ser'ezno.
       at him.GEN.M with her.INST.F serious.N
       'He is serious about her.'

b. U tebja naprjaženno s intellektom.
   at you strained.N with intellect
   'You're not too bright.'
c. U nego ploxo s pamjat'ju (s nervami).'
   at him bad:N with memory with nerves
   'He is having touble with his memory (nerves).'
d. U nego točno s golovoj ne v porjadke.
   at him precisely with head NEG in order
   'He is not quite right in the head.'
e. U nix s ljubovnymi delami ne skladyvalos'.
   at them with love matters/affairs NEG take-shape:N.SG
   'Their love lives were not going well.'
f. U nee bylo nevažno so zdorov'em.
   at her was:N not-well.N with health
   'Her health was not very good.'
g. U nas tugo s gorjučim.
   'We are hard-pressed for fuel.'
h. V kvartire u nego s mebel'ju nebogato.
   in apartment at him with furniture not-rich
   'He doesn't have much in the way of furniture in his apartment.'

USO sentences constitute evidence that there are I-Ss that cannot be represented in terms of a V's A-S alone: the predicate adjectives and other predicators (e.g., *ne skladyvalos'* 'not take-shape' in (37e)) that head it do not encode this construction in their diatheses; neither do the two prepositions, *u*+genitive and *s*+instrumental, that are an integral part of USO I-Ss. The fact that the USOs in (37) exist in colloquial Russian but not in other languages can be captured in diathesis-based theory as follows. They are represented in the lexicon of Russian as an impersonal construction, which can be conceived of as an "abstract" diathesis that is not "headed" by any specific lexical item or suffix (V = a semantically appropriate predicator)—for example,[21]

(38) $\{-\wedge -\}_1 \ \{j\wedge [u \ N_{GEN}]\}_2 \ \{k\wedge [s \ N_{INST}]\}_3 \ \{-\wedge V\text{-}o\}_4$

2.12 Conclusions

I have argued that the analysis and classification of I-Ss in Russian and, I assume, other languages, should be based on a typology of diatheses that project I-S. The difference between *impersonal verbs* like *tošnit'* and rogue impersonal predicators like *nakureno* (*V komnate nakureno* 'The-room is all smoked up'; see note 18), which are at one end of our typology, and the USO construction, which is at the opposite end, is a matter of degree, not kind. I have argued that all types of Russian I-Ss require some degree of lexical specification. This hypothesis depends on argumentation that a number of productive constructions assumed in traditional grammar to be impersonal actually have oblique-case theta subjects and lack the thetic semantics of true impersonals, and, therefore, are personal (see the modal-infinitive sentences in section 2.8 and the negated existential sentences in section 2.6).

Notes

1. Readers familiar with Relational Grammar will notice that many of RG's insights and mechanisms have been incorporated into the diathesis theory on which this analysis of impersonal sentences is based, but the action has been shifted from syntax to argument structure.

2. The neuter singular suffix -*o* in (1b) is used when there is no nominative subject for the verb to agree with (see Babby 1996; Lavine 2000). ACC = accusative, ADV = adverb, DAT = dative, F = feminine, GEN = genitive, infP = infinitive clause, INST = instrumental case, LOC = locative expression, M = masculine, N = neuter, NEG = negation, NOM = nominative, PI = predicate instrumental case, PL = plural, PRED = predicate, SG = singular. (1b) is not an *impersonal passive* (see Trask 1993).

3. Unergative Vs are monadic verbs whose argument is external in A-S and syntax. Unaccusative Vs are monadic verbs whose argument is internal in A-S and external in syntax. See Harves 2002.

4. Braces (curly brackets) indicate arguments; the subnumber "1" denotes the leftmost, "external" argument in V's diathesis, which projects to syntax as its (VP-external) subject; read "^" as "is linked to in V's diathesis"; "⇒" denotes projection from diathesis to syntax; ">" denotes a diathetic operation; and "→" is a syntactic operation. The subnumbers have an expository function only.

5. The Russian grammatical tradition recognizes *logical subject* (*sub"ekt*), which is in boldface in the following example: **U nego** *zabolela golova* (*zastučalo v golove*) '(lit.) **at him** began-to-hurt the-head$_{NOM}$ = his head began to hurt (began-to-knock in the head$_{LOC}$ = his head began to pound)' (see Kokorina 1979). This example shows that the logical subject may be neither the theta, syntactic, nor morphological subject: *u nego* is an adjunct from the point of view of argument structure and syntax. While logical subject corresponds to an important intuition about the organization of Russian sentences, it is still poorly defined and will play no role in what follows. See Williams 2003, 81; Lavine 2000, 51–52; Napoli 1989, 8.

6. The nominative case assigned to subject NP in (5b) and (6) is "abstract" nominative case and the subject NP thus involves a *mismatch* between the NP's *abstract* nominative case and its head's quirky *morphological* case, which is assigned by the attributive prepositional quantifier (see Babby 1987).

7. Only subject NPs agree with the verb in Russian.

8. [$_{CP}$ *komu*$_{DAT}$ [$_{infP}$ t$_N$ *pobespokoit'sja* [$_{PP}$ *o bytovyx melločax*]]] is the subject of *najdetsja*; see Babby 1999.

9. The following translation is a close approximation of (8)'s meaning: 'Finally she heard the sound of someone moving, of bare feet shuffling, of a shower's gurgling'.

10. *Train* in Russian is masculine (*poezd*); the *-o* suffix indicates nonagreement, which eliminates the possibility of pro-drop in (10).

11. For discussion and bibliography, see Papangeli 2004, 19. Keenan 1976 classifies these sentences as impersonal. Russian grammars classify them as "indefinite personal sentences."

12. We know the sentences in (15) have a null theta subject because it antecedes reflexives and controls nonfinite complements (see Babby 2009, chap. 3).

13. The direct object of negated transitive Vs can be genitive instead of accusative, but there is no evidence that 2-to-3 demotion occurs; see (26a).

14. Since *tošnit'* has an accusative direct object but does not assign an external theta role, it has precisely the properties that Burzio's Generalization predicts do not coexist. If there were a null expletive in (20b), it would satisfy the sentence's EPP requirement and the direct object's left displacement, which creates the neutral word order, would be unmotivated.

15. Compare *Ot nix nikuda ne det'sja* 'You can't hide from them' (modal) ∼ *Ot nix nekuda det'sja* 'There is no place to hide from them' (existential). See Babby 1999 for an analysis of the latter.

16. Sentences like the following provide evidence that the dative subject in modal-infinitive sentences is an argument of the modal head m (note that *potušiš'* 'extinguish' in (i) is a *finite* form of the verb with a modal interpretation, not an infinitive):

(i) Ploščad'   požara byla takoj,   čto **odnomu**   ne potušiš'.
    area:NOM.F fire:GEN was:F such.PL.F that alone:DAT.M NEG extinguish.2ND.SG
    'The fire was so big that you (=one) could not put it out alone.' (*Izvestija* 7, no. 23 (1981): 6)

Assuming that the modal meaning of finite *ne potušiš'* 'is not able to extinguish' is to be explained by head moving the lexical verbal head to the head of mP, the dative case of *odnomu* in (i) can be explained as agreement with the putative (null) dative subject in spec-mP. When *potušiš'* has simple future (nonmodal) meaning, *odin* is predictably nominative, not dative, since the mP is not present. The mP in (i) can be schematically represented as $[_{mP} nP_{i.DAT.M.SG} [_{m'} \textbf{[odnomu}_{DAT.M.SG}] [_{m'} [_m \textit{ne potušiš'}] [_{VP} \ldots t \ldots]]]$.

17. A "labile" verb can be used either transitively or intransitively (e.g., *He loves to eat* ∼ *He loves to eat knishes*).

18. Cf. i. Ob   ètoj istorii ne zabyvalos'.
           about this incident NEG forgot+o+sja
       ii. Ob   ètoj istorii ne bylo zabyto
           about this incident NEG was forgot+t (= en)+o
           'This incident was not forgotten about ((lit.) about this incident was not forgotten).'

Zaplačeno 'paid for' in *Za vse*$_{ACC}$ *uže zaplačeno* '(lit.) For everything has already been paid' has been reanalyzed as an impersonal predicator and is thus not a productively formed impersonal *-en-o* participle of *zaplatit'* 'to pay'. See also impersonal *nakureno* 'all smoked up'.

19. In other words, *Emu ne spitsja* is not a "transform" of *On ne spit* (i.e., *on* → *emu*): *on*$_{NOM}$ is an argument of *spit*, whereas *emu*$_{DAT}$ is an adjunct licensed by the impersonalization of the diathesis that projects *On spit* and the peripheralization of V's arguments associated with thetic semantics.

20. Adjectives affixed with -*o* in (37) are impersonal predicate adjectives, not the homophonous adverbs. I refer to this type of I-S as the USO construction since the prepositions *u* and *s* are part of this construction and -*o* is the nonagreement suffix.

21. See Goldberg 1995 for discussion of AS in the Construction Grammar framework.

References

Babby, L. H. 1980. *Existential sentences and negation in Russian*. Ann Arbor, MI: Karoma.

Babby, L. H. 1985. Prepositional quantifiers and the direct case condition in Russian. In M. Flyer and R. Brecht, eds., *Issues in Russian morphosyntax*, 91–117. Los Angeles: UCLA Slavic Studies.

Babby, L. H. 1987. Case, prequantifiers, and discontinuous agreement in Russian. *Natural Language and Linguistic Theory* 5:91–138.

Babby, L. H. 1994. A theta-theoretic analysis of adversity impersonal sentences in Russian. In S. Avrutin and S. Franks, eds., *Formal Approaches to Slavic Linguistics 2: The MIT meeting (1993)*, 25–67. Ann Arbor: Michigan Slavic Publications.

Babby, L. H. 1996. Inflectional morphology and theta role suppression. In J. Toman, ed., *Formal Approaches to Slavic Linguistics 3: The Maryland Meeting (1994)*, 1–34. Ann Arbor: Michigan Slavic Publications.

Babby, L. H. 1998. Subject control as direct predication: Evidence from Russian. In Ž. Bošković, S. Franks, and S. Snyder, eds., *Annual Workshop on Formal Approaches to Slavic Linguistics: The Connecticut Meeting (1997)*, 17–37. Ann Arbor: Michigan Slavic Publications.

Babby, L. H. 1999. Infinitival existential sentences in Russian. In T. H. King and I. Sekirana, eds., *Formal Approaches to Slavic Linguistics 8*, 1–21. Ann Arbor: Michigan Slavic Publications.

Babby, L. H. 2009. *The syntax of argument structure*. Cambridge: Cambridge University Press.

Chierchia, G. 1995. The variability of impersonal subjects. In E. Bach, E. Jelinek, A. Kratzer, and B. H. Partee, eds., *Quantification in natural languages*, 107–143. Dordrecht: Kluwer.

Galkina-Fedoruk, E. M. 1958. Bezličnye predloženija v sovremennom russkom jazyke. Izdatel'stvo Moskovskogo Universiteta.

Goldberg, A. 1995. *A construction grammar approach to argument structure*. Chicago: University of Chicago Press.

Harves, S. 2002. Unaccusative syntax in Russian. Doctoral dissertation, Princeton University.

Keenan, E. 1976. Towards a universal definition of "subject." In C. Li, ed., *Subject and topic*, 303–333. New York: Academic Press.

Kokorina, S. I. 1979. O semantičeskom sub"ekte i osobennostjax ego vyraženija v russkom jazyke. Izdatel'stvo Moskovskogo Universiteta.

Kozinskij, I. Š. 1983. O kategorii "podležaščee" v russkom jazyke. Moskva: Institut Russkogo Jazyka AN SSSR.

Kuroda, S. Y. 1972. The categorical and thetic judgement (evidence from Japanese syntax). *Foundations of Language* 2:153–185.

Lavine, J. A. 2000. Topics in the syntax of nonagreeing predicates in Slavic. Doctoral dissertation, Princeton University.

McCloskey, J. 1997. Subjecthood and subject position. In L. Haegeman, ed., *Elements of grammar: Handbook of generative syntax*, 197–235. Dordrecht: Kluwer.

Mel'čuk, I. A. 1974. O sintaksičeskom nule. In A. A. Xolodovič, ed., *Tipologija passivnyx konstrukcij: diatezy i zalogi*, 343–361. Leningrad: Nauka.

Napoli, D. J. 1989. *Predication theory*. Cambridge: Cambridge University Press.

Papangeli, D. 2004. *The morphosyntax of argument realization: Greek argument structure and the lexicon-syntax interface*. Utrecht: LOT Publishers.

Perlmutter, D. 1983. Personal vs. impersonal constructions. *Natural Language and Linguistic Theory* 1:141–200.

Perlmutter, D., and J. Moore. 2002. Language-internal explanation: The distribution of Russian impersonals. *Language* 78:619–650.

Rothstein, S. D. 1985. *The syntactic forms of predication*. Bloomington: Indiana University Linguistics Club.

Rothstein, S. D. 2001. *Predicates and their subjects*. Dordrecht: Kluwer.

Šeljakin, M. A. 1993. Spravočnik po russkoj grammatike. Moskva: "Russkij Jazyk."

Trask, R. L. 1993. *A dictionary of grammatical terms in linguistics*. New York: Routledge.

Trofimov, V. A. 1957. Sovremennyj russkij literaturnyj jazyk: morfologija. Izd. LGU.

Williams, E. 1994. *Thematic structure in syntax*. Cambridge, MA: MIT Press.

Williams, E. 2003. *Representation theory*. Cambridge, MA: MIT Press.

Zubizarreta, M. L. 1987. *Levels of representation in the lexicon and in the syntax*. Dordrecht: Foris.

3 Romanian as a Two-Gender Language

Nicoleta Bateman and Maria Polinsky

3.1 Introduction

The goal of this chapter is to argue that Romanian has two genders, rather than three as traditionally proposed, and in doing so to provide a comprehensive synchronic account of gender assignment in Romanian. The main argument is that gender categories can be predicted in Romanian based on semantic and formal features, and therefore that nominal classes need not be specified in the lexicon. Rather, within each number there is a binary distinction of gender classes that, once determined, lead to straightforward categorization of nouns.

Following Charles Hockett (1958, 231), "Genders are classes of nouns [systematically] reflected in the behavior of associated words."[1] This "behavior" is manifested in *agreement*, which we define as covariation between the form of the trigger (noun) and the form of the target (such as adjectives and articles). Thus, particular noun forms will co-occur with particular attributive and predicate adjective forms in the singular and in the plural.

Gender categorization and assignment is a fascinating phenomenon that brings together morphology, phonology, syntax, and simple semantic structures, so understanding categorization in a particular language offers us a glimpse into several levels of linguistic representation. Gender assignment provides a window into lexical access (which is one of the primary motivations for categorization—see Levelt 1989) and morphosyntactic integration, where the knowledge of a relevant gender contributes to reference identification and tracking. Romanian is particularly intriguing because of its complicated gender system, which stands out among the systems of the other Romance languages. Be it the result of the conservative preservation of the Latin three-gender system or the innovation of a third gender under heavy Slavic influence, Romanian is often cited as the unique three-gender language of the Romance group.

This chapter investigates this uniqueness further and brings Romanian more in line with the other, more mundane two-gender languages of its group. Specifically, we propose that Romanian has two noun classes (genders) in the singular and in the plural, but the actual division of nouns into classes in the singular is different from their division into classes in the plural. This lack of class isomorphism between the singular and the plural is the main reason why many researchers have analyzed Romanian as a three-gender system. Once we can get past the assumption that such an isomorphism is necessary, the two-gender composition of Romanian becomes much more apparent. As in many other Indo-European languages, Romance languages in particular, gender assignment is determined semantically for a small subset of nouns and by formal properties of the nouns themselves, namely noun endings, for the majority of the nominal lexicon. Since our analysis is synchronic in nature and addresses the current state of Romanian, we will not offer any new insights into the preservation of the Latin gender system or the role of the Slavic superstrate (beyond a short discussion of the existing analyses). These issues are beyond the scope of this chapter and must be addressed independently.

The chapter is organized as follows. In section 3.2 we introduce the relevant data, which lead to the main questions concerning the analysis of Romanian gender addressed in this chapter. In section 3.3 we present and analyze the principal existing analyses of Romanian gender. While we disagree with these analyses, each offers important insights, and our own proposal builds on those insights. Section 3.4 outlines our proposal for analyzing Romanian as a two-gender system, showing that such a system can account for the Romanian patterns in a more straightforward manner. Section 3.5 provides an evaluation metric comparing our analysis with the other analyses of Romanian gender, demonstrating that our proposal fares better on virtually all criteria. We provide conclusions and identify areas for further research in section 3.6.

3.2 The Problem

3.2.1 Data

Traditional analyses of Romanian recognize three genders: masculine, feminine, and neuter (Graur, Avram, and Vasiliu 1966; Mallinson 1986; Rosetti 1965, 1973; Corbett 1991; Chitoran 1992, 2002, among others). Gender is expressed through agreement on attributive adjectives, predicate adjectives, demonstratives, articles and other determiners, and the numerals "one" and "two." For the sake of simplicity, we use only adjectives to illustrate the agreement patterns. As table 3.1 shows, there is significant syncretism in agreement: masculine and neuter nouns take identical agreeing forms in the singular, and feminine and neuter nouns take identical agreeing forms in the plural.[2]

This syncretism in agreement is matched by syncretism in the number paradigm: masculine and neuter nouns are indistinguishable in the singular, illustrated in (1) as the neutralization of the masculine/neuter distinction, while neuter and feminine

Table 3.1
Noun-adjective agreement in Romanian

	Singular		Plural	
Masculine	trandafir rose.M	frumos beautiful.M	trandafiri rose.M	frumoși beautiful.M
Neuter	palton coat.N	frumos beautiful.M	paltoane coat.N	frumoase beautiful.F
Feminine	casă house.F	frumoasă beautiful.F	case house.F	frumoase beautiful.F

Table 3.2
Syncretism of plural forms

	Singular	Plural		Gloss
Masculine	copac	copac-**i**	[kopatʃʲ]	tree
	sabot	sabot-**i**	[sabotsʲ]	clog (shoe)
	colac	colac-**i**	[kolatʃʲ]	bread roll
	codru	codr-**i**	[kodri]	field
Neuter	teatru	teatr-**e**	[teatre]	theater
	clopot	clopot-**e**	[klopote]	bell
	dulap	dulap-**uri**	[dulapurʲ]	cabinet
	acvariu	acvari-**i**	[akvarij]	aquarium
Feminine	casă	cas-**e**	[kase]	house
	para	para-**le**	[paréle]	money
	blană	blăn-**uri**	[blənurʲ]	fur
	inimă	inim-**i**	[inimʲ]	heart

nouns are indistinguishable in the plural, shown in table 3.2. These patterns are consistent across cases, with masculine and neuter nouns taking the same case markers in the singular, and neuter and feminine nouns taking the same case markers in the plural. (See appendix A for examples.)

(1) *Neutralization of masculine/neuter distinction (nominative singular definite)*
  a. sabotul   [sabot-**ul**]   'the clog' (shoe) ⎫
  b. cartoful   [kartof-**ul**] 'the potato'   ⎬ MASCULINE
  c. blocul   [blok-**ul**]   'the block'   ⎫
  d. norocul   [norok-**ul**]   'the (good) luck' ⎬ NEUTER
  e. gardul   [gard-**ul**]   'the fence'   ⎭

As table 3.2 shows, there are three main plural markers, *-i*, *-e*, and *-uri*,[3] with an additional marker *-le*, which occurs on a small set of feminine nouns that end in a stressed *-á* or *-eá* (*cafea* ~ *cafele* 'coffee', *basma* ~ *basmale* '(head)scarf', *stea* ~ *stele* 'star'). The *-le* marker is fully predictable, and we will therefore focus on the three main plural markers, because these are shared among the genders. *-e* and *-uri* do not appear on masculine nouns, but *-i* appears on nouns from all three genders. We will show, however, that there are actually two separate *-i* markers, one that marks traditional masculine nouns, and another that marks traditional feminine and neuter nouns.

Given these facts, the challenge of Romanian gender can be articulated as follows: Romanian seems to have *three* genders in the lexicon: masculine, feminine, and neuter. However, there are only *two* agreement patterns in the singular and the plural: masculine and feminine. Neuter nouns do not have their own dedicated marking, and they do not have their own agreement pattern. The mapping from singular to plural is not one-to-one: neuter nouns follow the masculine pattern in the singular and the feminine in the plural. Given that gender is expressed through agreement, this begs the question of whether Romanian has three genders, or just two.

3.2.2 Gender Assignment: Two or Three Genders?

As is the case with gender in most languages, Romanian gender has a semantic core that accounts for the assignment of animate nouns to the masculine and feminine genders based on natural gender (Graur, Avram, and Vasiliu 1966; Mallinson 1986). Inanimate nouns, however, are distributed among all three genders. While there is little disagreement with respect to the semantic basis for gender assignment of animate nouns in Romanian, the factors determining gender assignment for inanimate nouns remain unclear.

The syncretism in the agreement and number paradigm described in the previous section is a vexing problem that many linguists and grammarians have grappled with since the eighteenth century. Syncretism is not uncommon in the world's languages (for instance, Corbett 1991 describes several languages that show a mismatch between the number of *controller* (lexical) genders and *target* (grammatical) genders). However, the syncretism exhibited in Romanian is of a different nature: it applies to an entire class, not a subset within a particular gender. Within a typical syncretism, which covers just a subset within a class (see Corbett and Fraser 1993; Baerman 2004; Stump 2001; among many others),[4] a learner has independent evidence that the relevant class stands on its own. In the case of full-class syncretism no such evidence is available to a language learner and it is impossible to identify the criteria that separate class X from the (syncretic) class Y.

There are at least two possible approaches to the Romanian facts outlined above:

- *Three-gender system (traditional analysis)*[5] Romanian nouns are lexically classified into three genders (or on a modification of such analysis, three *controller* genders) that map onto two agreement patterns (*target* genders). One agreement pattern is used in the singular, and the other in the plural.

• *Two-gender system (as proposed here)* Romanian nouns are not lexically specified for gender. There are two genders and two agreement patterns in the singular and the plural. Class membership is determined by formal cues and a small semantic core. Agreement is straightforward once class membership is determined, by mapping noun class directly to a set of agreeing forms.

Our proposal relies on formal features of Romanian nouns, specifically the singular and plural noun endings. Recall that we define agreement as covariation between the form of the noun (trigger) and that of the adjective (target). We capitalize on the fact that particular noun forms co-occur with particular adjective forms; thus gender specification on the noun is not necessary. In the singular these are the endings of the nominative indefinite form, and in the plural these are the plural markers -*i*, -*e*, and -*uri*. This hypothesis maintains a close relationship between the rules of plural formation and those of gender assignment and agreement. This is a welcome result given that speakers must know how to form the plural regardless of the division of the nominal lexicon into genders. Thus the same factors relevant for plural formation are indirectly relevant for predicting gender assignment and agreement in the plural. As a result, this analysis is more parsimonious than a three-gender analysis that does not capitalize on the forms of the plural to determine agreement. A three-gender analysis has a more complex nominal lexicon, and needs to be supplemented with complex gender-mapping rules between the singular and the plural.

In the next section we review three prior three-gender analyses of Romanian, and two prior two-gender analyses. The first two-gender proposal is by Hall (1965), who argues that "neuter" nouns are not a separate grammatical gender, but rather belong to different inflectional classes in the singular and the plural. His arguments, although not fully developed, lend themselves to the same type of analysis as the one proposed in this chapter. The second proposal is a development of Farkas's (1990) analysis into a two-gender account. We show that although it captures the attested agreement patterns, it raises several learnability questions and is in some ways very similar to three-gender analyses.

3.3 Previous Analyses of Romanian Genders

3.3.1 Three-Gender Analyses

In this section we present the main three-gender analyses of Romanian. The treatment of Romanian as a three-gender language is motivated on the one hand by historical considerations, and on the other by the need to establish a systematic mapping between genders and declensional classes (Graur, Avram, and Vasiliu 1966), or between controller and target genders (Corbett 1991).

3.3.1.1 Origins of the Romanian Neuter Much has been written about the source of the Romanian *neuter*. The two main possibilities are that the Romanian three-gender system was inherited from Latin or was reintroduced after the loss of the Latin neuter gender. The resolution of this debate is beyond the scope of this chapter, but we will provide synopses of the opposing views below.

Although Romanian developed from Latin, some scholars have disputed the idea that the neuter gender in Romanian has continued naturally from Latin. Since the Classical Latin neuter class became smaller in Vulgar Latin, which eventually gave rise to the two-gender modern Romance languages (French, Italian, Spanish, etc.), these scholars believe that the Romanian "neuter" does not simply continue from Latin (Mallinson 1986, 246). Rather, a "reinvention" or "rebirth" is proposed for this "gender," either because of a desire to express a distinction between "animate" and "inanimate" (Rosetti 1965, 84–88), or because of contact with the South Slavic three-gender superstrate (Rosetti 1965, 88; Petrucci 1993). According to Rosetti, the desire to distinguish animacy from inanimacy acted as a force that drew from the resources already available in the language (i.e., masculine singular and feminine plural endings) to create the neuter gender. Thus, under this account, the neuter was created to be *the gender for inanimates*; although not all inanimates were drawn into the neuter, there are *no animates* that are neuter (Rosetti 1965; Petrucci 1993).[6]

Other scholars have proposed that the Romanian gender system is continued directly from the Latin system, possibly due to contact with the three-gendered Slavic languages (Petrucci 1993, 174). Petrucci refutes the reinvention of the neuter based on Slavic influence, and finds no evidence indicating that contact with the Slavic languages affected the development of the Romanian gender system. Since there is no evidence of "ambigeneric" nouns—nouns that exhibit masculine morphology in the singular and feminine morphology in the plural—in the history of Slavic, Petrucci argues that the Romanian "neuter" could not have been borrowed from Slavic. Due to evidence of ambigeneric nouns in other Romance languages, including Italian, Dalmatian, early French and Provençal, Petrucci claims that this is a Romance-internal phenomenon (Petrucci 1993, 175–176). Further, South Slavic neuter borrowings into Romanian are mostly treated as feminines. For example, the South Slavic neuter nouns [tʃudo] 'miracle' and [sito] 'sieve' were borrowed as *ciudă* [tʃudə] 'envy' and *sită* [sitə] 'sieve' respectively, both of which are feminine (Petrucci 1993, 179). The facts described here strongly suggest that if there is a Romanian "neuter," it is not a result of Slavic influence.

3.3.1.2 Three-Gender Analyses of Romanian Most synchronic analyses of Romanian have relied on semantics to distinguish three genders: *masculine* for animate nouns denoting males, *feminine* for animate nouns denoting females, and *neuter* for inanimate nouns. This traditional view is that found in the Academy Grammar (Graur, Avram, and Vasiliu 1966). Corbett's (1991) and Farkas's (1990) analyses of Roma-

Romanian as a Two-Gender Language

Table 3.3
Romanian declensional classes (compiled from Graur, Avram, and Vasiliu 1966, 81–82)

I F/M	-ă	-a/-ea[1]	-á/-eá	Special cases[2]		
	casă 'house' (f)	Toma (m)	para 'money' (f)	zi 'day' (f)		
	tată 'father' (m)	Mircea (m)	lulea 'pipe' (f)	tanti 'aunt' (f)		

II	M	-u/-w	-j/-Cʲ	-C			
		codru 'field'	tei 'lime tree'	nuc 'walnut tree'			
		bou 'ox'	ochi [okʲ] 'eye'				
	N	-u/-w	-i/-j/-Cʲ	-C	-o	-ú	
		lucru 'thing'	alibi 'alibi'	amurg 'dusk'	apropo 'by the way'	atu 'ace'	
		cadou 'gift'	pai 'straw'				
			ochi [okʲ] 'fried egg'				

III F/M/N	-e			Special cases		
	sare 'salt' (f),			weekdays in		
	soare 'sun' (m),			-Cʲ and -j (f)		
	nume 'name' (n)					

1. The -a and -ea endings on masculine nouns appear only on proper names.
2. These are the only singular feminine nouns ending in [-i].

nian gender each represent a step forward in the understanding of the Romanian system. Each of these analyses is discussed below.

Graur, Avram, and Vasiliu (1966, 57) state that in Romanian grammatical gender corresponds "in principle" to natural gender, which translates primarily into the male/female/inanimate distinction, though this is "often not respected." In addition, they indicate that each noun gender corresponds to particular noun endings in the nominative singular indefinite form (p. 60). These endings are later merged to describe three "traditional declensional classes" in Romanian, which suggests that declensional classes and genders should correspond to one another in some unambiguous way. As table 3.3 shows, this is obviously not the case for Romanian: each declension contains nouns from more than one gender, showing a high degree of overlap in singular endings, particularly among neuter and masculine nouns (declension II).

Graur, Avram, and Vasiliu (1966) note that although Romanian nouns can be separated into the three declensional classes introduced above, "it would be more accurate to decline nouns based on their gender rather than their declensional class ... there is a declension for masculine nouns and one for feminine nouns, [with] the neuter nouns following the masculine in the singular, and the feminine in the plural"

(p. 82; our translation). This statement accurately describes the division of Romanian nouns assuming the gender of a noun is clear. However, if we consider the fact that inanimate nouns are not exclusively assigned to the "neuter" gender, then this statement says nothing about how one can predict which inanimate nouns should "follow the masculine in the singular and the feminine in the plural."

Attempts at setting up formal distinctions, such as the declensional classes described in table 3.3, lead to circular arguments: the declensional classes outlined above overlap greatly with the noun genders, which is why Graur, Avram, and Vasiliu (1966) suggest that the various singular and plural nominative/accusative and genitive/dative case forms should be derived based on the gender rather than the declensional class of the noun. At the same time gender classes are defined semantically, and, as we have shown above, semantic gender distinctions do not account for all of the nouns.

Corbett (1991, 105) states that "gender agreement provides the basis for defining gender and establishing the number of genders in a given language." He adopts Zaliznjak's (1964, 30) notion of "agreement class" in order to determine the number of genders in a language: nouns are in the same agreement class if, given the same conditions (e.g., same case/number, agreement domain and target), they take the same agreement form (Corbett 1991, 147–148). Corbett argues that although Romanian has three agreement classes, corresponding to the patterns of agreement for each of the three traditional genders, these three agreement classes are not necessarily genders as they are in other languages, such as German or Latin. Stating that Romanian has three genders implies that agreement on targets (adjectives, demonstratives, etc.) shows a three-way distinction, which is not the case.

To solve this problem Corbett introduces the concepts of *controller* and *target* genders. Controller genders are those into which nouns are divided, and target genders are those marked on adjectives, demonstratives, numerals, and so on (pp. 150–152). Romanian, then, has three controller genders and two target genders, corresponding to the traditional three genders and two agreement patterns, respectively. This is represented schematically in (2).[7] For example, controller gender I ("masculine") triggers agreement in -*i* on a plural adjective target, while controller gender III ("neuter") triggers agreement in -*e* on the same target:

(2) *Gender mapping in Romanian*

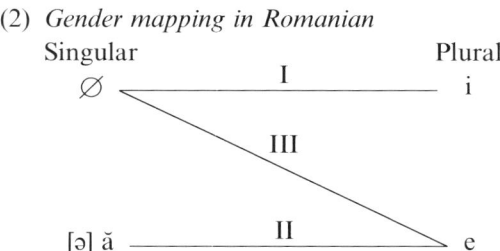

Corbett's account is theoretically more sophisticated than the previous descriptions of the Romanian gender system, and it is superior in that it formalizes the behavior of Romanian nouns. It posits three classes of nouns marked in the lexicon—the controller genders—and agreement mapping rules from the singular to the plural in the syntax, as represented in (2). This is attractive because it avoids the need to provide that one gender (neuter) patterns with another gender in the singular, and with a different gender in the plural. Instead, the three controller genders have mapping rules that map each of them to the same two target genders. However, this account still requires a three-to-two mapping between genders and agreement patterns, which is essentially the account provided in Graur, Avram, and Vasiliu (1966).

Finally, we turn to Farkas's (1990) analysis. Farkas's main purpose is not to decide whether Romanian has two genders or three, but rather to account for a case of apparent feature mismatch ("disagreement") in Romanian.[8] She provides a rule-based account for Romanian gender, assuming a three-way distinction using a single gender feature, [±fem]: traditional "masculine" nouns are [−fem], "feminine" nouns are [+fem], and "neuter" nouns are underspecified for gender. The patterning of the neuter nouns with masculines in the singular and feminines in the plural is obtained via feature filling rules, whereby nouns that are underspecified for the Romanian gender feature are assigned [−fem] values in the singular and [+fem] values in the plural. Farkas proposes two feature-filling rules to account for this pattern. First, she proposes the *Feature Co-occurrence Restriction* rule, given below in (3), which provides that a noun that is underspecified for gender will be assigned a [+fem] value in the plural.

(3) *Feature Co-occurrence Restriction* (FCR) *rule*
    $[\langle[+N], [-V]\rangle [+pl]] \to [+fem]$

To account for the patterning of underspecified nouns in the singular, Farkas proposes a feature filling rule, the *Feature Specification Default* rule, given below in (4), which states that the default gender specification is [−fem]:

(4) *Feature Specification Default* (FSD) *rule*
    $[\quad] \to [-fem]$

Farkas's analysis differs significantly from the other two described above. In particular, it avoids the syncretism in gender classification by positing an underspecified noun class for traditional neuters. This noun class, together with the feature filling rules FCR and FSD predict that neuter nouns will be masculine in the singular, feminine in the plural. This analysis maintains the stability of traditional masculine and feminine nouns which do not change gender class between the singular and the plural. However, the major drawback of this account is that it still does not predict what determines gender classification in the first place, namely which noun will be [−fem].

[+fem], or underspecified for [±fem]. As a consequence, much of the classifying work is accomplished through the use of diacritics, whose overabundance in the system poses a serious learnability challenge—the learner is expected to do a lot of rote memorization.

In summary, the three-gender analyses in Graur, Avram, and Vasiliu 1966 and Corbett 1991 make the right generalizations with respect to agreement patterns; however, they do so in a purely descriptive fashion. The main problem with these accounts is that they lack predictive power with respect to agreement. They simply stipulate that mapping between three genders and two agreement patterns involves either "neuter" nouns patterning with "masculines" in the singular and with "feminines" in the plural (Graur, Avram, and Vasiliu 1966), or one of the controller genders mapping on to one target gender in the singular, and to another in the plural (Corbett 1991). Farkas's (1990) analysis makes an important contribution regarding the predictability of the *behavior* of nouns, namely that masculines and feminines stay as such, but that neuters pattern with the masculines in the singular and with the feminines in the plural. Even so, this analysis does not provide a way of predicting noun classification, which is ultimately what we want to know. Given the lack of predictive power at different levels of these analyses, we now turn to alternative two-gender accounts of Romanian.

3.3.2 Two-Gender Analyses

In this section we discuss the precursors to the two-gender analysis of Romanian that we develop in section 3.4. Although the proposals discussed here have not been completely worked out by their respective proponents, they maintain that the nominal lexicon of Romanian can be described as a two-gender system. Hall (1965) bases his argument for two genders on the syncretism in the number paradigm of Romanian, and Farkas (1990) on the syncretism in agreement patterns. Both accounts seem to be more economical than the three gender accounts described above. Economy is achieved through a simpler nominal lexicon, as well as more straightforward agreement rules. There are two classes of nouns mapping onto two agreement patterns in both the singular and the plural. We show, however, that while Hall's account is compatible with our own two-gender analysis, an account based on Farkas 1990 is more compatible with a three- rather than a two-gender analysis.

One of Hall's (1965) arguments against the "neuter" as a synchronic grammatical gender is that it lacks its own morphological markers in both the singular and the plural, therefore the "neuter" is lost syntactically (this argument has been mentioned by several others, including Corbett 1991 and Cobeț 1983–1984, 93). We understand this argument to mean that if gender is relevant for agreement, which is part of syntax, then there should be as many genders as there are agreement patterns. In addition, Hall argues that there is no semantic basis for this "gender": "neuter" nouns are defined semantically as inanimate, but inanimates are distributed across the feminine and the masculine genders as well.

Hall's main argument for a two-gender system of Romanian is based on the number syncretism given in table 3.2. He proposes that "neuter nouns" are better described as *heteroclites*, "in that their chief characteristic is that they always belong, not necessarily to different grammatical genders, but to different inflectional classes in the plural as opposed to the singular" (Hall 1965, 427). This observation will be crucial for our own proposal, since we will argue that the declensional class of nouns in the singular and in the plural, and thus the actual singular and plural forms of nouns, determines agreement.

As already discussed, Farkas (1990) provides an alternative three-gender account of Romanian nouns. As Farkas herself mentions in a footnote, her analysis lends itself to a two-gender interpretation of Romanian by assuming the privative opposition [+fem] versus underspecified [0fem] (Farkas 1990, 543, note 9). With this contrast, only feminine nouns are specified for gender (as [+fem]), while all other nouns are underspecified with respect to gender, providing a two-way underlying distinction. Using this as a starting point we will develop Farkas's possible two-gender analysis of Romanian.

Recall that in her three-gender analysis Farkas utilizes a *Feature Co-occurrence Restriction* rule that accounts for the behavior of some of the underspecified nouns (traditional neuters) that appear to be feminine in the plural. This is repeated here for convenience, and states that underspecified plural nouns will be feminine.

(5) *Feature Co-occurrence Restriction* (FCR) *rule*
    $[\langle[+N], [-V]\rangle [+pl]] \rightarrow [+fem]$

This same rule can be applied to the possible two-gender analysis suggested, [fem]/underspecified. The key to this account is that only a subset of the underspecified nouns must undergo the FCR rule, namely all traditional "neuters." Farkas suggests that in order for only these nouns (and not traditional "masculines") to undergo rule (5), they would have to be marked with a diacritic that triggers the rule. Details about the exact specifications of the diacritic are not provided, except for its function as the rule trigger. With rule (5) and the diacritic in place, gender agreement follows the expected patterns. In the singular [+fem] nouns trigger agreement in *-ə* on adjectives, and underspecified nouns trigger agreement in ∅; in the plural [+fem] nouns trigger agreement in *-e* on adjectives, while underspecified nouns trigger agreement in *-i* (the same patterns used by Corbett 1991, 152, cf. (2)). The only underspecified nouns in the plural are traditional "masculine" nouns, since all of the "neuters" are [+fem] in the plural as a result of rule (5).

Therefore, under this account the lexicon contains nouns that are [+fem] and nouns that are underspecified for gender; among the latter there are nouns that are marked with a diacritic (traditional neuters) and nouns that are not (masculines). The problem with such an account is the use of the diacritic: it must be present on *every* traditional neuter noun. This class of nouns consists of nearly a third of all Romanian nouns, according to counts in Dimitriu 1996, 129, therefore the diacritic is equivalent to maintaining a third gender. Furthermore, the only function of the diacritic is to trigger the application of the FCR rule. This gives diacritics a greater power than they are intended to have, since they are features that attach to a particular lexical item or a *small* group of lexical items and whose main function is to signal exceptional behavior with respect to some grammatical process. This is technically equivalent to rote learning of exceptional words, which means that the categorization of roughly a third of Romanian nouns would have to be rote-learned under such analysis.

3.4 Proposed Two-Gender Analysis

With the foregoing background, it is time to turn to our own analysis of Romanian gender. We propose that Romanian has two noun classes in the singular and in the plural, and that this categorization is not lexically specified. The division of nouns into classes in the singular is different from their division into classes in the plural. Class assignment is determined by the ending of the noun in the singular and the plural, semantic core notwithstanding. Once class membership is established for singular and plural nouns, agreement proceeds very straightforwardly. For a few subsets of exceptional nouns, as discussed in section 3.4.2.1, this analysis still appeals to diacritics, but the number of diacritic-bearing nouns is kept small. Furthermore, the diacritics used in our analysis serve two functions: they determine the plural form of the noun, and they therefore predict gender agreement. In what follows we outline the details of class membership in the singular and in the plural, and then discuss how agreement works in a two-gender system.

3.4.1 Class Membership in the Singular

It is clear in all analyses of Romanian that masculine and neuter nouns are indistinguishable in the singular, both in their form (endings) and in their agreement pattern. Our analysis capitalizes on this lack of distinction and groups masculine and neuter nouns into a single class, separate from feminine nouns. Were it not for the plural, this would be the natural categorization of Romanian nouns and no controversy with respect to number of genders would exist.

We propose that there are two noun classes in the singular, and for the sake of simplicity, we call them class A and class B. Class A includes traditional feminine

Table 3.4
Class A and class B nouns

Class A			Class B		
boabă	[boabə]	'type of bean; grain'	buchet	[buket]	'bunch, bouquet'
umbră	[umbrə]	'shade, shadow'	borcan	[borkan]	'jar'
ghiară	[gjarə]	'claw'	buzunar	[buzunar]	'pocket'
casă	[kasə]	'house'	ficat	[fikat]	'liver'
cifră	[tʃifrə]	'number'	fior	[fior]	'shiver'
suliță	[sulitsə]	'spear; type of sword'	cartof	[kartof]	'potato'
culoare	[kuloare]	'color'	călcâi	[kəlkij]	'heel'
răbdare	[rəbdare]	'patience'	plai	[plaj]	'poetic land'
baie	[baje]	'bath'	cui	[kuj]	'nail'
ureche	[ureke]	'ear'	pârâu	[pɨriw]	'stream'
cheie	[keje]	'key'	panou	[panow]	'panel'
părere	[pərere]	'opinion'	taxi	[taksi]	'taxi'
sete	[sete]	'thirst'	alibi	[alibi]	'alibi'
			manto	[manto]	'coat'
			codru	[kodru]	'field'

nouns, and class B includes traditional masculine and neuter nouns. Class membership is determined based on a semantic core and formal cues. Animate nouns are assigned class based on natural gender, with those denoting females in class A and those denoting males in class B. Some smaller semantic subclasses include the names of trees, which are in class B, and abstract nouns, which are in class A. The formal cues that determine class membership are the final segment of the nominative indefinite form of the noun. Class A includes nouns that end in -ə or -e, and class B includes nouns that have all other endings (consonant, -i, -o, -u).[9] As is often the case when semantic features compete with formal features, the semantic features override the formal ones (Corbett 1991, 41); this particular ranking of features is also attested for other Romance languages (Corbett 1991, 58; Tucker, Lambert, and Rigault 1977; Harris 1991). Table 3.4 provides examples of nouns in each class.

3.4.2 Class Membership in the Plural

Traditional analyses assume that gender class determines a noun's plural form, while we take the opposite stance, namely that plural forms determine gender class. Our position is supported by the fact that in traditional three-gender analyses there is limited predictability of plural endings for nouns in the same class, clearly showing that gender specification alone does not predict plural form. For example, although the majority of traditional feminine nouns ending in -ə form the plural in -e (6a,b), quite a few form the plural in -i, as shown in (6c–e):

(6) a. fată—fete   'girl'
    b. masă—mese   'table'
    c. bucată—bucăți   'piece, chunk'
    d. ușă—uși   'door'
    e. flacără—flăcări   'flame'

In fact, with the exception of traditional masculines, all of which take the plural marker -*i*, there are very few feminine and neuter nouns for which gender classification alone can predict plural form. For example, feminine nouns ending in -*e* take the -*i* plural marker seen above. As we mentioned previously, there are also feminine nouns ending in stressed -*á* or -*eá* that take the -*le* plural marker, and there are neuter nouns ending in a stressed -*í* and borrowings from French ending in -*ou* that take -*uri* in the plural. Notice that in each of these cases the plural ending is determined by the noun's ending rather than its gender class, which supports our claim that the plural forms determine class membership in the plural, rather than the other way around.

We propose that there are two noun classes in the plural: class C and class D. Class C includes traditional masculine nouns, and class D includes traditional feminine and neuter nouns. As is the case with singular nouns, class membership is determined based on semantic and formal cues. Nouns denoting males and trees are in class C, and nouns denoting females and abstract nouns are in class D. The formal cues that determine class membership are the plural noun endings, *which are the actual plural markers*. We show evidence below for Romanian possessing two plural markers in -*i*, noted here as -i_1 and -i_2. Plural nouns ending in -i_1 are assigned to class C, while nouns taking all other plural markers (-*e*, -*uri*, -i_2) are assigned to class D. Given the close connection between class membership and plural markers, our analysis must include rules of plural formation. We show that the form of the plural—the selection of the plural marker—is predictable from formal and semantic features, and we can immediately classify nouns into classes C and D based on the plural form. Once this classification takes place, agreement proceeds straightforwardly.

Our argument for the existence of two plural markers in -*i* is based on both diachronic and synchronic factors. First, the -*i* plural marker of traditional masculine nouns and the -*i* plural marker of feminine and neuter nouns have different origins, as shown in table 3.5.[10] Although the origins of the feminine -*i* plural marker are disputed, and we will not take a position here with respect to the marker's likely source, it is clear that it is not a matter of simple phonetic development from Latin. The Latin second declension nominative plural ending -*ī* produced Romanian -*i* by regular sound change, while the Latin first declension nominative plural ending -*ae* produced Romanian -*e*, which is the plural marker for the majority of traditional

Table 3.5
Comparison of Latin and Romanian forms

	Latin	Development	Romanian		
	Singular	Plural	Plural		Gloss
Masculine	*socer*	*-ī* >	socr-i	[sokri]	'in-law'
	oculus	*-ī* >	och-i	[okʲ]	'eye'
Feminine	*barba*	*-ae* →	bărb-i	[bərbʲ]	'beard'
	fuga	*-ae* →	fug-i	[fudʒʲ]	'run, jog'
	lingua	*-ae* →	limb-i	[limbʲ]	'tongue, language'

feminine nouns. Thus, one *-i* is a direct reflex of Latin *-ī* ($-i_1$), and the other ($-i_2$) is not.

Second, the synchronic behavior of *-i* indicates two separate markers: they combine with different noun stems in systematic ways. Speakers do not have access to diachronic information, but they do have access to the singular form of the noun. $-i_1$ combines with nouns that denote a male or a tree, and those that end in a consonant or *-u* (class C nouns). $-i_2$ combines with nouns that denote females or abstract nouns, and those that end in *-ə*, *-e*, or *-ju* (class D nouns). Given that the synchronic motivation is uncovered via morphophonological analysis, we use a single *-i* when establishing plural formation rules, to which we now turn.

3.4.2.1 Rules of Plural Formation To establish the rules of plural formation we utilized Ross Quinlan's C4.5 Decision Tree algorithm, the details of which are not crucial here (see appendix E). Let us just mention that this algorithm takes input features and categorizes data according to those features that have the highest predictive power. We found that the following elements are indicative of the plural marker selected by each noun:

- The final segment of the nominative singular indefinite form
- The noun's semantics (masculine, tree)
- The mono- versus polysyllabicity of the singular (indefinite) noun
- The presence and character of a root diphthong[11]

The rules of plural formation are given in (7) in the form of the decision tree obtained from the algorithm, because this is the most straightforward presentation. We should note that this does not constitute a complete account of plural formation rules for all nouns, since the cues determining plural marker selection for certain nouns have thus far been less transparent, as we discuss shortly.

(7) *Rules of plural formation*
    Are there masculine semantic features?

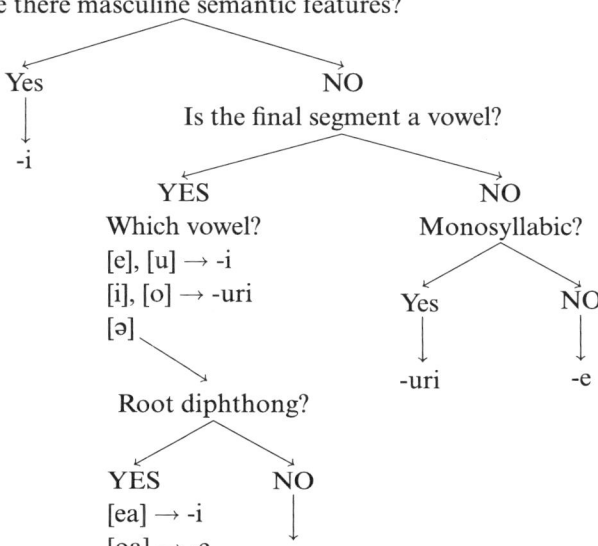

The algorithm in (7) shows how the formal and semantic features rank with respect to each other in determining the choice of plural marker. Note that the first cut is based on simple semantic properties—whether the noun denotes an animate male or a tree—thus reflecting the tendency for (typically coarse-grained) semantic features to override formal ones, as we noted in section 3.4.1. Beyond this primary distinction, which is presumably subject to rote learning, formal features predict the plural form of the noun and indirectly predict class membership. The *-i* plural markers are collapsed in (7), but recall that there are two such markers, $-i_1$ and $-i_2$, according to the type of stem each attaches to. If the noun ends in a consonant or *-u* then this marker is $-i_1$; otherwise it is $-i_2$.

The plural of a small number of class B nouns is not predicted by these rules. Some of these nouns are independent lexical items, but most can be subdivided into several small semantic categories. Under our proposal, all are marked with a diacritic specifying the plural marker they will take, but not their gender.[12] Since plural formation is independently needed, these subclasses of nouns have to be exceptionally marked under any analysis of Romanian and thus constitute a special case *not* just for our analysis. The following semantic categories also form the plural in $-i_1$ (Graur, Avram, and Vasiliu 1966, 58; Petrucci 1993, 188):

- The names of letters of the alphabet: [doj de a] 'two *as*', [doj de tʃe] 'two *cs*'
- The names of musical notes: [doj de la] 'two *las*', [doj de mi] 'two *mis*'

- The names of months: [un januarije] 'a (month) of January'
- Most names of numbers: [un patru] 'a four', [doj de zetʃe] 'two tens'
- (Most) names of mountains and cities: *Ceahlăii* [tʃeahləjj] 'the Ceahlăus' (mountain, pl.), *Iașii* [jaʃij] 'the Iașis' (city, pl.)
- Some names of plants and flowers: *trandafiri* [trandafirʲ] 'roses' *boboci* [bobotʃʲ] 'buds'

Nouns from these semantic categories could have been included in our decision tree; however, they were left out for two reasons. First, since the initial decision relates to the presence or absence of masculine semantics, the plural forms for these nouns would have been correctly predicted; thus including them would have cluttered the algorithm needlessly. Second, these classes are very small, and most of the types of nouns they include (except for plants and flowers) do not usually lend themselves to being used in the plural. When they *are* used in the plural, they tend to form the plural in exceptional ways that do not actually change the form of the singular noun—for example, 'two *a*s' is made plural in a construction such as *doi de a* [doj de a] 'two of a'. Thus, our analysis does still make use of diacritics, but their use is much more limited than it would be under a proposal such as our development of Farkas's (1990) two-gender account, and furthermore, this diacritic serves the purpose of determining plural form and indirectly agreement.

Our proposed rules of plural formation are consistent with those in Perkowski and Vrabie 1986 as well as Vrabie 1989, 2000, which provide a much more detailed account of plural formation for Romanian nouns. They propose additional semantic subclasses within each nominal class, and also rules based on phonological characteristics of the nouns in the singular, in a similar vein to what we propose in this chapter. Their findings support our analysis that once plural forms can be predicted, noun classification and agreement follow in a straightforward fashion.[13]

With the above plural formation rules in place, we can categorize nouns into two classes in the singular and in the plural, as follows:

Singular
Class A: nouns ending in -ə and -e
Class B: everything else

Plural
Class C: nouns ending in -i_1
Class D: everything else

Having established these noun classes, we now turn to agreement in a two-gender system.[14]

3.4.3 Agreement in a Two-Gender System

We remind the reader that we define agreement as covariation between the form of the trigger and the form of the target. Different agreement targets show different agreeing forms, but crucially, agreement with a particular noun class is consistent for all agreement targets (adjectives, numerals, demonstratives, and so on). The only difference among these agreement targets is the actual agreement marker. For illustrative purposes, in (8) we show the covariation in agreement between a noun and its attributive adjective, and we provide examples in (9). For example, when a singular noun ends in -ə or -e, an adjective modifying the noun will end in -ə.[15]

(8) *Covariation in agreement markers*

	Noun ending	Adjectival ending
Singular	-ə, -e	-ə
	-C, -u, -i, -o	-∅, -u
Plural	-e, -uri, -i$_2$	-e
	-i$_1$	-i

(9) a. *felie bună*   feli-e bun-ə   'good slice'
                       slice good
    b. *gard bun*   gard bun-∅   'good fence'
                       fence good
    c. *mese bune*   mes-e bun-e   'good tables'
                       table good
    d. *felii bune*   feli-i$_2$ bun-e   'good slices'
                       slice good
    e. *codru bun*   codr-u bun-∅   'good field'
                       field good
    f. *cordi buni*   codr-i$_1$ bun-i [bun^j]   'good fields'
                       field good

Agreeing forms (endings that appear on agreement targets) can be divided into two sets, as shown in table 3.6 (see appendix D for further discussion of agreement with demonstratives). The first set, set I, contains agreeing forms that occur with class B singular nouns and class C plural nouns, while set II contains agreeing forms that occur with class A singular nouns and class D plural nouns. With the noun classes and the agreeing sets in place, we establish the agreement rules listed in table 3.7, matching noun class to sets I or II. The examples in table 3.8 illustrate how agreement proceeds straightforwardly in this two-gender system. We include details about class membership determination (noun endings).

Table 3.6
Agreeing forms

Set	Singular				Plural			
	Indef./ 'one'	Def. art.	Adj/ dem	Derived adj.	'two'	Def. art.	Adj/ dem	Derived adj.
I	un/unu	-le/e#_ -ul	∅ -u	-u [denominal]	doj	-i	-i	-i [denominal]
II	o/una	-a	-ə	-e [deverbal] [denominal]	dowə	-le	-e	-i [denominal]

Table 3.7
Agreement rules

Noun class	Agreeing form
A	Set II, singular
B	Set I, singular
C	Set I, plural
D	Set II, plural

Table 3.8
Agreement in a two-gender system

Noun form	Noun ending	Noun class	Agreeing form	N-adjective pair		Gloss
masă table.sg	-ə	A	Set II, sg.	mas-ə table.sg	bun-ə good.sg	good table
felie slice.sg	-e	A	Set II, sg.	feli-e slice.sg	bun-ə good.sg	good slice
gard fence.sg	-C	B	Set I, sg.	gard fence.sg	bun-∅ good.sg	good fence
mese table.pl	-e	D	Set II, pl.	mes-e table.pl	bun-e good.pl	good tables
felii slice.pl	-i$_2$	D	Set II, pl.	feli-i slice.pl	bun-e good.pl	good slices
garduri fence.pl	-uri	D	Set II, pl.	gard-uri fence.pl	bun-e good.pl	good fences
codri field.pl	-i$_1$	C	Set I, pl.	codr-i$_1$ field.pl	bun-i good.pl	good field

In this section we have shown that with a small set of formal features and a minimal semantic core we can classify Romanian nouns into two classes in the singular and in the plural, and that once this classification is settled, agreement proceeds very straightforwardly pursuant to agreement rules. The principal contribution of our analysis concerns the classification of nouns in the plural, because it is in this paradigm that the gender controversy resides for Romanian. Our analysis is symmetrical in that for both numbers we rely on the form of the noun to determine class membership. In the singular, the ending of the singular noun determines whether nouns will be in class A or B, and in the plural the ending of the plural noun, which happens to be the plural marker, determines whether nouns will be in class C or D. To this end we have provided rules of plural formation, which are dependent on a small set of formal and semantic cues. Once we know the plural forms we can classify nouns into classes. This is the first time that such an analysis has been proposed for Romanian, capitalizing on rules of plural formation to determine class membership and, indirectly, agreement in the plural. This is an important result, because speakers must know how to form the plural regardless of gender, and the fact that they can use the same information for gender agreement makes this analysis more plausible. Basically, our analysis utilizes information that is independently available, without creating a burden on the language learner and introducing additional categories that may require more motivation.

3.5 Evaluating the Analyses

It is now time to bring together the analyses considered here to determine which of them best explains the Romanian gender system. Both two- and three-gender analyses rely on the same semantic core for noun categorization: nouns denoting males, females, trees, abstract nouns, and a few others such as names of cities and mountains. Beyond this semantic core, traditional three-gender analyses do not have a principled way of categorizing nouns. Even Farkas's (1990) three-gender account, which differs from the other three-gender accounts discussed here, does not have a means of predicting class membership. In all such accounts, feminine nouns are formally identified by the same features as in our proposal, namely the final vowels -*e* and -*ə* in the singular, but masculine and neuter nouns are classified arbitrarily as masculine and neuter, since they are indistinguishable from each other in the singular.[16] Their formal features would classify them as the same gender. The proposed two-gender analysis uses this generalization and classifies nouns into two classes in the singular and the plural, and these classes express the natural division of nouns based on their form, as well as their relationship to agreement: the same noun forms trigger the same agreement.

Our analysis is more parsimonious, because speakers need only look to a small set of semantic features and to the form of the noun in the singular and the plural in

Table 3.9
Agreement in a two-gender system

	Singular		Plural		
A	trandafir rose palton coat	frumos beautiful frumos beautiful	trandafiri rose paltoane coat	frumoși beautiful frumoase beautiful	C
B	casă house	frumoasă beautiful	case house	frumoase beautiful	D

Table 3.10
Agreement in a three-gender system

	Singular		Plural	
Masculine	trandafir rose.M	frumos beautiful.M	trandafiri rose.M	frumoși beautiful.M
Neuter	palton coat.N	frumos beautiful.M	paltoane coat.N	frumoase beautiful.F
Feminine	casă house.F	frumoasă beautiful.F	case house.F	frumoase beautiful.F

order to determine agreement. Tables 3.9 and 3.10 compare how agreement works in a two- versus a three-gender system. Notice that in the two-gender system noun forms that trigger the same agreement are in the same noun class. The behavior of the traditional neuter nouns is emergent, which is to be expected given the form of these nouns in the singular and in the plural. There is no need to mark a separate third gender. This is a generalization that cannot be captured in a three-gender analysis. Table 3.11 allows for a simple evaluation metric of the two types of analyses. It includes the following criteria:

• *Rote memorization* In any linguistic analysis, the more we can predict, the smaller the burden on the language learner. This criterion evaluates how much of nominal categorization is predictable, and how much must be memorized (i.e., via the use of diacritics).

• *Semantics* Semantic distinctions in categorization are learned relatively early (e.g., Karmiloff-Smith 1979; Snyder and Senghas 1997; Suzman 1999), but these distinctions are never fine-grained—they typically cover the difference in natural gender and animacy, thus corresponding to the conceptual categories learned in early cognitive development (Mandler 2000). Beyond these coarse-grained features, overreliance

Table 3.11
Comparison of the analyses

Criterion	Proposed 2-G analysis	Farkas's 2-G analysis	Farkas's 3-G analysis	3-G analyses
Rote memorization (diacritics)	minimal	up to 30% of the lexicon ("diacritics")	up to 30% of the lexicon	up to 30% of the lexicon
Contribution of semantics	minimal (small semantic core)	minimal (small semantic core)	minimal (small semantic core)	overgenerates (in some analyses)
Predictive power of singular noun endings	very high	unclear	unclear	unclear
Predictive power of the plural form	high	nonexistent	nonexistent	nonexistent
Mapping from trigger to target	direct	direct	direct	complex
Parallelism with other Romance gender systems	yes	yes	no	no

on semantics in determining gender categories greatly increases the neuter gender class in some three-gender analyses (Graur, Avram, and Vasiliu 1966), because there are many nonneuter inanimate nouns (see the discussion in section 3.3.1.2, where Graur, Avram, and Vasiliu (1966) acknowledge that using semantics works "in principle").

• *Noun forms* This criterion evaluates how much we can predict based on the formal characteristics of nouns, both singular and plural. In our account we rely heavily on form to categorize nouns, while in three-gender accounts it is unclear how much of a role noun form plays (presumably none at all in the plural, and perhaps some in the singular—that is, feminine nouns end in -ə or -e). In Farkas's (1990) two-gender account we can assume that singular forms do play a role, because feminines are separated from other nouns, which are underspecified, but plural forms are not predicted and play no role.

• *Agreement* (mapping from trigger to target) In traditional three-gender analyses there is a complex mapping of agreement trigger to target, with neuter nouns mapping to masculine agreement in the singular and feminine in the plural. In two-gender accounts this mapping is straightforward.

• *Parallelism with other Romance systems* Other Romance languages such as French and Spanish have two lexically specified nominal classes in the singular and plural. Our account brings Romanian closer to the rest of Romance at this surface level. At the lexical level, Romanian is different from other Romance languages, with no lexically determined noun classes.

Our proposal clearly fares better overall. It requires less rote learning and relies on fewer diacritics than any of the analyses considered here. The diacritics we have to use are minimal and serve a dual purpose, indicating the choice of plural marker and indirectly predicting class membership and agreement. In a three-gender analysis and in Farkas's two-gender analysis, the neuter gender would have to be marked with diacritics to separate it from the masculine, and this gender comprises roughly 30 percent of the nominal lexicon of Romanian (Dimitriu 1996). Semantic features play a role in both types of analyses, but in some analyses (Graur, Avram, and Vasiliu 1966) semantics overgenerates. Noun endings in the singular and the plural have high predictive power in the proposed two-gender system that makes use of independently needed morphophonemic rules (plural formation). In three-gender systems such rules are not capitalized on, making these systems less parsimonious. With respect to agreement, three-gender systems, with the exception of Farkas (1990), present us with an intricate mapping from agreement trigger to target, while in the two-gender system this mapping is straightforward. And finally, on a less important dimension, our proposal brings the nominal system of Romanian closer to other Romance languages at the surface level, where nouns are categorized in only two classes.

3.6 Conclusions and Outstanding Questions

This chapter has presented and analyzed core principles of gender assignment in Romanian, arguing that a two-gender system, as in other Romance languages, adequately accounts for the principles of gender categorization in this language.

The starting point for our investigation is the questionable status of the neuter gender in traditional analyses of Romanian. The neuter does not have its own markings or agreement pattern, being identical to the masculine in the singular and to the feminine in the plural in both these dimensions. Our analysis capitalizes on these facts and categorizes nouns into two classes in the singular and the plural. Nouns in each class share the same declension, namely noun endings (singular nominative indefinite for the singular, and plural markers for the plural). Because actual plural forms determine class membership in the plural, and indirectly agreement, we provide rules of plural formation that are established based on formal features of the nouns and a small semantic core. Gender agreement is straightforwardly predictable once the noun classes are established. Agreement rules map each of the two genders in the singular and the plural to a specific set of agreeing forms.

Our proposal provides a more economical system overall. First, we claim that there are only two genders in the singular and the plural, predictable based on a small semantic core and on formal properties of the nouns, namely the noun endings in singular and in the plural, as well as syllable count. Crucial to our account is that singular and plural gender assignment is established independently. Thus, unlike some other gendered languages, where the gender in the singular predicts the gender in the plural, and the plural form may not be directly relevant, in Romanian, the gender distinction in the plural is predicted from the form of the *plural*, not from the singular. A speaker of Romanian therefore needs to know the form of the plural in order to categorize the noun as belonging to one of the two available classes. But since the plural form is needed independent of gender, the morphological features dictating plural formation have a direct bearing on syntax. To our knowledge, ours is the first proposal maintaining a tight correlation between declensional class features (specifically, features determining plural formation) and agreement. By maintaining such a connection we are able to reduce the number of diacritics introduced in the lexicon.

In addition to reducing the memory load in the gender-learning process, the proposed analysis has a number of other advantages. By showing that Romanian has a two-gender system, we can bring it closer to all the other Romance languages in which nouns divide into only two classes. As a result of the two-way distinction proposed here, agreement mapping rules from two genders to two agreement patterns become more straightforward. Finally, the prospect of such an analysis creates new analytical possibilities for other gender systems: it is conceivable that complex gender systems of other languages could be simplified if gender and number are dissociated and the issue of gender classes is raised independently for each number.

Of course, some issues remain to be dealt with in the future. Two issues particular to Romanian call for further investigation. One of these is the high degree of variation in the choice of plural markers. For example, traditional neuter nouns *vis* 'dream' and *defileu* 'gorge' can have either the *-e* or the *-uri* plural markers, while traditional feminine nouns *monedă* 'coin' and *boltă* 'arch' can take either the *-e* or *-i$_2$* plural markers (see also Vrabie 1989, 401). There are no traditional masculine nouns that show this variation. It would be interesting to see the direction of this trend, but note that even with the variation the respective nouns remain in the same class, namely class D, so the analysis set forth in this chapter would continue to apply. Second, agreement with conjoined NPs (Farkas and Zec 1995; Sadler, 2006; Wechsler 2008) needs to be explored from the perspective of a two-gender system. While for combinations of male/female animate nouns there is virile agreement (agreement indexing features [+human, +male]), as in (10), agreement for different combinations of inanimate nouns shows different patterns. Only combinations of traditional masculine nouns result in a masculine agreeing form, while all other combinations result in a feminine agreeing form, as in (11).

(10) *Animate: Virile agreement*
  Pisica   și cainele   sunt uzi.
  cat.DEF[F] and dog.DEF[M] are wet.M.PL.
  'The cat and the dog are wet.'

(11) *Inanimate agreement*
   Gardul   și   scaunul   sunt albe.
   fence.DEF[N] and chair.DEF[N] are white.F.PL.
   'The fence and the chair are white.'

This chapter has concentrated on the analytical challenges particular to Romanian. However, we believe that the results achieved here, in keeping the gender system more parsimonious and in appealing to salient morphosyntactic cues readily available to young language learners, we have also touched on the general issues of morphological relevance that now await further exploration.

APPENDIX A

Case Markers

Romanian has five cases: nominative, accusative, genitive, dative, and vocative. The nominative and accusative (N/A) cases have the same form, as do the genitive and dative (G/D) cases. In the plural, genitive, dative, and vocative forms are the same for all nouns (the suffix *-lor* attached to the nominative/accusative plural form). The vocative case is mostly used with animate nouns. We provide the definite forms in the accompanying table.

	Singular			Plural			
	N/A	G/D	Voc	N/A	G/D	Voc	
M	brad-ul	bradul-ui	Bradule!	brazi-i	brazilor	Brazilor!	fir
N	gard-ul	gardul-ui	Gardule!	garduri-le	gardurilor	Gardurilor!	fence
F	mas-a	mes-ei	Maso!	mese-le	meselor	Meselor!	table

APPENDIX B

Traditional Masculine Nouns Ending in -*a*, -*ă* (most examples from Graur, Avram, and Vasiliu 1966, 82)

1. *tată*   'father'
2. *pașă*   'pasha'
3. *popă*   'priest'
4. *vlădică* 'messenger, guard (?)'

5. *papă* 'Pope'
6. *Toma, Mina, Zaharia, Mircea, Costea*—proper names in /-a/
7. *Dănilă, Păcală, Tândală, Nicoară*—proper names in /-ə/
8. *Gheorghiță, Petrică, Ionică, Costică, Jenică,* etc.—proper names formed with feminine diminutive suffixes /-itsə/ or /-ikə/

APPENDIX C

Traditional Feminine Nouns with Plural in -*uri*

1. *dulceață/dulcețuri*   'jam, preserves; types of jam, preserves'
2. *mâncare/mâncăruri*   'food/types of food'
3. *carne/cărnuri*   'meat/types of meat'
4. *mătase/mătăsuri*   'silk/types of silk'
5. *marfă/mărfuri*   'merchandise/types of merchandise'
6. *iarbă/ierburi*   'grass/types of grass'
7. *blană/blănuri*   'fur/types of fur'
8. *greață/grețuri*   'nausea/repetitive episodes of nausea; morning sickness'
9. *otravă/otrăvuri*   'poison/types of poison'
10. *sare/săruri*   'salt/types of salt'
11. *lână/lânuri*   'wool/types of wool' (also plural in *lâni* and *lâne*)
12. *gâlceavă/gâlcevuri*   'bickering'
13. *leafă/lefuri*   'wages'
14. *vreme/vremuri*   'weather; time (old times, old days)'
15. *gheață/ghețuri*   'ice'
16. *lipsă/lipsuri*   'lack'
17. *ceartă/certuri*   'fight, quarrel'
18. *treabă/treburi*   'work, task'

APPENDIX D

Demonstratives

D.A. and *N* in this table indicate demonstrative adjective and noun, respectively. *D.A. N* indicates that the demonstrative adjective precedes the noun, while *N D.A.* indicates the reverse. Dem. Pn indicates demonstrative pronoun.

	Singular		Plural	
SET	D.A. N	Dem. Pn and N D.A.	D.A. N	Dem. Pn and N D.A.
Set I	-∅	D.A. + a	-i	D.A. + a
Set II	-ə, -a	D.A. + a	-e	D.A. + a

Demonstratives show a specific pattern of behavior. There are four types of demonstratives: of proximity (e.g., *acest* 'this'), of proximity relative to another of the same kind (e.g., *cestălalt* 'this other one'), of distance (e.g., *acel* 'that'), and of distance relative to another of the same kind (e.g., *celălalt* 'that other one'). The proximity and distance demonstratives relative to another of the same kind share the same behavior, and the remaining two share a different behavior. The former have the same form both as pronouns and as demonstrative adjectives, while the latter do not. Consider the following examples:

	Single	Relative to another of same kind
Proximity	a. **acest** bărbat this.M man 'this man' b. *bărbatul* **acesta** man.DEF this.M 'this man' c. **acesta** this.DEF.M 'this one'	a. **cestălalt** bărbat this-other-one.M man 'this other man' b. *bărbatul* **cestălalt** man.DEF this-other-one.M 'this other man' c. **cestălalt** this-other-one.M 'this other one'
Distance	a. **acea** femeie that.F woman 'that woman' b. *femeia* **aceea** woman.DEF that.F 'that woman' c. **aceea** that-one.F 'that one'	a. **cealaltă** femeie that-other-one.F woman 'that other woman' b. *femeia* **cealaltă** woman that-other-one.F 'that other woman' c. **cealaltă** that-other-one.F 'that other one'

Notice that all forms of the demonstratives in the second column are identical within each gender. In addition, they have the typical endings that other adjectives have (e.g., zero for traditional masculine nouns, -ă [ə] for traditional feminine nouns). In the first column the pattern is different: the demonstrative adjective preceding the noun has the typical ending, while the demonstrative pronoun and the demonstrative adjective following the noun have the same form within each gender, and moreover they all end in -a. In fact, this -a ending appears for all such demonstratives, regardless of number/case and gender, but it is added to the regular ending corresponding to each noun class that the demonstrative modifies. Therefore, the demonstrative adjectives and pronouns are all based on the same regular form, to which the common -a ending is added for adjectives (when these follow the noun) and pronouns indicating a single referent (not relative to others of the same kind).

APPENDIX E

Computational Investigation

Ross Quinlan's C4.5 Decision Tree algorithm is a computer program that takes input features and constructs the best tree that classifies the data into the categories specified (class A or B for the singular, class C or D for the plural, and rules of plural formation). Here we present the methodology used in our analysis first for singular and plural noun classification, and then for rules of plural formation. In each case we used the same 1,950 nouns, drawn randomly from Juilland's (1965) frequency dictionary and from a noun list utilized for an electronic dictionary. Our goals were

- To test the reliability of the formal features in classifying nouns into two classes in the singular and in the plural. Our own observations showed that this should be done fairly easily, because the noun endings are clearly conducive to separating singular and plural nouns into two classes.
- To help identify some of the features that speakers rely on when selecting the plural marker.

Noun Classes in the Singular

In (1) we provide the features used in the decision tree for separating nouns into two classes in the singular. We ran the program twice: once with semantic features, and once without. In (2) we provide the decision tree when semantics features were used.

(1) *Singular, class A or B: Decision tree features and results*

Input features	Final segment type	consonant (includes semivowels) vowel	consonant (includes semivowels) vowel
	Segment value	vowel [ə, e, i, o, u] semivowel consonant	vowel [ə, e, i, o, u] semivowel consonant
	Semantics		male (♂), female (♀), tree (T), abstract (A), none
Accuracy		97.3%	98.6%

(2) *Decision tree, nouns in the singular*
   Is the final segment a consonant?

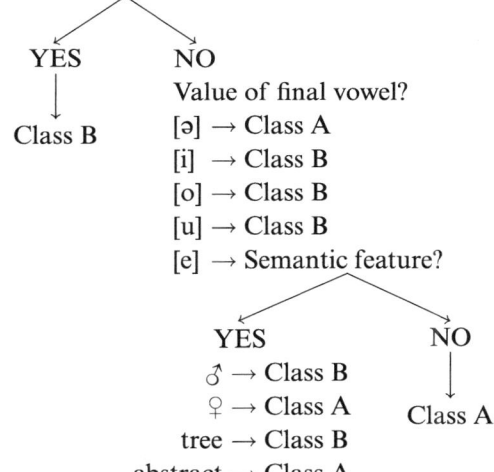

```
        YES           NO
         |         Value of final vowel?
      Class B      [ə] → Class A
                   [i] → Class B
                   [o] → Class B
                   [u] → Class B
                   [e] → Semantic feature?
                           YES            NO
                        ♂ → Class B        |
                        ♀ → Class A     Class A
                        tree → Class B
                        abstract → Class A
```

In this case, the program was able to correctly classify 98.6 percent of the nouns into two classes. The most important feature is formal, whether the final segment is a consonant or a vowel. If it is a consonant, then nouns are categorized in one class, and if it is a vowel, then the decision tree looks at the type of vowel. Vowels /-i, -o, -u/ are classified together in class B, /-ə/ in class A, and for /-e/ the decision tree looks to semantic features to make a determination. The remaining 1.4 percent of nouns are traditional masculine nouns that end in /-e/, a vowel typical of traditional feminine nouns, which is why the program erred toward classifying all nouns ending in /-e/ in the same class. When semantic features are excluded from the decision tree, the accuracy rate drops only slightly, to 97.3 percent. This is because some traditional masculine nouns end in vowels that are typical of traditional feminine nouns (i.e., *tată* 'father'), but semantic features trump formal ones in categorization when the two conflict.

Noun Classes in the Plural

In (3) we provide the features used in the decision tree for classifying nouns into two classes in the plural. We only included a single /-i/ plural marker. Synchronically there are two such markers, /-i$_1$/ and /-i$_2$/, as already discussed; however, because these have been identified via morphophonological analysis we included a single /-i/ in the algorithm.

(3) *Plural, class C or D: Decision tree features and results*

Input features	Semantics		male (♂), female (♀), tree (T), abstract (A), none
	Final segment value	consonant (C) semivowel (S) vowel [ə, e, i, o, u] (V)	consonant (C) semivowel (S) vowel [ə, e, i, o, u] (V)
	Final SV	[ju] none	[ju] none
	Plural marker	/-i/ /-e/ /-uri/	/-i/ /-e/ /-uri/
Accuracy		96.7%	98.7%

When all features are included, the decision tree can correctly categorize 98.7 percent of nouns. If semantic features are removed, the accuracy rate drops slightly to 96.7 percent. However, when semantic features are included they play an important role, as shown in the decision tree diagram in (4).

(4) *Decision tree, nouns in the plural*

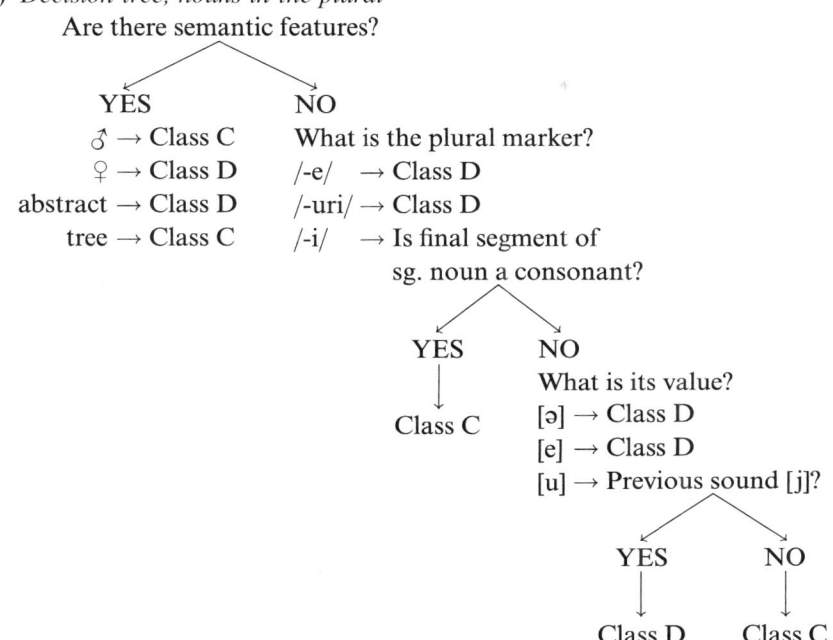

In this tree, semantic features make the first division of nouns. Thus, nouns that denote males and trees are in class C, and those that denote females and abstract nouns are in class D. Beyond the semantic core, it is the plural marker that determines class membership. Nouns that take the /-e/ and /-uri/ plural markers are in class D. For the /-i/ marker, the decision tree refers back to the singular form of the noun. This is to be expected, because this /-i/ represents two homophonous plural markers that combine systematically with different singular stems. If the singular noun ends in a consonant, then the plural form is categorized in class C, and if it ends in a vowel the nouns are categorized into classes C or D depending on the type of vowel. For the vowel /-u/ the decision tree further relies on the preceding segment, namely, if it is a semivowel /-j/. The distinctions in different types of the *-i* ending require some clarification for readers who are not entirely familiar with the Romanian data.

Recall that in the singular traditional masculine and neuter nouns are indistinguishable in form, and that /-u/ is a vowel characteristic of these nouns (or of class B nouns in our analysis). Since in our analysis traditional neuter nouns are classified with traditional feminine nouns, it is expected that speakers would need additional cues to classify those nouns that end in /-u/ in the singular and that take the /-i/ plural marker. Interestingly, all of these nouns end in [−ju] in the singular: *acvariu* [akvarju] 'aquarium', *planetariu* [planetarju] 'planetarium'. In (5) we summarize the synchronic distinction between the two different /-i/ plural markers. We present this here because this is where the distinction can be clearly laid out.

(5) *Synchronic /-i₁/ vs. /-i₂/ distinction*

Noun ending in the singular	Noun class in the plural	/-i/ type
-C (consonant)	C	/-i₁/
-ə, -e	D	/-i₂/
-ju	D	/-i₂/
-u (not -ju)	C	/-i₁/

To differentiate between the /-i/ that is suffixed to one noun form (-C or [-u]) versus the other ([-ə], [-e], [-ju]), we will label them /-i₁/ and /-i₂/. The first, /-i₁/, is for class C nouns (C or [-u] endings in the singular), and the second, /-i₂/, is for class D nouns ([-ə], [-e], or [-ju] endings in the singular). Hence, in the plural, semantic features and the plural marker predict class membership:

- /-i₁/ → class C
- /-e/, /-uri/, and /-i₂/ → class D

Rules of Plural Formation

In (6) we give the features used to establish the rules of plural formation for Romanian nouns. Semantic features are important in plural formation, so we do not include results for decision trees without semantic features.

(6) *Plural-formation decision tree features and results (/-i/, /-e/, /-uri/)*

Input features	Semantics	male (♂), female (♀), tree (T), abstract (A), none
	Syllable number	1 (one) 2 (polysyllabic)
	Final segment value	consonant (C) semivowel (S) vowel [ə, e, i, o, u]
	Singular root diphthong	[ea] [oa] none
Accuracy		79.50%

To save space, we do not repeat the decision tree here and refer the reader to the decision tree in (7) in section 3.4 of the chapter.

The accuracy rate for the rules-of-plural-formation decision tree is 79.5 percent, which is lower than the accuracy for noun categorization in the singular and the plural. The primary reason for this is the significant variation in modern Romanian with respect to plural marking. In (7) and (8) we give examples of nouns that can take two plural markers. These are traditional neuter nouns in (7) and examples of traditional feminine nouns in (8).

(7) /-e/ ~ /-uri/: Traditional neuter nouns

Singular	Plural	Gloss
vis	vise ~ vis**uri**	dream
defileu	defilee ~ defile**uri**	gorge
fus	fuse ~ fus**uri**	spinning needle

A Google search (www.google.com) returned the following results for the plural forms of these nouns:

- *vis* 'dream': 236,000 /-e/ and 23,000 /-uri/
- *defileu* 'gorge': 508 /-e/ and 236 /-uri/
- *fus* 'spinning needle': 967 /-e/ and 360 /-uri/

(8) /-e/ ~ /-i$_2$/: Traditional feminine nouns

Singular	Plural	Gloss
monedă	monede ~ monezi	coin
boltă	bolte ~ bolți	arch
coardă	coarde ~ corzi	rope

A Google search returned the following results for the plural forms of these nouns:

- *monedă* 'coin': 16,400 /-e/ and 532 /-i/
- *boltă* 'arch': 1,260 /-i/ and 371 /-e/
- *coardă* 'rope': 738 /-i/ and 523 /-e/

In (9) we summarize the direction of the errors made by the decision tree. Notice that most of the errors in classification occur between /-e/ and /-i/ and between /-uri/ and /-e/, which is exactly where one finds variation in selection of the plural marker.

(9) *Variation in plural-marker selection*

Plural marker	Classified as		
	/-e/	/-i/	/-uri/
/-e/	500	16	28
/-i/	**197**	**846**	22
/-uri/	**135**	7	**199**

Notes

We fondly dedicate this chapter to David Perlmutter, from whom we have both learned so much, and whose unwavering confidence in this project has been a constant source of inspiration to us. In his inimitable manner, David has often told us that the two-gender analysis of Romanian is as clear as daylight. We hope that our readers will concur in his assessment.

We are thankful to Ovidiu Bogdan, creator of a Romanian electronic dictionary, for providing us with a searchable noun file. www.castingsnet.com/dictionaries. For helpful discussions of this project, we are grateful to Eric Bakovic, Bernard Comrie, Grev Corbett, Donka Farkas, Jay Jasanoff, Andy Kehler, John Moore, Andrew Nevins, Keith Plaster, Sharon Rose, Steve Wechsler, and an anonymous reviewer. We regret that we were unable to take into account all of their excellent suggestions.

1. Noun class and gender are different terms denoting the same concept (Corbett 1991, 1); *class* and *gender* are used interchangeably in this chapter.

2. Romanian nouns inflect for one of five cases: nominative, accusative, genitive, dative, and vocative. The vocative case is quickly losing ground to the nominative, and the other four cases have only two distinguishing forms: nominative/accusative and genitive/dative forms (Graur, Avram, and Vasiliu 1966, 79). When inflecting for case, nouns can be singular or plural, and definite or indefinite. Definite forms have an enclitic definite suffix, while indefinite forms are preceded by a separate indefinite article.

3. These have various realizations according to the morphophonological rules of the language.

4. Syncretism has been a difficult issue for morphological theories and subject to heated debate. For our purposes, nothing hinges on a particular model of morphology with respect to syncretism—the crucial point, which no one seems to dispute, is that syncretic clusters occur within paradigms but do not span the entire class of nouns/paradigm.

5. Some early grammarians argued for as many as five genders (Eustatievici, Văcărescu, and Golescu as cited in Cobeț 1983–1984), whereas others argued for only two—*masculine* and *feminine*—either ignoring the neuters or saying that they are simultaneously masculine and feminine (Micu, Șincai, and others as cited in Cobeț 1983–1984). Arguments for only two genders arose in an attempt to be true to the etymological definition of *neuter* as "neither one nor the other of two," thus also explaining the lack of correspondence in content or form between the Romanian and Latin neuter genders (Cobeț 1983–1984, 92). A fourth gender has also been proposed—the "personal gender," which forms a subset of masculine and femi-

nine (Rosetti 1965, 85; Graur, Avram, and Vasiliu 1966, 59–60). The "personal gender" is expressed by adding the particle *pe* before proper names and names of personified animals:

(i) *Am   văzut-   o   pe Ioana*
   have.1s see.past—3s.f.clitic on Ioana
   'I saw Ioana.'

It parallels Spanish personal *a*; see

(ii) *Lo vi a Juan*
   'I saw Juan.'

6. The word *animal* 'animal' is neuter and it is animate. Mallinson suggests that this word could eventually be reinterpreted as masculine by a new generation of speakers (Mallinson 1986, 247). There are some collective nouns denoting groups of people, but not individuals, which are also neuter—that is, *popor* 'people', *tineret* 'youth'.

7. After Corbett 1991, 152, figure 6.1. (2) shows only the main agreement markers for each target gender: ∅ and *-i* for one, and *-ə* and *-e* for the other.

8. The notion of "disagreement" is used when the noun and the target have different genders. In Romanian when a demonstrative refers to an event it is feminine (*asta*), while the adjective describing the event is "masculine" (*uluitor*): *Asta*[fem] *e uluitor*[masc]. 'This is amazing.' See Farkas 1990 and Lumsden 1992 for discussion.

9. There is a subset of class B nouns (numbering around eighty) that end in /-e/. Of these, forty-seven are assigned to class B via semantics, and the remaining have to be marked with a diacritic as belonging to class B.

10. Many thanks to Ioana Chitoran for pointing this out and providing the examples. As used in table 3.5, ">" indicates development of the Romanian plural ending via regular sound change from the corresponding Latin form, while "→" indicates that the Romanian plural form was remade between Latin and Romanian.

11. We are grateful to Ioana Chitoran for discussion and comments regarding this feature. See Chitoran 2002 for further discussion.

12. We thank an anonymous reviewer for pointing out examples of lexical items that would need diacritics under our analysis. These are traditional masculine inanimate nouns such as *cercel* 'earring', *chilot* 'underpants'.

13. To mention just a few of these rules, by positing 47 minor distribution rules for the *-e* plural marker in the traditional neuter class, "as many as 2,857 di- and polysyllabic nouns [are saved] from arbitrariness" (Vrabie 1989, 407). These rules include very specific endings, such as *-ist*, *-ăț*, -cons + *ru*, which are beyond what we have attempted to accomplish in this chapter. Our goal has been to show that the plural can be predicted based on formal and semantic features, and that noun classification can be obtained based on the singular and plural forms. We believe we have accomplished that goal, and Perkowski and Vrabie's (1986) and Vrabie's (1989, 2000) rules for plural formation, while much more articulated, strongly support our analysis of the Romanian gender system.

14. As an anonymous reviewer pointed out, the stability of the correspondences between class D in the plural and class A in the singular, and also between class B in the singular and class C in the plural, should be captured in the complete analysis of the operation of Romanian gender. Our proposal correctly predicts classes to which a noun will belong in the singular

and the plural but does not currently attempt to formalize any correspondences between singular and plural classes.

15. Some adjectives are invariable in form for all genders, thus occurring in just one form in the singular and one form in the plural. Examples include the following:

verde [verde] 'green (all genders, sg)'
verzi [verz^j] 'green (all genders, pl)'

This is an example of low-level syncretism, which does not pose a problem for our analysis since most adjectives distinguish gendered forms.

16. Neuter nouns that have specific endings such as stressed -*i*, -*o*, or those borrowings from French that end in -*ow*, constitute small exceptional classes that can be identified as different from masculine nouns.

References

Baerman, Matthew. 2004. Directionality and (un)natural classes in syncretism. *Language* 80:807–827.

Chitoran, Ioana. 1992. Les Langues Romanes: Deux ou troix genres? (Le cas du roumain). *Les Langues Néo-Latines* 4:71–82.

Chitoran, Ioana. 2002. *The phonology of Romanian: A constraint-based approach*. New York: Mouton de Gruyter.

Cobeț, Doina. 1983–1984. Observații Privind Categoria Genului în Gramatica Românească de Pînă la Anul 1870. In *Annuaire de Linguistique et d'Histoire Littéraire* 29:1–99.

Corbett, Greville G. 1991. *Gender*. Cambridge: Cambridge University Press.

Corbett, Greville G., and Norman M. Fraser. 1993. Network morphology: A DATR account of Russian nominal inflection. *Journal of Linguistics* 29:113–142.

Dimitriu, C. 1996. *Gramatica Limbii Române Explicată*. Iași, România: Virginia Press.

Farkas, Donka. 1990. Two cases of underspecification in morphology. *Linguistic Inquiry* 21:539–550.

Farkas, Donka, and Draga Zec. 1995. Agreement and pronominal reference. In G. Cinque and G. Giusti, eds., *Advances in Roumanian linguistics* 10:83–101.

Graur, Alexander, Mioara Avram, and Laura Vasiliu, eds. 1966. *Gramatica Limbii Române*. 2nd ed. Vol. 1. Bucharest: Academy of the Socialist Republic of Romania.

Hall, Robert. 1965. The "neuter" in Romance: A pseudo-problem. *Word* 21:421–427.

Harris, James W. 1991. The exponence of gender in Spanish. *Linguistic Inquiry* 22:27–62.

Hockett, Charles F. 1958. *A course in modern linguistics*. New York: Macmillan.

Juilland, Alphonse G., P. M. H. Edwards, and Ileana Juilland. 1965. *Frequency Dictionary of Rumanian Words*. The Hague: Mouton.

Karmiloff-Smith, Annette. 1979. *A functional approach to child language*. Cambridge: Cambridge University Press.

Levelt, Willem J. M. 1989. *Speaking: From intention to articulation*. Cambridge, MA: MIT Press.

Lumsden, John S. 1992. Underspecification in grammatical and natural gender. *Linguistic Inquiry* 23:469–486.

Mallinson, Graham. 1986. *Rumanian*. Croom Helm Descriptive Grammars.

Mandler, Jean M. 2000. Perceptual and conceptual processes in infancy. *Journal of Cognition and Development* 1:3–36.

Perkowski, Jan L., and Emil Vrabie. 1986. Covert semantic and morphophonemic categories in the Romanian gender system. *The Slavic and East European Journal* 30(1):54–67.

Petrucci, Peter R. 1993. Slavic features in the history of Romanian. Doctoral dissertation, USC.

Rosetti, Alexandru. 1965. *Linguistica*. The Hague: Mouton.

Rosetti, Alexandru. 1973. *Brève Histoire de la Langue Roumaine des Origines à Nos Jours*. The Hague: Mouton.

Sadler, Louisa. 2006. Gender resolution in Rumanian. In Miriam Butt, Mary Dalrymple, and Tracy Holloway King, eds., *Intelligent linguistic architectures: Variations on themes by Ronald M. Kaplan*. Stanford, CA: CSLI.

Snyder, William, and Ann Senghas. 1997. Agreement morphology and the acquisition of noun-drop in Spanish. *Proceedings of the Annual Boston University Conference on Language Development* 21(2):584–591.

Stump, Gregory. 2001. *Inflectional morphology*. Cambridge: Cambridge University Press.

Suzman, Susan. 1999. Learn Zulu the way children do. *South African Journal of African Languages* 19:134–147.

Tucker, G. Richard, Wallace E. Lambert, and André A. Rigault. 1977. *The French speaker's skill with grammatical gender: An example of rule-governed behavior*. The Hague: Mouton.

Vrabie, Emil. 1989. On the distribution of the neuter plural endings in Modern Standard Romanian (MSR). *The Slavic and East European Journal* 33(3):400–410.

Vrabie, Emil. 2000. Feminine noun plurals in Standard Romanian. *The Slavic and East European Journal* 44(4):537–552.

Wechsler, Stephen. 2009. "Elsewhere" in gender resolution. In Kristin Hanson and Sharon Inkelas, eds., *The nature of the word: Studies in honor of Paul Kiparsky*. Cambridge, MA: MIT Press.

Zaliznjak, Andrej A. 1964. K voprosu o grammatičeskix kategorijax roda i oduševlennosti v sovremennom russkom jazyke. *Voprosy jazykoznanija* 4:25–40.

4   1-handed PERSONs and ASL Morphology

J. Albert Bickford

In American Sign Language (ASL) there is a suffix -PERSON that is used to derive nouns referring to people from verbs and occasionally other word classes, often with an agentive meaning. Common examples of signs that contain this suffix are listed in (1).

(1) a. TEACH + -PERSON   'teacher'

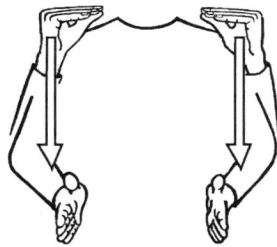

    b. SERVE + -PERSON   'waiter, server, servant'
    c. MANAGE + -PERSON   'manager, director'

The purpose of this chapter is to describe this suffix, in particular, to give an analysis of its two variant forms and their distribution. The most common form of the suffix is the same as the ASL noun PERSON, except that the suffix uses a B handshape while the independent noun is often initialized with a P handshape.[1] Accordingly, I call it the -PERSON suffix. This name is preferable to the more common label "agentive suffix," since the meaning that results from adding the suffix is not always agentive, especially when the root is not a verb. This can be seen in the examples listed in (2).

(2) a. CHRIST + -PERSON   'Christian'
    b. LIBRARY + -PERSON   'librarian'
    c. WRENCH + -PERSON   'mechanic, plumber'
    d. FARM[2] + -PERSON   'farmer'
    e. NEXT-TO + -PERSON   'neighbor'

This suffix is therefore unlike the English agentive suffix -er, which only attaches to verbs. Another way the ASL -PERSON suffix differs from English -er is that -er can be used to derive words for inanimate objects, such as 'stapler' or 'starter', whereas the ASL -PERSON suffix always derives a word that refers to a person. In fact, all grammatical uses of the -PERSON suffix that I am familiar with denote a person according to an established social role, most commonly an occupation. Thus, the suffix can only be appropriately used with a root whose meaning can be construed as characteristic of such a role. Sandler and Lillo-Martin (2006, 64–65) point out other differences, such as ASL forms like STUDY + -PERSON 'student' that do not correspond to an English word using -er (*studier).

The particular focus of this chapter is the existence of a 1-handed variant of the -PERSON suffix that occurs with certain roots. For example, 'lawyer' and 'mechanic' may be signed in either of two ways:

(3) 'Lawyer'
    a. LAW + -PERSON(2-handed)

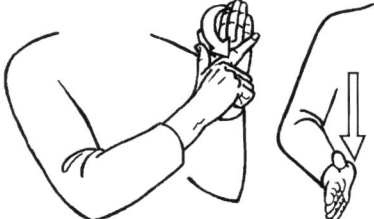

    b. LAW + -PERSON(1-handed)

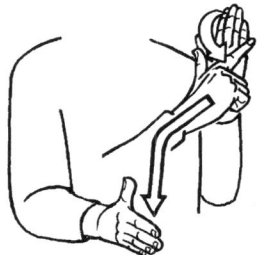

(4) 'Mechanic'
    a. WRENCH + -PERSON(2-handed)
    b. WRENCH + -PERSON(1-handed)

There is a fair amount of variation between signers in the use of the -PERSON suffix, in particular, in how much they use the 1-handed variant. One Deaf person I know never uses it; he consistently uses the 2-handed variant. Others use the 1-handed variant with some roots and the 2-handed variant with others. Some people can use either variant with certain roots, sometimes varying from one day to the next in which form they prefer.

Further, many signers have alternate ways of deriving an equivalent meaning. Some can use certain roots by themselves, without any suffix, with the meaning that would be expected if the -PERSON suffix were attached. For example, some Deaf people use signs like those listed in (5), especially in casual conversations with other Deaf people. Thus, the sign SERVE may also be used to mean 'server (in a restaurant)'. Mouthing an English word is sometimes used to distinguish which meaning is intended. These signers seem to have a rule of zero derivation that applies to some roots, as well as the rule that adds the -PERSON suffix to other roots, both of which produce the same change in meaning.

(5) a. LEAD   'lead'   'leader'
    b. SERVE   'serve'   'server'
    c. MANAGE   'manage'   'manager'
    d. LINGUISTICS 'linguistics' 'linguist'
    e. WRENCH   'wrench'   'plumber, mechanic'
    f. SWEEP   'sweep'   'janitor'

Some signers can also produce a noun referring to a person using the well-known nominalization process typified by the pair SIT vs. CHAIR (Supalla and Newport 1978)—modification of the movement of the root so that the derived noun has two short, tense, usually downward movements.[3]

(6) 'Leader' (alternate sign for some people, without -PERSON suffix)[4]

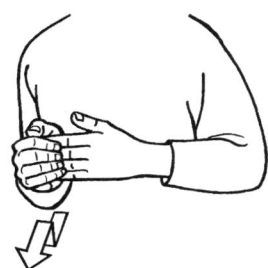

Thus, there is considerable variation in the use of the -PERSON suffix—in its form, in the roots that it is used with, and in the morphological alternatives for expressing the same meaning. This is not particularly surprising, given that these morphological processes are clearly derivational, not inflectional. I make the standard assumption (following Jackendoff 1975) that each derived form containing the -PERSON suffix is listed explicitly in a signer's lexicon, even when derivable by a general word-formation rule. Thus, signers may differ (1) in whether they have a particular derived form in their personal lexicon and (2) in the specific morphological process used to derive that form. They may even (3) have derived forms in their lexicon that apparently use the -PERSON suffix but that do not completely conform to the general rule. For example, the derived word for 'student' occurs with at least three different variants of the -PERSON suffix, as shown in (7). Although the first two forms conform to the general patterns already noted, (7c) is idiosyncratic. In it, the handshape of the suffix is 5 with palm facing down, not B with palm facing inward.[5]

(7) 'Student'
    a. LEARN + -PERSON(2-handed: BB)

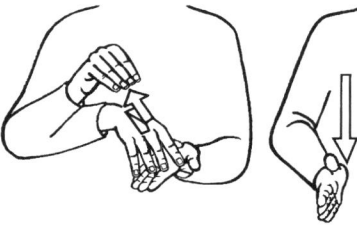

    b. LEARN + -PERSON(1-handed: B)

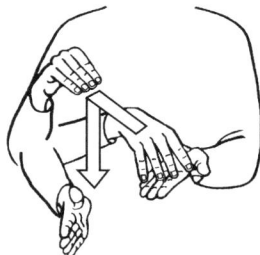

    c. LEARN + -PERSON(1-handed: 5)

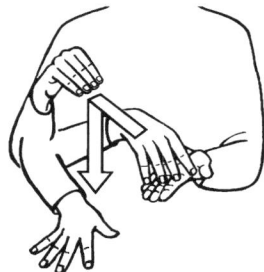

Despite the idiolectal variation in the use of the -PERSON suffix, there are consistent regularities for all signers that should be captured in a general analysis of it. These are listed in (8). The form of the suffix depends on the phonological class of the root, according to the classes originally noted by Battison (1978) and described in various ways in more recent work. I will use van der Hulst's (1996) labels for these classes, describing them as "BALANCED" and "UNBALANCED" signs.

(8) *Phonological class of the root* *Form of the -PERSON suffix*
    a. Both hands move and have identical handshapes.
       Battison 1978: "Type I"
       Sandler 1993: "echo articulator" or "E2"
       van der Hulst 1996: "BALANCED"

The 1-handed variant of the -PERSON suffix is never used.

    b. Weak hand does not move and its handshape is either identical to the strong hand or restricted to a small set of unmarked handshapes.
       Battison 1978: "Type II/III"
       Sandler 1993: "h2-place" or "2P"
       van der Hulst 1996: "UNBALANCED"

If the suffix may be used with the root, either variant of the suffix may occur (depending on the signer and the root). When the 1-handed variant is used, the weak hand stays in one place through both the root and suffix.

Rule (8a) states that with balanced roots, the 1-handed variant is never used. Consider the balanced root MANAGE. When the -PERSON suffix is added to it, only the 2-handed variant is possible, as indicated in (9).

(9) 'Manager'
    a. MANAGE + -PERSON(2h)   b. *MANAGE + -PERSON(1h)

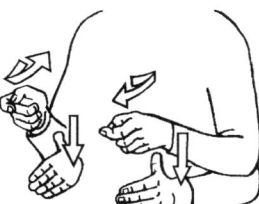 

Rule (8b) states that with unbalanced roots, either variant may be used. It also points out that the 1-handed variant of the suffix is not, strictly speaking, 1-handed. Consider again the example of the unbalanced root LAW, given in (3b). In the 1-handed variant, the weak hand remains in front of the shoulder throughout both the root and the suffix. That is, this variant of the suffix is also unbalanced, and its weak handshape is the same as in the root.

Example (10) is a particularly interesting example of the variation described in (8). I was asking one consultant about which form of the suffix she would use to sign INTERPRETER. When she tried out the 2-handed version of the suffix, both hands moved in the root. When she tried the 1-handed version of the suffix, the weak hand of the root was motionless, an instance of what Padden and Perlmutter (1987) call Weak Freeze. Eventually, she found both combinations acceptable. This is completely consistent with the generalization in (8)—although the root exists in both balanced and unbalanced (Weak Freeze) forms, the 1-handed version of the suffix is only possible with the unbalanced form.[6]

(10) 'Interpreter'
    a. INTERPRET + -PERSON(2h)

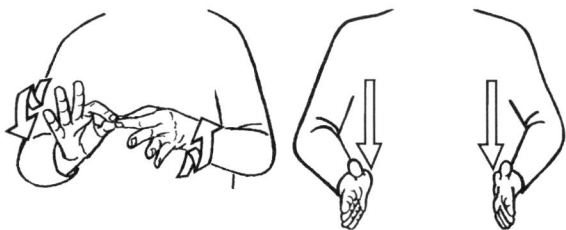

    b. INTERPRET(with Weak Freeze) + -PERSON(1h)

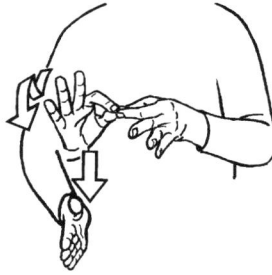

The progressive assimilation of handshape that occurs in the 1-handed version of the -PERSON suffix appears to be an instance of what has been called Weak Hand Spreading. This process has been noted by Liddell and Johnson (1986), Sandler (1993), and van der Hulst (1996, 140), among others. However, Weak Hand Spreading is normally assumed to be blocked by 2-handed signs (compare, for example, Nespor and Sandler's (1999, 163) work on prosody in Israeli Sign Language). So, it is not clear why spreading would occur onto an apparently 2-handed sign like the -PERSON suffix. It appears as if the spreading features have actually displaced its weak handshape features.

Brentari and Goldsmith (1993, 35) make a brief mention of these facts. Their account of the variation seems to be that the -PERSON suffix has two lexical forms, a 1-handed form and a 2-handed form, either of which can be used with certain roots. When the 1-handed form is used, the weak hand can spread from the root; when the 2-handed form is used, spreading of the weak hand is blocked.

However, an analysis like this does not explain why the 1-handed form never occurs with balanced roots. It would also be preferable to have an analysis in which there was only a single lexical form for the -PERSON suffix, with the different observed phonetic forms resulting from the interaction of general principles. I present one such analysis here, in a schematic form that is compatible with several different sets of theoretical assumptions about the phonological structure of ASL.

Suppose that the lexical form of the -PERSON suffix is underspecified for the weak hand, indicating only that the weak hand is involved in the sign but saying nothing about its handshape, orientation, motion, or location. This is represented in (11), following what van der Hulst (1996, 136) proposes for all balanced signs. (In these diagrams, many details of the feature geometry are not crucial to the analysis, as discussed later in this chapter.)

(11) *Lexical form of -PERSON suffix*

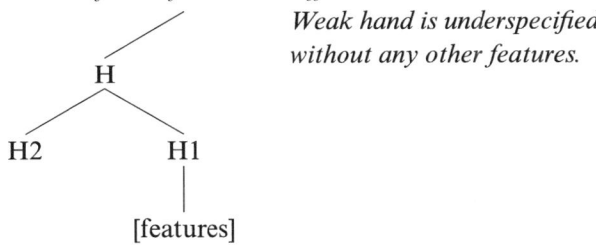

Weak hand is underspecified, without any other features.

When the -PERSON suffix is attached to an unbalanced root, such as LAW or WRENCH, one of two things can happen. One is that the features of the weak hand of the root[7] can spread to the weak hand of the suffix, resulting in the 1-handed variant of the suffix. This is illustrated in (12).

(12) *Weak Hand Spreading with unbalanced roots*

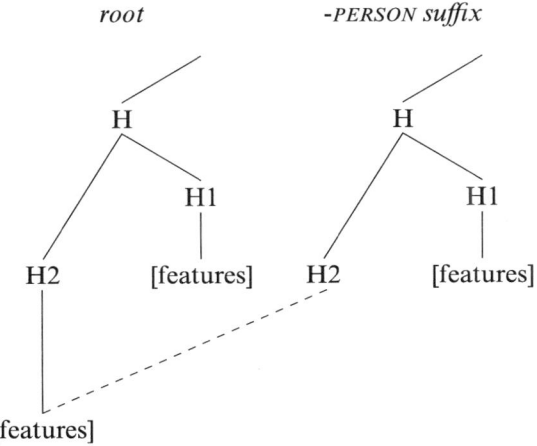

Weak-hand features of unbalanced root spread to suffix, resulting in 1-handed variant.

The other possibility is that the features do not spread, as illustrated in (13). If so, then again following van der Hulst, I assume the strong hand's features spread to the weak hand. This results in the 2-handed variant of the suffix.

(13) *Weak Hand Spreading need not apply with unbalanced roots*

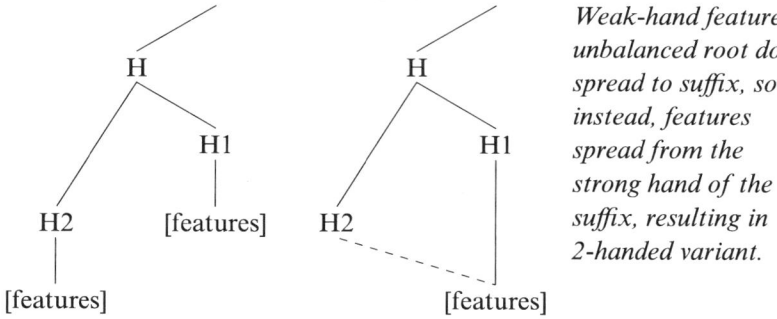

Weak-hand features of unbalanced root do not spread to suffix, so instead, features spread from the strong hand of the suffix, resulting in 2-handed variant.

This analysis, then, assumes that Weak Hand Spreading is optional, at least with this suffix, and this is why unbalanced roots may take either the 1-handed or 2-handed variant of the suffix. Remember, though, that individual signers may lexicalize only one of the two possibilities for a given root.

What happens when the -PERSON suffix is attached to a *balanced* root, such as TEACH or MANAGE? In this case, the weak hand of the root is also underspecified, as illustrated in (14). There are no features to spread from the weak hand of the root to the suffix. As a result, in both morphemes, the weak hand surfaces as a copy of the strong hand. The only form of the suffix that can occur is the 2-handed one.

(14) *Weak Hand Spreading does not occur with balanced roots*

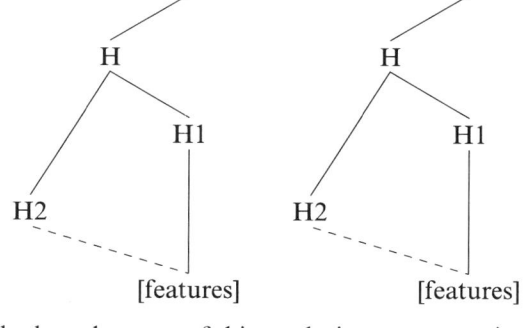

There are no weak-hand features to spread from a balanced root, resulting in only the 2-handed variant.

The key elements of this analysis are summarized in (15).

(15) *Summary: Key elements of the analysis*[8]
   a. In balanced signs in general, and in the -PERSON suffix in particular, the weak hand is not specified for any features, only that it is involved in the sign.

b. Weak Hand Spreading (or some process very much like it) applies optionally, spreading weak-hand features from the root to the suffix.
c. The spreading can only happen from unbalanced roots, because they are the only ones that have features specified for the weak hand.
d. If a weak hand does not get its features by Weak Hand Spreading, it gets them from the strong hand.

An analysis such as this is most obviously compatible with a theoretical approach like van der Hulst's, in which the weak hand is always represented phonologically as an articulator, in both balanced and unbalanced signs. However, it can also be adapted to an approach such as that presented by Sandler (1993), which represents the weak hand differently in balanced and unbalanced signs. In balanced signs, the weak hand is an articulator, as in van der Hulst's approach. This can be seen on the suffix in (16). However, in unbalanced signs (which she calls "h2-place" or "2P" signs), the weak hand appears in the feature tree as a place, not an articulator. This can be seen on the root in (16), where only the strong hand appears as an articulator. Under these assumptions, Weak Hand Spreading involves only place features, not handshape features. If it applies in (16), an anomalous structure results in which the suffix has two specifications for the weak hand, one as part of the place features for the sign, the other as an articulator.

(16) *Alternate analysis of (12), under the assumption that in unbalanced signs, the weak hand is a place*

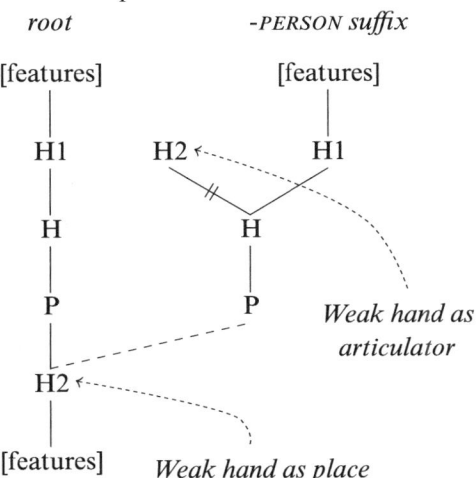

Spreading of weak-hand features causes the weak handshape as an articulator to delink, resulting in the 1-handed variant of the suffix.

Now, clearly, a theoretical approach like Sandler's that allows the weak hand to be treated as either an articulator or a place must have within it some principle that rules out any structure in which the weak hand is treated as both articulator and place. (Otherwise, a structure could result in which the weak hand is assigned two different and contradictory sets of features, one set as an articulator and the other as a place.) However this principle is stated, it presumably applies in a case like (16) to delink the underspecified articulator node for the weak hand. In the resulting structure, then, the weak hand is treated as a place in both root and suffix, yielding the 1-handed variant of the suffix, as desired. (As for situations in which Weak Hand Spreading does not occur, an analysis following Sandler's approach works the same way as outlined earlier—the weak hand gets its features from the strong hand.)

Thus, this analysis can be incorporated into either theoretical approach for representing the weak hand in unbalanced signs. Its correctness is therefore independent of whether one regards the weak hand in unbalanced signs as an articulator or as a place.

In summary, the variation between 2-handed and 1-handed forms of the ASL -PERSON suffix can be accounted for in a unitary analysis if one assumes that balanced signs such as this suffix do not specify any handshape features for the weak hand, only that the weak hand is involved in the sign. The independently needed rule of Weak Hand Spreading then optionally applies when the suffix attaches to an unbalanced root, supplying handshape features to the weak hand of the suffix from the weak hand of the root. If Weak Hand Spreading does not apply to an unbalanced sign, or if the root is a balanced sign with no weak-hand features to spread to the suffix, then the weak-hand features are supplied from the strong hand. This analysis explains why the 1-handed variant does not occur with balanced signs.

Notes

The paper on which this chapter is based was presented at the annual meeting of the Linguistic Society of America, Boston, January 10, 2004. David Perlmutter heard the paper and afterward encouraged me to submit it for publication (not knowing it was already planned for inclusion in this book). He also commented that he could see a lot of himself in it, which is certainly not accidental, because it was my privilege to have him as my dissertation director. His comments reassured me that this chapter would indeed be a fitting tribute to him and to the profound influence he has played in my professional life. Thank you, David—your influence continues, and it continues to be appreciated!

I would also like to thank my Deaf friends (who have asked not to be identified publicly) who took time to share with me their use of this suffix and who continue to help me understand their language. Finally, thanks to Rachel Channon for helpful comments on an earlier version of the chapter and to Alice Paschal for drawing the diagrams of the data.

1. Supalla (1998) discusses the historical relationships of these forms. Even today, some signers use the B handshape in the independent noun as well as the suffix. For them, what I call a suffix here could perhaps be analyzed as a root—that is, the derived nouns could be analyzed as compounds that include the noun PERSON. One might also argue that, because compounding is a well-established and ubiquitous process in ASL, it would be better to consider this process as an instance of compounding, not suffixation. On the other hand, suffixa-

tion is not unknown in ASL—for example, in the thumbs-up suffix used to derive comparative forms of certain adjectives such as BETTER. Aronoff, Meir, and Sandler (2005) discuss the existence of sequential affixation in signed languages and specifically consider -PERSON as a suffix (p. 312). Sandler and Lillo-Martin (2006, 64–65) mirror this discussion, adding criteria for distinguishing compounds from affixes. Some of the reasons for analyzing -PERSON as a suffix are its productivity and the degree of morphophonemic variation (which is more extensive than is typical of compounding and also somewhat idiosyncratic). Ultimately, though, the analysis of -PERSON as suffix versus root does not make any material difference to the analysis presented in this chapter.

2. Unlike English *farm*, ASL FARM can only be used as a noun.

3. This same tense, restrained movement, or something similar to it, may be observed with some of the signs listed in (5).

4. Signers also differ in whether the strong hand grasps the weak hand in LEAD and LEADER; for some signers the weak hand grasps the strong one. HELP and HELPER show similar variation; for most signers the strong hand is on top as the A hand, while for some signers the strong B hand lifts the weak A hand (apparently a retention from the older form of the sign in which the strong hand lifts the elbow).

5. This is possibly an assimilation to the first handshape of the root, although it is puzzling that the suffix would assimilate to the first handshape of the root and not to the second. This same 5 handshape with palm down in the suffix also occurs in one variant of PREACH + -PERSON 'preacher, pastor'. PREACH is a one-handed sign, so in one sense it is not surprising that the -PERSON suffix would be one-handed. Yet, other one-handed signs, like LIBRARY, generally take the regular 2-handed variant of the suffix (with the B handshape). It could simply be that this 1-handed, 5-handshape, palm-down variant is an idiosyncratic form historically derived from the -PERSON suffix but synchronically distinct from it.

There is also variation in the pronunciation of the root LEARN, and accordingly of the derived noun STUDENT. In addition to the form illustrated here, there is a hypercorrect form in which the strong hand moves all the way to the ipsilateral side of the forehead, usually followed in STUDENT by the 2-handed variant of -PERSON, thus similar to (7a). This form is primarily used when teaching ASL or in other situations highly influenced by English. There is also an idiomatic variant of STUDENT that is like (7c), but it uses a flattened O throughout the root LEARN, rather than starting as a 5-hand and closing to flattened O. (I have not observed this form when LEARN is used by itself as a verb.) Interestingly, this change in the root destroys the environment that supposedly conditions the assimilation of the suffix to a 5-hand, further reinforcing the suggestion that (7c) is a lexicalized variant of the derived noun not derivable by synchronic rules.

6. Padden and Perlmutter (1987, 368) suggested that Weak Freeze may be postlexical, but did not find evidence for this position, nor, for that matter, for the distinction between lexical and postlexical rules at all. The form in (10b) bears on this issue. To derive it, Weak Freeze must precede Weak Hand Spreading. If Weak Freeze is postlexical, so is Weak Hand Spreading, and conversely, if Weak Hand Spreading is lexical, so is Weak Freeze. Inasmuch as both rules apply only within words, not across word boundaries, this suggests that both should be considered lexical rules (if the distinction between lexical and postlexical is to be made at all).

7. It is not important for this chapter how the weak hand's features are specified. Rachel Channon (2004) has proposed that the weak handshape in most cases can be predicted based on the strong handshape, the portion of the weak hand that is contacted by the strong hand,

and perceptual requirements that the weak handshape be sufficiently distinct. Under her proposal, in most cases the only features that need to be specified for the weak hand in an unbalanced sign are that (1) the weak hand be involved in the sign, and (2) the portion of the weak hand that is contacted.

8. The assumptions in (15b–d) are consistent with a more general assumption that features may spread in only two ways: (1) between adjacent syllables if the spreading involves corresponding nodes (e.g., from H2 in one syllable to H2 in the next), or (2) within one syllable from the strong to the weak hand. I know of no data that would suggest that H1 features may spread directly to H2 of an adjacent syllable. Conceivably, the two allowed types of spreading may occur at different times (in a derivational model of morphology) or even in different components of the grammar (e.g., Weak Hand Spreading as a lexical rule and spreading from the strong to the weak hand in a postlexical rule; see also note 6).

References

Aronoff, Mark, Irit Meir, and Wendy Sandler. 2005. The paradox of sign language morphology. *Language* 81(2):301–344.

Battison, Robbin. 1978. *Lexical borrowing in ASL*. Silver Spring, MD: Linstok Press.

Brentari, Diane, and John A. Goldsmith. 1993. Secondary licensing and the nondominant hand in ASL phonology. In Geoffrey Coulter, ed., *Phonetics and Phonology 3: Current issues in ASL Phonology*, 19–41. New York: Academic Press.

Channon, Rachel. 2004. The weak hand rule: A reformulation of the symmetry and dominance conditions. Poster presentation, Theoretical Issues in Sign Language Research 8, Barcelona.

Jackendoff, Ray. 1975. Morphological and semantic regularities in the lexicon. *Language* 51:639–671.

Liddell, Scott K., and Robert E. Johnson. 1986. American Sign Language compound formation processes, lexicalization, and phonological remnants. *Natural Language and Linguistic Theory* 4:445–513.

Nespor, Marina, and Wendy Sandler. 1999. Prosody in Israeli Sign Language. *Language and Speech* 42:143–176.

Padden, Carol, and David Perlmutter. 1987. American Sign Language and the architecture of phonological theory. *Natural Language and Linguistic Theory* 5:335–375.

Sandler, Wendy. 1993. Hand in hand: The roles of the nondominant hand in sign language phonology. *Linguistic Review* 10:337–390.

Sandler, Wendy, and Diane Lillo-Martin. 2006. *Sign language and linguistic universals*. Cambridge: Cambridge University Press.

Supalla, Ted. 1998. Reconstructing early ASL grammar through historical films. Conference presentation, Theoretical Issues in Sign Language Research 6, Washington, DC.

Supalla, Ted, and Elissa Newport. 1978. How many seats in a chair? The derivation of nouns and verbs in American Sign Language. In P. Siple, ed., *Understanding language through sign language research*, 181–214. New York: Academic Press.

van der Hulst, Harry G. 1996. On the other hand. *Lingua* 98:121–143.

5 Six Arguments for *Wh*-Movement in Chamorro

Sandra Chung

5.1 Introduction

Since Seiter 1975, it has been known that constituent questions in many of the verb-initial Austronesian languages are headless-relative clefts (henceforth, HRCs)—complex sentences in which the interrogative phrase serves as a nonverbal predicate and the rest of the sentence serves as its subject, a headless relative clause. (See, e.g., Potsdam 2004 and Paul and Potsdam 2004 on Malagasy; Bauer 1991 on Maori; Georgopoulos 1991 on Palauan; Seiter 1975 on Tagalog and six other Philippine languages; and Aldridge 2004 on Tagalog and Seediq.) In these languages, Greenberg's (1963) claim that VSO languages always place their interrogative phrases at the left (the first half of his Universal 12) is satisfied not by *wh*-movement of these constituents, but by virtue of the fact that interrogative phrases can be predicates, and predicates are clause-initial. The observation leads to a speculation, one explored in different ways by, for example, Adger and Ramchand 2005 and Oda 2005. Could it be that *wh*-movement of interrogative phrases is systematically lacking in verb-initial languages, just as it has been claimed to be systematically lacking in SOV languages (the second half of Universal 12)? If so, the typological distribution of *wh*-movement would be narrower than is often supposed, and a host of other issues would immediately arise.[1]

This chapter brings evidence to bear on this speculation from Chamorro, a verb-initial Austronesian language spoken in the Mariana Islands. Some constituent questions in Chamorro can be analyzed either as HRCs or as derived directly by *wh*-movement of the interrogative phrase. I show that other types of Chamorro questions are not structurally ambiguous in this way: these other questions cannot be analyzed as HRCs, but must instead be derived by *wh*-movement of the interrogative phrase. More generally, there are types of focus constructions in Chamorro that cannot be analyzed as HRCs, but must instead be derived by *wh*-movement of the focus. The demonstration reveals that there are verb-initial languages—and, for that matter, Austronesian languages—that can satisfy Greenberg's Universal 12 via straightforward *wh*-movement.

5.2 Preliminaries

Chamorro is a null-argument language in which the predicate can be of any category type. When the predicate is a verb or an adjective, it can be followed by its arguments in any order, but the unmarked word order is Predicate Subject Complements—that is, VSO, as in (1a).

(1) a. Ha-konfitma i kotti i intensión i Covenant Agreement.
 AGR-confirm the court the intension the Covenant Agreement
 'The court confirmed the intention of the Covenant Agreement.' (*Saipan Tribune*, September 1, 2000)
 b. Hägas ha-läknus ennao siha na planu si Speaker Benigno R. Fitial.
 long.ago AGR-present that PL L plan UNM Speaker Benigno R. Fitial
 'Speaker Benigno R. Fitial presented those plans long ago.' (*Saipan Tribune*, September 14, 2000)

When the predicate is a noun or preposition, the entire predicate phrase (DP or PP) precedes the subject, as in (2).

(2) a. Ti médiku esti siha na siñoris.
 not doctor this PL L gentlemen
 '[The public is fortunate that] these gentlemen are not doctors.' (*Saipan Tribune*, June 8, 2000)
 b. Ginin i asagua-ña gi fine'nena dos haga-ña.
 from the spouse-AGR LOC first two daughter-AGR
 'Two of his daughters were from his first wife.' (Cooreman 1982, 8)

DPs are inflected for case via a proclitic at their left edge. There are three morphological cases—unmarked, oblique, and local—whose realizations are different for pronouns, proper names, and common nouns.

(3) Duranti-n ädyu na tiempu [änai sigi i dos di um-äpatti ni pigua' _],
 during-L that L time COMP keep.on the two AGR-divide OBL betelnut
 guäha un patgun [mamómokkat _ gi chälan].
 AGR.exist a child WH[nom].AGR.walk.PROG LOC road
 'During that time when they were dividing the betelnuts, there was a child who was walking on the road.'

Of special interest here is the internal structure of DP. DPs consist of a determiner, followed by an NP and then by a possessor. Relative clauses and other modifiers can occur adjoined to the left or to the right of an NP.

(4) a. i   hägas   songsung [nai   d*um*ángkulu gui' yan mañe'lu-ña _]
the long.ago village   COMP AGR.big   he with siblings-AGR
'the long-ago village in which he grew up with his brothers and sisters'
(*Saipan Tribune*, June 15, 2000)
b. gi   todu [nai   s*um*aonao   _] na programa-n radio
LOC all   COMP AGR.participate   L program-L radio
'in all radio programs in which he has participated' (*Saipan Tribune*, June 25, 2000)

As (3) and (4) show, relative clauses contain a DP gap (represented by an underline) but no overt relative pronoun. Nonetheless, the dependency between the gap and the head NP meets the standard criteria for *wh*-movement: it holds across an apparently unbounded distance, observes islands, and exhibits strong crossover effects (see Chung 1998, 214–221). The only open question is what element it is, exactly, that has been moved. I will arbitrarily assume that the answer is not the head NP, but rather a null DP operator, *O*, which can serve various grammatical functions but must undergo *wh*-movement to the specifier of the highest C in the relative clause. This null operator can serve as a DP argument, or as any of the adjuncts realized as DPs in the oblique or local case—specifically, instruments, manner phrases, or locations in time or space.²

Finally, the head NP of a relative clause can itself be null, in which case it contributes no descriptive content. In such cases, certain complementizers that realize the highest C of the relative clause are also unpronounced (see Chung 1998, 231–234, for the details). Compare

(5) a. Um-äsudda' häm yan i   palao'an [*O* ni   kinenne'-ña   si
AGR-meet   we with the woman   COMP WH[obj].take-AGR UNM
Manuel _ pära i   giput].
Manuel   to   the party
'I met the woman who Manuel took to the party.'
b. Esta   ti   máfattu   gi   banda-n [*O* änai   man-gaigi todu i
already not AGR.arrive.PROG LOC side-L   COMP AGR-be.at all the
manbihu _].
old.ones
'He hadn't yet gotten to the place where all the old men were.' (Cooreman 1983, 65)

(6) a. Um-äsudda' häm yan i   [*O* kinenne'-ña   si   Manuel _ pära i
AGR-meet   we with the   WH[obj].take-AGR UNM Manuel to   the
giput].
party
'I met the one who Manuel took to the party.'

b. D*um*imu guihi   [*O* änai gaigi   si   tata-ña   yan si
   AGR.kneel LOC.that   COMP AGR.be.at UNM father-AGR and UNM
   nana-ña   _].
   mother-AGR
   'They knelt where his father and his mother were.' (Cooreman 1983, 71)

I will refer to a relative clause whose head NP is null as a *headless relative* (HR).

5.3 The Issue

Greenberg's (1963, 111) Universal 12 states:

If a language has dominant order VSO in declarative sentences, it always puts interrogative words or phrases first in interrogative word questions; if it has dominant order SOV in declarative sentences, there is never such an invariant rule.

Consistent with Universal 12, Chamorro always places its interrogative phrases at the left. These interrogative phrases are typically DPs or PPs; if they serve as adjuncts or arguments, they cannot occur in situ.[3] Consider the constituent questions below.

(7) a. Hayi siña l*um*a'la'   _ gi $3.05 gi   ora   na suetdu?
       who? can WH[nom].AGR.live   LOC $3.05 LOC hour L   salary
       'Who can live on an hourly wage of $3.05?' (*Saipan Tribune*, November 28, 2000)
    b. Pära manu guätu   na   un-konni' si   Rita _ ?
       to   where? over.there COMP AGR-take UNM   Rita
       'To where did you take Rita?'
    c. Hafa malago'-mu?   _ ?
       what? WH[obl].want-AGR
       'What do you want?'
    d. Hafa na   guäha   giya Obyan ädyu i   latte stone _ ?
       what? COMP AGR.exist LOC Obyan that the latte stone
       'Why would there be those latte stones at Obyan?' (Cooreman 1983, 8)

As expected, the dependency between the interrogative phrase and the gap in constituent questions exhibits the familiar properties of *wh*-movement (see Chung 1998, 208–214).

It is immediately apparent that questions of type (7) could, in principle, be analyzed in two ways: as constructions in which the interrogative phrase has undergone *wh*-movement, as shown schematically in (8), or as HRCs (headless-relative clefts)—complex sentence types in which the interrogative phrase is a higher nonverbal predicate and the remainder, its subject, is an HR, as sketched in (9).

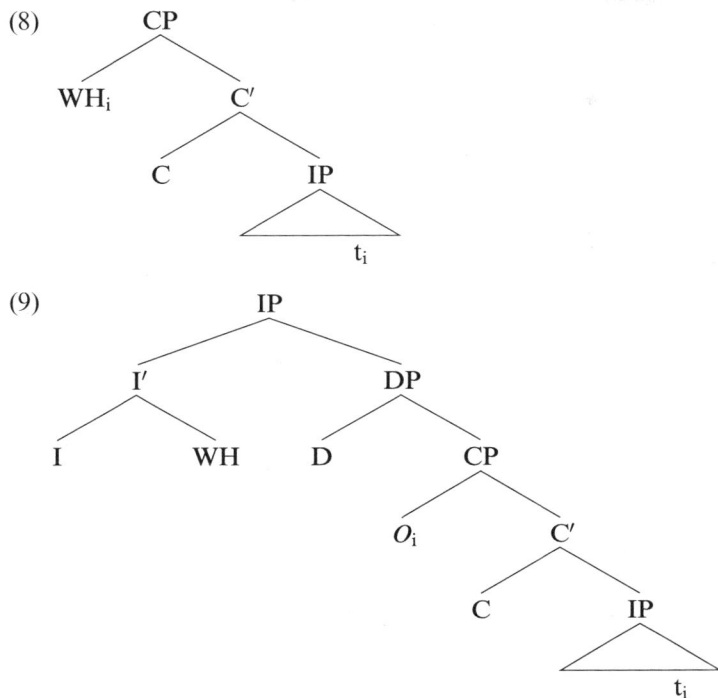

The availability of the HRC analysis follows from the fact that each of its parts is known independently to be available. As shown in section 5.2, Chamorro has HRs. The language also permits interrogative phrases to serve as predicates of clauses, as can be seen from (10).

(10) a. Hayi hao?
       who? you
       'Who are you?'
    b. Hafa i   óttimu na che'chu'-ñiha?
       what? the last   L job-AGR
       'What was their last job?'
    c. Pära hayi i   [O fina'tinas-mu   _] titiyas?
       for who? the WH[obj].make-AGR   tortillas
       'For whom were the tortillas that you made?'

Further, because constituent questions in Chamorro can be viewed as a subtype of focus (or cleft) construction, the choice between a simple *wh*-movement analysis and an HRC analysis arises for the focus construction as well. In the focus construction, the focus—typically a contrastive DP or PP—occurs at the left and is resumed by a gap. Consider

(11) a. Todu i   dos um-aluk   _ na   bunitu   esti na na'an.
       all the two WH[nom]-say   COMP AGR.pretty this L name
       '*Both of them* said that this name was beautiful.' (Cooreman 1983, 78)
   b. I   botu-mu míbali   _ !
      the vote-AGR WH[nom].AGR.valuable
      'It's *your vote* that counts!' (*Saipan Tribune*, October 1, 1997)
   c. Ginin i   finu' Juan na   ma-tungu'   as nana-ña   yan
      from the word Juan COMP AGR.PASS-know OBL mother-AGR and
      tata-ña   _ .
      father-AGR
      'It was from *Juan's words* that it was known by his mother and father.'
      (Cooreman 1983, 86)
   d. I   hälum guma' ha' nai siña man-laoya   hit _ .
      the inside house EMP COMP can AGR-walk.around we
      'We can wander around *only inside the house*.' (*Ginen i Obispo*, March 7, 1999)

As before, the dependency between the focus and the gap meets the familiar criteria for *wh*-movement. The analytic issue is whether the focus has itself undergone *wh*-movement, or is instead the predicate of an HRC.

Exactly this issue is raised and then resolved for English *wh*-clefts by Hankamer (1974), and for English *it*-clefts by Pinkham and Hankamer (1975). Hankamer and Pinkham establish that certain instances of clefts must be derived by *wh*-movement of the focus, others must be HRCs, and still others can be analyzed either way. Their demonstration relies on two types of arguments that will prove useful in what follows. First, if the focus could not independently serve as the predicate of a clause, it cannot be the predicate of an HRC, but must instead have reached its surface position via *wh*-movement. Second, if the focus exhibits connectivity effects linking it to the remainder of the sentence (henceforth, the remainder), it must have undergone *wh*-movement. But if connectivity might have held but does not, the focus must be the predicate of an HRC. I now bring these and other types of arguments to bear on the analysis of the Chamorro constructions in (7) and (11).

5.4 Evidence

This section gives six arguments that certain types of constituent questions and focus constructions in Chamorro must involve *wh*-movement of the interrogative phrase or focus. The combined weight of the evidence makes it clear that direct *wh*-movement is a live option in this language. Evidence is presented from an impossible type of predicate in 5.4.1, from two sorts of connectivity in 5.4.2 and 5.4.3, from sluicing in 5.4.4, from negative concord in 5.4.5, and from a specificity effect in 5.4.6.

5.4.1 An Impossible Type of Predicate

Although Chamorro allows predicates of clauses to be of any major category types, it—curiously—does not permit them to be DPs in the locative case. Compare the PP predicate in (12a) with the locative DPs in (12b–c).[4]

(12) a. Ginin as Juan i katta.
       from OBL Juan the letter
       'The letter was from Juan.'
   b. *Gi petta i ispehus.
       LOC door the mirror
       'The mirror is on the door.'
   c. *Gi hilu' lamäsa magagu-mu.
       LOC top table clothes-AGR
       'Your clothes are on top of the table.'

The only predicates that the language has for denoting location in space are verbs; for instance, the verb *gaigi* 'be at (a location)'.

(13) a. Gaigi gi petta i ispehus.
       AGR.be.at LOC door the mirror
       'The mirror is on the door.'
   b. Gaigi magagu-mu gi hilu' lamäsa.
       AGR.be.at clothes-AGR LOC top table
       'Your clothes are on top of the table.'

Nonetheless, interrogative phrases can occur in the locative case, as the constituent questions in (14) show.

(14) a. Gi manu ni man-ma'a'ñao i famagu'un mañ-aga _ ?
       LOC where? COMP AGR-afraid the children INFIN.AGR-stay
       'Where are the children afraid to stay?'
   b. Giya hayi nai ha-dipépendi gui' si Juan _ ?
       LOC who? COMP AGR-depend.PROG himself UNM Juan
       'Who does Juan depend on?'

More generally, focused phrases can occur in the locative case (Chung 1998, 272).

(15) a. Gi hilu' lamäsa nai ha-po'lu si Sally i nä'yan siha _ .
       LOC top table COMP AGR-put UNM Sally the dish PL
       'Sally put the dishes *on top of the table*.'
   b. Gi tatti-n ädyu na dos amku' na du*mi*mu i dos _ .
       LOC behind-L that L two old.one COMP AGR.kneel the two
       'It was behind those two old people that the two knelt.' (Cooreman 1983, 71)

Given that DPs in the locative case cannot be predicates of clauses, examples of the type (14–15) cannot be HRCs. Instead, they must be derived directly by *wh*-movement of the interrogative phrase or focus, as shown in (8).

5.4.2 Connectivity in Selectional Restrictions

A predicate's selectional restrictions are generally believed not to extend past its own maximal projection. This locality prevents the verb of the relative clause in English examples like (16) from imposing any selectional restrictions on the constituent following the copula.

(16) a. The island where they went for their vacation was Tinian.
    b. The island where they stayed during their vacation was Tinian.
    c. *The island where they went for their vacation was to Tinian.

In (16), the subject DP contains a relative clause modifier—either *where they went for their vacation* or *where they stayed during their vacation*. The point is that the verb inside the relative clause has no impact on the phrase following the copula (*Tinian*). If the verb of the relative clause could impose selectional restrictions on this phrase, one might expect (16c) to be grammatical, but it is not.

Consider now the fact that in the English *wh*-clefts in (17), the focus conforms to selectional restrictions imposed by the verb in the remainder.

(17) a. Where they went for their vacation was to Tinian.
    b. Where they stayed during their vacation was on Tinian.
    c. *Where they stayed during their vacation was to Tinian.

This connectivity is evidence that the focus in these examples must have undergone *wh*-movement (see Pinkham and Hankamer 1975, 430).

Chamorro exhibits the same sort of connectivity. In the constituent questions below, the interrogative phrase clearly conforms to selectional restrictions imposed by the verb in the remainder. The interrogative phrase in (18a) must be a goal, not a location, because *konni'* 'take' selects a goal; the interrogative phrase in (18b) must be a location, not a goal, because *po'lu* 'put' selects a location (compare (18c)).

(18) a. Pära manu guätu   nai   ma-konni' si   Miguel _ ?
        to   where? over.there COMP AGR-take   UNM Miguel
        'To where did they take Miguel?'
    b. Manu guätu   nai   ma-po'lu i   famagu'on-ta _ ?
        where? over.there COMP AGR-put   the children-AGR
        'Where did they leave our children?'
    c. *Pära manu guätu   nai   ma-po'lu i   famagu'on-ta _ ?
        to   where? over.there COMP AGR-put   the children-AGR
        'To where did they leave our children?'

Similarly, the focused phrase in the constructions in (19) conforms to selectional restrictions imposed by the verb in the remainder.[5]

(19) a. Ginin Guam nai pära u-fattu si Ramon _ agupa'.
from Guam COMP FUT AGR-arrive UNM Ramon tomorrow
'It's from Guam that Ramon will arrive tomorrow.'
 b. I hilu' lamäsa na u-po'lu i lepblu si Juan _ .
the top table COMP AGR-put the book UNM Juan
'It's on top of the table that Juan will put the book.'

These patterns argue that the interrogative phrase or focus in these examples must have undergone *wh*-movement.

5.4.3 Connectivity in Antecedent-Pronoun Relations

For a different argument from connectivity, I turn next to the architecture of antecedent-pronoun relations.

Antecedent-pronoun relations in Chamorro must conform to both universal and language-particular restrictions. For instance, Principle C of the Binding Theory must be observed. One consequence of this principle is that a full DP cannot antecede a pronoun that c-commands it. Consider the examples below, in which the relations symbolized by coindexing are excluded by Principle C.[6]

(20) a. H*um*anao gui'$_{j, *i}$ pära i lanchu-n Juan$_i$ gi Sábalu.
AGR.go he to the farm-L Juan LOC Saturday
'He$_{j, *i}$ went to Juan's$_i$ farm on Saturday.'
 b. Ha-ipi' *pro*$_{j, *i}$ i niyuk ni machetti-n Pedro$_i$.
AGR-split the coconut with machete-L Pedro
'He$_{j, *i}$ split the coconut with Pedro's$_i$ machete.'

Over and above this, Chamorro imposes the demand that a full DP either c-command, or else occur to the left of, any pronoun that it antecedes (see Chung 1998, 73–80). This requirement can be seen at work in the following.

(21) a. Ha-latchai i nä'-ña *pro*$_i$ i taotao$_i$.
AGR-consume the food-AGR the person
'The man$_i$ had consumed his$_i$ food.' (Cooreman 1983, 80)
 b. In-kenni' i famagu'on-ña *pro*$_{j, *i}$ pära i gima' Mr. Reyes$_i$.
AGR-take the children-AGR to the house Mr. Reyes
'We took his$_{j, *i}$ children back to Mr. Reyes'$_i$ house.'

In each of these examples, a full DP is attempting to antecede a possessor pronoun that occurs to its left. The relation is legal in (21a), because the full DP is the subject, and therefore c-commands the rest of the clause, including the pronoun.[7] But in (21b), the c-command condition is not met, and so coindexing is ruled out.

How do antecedent-pronoun relations work in constituent questions and focus constructions? If these constructions were invariably HRCs, we might expect a full DP embedded in the interrogative phrase or focus to be able to antecede a pronoun embedded in the remainder. The coindexing would observe Principle C, since the pronoun—a subconstituent of the HR—would not c-command the name. It would also satisfy the Chamorro-specific requirement, since the name—a subconstituent of the interrogative phrase or focus—would occur to the left of the pronoun. Further, we might expect a full DP embedded in the remainder to be unable to antecede a pronoun embedded in the interrogative phrase or focus. In such a configuration, the Chamorro-specific requirement would be violated, since the name—a subconstituent of the HR—would neither c-command the pronoun nor occur to its left.

Neither of these predictions is correct. There are examples in which a full DP embedded in the interrogative phrase or focus *cannot* antecede a pronoun embedded in the remainder.

(22) a. Kuantu   gi tumobit Juan$_i$ esta   ha-fa'gasi   pro$_{j,*i}$ _ ?
        how.many? LOC car   Juan   already WH[obj].AGR-wash
        'How many of Juan's$_i$ cars did he$_{j,*i}$ wash?'
     b. I   machetti-n Pedro$_i$ ipe'-ña   pro$_{j,*i}$ _ ni niyuk.
        the machete-L Pedro   WH[obl].split-AGR   OBL coconut
        'He$_{j,*i}$ split the coconut with *Pedro's$_i$ machete*.'

There are also examples in which a full DP embedded in the remainder *can* antecede a pronoun embedded in the interrogative phrase or focus.

(23) a. Kuantu   gi tumobet-ña pro$_i$ esta   ha-fa'gasi   si Juan$_i$ _ ?
        how.many? LOC car-AGR   already WH[obj].AGR-wash   UNM Juan
        'How many of his$_i$ cars did Juan$_i$ wash?'
     b. Gi gima'-ña   pro$_i$ na   in-bisita   i   biha$_i$ _ .
        LOC house-AGR   COMP AGR-visit   the old.lady
        'It was at her$_i$ house that we visited the old lady$_i$.'

These patterns are connectivity effects—more precisely, reconstruction effects. To see this, suppose that Principle C must be satisfied under reconstruction, and that the Chamorro-specific requirement can be met under reconstruction as well. Suppose further that the interrogative and focused phrases in (22–23) have undergone *wh*-movement. Then the coindexing in (22) will be excluded by Principle C under reconstruction, as in (20). But the coindexing in (23) will be legal, because under reconstruction it respects both Principle C and the Chamorro-specific requirement; compare (21a).

The view that reconstruction effects arise only through movement is not universally held. Nonetheless, there is evidence from other languages that this view is correct as far as clefts in particular are concerned (see Hankamer 1974 on English *wh*-clefts). I therefore take the patterns just exhibited to argue that (22–23) are not HRCs; rather, the interrogative phrase or focus must have undergone *wh*-movement.[8]

5.4.4 Sluicing

Further evidence that Chamorro has some constituent questions that are not HRCs is provided by the ellipsis process known as sluicing.

Merchant (2001) establishes that sluicing in numerous languages conforms to the following generalization: exactly those languages that allow a preposition to be stranded under *wh*-movement also allow a preposition to be stranded in (the elided IP of) sluicing. English, for instance, can strand prepositions under *wh*-movement and in sluicing, as (24) shows, but French cannot strand prepositions in either construction.

(24) a. Who was she talking to?
     b. We know she was talking to someone, but we don't know [who _].

Merchant uses this generalization to argue that sluicing is derived by deletion of a fully articulated IP from which the interrogative phrase has been extracted by *wh*-movement.

Surprisingly, Merchant's generalization appears to make the wrong predictions about sluicing in the Austronesian language Malagasy. Potsdam (2003) observes that Malagasy cannot strand prepositions under *wh*-movement, but seems to be able to strand prepositions in the material elided by sluicing. Compare the Malagasy examples in (25).

(25) a. *Trano iza   no mitoetra amina i Rasoa?
        house which? PRT live.ACT in   Rasoa
        'Which house does Rasoa live in?' (Potsdam 2003, 13)
     b. Mitoetra amin' ny trano i Rasoa fa   hadinoko hoe   trano [iza _].
        live.ACT in   the house Rasoa but forget.1SG COMP house what?
        'Rasoa lives in a house but I forget which house.' (Potsdam 2003, 13)

Potsdam's account of this builds on the claim that sluices—and, in fact, all constituent questions—in Malagasy are HRCs (see Paul and Potsdam 2004). This means that the constituent elided by Malagasy sluicing is not an IP, but instead an HR, and the interrogative phrase that survives this ellipsis in (25b) is not the object of a stranded preposition, but the predicate of an HRC. Given that the elided HR in (25b) can be formed from an applicative clause in which no preposition has been stranded, the end result is that sluicing in Malagasy does not constitute a counter-example to Merchant's generalization after all.

Now, Chamorro does not permit overt prepositions to be stranded under *wh*-movement.

(26) a. Ginin hayi na   un-risibi   i   katta _ ?
         from who? COMP AGR-receive the letter
         'From whom did you receive the letter?'
    b. *Hayi un-risibi   i   katta ginin _ ?
         who? AGR-receive the letter from
         'Who did you receive the letter from?'

The language also has a version of sluicing.

(27) Mam-ómoksai   mannuk, lao ti   ta-tungu' [hafa na klasi _].
     AGR.AP-raise.PROG chicken but not AGR-know what? L type
     'He's raising chickens, but we don't know what kind.'

This makes it relevant to ask whether Chamorro resembles French in conforming straightforwardly to Merchant's generalization, or whether it resembles Malagasy in appearing, at least initially, to offer a counterexample. If Chamorro, like French, cannot strand a preposition in the elided IP of sluicing, this would be consistent with the claim that some constituent questions in the language—those in sluicing—are derived by *wh*-movement of the interrogative phrase. On the other hand, if Chamorro were to pattern like Malagasy in permitting sluicing constructions of the type (25b), we would have a reason to follow Potsdam and Paul in proposing that all constituent questions in the language, including sluices, were HRCs.

In fact, Chamorro cannot strand a preposition in the elided IP of sluicing (Chung 2006). Compare (28a), in which the preposition *ginin* 'from' has been pied-piped, with the ungrammatical (28b), in which the preposition has been stranded inside the ellipsis.

(28) a. Si Joe ha-hunguk i   istoria ginin guahu, lao ti   hu-tungu' [ginin
         UNM Joe AGR-hear   the story from me   but not AGR-know from
         kuantu   más na taotao _].
         how.many? more LNK person
         'Joe heard the story from me, but I don't know from how many others.'
    b. *Si Joe ha-hunguk i   istoria ginin guahu, lao ti   hu-tungu'
         UNM Joe AGR-hear   the story from me   but not AGR-know
         [kuantu   más na taotao _].
          how.many? more LNK person
         'Joe heard the story from me, but I don't know how many others.'

The contrast between this and the Malagasy pattern in (25) is striking. It is reinforced by the observation that Chamorro, like Malagasy, does have a potential source for (28b) that could in principle be analyzed as an HRC, and in which no overt preposition has been stranded. Consider (29), in which one could treat the interrogative phrase as a predicate and the remainder, as an HR with a locative DP gap.

(29) Si   Joe ha-hunguk i   istoria ginin guahu, lao ti   hu-tungu' kuantu
UNM Joe AGR-hear   the story from me   but not AGR-know how.many?
más   na   taotao [O nai   ha-hunguk _].
more LNK person   COMP AGR-hear
'Joe heard the story from me, but I don't know how many others he heard it (at).'

Why is it impossible to derive (28b) from (29) by eliding the apparent HR? The most straightforward answer is that Chamorro sluicing—like sluicing in many other languages, but unlike Malagasy sluicing—is unable to elide HRs. The important point is that, for whatever reason, sluicing *cannot* derive (28b) from (29). This strongly suggests that a Malagasy-style analysis that would treat all constituent questions as HRCs is inappropriate for Chamorro. Instead, at least some constituent questions in the language—namely, those truncated by sluicing—are derived by *wh*-movement of the interrogative phrase.

5.4.5 Negative Concord

Further evidence that not all focus constructions are HRCs comes from the workings of negative concord.

Sentential negation in Chamorro is expressed by means of elements that occur in the vicinity of the clause's left edge: the negative *ti* 'not' (see (30a)), various negative verbs (30b), and—in the focus construction—a negative focus (30c).

(30) a. Ti   siña hao um-iskuela   gi   más   tákkilu' na iskuela.
      not can you AGR-go.to.school LOC more high   L school
      'You couldn't go to school in a higher school.' (Cooreman 1983, 152)
   b. Taya'   néngkanu' guihi   na tiempu.
      AGR.not.exist food   LOC.that L time
      'There wasn't any food at that time.' (Cooreman 1983, 50)
   c. Ni unu siña ta-sokni   nu esti na chinätsaga.
      not one can AGR-blame OBL this L hardship
      'We can blame *no one* for this hardship.' (*Saipan Tribune*, December 15, 1998)

Importantly, elements that express sentential negation can license the appearance of other morphologically negative forms that do not contribute any (separate) negation to the semantics. This phenomenon, known as negative concord, is illustrated below.

(31) a. Ti hu-bisita ni   háyiyi ha'.
         not AGR-visit not anyone EMP
         'I didn't visit anyone.'

b. Ti in-li'i' si Dolores ni mánunu ha'.
   not AGR-see UNM Dolores not anywhere EMP
   'We didn't see Dolores anywhere.'
c. Esti na tronku-n nunu ti p*in*ätcha ni háfafa ha' na distrosu.
   this L tree-L banyan not AGR.PASS.touch not any EMP L disaster
   'This banyan tree was not touched by any destruction.' (Cooreman 1983, 176)
d. Taya' ni unu t*um*aitai ni háfafa ha'.
   AGR.not.exist no one WH[nom].read not anything EMP
   'There wasn't anyone who read anything.'

I will refer to the left-edge elements that express sentential negation in Chamorro as expressors of negation, and to the morphologically negative forms they license as negative concord phrases.

As in other languages (see Ladusaw 1992), c-command plays a crucial role in the licensing of negative concord: negative concord phrases in Chamorro must fall within the c-command domain of an expressor of negation. This can be seen from the contrast between (31) and (32). The negative concord phrases in (31a–c) are c-commanded and licensed by the negative *ti* 'not', a functional head whose c-command domain includes the verb phrase. The negative concord phrases in (31d)—both subconstituents of the DP complement of *taya'* 'not exist'—are c-commanded and licensed by this negative verb. But the negative concord subject in (32a) is not licensed, evidently because it falls outside the c-command domain of *ti*. And in (32b), one negative concord phrase c-commands the other, but neither is licensed, because there is no expressor of negation to serve as the licenser.[9]

(32) a. *Ti mattu nigap ni háfafa ha'.
        not AGR.arrive yesterday not anything EMP
        'Nothing arrived yesterday.'
     b. *Hagu, pära un-sangan ni háfafa ha' ni pära hayi put esti.
        you FUT AGR-say not anything EMP not to anyone about this
        'As for you, you're to say nothing to anyone about this.'

Observe now that in the focus construction, a negative focus can license negative concord in the remainder (see Chung 1998, 273).

(33) a. Ni unu l*um*i'i' _ si Dolores ni mánunu ha'.
        not one WH[nom].see UNM Dolores not anywhere EMP
        '*No one* saw Dolores anywhere.'
     b. Ni háfafa ha' ma-tätaitai _ ni unu giya hämi.
        not anything EMP WH[nom].AGR.PASS-read.PROG not one LOC us
        '*Nothing* had been read by any one of us.'

In order for the negative concord phrases in (33) to be licensed, they must fall within the c-command domain of the negative focus. But that could not happen if the focus were the nonverbal predicate of an HRC and the remainder were its subject, an HR, because the predicate phrase does not c-command the subject in Chamorro (see Chung 2005). One indication that this is so can be recovered from the preceding discussion. Recall from (31–32) that the negative *ti* c-commands the verb phrase but not the subject. If we assume (as seems reasonable) that predicate phrases occupy a uniform structural position in Chamorro whatever their category type, then it follows that predicate phrases more generally do not c-command the subject. The HRC analysis, then, arrives at an impasse.

The alternative is that the negative focus in these examples has undergone *wh*-movement, and therefore occupies the specifier of C—a position from which it c-commands the remainder. Under this analysis, the negative concord phrases in (33) will be c-commanded and licensed in a completely unexceptional way. The success of this account argues that in constructions of the type (33), the focus must have undergone *wh*-movement.

5.4.6 A Specificity Effect

My last argument for *wh*-movement in constituent questions and focus constructions is supplied by a Chamorro specificity effect.

In Chamorro, subjects that are external arguments and that surface within the clause must be specific, in the following sense (see Chung 1998, 102–106). They can be realized as pronouns, proper names, definite DPs, or DPs headed by the indefinite article *un* 'a, one', a numeral, or *pälu* '(contrastive) some'.

(34) a. Mang-onni' yu' lahyan na taotao pära taotao-hu.
AGR.AP-take I plenty L person for person-AGR
'I took many people as my subordinates.' (Cooreman 1983, 34)
b. Sigi di um-añangun i dos umäsagua.
keep.on AGR-whisper.to.ea.other the two married.ones
'The two married people kept on whispering.' (Cooreman 1982, 77)

But they cannot be realized as DPs headed by the null nonspecific article or by a (weak or strong) quantifier.

(35) a. *Mañ-áchalik lalahi.
AGR-laugh.PROG men
'Men laughed.'
b. *Ha-tungu' meggai na taotao si tata-hu.
AGR-know many L person UNM father-AGR
'Many people know my father.'

Subjects that are internal arguments are not similarly restricted, as (36) is intended to suggest.

(36) a. Änai ma-bäba, h*um*uyung   patgun.
       when AGR-open AGR.come.out child
       'When they opened it, a child emerged.' (Cooreman 1983, 107)
   b. Pära u-ma-na'i   todu i   mätai ni iyo-nña.
       FUT AGR-PASS-give all   the dead OBL possession-AGR
       'Every dead person should be given his belongings.' (Cooreman 1983, 9)

Unsurprisingly, subjects that are external arguments exhibit the specificity effect even when they are realized as HRs.[10]

(37) a. Áttilung i   *O* gaigi   _ gi halum kahita.
       AGR.black the   WH[nom].AGR.be.at LOC inside box
       'The thing that was in the box was black.'
   b. *Áttilung *O* gaigi   _ gi halum kahita.
       AGR.black WH[nom].AGR.be.at LOC inside box
       'A thing that was in the box was black.'

Subjects of DP predicates exhibit the specificity effect as well. This is expected, given that DP predicates are individual-level, and so their subjects are external arguments (see, e.g., Diesing 1992; Chierchia 1995).

(38) a. Lao ti mansiudadanu-n America lokkui' i   natibu   guini?
       but not citizens-L   America also   the indigenous here
       'But aren't the local people here also American citizens?' (*Saipan Tribune*, February 8, 2000)
   b. Í'isao esti i   *O* ginin   batchit   _ .
       sinner this the   IMPERF WH[nom].AGR.blind
       'This one who had been blind was a sinner.' (*Ginen i Obispo*, March 14, 1999)
   c. *Impleáo i gubietnu   meggai na taotao Sa'ipan.
       employee the government many   L   person Saipan
       'Many Saipanese people are government employees.'

With this information in hand, let us now turn to constituent questions and focus constructions in which the interrogative phrase or focus happens to be a DP. If these constructions are HRCs, their DP predicate ought to be individual-level, and so their subject, the HR, ought to be an external argument. The HR should therefore exhibit the specificity effect.

Chamorro does have examples that are consistent with this prediction. The HR in the constituent question in (39a) is headed by a demonstrative; the HR in the (apparent) focus construction in (39b) is headed by the definite article.[11]

(39) a. Hayi ädyu i   O pära u-fahani-n   maisa gui' _ present?
who? that the   FUT WH[nom].AGR-buy.for-L self   him   present
'Who is that one who's going to buy a present for himself?'
b. Bos palao'an i   O um-agang   huyung _ .
voice woman the   WH[nom]-call out
'What called out was *a woman's voice.*'

Examples of this sort, however, are clearly in the minority. In most types of constituent questions and focus constructions, the remainder is not headed by any overt determiner. This means that (in an HRC analysis) the remainder is an HR headed by the null nonspecific article, or else (in the *wh*-movement analysis) the remainder is a constituent not headed by D at all—in other words, IP. See the examples cited earlier, as well as

(40) a. Hafa gaigi   _ gi   tatti-n   petta-n gima'-ñiha.
what? WH[nom].AGR.be.at   LOC behind-L door-L house-AGR
'[Not even I know] what is behind the door of their house.' (*Saipan Tribune*, December 10, 1998)
b. Más ki   1,100 na bisnis   ma-huchum   petta-nñiha _ .
more than 1,100 L   business AGR.PASS-close door-AGR
'*More than 1,100 businesses* have closed their doors.' (*Saipan Tribune*, December 19, 1998)

Either way, the putative HR is not formally marked as specific—a pattern difficult to square with the predictions of the HRC analysis. In this sense, the specificity effect argues that the constructions in (40) are not HRCs; rather, they are derived by *wh*-movement of the interrogative phrase or focus.

One might wonder whether this line of reasoning could be defused. For instance, it might be suggested that because the remainder contributes to the common-ground presupposition of the question or focus construction, it is, in effect, understood as specific. While such a suggestion might seem reasonable, it would leave unexplained why simple DPs lacking an overt determiner cannot be understood as specific in examples like

(41) *Ha-na'ma'a'ñao yu' taklalo'-mu.
AGR-make.afraid me anger-AGR
'[What's wrong with anger of mine?]—Anger of yours frightens me.'

In other words, it would remain mysterious why a purely pragmatic approach to the specificity effect seems not to generalize beyond constructions of the type (40).

In short, the specificity effect offers evidence against an HRC analysis of the constructions in (40), and in favor of a *wh*-movement analysis.

5.5 Conclusion

I hope to have shown that overall, the most direct approach to constituent questions and focus constructions in Chamorro is also the right approach: these constructions can, and in many instances must, be derived by *wh*-movement of the interrogative phrase or focus. Among the constructions that must be derived by *wh*-movement are those in which the interrogative or focused phrase surfaces in the locative case (as in (14–15)), shows connectivity with the remainder ((18–19) and (22–23)), licenses negative concord (33), or is a DP (if the remainder is not introduced by any determiner; see (40)). Constructions that must be analyzed as HRCs do occur, but are not nearly as common; see (39). Finally, if the specificity evidence of 5.4.6 is taken seriously, the types of constructions that are structurally ambiguous, in that they are amenable to both analyses, are rather circumscribed: they involve interrogative or focused phrases that are (stage-level) PPs and do not fall into any of the other subclasses just mentioned.

From this (perhaps unremarkable) conclusion, two larger points emerge. First, there *are* verb-initial Austronesian languages—notably, Chamorro—whose constituent questions and focus constructions are not exclusively HRCs. Second, the existence of languages like Chamorro significantly increases the challenge of attempting to correlate verb-first order with the absence of *wh*-movement.

Notes

Many thanks to the Chamorro speakers who contributed to this work, especially Priscilla Anderson, Manuel F. Borja, Teresina Garrido, Ray P. Lujan, William I. Macaranas, Maria P. Mafnas, Maria T. Quinata, Anicia Tomokane, and the late Agnes C. Tabor. Thanks also to Judith Aissen and James McCloskey for comments. This chapter is dedicated to David Perlmutter, who taught me syntactic argumentation.

1. For instance, what property of verb-peripheral languages might cause *wh*-movement of interrogative phrases to be prohibited or dispreferred? What property of headless-relative clefts might make them appropriate for realizing constituent questions?

The following abbreviations are used in the morpheme-by-morpheme glosses: ACT = active, AGR = agreement, AP = antipassive, COMP = complementizer, EMP = emphatic, FUT = future, IMPERF = imperfect, INFIN = infinitive, L = linker, LOC = local morphological case, OBL = oblique morphological case, PASS = passive, PL = plural, PROG = progressive, PRT = focus particle, SG = singular, UNM = unmarked morphological case, WH = Wh-Agreement, nom = nominative, obj = objective, obl = oblique. Note that infixes in the Chamorro examples are italicized.

2. The null operator *O* cannot be the object of an overt preposition, because *O* cannot pied-pipe a preposition, and overt prepositions cannot be stranded (see section 5.4.4).

3. Interrogative phrases that are (nonverbal) predicates of clauses always occur in situ. Note that for most speakers, multiple *wh*-questions are severely degraded.

4. Readers might wonder why (12b–c) could not be focus constructions in which the locative DP has been focused. There are (at least) two reasons. First, focused locative DPs are typically separated from the remainder of the sentence by an overt complementizer (compare (15)). Second, the DP in the remainder would have to be interpreted as a DP predicate, but DP predicates are individual-level, and therefore incompatible with locative phrases (see section 5.4.6).

5. The focused location in (19b) occurs in the unmarked morphological case because this is the default case for DPs that occur at the left edge of the clause. Consistent with this, the interrogative and focused phrases in (14–15) could also occur in the unmarked morphological case.

6. In this section (but not in other sections), null pronouns of relevance to the discussion are represented as *pro* in the Chamorro examples. For discussion of the distribution of null pronouns, see Chung 1998, 29–32.

7. Even if Chamorro's verb-initial order were assumed to be derived via VP raising, there would be a stage of derivation at which the subject—more precisely, the external argument—c-commanded the rest of the clause. For arguments against a VP-raising analysis of Chamorro clause structure, see Chung 2005.

8. Antecedent-pronoun relations can satisfy the c-command condition of the Chamorro-specific requirement under reconstruction. But, as might be expected, they cannot satisfy the precedence condition under reconstruction. See Chung 1998, 148–149.

9. Notice that none of the negative concord phrases in (32) are external arguments. Therefore, none of them would be independently excluded by the specificity effect to be discussed in section 5.4.6.

10. Irrelevantly, some speakers find (37b) grammatical if it is interpreted as 'A black thing was in the box'.

11. I say "(apparent) focus construction" because it is not obvious that any Chamorro constituent is being focused in (39b).

References

Adger, David, and Gillian Ramchand. 2005. Merge and move: Wh-dependencies revisited. *Linguistic Inquiry* 36:161–193.

Aldridge, Edith. 2004. Ergativity and word order in Austronesian languages. Doctoral dissertation, Cornell University.

Bauer, Winifred. 1991. Maori *ko* again. *Te Reo* 24:31–36.

Carnie, Andrew, Heidi Harley, and Sheila Ann Dooley, eds. 2005. *Verb first*. Amsterdam: John Benjamins.

Chierchia, Gennaro. 1995. Individual-level predicates as inherent generics. In G. N. Carlson and F. J. Pelletier, eds., *The generic book*, 176–223. Chicago: University of Chicago Press.

Chung, Sandra. 1998. *The design of agreement: Evidence from Chamorro*. Chicago: University of Chicago Press.

Chung, Sandra. 2005. What fronts? On the VP-raising account of verb-initial order. In Andrew Carnie, Heidi Harley, and Sheila Ann Dooley, eds., *Verb first*, 9–29. Amsterdam: John Benjamins.

Chung, Sandra. 2006. Sluicing and the lexicon: The point of no return. In Rebecca T. Cover and Yuni Kim, eds., *Proceedings of the Thirty-First Annual Meeting of the Berkeley Linguistics Society*, 73–91. Berkeley: Berkeley Linguistics Society, University of California.

Cooreman, Ann. 1982. *Chamorro texts*. Ms., University of Oregon, Eugene.

Cooreman, Ann. 1983. *Chamorro texts*. Ms., Saipan, U.S. Commonwealth of the Northern Mariana Islands.

Diesing, Molly. 1992. *Indefinites*. Cambridge, MA: MIT Press.

Georgopoulos, Carol. 1991. *Syntactic variables: Resumptive pronouns and A'-binding in Palauan*. Dordrecht: Kluwer.

Greenberg, Joseph H. 1963. Some universals of grammar with particular reference to the order of meaningful elements. In J. Greenberg, ed., *Universals of language*, 73–133. Cambridge, MA: MIT Press.

Hankamer, Jorge. 1974. On the non-cyclic nature of Wh-clefting. In M. W. Lagaly, R. A. Fox, and A. Bruck, eds., *Papers from the Tenth Regional Meeting of the Chicago Linguistic Society*, 221–233. Chicago: Chicago Linguistic Society.

Ladusaw, William. 1992. Expressing negation. In C. Barker and D. Dowty, eds., *Proceedings of the Second Conference on Semantics and Linguistic Theory*, 237–259. Columbus: Department of Linguistics, Ohio State University.

Merchant, Jason. 2001. *The syntax of silence: Sluicing, islands, and the theory of ellipsis*. Oxford: Oxford University Press.

Oda, Kenji. 2005. V1 and *wh*-questions: A typology. In Andrew Carnie, Heidi Harley, and Sheila Ann Dooley, eds., *Verb first*, 107–133. Amsterdam: John Benjamins.

Paul, Ileana, and Eric Potsdam. 2004. Sluicing without *wh*-movement in Malagasy. Delivered at CLS 40.

Pinkham, Jessie, and Jorge Hankamer. 1975. Deep and shallow clefts. In R. E. Grossman, L. J. San, and T. J. Vance, eds., *Papers from the Eleventh Regional Meeting of the Chicago Linguistic Society*, 429–450. Chicago: Chicago Linguistic Society.

Potsdam, Eric. 2003. Ellipsis identity and Malagasy sluicing. Delivered at NELS 33.

Potsdam, Eric. 2004. *Wh*-questions in Malagasy. Delivered at AFLA 11.

Seiter, William. 1975. *Information questions in Philippine languages*. Ms., University of California, San Diego.

6 On the Existence (and Distribution) of Sentential Subjects

William D. Davies and Stanley Dubinsky

6.1 Introduction

This chapter principally concerns the status and distribution of sentential subjects, as in (1), and to a lesser extent, the relation of (1) to the extraposition construction shown in (2).[1]

(1) That John left early disappointed us.

(2) It disappointed us that John left early.

We will show that some long-standing assumptions about the distribution of nonnominal subjects (going back to Koster 1978 and Stowell 1981) are incorrect, and that the distribution of these subjects is broader than previous analyses have acknowledged. We suggest that previous conclusions about this class of data were driven by facts whose explanation likely lies outside the realm of syntactic structure. While much of the debate about the status of sentential subjects occurred twenty to thirty years ago, the issue is still quite relevant, inasmuch as a number of current syntax textbooks still present what turn out to be questionable analyses of these structures (see Culicover 1997; Haegeman and Guéron 1999; Lasnik 1999, 1995; and Radford 1997). This is, to some degree, surprising, especially given the fact that the Case-theoretic explanations for the facts have declined in importance with the paradigm shift from Principles and Parameters (i.e., GB) to the Minimalist Program. What follows is an attempt to lay out previously established facts as well as some new ones, to call attention to long-standing misconceptions about sentential subjects, to distill the correct generalization for subject positions in English, and to point to potential sources of new data on the topic.

6.2 The Background

Rosenbaum 1967 presented one of the earliest accounts of (1) and (2) in the transformational literature. There, all sentential subjects are generated as complements to a subject pronoun *it* such that (1) and (2) have the same underlying structure, given in (3).

(3) [$_{NP}$ it [$_S$ that John left early]] disappointed us

In (1), according to Rosenbaum, the pronoun deletes, leaving the S in subject position dominated by a headless NP projection. In (2), the S extraposes to the right, leaving the pronoun *it* stranded in subject position (Delahunty 1981 and Iwakura 1978 propose similar analyses). Emonds 1970 (and 1972) noted several ways in which sentential subjects do not behave like ordinary NP subjects, and pointed out a number of problems with Rosenbaum's extraposition approach. Among other things, he notes that extraposition is obligatory (i) in subordinate clauses (4)–(5) and (ii) in the context of subject-aux inversion regardless of whether there is a questioned NP (6)–(7), and that (iii) clausal subjects are ungrammatical in the presence of other topicalized elements (8).

(4) a. *I think that that John left early disappointed them.
    b. I think that it disappointed them that John left early.

(5) a. *Although that the house is empty may depress you, it pleases me. (Koster 1978, (2b))
    b. Although it may depress you that the house is empty, it pleases me.

(6) a. *Did that John showed up please you? (Koster 1978, (3a))
    b. Did it please you that John showed up?

(7) a. *Who did that John left early disappoint?
    b. Who did it disappoint that John left early?

(8) a. *Such things, that he reads so much doesn't prove. (Koster 1978, (5b))
    b. Such things, it doesn't prove. (Koster 1978, (4b))

Concerned as he was with the coherence of the phrase structure component of the grammar and the capacity of overgeneration presented by rewrite rules of the form XP → YP (e.g., NP → S), Emonds proposed that sentential subjects are base-generated in an adjunct position and then "intraposed" into subject position by a rule of Subject Replacement (Brame 1976 proposes a similar analysis).

Emonds's 1976 analysis reverses the direction of movement he proposed earlier. Reacting perhaps to Postal's (1974) assertion that the intraposition analysis does not properly represent the semantics of the sentence at D-structure, Emonds replaces intraposition with extraposition and claims that sentential subjects such as in (1) are topicalized at S-structure. Observing as he did earlier that there is a correlation in the distribution of topics and sentential subjects, he states that "nongerund clauses will appear only in extraposition and topicalization NP positions" (p. 127). That is, where topics cannot appear, sentential subjects also cannot appear. His proposal for the D-structure of (1) and (2) is thus quite similar to that of Rosenbaum, except that the former is claimed to have a null pronoun in the base. For Emonds, sentential subjects (and complements) are generated under an NP node with an empty N head, as shown in (9).

(9) a. [$_{NP}$ ∅ [$_S$ that John left early]] disappointed us
    b. I hate [$_{NP}$ ∅ [$_S$ that they left early]]

These sentential arguments must be moved out of their base position in order for the sentence to be grammatical. Extraposition (i.e., rightward movement) results in an expletive *it* in the argument position, as in (10). Topicalization, as in (11), results in erasure of the empty head.

(10) a. [$_{NP}$ it] disappointed them [$_S$ that John left early]
     b. I hate [$_{NP}$ it] [$_S$ that they left early]

(11) a. [$_S$ that John left early] [$_{NP}$] disappointed them
     b. [$_S$ that they left early] I hate [$_{NP}$]

Movement of the sentential subject out of its D-structure position is, in either case, obligatory and the ungrammaticality of (7a), for example, is due in Emonds's account to the sentential subject remaining in the subject position over which the auxiliary must move.

Koster 1978, building on Emonds's observations, proposes that sentential subject clauses such as in (1) occupy a "satellite" position outside the main clause, and are therefore outside the domain of the subject-aux inversion rule at all levels of structure. Koster attempts to derive this from PS rules, stating that subject position is defined as an NP position and that his proposal to have sentential subjects occupy a "satellite" position from the outset does away with dubious (exocentric) rules such as NP → S. Under his analysis, (5a) is ungrammatical because the "satellite" clause cannot be subordinate to the complementizer *although*. In (6a) and (7a), the auxiliary *did* has moved across the "satellite" position rather than the subject position as in (6b) and (7b). In (8a), *such things* and *that he reads so much* compete for the same (topicalized) position.

Stowell (1981) also adopts the position that exocentric phrase structure (PS) rules are automatically ruled out by any theory that incorporates principles of X-bar syntax, and goes on to propose a theory-internal principle (in the Principles and Parameters/GB framework) to motivate the analysis proposed in Koster 1978. While the prohibition of exocentric PS rules can, by itself, preclude a sentential subject immediately dominated by NP, it does not explain why the canonical subject position appears to exclude Ss themselves.

In keeping with the GB position of explaining the distribution of arguments (partly) in terms of Case assignment principles, Stowell (1981) proposes the Case-Resistance Principle (CRP), given in (12).

(12) *Case-Resistance Principle* (CRP)
Case may not be assigned to a category bearing a Case-assigning feature.

According to Stowell, because [+Tense] is a Case-assigning feature that is responsible for nominative Case, tensed sentential subjects may not themselves be assigned Case. The CRP thus predicts that the tensed subject in (13a) must occupy some position other than the canonical subject position, while the infinitival subject in (13b) may occur in this position.

(13) a. [that John left early] [e disappointed us]
b. [[for John to leave early] would disappoint us]

The table in (14) summarizes the several analyses of sentential subjects (SSs) presented here.

(14)

	Rosenbaum 1967	Emonds 1970	Emonds 1976	Koster 1978
SSs are D-structure subjects	yes	no	yes	no
SSs are S-structure subjects	yes	yes	no	no

6.3 It Is Not a Case of Case

While sporadic challenges for particular languages have appeared from time to time (e.g., Chung 1991), Stowell's CRP has remained conventional wisdom, and is adopted in some recent texts (Culicover 1997, 51–52; Radford 1997, 297). Presumably, the CRP should also exclude VPs and PPs from Case-bearing positions, since both V and P are categories that bear an accusative Case-assigning feature. We would thus expect VPs, PPs, and tensed CPs all to avoid the Case-marked subject position, in contrast with NPs and APs.[2] Thus, according to Stowell, neither the clausal subject in (1) nor the PP subjects in (15) occupy the same position as the NP subject in (2).

(15) a. On the porch would be a good place to leave the toys.
b. On the porch reminds me of a good place to leave the toys.

A casual examination of the distribution of PP subjects shows it to be patently false. In contrast with (6a), (16) is perfect.[3]

(16) a. Would on the porch be a good place to leave the toys?
b. Does on the porch remind you of a good place to leave the toys?

Additionally, VPs and IPs, both of which are [−N] categories, can also occur in these constructions as in (17) and (18).[4]

(17) a. Why does eat pizza seem to be all he wants to do?
 b. Does wait and see sound like what they were willing to do?

(18) a. Would to leave early really reflect poorly on us all?
 b. When does to let sleeping dogs lie strike you as the best course of action?

Thus, Stowell's proposed CRP cannot be maintained. Further, a careful examination of clausal subjects indicates that the distribution of these too is wider than what Emonds and Koster have claimed. The examples in (19) are not nearly as bad as (6a) and (7a).

(19) a. To whom is that pigs can fly most surprising?
 b. Is that I am done with this homework really amazing? (Naturally occurring datum)

Crosslinguistic considerations also call into question any appeal to Case resistance as an adequate explanation of the English data. In his careful study of sentential arguments in a wide variety of languages, Dryer (1980) demonstrates the crosslinguistic tendency for both sentential subjects and sentential objects to occur in clause-final position and a secondary tendency (especially in SOV languages) for these elements to occur in clause-initial position. On the face of it, then, it might appear that such data are consistent with a Case-resistance explanation. However, these are merely robust tendencies. Dryer provides copious evidence that clause-internal sentential complements are dispreferred but definitely not disallowed. For example, in SOV languages, sentential objects frequently occur in the canonical object position (that is, sentence internally, following the subject and preceding the verb). While there are some SOV languages in which sentential objects obligatorily follow the verb—Dryer cites Persian and Turkish as examples of these—many more SOV languages (e.g., Choctaw and Japanese) do allow clause-internal sentential objects. Under the simplest set of assumptions, these sentential objects occur in canonical object position, a Case position. Given that very few languages absolutely require their sentential objects to occur in clause-final (or clause-initial) position, crosslinguistic data provide yet another challenge to Case resistance.

Chamorro provides empirical evidence that sentential arguments can occur in Case positions. Chung (1991) argues explicitly that CP subjects and objects in Chamorro take case and that the Case Resistance Principle cannot be operable in this language; she limits her argument to Chamorro. Evidence for this comes from a system of what she calls "*wh*-agreement," in which the morphology on a verb reflects the grammatical function of a *wh*-phrase that has moved across it. In (20), the subject is questioned and the *um* affix marks *wh*-agreement on the root *istotba*. In (21), the direct object is questioned, which results in a nominalization of the clause (indicated by the *ña* possessive suffix); here, the affix *in* marks the *wh*-agreement.

(20) Hafa$_i$, *um*istotba   hao t_{i_i}? (Chung 1991, (15b))
      what Infl.disturb.Prog you
            [Wh.nomin]
      'What is disturbing you?'

(21) Hayi$_i$, ch*in*iku-*ña* si Dolores t_{i_i}? (Chung 1991, (17b))
      what kiss-Agr   the D
            [Wh.obj]
      'Who did Dolores kiss?'

In simplex clauses, Chung formulates this in terms of the verb agreeing in Case with a clausemate that is a *wh*-trace.

In long-distance questions, the verb of the clause in which the extracted element originates takes agreement reflective of the grammatical function of the extracted element, but higher verbs take agreement that reflects the grammatical function of the clause from which the element is extracted. Thus, in (22), the embedded clause is nominalized because its direct object has been extracted. However, the higher verb takes the *um* affix: this is because the clause from which the element is extracted is the subject.

(22) Hafa$_i$ *um*istotba hao [ni   malago'-*ña* i   lahi-mu t_{i_i}?
      what Infl.disturb you Comp want-Agr   the son-your
            [Wh.nomin]   [Wh.obj]
      'What does it disturb you that your son wants?' (Chung 1982, (45a))

This contrasts with the situation when a subject has been extracted from a sentential subject, as in (23), where the verbs of both clauses take the *um* affix.

(23) Hayi na lahi$_i$, *um*istotba si Jose [ni   b*um*isita t_{i_i}
      who L boy   Infl.disturb the J   Comp Infl.visit
                  [Wh.nomin]   [Wh.nomin]
      haga-ña]? (Chung 1991, (23a))
      the daughter-his
      'What boy does it disturb Jose visited his daughter?'

As Chung argues, inasmuch as *wh*-Agreement is a manifestation of Case agreement and CPs trigger *wh*-Agreement, we must conclude that CPs in argument positions bear Case.

Levin and Massam (1986) also argue for the assignment of Case to CPs in Niuean. They note that some Niuean verbs with sentential complements take absolutive subjects while others take ergative subjects. Among the verbs with ergative subjects are *iola* 'know', *manatu* 'think, wonder', *talahuaua* 'say', and others.⁵ In (24), the matrix subject *kau kaihā* 'thieves' takes the ergative case particle *he*.

(24) Ne kitia **he kau kaihā** kua mate tuai e   molī he fale.
     PST see ERG group thief PERF die PERF ABS lamp in house
     'The thieves saw that the lamp in the house had gone out.'

Levin and Massam explicitly argue against analyzing the clausal complements as NPs on the basis of extraction facts. They also propose that sentential subjects of predicates such as *hangahanga* 'appear', *lata* 'be right', *mitaki* 'good', and others occur in subject position, accounting for the impossibility of Raising-to-Subject with these predicates, as opposed to predicates such as *maeke* 'be possible' and others that allow Raising. Levin and Massam conclude that these facts from Niuean provide evidence against Safir's (1982) hypothesis that sentential complements cannot be assigned Case.

6.4 Alternative Explanations

Two of the arguments brought forth by Emonds and Koster against the existence of sentential subjects include structures that are crosslinguistically marked. These are the arguments based on the degraded nature of sentential subjects that occur inverted with auxiliaries in questions (6a) and (7a), and sentential subjects that follow a topicalized NP (8a).⁶

(6) a. *Did that John showed up please you? (Koster 1978, (3a))

(7) a. *Who did that John left early disappoint?

(8) a. *Such things, that he reads so much doesn't prove. (Koster 1978, (5b))

In each of these structures, the sentential subject occurs internal to the clause—that is, neither in clause-initial nor clause-final position. Recall that Dryer (1980) demonstrates that the preferred position of sentential arguments (both subjects and complements) is clause-final position. He further demonstrates that, despite the fact that clause-internal sentential arguments can occur (especially objects in SOV languages), this position is greatly dispreferred crosslinguistically, with some languages (e.g., Persian and Turkish) seemingly banning them entirely. This fact thus adds a confounding factor to the data marshaled as evidence against sentential subjects (and sentential arguments in Case-marked positions as a whole).⁷ But as demonstrated above, the evidence against the existence of sentential subjects is questionable.

The distribution of nonnominal subjects clearly precludes the Case-theoretic explanation that has been advanced for it, and leads to the conclusion that other, nonsyntactic, factors have significantly clouded the picture. Having shown that sentential (or clausal) subjects do exist, we will now consider why they are kind of weird and so often avoided, and examine some of the nonsyntactic explanations for their distribution. Grosu and Thompson 1977 (G&T) reached similar conclusions with respect to then-current theoretical assumptions of syntactic theory, asserting that "neither Generative Semantics nor the Extended Standard Theory can provide an interesting (or even adequate) account of [the distribution of NP clauses]" (p. 139). They went on to suggest that the problems associated with this distribution "can be illuminated only by appealing to certain principles of language processing... even though no sufficiently detailed or precise theory of language processing is available at the moment" (p. 139). While Dryer (1980) showed the G&T solution to be unsuccessful overall, it is clear that they were on the right track. Some recent work appears to provide better explanations for the distribution of sentential subjects. In particular, we think that their distribution may be better explained in terms of prosody and phrasal weight (Erdmann 1988) or processing factors, such as the "integration cost component" of Gibson's (1998) Syntactic Prediction Locality Theory (SPLT). It is also evident that at least some of the data types presented by Koster were "red herrings," whose acceptability was severely degraded by "garden-path" processing difficulties.

6.4.1 Weight

As Delahunty (1983, 383) suggests, the relative unacceptability of many of Koster's examples may simply be a consequence of "the relative 'weights' and perhaps prosody" of the relevant constituents. Compare the unacceptable subject-auxiliary inversion example (25a) from Koster with the relatively acceptable structural analog (25b) from Delahunty.

(25) a. *Did that John showed up please you? (Koster 1978, (3a))
 b. To what extent did that Fred failed to show up anger those of his devoted fans who had waited by the stage door since dawn of the previous day? (Delahunty 1983, (11))

In Koster's example the sentential subject is twice the length (in syllables) of the matrix predicate, while in Delahunty's example, the six-word sentential subject is followed by an eighteen-word matrix predicate.

Erdmann (1988) confirms this. He extracted from linguistic corpora data showing the relative distribution of CP and IP (infinitival) in situ versus extraposed subjects. In these corpora, he found that the frequency of extraposition is extremely high with adjectival main-clause predicates (e.g., *is surprising*). In his data, 92.04 percent of CP subjects and 95.07 percent of IP subjects extraposed. This is not surprising given the tendencies that Dryer and G&T report. However, when the weight of the predicate VP was considered, it was found to play a significant role in determining when extraposition was avoided. With CP subjects in clause-initial subject position, the adjectival predicate was "light" 56 percent of the time and was "heavy" 44 percent of the time. In contrast, when CP subjects were extraposed, the adjectival predicate was "light" 88 percent of the time and "heavy" 12 percent. Figures are comparable for IP subjects (though slightly less dramatic). What this suggests is that extraposition is decreasingly motivated as the VP over which it moves becomes heavier. In results garnered from a corpus-based study, Wasow (1997) reports that the effect of phrasal weight in inducing heavy NP shift is linked to the relative weight of the two constituents, the second phrase being approximately three times heavier than the first (by any relevant measure).

It is reasonable therefore to suspect that the unacceptability of Koster's subject-auxiliary inversion example in (25a) has more to do with the sentential subject being twice as long as the following predicate (four words to two words), than with any violation of grammatical constraints.

6.4.2 Memory and Parsing Impediments

Section 6.4.1 discussed the role of phrasal weight in determining the placement of these phrases primarily from the perspective of production. There is also some indication that both memory limitations and parsing ambiguity play a role, from a processing perspective, in rendering unacceptable center-embedded sentential subjects.

In both G&T 1977 and Dryer 1980, the dispreference for clause-internal CPs (such as those produced in English by CP-Aux inversion) is explicitly tied to Fodor, Bever, and Garrett's (1974) explanation of the unacceptability of multiple center-embedding. Dryer's comment on this is as follows: "If we assume that clauses are the fundamental units of sentence processing, and that material is emptied from short term memory at clause boundaries, clause-internal sentential NPs will interrupt the processing of the main clause" (p. 161).

Hawkins (1994) proposes his Early Immediate Constituent principle to account for word-order tendencies observed in both production and perception studies. Based on the reported data, he claims that "the human parser prefers linear orders that maximize the IC-to-non-IC ratios of constituent recognition domains" (p. 77). Where extraposed and nonextraposed sentential subjects are concerned, this means that extraposed sentential subjects are preferable and easier to process than nonextraposed sentential subjects.

(26) a. [$_S$ [it] [pleased you]] [that John showed up]
     b. [$_S$ [that John showed up] [pleased you]]

In (26a), the three-word string *it pleased you* forms an S dominating the immediate constituents *it* and *pleased you*. In (26b), the first three words *that John showed* do not form an IC.

Eye-tracking experiments conducted by Frazier and Rayner (1988) indicate that sentential subjects were harder to process than their extraposed sentential subject analogs. For two experiments—one in which test sentences were given without a context and one in which they were contextualized—they report that reading times for the stimuli with sentential subjects were significantly longer than those with extraposed sentential subjects. This finding again appears to point to the importance of 'weight'.

However, some preliminary data, collected by Widmann (2005), suggests that the relative weight of sentential subjects and their predicates may play a less critical role in speakers' acceptability judgments in certain contexts than the absolute length of the center-embedded sentential subject. In two experiments, each presenting a different center-embedding context, speakers judged most acceptable center-embedded subjects that were neither too long nor too short.

Widmann's experiments tested subject-auxilary inversion contexts, as in (27a), and subordinate-clause contexts, as in (27b).

(27) a. Does that the parent wanted to come home cause any problem for the older children?
b. Although that the parent wanted to come home caused problems for the older children, it was not a terrible inconvenience.

In manipulating the length of the embedded sentential subject and the following predicate (four versus ten words; ten versus four words; seven versus seven words), experimental results indicated that speakers judged significantly more acceptable, embedded sentential subjects that were neither overly long nor overly short (i.e., seven-word sentential subjects were preferred over both four- and ten-word sentential subjects).

While further experiments are needed to confirm these results, an initial hypothesis put forward is that long sentential subjects (i.e., ten words) may tax short-term memory resources in the manner described by Dryer (above). Conversely, overly short center-embedded sentential subjects (i.e., four words) do not permit the parser sufficient time to recover from the initial misanalysis triggered by the first two words of (27a) and (27b). In reading *does that*... or *although that*..., it is hypothesized that the parser initially posits the following structure:

(28) a. [$_{CP}$ does [$_{IP}$ [$_{NP}$ that...
b. [$_{CP}$ although [$_{IP}$ [$_{NP}$ that...

The next two disambiguating words, *the parent*, force the parser to backtrack and reanalyze the structure as containing a center-embedded CP:

(29) a. [$_{CP}$ does [$_{CP}$ that [$_{IP}$ [$_{NP}$ the parent...
b. [$_{CP}$ although [$_{CP}$ that [$_{IP}$ [$_{NP}$ the parent...

In the four-word sentential subject context (e.g., *that the parent came*) there is not sufficient time following the disambiguating region for the parser to recover, before it must begin to parse the rest of the sentence. Hence, the seven-word sentential subjects, which permitted such recovery but did not overly tax memory, were judged significantly more acceptable. These results, if confirmed by further experimentation, are important in that they indicate that (1) more is at play than just the relative weight of constituents, and (2) parsing factors affecting acceptability judgments might be distinct from factors determining preferences in production.

Here again, we are led to the conclusion that the unacceptability of sentences used by Koster as evidence against the "existence of sentential subjects" is more likely the result of psycholinguistic factors than of grammatical principles.

6.4.3 Integration Costs

Another processing factor that can contribute to variation in the acceptability of clause-internal CPs is the integration of new referents into the discourse. As Gibson (1998, 16) points out, "Elements which cause...integration cost...are words introducing new discourse referents.... Doubly nested RC structures are easier to process when a first- or second-person pronoun (an indexical pronoun) is in the subject position of the most embedded clause, as compared with similar structures in which a proper name, a full NP or a pronoun with no referent is in the subject position of the most embedded." This is presumably a factor in rendering the relative clause in (30a) less acceptable than the one in (30b).

(30) a. ?The lawyer the banker irritated sued him.
    b. The lawyer I irritated sued me.

Similar (though weak) effects show up in sentences containing clause-internal CPs, where (31a) is somewhat worse than (31b).

(31) a. Did that players slipped on the ice truly worry the coach?
    b. Did that I finished on time really impress the teacher?

Confirmation of such differences would require experimental data.

6.5 Repercussions for Syntactic Theory

Thus far we have presented reasons to eschew a syntactic explanation for the distribution of sentential subjects, providing evidence against previous syntactic analyses of such and pointing to other, nonsyntactic factors that govern their distribution. One might ask at this point (if one has not already), why we (as syntacticians) are so exercised about this issue. There are two answers. First, we think that ignoring the sort of factors discussed in section 6.4 is bad for the pursuit of syntactic analysis generally, inevitably leading to very weak (or very wrong) arguments for an analysis. Second, the "received wisdom" of the CRP in syntactic circles has stood in the way of improved accounts of subject properties in English (and other languages). We will take up these issues in turn.

6.5.1 Garden-Path Obstacles to Linguistic Inquiry

Not only do prosodic and processing factors provide a reasonable alternative to the Case-theoretic explanation of the distribution of sentential subjects, but they also can help to illuminate the extreme weakness of some of the syntactic arguments that have been put forward in favor of Case-theoretic explanations. For example, one of Koster's (1978) arguments against sentential subjects involved showing that they could not appear with a preceding topicalized phrase. Koster's illustration of this is given in (32).

(32) *Such things, that he reads so much doesn't prove. (Koster 1978, (5b))

This is an undeniably unacceptable sentence. But it appears that the "ungrammaticality" of (32) is not a function of the incompatibility of sentential subjects and topics. Example (33a) is almost equally unacceptable, differing from (32) only in having a head noun dominating the sentential subject, and (33b) should be grammatical if the unacceptability of (32) were merely due to extraposition not having applied.

(33) a. *Such things, the fact that he reads so much doesn't prove.
    b. *Such things, it doesn't prove that he reads so much.

Since (33a) contains a complex NP subject rather than a sentential subject, Koster's analysis provides no account for its unacceptability, and since (33b) has an extraposed sentential subject, it would appear that the unacceptability of (32) is not due to the subject clause occupying any "satellite" position. We would instead argue that the unacceptability of (33a) and (33b) relates to factors that make it difficult to parse. The fact is that outside of some very well-rehearsed examples such as "Beans, I like," topicalized structures in English are usually slightly less acceptable than non-topicalized structures, because they are highly stylized sentences. (In fact, in our experience it is not unusual to find that students in an introductory syntax class initially judge topicalization structures as unacceptable.) So consider the pair in (34).

(34) a. Few people debate such things.
    b. Such things, few people debate.

The relative unacceptability of (33a) compared with (34b) might be due to the heavy NP in subject position in combination with the relatively marked topicalization order. For those who find (32) even less acceptable than (33a), we might add the problem of a garden-pathing. A common noun (such as *things*) with a following *that*-clause is generally parsed as a relative clause. The problem one confronts in parsing (32) is the fact that this initial parse will prove unsuccessful, and the processor will have to backtrack and revise the initial analysis (if that is even possible, given the other confounds). In addition, the sentence in (32), as well as that in (33a), suffers from the problem of weight. The predicate *doesn't prove* is very light (in Erdmann's terms) when compared with the subject *(the fact) that he reads so much*. When these confounding factors are removed, topicalization combined with a sentential subject improves in acceptability, as seen in example (35). Here the relative-weight confound has been ameliorated, in that the predicate *bothers to no end* is slightly heavier than the subject *that John's a fool*.

(35) a. Ted, that John's a fool bothers to no end, not Horatio.
  b. The instructor, that John's a fool bothers to no end, not the TA.

While neither sentence in (35) is particularly acceptable, we find (35b) worse than (35a), and would conjecture that this may be due to the garden-path tendency to initially analyze the string *the instructor that* as an NP followed by a relative clause. Sentence (35a), in contrast, does not suffer from this effect.

6.5.2 Back Toward a Better Analysis of Sentential Subjects

The arguments of Koster 1978 and Stowell 1981 are inconsistent with an analysis of subjects such as was proposed in Lees 1960 and Rosenbaum 1967 and was adopted in many subsequent works (e.g., Chomsky 1973; Emonds 1976; and Delahunty 1983, to name a few). Both Lees and Rosenbaum (and those who followed) analyzed sentential subjects as having an NP node immediately dominating an S.[8] In recent papers (Davies and Dubinsky 1999, 2001), we have presented new evidence suggesting that Lees and Rosenbaum were closer to the mark than has since been thought, at least with respect to the syntax of sentential subjects. The arguments presented in our papers support the notion that a range of languages, including English, have a syntactic requirement that all subjects be DPs—importantly, this induces a DP node dominating non-NP subjects. Under this analysis, sentential subjects have the structure shown in (36).

(36) [$_{DP}$ $\varnothing$ [$_{CP}$ that Shelby lost it]] is quite apparent

Four types of arguments support this analysis. First, non-NP subjects undergo obligatory raising, a fact that Delahunty (1983) also cites in arguing for the NP-hood of sentential subjects. In (37) *that Shelby lost it* has raised to be matrix subject, something that would be quite anomalous if the clause were "resistant" to Case.

(37) [$_{CP}$ that Shelby lost it]$_i$ appears [t$_i$ to be true]

Second, sentential subjects can trigger subject agreement on the verb, as observed by McCloskey (1991, 564) and shown in (38).

(38) [$_{CP}$ [$_{CP}$ that the march should go ahead] and [$_{CP}$ that it should be canceled]] have been argued by the same people at different times.

Third, a manner of licensing the quantificational adverb *equally* is via a plural NP or an NP with a mass noun as head. Conjoined CPs in subject position can license *equally*, as (39a) shows, while nonsubject CPs cannot (39b).

(39) a. That he'll resign and that he'll stay in office seem at this point equally possible. (McCloskey 1991, 564)
 b. Dale thought that Dana left and that Terry wouldn't come (*equally).

Finally, sentential subjects can host emphatic reflexives, as in (40a), while sentential complements cannot (40b).

(40) a. That there were twenty-five miles to go was itself enough to discourage Edwin.
 b. Edwin hoped that there were less than twenty-five miles to go (*itself).

However, this is not true only of sentential subjects: *all* non-NP subjects exhibit these properties. PP subjects and AP subjects also undergo obligatory raising (41), can trigger verb agreement (42), and license *equally* (43). Additionally, PPs can host emphatic reflexives, but only when they are subjects (44a).[9]

(41) a. [$_{PP}$ under the bed]$_1$ appears [t_1 to be a good place to hide]
 b. [very tall]$_1$ appears [t_1 to be just how he likes his bodyguards]

(42) a. [$_{PP}$ [$_{PP}$ under the bed] and [$_{PP}$ in the fireplace]] are not the best (combination of) places to leave your toys (Levine 1989, 1015)
 b. [$_{AP}$ [$_{AP}$ very brawny] and [$_{AP}$ very studious]] are what Cindy aspires to be

(43) a. Under the bed and in the closet equally remind me of that game of hide-and-seek we played.
 b. Very tall and quaintly studious equally bring to mind my sixth-grade science teacher.

(44) a. Under the bed and in the closet are themselves reasonable places to stash the cash.
 b. We stashed the cash under the bed and in the closet (*themselves).

As these data demonstrate, all non-NPs exhibit NP-like properties just when they are in subject position. This fact has been overlooked both in analyses that take sentential subjects to be subjects as well as in analyses that claim that they are not so. Thus the lexical category of a subject makes no difference to its distribution in English because all subjects are contained in DP projections (although, as argued in Davies and Dubinsky 2001, this is not the case for some other languages, such as Bulgarian).

Therefore, ironically perhaps, at one level we must concur with Koster's claim that "sentential subjects don't exist" in English—but not for the reasons Koster advanced. Rather, sentential subjects do not exist in English because English admits only DP subjects. This fact lends support to the notion that the explanation for the idiosyncratic behavior of English sentential subjects lies outside the domain of syntactic structure, most likely in the domain of language processing

Notes

For helpful comments, questions, and feedback on the content of this chapter, we thank Frederick Newmeyer, Maria Polinsky, Roumyana Slabakova, as well as audiences at the LSA Annual Meeting 2001, Northeastern Linguistics Society 2001, Southeastern Conference on Linguistics 2000, Eastern States Conference on Linguistics 1999, Chicago Linguistics Society 1998, Western Conference on Linguistics 1999, the University of Iowa, and the University of South Carolina, where portions of this chapter were presented.

1. The following abbreviations are used in the glosses, beginning with example (20): Wh.nomin = nominative *Wh*; Wh.obj = objective *Wh*; Infl = inflection; Prog = progressive; Agr = agreement; Comp = complementizer; PST = past, ERG = ergative, PERF = perfective, ABS = absolutive.

2. Safir (1983) suggests that PP and AP subjects are "honorary NPs" and thus raise, as in example (i), but does not distinguish between them in terms of their capacity to either assign or receive Case.

(i) a. Angry/unwanted is a terrible way to feel.
  b. To the moon seems to be a good place to go.

3. Stowell (1981) notes that PPs may be subjects in copular constructions, and limits their occurrence to that. His data (p. 268):

(i) a. [under the chair] is a nice place for the cat to sleep (Stowell 1981, (27))
  b. is [under the chair] a nice place to for the cat to sleep?

(ii) a. *[under the chair] pleased the cat (Stowell 1981, (28))
  b. *did [under the chair] please the cat?
    (cf. Did it please the cat under the chair?)

He speculates that perhaps the copula might have a special property that allows nominative case to "be absorbed or deflected away from subject position" and must also stipulate that (iia) cannot be due to topicalization because for some reason "reconstruction is obligatory in LF for PP arguments" (p. 269) and the CRP holds at all levels of grammar.

Notice as well that this purported special property of the copula does not, as it should, rescue sentential subjects from the CRP. This is seen here in (iii).

(iii) is [that the cat is under chair] ok with you?

Example (iii) is no better, and no worse, than other subject-aux inversion examples with other verbs and modals.

4. Of course, under Stowell's account, it might be claimed that the CRP does not apply to nonfinite IPs because they are [−tense]. However, under more recent theories of phrase structure (e.g., Grimshaw 1991), IP is just an "extended projection" of VP and shares its lexical category features [+V, −N]. Additionally, we note that the sentences in (18) are awkward,

and the status of their acceptability may not differ significantly from comparable sentences with tensed CP subjects. Reasons for this are addressed below.

5. Among the predicates taking absolutive subjects are *amanaki* 'hope', *manako* 'want', *piko* 'believe', and others.

6. In the remainder of the chapter, we forgo indicating degrees of acceptability on any examples that we generate. While there are important differences in acceptability that we will point to, these differences are relative, not absolute. Data cited from other sources are reproduced with the acceptability judgment of the source.

7. This dispreference led to a number of syntactic proposals that would rule out internal sentential subjects in English such as Ross's (1973) Internal S Condition and Kuno's (1973) constraint that subject sentences can only appear in sentence-initial position.

8. Lees and Rosenbaum also analyzed sentential complements of verbs as having NP immediately dominating S. This was abandoned within Extended Standard Theory in Chomsky 1973 so that extraction from sentential complements would not violate subjacency. The resulting asymmetrical analysis of sentential subjects and objects, as formulated in Chomsky 1973, is a view we argue to be essentially correct (Davies and Dubinsky 1999, 2001).

9. Because emphatic reflexives can only be used with phrases whose denotation is definite, AP subjects, which are properties, do not share this NP-like trait.

References

Brame, M. 1976. *Conjectures and refutations in syntax and semantics*. New York: North Holland.

Chomsky, N. 1973. Conditions on transformations. In S. Anderson and P. Kiparsky, eds., *A Festschrift for Morris Halle*, 232–286. New York: Holt, Rinehart and Winston.

Chung, S. 1982. Unbounded dependencies in Chamorro grammar. *Linguistic Inquiry* 13:39–77.

Chung, S. 1991. Sentential subjects and proper government in Chamorro. In C. Georgopolous and R. Ishihara, eds., *Interdisciplinary approaches to language*, 75–99. Dordrecht: Kluwer.

Culicover, P. 1997. *Principles and parameters: An introduction to syntactic theory*. Oxford: Oxford University Press.

Davies, W. D., and S. Dubinsky. 1999. Sentential subjects as complex NPs: New reasons for an old account of subjacency. *Papers from the Thirty-Fourth Regional Meeting, Chicago Linguistic Society*, 83–94. Chicago Linguistic Society, University of Chicago.

Davies, W. D., and S. Dubinsky. 2001. Functional architecture and the distribution of subject properies. In W. D. Davies and S. Dubinsky, eds., *Objects and other subjects: Grammatical functions, functional categories, and configurationality*, 247–279. Dordrecht: Kluwer.

Delahunty, G. 1981. *Topics in the syntax and semantics of English cleft sentences*. Bloomington: Indiana University Linguistics Club.

Delahunty, G. 1983. But sentential subjects do exist. *Linguistic Analysis* 12:379–398.

Dryer, M. 1980. The positional tendencies of sentential noun phrases in universal grammar. *Canadian Journal of Linguistics* 25:123–195.

Emonds, J. 1970. Root and structure-preserving transformations. Doctoral dissertation, MIT.

Emonds, J. 1972. A reformulation of certain syntactic transformations. In S. Peters, ed., *Goals of linguistic theory*, 21–62. Englewood Cliffs, NJ: Prentice Hall.

Emonds, J. 1976. *A transformational approach to English syntax: Root, structure-preserving, and local transformations.* New York: Academic Press.

Erdmann, P. 1988. On the principle of "weight" in English. In C. Duncan-Rose and T. Vennemann, eds., *On language*, 325–339. London: Routledge.

Fodor, J., T. Bever, and M. Garrett. 1974. *The psychology of language: An introduction to psycholinguistics and generative grammar.* New York: McGraw-Hill.

Frazier, L., and K. Rayner. 1988. Parameterizing the language processing system: Left versus right branching within and across languages. In J. A. Hawkins, ed., *Explaining language universals*, 247–279. Oxford: Blackwell.

Gibson, E. 1998. Linguistic complexity: Locality of syntactic dependencies. *Cognition* 68:1–76.

Grimshaw, J. 1991. Extended projections. Unpublished manuscript, Rutgers University.

Grosu, A., and S. Thompson. 1977. Constraints on the distribution of NP clauses. *Language* 53:104–151.

Haegeman, L., and J. Guéron. 1999. *English grammar: A generative perspective.* Malden, MA: Blackwell.

Hawkins, J. A. 1994. *A performance theory of order and constituency.* Cambridge: Cambridge University Press.

Iwakura, K. 1978. On root transformations and the structure preserving hypothesis. *Linguistic Analysis* 4:321–364.

Koster, J. 1978. Why subject sentences don't exist. In S. Jay Keyser, ed., *Recent transformational studies in European languages*, 53–64. Cambridge, MA: MIT Press.

Kuno, S. 1973. *The structure of the Japanese language.* Cambridge, MA: MIT Press.

Lasnik, H. 1995. Last resort. In S. Haraguchi and M. Funaki, eds., *Minimalism and linguistic theory*, 1–32. Tokyo: Hituzi Syobo.

Lasnik, H. 1999. *Minimalist analysis.* Malden, MA: Blackwell.

Lees, R. 1960. *The grammar of English nominalizations.* The Hague: Mouton.

Levin, J., and D. Massam. 1986. Classification of Niuean verbs: Notes on case. In P. Geraghty, L. Carrington, and S. A. Wurm, eds., *FOCAL I: Papers from the Fourth International Conference on Austronesian Linguistics*, 231–244. Canberra: Australian National University.

Levine, R. 1989. On focus inversion: Syntactic valence and the role of a SUBCAT list. *Linguistics* 17:1013–1055.

McCloskey, J. 1991. There, it, and agreement. *Linguistic Inquiry* 22:563–567.

Postal, P. 1974. *On Raising.* Cambridge, MA: MIT Press.

Radford, A. 1997. *Syntactic theory and the structure of English: A minimalist approach.* Cambridge: Cambridge University Press.

Rosenbaum, P. 1967. *The grammar of English predicate complement constructions.* Cambridge, MA: MIT Press.

Ross, J. R. 1973. The same side filter. *Papers from the Ninth Regional Meeting, Chicago Linguistic Society*, 549–566. Chicago Linguistic Society, University of Chicago.

Safir, K. 1982. Syntactic chains and the definiteness effect. Doctoral dissertation, MIT.

Safir, K. 1983. On small clauses as constituents. *Linguistic Inquiry* 14:730–735.

Stowell, T. 1981. Origins of phrase structure. Doctoral dissertation, MIT.

Wasow, T. 1997. Remarks on grammatical weight. *Language Variation and Change* 9:81–105.

Widmann, C. 2005. Factors at play in determining the acceptability of sentential subjects in English: The role of constituent relative weight. Unpublished manuscript, University of South Carolina.

7 Syntax and Semantics of Polish Emotion Verbs: A Corpus Study

Katarzyna Dziwirek

7.1 Introduction

This chapter offers several new generalizations about how Polish (and to a lesser degree English) speakers conceptualize emotions and how these conceptualizations translate into the morphology and syntax of emotional expression in the two languages. The data cited here comes from the Polish and English Language Corpora for Research and Applications (PELCRA), the Longman Corpus of Contemporary English, and the British National Corpus (BNC). PELCRA contains the Polish National Corpus (PNC), which mirrors the BNC in terms of genres and its coverage of written and spoken language. PELCRA has over 150,000,000 words of running text, out of which 100 million represent a balanced corpus, partly POS tagged. The Polish data cited here comes from the PELCRA sampler, which contains 10 million word tokens of twentieth-century Polish, though most of it has been checked against the entire PELCRA corpus.

The chapter is organized into three parts. In the first section I look at the correspondence between emotional expression and parts of speech. The second section considers the complements of Polish emotion verbs. In the last section I discuss the syntax and semantics of complex sentences with emotion predicates.

7.2 Emotions and Parts of Speech

My interest in emotions and parts of speech was initially inspired by Wierzbicka's (1995) observation that Slavic languages prefer to express "feeling emotions" with intransitive, often reflexive, verbs while English tends to use far more copular constructions with adjectives and participles. This, according to Wierzbicka, reflects both a semantic and a cultural difference between Slavic and English. The semantic difference is that "adjectives ... designate passive states, not active emotions to which people 'give themselves' more or less voluntarily" (p. 226), while emotions expressed by "reflexive verbs such as [Russian] *bojat'sja* 'to be afraid' ... are treated not as arising by themselves but by the speaker's conscious thoughts about the event" (p. 229). Thus, in a sense, by using reflexive verbs the Slavic speakers are manufacturing the emotion within themselves. The cultural difference is stated by Wierzbicka (1995, 226–227) as follows: "I believe that this [use of adjectives in English] is not 'accidental', but reflects an important feature of Anglo-Saxon culture—a culture which tends to view behavior described disapprovingly as 'emotional' with suspicion and embarrassment.... Their culture encourages them to be *glad* rather than *rejoice*, to be *sad* rather than to *pine*, to be *angry* rather than to *fume* or *rage*, and so on." By contrast, Slavic speakers value emotional expression and, so to speak, "do it with verbs."

To check Wierzbicka's assertion I divided the emotional field into six broad categories: ANGER, FEAR/WORRY, DISLIKE/DISGUST/HATE, SADNESS/WORRY/UNHAPPINESS, LIKE/LOVE/PLEASURE/SATISFACTION, and JOY/HAPPINESS/ENJOYMENT. I am aware that this does not cover the entire emotional field and that there are a lot of "leakages"—for example, between JOY, HAPPINESS, and LIKE/SATISFACTION/PLEASURE; between WORRY and FEAR; between WORRY and SADNESS; and so on. These are not set, unchangeable categories, nor, of course, are the English terms stand-ins for emotional universals (which is why I use small caps to refer to them); this is just a starting point for a classification. The data can be found in appendix A.

Looking at the set of basic verbs, adjectives, and participles in each language,[1] I find that, indeed, Polish speakers tend to have a larger repertoire of intransitive, often reflexive verbs to express their feelings, while English speakers have more numerous adjectives and participles at their disposal.[2]

All emotions
Intransitive verbs   Polish: 31   English: 23
Adjectives/participles   Polish: 45   English: 105

The actual number of Polish verbs is most likely much higher due to the fact that Polish has a large number of verbal prefixes that combine with the basic verbal stem to create shades of meaning (cf. *lękać się, przelęknąć się*, and *wylęknąć się*, which can all be translated as 'afraid/frightened'). Of the thirty-one Polish verbs in our sample, twenty-four are reflexive.[3]

The adjective/participle data also reveal some interesting patterns. First of all, consistent with the second half of Wierzbicka's observation, English numbers are indeed much larger. In part, it is because English has more transitive verbs and thus more passive participles, which can be used in the adjectival function.

Second, in most semantic fields there are adjectives/participles that indicate both "causing" and "feeling" the emotion. The number of "feeling" adjectives and participles tends to be larger than "causing" participles. The only exception is the DISGUST/DISLIKE field, where I could find no Polish adjectives that describe feeling these emotions. In Polish, they must be expressed with verbs.

Finally, the data reveal that the domain of FEAR has the largest number of adjectives that describe a permanent condition or trait. While other emotional domains also have adjectives that describe traits (e.g., *a loving husband, a happy child*), most emotion adjectives tend to be transitory and describe temporary states. FEAR's unique status is also reflected by the fact that it is the only emotion that has a noun describing a person in its grip: *coward* in English and *tchórz* in Polish. There are no nouns describing people who are habitually happy, angry, and so on, though there are the fairly recent English *worrier* and possibly *hater*.

The survey presented in appendix A is, of course, imperfect, and the numbers are not absolute, yet there are some interesting initial conclusions, beyond confirming Wierzbicka's observation regarding parts of speech. FEAR and SADNESS appear to be the most elaborated domains in both languages. Polish has twenty-three verbs and adjectives/participles referring to feeling FEAR, English has twenty-five, and FEAR-causing verbs are the most numerous among the transitive verbs (with thirteen for Polish and sixteen for English).

FEAR-related verbs
Feeling FEAR (verbs and adjectives)   Polish: 23   English: 25
Causing FEAR (verbs)   Polish: 13   English: 16

The domain of SADNESS, though elaborated in both languages, shows a contrast between them as well. There are twenty-two verbs and adjectives/participles referring to feeling sad in Polish, and thirty-five in English, whose speakers chose to name more shades of this emotion.

Feeling SADNESS
Verbs and adjectives/participles   Polish: 22   English: 35

It is a sobering finding that both languages have singled out fear and sadness for cultural elaboration, but a finding in keeping with recent findings that languages tend to have more words for negative emotions and thoughts than for positive ones (see Schrauf and Sanchez 2004).

The confirmation that Polish tends to express "feeling" emotions with intransitive, often reflexive, verbs, while English uses more copular constructions, has immediate consequences for teaching. In teaching Polish, we must focus on automatizing the verbs. The reverse is true for teaching English to Polish students.[4] Thus, to conclude, emotions can indeed be expressed with different parts of speech in different languages, and this needs to be taught early and often.[5]

7.3 Clause-Level Syntax of Polish Reflexive Emotion Verbs

7.3.1 Differences: Complements and Counterparts

Since reflexive verbs are such a prevalent way to talk about emotions in Polish, their structure requires closer scrutiny. In general, there appears to be little that all of them have in common, besides their reflexive nature. Some require a complement,[6] others do not. For some, the complement is an NP, for others a PP. If it is an NP, the complement can be instrumental, genitive, or, for one verb only, dative.[7] If it is a PP, a variety of prepositions are used. These are lexical differences quite similar to the differences in prepositional phrases that English emotion predicates select as their complements (cf. *angry AT, furious WITH, to worry ABOUT, to long FOR*, etc.). Another area of difference is that some of the verbs have nonreflexive, "causative" counterparts based on the same root (e.g., *rozzłościć się* 'to get angry' and *rozzłościć kogoś* 'to make someone angry'), while others do not.[8]

ANGER reflexive verbs. All of these verbs are compatible with PP *na* + ACC indicating cause of anger, and all, with the exception of *pieklić się*, have nonreflexive counterparts. Examples include *(roz)złościć się, wściekać się, (roz)(po)gniewać się, oburzyć się, (z)irytować się, pieklić się, rozjuszyć się*, and *(roz)sierdzić się*.

FEAR reflexive verbs. These verbs fall into two broad groups. Members of the first group have GEN complements and no causative counterparts: *bać się, obawiać się, lękać się, przelęknąć się*. Those in the second group have INST complements and causative counterparts: *zaniepokoić się, przerazić się*. *Przestraszyć się* falls between the two groups; it requires a GEN complement but has a causative counterpart.

SADNESS/WORRY reflexive verbs. These verbs all have INST cause/source and causative counterparts. Examples include *martwić się, trapić się*, and *smucić się*.

LIKE/LOVE reflexive verbs. Items in this category defy easy classification. Those that have NP complements tend to take INST source and have causative counterparts—for instance, *rozkoszować się* + INST, *zachwycać się* + INST, 'to delight in' or *zadowalać się* + INST 'to be satisfied with'. Others choose a variety of PP complements and do not have causative counterparts. Examples include *zakochać się w* + LOC 'to fall in love with', *lubować się w* + LOC 'to take pleasure in', *przywiązać się do* + GEN 'to become attached to', and *przyjaźnić się z* + INST 'to be friends with'. In this domain we also find the one Polish dative experiencer verb that appears in personal clauses. Like Italian *piaccere*, Russian *nravit'sja*, German *gefallen*, Spanish *gustar*, and so on, the Polish verb *podobać się* takes the liked entity as its agreement-determining subject while the experiencer appears as a dative NP. It does not have a causative counterpart.

JOY reflexive verbs. Some of these verbs can have either INST or *z* + GEN complements and causative counterparts: *cieszyć się, radować się* 'to rejoice'. Others do not take complements and do not have causative counterparts: *weselić się* 'to be merry'.

Table 7.1
Morphosyntactic properties of Polish reflexive emotion verbs

Emotion	NP complement	PP complement	causative counterpart
Anger		na + ACC	yes
Fear			
(a)	GEN		no
(b)	INST		yes
Sadness/worry	INST		yes
Like/Love			
(a)	INST		yes
(b)		w + LOC	no
(c)		do + GEN	no
(d)		z + INST	no
Joy	INST	z + GEN	yes
Disgust	INST		yes
Surprise	DAT		yes

DISGUST. There is only one reflexive verb in this domain. *Brzydzić się* requires an INST complement, and its closest causative counterpart *obrzydzić* is a ditransitive verb (DAT ACC 'to make something abhorrent/disgusting to someone').

SURPRISE. Again this domain is limited to a single reflexive verb. *Dziwić się* requires a DAT complement; it has a causative counterpart. The data are summarized in table 7.1. The table shows that few absolute predictions are possible. We cannot say that if a verb selects an NP complement, it will have a nonreflexive causative counterpart, since a group of FEAR verbs contradicts that. We cannot say that if a verb selects a PP complement it will not have a nonreflexive causative counterpart, because the ANGER verbs contradict that claim. We cannot determine what PP or what case NP emotion verbs will select to mark their reasons/sources. The only generalization that can be made on the basis of table 7.1 is that if a verb selects an INST complement, it will have a nonreflexive causative counterpart. This is suggestive of a common argument structure for both reflexive and nonreflexive verbs, and a syntactic reevaluation that might relate the two, but it is a matter for further study, which should include cognitive as well as emotion verbs.[9]

7.3.2 Similarities: Why Are Many, But Not All, Polish Emotion Verbs Reflexive?

A "true" reflexive verb suggests that the agent and patient of the action, or the subject and object of the sentence, are one and the same entity. From that, can we extrapolate, as Wierzbicka does, that Polish speakers are manufacturing the emotions conveyed by reflexive emotion verbs within themselves? Can we assume that they are both the producers and the experiencers of the emotion?

Yes and no. First, let us note that there are contexts where the "reflexive" particle *się* is used that have little to do with its reflexive meaning (the impersonal *się* construction, to name just one).[10] How can we tell if the presence of the reflexive particle is an instance of "true" reflexive meaning or not?

Next, consider that there are quite a few intransitive emotion verbs that are not reflexive in Polish (23 percent in our sample; e.g., *szaleć* 'to rage', *rozpaczać* 'to despair'). What of these emotions? Why would they not be manufactured within the speakers? This has been a long-standing problem in Polish linguistics. For if we posit an analysis that explains the reflexive nature of intransitive emotion verbs, why should it not apply to all intransitive emotion verbs? Up to now, lexical stipulation has been the less-than-satisfactory explanation.

One of the most valuable lessons I learned from David Perlmutter concerns different levels of explanation in linguistics—for example, that a solution that makes sense in terms of the current theory's formalism might not in fact be explanatory at all. Looking for broad generalizations that might not fit into the prevailing theoretical frameworks but that capture an essential insight about a linguistic problem, is much more worthwhile.

I believe that I have found such a generalization regarding the question posed in this section. The answer to the puzzle of Polish reflexive and nonreflexive intransitive emotion verbs cannot be found by looking at verbs alone. Dziwirek and Lewandowska-Tomaszczyk 2003 examined collocations of Polish emotion nouns and discovered a striking pattern with regard to how Polish speakers conceptualize emotions.

Polish emotion nouns appear to be divided into two nearly mutually exclusive sets. Some are seen as inherent in individuals and thus as part of human nature (albeit possibly in a dormant state), while others are perceived as external. This discovery is based on the collocations of the emotion nouns with some crucial verbs: you can awaken (*wzbudzić/obudzić*) or call forth or stir (*wywołać*) the internal emotions, and fall into (*wpaść w*) the external ones.[11]

Consider table 7.2. The relevant contrast is between the third column (*wpaść w*) and the fourth and fifth columns taken together. Some nouns show clear preferences for *wzbudzić* or *wywołać*, but there is also considerable overlap between them and, crucially, a striking degree of contrast between the two together and *wpaść w* (the third column).

The patterns in the table are not absolute—they are limited by the available data—yet we believe they reveal some real generalizations. While it might be possible for a Polish speaker to say *wpaść w oburzenie* 'fall into indignation', even though there are no examples of this type in our sample, the vast majority of the zeros in the table represent true impossibilities. For example, no Polish speaker would say *wpaść*

Table 7.2
Collocation patterns of Polish emotion nouns

Noun	English translation	X *wpaść w* + emotion	*wzbudzić* emotion *w* X	*wywołać* emotion *w* X
agresja	aggression	0	1	3
amok	amok	2	0	0
apatia	apathy	1	0	0
depresja	depression	9	0	0
desperacja	desperation	1	0	0
ekstaza	ecstasy	2	0	0
emocje	emotions	0	13	8
entuzjazm	enthusiasm	0	4	5
euphoria	euphoria	3	1	0
frustracja	frustration	0	1	2
furia	fury	9	0	1
gniew	anger/wrath	19	1	0
groza	terror, dread	0	0	2
hysteria	hysterics	9	0	0
(dobry) humor	(good) mood	11	0	0
irytacja	vexation	0	0	1
lęk	fear, anxiety	0	0	4
litość	pity/compassion	0	5	0
miłość	love	0	2	0
nadzieje	hopes	0	4	0
namiętność	passion	0	1	2
(zły) nastrój	(bad) mood	2	0	0
nerwica	neurosis	1	0	0
niechęć	aversion	0	2	3
niedowierzanie	disbelief/distrust	0	2	0
nienawiść	hate	0	2	0
niepokój	anxiety	0	6	5
niesmak	mild disgust	0	1	1
nieufność	distrust	0	3	0
nostalgia	nostalgia	0	0	1
obawa	anxiety	0	2	5
obłęd	madness	6	0	0
obrzydzenie	strong disgust	0	0	1
oburzenie	indignation	0	5	9
optymizm	optimism	0	3	0
panika	panic	26	0	6
podenerwowanie	nervousness	1	0	0
podniecenie	excitement	0	0	2
podrażnienie	irritation	0	0	1
podziw	admiration/wonder	0	6	1

Table 7.2
(continued)

Noun	English translation	X *wpaść w* + emotion	*wzbudzić* emotion *w* X	*wywołać* emotion *w* X
popłoch	panic	4	0	2
poruszenie	agitation	0	1	0
pożądanie	desire	0	2	0
przerażenie	terror	2	1	0
radość	joy	0	2	1
rozczulenie	tenderness/pity	2	0	0
rozgoryczenie	embitterment	0	0	1
rozpacz	despair	11	0	1
starch	fear	1	0	1
stress	stress	0	0	1
szacunek	respect	0	1	0
szał	fury/rage	17	0	0
szok	shock	1	0	9
tęsknota	hankering/nostalgia	0	2	0
tkliwość	tenderness/love	0	2	0
trwoga	fear/alarm	1	0	0
(różne) uczucia	(various) feelings	0	12	10
ufność	trust	0	2	0
uznanie	appreciation	0	3	0
wątpliwości	doubts	0	2	0
współczucie	empathy	0	2	0
wstręt	disgust/revulsion	0	2	0
zachwyt	enchantment/rapture	2	7	0
zaduma	pensiveness	4	0	0
zainteresowanie	interest	0	15	2
zamyślenie	reverie	3	0	0
zapał	ardor	0	1	0
zaufanie	trust	0	3	0
zdumienie	amazement/wonder	1	0	1
zdziwienie	surprise	0	3	0
zgorszenie	outrage	0	2	0
zgroza	horror	0	2	0
złość	anger	4	0	2
zmieszanie	embarassment	0	1	0
zniechęcenie	dejection	1	0	1
zwątpienie	doubt/hoplessness	1	0	1
żal	sorrow	1	0	0
żądza	lust	0	1	0

w tęsknotę, tkliwość, niechęć 'fall into yearning, tenderness, aversion'. Examples of data with the relevant verbs are in appendix B. As our translations demonstrate, there are often no direct equivalents of these expressions in English.

How do we characterize the two sets of emotions in Polish: those viewed as internal to human beings or groups of human beings and those perceived by Polish speakers as external? After considering previous analyses of similar constructions,[12] we determined that even though it is a cognate of the Russian *vpast' v*, the Polish expression *wpaść w* seems to more closely resemble the Russian expression *prijti v* 'come/arrive at an emotion', at least as described by Mostovaja 1998. Unlike with *vpast' v*, emotions used with *wpaść w* are not necessarily negative. (The Polish version of the 'righteous anger' sentence in note 12 is perfectly plausible: *Wpadł w słuszny gniew*.) Rather, the emotions used with *wpaść w* in Polish tend to be very intense, last for a relatively short time, and, most crucially, can be expected to be *overtly expressed by a person's physical demeanor*. The latter, in our opinion, is the key element of the Polish construction *wpaść w* + emotion. *Amok, apatia, depresja, desperacja, ekstaza, histeria, dobry/zły humor/nastrój, obłęd, panika, szał, trwoga,* and so on all have bodily correlates. When you are *amok, ecstatic, hysterical, mad, panicking*, and so forth, you behave in a certain way so that people can tell what you are feeling. Similarly, when you feel *apathy, depression*, or *dread*, these feelings tend to be clearly discernible. These are emotions or states you wear on your sleeve, so to speak, and cannot hide from others.

In contrast, emotions compatible with *wzbudzić* 'to awaken' and *wywołać* 'to call forth' do not necessarily have an overt physical manifestation. Some might be behaviorally externalized, hence the area of overlap between the two sets, but crucially, they can also be physically covert and lie dormant within a person.

This insight into how Polish speakers categorize emotions, based on collocations of emotion nouns, turns out to have consequences for verbs as well. As mentioned above, Polish has both reflexive and nonreflexive intransitive verbs. Verbs derived from the same roots as those emotions perceived as external are typically nonreflexive:

(1) wpaść w szał   szaleć   'to rage'
    wpaść w histerię   histeryzować   'to be hysterical'
    wpaść w panikę   panikować   'to panic'
    wpaść w rozpacz   rozpaczać   'to despair'

The opposite is also true. If an emotion seen as innate and thus one that can be awakened within a person has a corresponding verb, this verb will most likely be reflexive. Verbs based on the same roots as nouns that can never be used with *wpaść w* are always reflexive:

(2) *wpaść w zdziwienie   zdziwić się   'to be surprised'
    *wpaść w zainteresowanie zainteresować się   'to become interested'
    *wpaść w entuzjazm   entuzjazmować się   'to enthuse'
    *wpaść w niepokój   niepokoić się   'to be uneasy/anxious'

So it appears that a generalization of how Polish speakers conceptualize emotions based on collocations of emotion nouns, turns out to be relevant to the explanation of why some intransitive Polish emotion verbs are reflexive while others are not. Polish speakers seem to categorize emotions into two almost mutually exclusive sets. One group is seen as present inside individuals. These are the internal emotions that can be awakened and also possibly triggered by the speakers themselves (hence allowing/requiring reflexive verbs). Thus the reflexive particle that accompanies these verbs does in a sense mark the fact that they can be self-induced.[13] Emotions in the other group are perceived as external pitfalls one can fall into and do not allow a reflexive conceptualization.

This folk classification covers the vast majority of the data but is not absolute, because unsurprisingly, some emotions seem to hover on the edge—for example, ANGER words. ANGER nouns can occur with both types of verbs (*wpaść w* and *wzbudzić/wywołać*) and ANGER verbs have reflexive and causative versions. Consider, though, that ANGER-type emotions are complex and can be very distinct: they might or might not involve offenders/wrongdoers, can be public or private, justifiable or irrational, and so on. Most emotions have fewer variables and fall squarely into either the internal (*wzbudzić/wywołać* and reflexive intransitive verbs) or the external (*wpaść w* and nonreflexive intransitive verbs) category.

7.4 Syntax and Semantics of Complex Sentences with Emotion Predicates

In this section I briefly summarize findings regarding complex sentences with emotion verbs as main predicates. Some of this research was first reported in Dziwirek and Lewandowska-Tomaszczyk 2003 and Dziwirek 2004.

7.4.1 Clausal Complements of Intransitive Verbs

Clausal complements of intransitive emotion verbs are summarized in table 7.3. Some sample sentences will be useful. Sentence (3) illustrates *że* clauses.

(3) Lubiszewscy **cieszą się, że** budowa jest już za nimi.
    'The Lubiszewscys are glad that the construction is behind them.'

An example of an infinitive clause can be seen in (4).

(4) Zawodnicy **boją się przyjeżdżać** do centrum treningowego.
    'The players are afraid to come to the training center.'

Syntax and Semantics of Polish Emotion Verbs

Table 7.3
Clausal complements of Polish emotion verbs

	bać się "to be afraid"	*martwić się* "to worry"	*cieszyć się* "to be glad"
number of examples	1,421	338	1,304
complex sentences (cs)	580 (40%)	89 (23%)	301 (23%)
że that-clauses	275 (47% of cs)	46 (52% of cs)	265 (88% of cs)
infinitives	234		
żeby lest-clauses	55	4	
czy if-clauses	16	14	
wh-questions		10	26 (also *bo*)
to clauses		15	10

Here is an example of a *żeby* clause.

(5) Mama zawsze bardzo **się martwiła, żeby** ta kartka nie zginęła.
'Mom always worried lest his piece of paper go astray.'

Czy clauses occur in examples like (6).

(6) **Boją się jednak, czy** zdążą.
'They are afraid lest they be late.'

Sentence (7) illustrates *wh*-questions.

(7) Mukesh **martwi się, co** będzie, kiedy ktoś z rodziny zachoruje.
'Mukesh worries what will happen if one of the family should become ill.'

7.4.1.1 Findings Regarding the Complement Type
The patterns revealed by the corpus data include the following observations and generalizations.

• *Że* 'that' complements are allowed only in the three semantic fields exemplified above (FEAR, WORRY, and JOY) in Polish.[14] In all three they are the most frequent type of complex construction. No *że* complements were found with ANGER verbs (e.g., *złościć się, wściekać się*) in the 10 million PELCRA Sampler, and only a few in the 150 million PELCRA Corpus, yet such complements are frequent in English.

• In Polish, in the three fields examined here, only FEAR as exemplified by *bać się* allows infinitival complements. This contrasts with English, where infinitives are frequent with *glad* and *happy*, the counterparts of *cieszyć się*. However, many instances of *glad/happy* with infinitives were found to be politeness routines, rather than true expressions of emotions. (Saying *I would be glad/happy to help/do it/take that on* does not necessarily imply gladness or happiness.)

• *Żeby* complements are only found with verbs expressing "negative" emotions and are always negated. They correspond to the English "lest" complements and thus are incompatible with sunny, positive feelings such as JOY and HAPPINESS. This makes perfect sense for *lest* but is unexpected with *żeby*. Unlike *lest*, *żeby* does not have negation as part of its meaning, and its use with negative emotion verbs is unique. This is a subject for further research.

7.4.1.2 Findings Regarding the Meaning of Complement Clauses

Key findings include the following:

- The three verbs examined here and others like them are polysemous and can be construed as mental verbs as well as emotion verbs. This seems to contradict Wierzbicka's claim that all reflexive emotion verbs have a thinking component (which adjectives lack), since the thinking component is associated with the possibility of *że/żeby* complement clauses and, for example, *złościć się* 'to be angry' does not occur with such clauses in our sample. These findings would suggest that only *some* senses of *some* reflexive emotion verbs involve thinking (see Dziwirek and Lewandowska-Tomaszczyk 2005 for discussion of the different senses of *bać się*).
- Another finding is that, unsurprisingly, most of our fears and worries concern the future, and the overwhelming majority of the complements of *bać się* 'to be afraid' and of *martwić się* 'to worry' are future oriented. This is not the case with *cieszyć się* 'to be glad/happy': we can be glad because things are the way they are or because they have already happened.
- Finally, regarding the function of complex sentences with emotion predicates, we observe that English, much more than Polish, extends emotion expressions into politeness routines. Locutions like *I am afraid that...*, *I fear that...*, *I'd be glad/happy to...*, as well as *I hate to interrupt* and *I would like/love to help*, do not convey the literal meaning of the emotion. Their Polish counterparts are not used in this function nearly as much.

7.4.2 Transitive "Feeling" Verbs

In the survey of emotional parts of speech I noticed that in most emotion domains transitive verbs mean 'to cause the emotion' (*(roz)złościć kogoś* 'to anger someone', *(z)martwić kogoś* 'to sadden/worry someone', etc.), but not so in the LIKE/LOVE and DISLIKE/HATE fields (table 7.4). Here transitive verbs, like the intransitive ones, mean 'to feel the emotion'—for example, the subjects of both *kochać się* 'to be in love' and *kochać* 'to love' are the experiencers of the emotion. These fields are also where we find many infinitival (subject control) complements in both languages, though much more frequently in English.[15] There is a significant difference between the two fields in Polish with respect to infinitival complements as well.

A few sample sentences will illustrate the preceding points. Sentence (8) includes an infinitival construction.

Table 7.4
Clausal complements of transitive emotion verbs

	uwielbiać "to love/adore"	nienawidzić "to hate"	nie znosić "can't stand"	nie cierpieć "can't bear"
number of examples	214	362	162	108
complex sentences (cs)	56 (24%)	6 (1.6%)	9 (6%)	3 (3%)
że clauses				
infinitives	53 (95% of cs)	4	4	1
żeby clauses			1	1
czy clauses				
when-clauses	3	2	4	1
to-clauses				

(8) Bukowina, Michałów, to wspaniałe miejsca. **Uwielbiamy tu przyjeżdżać.**
'Bukowina, Michałów, they are wonderful places. We love coming here.'

A *żeby* clause is demonstrated in (9).

(9) A nade wszystko **nie znosił, by** się co w domu zmieniało.
'But most of all he hated for anything to change at home.'

The following is an example of a *when* clause.

(10) **Nienawidzę, gdy** wyją syreny. Boję się.
'I hate it when the sirens are wailing. I'm afraid.'

The verb *uwielbiać*, which has assumed a new dominance in the Polish language, is the closest equivalent of the English 'to love/adore', as in *I love/adore movies, ice cream, chocolate*, and so on. It has the same "over-the-top" quality, though its original meaning 'to adore' is still preserved in religious contexts. The fact that it is so often used with infinitive complements, suggests its closeness to English 'enjoy', which is typically coupled with an activity: *I enjoy bowling, singing, skiing, etc.*

The Polish verb *kochać* 'to love', not included in table 7.4, merits a study of its own. It is very rarely used in direct statements to the addressee. Polish *Kocham cię* 'I love you' is reserved for very serious, emotionally laden, romantic contexts and is not used lightly, the way *I love you* seems to be in (American?) English. It is uttered by Polish people very rarely, possibly only a few times in their lifetime.

The three main Polish verbs for expressing strong negative emotions in the DISLIKE/ HATE domain—*nienawidzić* 'to hate', *nie znosić* 'can't stand/bear', and *nie cierpieć* 'can't stand'—appear to be very concrete and very transitive, and rarely occur with complement clauses. It is clear that Polish does not work the same way as English does here: *nienawidzić, nie znosić,* and *nie cierpieć* tend to convey negative feelings toward a person, an object, or an abstract quality/concept. There are also no semantic extensions of these verbs to politeness formulas as in the English *I hate to bother you, but*..., *I hate to interrupt, but*..., or *I hate to say this, but*....

In summary, transitive verbs in the LIKE/LOVE and DISLIKE/HATE fields mean 'to feel' rather than 'to cause' an emotion in both languages. None of them allow *że/that* complement clauses, but the two fields differ from one another when it comes to infinitives. *Uwielbiać* frequently occurs with infinitival complements and often refers to activities; *nienawidzić, nie znosić*, and *nie cierpieć* tend to refer to concrete objects, people, or ideas and allow few complement clauses.

7.5 Conclusions

This chapter offers several empirical findings and calls attention to previously unnoticed facts and correlations. The study of Polish and English emotional expressions and parts of speech reveals a number of similarities and differences between the two languages. Our data support Wierzbicka's (1995) observation that Slavic languages tend to express "feeling" emotions with intransitive, often reflexive, verbs while English uses far more copular constructions with adjectives and participles. In both languages the FEAR and SADNESS domains are the ones with the most elaborated vocabulary.

Polish intransitive emotion verbs select a wide variety of complements and the only regularity found in this area is that INST complements of intransitive reflexive verbs correlate with the presence of a causative counterpart. The main contribution of the chapter lies in providing an explanation of why some Polish intransitive verbs are reflexive, while others are not. Building on the findings of the study of Polish emotion nouns in Dziwirek and Lewandowska-Tomaszczyk 2003, I show that the insight into how Polish speakers conceptualize emotions extends to verbs as well. Polish emotions appear to be divided into two almost mutually exclusive sets. Some are seen as present inside individuals and thus part of human nature, while others are perceived as external. The former are reflexive (since they can be self-triggered), the latter are not.

Like intraclausal complements, sentential complements typically refer to a source or reason for the emotion. They are less common than intraclausal complements. At most, complex sentences comprise 40 percent of all examples (*bać się* 'to be afraid'), while only 1.6 percent of sentences with *nienawidzić* 'to hate' have clausal complements. Finite *że/that* complements are less frequent with emotion verbs in Polish (cf. ANGER verbs in English), as are infinitives (cf. HATE verbs in English). In both languages complements of negative emotion verbs of the FEAR and WORRY type are usually future oriented and allow *żeby/lest* constructions.

Finally, corpus studies such as the present study have wide-ranging implications for different fields of linguistics and for language teaching, because they illuminate the nuances in the meaning of different verbal complements and reveal patterns, frequencies, and regularities not observable without considering large sets of data.

APPENDIX A

Basic intransitive verbs (to feel the emotion)

	Polish	English	Comments
ANGER	8	5	all P verbs reflexive
FEAR/WORRY	10	5	9 P verbs reflexive + *panikować*
SAD	8	12	4 P verbs reflexive, 4 not
LIKE/LOVE	10	3	9 P verbs reflexive + *sympatyzować*
JOY	3	3	all P verbs reflexive
DISLIKE/DISGUST	2	0	1 reflexive, 1 dative experiencer

ANGER P: (roz)złościć się, wściekać się, (roz)gniewać się, oburzyć się, (z)irytować się, pieklić się, rozjuszyć się, sierdzić się, E: to fret, to rage, to rave, to storm, to rampage
FEAR/WORRY P: bać się, obawiać się, lękać się, (za)niepokoić się, (za)trwożyć się, przestraszyć się, wylęknąć się, przelęknąć się, przerazić się, panikować, E: to fear, to dread, to worry, to startle, to panic
SAD/UNHAPPY P: (z)martwić się, (s)trapić się, zwątpić, rozpaczać, (za)smucić się, zniechęcać się, tęsknić, żałować, E: to grieve, to worry, to despair, to hanker, to long, to pine, to yearn, to crave, to miss, to regret, to mourn, to pity
LIKE/LOVE/PLEASURE P: (za)kochać się, lubować się, przywiązać się, przyjaźnić się, sympatyzować, rozkoszować się, zachwycać się, zadowalać się, zachęcać się, podobać się, E: to symphatize, to love, to care
JOY/HAPPINESS P: (u)radować się, (u)cieszyć się, weselić się, E: to rejoice, to enjoy oneself, to make merry
DISLIKE/DISGUST P: brzydzić się, obrzydnąć, E: 0

Transitive verbs

	Polish	English	Meaning
ANGER	8	8	to cause the emotion
FEAR	13	16	to cause the emotion
SAD	9	10	to cause the emotion
*LIKE/LOVE	6	6	to FEEL the emotion
JOY	6	5	to cause the emotion
*DISLIKE/DISGUST	7	11	to FEEL the emotion

ANGER P: (roz)złościć, (roz)gniewać, oburzyć, (z)irytować, (roz)drażnić, rozwścieczyć, rozjuszyć, rozsierdzić, E: to anger, to incense, to irritate, to vex, to exasperate, to infuriate, to annoy, to enrage

FEAR/WORRY P: niepokoić, przestraszyć, straszyć, zastraszyć, nastraszyć, (s)terroryzować, przerazić, zaalarmować, zatrwożyć, (z)martwić, (za)grozić, spłoszyć, onieśmielać, E: to bother, to alarm, to upset, to worry, to perturb, to frighten, to scare, to startle, to terrify, to threaten, to menace, to intimidate, to bully, to terrorize, to horrify, to dismay

SAD/UNHAPPY P: unieszczęśliwić, przygnębić, zasmucić, (z)martwić, zdeprymować, zniechęcić, (s)trapić, przytłoczyć, przybić, E: to distress, to depress, to dishearten, to dispirit, to sadden, to afflict, to discourage, to pain, to crush

LIKE/LOVE P: (po)lubić, uwielbiać, kochać, uwielbić, (u)miłować, upodobać sobie, E: to like, to enjoy, to love, to adore, to worship, to cherish

JOY/HAPPINESS P: (u)radować, (u)cieszyć, (u)szczęśliwić, rozradować, rozweselać, E: to gladden, to delight, to gratify, to please, to exhilarate

DISLIKE/DISGUST P: obrzydzić, obmierzić, mierzić, odpychać, nienawidzić, nie znosić, nie cierpieć, E: to repel, to disgust, to sicken, to dislike, to detest, to loathe, to hate, to execrate, can't bear, can't stand, to abhor

Adjectives and participles

	Polish	English	Meaning
ANGER	9	13	to feel the emotion
	2	4	to cause the emotion
FEAR	5	13	to cause the emotion
	4	6	to habitually feel the emotion–trait)
	9	14	to feel the emotion–state
SAD	14	28	to feel the emotion
LIKE	7	14	to feel the emotion
	7	11	to cause the emotion
JOY	5	11	to feel the emotion
			to cause liking and similar emotions
DISLIKE/DISGUST	7	18	to cause the emotion
	0	5	to feel the emotion

ANGER (feel) P: zły, wściekły, oburzony, zagniewany, zirytowany, rozjuszony, rozdrażniony, gniewny, rozzłoszczony, E: angry, cross, exasperated, furious, peevish, mad, indignant, irritated, annoyed, vexed, enraged, infuriated, incensed

ANGER (cause) P: irytujący, oburzający, E: irritating, annoying, exasperating, infuriating

FEAR (feel) P: zastraszony, przestraszony, przerażony, niespokojny, przelękniony, wylękniony, zaniepokojony, onieśmielony, trwożny, E: intimidated, frightened, scared, afraid, awestruck, terrified, anxious, upset, uneasy, restless, ill at ease, disquieted, fretful, disturbed

FEAR (trait) P: strachliwy, tchórzliwy, lękliwy, bojaźliwy, trwożliwy, E: timid, fearful, cowardly, fainthearted, timorous, cowardly

FEAR (cause) P: niepokojący, zastraszający, przeraźliwy, przerażający, zatrważający, E: alarming, distressing, disquieting, intimidating, horrifying, appalling, frightening, scary, startling, dismaying, upsetting, worrying, terrifying, menacing

SAD/WORRIED (feel) P: nieszczęśliwy, niepocieszony, strapiony, zrozpaczony, stroskany, zdesperowany, zdeprymowany, przybity, zniechęcony, zmartwiony, zatroskany, przygnębiony, smutny, zasmucony, E: wretched, unhappy, miserable, distressed, inconsolable, disconsolate, dejected, brokenhearted, hopeless, desperate, despairing, in despair, worried, saddened, depressed, downcast, dispirited, despondent, discouraged, disheartened, sad, sorrowful, cheerless, tearful, mournful, griefstricken

LIKE/LOVE (feel) P: kochający, przywiązany, oddany, zamiłowany, zakochany, błogi, zadowolony, E: loving, affectionate, fond, attached, kind, devoted, caring, enamored, infatuated, in love, satisfied, pleased, content

LIKE/LOVE (cause) P: zachwycający, rozkoszny, przyjemny, miły, sympatyczny, ujmujący, zachęcający, E: admirable, delightful, entrancing, lovely, enjoyable, pleasing, gratifying, engaging, winsome, stimulating, tempting

JOY (feel) P: uradowany, radosny, szczęśliwy, rad, wesoły, E: glad, delighted, rejoicing, joyful, gay, happy, exhilarated, blissful, pleased, merry

DISGUST/DISLIKE (feel) P: 0, E: disgusted, sickened, repelled, nauseated, repulsed

DISGUST/DISLIKE (cause) P: obrzydliwy, odrażający, wstrętny, nienawistny, obmierzły, ohydny, odpychający, E: abominable, hideous, foul, disgusting, loathsome, sickening, nauseating, detestable, vile, beastly, repulsive, repugnant, hideous, repellent, odious, execrable, hateful

APPENDIX B

Wpaść w 'to fall into'

Czasem przysypia, to znów **wpada w euforię**.
Sometimes he falls asleep; sometimes he shows signs of euphoria.

Ale nigdy nie **wpadł w taki gniew** jak teraz, gdy ją znów zobaczył.
But he never got so angry as now, when he saw her again.

I na przemian to **wpadał w strach**, to bawił się jak dziecko.
And he alternately acted terrified or played like a child.

Jussi Lehtinen: **Wpadłem w panikę.**
Jussi Lehtinen: I panicked.

Wzbudzić 'to awaken/to stir'

Ale obecnie wspólna niedola **wzbudziła w nim uśpioną tkliwość.**
But now, their shared plight caused a dormant tenderness to stir in him.

W dyskusji „Gazety" **żywe emocje wzbudził** sam feminizm.
In the discussion in Gazeta, the notion of feminism itself stirred strong emotions.

Początek spotkania **wzbudził niepokój** bytomskich kibiców.
The beginning of the match caused Bytom fans anxiety.

Jak żmija w stosunku do tych, którzy **wzbudzili w nim nieufność.**
He was like a snake toward those who caused his mistrust.

radości jaką przybycie księcia z Zadnieprza we wszystkich sercach **wzbudziło**,
joy, which stirred in everyone's heart at the arrival of the prince from Zadnieprze.

Wywołać 'to call forth/to stir'

Przygotowana jako dyplom, **wywołała spore poruszenie.**
[The work], prepared as an MA thesis, caused quite a stir.

Słuchane dziś, **wywołują uczucie nostalgii.**
When you listen to them today, they cause a feeling of nostalgia.

Początkowo sprawa nie **wywołała u nas entuzjazmu.**
Initially, this did not stir enthusiasm in us.

Celem pornografii jest **wywołanie podniecenia.**
The goal of pornography is to excite.

Ale to nie jedyny powód **wywołujący we mnie rozgoryczenie.**
But this is not the only reason I am bitter.

Notes

1. The procedure I adopted has been as follows: I checked words in a given semantic field in the Polish-English dictionary, then checked all translations in the English-Polish dictionary, then checked all the new words in the Polish-English dictionary, and so on. I then confirmed that all the words were "common" Polish words (occurred in the PELCRA Sampler at least

100 times—that is, 100 per 10 million. Most items had a much higher frequency. For the most part, I excluded metaphorical expressions. This might seem a little arbitrary at times (e.g., I include *piekłić się* 'to fume' (lit. 'to hell') in the set of anger words, though not expressions like *żółć go zalała* 'he was flooded by bile', etc.), but the focus of this study is on basic parts of speech.

2. The contrast between the two languages is particularly striking in some domains. For example, Polish has twice as many basic intransitive verbs (types, not tokens) in the FEAR and WORRY domain as English, and English does not have any intransitive verbs that mean 'to be/feel disgust(ed)'.

3. The expression "reflexive verb" needs to be clarified. It is used here as a label for Polish verbs whose basic form includes the reflexive clitic *się*. This term is not meant to suggest that the verbs in question are semantically reflexive (i.e., imply identity of the agent/patient, subject/direct object). It is a characterization of their morphosyntactic realization (that they must co-occur with *się*), though clearly, for Wierzbicka the presence of *się* with emotion verbs is semantically relevant, because it suggests that the speakers are "manufacturing the emotion within themselves."

4. Student errors are a good indication that this is an area that requires improvement. Unless verbs like *cieszyć się* 'to be glad/happy' are introduced early on and practiced extensively, students of Polish invariably say *Jestem szczęśliwy* (lit. 'I am happy'), which is not appropriate since it refers to an exalted type of happiness, not everyday gladness/satisfaction, and may be uttered by Poles on momentous occasions (e.g., their wedding day). This pattern holds with many basic emotional expressions, including *martwić się* 'to be worried', *bać się* 'to be afraid', *wściekać się, złościć się* 'to be angry', *dziwić się* 'to be surprised', and so on.

5. One might expect to find differences between English and Polish with regard to the use of adverbs for expressing emotions. English does not employ adverbs in this function except as modifiers of verbs/actions (*She sighed contentedly*). In Polish, constructions with adverbs (or impersonal adjectives) in conjunction with dative experiencers are used for expressing involuntary bodily states (e.g., *Zimno mi* 'I am cold' (lit. 'To me is cold')) and mental/cognitive states (*Trudno mi to zrozumieć* 'It is difficult for me to understand'). Yet we find few instances of this construction with emotions in Polish. The only examples come from the fields of joy and sadness:

(i) Wesoło mi.
   'I feel/am merry.'

(ii) Błogo mi.
   'I feel blissful.'

(iii) Smutno/Przykro mi.
   'I am sad/sorry.'

(iv) Tęskno mi.
   'I feel homesick/nostalgic.'

Adverbs seem to be used to express involuntary emotions much more frequently in Russian (see Wierzbicka 1999, 42). I suspect that this contrast between Polish and Russian might be connected to the finding, discussed in the next section, that many emotions are conceptualized by Polish speakers as dwelling within them. Thus, even though they are often externally triggered, many emotions are seen as internal to human beings and cannot perhaps be perceived as involuntary.

6. I am using this term in a most general, atheoretical sense, of a noun phrase or a prepositional phrase needed to complete their meaning (most often a cause or source of the feeling).

7. The case abbreviations are ACC = accusative, DAT = dative, GEN = genitive, INST = instrumental, LOC = locative, NOM = nominative. Other abbreviations include SG = singular, PL = plural, REFL = reflexive, 1 = first person, 2 = second person, and 3 = third person.

8. Overall the causative counterparts are much less frequent than the reflexive ones. For example, in our sample of 1,304 sentences with the verb *cieszyć*, 1,286 were with *cieszyć się* (reflexive) 'be happy/glad' and 18 with *cieszyć* (causative) 'make happy/glad'. Out of 338 examples with *martwić*, 330 involved *martwić się* (reflexive) 'to worry/be worried about' (as in *I worry about John/I am worried about John*) and only 8 were examples of *martwić* (causative) 'to (make) worry' (as in *John worries me*.) Thus, despite the much studied parallels between the two versions of the so-called psych verbs, the reality, at least in Polish, is that the reflexive, noncausative verbs are overwhelmingly more common.

9. Polish nonreflexive intransitive emotion verbs also select a variety of NP and PP complements but never an INST NP. They also do not have causative counterparts.

10. Consider the verb *myśleć* 'to think' in (i) and (ii):

(i) My myślimy.
we-NOM think-1PL
'We think.'/'We are thinking.'

(ii) Dobrze się nam dziś myśli.
well REFL us-DAT today thinks-3SG
'We are able to think well today.'

Myśleć is not normally reflexive (as shown in (i)) and occurs with the reflexive particle *się* in (ii) in the context of a dative subject and a qualifying adverb. For a detailed analysis of this construction see Dziwirek 1994.

11. Other verbs that can be used with Polish emotion nouns are as follows: X feels Y = *odczuwać, czuć*; X has Y = *mieć, żywić*; Y takes over X = *ogarnąć, opanować, wstępować w*; Z leads X to Y = *wprawić w, wpędzić w, doprowadzić do, przywieść do*.

12. Radden (1998) and Pena Cervel (2003) argue that English prepositional expressions of emotions containing the preposition *in* like the following

(i) I am in love.

(ii) She trembled in fear.

(iii) He cried out in anger/distress/sorrow/despair, etc.

(iv) *Tremble/cry out in worry, sadness, disappointment.

(v) *Tremble/cry out in joy, happiness.

are variations of the container metaphor, whereby only emotions strong enough to overpower people to the extent that they are no longer in control of their actions can be expressed in this way (hence, *not* tremble/cry out in worry, sadness, disappointment). These typically negative and very intense emotions engulf the experiencers, who cannot control their reactions.

Mostovaja (1998) claims that the container metaphor is not explanatory enough and proposes a more nuanced analysis of the Russian (in/into/*v*) prepositional expressions of emotion including *pogruzit'sja v* 'to sink into an emotion', *prijti v* 'to come into an emotion', and *vpast' v* 'to fall into an emotion'. Mostovaja suggests that for Russian speakers *vpast' v* 'to fall into an emotion' is associated with an image of falling into a hollow container. The emotion can be introverted or extroverted and can last for a long or a short time, but it is seen as "bad" or "wrong" by the speaker and so evokes disapproval. Thus it is possible to say:

(vi) Vpal v paniku/strax.
 'He panicked/ became overwhelmed by fear.' (Lit. 'He fell into panic/fear.')

but not

(vii) *Vpal v spravedlivyj gnev.
 'He fell into righteous anger.'

13. Though possibly in different ways for those verbs that do and do not have nonreflexive causative counterparts (e.g., *rozzłościć się* 'to get angry' versus *bać się* 'to be afraid').

14. This raises a question as to the grammatical relation of *że* clauses. Recall that in simple clauses *bać się* takes a GEN NP complement, *martwić się* an INST NP complement, and *cieszyć się* either INST NP or *z* + GEN PP.

15. Here, English also allows "for-to" infinitive complements (*I hate/love for him to X*), which have no infinitival counterparts in Polish (subjunctive clauses convey this meaning).

References

Athanasiadou, Angeliki, and Elżbieta Tabakowska, eds. 1998. *Speaking of emotions: Conceptualisation and expression*. New York: Mouton de Gruyter.

Dziwirek, Katarzyna. 1994. *Polish subjects*. New York: Garland.

Dziwirek, Katarzyna. 2004. Cultural diversity in expressions of emotions: Teaching and research. Paper presented at the Cultural Diversity and Language Education Conference, University of Hawaii.

Dziwirek, Katarzyna, and Barbara Lewandowska-Tomaszczyk. 2003. Syntax and semantics of Polish and English expressions of emotions: A corpus study. Paper presented at the AATSEEL Conference, San Diego.

Dziwirek, Katarzyna, and Barbara Lewandowska-Tomaszczyk. 2005. Syntax and semantics of Polish and English complex expressions of emotions: A corpus study of FEAR expressions. Paper presented at the Annual Meeting of PALC (Practical Applications in Language and Computers), Łódź, Poland.

Landsberg, M., ed. 1995. *Syntactic iconicity and linguistic freezes*. Berlin: Mouton de Gruyter.

Mostovaja, Anna D. 1998. On emotions that one can "immerse into," "fall into," and "come to": The semantics of a few Russian prepositional constructions. In Angeliki Athanasiadou and Elżbieta Tabakowska, eds., *Speaking of emotions: Conceptualisation and expression*, 295–330. New York: Mouton de Gruyter.

Pena Cervel, M. Sandra. 2003. *Topology and cognition: What image-schemas reveal about the metaphorical language of emotions*. Munich: Lincom Europa.

Radden, Gunter. 1998. The conceptualization of emotional causality by means of prepositional phrases. In Angeliki Athanasiadou and Elżbieta Tabakowska, eds., *Speaking of emotions: Conceptualisation and expression*, 273–294. New York: Mouton de Gruyter.

Schrauf, Robert, and Julia Sanchez. 2004. The preponderance of negative emotion words in the emotion lexicon: A cross-generational and cross-linguistic study. *Journal of Multilingual and Multicultural Development* 25(2):266–284.

Wierzbicka, Anna. 1995. Adjectives vs. verbs: The iconicity of part-of-speech membership. In M. Landsberg, ed., *Syntactic iconicity and linguistic freezes*, 223–245. Berlin: Mouton de Gruyter.

Wierzbicka, Anna. 1999. *Emotions across languages and cultures: Diversity and universals.* Cambridge: Cambridge University Press.

8 Term Relations and Relational Hierarchies

Patrick Farrell

8.1 Introduction

Outside of Relational Grammar (RG), it is widely assumed that there are only "surface" grammatical relations (GRs) that come in a small variety, at least if GRs of the "subject" and "direct object" kind are distinguished from semantic roles, such as agent and instrument. The question I wish to explore in this chapter is what kind of monostratal theory of GRs might suffice to adequately account for an interesting range of GR phenomena.

Putting aside the question of strata, five fundamental assumptions about GRs in RG (Perlmutter 1983; Perlmutter and Rosen 1984) are first, that there is a basic difference between oblique and term (i.e., core) relations; second, that the term relations are ranked relative to each other with respect to relative syntactic prominence or accessibility to syntactic processes, such that numbers showing this ranking can be used to formally designate the relations; third, that continuous segments of the GR hierarchy form natural classes (e.g., 1–2–3 = terms; 1–2 = nuclear terms; 2–3 = object terms); fourth, that the traditional subject (= 1), direct-object (= 2), and indirect-object (= 3) categories are the only term relations; and fifth, that the three term relations are universally instantiated and have the same prototypical members across languages (i.e., in a basic transitive active clause the agent is 1, the patient is 2, and a recipient, if present, is 3).

RG manages in the face of the array of different GR categories that languages exhibit by capitalizing on defined categories that emerge from multistratal analyses of clause structure, such as "1 in some stratum and final term" (= working 1) and "2 in some stratum and not a distinct final term" (= acting 2). To compensate for the lack of such categories in a monostratal theory, I adopt the first three assumptions of RG but abandon both the fourth and fifth. That is, I question both the idea that the term relations are limited to no more than three, as does Postal 1990 for other reasons and without abandoning strata, and the idea that there is some crosslinguistically invariant basis for determining either their content or, where content is the same, their ranking with respect to each other. The grammatical relation typology envisioned is as follows:

(1) *GR hierarchy*
 [TERM 1 > 2 > (3 > ... n)] > oblique

Not only are an indeterminate number of term relations available, but how they are defined is subject to crosslinguistic variation of an uncertain range. Just as the highest-ranking GR can have different semantic prototypes in different languages (macroagent, for example, in syntactically accusative languages and macropatient in syntactically ergative languages—see section 8.2), the other GRs can too. The 2 category may be defined by the macropatient semantic role in one accusative language but may not even include the macropatient role in another. Within this vision of GRs, numbers are truly appropriate designations of term relations and the traditional subject, object, and indirect-object concepts bear no crosslinguistically meaningful relationship to the numbers that languages use.

8.2 Term Relations and Ergativity

Even independently of the question of strata, the idea that in all languages the dependent with the macroagent role (henceforth A) and the dependent with the macropatient role (henceforth P) in a basic active clause are 1 and 2 respectively runs into difficulties in the characterization of syntactically ergative languages such as Dyirbal (Dixon 1979, 1994), Sama (Foley and Van Valin 1984), and Inuit (Bittner and Hale 1996). Consider, for example, the constraint on relativization in Inuit, illustrated by the following examples (from Bittner and Hale 1996).[1]

(2) a. [arna-p   [_   ani-sima-su-p]]   angut
      woman-ERG$_i$ *Abs pivot$_i$* go.out-PERF-RELAT.INTR-ERG man
      aku-v-a-a
      see-IND-TR-3SGA.3SGP
      'The woman who had gone out saw the man.'
  b. [arna-t   [_   miiqqa-p isiginnaa-ga-i]]
      woman.ABS-PL$_j$ *Abs pivot$_j$* child-ERG watch-RELAT.TR-3SG.PL
      mirsur-p-u-t
      sew-IND-INTR-3PLS
      'The women the child is watching are sewing.'

Ergative case marking is used only for the A in a transitive clause. Absolutive case marking is used for the P in a transitive clause and the single syntactically privileged dependent in an intransitive clause (S), which may be either A-like or P-like semantically. Verbs are inflectionally cross-referenced with the A, P, and S dependents. The constraint of interest on relativization is that the pivot (i.e., the omitted element in the relative clause) must be the dependent that would be case-marked absolutive: the P in a transitive clause, as illustrated by (2b), or the S in an intransitive clause, as illustrated by (2a). Relativization is not the only syntactic phenomenon that privileges the absolutive dependent and excludes the ergative dependent. In infinitival clauses, for example, only one dependent triggers agreement and this is the P in transitive clauses and the S in intransitive clauses. Similarly, only the absolutive dependent can be the controller of a subordinate adjunct clause.

Now, if one assumes that GRs are defined in terms of A, P, and S in the same way across languages and that the definitions are the accusative one shown in (3), the constraints on relativization, agreement in infinitival clauses, and control of subordinate clauses in Inuit are not adequately characterized in terms of GRs.

(3) *Typical accusative definition of highest GRs*
    1   > 2
    A/S P

It is not possible to state the constraints in question in terms of either a particular GR or a continuous segment of the GR hierarchy, since the category of absolutive dependents includes all 2s and only some 1s. It is possible, of course, to define a special GR and state the constraint in terms of this defined relation. That is, one could say, as in RG, that only the lowest-ranking nuclear term in a clause (where only 1 and 2 are nuclear terms) can be the privileged dependent. One problem with this general approach to syntactically ergative languages, noted long ago by Johnson 1974, is that it portrays them as having their highest-ranking GR in basic transitive clauses actually outranked in terms of overall syntactic privilege in the language and, in particular, in terms of relativization, which otherwise appears to never preclude the most prominent GR from the class of possible pivots (Keenan and Comrie 1977). A second problem is that special definitions of GR categories such as "1 of a transitive clause" (= ergative dependent) and "lowest-ranking nuclear term" (= absolutive dependent) opens up the possibility of such equally natural but apparently nonoccurring GR categories as "nuclear term of a transitive clause" (= category of dependents including the A and P of transitive clauses but excluding the S of intransitive clauses).

An alternative way of looking at syntactically ergative languages is that they simply have a different definition of GRs, such as the following:

(4) *Ergative definition of highest GRs*
    1 > 2 > 3
    P S A

Under this characterization of GRs in Inuit, absolutive case is used for the 1–2 segment of the GR hierarchy and this same class of dependents is syntactically privileged with respect to various syntactic phenomena—by virtue of its high ranking.

This characterization of ergative languages follows, in essence, the approach of Role and Reference Grammar (Van Valin and La Polla 1997; Van Valin 2006) and recent Transformational Grammar (Bittner and Hale 1996; Ura 2000), insofar as it claims that what primarily differs in syntactically ergative languages is that the P of a transitive clause is designated as the most privileged dependent. It differs in assigning a distinct GR to the S of intransitive clauses. One virtue of explicitly recognizing a distinct GR for the S category of dependents is that it makes it possible to easily characterize both GR phenomena that work in terms of P and S and those that work in terms of A and S—that is, the continuous segment 2–3 on the GR hierarchy, which syntactically ergative languages appear to always utilize in some way. In Inuit, for example, the antecedent of a reflexive pronoun must be a dependent in the 2–3 segment of the hierarchy (i.e., S/A), as illustrated by the following examples from Ura 2000:

(5) a. *Junna   immi*-nut tatigi-v-u-q
       Junaa.ABS self-DAT   trust-IND-INTR-3SGS
       'Junna trusts in self.'
    b. *Junna*-p   Kaali   *immi*-nik uqaluttuup-p-a-a
       Junna-ERG Kali.ABS self-INSTR tell-IND-TR-3SGA.3SGP
       'Junna$_i$ told Kali$_j$ about self$_{i/*j}$.'

In (5a) the antecedent of the reflexive pronoun is the absolutive dependent (i.e., the S or 2); in (5b) only the A (or 3) and not the P (or 1) can be the antecedent. At the same time, such an unnatural class of GRs as "A/P but not S" is correctly characterized as unnatural by virtue of the fact that the GRs 1 and 3 (without 2) do not form a continuous segment of the GR hierarchy.[2]

Morphologically ergative languages might define the highest-ranking GRs as follows:

(6) *Alternative ergative definition of highest GRs*
    1 > 2 > 3
    A   S   P

As in syntactically ergative languages, the most privileged GR category is the 1–2 segment of the hierarchy. However, this happens to be the same as the 1 category of the typical accusative hierarchy, as shown in (1). Morphologically ergative languages just happen to use the 2–3 segment of the hierarchy for at least some aspect of GR marking (typically case marking). The phenomenon known as split ergativity occurs when the 2–3 segments and the 1–2 segments, of either (4) or (6), are both used for different aspects of GR marking (verb agreement or case marking) or for the same aspects under different conditions (e.g., main versus subordinate clauses).

A tripartite language, the existence of which provides strong evidence for the idea that each of A, S, and P can define a distinct GR, is one that utilizes either (4) or (6) and whose GR-marking system explicitly distinguishes 1, 2, and 3, rather than collapsing 2 with either 1 or 3. Consider, for example, the case-marking system of Nez Perce, illustrated by the following examples (from Rude 1985, via Mithun 1999, 229):[3]

(7) a. x̣áx̣aas-nim hitwekíice
grizzly-ERG he is chasing
'Grizzly is chasing me.'
b. x̣áx̣aac hiwéhyem
grizzly he has come
'Grizzly has come.'
c. ʔóykalo-m titóoqan-m páaqaʔancix   x̣áx̣aas-na
all-ERG   people-ERG they respect him grizzly-ACC
'All people respect grizzly.'

Assuming the ergative GR hierarchy in (6), 1s (= As of transitive clauses) are case-marked ergative, as with 'grizzly' in (7a) and 'all people' in (7c); 3s (= Ps of transitive clauses) are case-marked accusative, as with 'grizzly' in (7c); and Ss are unmarked, as with 'grizzly' in (7b).

Finally, as shown in section 8.4, the idea that there can be three distinct GRs for the range covering A, S, and P is useful for characterizing some kinds of split-intransitive (split-S) languages, which can have a GR hierarchy such as (6) but that differ in the precise definition of the 1 and 2 categories, putting A and A-like Ss into the 1 category and only P-like Ss into the 2 category.

8.3 "Object" Relations

Having established that it is at least reasonable to claim that the GRs at the top end of the GR hierarchy, and in particular, the GR category 1, may be defined in different ways across languages, it is worth considering how languages may vary with respect to the full set of term relations. The claim I wish to make is that there are more alternative definitions and rankings of "object" relations across languages than those that are typically recognized.

In an influential paper on the typology of object categories Dryer (1986) posits a difference between two basic language types that yields something like an ergative-versus-accusative contrast in the domain of objects. In one kind of language, a category of dependents with recipient as prototype is folded into a larger category of "primary object," which also includes the object of a simple transitive clause (P). The other object in ditransitive clauses (P2) is a "secondary object." In the alternative basic type of language the category with recipient as prototype is the standard "indirect-object" category and patient-type dependents in both ordinary transitive clauses and transitive clauses with indirect objects are folded into a single category of direct objects. Using only numbers and ranking for GRs, these types of languages can be characterized with the following alternative definitions of the object range of the GR hierarchy, as shown for typical accusative languages in (8) and (9).[4]

(8) *Definition of GRs in indirect-object accusative language*
    1   > 2   > 3   > Oblique
    A/S   P/P2   Rec

(9) *Definition of GRs in primary-object accusative language*
    1   > 2   > 3   > Oblique
    A/S   Rec/P   P2

Portuguese provides an example of what is apparently an indirect-object language, as illustrated by the following examples.

(10) a.   Eles venderon a   casa   (a uma mulher)
            they sold.3PL the-SG.FEM house to a   woman
            'They sold the house (to a woman).'
      b.   Eles a   venderon (a ela)
            they 3SG.FEM.ACC sold.3PL   to her
            'They sold it(FEM) (to her).'
      c.   A casa (lhe)   foi vendida por eles
            the house 3SG.DAT was sold   by them
            'The house was sold (to him/her) by them.'
      d.   *A mulher foi   vendida uma casa   por eles
            the woman was sold   a   house by them
            'The woman was sold a house by them.'

A dependents (in active clauses) determine verb agreement and can only be expressed as full pronouns. Rec dependents, or 3s, require the preposition *a* 'to' when nonpronominal and are otherwise expressed as a bound dative pronominal form (*lhe*) in a preverbal slot. Patient-type dependents, or 2s, can be expressed as a gender-agreeing bound pronoun, which takes an accusative form in the third person. 2s and 3s are differentiated from obliques and 1s by the fact that they alone can be the pivot in the *se* reflexive/reciprocal construction (not shown here); 2s are differentiated from 3s not only by pronominal differences, but also in that only 2s can be the 1 in the passive construction, whether or not a recipient is present in the clause as shown by (10c,d).

Yaqui (Yuto-Aztecan) has properties characteristic of a primary-object language, as illustrated by the following examples, from Van Valin 2001:

(11) a.   Joan   Peo-ta   ʔuka   vaci-ta   miika-k
            Juan.NOM Pedro-ACC DET.ACC corn-ACC give-PERF
            'Juan gave Pedro the corn.'

b. Peo ʔuka vaci-ta miik-wa-k
Pedro-NOM DET.ACC corn-ACC give-PASS-PERF
'Pedro was given the corn.'
c. *uʔu vaci Peo-ta miik-wa-k
DET.NOM corn-NOM Pedro-ACC give-PASS-PERF
'The corn was given Pedro.'

Both Rec and P2 are marked the way that Ps are in monotransitive clauses. However, only the Rec in a ditransitive clause is able to be promoted to 1 in the passive construction. Given the GR definitions in (9), accusative case marking works for the 2–3 segment of the hierarchy but promotion to 1 is restricted to 2s.

In what follows I look at three languages, which might appear to be simple primary-object or indirect-object languages, and show that all of these arguably have more than two "object" GRs and that they are defined in different ways in each. Taba can collapse P, P2, and Rec into two categories but has a third kind of object term relation for instrument or locative dependents. Italian, which would seem to be a straightforward indirect-object language, actually exemplifies a kind of language with so-called dative subjects or I-nominals (Moore and Perlmutter 2000). As such, in addition to Rec and P GRs, a distinct experiencer GR, which has some of the privileges of 1s in addition to properties of Rec and P dependents, must be recognized. English, on the other hand, arguably has four distinct term relations lower than 1, defined in terms of the Ben(eficiary), Rec, P, and P2 categories.

8.4 Taba

Taba, as described by Bowden 2005, is a mixed accusative/split-intransitive Austronesian language in which the properties and behaviors that distinguish A and P dependents are sometimes manifested in the same way across both transitive and intransitive clauses. In the following examples, the A of transitive (12a) and intransitive (12b) clauses is cross-referenced with a proclitic on the verb, whereas the P of an intransitive clause (12c) is not.

(12) a. i n=wet yak
3SG 3SG=hit 1SG
'He hit me.'
b. i n=alhod.
3SG 3SG=run
'He is running.'
c. mot i
die 3SG
'It died.'

The A versus P distinction is also manifested with nonclitic pronouns. Only a pronominal A can precede the V; a P follows, whether in a transitive clause, as in (12a), or an intransitive one, as in (12c). The category S is nevertheless relevant in the grammar, since if either the A or S is a full NP, it must precede the verb (independently of the A/P distinction), whereas a non-S P generally follows:

(13) a. Oci n=wet yak
    Oci 3SG=hit 1SG
    'Oci hit me.'
  b. Oci n=alhod
    3SG 3SG=run
    'Oci is running.'
  c. ubang da blongan
    fence DET be.long
    'The fence is long.'
  d. n=pun babang da
    3SG=kill moth DET
    'She's killing the moth.'

Thus, following the same kind of logic applied to ergative languages above, the top end of the GR hierarchy in Taba (and other such languages) must be as follows, with the understanding that S_a is the macroagent of an intransitive clause and S_p is the macropatient of an intransitive clause.[5]

(14) *Definition of highest GRs in mixed accusative/split-S language*
    1   > 2 > 3
    A/S_a S_p P

The grammar of the phenomena discussed thus far is that verbal proclitics are necessarily cross-referenced with 1s, only pronominal 1s precede the verb, and if a clause has a full NP in the 1–2 segment of the hierarchy, this NP must precede the verb.

Now, with respect to the traditional "object" categories of the language, which would be the terms 3 and below on the hierarchy, Taba appears at first to be a routine primary-object language, as evidenced by the following examples.

(15) a. n=goras   kapaya ada kobit
    3SG=shave papaya with knife
    'She deseeded the papaya with a knife.'
  b. Banda n=ot-ik   yak yan
    Banda 3SG=catch-APPL 1SG fish
    'Banda gave me some fish.'

In a monotransitive clause such as (15a) the P must be right-adjacent to the verb, with any oblique dependents, which are adpositionally marked, following. In a ditransitive clause headed by a verb meaning 'give,' such as 'catch' with an applicative affix, as shown by (15b), the Rec, which is not adpositionally marked, is necessarily right-adjacent to the verb.[6] Thus, Rec and P appear to form a primary-object category and, based on the linear-order constraint, the P2 in a clause with a macro-recipient argument is a secondary object. Or, alternatively, Rec defines a distinct GR category (3) and P and P2 are collapsed into another (4) and postverbal term order is determined by the hierarchy. Lacking evidence to decide between these analyses, I will assume the latter one here.[7]

The complication shows up in other kinds of "promotion-to-object" clauses. For example, an alternative way of expressing the propositional content of (15a) is (16), which has the same applicative suffix added to the verb as in (15b) and the instrumental dependent expressed without an adposition—something that is only possible if the applicative suffix is expressed.

(16) n=goras-ak kapaya kobit
 3SG=shave-APPL papaya knife
 'She deseeded the papaya with a knife.'

(17) a. Mina n=yol woya
  Mina 3SG=take-APPL water
  'Mina is taking water.'
 b. Rauf n=yol-o wola ai coat=so
  Rauf 3SG=take-APPL rope firewood CLASS=one
  'Rauf removed the rope from the firewood.'

(18) a. Bib n=sung um li
  Bib 3SG=enter house LOC
  'Bib entered into the house.'
 b. Bib n=sung um
  Bib 3SG=enter house
  'Bib entered the house.'
 c. Bib n=sung-ak Nou um
  Bib 3SG=enter-APPL Nou house
  'Bib entered the house with Nou.'

In (17b) an applicative suffix is added to the verb *yol* 'take' to indicate that its source argument is overtly expressed, again without an adposition. The contrast between (18a) and (18b) shows that the goal argument of *sung* 'enter' can be expressed either with or without an adposition. Example (18c) shows that with the applicative suffix an additional P-type argument can be added to a clause with *sung*, yielding a kind of double-object construction. The constituent-order generalization is that locative (including source and goal) and instrument applied objects follow any other. They also differ with respect to syntactic privilege. P/P2 and Rec objects, whether in double-object scenarios or not, can optionally undergo object fronting in clauses with no full NP with GR 1, whereas locative and instrument objects cannot:

(19) a. kolai da l=pun-ak peda
 snake DET 3PL=kill-APPL machete
 'They killed the snake with a machete.'
 b. mon da meu h=wet
 man Det 2SG 2SG=hit
 'You hit that man.'
 c. pipis lloci l-ha-tada-k i
 money much 3PL-CAUS-PRESENT-APPL 3SG
 'They gave him a lot of money.'
 d. *peda n=pun-ak i
 machete 3SG=kill-APPL 3SG
 'He killed it with a machete.'
 e. *um da n=sung
 house DET 3SG=enter
 'She entered the house.'

There is thus a third kind of object, in addition to those defined by Rec and P/P2. The different kinds of object are ranked relative to each other and can be defined as follows: Rec (= 3), P/P2 (= 4), and locative/instrumental (= 5). 5s are systematically more like obliques than the other terms, not only in that they cannot undergo object fronting but also in that they can generally optionally be marked with an adposition, as illustrated in (20). In this example, the applicative suffix (which characteristically indicates termhood) co-occurs with an adposition (which characteristically indicates obliqueness).

(20) n=goras-ak kapaya ada kobit
 3SG=shave-APPL papaya with knife
 'She deseeded the papaya with a knife.'

The GR hierarchy for Taba and its grammar for the phenomena discussed here are as follows:[8]

(21) *Definition of GRs in Taba*
 1 > 2 > 3 > 4 > 5 > Oblique
 A/S_a S_p Rec P/P2 Instr/Loc
 Grammar
 1 Determines features of verbal proclitic
  If pronominal precedes verb
 1 → 2 Obligatorily preverbal if full NP
 3 → 4 Can undergo object fronting

5		Can be marked with adposition
Obl		Must be marked with adposition
3 → Obl		(By default) follow verb in order determined by ranking

It is worth considering a standard multistratal RG analysis of Taba, since it would require, at least in some measure, the same move as the proposed analysis with respect to the issue of the alignment of semantic roles and GRs. The alignment of intial GRs and semantic roles would be as follows:

(22) *Definition of initial GRs (all languages)*
  1   > 2   > 3   > Oblique
  A/S_a P/S_p Rec   all others

The surface GRs of the initial terms would be accounted for by having the S_p advance to 1 (by "unaccusative" advancement) and the Rec advance from 3 to 2, causing the initial 2 to become a chômeur. The S_p would be excluded from determining the features of the verbal proclitic, for example, because this phenomenon would be constrained to work only with consistent 1s (i.e., dependents bearing the 1 relation in all strata). The tricky matter is how to characterize the instrument and locative terms, since applicative constructions are usually analyzed as having obliques advance to 2. Since the Taba constructions have the advanced obliques behaving in a less termlike way than the initial 2s, the only possible analysis, it would seem, is to claim that the advancement is to 3, a GR that is conveniently available, since initial 3s are always final 2s. Such an analysis reveals the frailty of the claim that notions such as "indirect object" have a universal semantic motivation. Under the analysis in question, there would be no consistent 3s in Taba and the "natural" class of "dependents bearing the 3 relation" would include macrorecipients, which are not surface 3s, and some locatives and instruments, which are surface 3s only because 3 is a term relation other than 2 that is not otherwise being used on the surface. If such analyses are allowed, the relationship between numbers and the surface GR categories that languages happen to use is ultimately arbitrary, as claimed in the proposed analysis.

8.5 Italian

Italian is an accusative language, much like Portuguese, as it is portrayed above. Thus, A, P, and Rec dependents differ in terms of case and verb agreement properties, as illustrated by the following examples:

(23) a. I   bambini   hanno   dato la   chiave a Giovanni
       the-PL.MASC child-PL have-3PL given the-SG.FEM key   to Giovanni
       'The children gave the key to Giovanni.'

  b. Egli l'hanno   dato a Giovanni
    they 3SG.ACC-have-3PL given to Giovanni
    'They gave it to Giovanni.'
  c. Egli gli   hanno dato la chiave
    they 3SG.MASC.DAT have-3PL given the key
    'They gave him the key.'

The A, P, and Rec dependents have full, bound (proclitic) accusative, and bound (proclitic) dative pronominal forms, respectively; and only the A determines person/number verb agreement. P and Rec dependents share the property of being able to be *si* reflexive/reciprocal pivots, but only a P can be the 1 in the passive construction:

(24) a. I bambini si sono dati   le mani
    the child-MASC.PL REFL.3 be-3PL given-MASC.PL the hands
    'The children gave each other their hands.'
  b. Egli si sono bacciati
    they REFL.3 be-3PL kissed
    'They kissed each other.'
  c. La chiave è stata   data   a Giovanni
    the key be-3SG been-SG.FEM given-SG.FEM to Giovanni
    'The key was given to Giovanni.'
  d. *Giovanni è stato   dato   la chiave
    Giovanni be-3SG been-SG.MASC given-SG.MASC the key
    'Giovanni was given the key.'

The fact of most interest is that there is a class of psychological predicates, including *piacere* 'like', *sembrare* 'seem', *mancare* 'lack', and several others, whose experiencer dependent is expressed as an apparent "object," being marked by the 'to' preposition or expressed as a dative proclitic and not being a verbal agreement controller, as the following examples (adapted from Perlmutter 1984) show:

(25) a. Gli   piacciono le sinfonie di Beethoven
    3SG.DAT like-3PL the symphonies of Beethoven
    'He likes Beethoven's symphonies.'
  b. Ai bambini non manca energia
    to.the child-PL NEG lack-3SG energy
    'The children don't lack energy.'

Further evidence for considering this kind of experiencer dependent to be a non-1, despite the English translations of the sentences above, comes from the fact that it can be a reflexive pivot:[9]

(26) I bambini si piacciono molto
   the children REFL.3 like-3PL a lot
   'The children like each other a lot.'

At the same time, however, unlike Rec and P dependents, this kind of experiencer is able to control the missing 1 of adverbial clauses of various kinds, which only the 1 of a main clause can otherwise do, as shown by the following examples adapted from Perlmutter 1984:

(27) a. $\emptyset_{i/*j}$ essendo appena tornata/*o   in città, Maria$_i$ ha
         being   just   returned-SG.FEM/SG.MASC to town Maria has
         telefonato a   Giorgio$_j$
         phoned   to Giorgio
         'Having just returned to town, Maria called Giorgio.'
   b. $\emptyset_i$ avendo lavorato tutta la   giornata, gli$_i$ manca energia
         having worked all   the day   3SG.DAT$_i$ lacks   energy
         'Having worked all day, he lacks energy.'

As Perlmutter carefully shows, the condition on the controllers cannot be stated in semantic terms, since dative experiencers and all kinds of 1s, even the stimulus dependent of psychological verbs in the right context, can be controllers:

(28) $\emptyset_{i/j}$ essendo appena tornata/o   in città, Claudia$_i$mi$_j$ pareva
         being   just   returned-SG.FEM/SG.MASC to town Claudia 1SG seemed
         più   bella   del   solito
         more beautiful than usual
         'Having just returned to town, Claudia seemed more beautiful to me than usual.' (*Ambiguous*)

The relational hierarchy for Italian and the conditions on the grammatical phenomena considered here can be summarized as follows:[10]

(29) *Definition of GRs in Italian*
     1   > 2   > 3   > 4   > Oblique
     A/S   Exp   Rec   P/P2
     Grammar of phenomena considered above
     1   Determines verb agreement
              Has full pronominal form
     1 → 2   Can control adverbial clauses
     2 → 4   Can be a *si* reflexive/reciprocal pivot
     2 → 3   Has dative pronominal clitic form
              Marked with preposition *a* when not pronominal
     4   Has accusative pronominal clitic form
              Can be 1 in passive construction

The RG analysis of Italian differs significantly in that it assumes that the experiencer dependents of verbs like *piacere* and *mancare* are initial 1s that demote to 3.

They behave like "indirect objects" because they are final 3s. They can control adverbial clauses, like final 1s, because of their initial 1hood. The constraint is stated by Perlmutter in terms of the notion "working 1"—that is, dependents that are both a 1 in some stratum and a final term. The importance of the analysis proposed here is not that it improves in any way on the standard RG analysis; rather, it is that it shows a novel, monostratal way of dealing with a phenomenon on which one of the strongest cases for the multistratal approach to GRs can be built.

8.6 English

English appears to be an accusative primary-object language. The following examples illustrate, in brief, the accusative nature of the language:

(30) a. The boy likes them/*they
   b. They like/*likes the boy
   c. They are sleeping
   d. They are fading

(31) a. He$_i$ seems [___$_i$ to like the boy]
   b. The boy seems [___$_i$ to be sleeping]
   c. The sofa seems [___$_i$ to be fading]
   d. *The boy$_i$ seems [him to like ___$_i$]

Independently of the meaning of intransitive verbs or any factors of animacy or semantic role, the A/S dependent in basic active clauses contrasts with the P dependent in various ways: it is the only possible nominative pronoun (e.g., *they* versus *them* in (30a)); it alone can and must appear preverbally; it alone determines the inflectional form of the first verbal element (e.g., *are* versus *is* indicates plural third person 1 in (30c–d) and *likes* versus *like* indicates singular third person 1 in (30a)); and it alone can be the pivot in raising constructions of the type that the verb *seem* participates in, as shown by the examples in (31).

Like Yaqui, discussed in section 8.3, English can have up to two postverbal NPs that are not marked with a preposition and that are not distinguished in any way from each other in terms of overt GR marking.

(32) a. The boy gave the girl a present.
   b. Smith asked the teacher a question.
   c. He sent me them.

Moreover, as the following examples show, in double-object clauses the macro-recipient type of object is the one that behaves most like the P in a monotransitive clause, because it and not the P2 must come first in terms of linear precedence (33).

Also, at least for many speakers (indicated by the % notation), it is the only one that can be expressed as the 1 in the passive construction, as indicated by the contrast between (34) and (35) (see, for example, Czepluch 1982; Postal 1986, 58; Siewierska 1991, 97; Ura 2000, 244).

(33) a. *The boy gave a present the girl.
b. *The girl asked a question her teacher.

(34) a. The boy was liked by everyone.
b. The girl was given a present (by the boy).
c. I was asked a question (by the students).

(35) a. %A present was given the girl (by the boy).
b. %A question was asked me (by the students).

However, for many speakers, particularly those that do not accept sentences such as those in (35), the beneficiary subtype of first object cannot be the 1 in a passive construction:

(36) a. %The woman was bought a car by her husband.
b. %We were sung a song by the children.

Unlike in what might be considered a pure primary-object language, English allows in most cases an alternative oblique realization of the first object:

(37) a. The boy gave a present to the girl.
b. Smith asked a question of the teacher.
c. The bartender poured another drink for me.

The nature of the relationship between the alternative constructions has been a much discussed and controversial topic. I have nothing to add to it here, although I assume, of course, an analysis without GR revaluation, as in Pinker 1989, for example. Beyond the ability to be alternatively expressed as a term, the prepositionally marked dependents in (37) have the syntactic properties of obliques in general (Farrell 2005b, 28–38), which is why I assume here that they are obliques.

Now, beyond their marking properties (no adposition, nonnominative pronoun), and their ability to be the 1 in the passive construction for some speakers, all objects share the property of normally having to precede any oblique dependent, as illustrated by the following examples:

(38) a. I built (my mother) a house with my own hands.
b. *I built (my mother) with my own hands a house.

(39) a. She sent (the mayor) a response via e-mail.
b. *She sent (the mayor) via e-mail a response.

Recipient dependents expressed as obliques, by contrast, can generally either precede or follow other obliques:

(40) a. I sent a response to the mayor via e-mail.
    b. I sent a response via e-mail to the mayor.

All objects also share the property of being able to precede the discontinuous Prep(osition) of a V(erb)-Prep lexeme, as illustrated by (43), unlike obliques (see Farrell 2005a and references cited there), as illustrated by (41b) and (42b).[11]

(41) a. The boy *gave* the present *back* to her.
    b. *The boy *gave* the present to her *back*.

(42) a. He *ended up* with her.
    b. *He *ended* with her *up*.

(43) a. The boy *gave* her the present *back*.
    b. The boy *gave* her *back* the present.

However, the grammar of V-Prep lexemes also distinguishes between different types of objects. For example, for many speakers at least, V-Prep discontinuity is obligatory with the first object of ditransitive clauses but not the P of monotransitive clauses (with or without an oblique dependent):

(44) a. %The boy *gave back* the woman the present.
    b. The boy *gave* the woman *back* the present.
    c. The boy *gave back* the present (to the woman).

Another phenomenon in the grammar of English that differentiates the object categories is *tough* movement. As is well known (e.g., Larson 1988; Siewierska 1991, 97), whereas the P of a monotransitive clause can be the pivot in the *tough*-movement construction (45a–b), as can obliques in general (45c–d), the first object in a ditransitive clause cannot (45e).

(45) a. People like these are difficult not to like.
    b. This will be easy to send to her.
    c. People like these are easy to give things to.
    d. He is difficult to do anything with.
    e. *People like these are easy to give things.

Furthermore, the P2 in a ditransitive clause can also be a *tough*-movement pivot:

(46) a. Presents like these are easy to give people.
    b. This one will be easy to send you.
    c. This is a question that will be hard to ask you.

The GR categories of relevance to the phenomena discussed above and their grammar can be summarized as follows:

(47) *Definition of GRs in English*
    1   > 2   > 3   > 4 > 5   > Oblique
    A/S   Ben   Rec   P   P2
Grammar of phenomena considered above
    1   Precedes verb
                Determines verb agreement
                Pivot in raising construction
                Nominative pronominal form in tensed clauses
    1 → 5   Not marked with preposition
    2 → Obl   (By default) follow verb in order determined by ranking
    2 → 5   Allow Prep of V-Prep lexemes to follow
    2 → 3   Require Prep of V-Prep lexemes to follow (%)
    2 → 5   Realizable as 1 in passive construction (%)
    3 → 4   Realizable as 1 in passive construction (%)
    4 → Obl   Can be *tough*-movement pivot

According to the standard RG analysis of English objects, there are, of course, only two surface object GRs: 2 and 3. The 3 relation, however, is reserved for *to*-marked recipients, analyzed here as obliques. Thus, P, Rec, and Ben objects are all final 2s, the latter having undergone optional 3-2 and Ben-2 advancement, respectively, causing the P2 to demote to chômeur. All of the necessary distinctions can be drawn. Rec and Ben final 2s are (different kinds of) advancees to 2; the P of a monotransitive clause is a consistent 2; and the P2 is a 2-chômeur. The proposed analysis is preferable, however, in the following ways. First, it allows the constraint on *tough* movement to be stated in maximally general terms: dependents bearing the GR 4 and below on the GR hierarchy are eligible. Under the RG analysis, the constraint needs to be stated in terms of final GRs, since the 1-chômeur of the passive construction is eligible (*People like that are easy to be tricked by*). Thus, dependents bearing the final relation 2 or below are eligible, *except* if they have advanced to 2. A second advantage of the proposed analysis is that it allows a generalization to be captured concerning when a dependent is not marked by a preposition—that is, if it is a term. Since final GRs are what matter (as evidenced by what happens with the initial 1s of the passive construction, for example) and P2s are necessarily analyzed as final chômeurs, which are nonterms, they do not form a natural class with final 1s and 2s. Finally, the proposed analysis makes it possible to state a generalization concerning postverbal constituent order—that is, postverbal terms precede obliques and are ordered according to rank on the hierarchy. Since P2s are analyzed as chômeurs, which are ordered below (or with) obliques on the RG hierarchy, they must be seen as exceptional in their behavior.

8.7 Conclusion

If one takes seriously the idea that term GRs are the core categories implicated by the inflectional marking systems of languages and/or other syntactic phenomena as well as the idea that dependents cannot bear multiple GRs, languages must be viewed as having different numbers and kinds of GR categories. Moreover, these categories do not necessarily correspond in any straightforward way to traditional GRs such as subject, direct object, and indirect object, although the semantic-role categories that are often designated unwittingly by these expressions do figure prominently in language-specific definitions of GRs.

Theories that posit a limited set of predetermined GR categories for term relations need to have recourse to semantic-role information or "initial/logical" GR information and strata in order to account for the wide variety of GR categories that syntactic phenomena are demonstrably sensitive to. In RG, for example, Rec and P surface "direct objects" in English are differentiated by their initial GRs. Since these are hypothesized to be determined by semantic roles, semantic roles are utilized, indirectly, to define subcategories of the predetermined surface GRs. The approach to term GRs envisioned here differs in that it eliminates the need for this kind of subcategorization, since there are no predetermined GR categories. Language-specific term GRs that are implicated by syntactic phenomena are simply recognized as separate basic-level categories from the outset, eliminating the need for stratal representations of GRs or GR semantic subcategorization of some other kind. What is mainly needed in addition is GR ranking and the kind of supercategorization of continuous segments of the ranking hierarchy that emerges from this, both of which are also used in RG and other theories, and are presumably indispensable. Naturally, whether this vision of GRs is capable of being fashioned into a comprehensive theory capable of handling a wider array of the GR phenomena found across languages remains an open question. This much, however, should be clear: there exist at best shaky empirical grounds for maintaining that languages are constrained to having a small set of surface GRs that correspond to the parochial notions of subject, object, and indirect object.

Notes

Thanks are due to John Moore and an anonymous reviewer for helpful comments on an earlier version of this chapter and, of course, to David Perlmutter, whose incomparable research and teaching have provided endless inspiration.

1. Abbreviations in glosses include 1, 2, 3 = first, second, third person; A = macroagent; ABS = absolutive; ACC = accusative; APPL = applicative; CAUS = causative; DAT = dative; DET = determiner; ERG = ergative; FEM = feminine; IND = indicative; INTR = intransitive; INSTR = instrument(al); LOC = locative; MASC = masculine; NOM = nominative; NEG = nega-

tive; P = macropatient; PASS = passive; PERF = perfective; PL = plural; PST = past; RELAT = relative clause; S = privileged argument of intransitive verb; SG = singular; TR = transitive.

2. Of course, if there can be alternative GR definitions and alternative hierarchies, one could ask what precludes 1 = S, 2 = A, 3 = P, for example. Presumably the fact that S is a category that includes both As and Ps makes it semantically anomalous for S not to be put either in the same category as A or P or in a category that is between the two categories that it straddles.

3. Although tripartite case-marking systems such as this are rare, they have also been claimed to occur in the Australian languages Wangkumara and Galali (Dixon 1994, 41).

4. I am thinking here of Rec(ipient) as macrorecipient, or a supercategory of semantic roles (with an uncertain and crosslinguistically variable range of members) with the recipient in a transfer-of-possession as prototype, essentially what is often simply characterized as "indirect object" in much descriptive and typological work and initial 3 in RG. I am thinking of P2 as the most patientlike participant in a clause with more than one "object"—that is, roughly the typical object theta in Lexical-Functional Grammar or 2 chômeur (with term behavior) in Relational Grammar.

5. As Bowden notes, one cannot reduce the grammar of Taba to universal semantic categories, because A and P are language-specific semantic categories in terms of which the syntactically relevant GRs are defined. By way of example, based on syntactic behavior a human-referring argument of a 1-place verb is in the A category in Taba, independently of verb meaning (i.e., even with a verb such as 'die' or 'be big'). This does not, however, mean that the A versus P distinction can be reduced to human versus nonhuman, because inanimate arguments can be in the A category in cases such as 'The eruption didn't kill people'.

6. Bowden only gives examples of objects of the Rec kind that are pronominal, but explicitly claims that these must always precede P2 objects (see note 8).

7. The claim here is that Taba is actually an indirect-object language, with respect to the Rec, P, and P2 categories. However, the GR defined by Rec outranks that defined by P/P2.

8. This analysis is only partially similar to that proposed by Bowden, who calls objects "undergoers" and distinguishes four types: first undergoers (Rec and P in clauses with no Rec), second undergoers (instrument object, locative object, and P in clauses with Rec), close undergoers (Rec and P in all clauses), and remote undergoers (instrument and locative). I essentially simply factor out Rec and P as prototypes of separate categories and allow GR-ranking to account for the linear order that Bowden uses the first versus second distinction for. Of course, one could say that Rec and P are in the same GR category (3, for example) and that Rec 3s must precede P 3s. But this is not a different analysis: a special category of Rec object is recognized as having a distinct kind of grammatical privilege. The virtue of the proposed analysis is that the linear-order constraint, which is needed for P objects versus locative and instrumental objects anyway, can be stated simply as one GR-hierarchy constraint.

9. And see Perlmutter 1984 for various other reasons, omitted from the discussion here only for the sake of brevity.

10. This analysis implicitly rejects the analysis of split intransitivity in Italian adopted in Perlmutter 1989 and much other RG work, which would be difficult to handle along the same lines as is suggested for Taba. Fortunately, as in English (Farrell 2005b, chap. 3), a purely semantic account of the phenomena claimed to motivate unaccusativity may be viable or even preferable for Italian (Van Valin 1990).

11. However, P2s are less happy and sometimes quite unhappy with a following preposition, unlike the object of a corresponding monotransitive clause (e.g., *He set me up a table* is highly preferable to *He set me a table up*, whereas *He set a table up for me* is as good as *He set up a table for me*). The more obliquelike behavior of the P2 with respect to this phenomenon is consistent with the analysis proposed here, although why there should be differences across V-Prep lexemes is unclear.

References

Bittner, Maria, and Ken Hale. 1996. Ergativity: Towards a theory of a heterogeneous class. *Linguistic Inquiry* 27:531–604.

Bowden, John. 2005. Taba as a "split-O" language: Applicatives in a split-S system. RSPAS Working Papers in Linguistics. http://rspas.anu.edu.au/linguistics/WP/Bowden2.html.

Czepluch, Hartmut. 1982. Case theory and the dative construction. *Linguistic Review* 2:1–38.

Dixon, R. M. W. 1979. Ergativity. *Language* 55:59–138.

Dixon, R. M. W. 1994. *Ergativity*. Cambridge: Cambridge University Press.

Dryer, Matthew S. 1986. Primary objects, secondary objects, and antidative. *Language* 61:808–845.

Farrell, Patrick. 2005a. English verb-preposition constructions: Constituency and order. *Language* 81:96–137.

Farrell, Patrick. 2005b. *Grammatical relations*. Oxford: Oxford University Press.

Foley, William A., and Robert D. Van Valin, Jr. 1984. *Functional syntax and universal grammar*. Cambridge: Cambridge University Press.

Johnson, David E. 1974. Toward a theory of relationally-based grammar. New York: Garland. (Doctoral dissertation, University of Illinois at Urbana-Champaign.)

Keenan, Edward L., and Bernard Comrie. 1977. Noun phrase accessibility and universal grammar. *Linguistic Inquiry* 8:63–100.

Larson, Richard K. 1988. On the double object construction. *Linguistic Inquiry* 19:335–391.

Mithun, Marianne. 1999. *The languages of Native North America*. Cambridge: Cambridge University Press.

Moore, John, and David M. Perlmutter. 2000. What does it take to be a dative subject? *Natural Language and Linguistic Theory* 18:373–416.

Perlmutter, David M. 1983. *Studies in relational grammar 1*. Chicago: University of Chicago Press.

Perlmutter, David M. 1984. Working 1s and inversion in Italian, Japanese, and Quechua. In David M. Perlmutter and Carol Rosen, eds., *Studies in relational grammar 2*. Chicago: University of Chicago Press.

Perlmutter, David M. 1989. Multiattachment and the unaccusative hypothesis: The perfect auxiliary in Italian. *Probus* 1:63–119.

Perlmutter, David M., and Carol Rosen, eds. 1984. *Studies in relational grammar 2*. Chicago: University of Chicago Press.

Pinker, Stephen. 1989. *Learnability and cognition: The acquisition of argument structure*. Cambridge, MA: MIT Press.

Postal, Paul M. 1986. *Studies of passive clauses*. Albany: State University of New York Press.

Postal, Paul M. 1990. French indirect object demotion. In P. M. Postal and B. D. Joseph, eds., *Studies in relational grammar 3*, 104–200. Chicago: University of Chicago Press.

Rude, Noel. 1985. Studies in Nez Perce grammar and discourse. Doctoral dissertation, University of Oregon.

Siewierska, Anna. 1991. *Functional grammar*. London: Routledge.

Ura, Hiroyuki. 2000. *Checking theory and grammatical functions in universal grammar*. Oxford: Oxford University Press.

Van Valin, Robert D. Jr. 1990. Semantic parameters of split intransitivity. *Language* 66:221–260.

Van Valin, Robert D. Jr. 2001. The role and reference grammar analysis of three-place predicates. Ms., SUNY Buffalo. http://linguistics.buffalo.edu/research/rrg/vanvalin/papers/3-placepreds.pdf.

Van Valin, Robert D. Jr. 2006. *Exploring the syntax-semantics interface*. Cambridge: Cambridge University Press.

Van Valin, Robert D. Jr., and Randy J. La Polla. 1997. *Syntax: Structure, meaning, and function*. Cambridge: Cambridge University Press.

9 Constraints on Verb Stem Stacking in Southern Tiwa

Donald G. Frantz

Complex verb stems in the Southern Tiwa language[1] may include more than one verb stem. Whether this is described as "verb incorporation" or the result of "clause union," it is productive. Some such complex stems include what might be called "derivational suffixes" such as *'am* 'cause' or *mi* 'go to do', which are necessarily the Head of a complex verb stem. I treat these "suffixes" as bound stems that must be the Head of a complex stem. But there are also many more complex stems whose Head may alternatively occur with a (surface) clausal complement, as will be shown in (7)–(21).

Though the phenomenon of verb stacking is common in the language, one cannot, of course, stick verbs together willy-nilly. The purpose of this chapter is to consider the nonsemantic constraints involved. As I will show, the major constraint can be seen to be similar to, but stronger than, that proposed by Mark Baker (1996) for polysynthetic languages.

9.1 Background

All Southern Tiwa verbs have an agreement prefix that reflects features of from one to three morphosyntactic arguments, as described in Frantz 1995; the three are ERG, ABS, and DAT. The Head of each verb stem, whether the stem is simplex or complex, determines the arguments that the stem takes. The prefix shapes are a function of person, number, and morphological category of a verb's arguments;[2] hence, the three morphosyntactic argument types are defined by the prefix sets. Nominals functioning as morphosyntactic arguments are not themselves case-marked in Southern Tiwa. In the examples I include, the verb prefixes are glossed in the same manner as in other publications on Southern Tiwa—that is, the features reflected in the prefix are indicated according to the following schema: (ERG:)(DAT/)ABS.

9.2 Multiplex Verb Stems

These are very common in Southern Tiwa. I begin by presenting examples that do not have biclausal counterparts (in all complex stem examples, I have put the stem in boldface):[3]

(1) A-**si-'am**-ban 'u-ide.
    2SG:A-**cry-cause**-past child-SG
    'You made the child cry.'

(2) Yede bi-musa-**miki-'am**-hi euwa-n.
    that 1SG:B-cat-**feed-cause**-FUT young^man-PL
    'I will make the young men feed that cat.'

Examples (1) and (2) make use of causative *'am*, which takes an agent, a patient, and a logical clausal complement as arguments.[4] The logical subject of the complement is coreferential with the patient argument of the causative. Observe in (2) that if the complement has a logical object (in this case *yede musa*), the Head of that argument is necessarily incorporated.[5] The agreement prefix on the verb reflects person and number of the agent of the causation as an ERG and of the patient (= logical subject of the complement) as ABS.

Examples (3), (4), and (5) are similar, but use a different causative (*w*)*i* that also takes an agent, an experiencer/patient, and clausal complement. Here again the subject of the complement is coreferential with the patient argument, and if the complement is intransitive, the agreement facts are the same as in (1). However, if the complement has a logical object, it is realized as ABS, and the experiencer/patient argument of the causative will be realized either as an oblique (marked by enclitic postposition *'ay*), as in (4), or as a DAT, as in (5):

(3) Ti-**cheuat-i**-ban.
    1SG:A-**enter-cause**-past
    'I led him in.'

(4) Bi-khwian-**mu-wi**-ban u-ide-'ay.
    1SG:B-dog-**see-cause**-past child-sg-LOC
    'I showed the dogs to the child.'

(5) Tam-khwian-**mu-wi**-ban 'u-ide.
    1SG:A\B-dog-**see-cause**-past child-SG
    'I showed the dogs to the child.'

Example (6) involves the bound stem *mi* 'go'. It takes a clausal argument as well, the logical subject of which will be coreferential with the subject of 'go'. Unlike the causatives, this bound stem does not take an additional argument, so the resultant complex stem is intransitive. (Recall that the Head of the verb determines its argument structure.) In (6), the verb takes an agreement prefix that reflects the features of the nonclausal argument of *mi* 'go', as an ABS.

(6) Te-pî-**sheu-mi**-we.
 1SG-deer-hunt-go-PRES
 'I'm going to hunt deer.'

Next are complex stems that have biclausal counterparts; I present the biclausal variant followed by the monoclausal form:

(7) Hliawra-n bi-mache-'ay yedin ibi-diru-k'ar-him'ay.
 lady-PL 1SG:B-accomp-past those 1PL:B-chicken-eat-purpose
 'I was eating those chickens with the ladies.'

(8) Hliawra-n yedin bi-diru-**kar-mache**-'ay.
 lady-PL those 1SG:B-chicken-eat-accomp-past
 'I was eating those chickens with the ladies.'

Comparing (7) and (8), note that the former has two distinct verbs, both of which have agreement prefixes as well as verb suffixes, while in (8) there is only one verb, the stem of which is made up of the stems of both verbs of (7). The logical object of *k'ar* 'eat' (the ABS in (7)) is incorporated in the verb of (8), but it is not reflected in the agreement prefix; the prefix reflects only the ERG and ABS arguments of *mache* 'accompany'. (The verb 'eat' has the shape *kar* in (8) rather than the shape *k'ar* as in (7). Many roots have a suppletive form when not the morphological Head of the stem.) Examples (9) and (10) are similar to (7) and (8), except that the Head of the stem is *chachi* 'order':

(9) Ti-chachi-ban u-p'akhu-kha-hi-'i
 1SG:A-order-past A:C-bread-bake-FUT-SUB
 'I ordered her to bake bread.'

(10) Ti-p'akhu-**kha-chachi**-ban.
 1SG:A-bread-bake-order-past
 'I ordered her to bake bread.'

Comparing (11) and (12), we see that *t'am* 'help' takes three arguments: ERG, DAT, and ABS, as reflected in the prefix. The ABS argument is a phonologically and semantically "empty" argument (Frantz 2008) belonging to the morphological category C. The DAT is coreferential with the logical subject of the second clause in (11). When the verb stems are combined, as in (12), the complex stem has the same arguments reflected in the prefix, but the logical object of *miki* 'feed' cannot be reflected in the prefix; it is necessarily incorporated.

(11) Tow-t'am-ban   ∅-musa-miki-hi-'i.
    1SG:A\C-help-past A:A-feed-FUT-SUB
    'I helped him feed the cat.'

(12) Tow-musa-**miki-t'am**-ban.
    1SG:A\C-cat-feed-help-past
    'I helped him feed the cat.'

Examples (13) and (14) are similar to (11) and (12), except that *hwêyu* 'allow' has an "empty" A as ABS:

(13) Ta-na-hwêyu-ban   u-p'akhu-kum-t'a-hi-'i.[6]
    1SG:A\A-q-allow-past A:C-bread-sell-do-FUT-SUB
    'I let her sell the bread.'

(14) Ta-na-p'akhu-**kum-hwêyû**-ban.
    1SG:A\A-q-bread-sell-let-past
    'I let her sell the bread.'

Examples (15)–(21) are other sets of sentences showing simplex versus complex verb stems:

(15) Ku-na-pi-m   (hi'a) a-feuari-hi-'i.
    2SG:C-q-know-PRES COMP 2SG-cry-FUT-SUB
    'You know how to dance.'

(16) Ku-(na-)**feuar-pi**-m.
    2SG:C-q-dance-know-PRES
    'You know how to dance.'

(17) U-na-musa-**miki-pi**-m.
    A:C-q-cat-feed-know-PRES
    'He knows how to feed the cat.'

(18) Te-na-kheuap-a te-t'arat'a-hi-'i.
    1SG-q-like-PRES 1SG-work-FUT-SUB
    'I like to work.'

(19) Te-na-**t'arata-kheuap**-a.
    1SG-q-work-like-PRES
    'I like to work.'

(20) A-na-kheuap-'an   a-diru-k'ar-hi-'i.
    2SG-q-like-PRESHAB 2SG:A-chicken-eat-FUT-SUB
    'You like to eat chicken.'

(21) A-(na-)diru-**kar-kheuap**-'an.
2SG-q-chicken-eat-like-PRESHAB
'You like to eat chicken.'

Some other verbs that may occur either in clauses with a surface complement clause or as the Head of a verb with verb incorporation are *beaw* 'want', *khîwî* 'try', *pî* 'learn to', *p'ay* 'forget to', and *far* 'finish'.

9.3 Multiplex Verb Stems of More Than Two Roots

The semantics of these verbs as Head of complex stems suggests that they should be able to have complements made up of complex stems, and so incorporate those complex stems to result in stems made up of more than two simplex stems. And some such stems are possible:

(22) Ti-na-**kar-pî-khîwî**-we.
1SG:A-q-eat-go-try-PRES
'I'm trying to go eat.'

(23) In-na-shuth-**pe-pî-peche**-ban.
1SG\A-q-shirt-make-learn-decide-PAST
'I decided to learn to make shirts.'

(24) Ta-na-p'ahwe-**kum-pî-hwêyu**-ban.
1SG:A-q-egg-buy-go-allow-past
'I let him go buy eggs.'

Yet, many logically possible combinations are simply unacceptable; consider the following:

(25) *Te-na-**pî-wi-beaw**-a.
1SG-q-learn-cause-want-pres
'I want to teach him.'

(26) *In-na-p'ahwe-**kum-pî-hwêyu-peche**-ban.
1SG\A-q-egg-buy-go-allow-decide-past
'I decided to allow him to go buy eggs.'

The unacceptable combinations have one thing in common: there are arguments of one or more component verb stems that are not reflected in the verb prefix. This in turn is due to the fact, stated earlier, that only the arguments of the Head are reflected in the agreement prefix. For example, the Head *beaw* 'want' in 'I want to teach him' takes an ABS and a complement as its only arguments. So only the "wanter" can be reflected in the verb prefix; the "causee" (of 'cause to learn') cannot trigger agreement. In the example glossed 'I decided to allow him to go buy eggs', *peche* 'decide', which is Head of the complex stem, takes the experiencer as DAT and an empty A as ABS as its morphosyntactic arguments; hence the "allowee" (who is also agent of 'go' and 'buy'), not being an argument of 'decide', cannot trigger agreement.

Thus it appears that if any argument of a verb stem in a complex stem cannot be reflected in the verb prefix, that verb is ungrammatical. However, there are many examples presented earlier that show that this is not the whole story. Note, for example, that 'cat' in (2), (12), and (17) is not a morphosyntactic argument of the Head of the verbs in those examples and so is not reflected in the verb prefixes, yet the sentences are acceptable. What such examples have in common is that the noun Head of such arguments is incorporated in the verb.

9.4 Summary to This Point

The arguments of the component roots of Southern Tiwa verbs must be reflected in the agreement prefix or have their Head noun incorporated. These two together can be restated as a constraint that arguments be represented morphologically in the verb. This is a stronger version of Baker's "morphological visibility" constraint on polysynthetic languages, which referred to morphosyntactic arguments only.

(27) *In-na-**miki-hwêyu-peche**-ban   'î.
    1sg\A-q-feed-allow-decide-past 2
    'I decided to let him feed you.'

Examples such as (27) are bad because the only way to meet this stronger MVC would be to incorporate the head of the object argument of the lower verb, but such incorporation is blocked by the constraint that first- and second-person pronouns cannot be incorporated; in (27), the object that would need to be incorporated is second-person pronoun, and so it is bad.[7]

9.5 Null Pronouns as Arguments

Things get even more interesting if the Head of such a nominal is null by virtue of being in a context where it would otherwise be redundant. First, to see that a null pronoun as a morphosyntactic argument (in this case ABS) is reflected in the verb prefixes, compare (29) with (28):

(28) Tow-(na)b'akhu-wia-ban.
    1sg:B\C-bread-give-past
    'I gave breads to them.'

(29) Tow-wia-ban.
    1SG:B\C-give-past
    'I gave them to them.'

Now, compare (2), repeated here, with (30). The latter is well formed, even though the object of *miki* 'feed' is not reflected in the morphology:

(2) Yede bi-**musa-miki-'am**-hi   euwa-n.
    that 1SG:B-**cat-feed-cause**-FUT young^man-PL
    'I will make the young men feed that cat.'

(30) (Yede) i-**miki-'am**-hi   euwa-n.
    that   1SG:B-**feed-cause**-FUT young^man-PL
    'I will make the young men feed {it, (that)}.'

So it is all right to have an object of the lower verb unreflected in the verb morphology, just in case the head of the object nominal would be incorporable if nonnull. Baker (1996) would explain cases such as (30) by saying that the verb has a null "cognate" object incorporated (see Baker 1996, 208ff.), but I prefer to say that incorporation is vacuous (i.e., its effect cannot be seen) in such cases. Now, one might object that these are simply two ways of describing the same thing. But they are not; null cognate object incorporation would need additional constraints to rule out its use to save examples such as (27). Furthermore, the possibility of a stranded demonstrative points away from a cognate object analysis, since Baker apparently assumes that a cognate object represents an entire nominal, not just its Head.

Similarly, we can now explain the cases where incorporation is blocked by apparent extraction of a focused (topicalized?) nominal without resulting in an ungrammatical sentence, as in (31):

(31) Yede 'u'u-de, bey-hwea-'am-ban.
    that baby-SG 2SG:1SG-carry-cause-past
    'You made me carry **that baby**.'

The object of 'carry' is a null pronoun because an overt nominal would be redundant in the context of the focused nominal. So obligatory incorporation of the null head is vacuous.[8]

9.6 Conclusion

Only the Head of a verb stem in Southern Tiwa can license surface arguments.[9] Verb agreement prefixes reflect only licensed arguments. These constraints, combined with a stronger version of Baker's morphological visibilty constraint (see (32)), rule out the grammaticality of complex stems in which any argument of a component verb other than the Head is not incorporated. Apparent exceptions are verbs whose unlicensed arguments are null pronouns in a situation where a nonnull nominal would be incorporated.

(32) *Complex Verb Stem Constraint*
The arguments of the component stems of Southern Tiwa verbs must either be reflected in the agreement prefix or be incorporable according to the rules stated in Frantz 1995, 90–92.

Notes

1. Southern Tiwa is a language of the Kiowa-Tanoan family. It is spoken primarily in a pueblo south of Albuquerque, NM. As I have stated in earlier papers, I am deeply indebted to Barbara Allen and Donna Gardiner as coresearchers. Of course I am also indebted to several very helpful native speakers of the language, whose names I withhold for cultural reasons.

I have been remiss in earlier papers in not expressing the extent to which David Perlmutter helped to guide our research on Southern Tiwa. His many discussions with us over a period of years, proposing working hypotheses that were based on what seemed to us like uncanny insights, made our research exciting and rewarding. I hope this belated acknowledgment will at least partially make up for my earlier failure to give him the credit he deserved.

2. For purposes of verb agreement, the two numbers (singular and plural) and three noun classes (i, ii, and iii) are combined as follows to yield three agreement categories, A, B, and C:

A = iSG or iiSG; B = iPL or iiiSG; C = iiPL or iiiPL

3. Abbreviations utilized in glosses are: 1 = first person, 2 = second person, COMP = complementizer, FUT = future, LOC = locative, PL = plural, PRES = present, PRESHAB = habitual present, SG = singular, SUB = subordinator.

4. See Alsina 1992 regarding the claim that such a derivational causative morpheme has more than an Agent and complement as arguments.

5. Incorporation takes place unless the nominal in question is first or second person, putatively because incorporees must be lexical heads. However, since there are emphatic first- and second-person pronouns, which surely are "lexical" in any common usage of that term, yet are never incorporated, it must be something else about them that prevents their incorporation. The constraint is apparently specifically that no item that is linked to speaker or addressee referents on the referential dimension can be incorporated.

6. The root *kum* is apparently never the Head of a verb; hence it is shown with *t'a* 'do' in this example. Note that *t'a*, which can bring its own argument requirements and is usually intransitive, here is a "light" verb, and the complex verb has the argument structure of *kum*.

7. I included a similar example in Frantz 1995, 89 (23), unstarred; however, my latest (much younger) consultant rejects it. It may be that speakers differ where speech act participants are concerned. This bears further investigation.

8. This treatment may be a problem for a GB analysis, since both extraction and incorporation leave traces. I have shown elsewhere (Frantz 1991) that null pronouns can be replaced by an emphatic pronoun, but traces cannot; yet an emphatic pronoun is not completely ruled out in (31); consider the following example:

Yede 'u'u-de, bey-hwea-'am-ban   (% âwa)
that baby-SG 2SG:1s-carry-cause-past 3SG
'That baby, you made me carry it.'

9. Baker (1996, 395 n. 37) words this same observation about Southern Tiwa as follows: "Apparently, a complex verb cannot inherit the argument structure of its nonhead in this language."

References

Allen, Barbara J., Donald G. Frantz, Donna B. Gardiner, and David M. Perlmutter. 1990. Verb agreement, possessor ascension, and multistratal representation in Southern Tiwa. In P. Postal and B. Joseph, eds., *Studies in Relational Grammar 3*, 321–384. Chicago: University of Chicago Press.

Alsina, Alex. 1992. On the argument structure of causatives. *Linguistic Inquiry* 23(4):517–555.

Baker, Mark C. 1996. *The polysynthesis parameter*. New York: Oxford University Press.

Frantz, Donald G. 1991. Null heads and noun incorporation in Southern Tiwa. *Papers from the Special Session on American Indian Linguistics*, 32–50. Berkeley: Berkeley Linguistics Society.

Frantz, Donald G. 1995. Southern Tiwa argument structure. In C. S. Burgess, K. Dziwirek, and D. B. Gerdts, eds., *Grammatical relations: Theoretical approaches to empirical questions*. Stanford, CA: Center for the Study of Language and Information.

Frantz, Donald G. 2008. Empty arguments in Southern Tiwa. Ms.

10 Three Doubling Constructions in Halkomelem

Donna B. Gerdts

10.1 Introduction

Perhaps one of the most important legacies of the theory of Relational Grammar is the recognition that argument structure positions such as subject and object are highly constrained in both their semantics and their syntax. The Stratal Uniqueness Law (Perlmutter and Postal 1983) limits the positions associated with a single verb to one each of the term relations (subject, object, and indirect object). Furthermore, the Motivated Chômage Law (Perlmutter and Postal 1983) stipulates that a nominal cannot give up its status as an argument unless some other nominal is brought in to occupy that position. This highly constrained view of "rule interaction" has held up well to various empirical challenges, and has been incorporated into most modern theories of syntax.

One class of constructions that Relational Grammar handles quite elegantly involves the arrival of an NP to an object position—advancements (as in applicatives), unions (as in causatives), and ascensions (as in subject-to-object raising). The new object usurps the object relation, placing the notional object (the patient) *en chômage*, thus providing an empirical basis for the Motivated Chômage Law. However, another class of constructions has proven problematic for a theory of chômage: in antipassive constructions not only does the notional object not occupy the object position, but neither does any other NP, and thus the surface syntax of an antipassive construction is intransitive.

We can see this by comparing a transitive clause (1a) with an antipassive clause (1b) in Halkomelem, a Salish language spoken by around one hundred elders in southwestern British Columbia:[1]

(1) a. naʔət qʷəs-t-əs   t⁰ə ƛ̓eləm̓ sce:łtən.
       AUX go.in.water-TR-3ERG DT salted salmon
       'He/she put the salted fish in water.'

b. na?ət qʷs-els ?ə t⁰ə ƛ̓eɬəm̓ sce:ɬtən.
   AUX go.in.water-ACT OBL DT salted salmon
   'He/she soaked the salted fish.'

As Gerdts (1988) points out, the object in a transitive clause appears as a simple DP as in (1a), not as an oblique-marked DP (with the oblique preposition *?ə*) as in (1b). Furthermore, Halkomelem verb morphology transparently represents the difference between transitive and intransitive clauses: (i) the third-person ergative in (1a) determines agreement (*-əs*), but the third-person absolutive in (1b) is zero-marked; and (ii) the transitive verb in (1a) is overtly marked by a transitive suffix (*-t*), while the intransitive verb in (1b) is marked instead with the antipassive suffix (*-els*).

The seemingly unmotivated chômage of an object is not limited to antipassive constructions. In this chapter, I discuss three additional constructions in which the notional object appears as an oblique-marked DP rather than as the syntactic object. These are constructions with lexical suffixes (2), denominal verbs (3), and cognate objects (4).

(2) nem̓ č   nəw̓=əĺcəp   ?ə kʷθə syaḷ!
    go 2SUB bring.in=firewood OBL DT firewood
    'Go bring in the firewood!'

(3) nem̓ cən c-kʷəmləxʷ   ?ə kʷθə x̌peỷ kʷəmləxʷ.
    go 1SUB VBL-get.roots OBL DT cedar root
    'I'm going to get cedar roots.'

(4) t̓iləm cən ce? ?ə kʷ s-t̓iləm.
    sing 1SUB FUT OBL DT N-sing
    'I will sing a song.'

What these three types of examples have in common is that an element inside the predicate is doubled by the head noun in the oblique-marked DP. Thus I refer to these collectively as "doubling" constructions.

Before turning to these constructions, I first review in section 10.2 some examples of what would be considered in RG terms to be the motivated chômage of an object NP. I briefly illustrate the properties of the final object versus the chômeurized object, which appears as an oblique-marked DP, in several constructions. A key piece of evidence is extraction: chômeurized objects are extracted differently from both direct objects and oblique nominals. In section 10.3, I turn to a discussion of the syntax and semantics of doubling constructions, showing that the oblique-marked DPs in these constructions align with the chômeurized objects discussed in section 10.2. Examination of these constructions leads to the conclusion that objects may be chômeurized not only if another NP takes on the object role, but also if there is some predicate-internal reference to the nominal. I briefly explore the limits of the phenomena that fall under this umbrella in section 10.4, where I return to the issue of antipassive constructions. I conclude with some brief remarks on the syntax and semantics of doubling constructions and their implications for the morphology-syntax interface in section 10.5.

10.2 Extra Objects

Halkomelem Salish is, in the parlance of Mapping Theory, a 2-MAP language (Gerdts 1992, 1998b). That is, at most two positions are morphosyntactically licensed in the surface syntax. In Halkomelem monotransitive clauses, the agent and patient will link to the two MAPs.

(5) niʔ q̇ʷaqʷ-ət-əs tᶿə swəẏqeʔ tᶿə speʔəθ.
    AUX club-TR-3ERG DT man   DT bear
    'The man clubbed the bear.'

(6) niʔ cən q̇ʷaqʷ-ət tᶿə speʔəθ.
    AUX 1SUB club-TR DT bear
    'I clubbed the bear.'

(7) niʔ q̇ʷaqʷ-əθamš-əs tᶿə swəẏqeʔ.
    AUX club-TR:1OBJ-3ERG DT man
    'The man clubbed me.'

This means that any clause has at most two direct arguments, which in Halkomelem are determiner phrases (DPs) or their equivalent in subject or object pronominal marking.[2]

But what happens when there are more than two NPs competing for the MAPs, as for example in ditransitives (8), benefactive applicatives (9), or causatives based on transitive verbs (10)?

(8) nem̓ cən sam̓-əs-t łə słeniʔ ʔə θə nə snəxʷəł.
    AUX 1SUB sell-DAT-TR DT woman OBL DT 1POS canoe
    'I'm going to sell my car to the woman.'

(9) niʔ q̇ʷəl-əłc-t-əs łə nə ten łə słeniʔ ʔə kʷθə səplil.
    AUX bake-BEN-TR-3ERG DT 1POS mother DT woman OBL DT   bread
    'My mother baked the bread for the woman.'

(10) nem̓ cən məkʷ-stəxʷ tᶿə sƛ̓iʔƛ̓qəł ʔə tᶿə q̇əyemən, nem̓ ʔə tᶿə k̓ʷaƛ̓kʷa
     go 1SUB pick.up-CS DT child   OBL DT shell   go OBL DT salt.water
     cəwmən.
     seashore
     'I'm going to get the boy to pick up seashells by the seashore.'

Halkomelem is what Dryer (1986) calls a primary/secondary object language. In case of competition, the patient always loses the object slot to some other nominal. Thus, in examples like those above, the dative (8), benefactive (9), or causee (10) is a direct argument, which appears as a DP, as in the above examples, or a pronominal object, as in the following:

(11) niʔ ʔam-əs-θamš-əs ʔə kʷθə pukʷ.
AUX give-DAT-TR:1OBJ-3ERG OBL DT book
'He gave me the book.'

(12) niʔ q̓ʷəl-əłc-θamš-əs ʔə kʷθə sce:łtən.
AUX bake-BEN-TR:1OBJ-3ERG OBL DT salmon
'He baked the salmon for me.'

The patient, on the other hand, is framed as an oblique-marked DP.

Extraction, which is used in a variety of constructions, including relative clauses, *wh*-questions, clefts, and pseudo-clefts, provides additional evidence for the difference between the direct argument and the oblique-marked extra object in applied constructions.[3] As the following example shows, objects are extracted without the addition of any morphology to the verb:

(13) a. niʔ č lem-ət kʷθə swəy̓qeʔ.
AUX 2SUB look.at-TR DT man
'You looked at the man.'
b. nił kʷθə swəy̓qeʔ [niʔ ləm-ət-axʷ].
3PRO DT man AUX look.at-TR-2SSUB
'It's the man that you looked at.'

As the following examples show, applied objects can also be extracted with no additional morphology:

(14) swiw̓ləs kʷθə niʔ ʔam-əs-t-əs ʔə kʷθə pukʷ.
boy DT AUX give-DAT-TR-3SSUB OBL DT book
'It's a boy that he gave the book to.'

(15) łwet k̓ʷə niʔ q̓ʷəl-əłc-t-axʷ ʔə kʷθə səplil?
who DT AUX bake-BEN-TR-2SSUB OBL DT bread
'Who did you bake the bread for?'

(16) łwet ceʔ k̓ʷə nem̓ məkʷ-stəxʷ-axʷ ʔə t⁰ə q̓əyemən?
who FUT DT go pick.up-CS-2SSUB OBL DT shell
'Who are you going to have pick up the shells?'

In contrast, the extra object can only be extracted via nominalization; the verb has a nominalizing prefix *s-* and the subject is expressed as a possessor:

(17) nił kʷθə pukʷ niʔ s-ʔam-əs-t-s   kʷθə swiẃləs.
     3PRO DT   book AUX N-give-DAT-TR-3POS DT   boy
     'It's the book that he gave the boy.'

(18) snəxʷəł kʷθə niʔ s-θəy-əlc-t-s   kʷθə swəẏqeʔ.
     canoe DT   AUX N-fix-BEN-TR-3POS DT   man
     'A canoe is what he fixed for the man.'

(19) stem ʔalə k̓ʷə niʔ ʔən̓ s-makʷ-stəxʷ t⁰ə sλ̓iʔƛ̓qəł?
     What INQU DT   AUX 2POS N-pick.up-CS   DT child
     'What did you have the child pick up?'

Direct extraction of the oblique-marked DP is ungrammatical:

(20) *nił   kʷθə pukʷ niʔ ʔam-əs-t-əs   kʷθə swiẃləs.
     3PRO DT   book AUX give-DAT-TR-3SSUB DT   boy
     'It's the book that he gave the boy.'

Not only do extra objects contrast with direct objects, they also contrast with true obliques. Like extra objects, true obliques are marked with the preposition ʔə:

(21) niʔ cən   q̓ʷaqʷ-ət ʔə kʷθən̓ šapəl-əł.
     AUX 1SUB club-TR   OBL DT:2POS shovel-PST
     'I hit him with your shovel.'

(22) yaθ   ʔəw̓ yə-x̌ʷan̓čənəm̓ ʔə təna še:ł.
     Always LNK SER-run(IMPF)   OBL DM road
     'He always ran on that road.'

They are also extracted via nominalization.

(23) nił   kʷθə ʔən̓-šapəl-əł niʔ nə   š-q̓ʷaqʷ-ət.
     3PRO DT   2POS-shovel-PST AUX 1POS N.O-club-TR
     'It's your shovel that I clubbed it with.'

(24) nił təna še:ł yaθ   ʔəw̓ š-x̌ʷan̓čənəm̓-s.
     3PRO DM   road always LNK N.O-run-3POS
     'It's this road that he always runs on.'

However, the nominalizing prefix used in oblique extraction is the prefix *š(xʷ)-* and not *s-*.[4]

In summary, there are two types of extraction in Halkomelem: direct extraction, which is used for the extraction of objects, and extraction through nominalization, which is used for oblique-marked DPs. Thus, the conditions for extraction can be summarized as follows:

(25) a. Objects are directly extracted.
     b. Oblique-marked DPs are extracted via nominalization.

i. Nominalization with *s-* is used to extract extra objects (themes of ditransitives, patients of causatives, etc.).
ii. Nominalization with *š(xʷ)-* is used to extract obliques (location, direction, instrument, manner, stimulus).

Following the terminology of Gerdts and Hukari (forthcoming), I refer to oblique-marked DPs of type i as oblique objects, thus distinguishing them from oblique-marked DPs of type ii, which I refer to simply as obliques.

As summarized in table 10.1, case marking and extraction taken together can be used to distinguish the three types of nonsubject nominals in Halkomelem.

10.3 Doubling Constructions

The constructions that I have discussed so far (ditransitives, applicatives, and causatives) are fairly typical of those found in many of the world's languages, especially in what Gerdts (1992) refers to as 2-MAP languages. But now the plot thickens. Halkomelem has many polysynthetic properties, including robust verbal affixation. Besides verbal affixes for transitives, applicatives, causatives, reflexives, reciprocals, middles, and desideratives, Halkomelem also has lexical suffixes (Gerdts 2003), which are suffixes that function like incorporated nouns, and verbalizing prefixes used to create denominal verbs (Gerdts and Hukari 2008).[5]

In many of the constructions formed with these affixes, not only is reference made to the nominal within the predicate complex, but often there is a freestanding DP making more precise reference to the same nominal. Thus, Halkomelem frequently shows "doubling" effects. The freestanding DP is typically packaged as an oblique-marked phrase—more precisely, an oblique object.

In this section, I show three constructions with doubling—lexical suffixes in section 10.3.1, denominal verbs in 10.3.2, and cognate objects in 10.3.3.

10.3.1 Lexical Suffixes

Halkomelem, like other Salish languages, has approximately one hundred lexical suffixes—suffixes with the meanings of nouns. Most of these bear little or no resemblance to freestanding nouns of the same or similar meaning:

Table 10.1
Properties of objects and obliques in Halkomelem

	Objects	Oblique objects	Obliques
Case marking	zero	preposition *ʔə*	preposition *ʔə*
Extraction	direct	via nominalization with *s-*	via nominalization with *š(xʷ)-*

(26) qələm̓   'eye'   =aləs   'eye'
     sx̌ən̓ə   'foot'   =šən   'foot, leg'
     telə́w̓   'arm, wing'   =ex̌ən   'arm, wing'
     leləm̓   'house'   =ew̓txʷ   'building, room'
     qeq   'baby'   =eyəɬ   'baby, child'
     celəš   'hand'   =cəs   'hand, finger'

In a few cases, however, the suffix is clearly a truncated form of the noun:

(27) θaθən   'mouth'   =(a)θən   'mouth, edge'
     məqsən   'nose'   =əqsən   'nose, point'
     təpsəm   'neck'   =əpsəm   'neck'
     təməxʷ   'land'   =məxʷ   'land, group of people'

So the generally held view is that lexical suffixes originated as N roots that occurred frequently in compounds, which were subsequently reduced to bound forms and later degraded to suffixes (Gerdts and Hinkson 1996; Kinkade 1998).

Lexical suffixes commonly appear in complex predicates. That is, they are attached to a verb stem, and the resulting compound functions syntactically as the main predicate of a clause (Gerdts 2003). One function of lexical suffixes is to refer to the patient of a semantically transitive verb:

(28) šk̓ʷ=əyəɬ   bathe=baby   'bathe a baby'
     sq̓=əlcəp   split=firewood   'split firewood'
     qʷs=ey̓ən   dip.into.water=net   'set a net'
     səw̓q̓=iw̓s   seek=body   'search for a lost person'
     ɬc̓=əlqən   cut=hair   'shear wool'

The clause can be syntactically intransitive, as can be seen by comparing the lexical suffix constructions in the (a) examples in (29)–(30) to the corresponding transitive clauses in the (b) examples in (29)–(30).[6]

(29) a. niʔ šk̓ʷ=əyəɬ   ɬə słeniʔ.
        AUX bathe=baby DT woman
        'The woman bathed the baby.'
     b. niʔ šak̓ʷ-ət-əs   ɬə słeniʔ ɬə qeq.
        AUX bathe-TR-3ERG DT woman DT baby
        'The woman bathed the baby.'

(30) a. ʔi: səq̓=əlcəp   kʷθən̓ mən̓ə?
        AUX:Q split(IMPF)=firewood DT:2POS offspring
        'Is your son chopping wood?'
     b. ʔi: seq̓-t-əs   kʷθən̓ mən̓ə   tθə syaɬ?
        AUX:Q split(IMPF)-TR-3ERG DT:2POS offspring DT firewood
        'Is your son splitting the firewood?'

The (b) clauses are transitive and thus their predicates have the -*t* transitive suffix and third-person ergative agreement, while the (a) clauses lack these. Furthermore, NPs in argument positions are always preceded by a determiner in Halkomelem.[7] In this respect, lexical suffixation parallels the type of noun incorporation that has become known in the literature as compounding noun incorporation (S. Rosen 1989; Gerdts 1998a). We see this for example in Chukchee (Muravyova 1998, 524–525):

(31) a. gəm-∅ tə-wala-mna-∅-g'ak.
 1-ABS 1SG.S-knife-sharpen-AOR-1SG.S
 'I sharpened the knife.' (Lit. 'I knife-sharpened.')
 b. gəm-nan walə-∅ tə-mne-∅-g'en.
 1-ERG knife-ABS:SG 1SG.S-sharpen.AOR-3SG.O
 'I sharpened the knife.'

The example of noun incorporation in (31a) is transparently intransitive, while the corresponding clause in (31b) is transitive, as seen by the difference in case marking on the subject.

Nevertheless, lexical suffixes can be doubled with a freestanding DP, which appears as an oblique-marked DP:[8]

(32) nem̓ č θəy=e?ɬ ?ə t⁰ən̓ šxʷ?am̓ət!
 go 2SUB fix=fabric OBL DT bed
 'Go make your bed!'

(33) nem̓ cən t̓q̓ʷ=e:n ?ə t⁰ə st⁰eqən.
 go 1SUB cut.off=plant OBL DT bulrush
 'I'm going to cut down the bulrushes.'

(34) nem̓ cən ɬəlq=ət⁰e? ?ə t⁰ə ləmətulqən.
 go 1SUB soak=fibre OBL DT wool
 'I'm going to dye the wool.'

Often the semantics of such constructions involves a hyponymous relationship between the lexical suffix and the DP: the lexical suffix refers to the nominal's type, while the DP refers to a particular instantiation. In this respect, lexical suffixation parallels classifying noun incorporation; see the following Mohawk example (Mithun 1984, 870):

(35) Tohka niyohserá:ke tsi nahe' sha'té:ku nikú:ti. rabahbót
 several so.it.year.numbers so it.goes eight of.them bullhead
 wahu-tsy-ahní:nu ki rake'níha.
 he-fish-bought this my.father
 'Several years ago, my father bought eight bullheads.'

The extraction evidence shows that the oblique-marked DP is an oblique object: it extracts via nominalization with the prefix *s-*.

(36) nił tᶿən šxʷʔamət niʔ nə s-θəy=eʔł.
     3PRO DT bed   AUX 1POS N-fix=fabric
     'It's your bed that I made.'

(37) nił tᶿə stᶿeqən ʔi nə s-t̕q̕ʷ=e:n.
     3PRO DT bulrush AUX 1POS N-cut.off=plant
     'It's the bulrush that I am cutting.'

(38) nił ceʔ təʔi ləmətulqən nə s-ɬəlq=ət̕ᶿeʔ.
     3PRO FUT DT wool   1POS N-soak=fibre
     'It's that wool that I will dye.'

We see then that the oblique-marked DP doubling the lexical suffix behaves like the extra object in a semantically ditransitive construction in Halkomelem.

10.3.2 Denominal Verbs

Some intransitive verbs in Halkomelem, such as *ł-tih* 'drink tea', *c-tiqiw* 'have/get a horse', or *txʷ-lələ́m* 'buy a house', are composed of a noun base (e.g., *tih* 'tea', *stiqiw* 'horse', *lələ́m* 'house') and a verbalizing prefix (*ł-* 'eat, drink, partake', *c-* 'have, get, make', *txʷ-* 'buy').[9] These forms appear in a denominal verb construction, where the patient of a transitive event corresponds to the head of the denominal verb (Gerdts and Hukari 2008).

(39) ʔewe:č   ł-tih-əxʷ?
     NEG:Q:2SUB VBL-tea-2SSUB
     'Won't you take tea?'

(40) ʔi ʔə yəxʷ ʔəw̓ c-tiqiw   kʷθən̓ səlsilə?
     AUX Q SUP LNK VBL-horse DT:2POS grandparent(PL)
     'Do you suppose your grandparents still have horses?'

(41) niʔ txʷ-lələ́m kʷθə nə stiwən.
     AUX VBL-house DT   1POS nephew
     'My nephew bought a house.'

The Halkomelem denominal verb construction is syntactically intransitive, as seen by comparing (41) above to the corresponding transitive clause in (42).

(42) niʔ ʔiləq-ət-əs   kʷθə nə stiwən kʷθə leləm̓s.
     AUX buy-TR-3ERG DT   1POS nephew DT   house-3POS
     'My nephew bought his house.'

The clause in (42) exhibits both transitive marking and ergative agreement, while the clause in (41) does not.

Nevertheless, denominal verbs can be doubled with an oblique-marked DP.

(43) niʔ   cən   ɬ-səplil   ʔə   kʷ pəpaṁ   səplil.
     AUX   1SUB VBL-bread   OBL DT swelling.up bread
     'I ate some yeast bread.'

(44) nem̓   cən   ɬ-pax̌ʷəm   ʔə   kʷθə *menthol* s-pax̌ʷəm.
     go   1SUB VBL-smoke   OBL DT   menthol   N-smoke
     'I'm going to smoke a menthol cigarette.'

(45) nem̓   cən   c-kʷəmləxʷ   ʔə   kʷθə x̌peẏ kʷəmləxʷ.
     go   1SUB VBL-get.roots OBL DT   cedar root
     'I'm going to get cedar roots.'

The oblique NP serving as the doubled object is an oblique object: it is extracted via nominalization with the prefix *s-*.

(46) niɬ   kʷθə pəpaṁ   səplil niʔ   nə   s-ɬ-səplil.
     3PRO DT   swelling.up bread   AUX   1POS N-VBL-bread
     'It's yeast bread that I ate.'

(47) niɬ   kʷθə *menthol* s-pax̌ʷəm   niʔ   nə   s-ɬ-pax̌ʷəm.
     3PRO DT   menthol   N-smoke   AUX   1POS N-VBL-smoke
     'It's a menthol cigarette that I smoked.'

(48) niɬ   kʷθə x̌peẏ kʷəmləxʷ   niʔ   nə   s-c-kʷəmləxʷ.
     3PRO DT   cedar root   AUX   1POS N-VBL-get.roots
     'It's cedar roots that I got.'

Semantically, there is often some overlap—but not complete identity—between the nominal base of the denominal verb and the oblique-marked DP.[10] True doubling is not possible, because this would be semantically vacuous. Rather, the DP gives some more precise detail about the N serving as the verb base. For example in (49), the determiner *θə* identifies the DP as feminine.

(49) c-sisəl̓ə   tᶿəwniɬ   tətəm̓ ʔə   θə   sisəl̓ə-s.
     VBL-grandparent(DIM)   DT:LNK:3PRO   wren   OBL DT   grandparent(DIM)-3POS
     'Wren had a grandmother.'

Also, we see that in (50) the DP includes an N modifier *sq̓ʷi:l̓məxʷ* 'blackberry' of the head *pay* 'pie'.

(50) nem̓ ɬ-pay   ʔə   kʷθə sq̓ʷi:l̓məxʷ pay niʔ   scə́c̓eʔ ʔə   kʷθə lətem.
     go   VBL-pie OBL DT   blackberry pie AUX   on   OBL DT   table
     'Go and have the blackberry pie that's on the table.'

The parallels between lexical suffix constructions and denominal verb constructions are obvious. Both involve an element within the verb complex that is doubled with an oblique object that overlaps with it semantically.

10.3.3 Cognate Objects

Nouns formed from verbs by means of the addition of the prefix *s-* are quite common in Halkomelem. One major pattern is nouns formed from unergative verbs (verbs that are intransitive and whose sole argument is an agent). The meaning of the noun is the concrete or abstract thing that is associated with the event denoted by the verb.[11]

(51)   qʷal   'speak'   sqʷal   'speech, words'
       tiləm   'sing'   stiləm   'song'
       tiwiʔəɬ   'pray'   stiwiʔəɬ   'prayer'
       ya:m   'order (v.)'   sya:m   'order (n.)'
       yays   'work (v.)'   syays   'work (n.)'
       ʔəɬtən   'eat'[12]   sʔəɬtən   'food'

None of the verbs in (51) allow the addition of the transitive suffix *-t* (*qʷalt, *tiləmət, *tiwiʔəɬt, *ya:mt,[13] *yayst, *ʔəɬtənət), and they cannot appear in transitive clauses with a DP object. Nevertheless, Halkomelem allows such intransitive verbs to appear in semantically transitive clauses in which the patient is expressed as an oblique-marked DP, which can be cognate with the verb itself:

(52) tiləm cən ceʔ ʔə kʷ s-tiləm.
     sing 1SUB FUT OBL DT N-sing
     'I will sing a song.'

(53) niʔ cən yays ʔə θə nə s-yays.
     AUX 1SUB work OBL DT 1POS N-work
     'I worked on my work.'

(54) tiwiʔəɬ cən ceʔ ʔə kʷθə s-tiwiʔəɬ ʔə təna sieʔ ʔə tᶿey.
     pray 1SUB FUT OBL DT   N-pray   OBL this now OBL that
     'I will say the prayer now.'

Crosslinguistically, languages differ as to whether they frame the cognate object as an argument or an adjunct (see Nakajima 2006 and the references there). Halkomelem has the ideal means for representing cognate objects—the oblique object, which has the semantics of an object but the syntax of a nonargument. Cognate objects are oblique objects: they extract via nominalization with the prefix *s-*.

(55) niɬ ɬə nə s-tiləm [nə s-tiləm ceʔ].
     3PRO DT 1POS N-sing 1POS N-sing FUT
     'It is my song that I will sing.'

(56) niɬ ɬə nə s-qʷal [nə s-qʷal ceʔ].
     3PRO DT 1POS N-speak 1POS N-speak FUT
     'It's my speech that I will speak.'

(57) nił   kʷθə nə   s-tiẃiʔəł [nə   s-tiẃiʔəł ceʔ ʔə   təńa steʔ ʔə   t⁰eẏ].
     3PRO DT   1POS N-pray   1POS N-pray   FUT OBL this now OBL that
     'It's my prayer I am going to say now.'

In these extraction examples, the predicate is a doppelgänger of the noun: the verb is nominalized with the *s-* prefix and so it exactly matches the noun that is derived from the verb with the same *s-* nominalizer.

The cognate object construction is the opposite of the denominal verb construction in the sense that the verb is more basic morphologically and the noun is derived. But semantically the two constructions are parallel: as in the denominal verb construction, oblique-marked DPs in the cognate object construction allow not only determiners, which anchor the NP in time and space, but also modifiers, which help establish the particular instantiation of the nominal:

(58) qʷal cən ceʔ ʔə   k̓ʷ ʔəxʷiń s-qʷal.
     speak 1SUB FUT OBL DT little N-speak
     'I will give a little speech.'

Moreover, the noun need not be one that is morphologically derived from the verb, as long as it satisfies the selectional restrictions of the verb.

(59) niʔ ʔəłtən θə słeniʔ ʔə   kʷθə səplil.
     AUX eat   DT woman OBL DT   bread
     'The woman ate the bread.'

(60) neṁ cən ya:m   ʔə   k̓ʷ qʷłeẏšən neṁ ʔə   t⁰ə qʷłeẏšən=eẇtxʷ.
     go 1SUB order:MID OBL DT shoe   go OBL DT shoe=building
     'I am going to order shoes from the shoe store.'

(61) niʔ cən tiləm ʔə   łə nə syəwən.
     AUX 1SUB sing OBL DT 1POS spirit.song
     'I sang my spirit song.'

In this respect, patients of intransitive verbs are no different than patients of transitive verbs.

In sum, what we see is that the cognate object construction belongs to a larger class of constructions—clauses with transitive semantics but intransitive syntax. This observation raises the broader issue of where to draw the line between doubling constructions and other syntactically intransitive clauses in Halkomelem, which in turn leads us to a discussion of antipassives.

10.4 Antipassive as a Case of Doubling?

Antipassives in Halkomelem (Gerdts and Hukari 2000b, 2005), as mentioned in the introduction, show this same pattern: they are semantically transitive since they involve an agent and a patient but are syntactically intransitive, as seen by comparing the transitive clauses in the (a) examples in (62)–(63) with their antipassive counterparts in the (b) examples in (62)–(63):

(62) a. ni? tə́m-ət-əs   tᶿə sləwəy̓.
       AUX pound-TR-3ERG DT cedar.inner.bark
       'He/she pounded on the inner bark of the cedar.'
    b. ni? tə́m-els   ʔə tᶿə sləwəy̓.
       AUX pound-ACT OBL DT cedar.inner.bark
       'He/she pounded on the inner bark of the cedar.'

(63) a. x̌ə́l-ət č   tᶿən̓   sne.
       write-TR 2SUB DT:2POS name.
       'Write your name.'
    b. ni? ʔə č wəł   x̌ə́l-els ʔə kʷθə nə pipə?
       AUX Q 2SUB already write-ACT OBL DT 1POS paper?
       'Did you write my letter/form already?'

The patient in the antipassive, if it is expressed, appears as an oblique-marked DP, which tests to be an oblique object: it extracts via nominalization with the prefix *s-*.

(64) stem k̓ʷə ni? ʔən̓-s-x̌ə́l-els?
     what DT AUX 2POS-N-write-ACT
     'What did you write?'

Unlike the three cases of doubling discussed in section 10.3, antipassives lack a precise reference to the nominal within the predicate complex; the only predicate-internal morphology in the above examples is the suffix *-els*, which Gerdts and Hukari (2000b) label as the "activity" suffix because it often adds a sense of habitual or routine activity to the event. This suffix is attached only to lexically transitive bases, so there is always some patient implied. In some cases the semantics of an unexpressed patient can be filled in via a cultural default:

(65) q̓pels   'collect' [when going around collecting money]
     wənels   'throw' [when throwing out money or blankets in the bighouse]
     łq̓els   'lay (it) down' [when making a down payment or donating blankets]
     yəqʷels   'burn' [ritual burning of the clothes of the deceased]
     pepək̓ʷəls   'smoking' [when smoking salmon for storing]
     λ̓əyq̓els   'push down' [when kneading bread]
     yək̓ʷels   'break' [when breaking old plates in ceremony for black faces]
     ləw̓els   '(shaman) working a cure', 'escape being guessed right on' [in the bone game]

Examples like these show that perhaps the best way to conceive of the antipassive morphology is that it functions like nonspecific object marking: it sketches the presence of a patient without giving it a role in the argument structure.

This view of antipassive morphology fits well with examples of Halkomelem antipassives in which there is an oblique object with the nonspecific determiner ($k^{'w}$), which evokes a generalized event with a nonindividuated patient, as is characteristic of antipassives in many languages (see Cooreman 1994 and the references there).

(66) ʔi: čekʷx̌-əls   θəṅ   mənə ʔə k̓ʷ sqəw?
     AUX:Q fry(IMPF)-ACT DT:2POS child OBL DT fry.bread
     'Is your daughter frying bread?'

(67) nem̓ t̓ˀəm̓q-els ʔə k̓ʷ q̓pəneʔtən!
     go   snip-ACT OBL DT ribbon
     'Go and snip a piece of ribbon!'

However, the nonspecific patient effect of the antipassive verb can be overridden; a specific patient anchored to a particular event in time and space can be expressed as an oblique object.

(68) niʔ cə   yək̓ʷ-els ʔə t̓ˀə nə   šeł.
     AUX CONF break-ACT OBL DT 1POS door
     'He broke down my door.'

(69) nem̓ cən ʔəƛ̓q-els ʔə ɬə nə   telə   tənni? ʔə ɬə telewtx̌ʷ.
     go 1SUB out-ACT OBL DT 1POS money from OBL DT bank
     'I am going to take my money out of the bank.'

(70) ʔi   cən ləm̓-els   ʔə t̓ˀəṅ   sʔit̓ˀəm.
     AUX 1SUB hem(IMPF)-ACT OBL DT.2POS dress
     'I am hemming your dress.'

The predicate signals that there is some patient involved, one that is intricately linked to the semantics of the verb, and the oblique phrase gives a more detailed statement of what that patient is. This might at first seem paradoxical, but it is exactly the type of double layer of semantics that is exhibited by the doubling constructions discussed above. Thus, antipassives can be seen to be both syntactically and semantically similar to doubling constructions.

10.5 Conclusion: The Syntax and Semantics of Doubling

A defining characteristic of polysynthesis is that reference to a nominal can be made within the predicate complex. Not only can grammatical features such as the person, number, and gender of the nominal be referenced by verb agreement in a head-marking language, but sometimes the nominal semantics itself can be referenced, either vaguely, as in the case of classificatory constructions, or more precisely, as in the case of denominal verbs. Nevertheless, what does not seem to appear within the predicate complex is reference to a nominal's deixis—its location in time and space. This is accomplished by means of the determiner element within a DP.[14]

Moreover, while predicate-internal morphology can only be used to refer to the nominal's type in a generalized way, the doubled external phrase can be used to express the particular kind or instantiation of a nominal. We see that the four constructions discussed above—lexical suffixes, denominal verbs, cognate objects, and activity antipassives—all have this characteristic. The external DP is used to elaborate more specifically the nominal sketched (either vaguely or more precisely) within the predicate. Furthermore, all of these constructions share a common property: the nominal sketched by the predicate is its internal argument (i.e., in the above examples, the patient of a semantically transitive verb).

The Halkomelem data raise the issue of the boundary between doubling constructions and other semantically transitive constructions, a topic that deserves further exploration. Suffice it to say that, in contrast to doubling constructions and antipassives, regular transitive sentences do not invoke a double layer of semantics, at least in Halkomelem. For example, third-person patients, although they are zero-marked and thus do not distinguish gender or number, nonetheless imply a specific object.

(71) niʔ cən kʷən-ət.
 AUX 1SUB take-TR
 'I took him/her/it/them/*something.'

Why would a language allow doubling constructions when fully transitive clauses without an extra predicate-internal element are available in most cases? In an ergative language such as Halkomelem, the answer seems clear: transitive clauses are reserved for events where the object has a high degree of discourse salience and semantic individuation. Intransitive constructions are used when the emphasis is on the event itself rather than the patient of the event, or where the patient of the event is integral to defining the action.

How do the Halkomelem constructions discussed relate to the starting point of the chapter—the legacy of Relational Grammar with respect to the Stratal Uniqueness Law and the Motivated Chômage Law? The Stratal Uniqueness Law, since it refers only to nominal arguments per se, is only relevant to doubling constructions if there is some presumption that the element within the predicate originates as an argument NP, as, for example, in the head movement analysis of noun incorporation in Baker 1988. If, on the other hand, the predicate-internal reference to the nominal is considered to originate as part of the predicate, then Stratal Uniqueness is irrelevant to doubling constructions.

The more serious challenge is to the Motivated Chômage Law. One approach is to assume that if the internal argument nominal is referred to by predicate-internal morphology, then the language may consider the object position to have been filled (or in Case-theoretic terms, Accusative case is absorbed), resulting in a surface intransitive clause. We see this in the case of morphological reciprocals and reciprocals crosslinguistically, which differ in this respect from object agreement morphology, as first pointed out by Perlmutter (1969). But as Chung and Ladusaw (2004) point out, predicate-internal reference to the nominal serves to restrict it but not necessarily to saturate it. Additional semantic facts relating to the nominal may be expressed in a freestanding DP. Since languages vary as to whether the presence of predicate-internal morphology results in intransitive syntax, they vary as to whether this DP is framed as a direct object or an adjunct.

Halkomelem has a ready-made strategy for expressing such DPs: they are oblique objects, as evidenced by the extraction data. Motivated chômage strictly defined would require the oblique object to be chômeurized by another NP. But what we see in the case of predicate-internal nominal morphology is that the internal argument can be self-chômeurizing. Or to put it another way, predicate-internal morphology referencing the nominal is a sufficient (though in some languages not a necessary) condition for the detransitivization of the clause.[15]

At the end of the day, since none of the doubling constructions, nor antipassive for that matter, involve the arrival of a new nominal to usurp the relation of the patient, it is easiest to claim that there is no actual chômage and therefore the Motivated Chômage Law is irrelevant. Not all "case-absorbing" constructions therefore relate to realignments in argument structure.

Notes

1. Data are given with symbols often used for Native American languages. Glottalization is marked with an apostrophe over the consonant, and labialization with a superscript w. The alveolar fricative is represented as $š$, the uvular fricative as $x̌$, and the lateral fricative as $ł$. The affricates are represented as t^θ (dental), c (alveolar), $č$ (palatal), and $\lambda̓$ (lateral).

The following abbreviations are used in glossing the data: ABS: absolutive, ACT: activity, AOR: aorist, AUX: auxiliary, BEN: benefactive applicative suffix, CONF: confirmative, CS: causative, DAT: dative applicative suffix, DIM: diminutive, DM: demonstrative, DT: determiner, ERG: ergative, FUT: future, IMPF: imperfective, INQU: inquisitive, LNK: linker, MID: middle, N: nominalizer, NEG: negative, O: object, OBJ: object, OBL: oblique, PL: plural, POS: possessive, PRO: pronoun, PST: past, Q: question, S: subject, SER: serial, SG: singular, SSUB: subordinate subject, SUB: subject, SUP: suppositive, TR: transitive, VBL: verbalizer, VPX: lexical prefix.

2. Halkomelem does not allow bare NPs in argument positions, though bare NPs appear as predicate nominals, appositives, and vocatives.

3. Gerdts 1988, 59ff discusses the structure of extractions and the nominalizations on which oblique extractions are based.

4. More precisely, there is an oblique prefix x^w- preceded by the nominalizing prefix s-. The s- changes to $š$- before x^w, and the x^w is lost (in Island Halkomelem dialects), except before glottal stop.

5. See Gerdts 1998a for a comparison of noun incorporation, lexical suffixation, and denominal verbs.

6. Lexical suffix constructions can also be transitive. For discussion, see Gerdts 2003 and Gerdts and Hinkson 1996, 2004a, 2004b.

7. See note 2.

8. Lexical suffix constructions of the classificatory type are also possible (Gerdts and Hinkson 1996, 2004a, 2004b). These constructions are surface transitives and the patient is the direct object.

(i) ʔəẃ hay kʷs xʷ-t̓əx̌ʷ=wil-t ct t⁰ə ləpat ʔi t⁰ə laʔθən.
 LNK only DT VPX-wash=vessel-TR 1PL.SUB DT pot and DT dishes
 'We only wash pots and plates.'

I do not discuss these constructions further here due to lack of space. The other doubling constructions discussed here do not have transitive counterparts.

9. The nominal prefix s- is omitted after c- and l- but not after tx^w- and $\lambda̓$-. Thus I conclude that a phonological rule of cluster simplification is at work in the former cases rather than a morphological restriction that requires the base to be a root.

10. Gerdts and Hukari (2008) argue that the base is an NP rather than an N.

11. See Gerdts 1991, 2006, as well as Gerdts and Hukari 2000a for a discussion of the unergative/unaccusative distinction in Halkomelem.

12. The verb ʔəłtən is used strictly as an intransitive verb. The patient, if there is one, is always an oblique object. Halkomelem also has a transitive verb for 'eat', ləyx̌t.

13. The root in this verb also occurs with the transitive suffix to form a semantically ditransitive verb yaːt 'order someone to do something'.

14. Several scholars have observed that incorporated nouns lack deictic properties. Farkas and de Swart (2003) note the semantic similarity between incorporated nouns and bare NPs.

15. Various accounts within Relational Grammar have been offered to explain the surface intransitivity of noun incorporation constructions and their ilk. Gerdts (1979), following a suggestion of Postal (1977), claims that noun incorporation constructions involve antipassive and thus incorporation is simply a way of packaging an object-chômeur. This analysis proved uninsightful for cases of classifying noun incorporation, since they show no evidence of detransitivization.

Alternatively, Gerdts (1987) suggests a multiattachment analysis parallel to the analysis given for reflexives (C. Rosen 1988). Detransitivization in compounding noun incorporation results from cancellation of the multiattached object arc. Surface transitivity in classifying noun incorporation results from the birth of an object arc. However, the multiattachment analysis does not accommodate the type of constructions discussed here, which are surface intransitive but nevertheless have a freestanding DP.

References

Baker, Mark C. 1988. *Incorporation: A theory of grammatical function changing*. Chicago: Chicago University Press.

Chung, Sandra, and William A. Ladusaw. 2004. *Restriction and saturation*. Cambridge, MA: MIT Press.

Cooreman, Ann. 1994. A functional typology of antipassives. In B. A. Fox and P. J. Hopper, eds., *Voice: Form and function*, 49–88. Amsterdam: John Benjamins.

Dryer, Matthew S. 1986. Primary objects, secondary objects, and antidative. *Language* 62(4):808–845.

Farkas, Donka F., and Henriëtte de Swart. 2003. *The semantics of incorporation: From argument structure to discourse transparency*. Stanford, CA: CSLI Publications.

Gerdts, Donna B. 1979. Object incorporation and transitivity. Paper presented at the 43rd International Conference of Americanists, Vancouver, BC.

Gerdts, Donna B. 1987. A union analysis of noun incorporation. Paper presented at the Third Biennial Conference on Relational Grammar, University of Iowa.

Gerdts, Donna B. 1988. *Object and absolutive in Halkomelem Salish*. New York: Garland.

Gerdts, Donna B. 1991. Unaccusative mismatches in Halkomelem Salish. *International Journal of American Linguistics* 57:230–250.

Gerdts, Donna B. 1992. Morphologically-mediated relational profiles. In *Proceedings of the Annual Meeting of the Berkeley Linguistics Society* 18:322–337. University of California, Berkeley.

Gerdts, Donna B. 1998a. Incorporation. In Andrew Spencer and Arnold M. Zwicky, eds., *The handbook of morphology*, 84–100. Oxford: Blackwell.

Gerdts, Donna B. 1998b. Mapping Halkomelem voice. In E. Czaykowska-Higgins and M. D. Kinkade, eds., *Studies in Salish linguistics: Current perspectives*, 303–323. The Hague: Mouton.

Gerdts, Donna B. 2003. The morphosyntax of Halkomelem lexical suffixes. *International Journal of American Linguistics* 69:345–356.

Gerdts, Donna B. 2006. Argument realization in Halkomelem: A study in verb classification. In *Proceedings of WSCLA XI, University of British Columbia Working Papers in Linguistics* 19:61–81.

Gerdts, Donna B., and Mercedes Q. Hinkson. 1996. Salish lexical suffixes: A case of decategorialization. In *Proceedings of the Conference on Conceptual Structure, Discourse and Language*, 163–176. Stanford: CSLI Publications.

Gerdts, Donna B., and Mercedes Q. Hinkson. 2004a. The grammaticalization of Halkomelem FACE into a dative applicative suffix. *International Journal of American Linguistics* 70(3):227–250.

Gerdts, Donna B., and Mercedes Q. Hinkson. 2004b. Salish numeral classifiers: A lexical means to a grammatical end. *Sprachtypologie und Universalienforschung* 57:247–279.

Gerdts, Donna B., and Thomas E. Hukari. 2000a. The dual structure of Halkomelem motion verbs. In *Proceedings of the Workshop on American Indigenous Languages 2000, Santa Barbara Working Papers in Linguistics* 10:33–46.

Gerdts, Donna B., and Thomas E. Hukari. 2000b. Stacked antipassives in Halkomelem Salish. In *Papers for the International Conference on Salish and Neighbouring Languages* 35:95–106. *University of British Columbia Working Papers in Linguistics.*

Gerdts, Donna B., and Thomas E. Hukari. 2005. Multiple antipassives in Halkomelem Salish. In *Proceedings of the Twenty-Sixth Annual Meeting of the Berkeley Linguistics Society, Special Session*, University of California, Berkeley, 51–62.

Gerdts, Donna B., and Thomas E. Hukari. 2008. Halkomelem denominal verbs. *International Journal of American Linguistics* 74:489–510.

Gerdts, Donna B., and Thomas E. Hukari. Forthcoming. *Halkomelem.* Munich: Lincom Europa.

Kinkade, M. Dale. 1998. Origins of Salishan lexical suffixes. In *Papers for the International Conference on Salish and and Neighboring Languages* 33:266–295. Seattle: University of Washington.

Mithun, Marianne. 1984. The evolution of noun incorporation. *Language* 60:847–894.

Muravyova, Irina A. 1998. Chukchee (Paleo-Siberian). In Andrew Spencer and Arnold M. Zwicky, eds., *The handbook of morphology*, 521–538. Oxford: Blackwell.

Nakajima, Heizo. 2006. Adverbial cognate objects. *Linguistic Inquiry* 37(4):674–684.

Perlmutter, David M. 1969. Derived intransitivity in syntax. Paper presented at the Fifth Regional Meeting of the Chicago Linguistic Society, Chicago.

Perlmutter, David M., and Paul M. Postal. 1983. Some proposed laws of basic clause structure. In D. M. Perlmutter, ed., *Studies in relational grammar 1*, 81–128. Chicago: University of Chicago Press.

Postal, Paul M. 1977. Antipassive in French. *Lingvisticae Investigationes: Revue Internationale de Linguistique Francaise et de Linguistique Generale* 1:333–374.

Rosen, Carol G. 1988. *The relational structure of reflexive clauses: Evidence from Italian.* New York: Garland.

Rosen, Sarah Thomas. 1989. Two types of noun incorporation: A lexical analysis. *Language* 65:294–317.

11 Origins of Differential Unaccusative/Unergative Case Marking: Implications for Innateness

Alice C. Harris

11.1 Introduction

It has recently been emphasized that some linguistic phenomena are best explained not by appeals to innateness, but as epiphenomena, results of their own history (Anderson 2004; Blevins 2004; Blevins and Garrett 1998; Garrett 2008); this view is sometimes referred to as "evolutionary." While there is much merit to this approach, it is surely not the case that all phenomena can be fully explained in this way. In previous work (Harris and Campbell 1995, chap. 8) I have supported the view that crosslinguistically many word-order harmonies can be elegantly explained as the reanalysis of a harmonizing expression, such as the relative order of noun and adposition resulting from the reanalysis of genitive and noun (see Greenberg 1963, 99, and many other authors, regarding this and other examples). I have proposed two new sources of such harmonies—the verb and auxiliary from complex sentences, and the comparative adjective and standard of comparison from the general position of the complements of adjectives (Harris 2000). Yet in both works I have shown that this is not the only source of word-order harmonies; while many word-order harmonies are epiphenomena, it would be a mistake to attribute all to this source. In the present chapter I argue that the subject case marking differential, too, is partly to be explained as the results of its own history of reanalysis, but that innate or acquired knowledge of unergative and unaccusative[1] verb classes also has a role to play in their explanation. I argue that differential case marking for unaccusative and unergative verbs cannot be entirely explained as an epiphenomenal result of diachronic change.

Differential unaccusative/unergative case marking is illustrated in the contrast between (1) and (2), where the unaccusative verb *darča* requires a subject in the so-called nominative case, while the unergative verb *itamaša* takes a subject in the so-called ergative case.[2]

(1) bavšv-i   darča   saxl-ši³ (Author's fieldnotes)
    child-NOM she.remained house-in
    'The child remained in the house.'

(2) bavšv-ma itamaša   ezo-ši (Author's fieldnotes)
    child-ERG she.played yard-in
    'The child played in the yard.'

In this chapter I compare the development of differential case marking in Georgian, Udi, and Batsbi (also known as Tsova-Tush or Bats), three languages of the Caucasus. Georgian is not related to the other two, and Udi and Batsbi are only distantly related. Differential case marking is innovative in all three and cannot be attributed to a shared protolanguage. The differential case marking developed in three completely different ways in the three languages.

If synchronic differential unaccusative/unergative phenomena are fully explained through their diachronic origins, the occurrence of an unaccusative/unergative distinction in languages around the world must be viewed as an epiphenomenon. On the other hand, if synchronic phenomena that distinguish unaccusative from unergative are not so explained, the distinction itself is most naturally ascribed to our innate language faculty. For example, if incorporation of an object by a transitive light verb, as in (3), fully accounts for the origins of the unergative/unaccusative distinction in Udi, the synchronic distinction is explained as the result of the reanalysis of such constructions. (This process is described in greater detail in section 11.2.)

(3) pačaγ-q'a ič   čubux arc-i   ixt'ilät-q'un-b-esa-i (Taral)
    king-and self's wife   sit-PTCPL conversation-3PL-DO-PRES-PAST
    'The king and his wife, sitting, were conversing.'

I argue that such a reanalysis is indeed part of the explanation in Udi, but that we must refer also to the generalization of the phenomenon within the natural class of unergative verbs. I suggest that the knowledge of this class is innate.

In this chapter I argue that there is no explanation of the origins of the case-marking differential in Batsbi that would attribute it to a similar reanalysis. I show that the differential in Georgian, as in Udi, is partly explained through the constructions from which it developed, but that those constructions cannot explain certain parts of their development. The availability of an innate distinction between unergative and unaccusative classes of verbs is one approach to completing the picture.

I begin by describing the origin of the case-marking differential in Udi in section 11.2; the differential in Udi is largely the result of its history. For this reason, it serves to show both the elegance of this method of explanation and its limitations. In section 11.3 I turn to Batsbi. I have written before on the origins of this distinction in Georgian (Harris 1985), and in section 11.4 I summarize that description. In section 11.5 I discuss the implications of these facts.

11.2 Udi

11.2.1 Description of the Origins of Differential Case Marking in Udi

Udi is a member of the Lezgian subgroup of the Nakh-Daghestanian (or North East Caucasian) languages, rather distantly related to its closest sisters. My examples come from the Vartašen dialect as spoken in the village of Okt'omber, but the other dialect, Nij, is substantially like it in terms of morphosyntax (Harris 2005).

Udi, like its sisters, inherited strictly ergative case marking, with the subject of a transitive marked with the ergative case and the subject of an intransitive and the direct object in the zero-marked nominative (absolutive) case. In Udi, some changes in case marking have been made, and, under the influence of Azeri, definite direct objects are now marked with the dative. In pre-Udi a large number of verbs could incorporate nouns, adjectives, adverbs, or (locative) preverbs; the number of incorporating verbs has sharply decreased, and the incorporating verbs, now light verbs, have become in part markers of verb categories (see Harris 2002, 2008). I refer to the combination of a light verb and an incorporated element as a complex verb.

There are only about eight light verbs; the basic meaning of a complex verb is expressed by the initial (or incorporated) element. In addition to classifying, the light verbs carry the tense-aspect-mood suffixes and in this sense make the word a verb.

Direct objects were often incorporated by transitive verbs, as in (3) and (4). Many of these complex verbs were reanalyzed as intransitives, and as a consequence there arose a group of intransitive verbs that occurred with ergative subjects.

(4) Luiza-n   udi-n   muz-in   äit-ne-p-e (Author's fieldnotes)
    Louisa-ERG Udi-GEN language-INST word-3SG-SAY-AORII
    'Louisa spoke in Udi.'

In Udi I identify a verb as an unergative if it requires an ergative case subject and does not subcategorize an object external to the verb, as in (4). I identify a verb as unaccusative if it is intransitive and requires that its subject be in the nominative case. Clearly these diagnostics would not work in all languages, but it emerges below that the verbs they identify correspond to the crosslinguistic sets of unergatives and unaccusatives, respectively.

The development from light verb to classifier in Udi is ongoing; these elements have a mixture of the properties of light verbs, on the one hand, and of merely classificatory morphemes, on the other. The properties that identify these as light verbs are the following: (i) Some, *b-* 'do', *bak-* 'be, become', and *p-* 'say, speak' can be used independently—that is, without an initial (incorporated) element. (ii) Many initial elements are also used independently, and thus some collocations are transparent, as are (3) and (4) above. (iii) A few verbs that are not light verbs occur with an incorporated element—for instance, *c'i-lax-* 'give a name to' (*c'i* 'name', *lax-* 'lay, place, put'), *c'ap-duɣ-* 'applaud' (*c'ap* 'applause', *duɣ-* 'hit, beat'). (iv) The light verb *p-* 'say, speak' is multiply suppletive, and the alternation of unrelated stems is required for this light verb, just as for the independent verb from which it derives.

The properties that suggest that these so-called light verbs have already been reanalyzed as mere classificatory elements are the following: (i) Some, namely *-d-*, *-(e)ɣ-*, *-č-*, and *-k'-*, cannot occur independently (without an initial element). (ii) Some initial elements cannot be used independently, and thus for some collocations one cannot identify a meaning for the light verb. An example is *fal-le-d-e* 'she swung, flourished, flapped', where neither the light verb nor the initial element can be glossed independently. (iii) As we see below, for those verbs that do have identifiable meanings, the meaning of the whole verb is often noncompositional. (iv) According to Wolfgang Schulze (personal communication), in the Baku dialect the verbs I have identified as unergatives occur with nominative subjects, in spite of the fact that the light verbs require an ergative case subject when used independently. Because of these conflicting characteristics, I believe that this change is ongoing and has affected some light verbs before others.

A summary of the ways in which light verbs classify complex verbs in Udi is given in (5).

(5) i. Inchoatives are marked with *-bak-*.
   ii. Other unaccusatives are marked with *-(e)ɣ-*.
   iii. Unergatives are marked with *-p-*.
   iv. Transitive verbs of inherently directed motion are marked with *-č-*.
   v. Transitive change-of-state verbs are marked with *-b-*.
   vi. Other transitives are marked with *-d-*, *-t'-*, or *-k'-*.

As an independent verb, *bak-* means 'be, become'; *-(e)ɣ-* cannot occur alone, but etymologically it is 'come, go'. As intransitive verbs, these inherited government of an nominative (absolutive) case subject, and all of the dozens of verbs formed with these take nominative case subjects today, with the exception of two transitives, *i-bak-* 'hear' and *aba-bak-* 'learn, know'.[4]

(6) šonor   qai-q'un-**bak**-sa (Taral)   Unaccusative
    they.NOM back-3PL-**BE**-PRES
    'They returned.'

(7) me biric'   c'or-**eɣ**-al-le (Recipe 4)   Unaccusative
    this rice.NOM drain-**GO**-FUTII-3SG
    'The rice will drain [in the collander].'

I assume that unaccusative verbs are formed with *-bak-* 'be, become' and *-eɣ-* 'go, come' because their meanings are compositionally related to the meanings of these light verbs. Thus, the fact that the light verbs that form these complex verbs are themselves intransitive, together with the fact that Udi inherited an ergative case system, explains the use of the nominative case with these unaccusatives.

The light verb -*p*- 'say' forms unergatives, it but also forms quite a few transitives; and conversely, the light verb -*b*- 'do, make' is especially associated with transitives but also forms many unergatives.

(8) xinär-en gölöš-ne-**p**-e (Author's fieldnotes)   Unergative
    girl-ERG dance-3SG-SAY-AORII
    'The girl danced.'

(9) nana-n   lek'er-ax⁵ xaxa-**p**-e (Author's fieldnotes)   Transitive
    mother-ERG dish-DAT break-SAY-AORII
    'Mother broke the dishes.'

(10) taral-en t'ik'-n-u   bui-ne-**b**-sa   xe-n-en (Taral)   Transitive
     Taral-ERG wineskin-OBL-DAT fill-3SG-DO-PRES water-OBL-INST
     'Taral fills the wineskin with water.'

(11) išq'ar-muɣ-on höjät-**b**-esa-i (Author's fieldnotes)   Unergative
     man-PL-ERG argue-DO-PRES-PAST
     'The men were arguing.'

Thus, the classifiers (light verbs) do not draw a sharp line between unergatives and transitives. On the other hand, very few unaccusatives are formed with -*p*- (e.g. *čur-p-* 'stand') or -*b*- (e.g., *port-b-* 'endure'), and it appears that no unergatives are formed with -*bak*- or -*eɣ*-.

It was natural for transitives to be formed with -*b*- 'do, make' because it is a part of the compositional meaning of change-of-state transitives (such as the verb *tämiz-b-* 'clean', from the adjective *tämiz* 'clean') and of transitives with an incorporated noun (e.g., *gom-b-* 'paint', from *gon* 'color'). 'Do, make' also forms a natural compositional part of unergatives such as *aš-b-* 'work' from the noun *aš* 'work, business'.

As (8–9) illustrate, as a light verb, -*p*- no longer means 'say' in many examples. As shown in Harris 2002, 202–206, this verb was probably first used in the expression of language and nonlanguage noises made with the mouth (e.g., *bifar-p-* 'curse' from the noun *bifar* 'curse', and *axšum-p-* 'laugh' from the noun *axšum* 'laughter'). This light verb was later extended to noises not made with the mouth (such as *gürü-p-* 'thunder') and to other verbs related to the mouth (e.g., *q'uč'-p-* 'swallow, gulp'), and finally to verbs unrelated semantically, such as *ači-p-* 'play'.

The fact that the transitives and unergatives in (8–11) are formed with light verbs that are themselves transitive explains the use of the ergative case with these complex verbs.[6]

There are few simplex verbs in the language (i.e., verbs lacking light verbs); (12) provides some examples.

(12) a. *Transitives*
      aq'- 'take, get, receive, buy'   *beγ*- 'see, look at'
      biq'- 'get, catch; build'   *box*- 'boil'
      ef- 'keep, hold'   *uγ*- 'drink'
      sak- 'push'   *(u)k*- 'eat'
 b. *Unaccusatives*
      ač- 'get lost'   *ayz*- 'stand up'
      bap'- 'reach, arrive'   *bi*- 'die'
      bit- 'fall, stay'   *bu*- 'be'

Note that because I identify a verb as an unergative only if it takes an ergative subject and does not subcategorize a direct object, we do not expect to find inherited unergatives in a language that inherited ergative case marking. Before incorporation and complex verbs became prevalent, all intransitive verbs would have taken nominative subjects, since there was no differential case marking for intransitive verbs.

11.2.2 Implications of the Origins of Differential Case Marking in Udi

The use of the ergative case for subjects of simplex transitives and the use of the nominative for subjects of simplex unaccusatives in Udi was inherited from the protolanguage. The use of the nominative in complex unaccusatives, such as those in (6–7), was continued because the new unaccusatives were formed with light verbs that were themselves intransitive. The use of the ergative for subjects of complex transitives was similarly continued because these were formed with light verbs that were themselves transitive. The use of the ergative with unergative verbs, such as those in (8) and (11), originated through the use of transitive light verbs and the reanalysis of the resulting complexes as intransitive. The transitive light verbs, *-p-* 'say' and *-b-* 'do', were a natural choice from a semantic point of view, as shown above. Thus the case-marking differential in complex verbs, by far the majority of verbs in the language, is clearly an epiphenomenon, a result of the history of complex verbs in Udi. Complex verbs provide an elegant explanation of split intransitivity in Udi.

There are, however, some loose ends that this does not explain. First, we have no explanation for the extension of *-p-* to form unergatives and some transitives entirely unrelated to its original meaning, 'say'. It is expected that the sphere of use of a grammatical morpheme of this kind will expand historically, and it is not at all surprising that it comes to be used with verbal meanings unrelated to 'say'. What is unexplained is why 'say' was extended only to verbs with the semantics of unergatives and transitives (with two exceptions described below). That is, why are there so many unergative and transitive verbs like those in (8) and (9) above, semantically unrelated to 'say', but only a tiny handful of unaccusative ones? For example, why was *-p-* 'say' extended to form *gölöš-p-* 'dance', rather than to *uk-eγ-* 'be eaten, be edible', when the latter might be seen as more semantically related? Complex verbs explain the origin of the case-marking differential only if the light verb is semantically motivated and requires, in the ergative input case system, the case used in the split case output system. We can only explain the fact that 'dance' is formed with the light verb 'say' by noting that this light verb, requiring an ergative subject, was extended to the classes of unergatives and transitives, and that this extension is thus based on these classes, which must be either innate or learned from the nature of actions. Thus, the synchrony-as-epiphenomenon explanation fails for all unergatives and transitives where the notion 'say' is not semantically motivated, a sizable portion of the verbal lexicon.

The other side of this problem is that there are a few unaccusatives formed with -*p*-.

(13) künj-i   sa   beγ-k'ena xinär   čur-**p**-i-ne (Taral)
corner-DAT one sun-like   girl.NOM stand-SAY-PTCPL-3SG
'In the corner stood a girl like the sun.'

(14) käix iša käravan   gal-[l]e-**p**-e (Taral)
dawn near caravan.NOM place-3SG-SAY-AORII
'Near dawn the caravan moved.'

How can we explain the use of the nominative case with complex unaccusatives formed with -*p*- 'say', if it is the subject case of the input light verb that determines the case of the output complex verb? Again, the case-marking differential can only be explained as epiphenomenal if the choice of light verb is semantically motivated, and the subject case of the new lexeme is explained by that of the light verb. In these examples, neither of the conditions is met. Thus, the case marking of the verbs in (13–14) cannot be explained as a result of their history. The fact that the derived verbal lexemes require a case other than that required by the light verb demonstrates the importance of a force other than history—reference to an innate or learned distinction between classes of verbs.

A further problem is related to the lack of inherited unergative verbs. I explained above that there cannot be any because of the way I identify them. However, there are likewise no simplex verbs that one would expect to be unergative in a language with differential case marking—with one possible exception.

(15) ek   t'i-ne-st'a[7]   düz-i (Author's fieldnotes)
horse.NOM run-3SG-PRES field-DAT
'The horse is running in the field.'

The verb 'run' might be expected to be unergative, but it requires a nominative case subject.[8] The case is easily explained as the inherited construction with this simplex intransitive verb. But how do we explain the general lack of inherited verbs of this type? That is, with this single exception, all verbs that might be expected on semantic grounds to be unergative have acquired a light verb and with it an ergative case subject. Although there are only some forty to sixty simplex verbs in the language, other things being equal, we would expect more of them to be like 'run'—of the semantic type expected to be unergative. This fact cannot straightforwardly be attributed to the history.

Can the Udi use of the ergative case with unergatives be attributed to Georgian influence? Udi speakers were already in the Transcaucasus at the earliest historical times and are known to have been in contact with Georgians. In recent centuries Udi speakers have had much closer contact with Azeri, a Turkic language, and Armenian (Indo-European), both entirely nominative-accusative. Then, in 1921 a group of Udis established a new village on Georgian territory. The construction at issue here is abundantly attested in nineteenth-century texts, long before the new village was founded. Palimpsest texts of Old Udi thought to be from approximately the eighth to the tenth century A.D. were discovered in 1975, but have not yet been published. Evidently these texts have the construction, but little information has been released as yet. In view of the apparent age of the construction and the lack of information about the extent of Udi contacts at that period, we can really say only that Georgian contact cannot be ruled out as an influence in the innovative Udi case marking.

11.3 Batsbi

Batsbi is a member of the Nakh or Vainakh subgroup of the Nakh-Daghestanian family; it is only very distantly related to Udi. Proto-Nakh-Daghestanian had true ergative case marking, and Proto-Nakh had the same. That is, in these protolanguages, subjects of transitives were marked with the ergative case, and direct objects and subjects of all intransitives with the nominative (absolutive) case. Batsbi, however, permits two different subject cases—ergative and nominative—for first- and second-person subjects of intransitive verbs.[9] Batsbi is unusual in that while there are unaccusatives that only take a nominative case subject, (16), and unergatives that only take an ergative subject, (17), many intransitive verbs may take a subject in either case, with a difference of meaning, as indicated in (18–19) (Holisky 1987). I assume that this is an example of conversion—that is, I assume that 'fell', for example, is an unaccusative verb from which a derived unergative can be formed without morphological marking on the verb form, other than that provided by the agreement marker.

(16) (so)   xe-n-mak   qac'-u-sŏ
 1SG.NOM tree-DAT-on hang-PRES-1SG.NOM
 'I am hanging in a tree.'

(17) (as)   daḣ y-apx-yail-n-as
    1SG.ERG PV CM-undress-AUX-AOR-1SG.ERG
    'I got undressed.'

(18) (so)   vož-en-sŏ
    1SG.NOM fell-AOR-1SG.NOM
    'I fell down, by accident.'

(19) (as)   vuiž-n-as (All, Holisky 1987, 105)
    1SG.ERG fell-AOR-1SG.ERG
    'I fell down, on purpose.'[10]

The independent subject pronoun is found only in emphatic contexts.

The development of the ergative/nominative subject case distinction in Batsbi involved (i) development of differential case marking on pronoun subjects, though they are not generally overt, (ii) cliticization of pronouns, then (iii) change of clitics into affixes. I begin with the inherited system of agreement.

From the protolanguages, Batsbi inherited a system of class (gender) agreement. Nouns are divided into some eight classes (Dešeriev 1953; Č'relašvili 1967), and some verbs, but not all, indicate class agreement. Agreeing verbs indicate the class of the subject of an intransitive, as illustrated in (20), or that of the direct object of a transitive, as in (21).

(20) a. vašŏ   **v**-axe^n 'Brother (**v**-class) left.'
     b. yašŏ   **y**-axe^n 'Sister (**y**-class) left.'
     c. bader   **d**-axe^n 'The child (**d**-class) left.'

(21) a. nanas vašŏ   **v**-ik'e^n 'Mother took brother (**v**-class).'
     b. nanas yašŏ   **y**-ik'e^n 'Mother took sister (**y**-class).'
     c. nanas bader   **d**-ik'e^n 'Mother took the child (**d**-class).'
(Holisky and Gagua 1994, 177)

In addition to the inherited system that is illustrated in (20) and (21), Batsbi developed an innovative suffixal agreement.[11] (22) lists the ergative and nominative case forms of the independent pronouns of Batsbi; the breve (˘) represents reduction of a vowel, a process that applies to word-final vowels (except *a*) in polysyllabic words.

(22)   *Nominative*   *Ergative*
    1SG   so   as
    2SG   ho   ah, ahŏ
    1EX   txo   atx, atxŏ
    2PL   šu   aiš, aišŭ (Data from Holisky and Gagua 1994, 173)

The first-person inclusive, *vai*, behaves differently (see Holisky and Gagua 1994, 173), and the demonstrative pronouns that are used for third-person reference also behave differently. Neither conditions suffixal agreement.

The independent pronouns are suffixed to verbs as illustrated in (23) and (24). The intransitives in (23) use the nominative case forms shown in (22), while the transitives in (24) show the ergative forms. Those in (23) are illustrated with the *d*-class prefix, but this varies according to class.

(23) a. d-a-sŏ 'I am'
     b. d-a-ħŏ 'you are'
     c. d-a-txŏ 'we are'
     d. d-a 'he/she/it is, they are'

(24) a. teše-as → tešes 'I believe it'
     b. teše-ah → teše 'you believe it'
     c. teše-atx → tešetx 'we believe it'
     d. teše-aišĭ → tešišĭ 'y'all believe it'
     e. tešĕ 'he/she/it/they believe it' (Holisky and Gagua 1994, 177)

Examples (25–27) provide illustrations of agreement with intransitive and transitive subjects in whole sentences.

(25) **so**   osi   **v-a-ra-sŏ** (Dict 24a)   Unaccusative
     I.NOM there CM-be-IMPF-1SG.NOM
     'I (male) was there.'

(26) **as**   sk'ol-i   v-ex-n-**as** (Author's fieldnotes)   Unergative
     I.ERG school-in CM-go-AOR-1SG.ERG
     'I (male) went to school.'

(27) p'ay   b-eyɫ-n-**as**   ħo^n (Author's fieldnotes)
     kiss.NOM CM-give-AOR-1SG.ERG you.DAT
     'I gave you a kiss.' 'I kissed you.'

The forms of the independent pronouns in (22) and the forms of the agreement markers derived from them, illustrated in (23–24), distinguish unaccusative from unergative in terms of case marking; this shows up most clearly in verbs like those in (16) and (17). As Holisky (1987) shows, the subject of intransitive verbs is differentially marked in Batsbi.

There is nothing in the history of Batsbi to explain why some intransitive verbs have subjects in the ergative (in first and second person), while others have subjects in the nominative. In particular, there is no marking of transitivity in the intransitive verbs that occur with ergative subjects, such as (17), (19), and (26). In other respects, case marking in Batsbi is essentially like that in its most closely related sisters, Chechen and Ingush (Nichols 1994a, 1994b).[12] There have been no syntactic changes that would lead naturally to this case marking (and agreement) split.

A different possibility is that split intransitivity might have diffused from Georgian. The Batsbi live in the village of Alvani in Georgia and have been in Georgia for centuries. All Batsbi are fluent in Georgian, and schooling has long been provided in Georgian. It is thus possible that the unaccusative-unergative case split described above (and more completely in Holisky 1987) is to be attributed in part to diffusion from Georgian. However, there are many differences, which pose problems for such an account. First, none of the morphology of case marking is borrowed from Georgian or is similar in structure to that in Geogian. Second, the Batsbi derivation of unergatives from unaccusatives and vice versa (or optional, alternating case), as illustrated in (18–19), is not found in Georgian. On the contrary, in Georgian a given verb strictly requires a subject in one case or another. Third, the Batsbi restriction to first and second persons is not found in Georgian; indeed, in Georgian, the case distinction is actually neutralized in the first and second persons, and the case differential shows up only in the third person. Fourth, the Georgian restriction of the case differential to certain tense-aspect-mood paradigms is not found in Batsbi. Finally, there is no specific evidence of diffusion. In spite of all these differences, we cannot rule out the possibility that transfer from Georgian is partly responsible for these patterns in Batsbi.

11.4 Georgian

Georgian is unrelated to Batsbi and Udi, but like them it inherited a system of true ergative case marking (Harris 1985 and sources cited there). Fortunately, the latter part of the change from true ergative case marking to differential case marking for intransitive verbs is attested.

There are no additional languages in contact with Georgian that could be responsible for differential case marking with intransitive verbs, so "the buck stops here." Georgian has had contact with languages of the Northwest Caucasian and Nakh-Daghestanian families, each with ergative marking except in Udi and Batsbi. It has had contact with the Turkic languages Azeri and Turkish, and with several Indo-European languages, including Greek, Armenian, Russian, and several Iranian languages. It was probably also in contact with Aramaic or other Semitic languages. The sister languages of Georgian have case marking related to that found in Georgian (see Harris 1985 for details); but Svan, Laz, and Mingrelian have been influenced by Georgian, not the other way around. There is no language other than Georgian itself to which the development of differential intransitive case marking can be attributed.

Harris (1985) shows that earlier stages of Common Kartvelian had ergative case marking, and that an antipassive was reanalyzed as basic in certain verb forms (Series I), leaving the ergative construction only in what is now known as Series II forms of the verb. In early Old Georgian, unergative verbs very seldom occur in Series II forms. This is due to the fact that unergatives are primarily atelic (Holisky 1981; Levin and Rappaport Hovav 1995) and so do not distinguish perfective versus imperfective aspect, while in Old Georgian Series II marked perfective aspect (Mač'avariani 1974; Schmidt 1963). The two were thus naturally incompatible. In Old Georgian, unergative verbs lacked forms in Series III. This chapter is limited to the development of the case-marking differential in Series II.

Unergative verbs are atelic and intransitive, but in Georgian and other languages some of them can take an optional direct object. Typically, an unergative verb with a direct object is telic. For example, 'dance' as an intransitive denotes an activity without an inherent end point, but 'dance the samba' is telic. 'Dance the samba' can be made perfective, while 'dance' ordinarily cannot. Thus the infrequent occurrences of unergatives in Series II in Old Georgian often have an object and so are actually transitive. For instance, *t'irili* 'cry' is ordinarily intransitive, but in (16) it has a direct object, *dac'uvay* 'burning'.

(28) [mat]   dait'ir-on dac'uva-y (Leviticus 10:6, G, cited by Abulaʒe 1973, 412b)
    they.ERG cry-3PL   burning-NOM
    'Let them bewail the burning'

(29) nu uk'ue(y) marxva-y   imarxet čem tvis (Zak 7, 5)
    whether   fasting-NOM you.fast me   for
    'whether you fasted (a fasting) for me'

(30) aγixil-n-a   tual-ni   zeca-d (Luke 9:16)
    look-them-he eye-PL.NOM heaven-TRANS
    'He looked up toward Heaven.'

A few unergative verbs, such as *marxvay* 'fast' in (29), could appear with a cognate object, which, like other direct objects, made the verb telic. And a very few unergative verbs could take a body part direct object, as illustrated in (30). These transitive constructions took ergative subjects and nominative case direct objects, just as other transitives did. The plural object (*tualni* 'eyes' in (30)) triggers plural agreement, *-(e)n*, limited to plural direct objects. These transitive constructions in Old Georgian may have made common the use of the ergative subjects with verbs that were ordinarily unergative, thus paving the way for the general use of ergative subjects with intransitive unergatives. Moreover, because Georgian permits widespread pro-drop for objects, as well as subjects, some examples of the kinds illustrated in (28–30) had no overt object and thus were indistinguishable from intransitives.

In Old Georgian, some unergatives were made telic through incorporation; a light verb, such as 'do, make' could incorporate the stem of the unergative verb, as in (31).

(31) ɣaɣad-q'o   q'ovel-man er-man (Joshua 6:20, M, cited by Abulaʒe 1973, 460b)
shout-make all-ERG   people-ERG
'All the people shouted, gave a shout.'

Like the optional direct object, the incorporated object construction in (31) makes it possible for the unergative to become telic, to be perfective, and to occur in the perfective Series II. At the same time, the unergative occurs in a transitive construction with an ergative subject. This construction was seldom used in the imperfective Series I; rather, a form such as *ɣaɣadebda* 'he was shouting, crying out'—with the same root but without *q'o* 'make, do'—was used.

Finally, some unergatives are the reflexive intransitive counterparts of transitive verbs. In Series II, there were four constructions in which such verbs could, in principle, occur; these are indicated in (32).

(32) a. ERG verb NOM
    b. ERG verb self-NOM
    c. NOM verb
    d. ERG verb

That is, the verb could occur (a) as a transitive, with ergative subject and nominative direct object, (b) as a grammatically transitive reflexive, (c/d) as a grammatically intransitive verb, also with reflexive semantics. Possibility (c), with a nominative subject, represents the inherited construction, while (d), with an ergative subject, represents a later development, probably influenced by (32b). The examples in (33) are from the modern language, and (34) provides similar examples from Old Georgian.

(33) a. deda-m   švil-i   dabana (Author's fieldnotes)   Modern Georgian
        mother-ERG child-NOM bathe
        'The mother bathed her child.'
    b. deda-m   t'an-i   daibana (Author's fieldnotes)
        mother-ERG body-NOM bathe
        'The mother bathed her body.'
    d. deda-m   daibana (Author's fieldnotes)
        mother-ERG bathe
        'The mother bathed [herself].'

(34) c. [ganis]uen-n-e-t (Mt 26:45, Birdsall 1971, 65)   Old Georgian
        rest-PL-AOR-PL
        'Rest [yourselves].'
    d. ganisuenos mis zeda sul-man   ɣmrt-isa-man (Isaiah 11:2)
        it.rest   him on spirit-ERG god-GEN-ERG
        'The spirit of God shall rest [itself] upon him.'

The point here is that a reflexive with an overt object, as in (32b, 33b), may have influenced the use of the ergative case in a reflexive without an overt object, as we see in (32d, 33d, 34d). The construction in (32d) is continued in Modern Georgian, both for the verbs illustrated here, and as a productive construction. (32c) is maintained in a few old verbs, such as *moemzada* 'he prepared', but is discontinued as a productive construction.

In the transition from Old Georgian to Modern Georgian, Series II ceased to be strictly associated with perfective aspect. In the modern language one finds both perfective and imperfective forms in both Series I and Series II. In this newer system, unergatives have become common in Series II.

The examples above suggest how optional direct objects, object incorporation, and reflexive constructions have contributed to the innovation of ergative case subjects for unergative verbs in Series II in Georgian. This change for unergative verbs marked the beginning of differential case marking for intransitives in Series II in Georgian. These three constructions may have established for the first time a pattern for the use of the ergative case with verbs that were otherwise intransitive.

The three constructions described here do not, however, explain how the ergative case marking was generalized to unergative verbs as a class. On the basis of evidence in Old Georgian, Modern Georgian, and sister languages, we believe that only a small number of unergatives could occur in transitive constructions similar to (28–30). On the same basis, it is reasonable to assume that only a small number of verbs occurred in reflexive constructions of the types illustrated above. It is possible that the Old Georgian texts, primarily biblical and hagiographical, do not represent the full extent of the use of the incorporated object construction.[13] Whatever its status in Old Georgian, it is not reasonable to attribute the introduction of the ergative with intransitives primarily to the incorporated object construction, since it was not continued into the modern language, while the use of ergative marking with unergatives was. In the modern language new Series II forms were based, not on the incorporated object construction, but on the stem of the unergative alone. For example, corresponding to *γaγad-q'o* in (31), the modern language has *i-γaγad-a* 'he cried out', and in this form there is no reflex of the light verb *q'o*.[14] All this means that the new unergative pattern—ergative subject with intransitive verb—was generalized from a small number of verbs to hundreds of regular unergatives (see Holisky 1981 on the regularity of this construction in Modern Georgian). There is no explanation for this generalization without recognizing the existence of unergatives as a natural class of verbs, either innate or learned.

11.5 Conclusion: Implications

Three languages in the Caucasus have developed in relatively recent times constructions in which case assignment distinguishes between unaccusative and unergative verbs. In Udi the mechanism is quite apparent; light verbs were paired with semantically appropriate incorporated elements, and the case assignment was determined by the light verb. After these were reanalyzed, unergatives were left with ergative subjects, while unaccusatives had nominative subjects. While this accounts for most of the facts, some residue can be explained only by appeal to an innate or acquired knowledge of the classes of unaccusative and unergative verbs. Georgian influence cannot be ruled out, although it is not apparent.

In Batsbi, on the other hand, there is no evidence of any comparable mechanism that introduced ergative subjects to intransitive sentences. Contact with Georgian may have played a role in the Batsbi change.

In Georgian, in spite of abundant evidence, the generalization of ergative subjects to all unergative verbs cannot be attributed to any specific construction. Several constructions played a role in "seeding" the innovative case marking, but none was widespread. Only a learned or hardwired sense of these verbs can explain the generalization of the innovative construction.

Several recent works (listed in the introduction) have explained the occurrence or distribution of some linguistic phenomena as the result of historical change. It is absolutely correct to do so, and innateness should be called on as the explanation only after all other possibilities have been exhausted. Nevertheless, the fact that many phenomena are the natural result of regular change does not mean that innate knowledge of language structure does not also play a role. I have shown here that explanation of differential case marking in these languages must make reference to knowledge of unaccusative and unergative verb classes.

Notes

This chapter is part of a project on diachronic morphology; the research for it was supported by the National Science Foundation under Grant Number BCS-0215523, by the Centre for Advanced Study in Oslo in 2005, and by a research assignment from SUNY Stony Brook 2004–2005. The chapter draws on earlier research supported by the National Science Foundation under Grants Number BNS-8217355 and SRB-9710085, and by the International Research and Exchanges Board under the ACLS-Academy of Sciences Exchange with the Soviet Union (1989). I am grateful to each of these organizations and to my consultants, Luiza Neshumashvili, Dodo Misk'alishvili, Nana Agasishvili, Tsatso Chik'vaidze, Bela Shavxelishvili, and Tsisnami Dingashvili.

1. On the terms *unergative* and *unaccusative*, see, for example, Perlmutter 1978. For a complete history of the Unaccusative Hypothesis, see Pullum 1988.

2. In this chapter I use *ergative* and *nominative* as the conventional names of two cases. In each language, the case called ergative was historically a true ergative but has come to have mixed use, for which there is no crosslinguistically standard name. In each language, the case called nominative was historically the absolutive.

3. Abbreviations used in glossing examples include the following: AOR aorist (Batsbi and Georgian), AORII aorist II (Udi), AUX auxiliary, CM (gender-) class marker, DAT dative, ERG

ergative, EX exclusive, FUTII future II, GEN genitive, IMPF imperfective, INST instrumental, NOM nominative, OBL oblique, PL plural, PTCPL participle, PRES present, PV preverb, SG singular, TRANS translative case. My glosses of Batsbi follow Holisky and Gagua 1994, but I use the symbols ⟨y⟩ for the palatal glide, ⟨h⟩ for the voiceless pharyngeal fricative, and breve (˘) for reduced vowels. Neither Udi nor Georgian distinguishes gender, and glosses use 'he' or 'she' indiscrimately. In Udi, light verbs are glossed with the meaning of the corresponding independent verb, DO, BE, GO, SAY, even where the meanings are not compositional. The imperfect is composed of the present suffix plus a clitic with a past sense and is glossed PRES-PAST. "Taral" is the title of a text I have recorded.

4. These are so-called inversion verbs and earlier governed a dative case experiencer and nominative case stimulus; today the subject is in the ergative.

5. Recall that definite direct objects are put in the dative.

6. Little is known of the nature of the remaining light verbs. Wolfgang Schulze has suggested (personal communication) that -d- may have meant 'give'. It is the productive formant of causatives and of some other transitive verbs, and we may assume that it derives from a transitive. The light verb -č- forms four transitive verbs: e-č- 'bring', la(y)-č- 'carry up', ba(y)-č- 'carry in', č'i-č- 'carry out'; ta-š- 'take' may be related. Similarly, -k'- forms a few transitives, and we may assume that both of these derive from transitive verbs.

7. The form t'i-ne-st'a may contain the root t'it'- 'run', which is regularly split by the agreement marker -ne-; the t' element then metathesizes regularly with s of the present tense marker, -sa. An alternative analysis is that this is from *t'i-ne-t'-sa, where -t'- is a light verb. The comparative evidence is weak, and the etymology is thus indeterminate at this time.

8. The sentence corresponding to (15), but with the ergative (-instrumental) case (ek-en), is grammatical, but it means 'He ran across the field by means of (i.e., on) a horse.'

9. A handful of verbs have this feature for third person, as well as first and second. See Holisky 1987 for further details.

10. There are other languages with a volitional/nonvolitional distinction marked by a case-marking differential, notably Northern Pomo, a Pomoan language of northern California (O'Connor 1986, 1992).

11. I assume here the correctness of Holisky and Gagua's statement that these are affixes, though nothing here hinges upon their being affixes, rather than clitics.

12. Batsbi also makes use of light verbs (or auxiliaries), but they may be less prevalent than in Udi (cf. Črelašvili 1990). Batsbi has two, dar 'make, do' and dalar, which intransitivizes verbs. While light verbs in Udi mostly incorporate nouns or adjectives, Batsbi dar and dalar mostly cooccur with verb roots; partly as a result of this, they develop in very different ways in the two languages. In particular, dalar is found with some intransitives of every type—those that take only nominative case subjects (e.g., k'ac'k'ar-dalar 'become smaller, shrink'), those that take only ergative subjects (e.g. prena(d)-dalar 'fly'), those that take a subject in either case (e.g., k'urč-dalar 'go by rolling, roll') (data from Holisky 1987). A very small number of intransitives in Batsbi are formed with dar 'do, make'. While one would expect them to take only an ergative subject, in fact more of those listed by Holisky (1987) fall into the category of intransitives that take only nominative case subjects, such as xauk'-dar 'be thirsty', than into the category that take only ergatives, with none in the category that takes either case. I conclude that light verbs did not play a role in the origin of differential case marking in Batsbi.

13. On the other hand, it is possible that this construction was somewhat artificial, originated through translation, and was limited to the written language.

14. The development of this morphology, which is characteristic of unergatives in Georgian, is discussed in Harris 1985, 347–350, and the entire transition is described in greater detail in chapter 14 of the same work.

References

Abulaʒe, Ilia. 1973. *ʒveli kartuli enis leksik'oni.* [Dictionary of the Old Georgian language.] Tbilisi: Mecniereba.

Anderson, Stephen R. 2004. Morphological universals and diachrony. In G. Booij and J. van Marle, eds., *Yearbook of morphology*, 1–17. Dordrecht: Foris.

Birdsall, J. N. 1971. Khanmeti fragments of the Synoptic Gospels from Ms. Vind. Georg. 2. *Oriens Christianus* 55:62–89.

Blevins, Juliette. 2004. *Evolutionary phonology: The emergence of sound patterns.* Cambridge: Cambridge University Press.

Blevins, Juliette, and Andrew Garrett. 1998. The origins of consonant-vowel metathesis. *Language* 74:508–556.

Č'relašvili, K'onst'ant'ine. 1967. Gramt'ik'uli k'lasebis raodenobis šesaxeb C'ovatušur enaši. [On the number of grammatical classes in the Tsova-Tush language.] In G. Axvlediani, A. Šaramiʒe, I. Imnaišvili, A. Urušaʒe, G. Šalamberiʒe, Š. ʒiʒiguri, and K'. Č'umburiʒe, eds., *Orioni: Ak'ak'i Šaniʒes*, 332–335. Tbilisi: Tbilisi State University Press.

Črelašvili [Č'relašvili], K. T. 1990. Dva tipa sprjaženija glagolov v bacbijskom jazyke. *C'elic'deuli* 17:61–64.

Dešeriev, Ju. D. 1953. *Bacbijskij jazyk.* Moscow: Akademija.

Garrett, Andrew. 2008. Paradigmatic uniformity and markedness. In Jeff Good, ed., *Linguistic universals and language change*, 125–143. Oxford: Oxford University Press.

Greenberg, Joseph H. 1963. Some universals of grammar with particular reference to the order of meaningful elements. In J. H. Greenberg, ed., *Universals of language*, 73–113. Cambridge, MA: MIT Press.

Harris, Alice C. 1985. *Diachronic syntax: The Kartvelian case.* Syntax and Semantics 18. New York: Academic Press.

Harris, Alice C. 2000. Word order harmonies and word order change in Georgian. In R. Sornicola, E. Poppe, and A. Sisha-Halevy, eds., *Stability, variation and change of word order patterns over time*, 133–163. Amsterdam: Benjamins.

Harris, Alice C. 2002. *Endoclitics and the origins of Udi morphosyntax.* Oxford: Oxford University Press.

Harris, Alice C. 2005. The status of person marking in Nij Udi. In D. Haug and E. Welo, eds., *Haptačahaptāitiš: Festschrift for Fridrik Thordarson*, 91–104. Oslo: Novus Forlag.

Harris, Alice C. 2008. Light verbs as classifiers in Udi. *Diachronica* 25, guest ed., Claire Bowern, 213–241.

Harris, Alice C., and Lyle Campbell. 1995. *Historical syntax in cross-linguistic perspective.* Cambridge: Cambridge University Press.

Holisky, Dee Ann. 1981. *Aspect and Georgian medial verbs*. Delmar, NY: Caravan Press.

Holisky, Dee Ann. 1987. The case of the intransitive subject in Tsova-Tush (Batsbi). *Lingua* 71:103–132.

Holisky, Dee Ann, and Rusudan Gagua. 1994. Tsova-Tush (Batsbi). In R. Smeets, ed., *The indigenous languages of the Caucasus, vol. 4: The North East Caucasian languages, part 2*, 147–212. Delmar, NY: Caravan Press.

Levin, Beth, and Malka Rappaport Hovav. 1995. *Unaccusativity: At the syntax-lexical semantics interface*. Linguistic Inquiry Monograph 26. Cambridge, MA: MIT Press.

Mač'avariani, Givi. 1974. Asp'ekt'is k'at'egoria kartvelur enebši. [The category of aspect in the Kartvelian languages.] *KESS* 4:118–141.

Nichols, Johanna. 1994a. Chechen. In R. Smeets, ed., *The indigenous languages of the Caucasus, vol. 4: The North East Caucasian languages, part 2*, 1–77. Delmar, NY: Caravan Press.

Nichols, Johanna. 1994b. Ingush. In R. Smeets, ed., *The indigenous languages of the Caucasus, vol. 4: The North East Caucasian languages, part 2*, 79–145. Delmar, NY: Caravan Press.

O'Connor, Mary Catherine. 1986. Semantics and discourse pragmatics of active case-marking in Northern Pomo. In S. DeLancey and R. R. Tomlin, eds., *Proceedings of the First Annual Meeting of the Pacific Linguistics Conference*, 225–246. Eugene: University of Oregon.

O'Connor, Mary Catherine. 1992. *Topics in Northern Pomo grammar*. New York: Garland.

Perlmutter, David M. 1978. Impersonal passives and the unaccusative hypothesis. *BLS* 4:157–189.

Pullum, Geoffrey K. 1988. Topic... comment: Citation etiquette beyond thunderdome. *NLLT* 6:579–588.

Schmidt, Karl Horst. 1963. Zu den Aspekten im Georgischen und in indogermanischen Sprachen. *BK* 15–16:107–115.

Smeets, Rick, ed. 1994. *The indigenous languages of the Caucasus, vol. 4: The North East Caucasian languages, part 2*. Delmar, NY: Caravan Press.

12 Underlying and Surface Grammatical Relations in Greek *consider* Sentences

Brian D. Joseph

12.1 Introduction

A hallmark of Relational Grammar (RG) has always been that it states syntactic generalizations directly in terms of grammatical relations rather than by reference to word order or to other sorts of configurational representations. Moreover, within RG, it has been a basic tenet that this reference to grammatical relations need not be restricted just to the superficial relations one can observe in the actual production of a sentence; rather reference to relations at different levels of syntactic analysis (known as "strata") is often needed.

In this tribute to David Perlmutter, I offer a brief analysis of some facts from Modern Greek in which reference to nonsuperficial grammatical relations—grammatical relations at a level other than the final stratum (roughly, the surface structure)—is needed. Moreover, this is so even in a sentence that appears to be "monostratal" in its syntax—that is, to have a rather "flat" syntactic structure with the syntax essentially read off of the surface, a sentence that seemingly can be generated just by a simple phrase structure rule.

The sentence type in question is illustrated in (1):[1]

(1) (eγo)   θeoro   ton jani   eksipno
    I/NOM consider/1SG the John/ACC smart/ACC.MASC.SG
    'I consider John smart.'

Such a sentence—with a verb *θeoro* 'consider'; an accusative NP object, *ton jani* 'John'; and an adjective *eksipno* 'smart' predicated of the object—might be argued to be a relatively flat structure, with *ton jani* governed by the verb and *eksipno* as an adjunct modifying *jani*. Indeed, accusative case marking on *ton jani* is expected for the object of a verb, and masculine accusative singular is the expected form of an adjective modifying a noun of that sort. Admittedly a small clause analysis could be entertained for such a sentence, but even that is not fully biclausal.

There are two fuller sentence types that (1) seems to be related to, with a complete clausal complement; these are given in (2):

(2) a. θeoro   pos o janis   ine   eksipnos
       consider/1SG COMP the John/NOM is/3SG smart/NOM.MASC.SG
       'I consider that John is smart.'
    b. θeoro   ton jani   pos ine   eksipnos
       consider/1SG the John/ACC COMP is/3SG smart/NOM.MASC.SG
       'I consider John to be smart.' (Lit.: 'I consider John that (he) is smart.')

Such sentences also contribute to the impression that (1) is a monostratal and basically flat (S ⇒ (NP) V NP) structure, since it is clear in (1) that there is no other verb besides *θeoro* and that moreover complement clauses with verbs are possible with *θeoro*.

The English parallel to (1) is given in (3):

(3) I consider John smart.

While (3) has been the object of considerable discussion in the literature as to a small-clause analysis (e.g., Stowell 1981, 1983) versus a predication analysis (e.g., Williams 1980, 1983), it nonetheless offers some evidence showing it to be monostratal.[2] In particular, English seems to allow *tough*-Movement on direct objects only with "nonderived" ("thematic") objects, as argued by Berman (1973),[3] and as demonstrated by the sentences in (4):

(4) a. *Mary is easy to give *e* presents
       (cf. Mary is easy to give presents to *e* / Presents are easy to give *e* to Mary)
    b. *John is hard to believe *e* to have committed that crime

Importantly, *tough*-Movement on *John* in (3) is perfectly grammatical, as in (5):

(5) John is easy to consider *e* smart

a fact suggesting that *John* in that sentence is a thematic (i.e., underlying) object of *consider*, and that English sentences like (3) therefore are monostratal and thus relatively flat in structure.

A consideration of some additional facts, however, reveals that the Greek sentence in (1) is different from its apparent English counterpart in (3) with respect to monostratalness and flatness of structure. That is, it turns out that there is a process in the language—one type of reflexivization—for which crucial reference must be made to the status of *ton jani* in (1) in terms of the grammatical relation it bears at different levels of analysis ("strata"). In this reference to multiple levels, *ton jani* must be specified as a superficial object that is underlyingly a subject, in RG terms, a final stratum 2 (object) that is also an initial-stratum 1 (subject). The structure of (1) is therefore more complex than its superficial form would suggest and more so too than the English (3).

12.2 Reflexivization in Greek

Greek has two types of reflexivization. There is a syntactic construction that makes use of the reflexive nominal *ton eafto* 'the self' with a possessive pronoun indicating the coreferent nominal in the reflexivization, as in (6):

(6) i maria xtipai ton eafto tis
 the Mary/NOM hit/3SG.ACT the self/ACC her
 'Mary is hitting herself.'

In addition, there is a morphological reflexive in which the coreferential linking is expressed through so-called nonactive verbal morphology, also known as medic-passive or middle voice forms.[4] In the case of 'hit', the equivalent to (6) using this morphological strategy would be (7a), and some other such reflexives are given in (7b) and (7c):

(7) a. i maria xtipjete
 the Mary/NOM hit/3SG.NON-ACT
 'Mary is hitting herself.'
 b. i maria plenete
 the Mary/NOM wash/3SG.NON-ACT
 'Mary is washing herself.'
 c. i maria kitazete s ton kaθrefti
 the Mary/NOM look-at/3SG.NON-ACT in the mirror/ACC
 'Mary is looking at herself in the mirror.'

While the syntactic reflexive is rather free in terms of what sorts of coreferesntial linkages can be expressed, Modern Greek morphological reflexivization is constrained such that only underlying (i.e., thematic) direct objects can be linked with coreferent subjects. In RG terms, this constraint would mean that only a final-level 2 that is also (simultaneously)[5] an initial 2 can be linked with a subject in this reflexivization strategy. The evidence for this constraint comes from the reflexivization possibilities in two constructions that have a "surface" (final-level) direct object that is a not an initial direct object and cannot be linked to a subject in a nonactive voice reflexive construction. Although presented in Joseph 2000, the relevant evidence is briefly recapitulated here.

First, in the Greek "Dative Shift" construction, illustrated in (8), the notional indirect object, corresponding to the prepositional phrase in (8a), occurs as a final-level direct object, a 2 in RG terms, marked with accusative case, as in (8b). However, this accusative-marked final 2, corresponding as it does to a semantic indirect object, is a noninitial 2, and, as (8c) demonstrates, it cannot be linked with the subject via the morphological reflexivization strategy—(8c) has only a passive reading and not a reflexive reading:

(8) a. ðiðasko   γramatiki   s ton jani
       teach/1SG.ACT grammar/ACC to the John/ACC
       'I teach grammar to John.'
    b. ðiðasko   ton jani   γramatiki
       teach/1SG.ACT the John/ACC grammar/ACC
       'I teach John grammar.'
    c. o janis   ðiðaskete   γramatiki
       the John/NOM teach/3SG.NON-ACT grammar/ACC
       'John is taught grammar.' / *'John teaches himself grammar.'

Second, the full complement structure with *θeoro* 'consider', given in (2) above, admits of an analysis whereby (2a) reflects the underlying structure more or less directly and (2b) is a "derived" structure, in which the surface accusative NP, the final-level 2, is a noninitial (i.e., nonthematic) object, taking on final 2 status as the result of what has elsewhere been called Subject-to-Object Raising (see Joseph 1976, 1990, 1992). Important for the argument here is the fact that this final (and noninitial) object cannot feed into the morphological reflexive strategy, as shown by the unavailability of a reflexive reading for (9b), where only a passive sense is possible for *θeorite*:

(9) a. θeoro   ton jani   pos ine   jeneos
       consider/1SG.ACT the John/ACC COMP is/3SG brave/NOM.SG
       'I consider John to be brave.'
    b. o janis   θeorite   pos ine   jeneos
       the John/NOM consider/3SG.NON-ACT COMP is/3SG brave/NOM.SG
       'John is considered to be brave.' / *'John considers himself to be brave.'

Furthermore, there is an instructive contrast between (9) and similar-appearing structures with *piθo* 'persuade', as given in (10). With *piθo* there is a postverbal accusative object that is an initial object (in (10a)), and in the nonactive voice (in (10b)), both a passive reading, as with *θeorite* in (9b), and a reflexive reading are possible:

(10) a. episa   ton jani   pos ine   jeneos
        persuaded/1SG.ACT the John/ACC COMP is/3SG brave/NOM.SG
        'I persuaded John that he is brave.'
     b. o janis   pistike   pos ine   jeneos
        the John/NOM persuaded/1SG.NON-ACT COMP is/3SG brave/NOM.SG

'John was persuaded that he is brave.' / 'John persuaded himself that he is brave.'

The reflexive possibility in (10b) is consistent with the constraint on nonactive voice reflexivization, because unlike *ton jani* in (9a), *ton jani* in (10a) is an initial (and final) 2.

12.3 Reflexivization in *consider* Sentences

With this constraint, it is now possible to test for the type of object that *ton jani* in (1) is. As (11) shows, the morphological reflexivization strategy based on the structure of (1) is ungrammatical—that is, in (11),

(11) o   janis   θeorite   eksipnos
     the John/NOM consider/3SG.NON-ACT smart/NOM.SG

only a passive interpretation 'John is considered smart' is possible and not a reflexive reading, '*John considers himself smart'. This fact means that *ton jani* in (1), even though clearly a final-stratum 2 (surface direct object), is not an initial 2, being rather a nonthematic object.[6] What its initial grammatical relation is perhaps is not clear, but it could well be an initial 1 (a subject), if sentence (1) above is taken to be a reduction in some way from the structures indicated in (2). In any case, though, given the constraint on the morphological reflexive, (11) fits in with a pattern of reflexivization possibilities in Greek focusing on final-stratum objects that are also initial-stratum objects; the morphological reflexive strategy is not possible with a final object that is a different initial-stratum grammatical relation, as in (8c), (9b), and (11).

It is important to note that the problem with reflexivization in (12) is not a semantic problem since the syntactic reflexive can be employed to provide a reflexive reading:

(12) θeoro   ton eafto   mu eksipno
     consider/1SG the self/ACC my smart/ACC.SG
     'I consider myself smart.'

Moreover, it is not a morphological problem since the nonactive form *θeorite* does occur, but only in a passive sense, not a reflexive sense.

12.4 Conclusion

The result of this discussion is that reference to multiple levels of grammatical relations is an essential part of the statement of nonactive voice reflexivization in

Greek—it operates with final 2s (roughly, surface direct objects) that are simultaneously initial 2s (underlying direct objects). No other combination of grammatical relations allows for this reflexivization strategy. While one could explore the possibility of stating this on a semantic basis in terms of the thematicity of the direct object to be linked with a coreferent subject, it is not clear that "theme" or "affected entity" is a coherent semantic notion; the entity hit or washed in (7a,b) clearly is affected in some way but is the entity persuaded in (10b) affected in the same way, or is the entity viewed in (7c) even affected at all? Most likely not, making a purely semantic characterization less compelling. Moreover, restricting the morphological reflexive to a layer of lexical derivation could produce the desired results. But the basic fact remains that there is a syntactic dimension to reflexivity in Greek in that the realization of argument structure in nonactive verbs is different from that seen with active verbs; furthermore, reflexivization participates in that argument reduction. Consequently, one way or another, reference to grammatical relations at different levels of analysis must be recognized to account for the full range of reflexivization facts in Greek.

Notes

This chapter was completed while I was a Special Visiting Fellow at the Research Centre for Linguistic Typology at La Trobe University in the Melbourne, Australia, area. I would like to thank its director, Bob Dixon, and its associate director, Sasha Aikhenvald, for kindly inviting me to spend some time at the Centre in the summer of 2006. It was a fitting place to write this tribute to David Perlmutter, because he always emphasized to me that linguistic theory was about accounting for the ways in which all languages are similar and the ways in which they are different, and this is a basic goal of linguistic typology as well.

What I present here is an application of an analysis that David helped me with years ago having to do with the interaction of raising and reflexivization in Modern Greek (some of my findings were published in the appendix to Joseph 1990). I happily dedicate the present piece to him.

1. Here is a key to the abbreviations used in glossing the examples: ACC = accusative, ACT = active, COMP = complementizer, MASC = masculine, NOM = nominative, NON-ACT = nonactive, SG = singular.

2. These facts from English and other aspects of the Greek sentence type here are discussed in greater detail and with a different goal in Joseph 2000.

3. Berman stated the constraint as follows: "Tough movement may move a noun phrase only from its position in underlying structure" (p. 39), and this can be interpreted as given here in terms of thematicity of the direct object.

4. These forms can have passive or, with plurals, reciprocal, meanings, as well as other functions irrelevant to the matter at hand here.

5. RG is a nonderivational framework (hence the "scare quotes" around terminology below like "derived" object, which are intended in a metaphorical sense), so it is not the case that an initial relation turns into a final one, but rather a given nominal has properties from its

initial status and its final (and other level) status at all points in the generation/interpretation of a sentence.

6. As discussed in Joseph 2000, this is different from the ostensibly parallel English sentence type, to judge from the facts in (4) and (5), but it seems one has to simply take each language on its own terms.

References

Berman, Arlene. 1973. A constraint on *tough*-movement. *Papers from the Regional Meeting of the Chicago Linguistic Society* 9:34–43.

Joseph, Brian D. 1976. Raising in Modern Greek: A copying process? *290r*: Harvard Studies in Syntax and Semantics* 2:241–278.

Joseph, Brian D. 1990. *Morphology and universals in syntactic change: Evidence from Medieval and Modern Greek*. Outstanding Dissertations in Linguistics Series. New York: Garland. (Expanded and updated version of 1978 Harvard University doctoral dissertation.)

Joseph, Brian D. 1992. Diachronic perspectives on control. In Richard Larson, Sabine Iatridou, Utpal Lahiri, and James Higginbotham, eds., *Control and grammatical theory*, 195–234. Dordrecht: Kluwer.

Joseph, Brian D. 2000. *consider* sentences re-considered in the light of Greek evidence. In Katerina Nicolaidis and Marina Mattheoudakis, eds., *Proceedings of the 13th International Symposium on Theoretical and Applied Linguistics, April 1999 (Festschrift for Prof. Athanasios Kakouriotis)*, 81–88. Thessaloniki: Department of English, Aristotle University.

Stowell, Tim. 1981. Origins of phrase structure. Doctoral dissertation, MIT.

Stowell, Tim. 1983. Subjects across categories. *Linguistic Review* 2:285–312.

Williams, Edwin. 1980. Predication. *Linguistic Inquiry* 11:203–238.

Williams, Edwin. 1983. Against small clauses. *Linguistic Inquiry* 14:287–308.

13 French Inchoatives and the Unaccusativity Hypothesis

Géraldine Legendre and Paul Smolensky

13.1 Introduction

In this chapter we examine certain properties of inchoative verbs in French. A central issue is the extent to which these properties are to be explained as consequences of syntactic distinctions, notably, that between unaccusative and unergative verbs (Perlmutter 1978). This line of attack has been pursued in Labelle 1992. One principal claim of the present chapter (section 13.4) is that this general approach is problematic because it proves impossible to ascertain the unaccusativity status of French inchoatives on the basis of empirical evidence alone. The other main claim is that the inchoative pattern in question can be explained by a simple nonstructural analysis, provided that grammatical competition among both syntactic expressions and semantic interpretations is properly construed (section 13.3). The phenomena to be explained are laid out in section 13.2.

Inchoativization in Romance frequently yields a verb marked with a reflexive clitic. In French, the process of deriving an inchoative verb denoting a change of state from a transitive causative one, however, yields three classes of alternating verbs. Class I, illustrated by *briser/se briser* 'break', exemplifies the general Romance pattern, while Class II, illustrated by *crever/crever* 'burst', exemplifies the English-like pattern. Class III involves triads composed of two alternative inchoatives—*casser/se casser/casser* 'break'—as illustrated in (1).

(1) a. Le vent a cassé la branche.
      'The wind broke the branch.'
   b. La branche s'est cassée.
      'The branch broke.'
   c. La branche a cassé.
      'The branch broke.'

Given that all inchoatives denote a change of state, their single argument bears the thematic role of patient in both (1b) and (1c). However, inchoatives may differ aspectually. A change of state may be punctual or not, homogeneous or not, and a language may choose to encode a distinction between the process of change itself and the resulting state. For example, Labelle (1992) argues that inchoative *casser* denotes an autonomous process of change while *se casser* denotes the effect of change on the final state. In section 13.3, we present an analysis in which aspect plays a central role.

On the basis of syntactic tests previously proposed for French, Labelle goes on to claim that all reflexive inchoatives are unaccusative while intransitive (i.e., nonreflexive) inchoatives are unergative, regardless of class membership. In particular, she argues that the contrast in (2) supports the conclusion that *se casser* is unaccusative while *casser* is unergative.

(2) a. Il s'en est cassé trois.
    b. *Il en a cassé trois.
       'There broke three of them.'

Only the reflexive inchoative is grammatical in impersonal constructions (henceforth ICs). In (2) *en* is a partitive clitic pronoun corresponding to the complement of the numeral. If ICs are sensitive to the unergative/unaccusative distinction, surely the pattern in (2) must be evidence that *se casser* is unaccusative while *casser* is unergative. Unfortunately, Labelle's assumption is faulty because French ICs do not pick out unaccusatives, as discussed extensively in Cummins 1996 and Legendre 1989, 1990. See section 13.4 for further discussion.

In addition, (2b) is perfectly grammatical under a referential reading of the subject pronoun *il*, with *en* standing for a direct object modified by the numeral *trois*, as in *trois branches* 'three branches'. As such, (2b) has the reading of *He broke three (of them)*. As a result, the ungrammaticality of (2b) cannot be fully understood without also explaining its grammaticality under an alternative interpretation.

We propose to investigate the three classes of inchoatives and the pattern in (2) from the perspective of a bidirectional version (Blutner 2000) of Optimality Theory (Prince and Smolensky [1993] 2004). Specifically, in section 13.3 we propose that simultaneous competition between both expressions and interpretations provides a simple account of the facts based on elementary principles of markedness, according to which the grammatically preferred interpretation of an inchoative is telic, and the grammatically preferred expression of an inchoative is reflexive.

We also reexamine, in section 13.4, the general claim that impersonal constructions and partitive *en*-cliticization are valid diagnostic tests for unaccusativity in French in light of two independently motivated corpus studies (Hériau [1976] 1980; Rivière 1981), ultimately reaching the same conclusion as in Legendre 1989. In doing so, we demonstrate that the preference for adjuncts and clitics *en* and *y* in ICs is tied to informational properties of presentational constructions rather than any syntactic distinction, including the one embodied in the Unaccusative Hypothesis. Finally, we consider the question of whether inchoative *casser* is unergative. We show that it is impossible to pinpoint its syntactic structure on the basis of syntactic tests like parti-

French Inchoatives and the Unaccusativity Hypothesis

cipial constructions and appeal to the Universal Alignment Hypothesis (Perlmutter and Postal 1984) to conclude that *casser*, like *se casser*, *se briser*, and *crever*, must be unaccusative.

13.2 Two Generalizations to Explain

13.2.1 Preservation of Lexical Aspect

While the class membership of a given verb may vary slightly across speakers, all speakers of French appear to have three classes of causative-inchoative alternations. Each class is equally heterogeneous in the sense that it includes punctual achievement verbs as well as telic durative verbs denoting transitions from one state into another with an inherent endpoint. Each class also includes durative verbs derived from adjectives, either directly, as in *gros* 'fat' and *grossir* 'put on weight' (Class II)—or via the addition of a prefix as in *léger* 'light' and *s'alléger* 'get lighter' (Class I)—or both (Class III).

(3) *Classes of inchoative verbs alternating with a transitive causative*
   a. Class I
      Punctual: *se briser* 'break'
      Durative: *s'améliorer* 'get better', *se calcifier* 'become chalky', *se détériorer* 'get worse', *se gâter* 'go bad', *s'alléger* 'get lighter', *s'assécher* 'dry out', *s'agrandir* 'get larger', *s'amaigrir* 'get thinner', *s'alourdir* 'get heavier'
   b. Class II
      Punctual: *crever* 'burst', *claquer* 'slam'
      Durative: *moisir* 'grow moldy', *flétrir* 'wither', *grossir* 'put on weight', *grandir* 'grow up', *maigrir* 'lose weight', *vieillir* 'age', *durcir* 'harden', *sécher* 'dry'
   c. Class III
      Punctual: *(se) casser* 'break', *(se) rompre* 'break up'
      Durative: *(se) cristalliser* 'crystallize', *(se) gonfler* 'swell (up)', *(se) muer* 'molt', *(se) tarir* 'dry up', *(se) rétrécir* 'shrink', *(se) noircir* 'blacken', *(s')épaissir* 'thicken', *(se) refroidir* 'cool (down)', *(se) ramollir* 'soften', *(se) ternir* 'tarnish, dull', *(s')aigrir* 'turn sour'

The most curious fact about this classificatory system is the existence of Class III and what might, at first glance, be interpreted as a case of optionality. In fact, the two variants—with and without *se*—are not identical aspectually (Labelle 1992; Ruwet 1972; Zribi-Hertz 1987). A first difference in aspectual meaning is revealed by telicity tests. Telic (but not atelic) verbs in French are compatible with the temporal paraphrase 'take amount of time x to finish doing something' and the phrase 'in amount of time x', which focus on the end of the time interval. The pattern established on the basis of (4) differentiates inchoative *se casser* from *casser* and other Class III inchoatives in (5)–(6).[1]

(4) a. Il a mis quinze minutes pour arriver à la gare.
       'He took fifteen minutes to arrive at the train station.'
   b. Il est arrivé à la gare en quinze minutes.
       'He arrived at the train station in fifteen minutes.'
   c. *Il a mis quinze jours à jouer.
       'He took two weeks to (finish) playing.'
   d. *Il a joué en quinze jours.
       'He played in two weeks.'

(5) a. La branche a mis dix secondes à se casser.
   b. *La branche a mis dix secondes à casser.
       'The branch took ten seconds to break.'
   c. La branche s'est cassée en dix secondes.
   d. *?La branche a cassé en dix secondes.
       'The branch broke in ten seconds.'

(6) a. La source a mis vingt ans à se tarir.
   b. *La source a mis vingt ans à tarir.
       'The source (of water) took twenty years to dry up.'
   c. La source s'est tarie en vingt ans.
   d. *?La source a tari en vingt ans.
       'The source dried up in twenty years.'

Specifying the final state reveals a further contrast in (7) that confirms the distinct temporal organization of inchoative *se casser* vs. *casser*. *Se casser* focuses on the endpoint itself (i.e., a state of being apart), while *casser* focuses on the transition itself and has the meaning of coming apart under stress and leading to an endpoint (Labelle 1992).

(7) a. *La branche a cassé en trois morceaux.
   b. La branche s'est cassée en trois morceaux.
       'The branch broke into three pieces.'
   c. *L'oiseau a mué en un monstre à cinq têtes. (Zribi-Hertz 1987, 334)
   d. L'oiseau s'est mué en un monstre à cinq têtes.
       'The bird turned into a five-headed monster.'
   e. *Le sel a cristallisé en milliers de grains minuscules.
   f. Le sel s'est cristallisé en milliers de grains minuscules.
       'The salt crystallized in thousands of tiny grains.'

As expected, the same tests show that transitive *casser*, *briser*, and so on as well as inchoative *se briser* (Class I) are telic.

(8) a. Le vent a mis dix secondes à casser la branche.
       'The wind took ten seconds to break the branch.'

b. Le vent a cassé la branche en trois morceaux.
'The wind broke the branch into three pieces.'
c. L'enfant a mis dix secondes à briser le vase.
'The child took ten seconds to break the vase.'
d. L'enfant a brisé le vase en mille morceaux.
'The child broke the vase into a thousand pieces.'

(9) a. Le vase a mis moins de trois secondes à se briser.
'The vase broke in less than three seconds.'
b. Le vase s'est brisé en mille morceaux.
'The vase broke into a thousand pieces.'

What is surprising, however, is that Class II inchoatives (those that do not have a reflexive inchoative counterpart), such as *crever* 'burst', behave differently. Aspectually speaking, *crever* behaves like inchoative *se casser* rather than *casser*. *Crever*, unlike *casser*, is telic both in its transitive and intransitive uses, as shown in (10). In other words, the aspectual shift observed with inchoative *casser* does not extend to inchoative *crever* and other Class II verbs. A generalization regarding the preservation of lexical aspect is formulated in (11).

(10) a. Le clou a crevé la roue en deux secondes.
'The nail pierced the wheel in two seconds.'
b. La roue a crevé en deux secondes.
'The wheel burst in two seconds.'
c. La roue a mis deux secondes à crever.
'The wheel took two seconds to burst.'

(11) *First generalization*
Lexical aspect is systematically preserved under inchoativization. Every alternating change-of-state verb has one and only one telic inchoative counterpart. The default one is the reflexive-marked inchoative (e.g., *se briser*). If the lexicon does not provide a reflexive option, a nonreflexive inchoative preserves the lexical aspect of its source (e.g., *crever*). When two inchoative options exist, such as *casser/se casser*, it is the reflexive one that is telic (like transitive *casser*); intransitive *casser* is atelic.

13.2.2 Blocking in Impersonal Constructions

It is well known that transitive verbs cannot occur in French ICs unless they are passivized (e.g., Kayne 1975; Legendre 1990; Postal 1986). Reflexive inchoatives are grammatical, but nonreflexive inchoatives systematically trigger a shift in interpretation from an impersonal interpretation of the subject pronoun *il* to a referential interpretation. This pattern is independent of class membership. *Crever* behaves just like *casser*.

(12) a. Il s'est cassé plusieurs branches.
'There broke several branches.'
b. Il a cassé plusieurs branches.
'He broke several branches.'/'*There broke several branches.'

(13) a. Il a crevé plusieurs roues.
'He pierced several wheels.'/'*There blew out several wheels.'
b. Il a claqué plusieurs portes.
'He slammed several doors.'/'*There slammed several doors.'

Just like *crever*, *éclater* 'burst' denotes a punctual change of state. However, contrary to *crever*, *éclater* does not have a transitive counterpart, at least in Modern French. As a result, the impersonal interpretation cannot be blocked and (14) is grammatical.

(14) Il a éclaté plusieurs bombes à Bagdad.
'There burst several bombs in Baghdad.'

(15) *Second generalization*
The existence of a transitive causative verb blocks the impersonal interpretation of a nonreflexive inchoative counterpart.

13.3 Superoptimality and Inchoatives

13.3.1 Empirical Pattern to Be Explained

In this section we sketch a simple analysis of the empirical generalizations presented in the previous section. The pattern instantiating these generalizations is summarized schematically in (16)–(17).

(16) NP (se) AUX V
    a. *casser* class
        ⟨se casser, +TE⟩   *⟨casser, +TE⟩
        *⟨se casser, −TE⟩   ⟨casser, −TE⟩
    b. *briser* class
        ⟨se briser, +TE⟩   ~~⟨briser, +TE⟩~~
        *⟨se briser, −TE⟩   ~~⟨briser, −TE⟩~~
    c. *crever* class
        ~~⟨se crever, +TE⟩~~   ⟨crever, +TE⟩
        ~~⟨se crever, −TE⟩~~   *⟨crever, −TE⟩

(17) il (se) AUX V NP
    a. *casser* class
        ⟨se casser, +IMP⟩   *⟨casser, +IMP⟩
        *⟨se casser, −IMP⟩ ⟨casser, −IMP⟩

French Inchoatives and the Unaccusativity Hypothesis

b. *briser* class
⟨se briser, +IMP⟩   ~~⟨briser, +IMP⟩~~
*⟨se briser, −IMP⟩   ~~⟨briser, −IMP⟩~~

c. *crever* class
~~⟨se crever, +IMP⟩~~   *⟨crever, +IMP⟩
~~⟨se crever, −IMP⟩~~   ⟨crever, −IMP⟩

(16) displays the grammaticality patterns for the three classes of verbs discussed in section 13.2 (exemplified by *casser*, *briser*, and *crever*) in a sentence frame such as *la branche (se)* AUX V (e.g., *la branche s'est cassée*). (17) shows the corresponding pattern for the same verb types but in a frame like *il (se)* AUX V *plusieurs branches*. These displays indicate the grammaticality of *expression-interpretation pairs*, where the sole dimension of interpretation that is considered in (16) is the telic/atelic contrast (+TE versus −TE), and in (17) the contrast between the nonreferential (impersonal: +IMP) and referential (−IMP) interpretations of *il*.

In (16)–(17), the pairs with an asterisk are ungrammatical in French, and those that are ~~struck through~~ are impossible because the lexical specifications defining the verb classes are violated: reflexivity (presence of *se*) is mandatory for *briser*, forbidden for *crever*, and optional for *casser*.

The principal features of the empirical pattern in (16) that we seek to explain are encapsulated in (18).

(18) *The contrast to be explained*
Considering the nonreflexive expressions in (16)–(17):
a. In (16), the grammatical interpretation is −TE with *casser*, but +TE with *crever*; but
b. In (17), the grammatical interpretation is −IMP with both *casser* and *crever*.

From the perspective we develop here, this contrast is of interest because in (18a) the existence of a reflexive counterpart appears to affect the interpretation of the nonreflexive—but this is not inevitably so, because in (18b) the existence of a reflexive counterpart has no effect on the nonreflexive's interpretation.

13.3.2 Idea of the Analysis

The formal explanation of (18) proves remarkably simple, but space limits prevent us from presenting it here. Stated informally, the basic idea is actually more cumbersome to express. Starting with the pattern (18a) displayed by telicity, the explanation we develop is summarized in (19). In the Optimality Theoretic framework in which this explanation is couched, "unmarked" is formalized as "more harmonic," with grammars determining the relative Harmonies of alternative structural descriptions, and grammatical structures being those with maximal Harmony (Goldsmith 1993;

Legendre, Miyata, and Smolensky 1990; Prince and Smolensky [1993] 2004; Smolensky, Legendre, and Tesar 2006).

(19) *Proposed explanation of (18a) (informal)*
  a. *Premises*
    i. The unmarked interpretation of an inchoative is telic.
    ii. The unmarked expression of an inchoative is reflexive.
  b. *Then,*
    i. In determining the expression for +TE, with *casser*, where reflexivization is lexically optional, the pair ⟨se casser, +TE⟩ meets both markedness conditions (19ai–ii) and is selected over ⟨casser, +TE⟩; this leaves the nonreflexive to be assigned the atelic interpretation (16a).
    ii. But with *crever*, the lexicon makes no reflexive available, and the sole expression available is assigned a +TE interpretation (16c), violating (19aii) but satisfying (19ai).
  c. *That is,*
    i. For the +TE interpretation favored for all inchoatives, there is competition between the reflexive and nonreflexive expressions for *casser*, but not for *crever*; the winner of the competition for *casser* is reflexive.
    ii. In interpreting the nonreflexive, for *casser* the reflexive is the unmarked expression for +TE and this makes −TE the grammatical interpretation of the nonreflexive.
    iii. For *crever*, however, the +TE interpretation has not been assigned to the (unavailable) reflexive expression, and the grammatical expression of +TE is then the nonreflexive, in conformity with (19ai).

In this explanation, syntactic expressions compete in determining the optimal expression for a given interpretation: +TE, in (19ci). This kind of competition is the *expressive optimization* that is standard in Optimality Theoretic syntax and phonology (Prince and Smolensky [1993] 2004; Legendre, Grimshaw, and Vikner 2001). However the explanation also requires competition among *interpretations* for determining the optimal interpretation of a given expression: the nonreflexive, in (19cii). This kind of *interpretive competition* is a central feature of OT semantics (Hendriks and de Hoop 2001). The proposed explanation requires *both* expressive and interpretive optimization: it requires *bidirectional OT* (Blutner 2000; Boersma 1998; Prince and Smolensky [1993] 2004, chap. 9; Smolensky 1996; Tesar and Smolensky 2000; Wilson 2001).

The type of pattern exhibited here is just the type predicted by the form of bidirectional OT employing *weak superoptimality* (Blutner 2000).[2] In this architecture, interpretive and expressive competition occur simultaneously in defining grammaticality.

French Inchoatives and the Unaccusativity Hypothesis

It is this simultaneous competition that makes possible the contrast between (19cii) and (19ciii), a contrast that critically depends simultaneously on two factors: the existence of a competing expression for +TE (the reflexive that is available for *casser* but not *crever*) and the existence of a competing interpretation for the nonreflexive (available for *crever* but not *casser*). The crucial inference is that *because* the grammatical expression of +TE is reflexive for *casser*, this interpretation is blocked for the nonreflexive.

How the account explains the impersonal pattern (18b) and its contrast with (18a) is informally sketched in (20).

(20) *Proposed explanation of (18b) (informal)*
   a. *Additional premises*
      i. Expletives are marked.
      ii. A clause is marked when its arguments cannot be accommodated by the argument structure of its verb; this has priority over the other relevant markedness conditions.
   b. *Then,*
      i. With *casser*, where reflexivization is lexically optional, in determining the expression for the impersonal interpretation +IMP, the pair ⟨se casser, +IMP⟩ is selected over ⟨casser, +IMP⟩ (17a) because of (19aii); for −IMP, ⟨casser, −IMP⟩ is selected over ⟨se casser, −IMP⟩ by (20aii).
      ii. But with *crever*, with no reflexive available, the competition reduces to that between the interpretations ⟨crever, +IMP⟩ and ⟨crever, −IMP⟩; now the − interpretation wins (17c) by (20ai), whereas for the telicity case the + interpretation wins by (19ai).

The conditions in (20a) are of course absolutely standard assumptions in one form or another; (20ai) is most familiar in the OT syntax literature as FULLINTERPRETATION (Grimshaw 1997). We assume that inchoative reflexivization with *se* absorbs the external argument of a transitive verb (Bouchard 1984; Marantz 1984; Grimshaw 1990), leaving only one argument position, and the sentence *il se* AUX V NP already has a full NP internal argument independently of *il*. So in the reflexive forms, *il* must be given an impersonal (expletive) interpretation to satisfy (20aii).

13.4 Inchoatives and the Unaccusative Hypothesis

In the proposed account of French inchoatives surface-opaque structural properties such as the unaccusative/unergative distinction do not play a role. In this section, we examine the structural issue further and conclude that a structural approach to the phenomena under investigation is independently problematic. In particular, we demonstrate that assigning an unergative structure to nonreflexive inchoatives is empirically unwarranted, contrary to the claim made in Labelle 1992. Unlike her, we do not abandon the Universal Alignment Hypothesis (Perlmutter and Postal 1984) or the Uniformity of Theta Assignment Hypothesis (Baker 1988), which determine the syntactic configuration of arguments (internal versus external) on the basis of their thematic role. Instead we turn to these theoretical principles to motivate an unaccusative analysis of all inchoatives.

The discussion is organized as follows. Section 13.4.1 shows that impersonal constructions can be distinguished solely on the basis of their discourse-pragmatic properties: existential ICs serve to introduce a new, not-yet-activated, entity in the world of discourse while event-reporting ICs merely introduce a new event. Both varieties are grammatical with all intransitive verbs, including those identified as unergative on the basis of their ungrammaticality in participial constructions (Legendre 1989). Furthermore, the enhancement effect of locative and partitive clitics (y, en) in ICs is shown to be related to their discourse-pragmatic status. Section 13.4.2 turns to the (possibly only remaining) syntactic test for unaccusativity in French, participial constructions. Aspectual restrictions (telicity) and structural restrictions (unaccusativity) are teased apart, leading to the conclusion that the status of internal argument is a necessary condition for appearing in participial constructions (in accord with Legendre 1989). However, the fact that the participle form of *casser* is grammatical in participial constructions does not conclusively prove that inchoative *casser* is unaccusative because the existence of transitive *casser* is sufficient to explain its grammaticality.

13.4.1 Impersonal Constructions and Partitive *en*-Cliticization

Despite claims to the contrary (e.g., Labelle 1992; Marandin 2001; Pollock 1986; Ruwet 1988), impersonal constructions (ICs) and partitive *en*-cliticization (*en*) are not restricted to internal arguments in French. Besides examples such as (21a–c)—discussed in Bouchard 1995, Cummins 1996, and Legendre 1989—two independent descriptive studies of French,[3] one based on modern literature (Hériau [1976] 1980) and the other, on a corpus of native-speaker elicitations (Rivière 1981), confirm that there are by and large no restrictions on intransitive verbs appearing in ICs.

(21) a. Il travaille des milliers d'ouvriers dans cette usine.
  'There work thousands of workers in this plant.'
 b. Pendant des siècles il a régné des tyrans sur cette petite île de l'Atlantique.
  'For centuries there reigned tyrants on this small Atlantic island.'
 c. Il dort un chat au coin du feu.
  'There sleeps a cat by the fireplace.'

In particular, Hériau ([1976] 1980) demonstrates that besides verbs of existence and appearance, traditionally held to be the verb classes that ICs are restricted to, his corpus contains unergative verbs like *saigner* 'bleed', *rêvasser* 'daydream', *répondre* 'answer', *bailler* 'yawn', *pleurer* 'cry', *crisser* 'crunch', *frissonner* 'shiver', *frémir* 'shudder', *baver* 'dribble', *poudroyer* 'rise in clouds', and *palpiter* 'pound'.

ICs do show certain affinities for verbs of existence, for clitic pronouns like partitive *en* and locative *y*, but these can be shown to be related to their discourse-pragmatic functions. In general, ICs give a presentational value to a previously unidentifiable entity, as shown by the indefinite restriction on the postverbal NP (Lambrecht 1994). Two types of presentational constructions can be differentiated but they crosscut the unaccusative/unergative distinction. As shown in (22), existential ICs have a consistently generic or habitual reading, which also explains their affinity with the present and past imperfective tenses, regardless of verb class. They can all be paraphrased as [*il y a... qui...*], as in *Il y a beaucoup d'enfants qui disparaissent sans laisser de traces* 'There are many children who disappear without leaving any clue'.

(22) a. Il disparaît trop d'enfants sans laisser aucune trace.
'There disappear too many children without leaving any clue.'
b. Il aigrissait deux litres de lait dans le frigo.
'There turned sour two quarts of milk in the fridge.'
c. Il gisait un homme sur le trottoir.
'There was lying a man on the sidewalk.'
d. Il bourdonnait des milliers d'insectes autour de nous.
'There hummed thousands of insects around us.'

Event-reporting ICs are also attested with all intransitive verbs. Examples (23a–c) are natural answers to present or nonpresent tense forms of the question *Que se passe-t-il?* 'What is happening?'

(23) a. Il sort des enfants de partout.
'There exit children from everywhere.'
b. Il brille mille étoiles dans le ciel ce soir.
'There shine a thousand stars in the sky tonight.'
c. Il bondissait des chiens de tous les côtés.
'There came out dogs from all directions.'

Unergative ICs are occasionally said to require or strongly favor a locative or temporal adjunct. As it turns out, this constraint does not operate across the board (for reasons that are still unclear) nor does it distinguish unergative from unaccusative ICs. The sentences in (24) exemplify bare unergative ICs, while those in (25) show that both syntactic classes can exhibit a strong preference for an adjunct (all bare variants are dispreferred if not readily ungrammatical). The reader may verify that this constraint crosscuts the existential versus event-reporting dimension.

(24) a. Il subsiste un doute. (Existential)
'There remains some doubt.'
b. Il a sonné cinq heures. (Event reporting)
'There struck five o'clock.'

(25) a. Il entre des étrangers dans la cour. (Event reporting)
'There enter strangers in the yard.'
b. Il meurt trop d'enfants dans le Tiers-Monde. (Existential)
'There die too many children in the Third World.'
c. En 1970 il conduisait moins de femmes que maintenant. (Existential)
'In 1970 there drove fewer women than nowdays.'
d. Hier à Bobino il chantait un artiste espagnol inconnu en France. (Event reporting)
'Yesterday at the Bobino concert hall there sang a Spanish singer previously unknown in France.'

According to Lambrecht 1994, a main function of ICs is to demote the agentivity of the referent and promote the presentational function of the structure. Further specification of an event in terms of the location or temporality of the universe of discourse (e.g., *mourir dans le Tiers-Monde*) can be understood as serving that main function. It spreads the focus over properties of the event that are typically backgrounded in canonical sentences rather than concentrating it on the referent of the postverbal NP in the absence of an adjunct. That an existential interpretation is also enhanced by a specification of the location or temporality of the universe of discourse is not surprising either. The locative or temporal PP anchors the state of affairs in the universe of discourse, adding a dimension beyond its mere existence.

A final characteristic of French ICs is that they favor locative adjuncts that are realized as clitic pronoun *y*, as shown in (26). This preference is also tied to their discourse status. ICs introduce new, nontopical information. Adding contrastive focus via *ne...que* 'only' or *surtout* 'mostly' always yields an improved IC, as (27) illustrates.

(26) a. Il y circule des voitures. (y = dans les rues pavées de la ville)
'There circulate cars there.' (there = on the cobbled city streets)
b. Il y pousse des fraisiers. (y = le long du sentier)
'There grow strawberry plants there.' (there = along the pathway)

(27) a. Dans les rues il ne rôdait que des créatures de rêve.
'In the streets there roamed only fantasy creatures.'
b. Il y pousse surtout des fraisiers.
'There grow mostly strawberry plants there.'

The *y* preference follows from a cognitive constraint limiting the number of inaccessible (new) referents that can be introduced at any one time in a clause to one (Lambrecht 1994, 170). Expressing a locative adjunct as *y* allows the cognitive constraint to be satisfied without losing the anchoring function of the locative. As a consequence, *y* does not detract from the focus on the existence of a particular state of affairs. By a similar reasoning process, the partitive clitic pronoun *en* should also enhance an IC—and it does. Most spontaneous elicitations of ICs naturally start as *Il en* V..., and many examples in Hériau ([1976] 1980) involve *en* rather than a full postverbal NP.

(28) a. Il y dort plusieurs chats.
   'There sleep several of them there.'
   b. Il en dort un au coin du feu.
   'There sleeps one of them by the fireplace.'

In sum, there is no empirical basis for claiming that French ICs are restricted to verbs whose argument is internal (e.g., unaccusative and passive). The factors that do or do not enhance particular instances of the construction, such as partitive *en* and locative *y*, are independent of any subclass of verbs and point to discourse-pragmatic constraints.

13.4.2 Participial Constructions and Unaccusativity

Participial constructions (PCs)—including predicative constructions, adnominal participial adjectives (APAs), and Participial Absolutes (PAs)—have been widely used as syntactic tests for unaccusativity in Romance (e.g., Legendre 1989; Perlmutter 1989; Rosen 1988). We reexamine them here in light of the telicity distinction introduced earlier to characterize the difference between inchoative *casser* versus *se casser*. The main types of PCs are exemplified with a transitive verb in (29).

(29) a. Le mur est peint.
   'The wall is painted.'
   b. Le mur peint hier (par X) a été détruit ce matin.
   'The wall painted yesterday (by X) was destroyed this morning.'
   c. (Une fois) le mur peint (par X),...
   '(Once) the wall painted (by X),...'

Only one argument may appear in PCs, which in turn imposes a restriction on transitive verbs. Only the internal argument may appear. The agent, if it appears at all, must surface as an adjunct, as shown in (29b–c).[4] The outcome is therefore homophonous with the passive form of transitive verbs, minus the auxiliary itself in APAs and PAs (see Legendre 1989 for further discussion).

Telic predicates freely appear in PCs, pointing to an additional constraint of an aspectual nature. This is clear from the contrast in definiteness that distinguishes the internal arguments in (30) and the telic interpretation of activity verbs like *peindre* 'paint' in conjunction with a definite direct object (Dowty 1979). The ungrammaticality of atelic activity verbs like *conduire la voiture pendant des heures* 'drive the car for hours' as well as of atelic stative verbs like *exister* 'exist', *durer* 'last', and *subsister* 'remain' appear to follow from the telicity constraint as well.

(30) a. Le mur peint en une heure,...
 'The wall painted in an hour,...'
 b. *Un mur peint en une heure,...
 'A wall painted in an hour,...'

(31) *La voiture conduite pendant des heures,...
 'The car driven for hours,...'

(32) a. *Les dinosaures existé(s),...
 'Dinosaurs existed,...'
 b. *La famine duré,...
 'Famine lasted,...'
 c. *Le doute subsisté,...
 'Doubt remained,...'

The behavior of two further subclasses of verbs complicates this picture. As is well known, atelic manner-of-motion verbs take on a telic interpretation when they appear with a specified goal, as shown in (33). However, the telic interpretation of *courir à l'école* 'run to school' does not render it grammatical in PCs. This shows that the one-argument constraint and the telicity constraint are not sufficient to characterize PCs in French. Arguably, (34a–b) are ungrammatical because *courir* (with or without a specified goal) is an unergative verb (Legendre 1989).

(33) a. *L'enfant a mis dix minutes à courir dans le parc.
 'The child took ten minutes to run in the park.'
 b. *L'enfant a couru dans le parc en dix minutes.
 'The child ran in the park for ten minutes.'
 c. L'enfant a mis dix minutes à courir à l'école.
 'The child took ten minutes to run to school.'
 d. L'enfant a couru à l'école en dix minutes.
 'The child ran to school in ten minutes.'

(34) a. *L'enfant couru dans le parc,...
 'The child run in the park,...'
 b. *L'enfant couru à l'école,...
 'The child run to school,...'

While telic *courir* is syntactically unergative, atelic *rester* 'stay' must be analyzed as unaccusative. This is because *rester*, contrary to other atelic verbs of state like *exister*, *durer*, and *subsister*, is grammatical in PCs, as shown in (35), in contrast with ungrammatical (32).

(35) Restée seule pendant des heures,...
 'Stayed alone for hours,...'

In sum, PCs are subject to three constraints, only two of which need to be satisfied by any grammatical sentence: (i) one argument only, (ii) internal argument only, and (iii) telic predicate only. As is clear from the patterns in (34) and (35), telicity is the weakest constraint. In general, telicity goes hand in hand with unaccusativity. Where it does not, as in (34) and (35), the structural property requiring an internal argument prevails.

Unfortunately, the discussion of PCs cannot inform the issue of whether inchoative *casser* is unergative or unaccusative because the participle *cassé(e)* is ambiguous between its three variants, including transitive *casser* and inchoative *se casser*. The mere existence of a transitive counterpart allows the three constraints to be satisfied, with the result that *casser* (along with all other inchoatives) is grammatical in all PCs.

(36) a. La branche est cassée.
 'The branch is broken.'
 b. La branche cassée a été enlevée.
 'The broken branch was removed.'
 c. Cassée en trois morceaux, la branche a été enlevée.
 'Broken into three pieces, the branch was removed.'

One cannot conclude either that inchoative *casser* is unergative on the basis of its auxiliary choice (*avoir* 'have') or its atelicity. On the one hand, *rester* is atelic, yet it is unaccusative, as shown above. On the other, verbs denoting a change of state that do not have a transitive counterpart—including *faner* 'fade', *éclore* 'hatch', and *périr* 'perish'—can be argued to be unaccusative on the basis of their grammaticality in PCs, yet they select *avoir*.

(37) a. Les oeufs sont éclos.
 'The eggs are hatched.'
 b. Il a voulu des oeufs éclos.
 'He wanted hatched eggs.'
 c. (Une fois) les oeufs éclos,...
 'Once the eggs hatched,...'
 d. Les oeufs ont éclos.
 'The eggs hatched.'

Auxiliary selection in the periphrastic past tense is tied to lexicoaspectual properties rather than syntactic properties of individual verbs, as argued in Sorace 2000, Legendre and Sorace 2003, as well as Legendre 2007a, 2007b.

Labelle's claim that nonreflexive inchoatives are unergative came at a high price. Assigning the status of internal argument to inchoative *se casser* and external argument to inchoative *casser* forced her to weaken the universal principle regulating the syntactic realization of thematic arguments known as the Universal Alignment Hypothesis (Perlmutter and Postal 1984) or the Uniformity of Theta Assignment Hypothesis (Baker 1988). This principle determines that the argument status of *casser* is identical in its three variants and internal. In other words, the U(T)AH—if it is undominated in French—forces an unaccusative analysis of inchoatives derived from transitives, irrespective of their morphology. The issue of whether the U(T)AH is ever violated in French is best left for future exploration. For now, we conclude that there is no reason, empirical or theoretical, to abandon the claim that all inchoatives are unaccusative in French.

Notes

1. In general, atelic verbs are compatible with an adverbial phrase spanning the duration of an interval (e.g., *pendant une heure* 'for an hour'), provided the time frame is pragmatically appropriate and the predicate denotes a nonpunctual event. The latter restriction is presumably the reason why *casser* is ungrammatical in *La branche a cassé pendant trois secondes 'the branch broke for three seconds'.

2. The reader is warned that in some works in OT semantics and pragmatics, '$a < b$' is used to mean 'a is more harmonic than b'; here we adopt the usage standard in OT (from Prince and Smolensky [1993] 2004), in which it means 'a is less harmonic than b'.

3. We thank Catherine Chvany for bringing Rivière's work to our attention.

4. The exception is the predicative construction—for example, *Le mur est peint* 'The wall is painted'. An adjunct *par*-phrase is ungrammatical presumably because this construction has a resultant state interpretation.

References

Baker, M. 1988. *Incorporation: A theory of grammatical function changing*. Chicago: University of Chicago Press.

Blutner, R. 2000. Some aspects of optimality in natural language interpretation. *Journal of Semantics* 17:189–216.

Boersma, P. 1998. *Functional phonology: Formalizing the interactions between articulatory and perceptual drives*. The Hague: Holland Academic Graphics.

Bouchard, D. 1984. *On the content of empty categories*. Dordrecht: Foris.

Bouchard, D. 1995. *The semantics of syntax*. Chicago: University of Chicago Press.

Cummins, S. 1996. Meaning and mapping. Doctoral dissertation, University of Toronto.

Dowty, D. 1979. *Word meaning and Montague grammar*. Dordrecht: Reidel.

Goldsmith, J. A. 1993. Harmonic phonology. In J. A. Goldsmith, ed., *The last phonological rule*. Chicago: University of Chicago Press.

Grimshaw, J. 1990. *Argument structure*. Cambridge, MA: MIT Press.

Grimshaw, J. 1997. Projection, heads, and optimality. *Linguistic Inquiry* 28:373–422.

Hendriks, P., and H. de Hoop. 2001. Optimality theoretic semantics. *Linguistics and Philosophy* 24(1):1–32.

Hériau, M. [1976] 1980. Le verbe impersonnel en français moderne. Doctoral dissertation, Université de Haute-Bretagne. Lille: Atelier de reproduction de thèses, Université de Lille III.

Kayne, R. 1975. *French syntax: The transformational cycle*. Cambridge, MA: MIT Press.

Labelle, M. 1992. Change of state and valency. *Journal of Linguistics* 28:375–414.

Lambrecht, K. 1994. *Information structure and sentence form*. Cambridge: Cambridge University Press.

Legendre, G. 1989. Unaccusativity in French. *Lingua* 79:95–164.

Legendre, G. 1990. French impersonal constructions. *Natural Language and Linguistic Theory* 8:81–128.

Legendre, G. 2007a. Optimizing auxiliary selection in Romance. In R. Aranovich, ed., *Split auxiliary systems: A cross-linguistic perspective*, 145–180. New York: John Benjamins.

Legendre, G. 2007b. On the typology of auxiliary selection. *Lingua* 117(9):1522–1540.

Legendre, G., J. Grimshaw, and S. Vikner, eds. 2001. *OT syntax*. Cambridge, MA: MIT Press.

Legendre, G., Y. Miyata, and P. Smolensky. 1990. Can connectionism contribute to syntax? Harmonic grammar, with an application. In M. Ziolkowski, M. Noske, and K. Deaton, eds., *Proceedings of the Chicago Linguistic Society* 26:237–252.

Legendre, G., and A. Sorace. 2003. Auxiliaires et intransitivité en français et dans les langues romanes. In Danièle Godard, ed., *Les langues romanes: Problèmes de la phrase simple*, 185–233. Paris: CNRS Éditions.

Marandin, J-M. 2001. Unaccusative inversion in French. In Y. d'Hulst, J. Rooryck, and J. Schroten, eds., *Romance Languages and Linguistic Theory 1999*, 195–222. Amsterdam: John Benjamins.

Marantz, A. 1984. *On the nature of grammatical relations*. Cambridge, MA: MIT Press.

Perlmutter, D. M. 1978. Impersonal passives and the unaccusative hypothesis. In *Proceedings of the Fourth Annual Meeting of the Berkeley Linguistics Society*, 157–189. Berkeley: University of California Press.

Perlmutter, D. M. 1989. Multiattachment and the unaccusative hypothesis: The perfect auxiliary in Italian. *Probus* 1:63–119.

Perlmutter, D. M., and P. M. Postal. 1984. The 1-advancement exclusiveness law. In D. Perlmutter and C. Rosen, eds., *Studies in relational grammar 2*, 81–125. Chicago: University of Chicago Press.

Pollock, J-Y. 1986. Sur la syntaxe de *en* et le paramètre du sujet nul. In M. Ronat and D. Couquaux, eds., *La grammaire modulaire*, 211–246. Paris: Editions de Minuit.

Postal, P. M. 1986. *Studies of passive clauses*. Albany: State University of New York Press.

Prince, A., and P. Smolensky. [1993] 2004. *Optimality Theory: Constraint interaction in generative grammar*: Technical report, Rutgers University and University of Colorado at Boulder, 1993. ROA 537, 2002. Revised version, Oxford: Blackwell, 2004.

Rivière, N. 1981. *La construction impersonelle en français contemporain*. Paris: Jean-Favard.

Rosen, C. 1988. *The relational structure of reflexive clauses: Evidence from Italian*. New York: Garland.

Ruwet, N. 1972. *Théorie syntaxique et syntaxe du français*. Paris: Editions du Seuil.

Ruwet, N. 1988. Les verbes météorologiques et l'hypothèse inaccusative. In C. Blanche-Benveniste, A. Chervel, and M. Gross, eds., *Mélanges à la mémoire de Jean Stéfanini*.

Smolensky, P. 1996. On the comprehension/production dilemma in child language. *Linguistic Inquiry* 27:720–731.

Smolensky, P., G. Legendre, and B. B. Tesar. 2006. Optimality theory: The structure, use, and acquisition of grammatical knowledge. In P. Smolensky and G. Legendre, eds., *The harmonic mind: From neural computation to optimality-theoretic grammar*, vol. 1, 453–544. Cambridge, MA: MIT Press.

Sorace, A. 2000. Gradients in auxiliary selection with intransitive verbs. *Language* 76:859–890.

Tesar, B. B., and P. Smolensky. 2000. *Learnability in optimality theory*. Cambridge, MA: MIT Press.

Wilson, C. 2001. Bidirectional optimization and the theory of anaphora. In G. Legendre, S. Vikner, and J. Grimshaw, eds., *Optimality-theoretic syntax*. Cambridge, MA: MIT Press.

Zribi-Hertz, A. 1987. La réflexivité ergative en français moderne. *Le Français Moderne* 55:23–54.

14 On the Analytic Expression of Predicates in Meskwaki

Philip S. LeSourd

14.1 Introduction

Verbs in Meskwaki (also known as Fox), an Algonquian language of Iowa, are frequently modified by one or more preverbal particles or *preverbs*, as illustrated in (1). Here and below, preverbs and the stems of the associated verbs are underlined.[1]

(1) a. K-îh=<u>anemi</u>   <u>owîwi</u>.
      2-FUT=continue have.wife.IND
      'You (sg.) will continue to have a wife.' (Michelson 1921, 64.8)
   b. Mêmêchiki=mekoho k-îh=<u>anemi</u>   peshikwi <u>âchimoh</u>-etî-pwa.
      surely=EMPH   2-FUT=continue straight tell-RECIP-22.IND
      'You will surely continue to tell each other in an upright fashion.'
      (Michelson 1921, 56.32–33)

Many of the same forms are used as modifiers of nouns and other particles—that is, as *prenouns* and *preparticles*.

  Both phonologically and syntactically, preverbs are independent words. A preverb-verb complex may accordingly be interrupted by one or more enclitic particles or by one or more "included" words or phrases, in the terminology of Bloomfield 1946, 103. Some typical examples are given in (2). The preverb *anemi* 'along, continuing' in (2a) is separated from the verb with which it is construed by the enclitic particle =*chîhi* 'it was discovered'. In (2b), the preverb *pwâwi* 'not' is separated from a following preverb by three enclitic particles and the pronoun *owiyêhani* 'someone (obv.)', the latter functioning as the subject of the verb with which both preverbs are construed.

(2) a. Peteki   êh=inâpi-chi,   êh=<u>anemi</u>=**chîhi**
       backward AOR=look.there-3.CONJ AOR=continue=it.was.discovered
       <u>anehkîhi</u>-nichi wîtêm-âchini.
       be.few-3'.CONJ accompany-3'/3.OBV.SG.PART
       'When he looked back, it turned out that his companions were few (lit., the one he accompanied was few).' (Jones 1907, 338.17)

b. **Êh**=pwâwi=**kêh**=**meko**='**pi**   owiyêh-ani   kashki pyênot-aminichi.
AOR=not=and=EMPH=REPORT someone-OBV.SG be.able come.to-3′/3IN.CONJ
'And it is said no one (obv.) could ever reach it.' (Michelson 1917, 52)

Dahlstrom (1987, 2000) demonstrates that the variety of material that may be included between a preverb and the verb with which it is associated precludes any analysis of such material as syntactically incorporated. Thus preverb-verb complexes are clearly phrasal in character.

Despite their syntactic status as phrases, preverb-verb complexes are treated in certain respects as units on a par with single words. For example, inflectional prefixes are added directly to a verb when no preverb is used, but are added to the first preverb in a preverb-verb complex. Thus the first-person prefix *ne-* is attached to *wâpam-* 'look at' in (3a), but is attached instead to the preverb *pyêchi* 'come' in (3b).

(3) a. **Ne**-wâpam-âwa.
1-look.at-1/3.IND
'I look at him.' (Jones 1911, 818)
b. **Ne**-pyêchi ke-tânes-a   wâpam-âpena.
1-come   2-daughter-PROX.SG look.at-11/3.IND
'We (exc.) have come to see your (sg.) daughter.' (Michelson 1917, 51)

Because preverb-verb complexes and simplex verbs receive parallel treatment in inflection, it has been a standard assumption in Algonquian linguistics since the pioneering work of Jones (1904, 1911) that preverb-verb sequences in Meskwaki are compounds of some kind. Michelson (1917, 50–52) suggested that such sequences are formed by "loose composition"—that is, through a process that derives compound stems whose members retain considerable syntactic independence. An analysis of preverb-verb complexes as compounds raises problems, however, for any theory of grammar that treats all syntactic words as independent lexical items and attributes the concatenation of words into phrases solely to principles of syntax. I will argue below that the evidence of inflection, in and of itself, provides only weak support for an analysis of preverb-verb complexes as lexical formations. Goddard (1988, 1990b, 2002) has called attention to several additional properties of Meskwaki preverbs, however, that pose a significant challenge for theories that postulate strict separation of syntax from lexicon.

Goddard's observations may be classified under three headings. First, the semantic interpretation of preverb-verb complexes does not always conform to their syntactic bracketing. In particular, a preverb may be construed with the initial component of the stem of the verb that it modifies, rather than with the stem as a whole, suggesting that preverb-stem combinations may function as bases for derivation. Second, certain preverbs are valence-bearing particles. A preverb-verb complex that includes one of these preverbs takes a complement that cannot occur with the modified verb when it is used alone: adding a preverb of this class to a verb serves to modify the verb's syntactic argument structure. Finally, certain morphological generalizations can only be stated if verb stems and preverb-verb complexes are parallel formations. Goddard concludes that the preverb-verb complexes of Meskwaki have the status of lexical items. If the concatenation of preverbs with verbs is accomplished in the syntax, he suggests, then lexical processes of Meskwaki must have access to the output of syntactic processes.

I argue here that Goddard's observations concerning the interpretation of preverbs do not, in fact, pose a problem for standard theories of the lexicon, since they can be given a purely semantic account along the lines of the analysis that Beard (1991) has proposed for comparable "bracketing paradoxes" in English. In essence, Beard argues that apparent bracketing paradoxes of the relevant kind simply reflect the fact that a modifier may be construed with a semantic component of the modified expression. As he demonstrates, such effects may be observed in English even in cases in which the modified expression is not morphologically complex. Since "bracketing paradoxes" can arise in the absence of bracketing, the semantic effects in question appear to be independent of syntactic or morphological structure.

Craig and Hale (1988) have argued that valence-changing preverbs in several languages of the Americas are derived from postpositions via syntactic head movement and adjunction—that is, by incorporation in the sense of Baker 1988. An analysis along these lines for Meskwaki derives a measure of support from the fact that the preverbs of the language may typically occur as independent adverbial particles as well. When a valence-bearing particle that ordinarily functions as a preverb is employed in this manner as an independent adverbial, it governs a complement of its own, which is to say that it functions as a postposition.

An incorporation analysis of the valence-changing preverbs of Meskwaki nonetheless faces two serious problems. First, postpositional phrases are systematically optional constituents of clauses, and are thus presumably to be analyzed as adjuncts. If incorporation may take place only from complement positions, as Baker argues, then postpositions cannot be the syntactic source of valence-changing preverbs in Meskwaki, since postpositional phrases are not complements in this language. Second, the preverbs in question are not, in fact, incorporated: preverbs and verbs in Meskwaki are syntactically independent words. I conclude, then, that the valence-changing properties of Meskwaki preverbs do indeed pose a problem for any theory of the lexicon that permits only single words to constitute lexical entries.

The morphological relationships that obtain between preverb-verb complexes and simplex verb stems provide a basis for another type of argument that preverb-verb combinations are lexical formations. Preverbs, as Goddard has noted, are derived from *initials*, morphemes or complexes of morphemes that also function as initial components of verb stems. Productive morphological processes derive initials from noun or verb stems or *themes*—that is, partly inflected stems. Final components of verb stems, or *finals*, may likewise be morphologically simple or complex. In particular, finals may be derived from verb stems.

As it happens, however, the derivation of finals from verb stems is not productive. Thus some verb stems are matched by finals, while others are not. For the most part, the effect of combining an initial with a stem is achieved by combining the initial with a final corresponding to the stem, provided that one exists. Thus the effect of combining an initial with a verb stem is usually achieved by deriving a unitary verb stem, if this is possible. On the other hand, if no final exists that can stand in for the stem in question, then the combination of an initial with a stem is instead made by deriving a preverb from the initial and employing it as a modifier of the stem. That is, the combination of an initial and stem takes the form of a preverb-verb complex, rather than a unitary verb stem, when this is the only option available for combining the two in a single predicate.

Clearly, then, preverb-verb complexes and unitary verb stems are in some sense parallel formations. Moreover, the fact that the use of a unitary stem is typically preferred, when one is available, can be described as a morphological blocking effect: the existence of a unitary verb stem ordinarily blocks the formation of a preverb-verb complex with the same meaning. Blocking relationships of this type routinely obtain among lexical formations (Aronoff 1976; Bochner 1993). Thus the participation of preverb-verb complexes in blocking is predicted if such formations are lexically derived.

Goddard (1988, 1990b, 2002) reasons that if both complex verb stems and preverb-verb complexes are lexically formed, then their parallel structure can be described in terms of a network of paradigmatic relationships among sets of such formations. An account that would take only verb stems to be lexically derived, leaving the concatenation of preverbs and verbs to be handled entirely in syntax, would provide no comparable way to state the systematic relationships that obtain among formations of the two kinds.

Goddard's reasoning in this matter seems to me to be compelling. I would like to suggest, however, that the properties of the preverb-verb complexes of Meskwaki that Goddard has identified do not require us to suppose, as he has argued, that the formation of lexical items in Meskwaki must be stated in terms of syntactically derived structures. This conclusion follows only if lexical entries are restricted to stating the properties of single syntactic words—that is, if only synthetic verb stems, and not their analytically expressed counterparts, may be represented in the lexicon. If analytically expressed predicates may be directly represented in lexical entries, as Ackerman and Webelhuth (1998) have suggested, then the preverb-verb complexes of Meskwaki may be analyzed as lexical formations on a par with simplex stems. Any generalization that covers predicates of both types may then be given a unitary statement as a lexical rule. I do not attempt to develop a formal theory of this kind here, however. The present chapter aims only to establish an outline of the phenomena that such a theory will need to accommodate.[2]

14.2 Preverbs and Inflection

Verbs in Meskwaki are inflected in twenty-six paradigms or *modes* (Dahlstrom 2000). These may be classified into three formal types or *orders*: the independent, conjunct, and imperative orders. The forms of the three types have complex and partly overlapping syntactic distributions. To a first approximation, we may think of independent forms as occurring in main clauses, while conjunct forms occur in subordinate clauses. Forms of the aorist mode of the conjunct order are regularly used in main clauses in hearsay narratives, however, and the negative mode used in ordinary main clauses is a conjunct formation. Imperative forms are used primarily in commands.

Two person-marking prefixes are employed in inflection in the independent order: first-person *ne(t)-* and second-person *ke(t)-*. (The allomorphs with *t* occur before vowels, those without *t* before nonsyllabics.) These prefixes index subjects in some forms, objects in others. As I have already noted, they are added directly to the verb if no preverb is used, but to the first preverb in a preverb-verb complex. Examples with the prefix *ke-* are given in (4). Note that the inflectional affixes, given in boldface, effectively bracket the preverb-verb complex, whether or not it is continuous.

(4) a. Pêhki=wîna=meko wîshikesiwen-i **ke-mîn-ene**.
 really=but=EMPH strength-IN.SG 2-give-1/2.IND
 'But I give you (sg.) great strength.' (Michelson 1927, 24.28)
 b. Nahi, châki=kohi **ke-pyêchi nân-ene-pwa**.
 hey all=certainly 2-come go.get-1/22-22.IND
 'Well, I have come to get you (pl.).' (Jones 1907, 52.7–8)
 c. **Ke-peshikwi**=châh=meko mani **wîtamô-ne-pwa** ...
 2-straight=so=EMPH this.IN tell-1/22-22.IND
 'I have told you (pl.) this in an upright manner.' (Michelson 1925, 136.8–9)

Other inflectional material is suffixal, including all of the affixes used in the conjunct and imperative inflectional systems. These suffixes are always added to the verb itself.

The prefixes used in independent inflection indicate only the person of the indexed participant (subject or object). Both person and number are marked by suffixes, but only for plural participants. In both (4b) and (4c), for example, the second-person prefix *ke-* and the second-person plural suffix *-pwa* function together to indicate that the object of the verb is second person and plural.

Two proclitic tense markers have distributions comparable to those of the personal prefixes—that is, they are added to the first preverb in a preverb-verb complex, but to the verb itself if no preverb is used.[3] These are the future proclitic *wîh*=, used both with independent and with conjunct forms, and the aorist proclitic *êh*=, used only in certain conjunct paradigms. The personal prefixes combine irregularly with the future proclitic, yielding the forms *nîh*= and *kîh*= for the first and second persons, respectively. The distribution of *wîh*= is illustrated in (5).

(5) a. Âkwi=kêh=êyîki **wîh**=<u>kemôtem</u>-akwini, kochîhi k-**îh**=<u>manetôwi</u>-pena.
not=and=also FUT=steal.from-12.NEG although 2-FUT=be.manitou-12.IND
'Likewise we (inc.) shall not steal it from them, although we (inc.) are to be manitous.' (Michelson 1921, 42.34–35)

b. K-**îh**=<u>wîshiki</u>=châh=meko <u>nenehkênet</u>-a.
2-FUT-strongly-so-EMPH think.of-2/3IN.IND
'You (sg.) must keep it firmly in mind.' (Dahlstrom 1987, 72)

An ablaut process known as *initial change* modifies short vowels in word-initial syllables in several paradigms of the conjunct type: *a* and *e* are replaced by *ê*, as is word-initial *i*; *o* is replaced by *wê*. The distribution of the sites at which initial change is carried out again parallels that of the personal prefixes: the first syllable of the first preverb in a preverb-verb complex is subject to ablaut; if no preverb is used, then the first syllable of the verb stem itself is affected. Examples are given in (6)–(7). The boldfaced items appear in their unchanged forms in the examples labeled (a) and in their changed forms in the corresponding examples labeled (b). Note that the first component of the verb stem is subject to change in (6b), where no preverb is used, while the first member of the preverb-verb complex bears change in (7b).

(6) a. takâwi=meko êh=<u>kashki</u> **ish**-iwen-ânichi
a.little=EMPH AOR=be.able thus-lead-3'/3'.CONJ
'he was able to take him a little ways in that direction' (Jones 1907, 202.15–16)

b. Îni='pi **êsh**-inâkê-chi mani nakamôn-i.
that=REPORT thus-sing-3.CONJ this.IN song-IN.SG
'That, it is said, is how he sang this song.' (Michelson 1927, 86.38)

(7) a. Nahi, **natawi**=nîhka mani mawi wâpat-âtâwe owâsîsani.
hey seek=EXCLAM this.IN go look.at-12/3IN.IMP nest
'Hey, let's try to go look at this nest!' (Dahlstrom 1987, 68)

b. **nêtawi** mani wêwênênet-akiki net-ahki-m-i.
seek this.IN control-33/3IN.PROX.PL.PART 1-earth-POSS-IN.SG
'the ones who sought to control my earth' (Dahlstrom 1987, 68)

Several preverbs in Meskwaki have a distinctly grammatical character. For example, the preverb *âmi* 'would, should' serves as "the regular substitution for the potential inflection in participles," or relative clause forms, since the suffixes that index a relativized constituent in such forms occupy the position in which a potential aspect marker would appear (Goddard 1988, 114). Thus *âmi* is used in (8a) with essentially the force of potential aspect. Compare the corresponding nonparticipial form in (8b), with potential inflection.

(8) a. **âmi** seswam-ech-i
would spray.on.by.mouth-X/3-IN.SG.PART
'that (in.) which he is to be sprayed with' (Goddard 1987, 110)
b. ... ahkowi='pi <u>och-ishim</u>-**enêha** wîtekôwa
in.the.rear=REPORT from-lay-X/3.POT owl
'... the owl should be laid behind (them), it is said' (Michelson 1921, 18.26–27)

The negative preverb *pwâwi* 'fail to, not' is involved in a complex set of relationships involving both inflectional affixes and independent particles. The negative particles *âkwi*, *kâta*, and *awita*, which do not have the syntax of preverbs, are "used for main clause indicative verbs, prohibitions, and potential verbs, respectively," while "all other types of verbs are negated by the preverb" *pwâwi* (Dahlstrom 1987, 70). As Bloomfield (1927, 210) notes, however, "the negative itself is negated by composition with" *pwâwi*, as shown in (9).

(9) Âkwi=kêhi wîh=<u>pwâwi</u> kehkênet-amanini.
not=and FUT=not know-2/3IN.NEG
'You (sg.) would not fail to know about it.' (Dahlstrom 1996b, 109)

It would appear, then, that the preverb *pwâwi* is not, strictly speaking, in complementary distribution with *âkwi* 'not'. Similarly, Goddard (1988, 114) notes that *âmi* 'would, should' does not function solely as a marker of potential aspect. Thus while some Meskwaki preverbs have clearly taken on grammatical functions, they do not appear to have the formal status of inflectional elements. Preverbs of this kind are the functional equivalents of inflectional morphemes, but not their formal equivalents.

Given that preverbs are not themselves inflectional elements, what can we conclude about their status from the way they are treated in inflection? It is clear that a suite of inflectional processes, including initial change as well as the addition of person-marking prefixes and tense-marking proclitics, target the left margin of the preverb-verb complex, thus treating such formations on a par with unitary verb forms. This observation is consistent with an analysis of preverbs as prior members in verbal compounds. Indeed, the treatment of preverbs in inflection has been widely cited as evidence that preverb-verb complexes in Meskwaki have a morphological status comparable to that of verbs (Dahlstrom 1987, 2000; Goddard 1988, 2002; Ackerman and LeSourd 1994; Ackerman and Webelhuth 1998; Crysmann 1999).

Given the mechanisms available for the analysis of inflection in contemporary syntactic theories, however, it is not clear that this conclusion must follow. Suppose that Meskwaki preverb-verb complexes are represented in syntax only as belonging to some phrasal category (say V-bar) in which preverbs are represented as verbal modifiers. Suppose, further, that we make the standard assumption that the minimal instantiation of the category in question consists of a verb alone, with no such modifiers. Now all that we will need to do to obtain the right distribution of inflectional material is to state this distribution in terms of phrasal constituents of the appropriate type. Under minimalist assumptions, for example, we might propose that a superordinate functional head bears inflectional features that need to be checked by some element within the constituent that includes the verb and its modifiers, either by raising or by agreement. We can then invoke Relativized Minimality, or some comparable principle, to ensure that only the highest element within this constituent that has the potential to bear the features in question is permitted to raise (or agree), and thus that only the highest such element can in fact bear the features in question in any derivation that does not crash. Assuming that left-to-right order reflects syntactic superiority, the highest such element will be the leftmost preverb if one is used, otherwise the verb itself.

Analogs of this sort of analysis in other frameworks can easily be imagined. It would seem, then, that the facts of inflection in Meskwaki tell us only that preverb-verb complexes and simplex verbs are parallel structures. The phenomena in question do not actually establish either that preverb-verb complexes have a status comparable to that of words or that such combinations are lexically formed.

14.3 Preverbs and Semantic Interpretation

Verb stems in Meskwaki, as in other Algonquian languages, may typically be analyzed into components, which may themselves be morphologically complex (Goddard 1990b). Each of these components belongs to one of three position classes: *initials* occur in stem-initial position, *medials* in stem-medial position, and *finals* in stem-final position. A stem ordinarily includes at least an initial and a final. Thus, for example, the stem *kîshk-eshw-* 'cut' that appears in the verb *kîshk-eshw-êwa* 'he cuts him (off, up)' consists of an initial *kîshk-* 'severed, cut off, cut through' plus a final *-(e)shw-* 'act on by cutting edge'. The stem of *kîshk-ikwê-shw-êwa* 'he cuts off his head' includes the same initial and final, here separated by the medial *-ikwê-* 'neck' (Goddard 1988, 60–61). Initials and finals are semantically diverse, while medials typically have concrete, nounlike meanings, as in the present example.

Components of verb stems may themselves be derived from stems or from themes (partly inflected stems), yielding derived stems of considerable internal complexity. In the following sentence, for example, the stem of the verb *otôtêweniw-âchim-âpi* 'they are said to have a village' consists of an initial *otôtêweniw-* derived from the stem *otôtêweni-* 'have a village', which is in turn based on *otôtêwen-*, a partly inflected form of the stem of the noun *ôtêwen-i* 'village' made by adding the third-person possessor prefix *ot-*. The final component of the stem 'tell about someone having a village' is *-âchim-* 'tell about'.

(10) Nekotahi   îniyêka   otôtêweniw-âchim-âpi.
     somewhere   those.PROX.ABS   have.village-tell.about-X/33.IND
     'It is said of them that they have a town somewhere.' (Goddard 1988, 71)

As Goddard (1988) notes, the initial component of a complex stem of this type is interpreted as representing a predicate that stands as the logical complement of the predicate represented by the final: in this case, the logical complement of 'it is said of them' is 'they have a village'. On the basis of this observation, he suggests that a sentence like (10) is derived from an underlying biclausal structure through the incorporation of the verb of the complement clause into the verb of the matrix clause.

In support of an analysis of (10) along these lines, Goddard points out that *nekotahi* 'somewhere', superficially an oblique complement of *otôtêweniw-âchim-* 'tell about someone's having a village', is interpreted as a complement only of the initial *otôtêweniw-* 'have a village': *nekotahi* 'somewhere' specifies the location of the village in question, not the location of the relevant event of speaking. (We will see in section 14.5 that locative expressions of the kind at issue here are indeed verbal complements and not adjuncts.) Thus, he concludes, the formation of complex stems that represent logically complex predicates presupposes the application of syntactic rules.

Such an analysis is possible, however, only if syntactic theory admits the type of restructuring operation that Goddard's proposal presupposes. This assumption has been widely challenged. The alternative, of course, is to postulate hierarchically organized semantic structures for individual lexical items. We can then formulate rules of word formation that will permit a derived word to inherit the semantic representation of its base as a component of its own lexical representation, together with an appropriately linked set of syntactic arguments. In the present case, the stem of *otôtêweniw-âchim-* 'tell about someone's having a village' will be associated, as a single lexical item, with a logical structure that includes a representation of the meaning of *otôtêweni-* 'have a village' as a component of its meaning and with a grammatical function structure that specifies that it takes a subject, an object, and a locative complement. That the locative complement is interpreted as situating the village in question, rather than an act of speaking, will then follow from the fact that the representation of this complement is tagged in the lexical entry for the complex stem as a logical argument of the component predicate. Thus both the complement-taking properties of a stem like 'tell about someone's having a village' and the semantic interpretation of the complements in question can readily be accommodated without postulating postsyntactic stem formation. The internally complex semantic structure of a verb like 'tell about someone's having a village' must be available to rules of semantic interpretation, but need not be available to the syntax.

Other interpretative properties of preverbs likewise suggest that syntactic structure does not always parallel semantic structure. Goddard (1988, 2002) points out, for example, that a preverb may function semantically to modify just the initial component of a verb stem, rather than the stem as a whole. Typical examples are given in (11)–(12).

(11) Êh=kîshi=meko nêsêw-itêhê-nichi o-kwis-ani.
AOR=completed=EMPH get.well-think-3OBV.CONJ 3-son-OBV.SG
'(The man's) son thought that (the man) was already well.' (Goddard 1988, 70)

(12) ...êh=pwâwi=mekoho nenoshê-hkâno-chi
AOR=not=EMPH hear-pretend-3.CONJ
'... and he played as if he was deaf' (Goddard 2002, 2)

The preverb in each of these examples is construed only with the first component of the stem of the verb that it modifies: 'he thought the man was already well', rather than 'his son already thought...'; 'pretended not to hear', rather than 'did not pretend to hear'. Thus the preverb-verb complexes in these examples present us with a type of "bracketing paradox." The interpretation indicated for the preverb-verb combination in (11), for example, suggests that its components are semantically grouped as shown in (13a); but the morphological and syntactic structure would appear be that shown in (13b).

(13) a. [kîshi nêsêwi]-têhê-
completed get well think
'think someone to have recovered'
b. kîshi [nêsêwi-têhê]-

In each of these, the initial component of the stem of the modified verb is itself derived from a verb stem: *nêsêw-* in (11) is based on *nêsê-* 'get well, survive'; *nenoshê-* in (12) is 'hear'. Goddard (2002, 3) notes, however, that comparable bracketing paradoxes arise in cases involving initials that are not derived from stems. In (14), for example, the preverb *pyêchi* 'come' takes scope only over the initial *nîs-* 'down, descend, lower'; but *nîs-* is an underived initial, not a stem.

(14) Îni êh=pyêchi nîs-ênet-amâni nîyawi.
then AOR=come descend-consider-1/3IN.CONJ myself
'Then I imagined myself coming down.' (Goddard 2002, 3)

Thus the problem posed by such bracketing paradoxes cannot in general be solved either by positing syntactic verb incorporation or by deriving preverb-verb complexes with complex verbs from preverb-stem combinations.

Examples of this type are problematic, of course, only if we maintain that a modifier of a word must take the interpretation of the word as a whole as its scope. If, on the other hand, a modifier may be construed with a *component* of the meaning of the modified expression, then the fact that a preverb may take only the initial in a following verb stem as its scope is unsurprising. Beard (1991) has presented just such an account of comparable bracketing paradoxes in English.

The relevant English cases include examples like those in (15) and (16).

(15) a. [nuclear] [physicist] 'a physicist who is nuclear (to some project)'
     b. [nuclear physic]ist 'someone who studies nuclear physics'

(16) a. [criminal] [lawyer] 'a lawyer who is criminal'
     b. [criminal law]yer 'someone who practices criminal law'

As Beard (1991, 196) observes, "These constructions seem to have, in addition to a wide scope reading [[Xx][Yy]], exemplified by (a), which parallels syntactic structure, a narrow scope reading [[Xx Y]y], exemplified in (b), which does not. Under the assumption...that semantic operations preserve syntactic structure, the narrow scope reading is not predicted."

Beard's analysis proceeds by rejecting this assumption. He proposes instead that modifiers are not interpreted with respect to the semantic representation of the modified expression, taken as a whole, but rather with respect to components or features of this semantic representation, a procedure that he calls "decompositional composition." In support of this approach, he notes that scopal ambiguities like those observed in (15) and (16) may arise even in cases in which the modified expression is not morphologically complex, as in (17) and (18):

(17) *old friend*
    a. 'friend who is old'
    b. 'member of an old friendship'

(18) *good athlete*
    a. 'athlete who is a good person (in any of several senses)'
    b. 'someone who is good as an athlete, plays a sport well'

Here the narrow-scope reading (b) is available even though no morphological component of the modified noun corresponds to the semantically modified component of its meaning. Beard's proposal, he argues, "reduces the wide scope and narrow scope readings of attribute phrases to a question of which feature is selected, in effect making all attribute composition the same and obviating the distinction between wide scope and narrow scope readings of attribute phrases" (p. 195). A consequence of his proposal, he concludes, is that "bracketing paradoxes of the *nuclear physicist* type cannot be used to test or compare the adequacy of competing syntactic or morphological theories" (p. 227).

An approach to semantic interpretation in Meskwaki along the lines of Beard's "decompositional composition" finds support in two other observations of Goddard's. First, Goddard (2002, 3) notes that "all verbal modifiers have access to stem-internal morphology, not just arguments and preverbs." In (19), for example, the adverbial particle *masâchi* 'barely' clearly does not form part of the preverb-verb complex, since the verb word itself serves as host for the aorist proclitic in this example. The particle is nonetheless construed here only with the initial *konakwîw-* 'get through', not with the verb stem as a whole: the reading is "thought that they barely got through their lives," not "barely thought that they got through...."

(19) Nâhka=meko **masâchi** êh=<u>**konakwîw**</u>-ênet-aki   metemôka
again=EMPH   barely   AOR=get.through-consider-3/3IN.CONJ old.woman
owîyâwâwi.
them
'And again the old lady thought that they barely passed through with their lives.' (Goddard 2002, 3)

Goddard (2002, 4) further observes that a preverb may be interpreted as modifying a word that is not part of the preverb-verb complex. Thus the preverb *kîshâkochi* 'as much as possible' in (20) functions as a modifier of the preparticle-particle complex *nâwi=meko nenoswahkiwe* 'in the middle of a buffalo herd', included here between preverb and verb.

(20) Êh=**<u>kîshâkochi</u>**=chîhi=meko   nâhka **nâwi**=meko
AOR=as.much.as.possible=it.was.discovered=EMPH again   middle=EMPH
nenoswahkiwe   shekishi-ki.
in.buffalo.herd lie-3.CONJ
'She found that she was again lying in the very center of a herd of buffalo.' (Goddard 2002, 4)

It seems clear, then, that semantic interpretation in Meskwaki is not in general limited to composing the readings of syntactic or morphological constituents. But if this conclusion is correct, then Goddard's observations concerning the interpretation of preverb-verb complexes do not in fact provide evidence that bears on the syntactic or lexical derivation of such formations.

14.4 Preverb-Verb Complexes as Bases for Derivation?

Goddard (2002, 2) maintains that a "compound stem" in Meskwaki—that is, a combination of a preverb and a stem—"enters into derivation like a simple stem, despite having one or more internal word boundaries." The arguments he presents in support of this position, however, are based entirely on semantic "bracketing paradoxes" of the kind that we have just surveyed. As we have observed, such arguments from semantic interpretation are problematic.

Potentially more interesting from this point of view are derived nominals in Meskwaki that appear to be based on preverb-verb combinations. It is a standard assumption of lexicalist theories of syntax that only lexical rules may carry out derivational operations that result in a change of syntactic category. Thus a demonstration that preverb-verb combinations may serve as bases for category-changing derivation would provide strong support for the view that such combinations are lexically formed. As it turns out, however, the available evidence on this point is equivocal, since the productivity of the patterns of derivation at issue is doubtful.

A typical example of a derived nominal of a relevant type is the form *menwi-mehtosêneniwi-wen-i* 'good life'. The stem of this nominal appears to be derived from the preverb-verb combination *menwi mehtosêneniwi-* 'live well' by the addition of the derivational suffix *-wen-*, which forms abstract nouns (cf. *menwi mehtosêneniwiwa* 'he lives well'). The preverb *menwi* is not ordinarily used as a prenoun, so an analysis of 'good life' as a prenoun-noun complex is excluded (Bloomfield 1927, 190). But if a category-changing derivational process may take preverb-verb combinations as its input, then the lexical status of preverb-verb complexes would appear to be assured. (Precisely this line of reasoning is pursued by Ackerman and LeSourd 1994; see also Crysmann 1999.)

The argument is not as strong as it might seem, however. It is not at all clear that nominalizations in which the base of derivation includes a preverb are productively formed. Thomason (2005, 435–437), who reports several examples of this type, suggests that they are best regarded as idiomatic expressions. It seems likely, then, that the examples in question are simply lexically listed forms, not forms that reflect that application of a derivational process. If so, then the evidence of these examples does not, in the end, support the conclusion that preverb-verb complexes are lexically derived predicates. To determine whether expressions of this kind have the status of lexical items, we will need to look elsewhere.

14.5 Valence-Changing Preverbs

As we observed in section 14.3, a typical verb stem in Meskwaki consists of an initial plus a final, with or without an intervening medial. A monomorphemic initial is a *root*. A small but grammatically important class of such initials, which Bloomfield (1946, 120) terms *relative roots*, function to introduce reference to a semantic domain, but do not themselves specify any point within that domain. The reference in question must therefore be specified by some other expression within the clause, which serves as the *antecedent* of the relative root. This expression may be a noun or pronoun, a particle, or a subordinate clause. As we will see below, the antecedent of a relative root functions as an oblique complement of a verb or preverb-verb complex. Unlike subjects and objects, which are freely omitted under appropriate discourse conditions, the antecedent of a relative root must ordinarily be overtly expressed, even if it is pronominal.[4]

Some examples may help to clarify the way relative roots are used. In (21) the root *in-* ~ *-en-* introduces reference to the semantic domain of manners. While it is convenient to gloss this morpheme as 'thus', it does not in itself have deictic force. The manner in question must be specified by an antecedent, here the pronoun *kotaki* 'other'. The root *ot-* 'from' in (22) introduces reference to the domain of sources. The antecedent in this case is the locative noun phrase *ayôh...nemâtesêheki* '(from) this knife of mine'.

(21) **kotaki** net-**en**-ênem-ekwa
 other 1-thus-think-3/1SG.IND
 'he (a manitou) has blessed me in a different way' (Goddard 1987, 111)

(22) ...wîh=**ot**-**en**-amêkwe ashkotêw **ayôh**=mekoho **ne-mâtesêh-eki**.
 FUT=from-by.hand-22/3IN.CONJ fire this.LOC=EMPH 1-knife-LOC
 '...then you (pl.) will get fire from my knife here.' (Michelson 1921, 46.17–18)

Other relative roots in Meskwaki include *tan-* 'there, at that place', *ahkw-* 'that far, to such a linear extent', *ahpîht-* 'that much, to such a degree', and *tasw-* 'so much, so many' (Goddard 1988, 64). The forms ending in *n* and *t* are subject to a rule by which *n* is replaced by *sh* and *t* by *ch* before *i*. Thus *tan-* appears as *tash-* in *tash-itêhê-wa* 'he thinks, expects there', while *in-* occurs as *ish-* in *ish-itêhê-wa* 'he thinks thus'.

Several other initials function like relative roots in introducing a verbal complement, but instead of oblique complements, they introduce complements of a type known as *secondary objects*, distinct from the *primary objects* of ordinary transitive verbs. Secondary objects function syntactically as second objects of ditransitive verbs and as complements of certain formally intransitive verbs. While primary objects are reflected in verbal inflection, secondary objects, like oblique complements, are not. Unlike obliques, secondary objects are freely omitted in null anaphora. Moreover, secondary objects typically follow the verb of a clause (in unmarked word order), while obliques usually precede it (Dahlstrom 1996b). One of the roots that introduce secondary objects is *kek-* '(together) with, having', illustrated in (23). The object introduced by *kek-* in this sentence is *onowahônwâwani* 'their fan', which occurs here in postverbal position as expected.

(23) Meshê='nah=wîna=mekoho êh=**kek**-ekâ-wâchi
 in.some.way=EMPH=but=EMPH AOR=having-dance-33.CONJ
 o-nowahôn-wâw-ani.
 3-fan-33-IN.SG
 'Indeed, they could only dance with their fans.' (Michelson 1925, 210.40–41)

The expressions of source, manner, location, and the like that stand as antecedents to relative roots are not objects, but they are nonetheless lexically selected complements and not adjuncts. For example, expressions of this kind cannot in general be added to clauses in which no relative root appears (Goddard 1988, 64–66, 1990a, 45–46).

The distribution of locative complements is typical in this respect. As Goddard (1990a, 45) notes, "Some verbs have this locative valence as an optional lexical feature; not surprisingly these verbs are ones that refer to actions that are inherently localized and durative." One such verb is *nepâ-* 'sleep'. As shown in (24a), forms of *nepâ-* may be used without a specification of location, but a locative expression may be added without any modification of the verb, as in (24b).

(24) a. Êh=wîseni-chi, êh=**nepâ**-chi.
　　　 AOR-eat-3.CONJ AOR-sleep-3.CONJ
　　　 'He ate, and he slept.' (Goddard 1990a, 45)
　　b. **Îyâhi**　　êh=**nepâ**-wâchi.
　　　 over.there AOR-sleep-33.CONJ
　　　 'They slept over there.' (Goddard 1990a, 45)

The use of such an expression is obligatory when the verb stem includes the relative root *tan-* 'there', except in a construction in which this root has a special aspectual force (Goddard 1990a, 45). Other verbs generally do not occur with locative phrases. This contrast is illustrated in (25). The verb *âchimoh-* 'tell, instruct', shown in (25a), does not occur with locatives. But a final derived from this stem may be added to *tan-*, giving *tan-âchimoh-*. The resulting verb requires the use of an expression to serve as an antecedent for the relative root, provided that *tan-* is given its usual spatial interpretation.

(25) a. Ôni='pi　　　o-shemîh-ani　êh=**âchimoh**-ekochi...
　　　 then=REPORT 3-niece-OBV.SG AOR=tell-3'/3.CONJ
　　　 'Then, they say, he was informed by his niece...' (Goddard 1990c, 166)
　　b. **Înah**=châh=nêh=wîna **tan-âchimoh**-âpi...
　　　 there=so=also=she　　location-tell-X/3.IND
　　　 'She too was instructed there...' (Goddard 1990c, 165)

This situation is unexpected if locatives are adjuncts, since adjuncts are typically optional. The observed distribution is expected, however, if locative phrases are complements, since the lexical properties of individual predicates (in particular, their meaning) determine the range of complements with which they may or must occur. The distribution of other types of oblique expressions is comparable to that of locatives. Thus obliques in general appear to be lexically selected complements in Meskwaki.[5]

The derivation of finals from stems is not productive. Thus not all stems may be directly suffixed to a relative root. Preverbs are productively derived from initials, however. In particular, preverbs are freely formed from relative roots. Thus the effect of combining a given relative root with a stem may be achieved, when no final corresponds to the stem, by employing a preverb derived from the root in question as a modifier of the stem. Only in this way can such a stem be employed with an oblique complement if the stem does not inherently bear a valence for a complement of the relevant type.

Consider, for example, the verb *peseshê-* 'listen', which does not, by itself, take locative complements. No final corresponds to this stem, so there is no way to form a unitary stem based on *tan-* and *peseshê-* which can take a locative complement. To achieve the effect of combining *tan-* with *peseshê-*, a preverb based on *tan-*, namely *tashi*, is instead employed to derive a preverb-verb complex. This complex as a whole, just like any stem based on *tan-*, now bears a valence for a locative complement. Thus it is the presence of the preverb *tashi* in the following example that licenses the appearance of the locative pronoun *înahi* 'there', phonologically reduced here to *înah*.

(26) "Asâmi=wêna **înah**=nêh=wîna **tashi** peseshê-wa," êh=i-chi=meko.
 really=in.fact there=also=he location listen-3.IND AOR=say-3.CONJ=EMPH
 '"But really, he listened there too," she insisted.' (Goddard 1990c, 165)

Verbs like 'sleep', on the other hand, which inherently bear a locative valence, neither form derivatives with *tan-* nor combine with *tashi* (Goddard 1990a, 45).

To put the same observations another way, *tashi* is a valence-changing preverb: using *tashi* as a modifier of a verb, we derive an expression—a preverb-verb complex—with a valence for one more complement than the verb itself licenses, namely, the locative complement that serves as the antecedent of the relative root *tan-* on which *tashi* is based. Preverbs based on the other relative roots of Meskwaki similarly function as valence-changing preverbs: each derives preverb-verb complexes that bear a valence for a complement that serves as the antecedent for the underlying relative root. Thus the preverb *ishi*, based on the relative root *in-* 'thus', derives preverb-verb complexes with a valence for a complement specifying manner, as shown in (27a). The preverb *ochi*, based on *ot-* 'from', derives preverb-verb complexes with a valence for a complement expressing a source, as shown in (27b).

(27) a. Awita=kêh owîyêha **kêkôhi** **ishi** myân-ênet-asa.
 not=and someone something thus bad-consider-3/3IN.POT
 'And no one would consider it bad in any way.' (Dahlstrom 1987, 70)
 b. **Manahka ochi** pyê-wa wêt-âpa-niki mahkwa.
 yonder from come-3.IND from-dawn-3OBV.IN.PART bear
 'A bear came from over there in the east.' (Dahlstrom 1987, 58)

We noted above that stems based on the root *kek-* 'with, having' take secondary objects, rather than oblique complements. Not surprisingly, then, the preverb *keki* derives preverb-verb complexes that bear a valence for a secondary object, as illustrated in (28). The secondary object corresponding to *keki* in this case is *nekoti mashishki* 'one herb' (used here in reference to tobacco); the verb *pakisen-* 'set down' by itself takes only a primary object. Note the characteristic postverbal position of the secondary object in this example, as opposed to the preverbal position of the locative complement *îyâhi* 'over there', introduced by the preverb *tashi*.

(28) Nekoti=châhi ne-**keki** pakisen-âwaki   **nekoti mashishki** wînwâwa
     one=for   1-having set.down-1/33.IND one   herb   they
     îyâhi   wîh=**tashi** kîshikenamâtiso-wâchi...
     over.there FUT=location raise.for.self-33.IN.SG.PART
     'For I have given them (lit., set them down having) one herb for them to raise for themselves over there...' (Michelson 1929, 50.8–10)

We see, then, that there are two types of valence-changing preverbs in Meskwaki: those based on relative roots and those based on roots that introduce secondary objects. Thus we find that the valence-changing preverbs of Meskwaki not only license the occurrence of complements, but determine the grammatical functions borne by those complements. Note, too, that a secondary object introduced by *keki* 'with, having' clearly has the status of an object of the associated verb, since the noun phrase in question is positioned with respect to the verb in (28), not with respect to the preverb. Thus the addition of the preverb truly does effect a change in the argument structure of a verb.

14.6 Against an Incorporation Analysis of Valence-Changing Preverbs

Craig and Hale (1988) propose that valence-changing preverbs in several Native American languages are derived from postpositions through syntactic incorporation —that is, by head movement and adjunction to a verb. An account along these lines deserves consideration for Meskwaki as well, since many of the valence-changing preverbs of the language also function as postpositions.

In fact, most of the particles that function as preverbs in Meskwaki may also occur outside the preverb-verb complex as adverbials. This is true, in particular, of particles like *ishi* 'thus' and *ochi* 'from' that are derived from relative roots. When such a particle is used as an independent adverbial, it takes its own complement, which then functions as the antecedent of the relative root on which it is based. In other words, when a particle of this type occurs outside a preverb-verb complex, it functions as a postposition, as illustrated in (29).[6]

(29) a. ... kâta nâhkachi kakâchim-iyêkani   [kêkôhi   'shi]_{PP} owîyêha
         not   also   joke.with-2/3.PROHIB something thus someone
      '... and do not in any way joke with anyone' (Michelson 1925, 68.10–11)
   b. mâne êh=nowiwen-emechi   [înahi   **ochi**]_{PP} mehtosêneniw-ahi
      many AOR-lead.out-X/3′.CONJ that.LOC from   person-OBV.PL
      'many people were carried out from that place' (Dahlstrom 1987, 58)

While examples like these lend initial plausibility to an incorporation analysis of valence-changing preverbs in Meskwaki, an account along the lines of Craig and Hale's proposal in fact encounters several problems.

Craig and Hale's analysis is formulated within the theory of incorporation developed in Baker 1988, which assumes a version of the Government-Binding framework. One of the principal claims of Baker's theory is that incorporation takes place only from governed positions—that is, from complements. As we have seen, the antecedents of relative roots in Meskwaki are complements, as an incorporation analysis would lead us to expect. But Craig and Hale's proposal requires more than this: the postpositional phrases from which incorporation takes place must also be complements. Yet postpositional phrases are systematically optional constituents of Meskwaki clauses. Thus there is little reason to believe that overt postpositional phrases in this language are ever complements.

Of course, we might postulate abstract postpositional phrases in governed positions to provide a source for the valence-changing preverbs of Meskwaki. Craig and Hale in fact propose just such an analysis of valence-changing preverbs in the Siouan language Winnebago. To adopt such a proposal for Meskwaki, however, is to abandon any attempt to relate the valence-changing preverbs of the language to the postpositions whose occurrence provided the initial motivation for pursuing an account based on incorporation. Moreover, Craig and Hale argue that the process of incorporation in Winnebago has the automatic consequence that a postpositional object becomes an object of the verb into which the postposition is incorporated. In Meskwaki, however, preverbs based on relative roots introduce oblique complements, not objects. Finally, there is no obvious sense in which the valence-changing preverbs of Meskwaki are incorporated. Like the other preverbs of the language, they are syntactically independent words. Overall, then, there appears to be little motivation for an incorporation account of the valence-changing preverbs of Meskwaki.

There is a more fundamental reason, however, why an incorporation analysis of valence-changing preverbs is inappropriate for Meskwaki. The relationship between initial components of verb stems and preverbs on the one hand and independent particles on the other that we have observed in the case of relative roots is not limited to valence-bearing initials. Such relationships are in fact quite typical for the whole class of initials, regardless of their semantic properties. Any account of valence-bearing roots that fails to relate their distribution to that of initials in general is surely defective.

Consider the root *kashk-* 'be able'. Like a relative root, *kashk-* may appear as the initial component of a verb stem, as the base of a preverb, or as the base of an independent particle. The first possibility is illustrated in (30a): here *kashk-* is the initial component of the stem *kashk-iht-* 'manage to do, get'. The particle *kashki* functions as a preverb in (30b), as shown by the fact that it hosts the aorist proclitic. In (30c), however, *kashki* can only be an independent particle, since here it follows the verb with which it is construed.

(30) a. ... îni   êhkwi **kashk**-iht-ôchi   êh=kanawi-chi.
      that.IN so.far be.able-do-3.IN.SG.PART AOR=speak-3.CONJ
      '... and that was as much as she could manage to say' (Jones 1907, 180.11)

   b. Êh=**kashki**=mekoho ânehkôchike-niki   ot-ôhkan-em-wâw-ani
      AOR=be.able=EMPH lengthen.out-3′IN.CONJ 3-bone-POSS-33-IN.PL
      êh=takwike-niki.
      AOR=grow.together-3′IN.CONJ
      'Their bones were able to lengthen out and grow together.' (Michelson 1921, 30.18–19)

   c. Pwâwi=kêhi='pî='na   âhkwamat-aka   **kashki**
      not=and=REPORT=that.AN be.sick-3/3IN.PROX.SG.PART be.able
      apenôhêha...
      child
      'But the child was one that had managed not to become sick...' (Goddard 1990c, 168–169)

Most other initials have similar distributions. To be sure, the particle derived from a given initial may occur more frequently in one function than it does in another. Thus *kashki* 'be able' is considerably more common as a preverb than it is as an independent particle. A typical initial, however, may occur either as a component of a verb stem or as the base of a particle. A typical particle based on an initial may function either as a preverb or independently.

The distribution of relative roots is like that of initials of any other kind. Thus it is not surprising that these roots occur both as initial components of verb stems and as bases for particles. Nor does the fact that particles based on such roots occur both as preverbs and as independent adverbials (postpositions) require any special explanation. The argument-inducing properties of relative roots follow from their meanings, which require them to take antecedents. When a particle based on a relative root occurs as the initial component of a verb stem, the verb itself bears a valence for an oblique complement to serve as such an antecedent. When a particle based on one of these roots occurs as part of a preverb-verb complex, the particle contributes the valence of the root to the argument structure of the complex as a whole. When the particle occurs as an independent adverbial, it takes its own complement and thus functions as a postposition. Roots like *kek-* 'with, having' that introduce secondary objects have properties somewhat different from those of relative roots (see note 6), but the valence-inducing character of the corresponding preverbs again follows from the meanings of the underlying initials. An incorporation analysis of valence-changing preverbs in Meskwaki is thus essentially beside the point. An analysis of valence-inducing initials along these lines will not contribute to an account of the distribution of initials of other types. An adequate general account of the distribution of initials, on the other hand, will leave no work for an incorporation analysis to do.

14.7 The Morphology of the Preverb-Verb Complex

As we have seen, verb stems in Meskwaki are built up from components: initials, medials, and finals. Components of any of these types may be morphologically complex. In particular, components may themselves be derived from stems. Some examples are given in (31).

(31) a. peshikw-âhkw-at-wi
       straight-wood-INTR-3IN.IND
       'it (log, stick, etc.) is straight' (Jones 1911, 795)
    b. mîhkem-ehkwêw-ê-wa
       court-woman-INTR-3.IND
       'he is courting' (Goddard 1990b, 456)
    c. atamêw-api-wa
       smoke-sit-3.IND
       'he smokes sitting' (Goddard 1990b, 457)

The stem of the verb in (31a) is based on a root and two other monomorphemic components. The initial in (31b) is derived from a transitive verb stem, the medial from a noun stem; compare *mîhkem-êwa* 'he courts her', *ihkwêw-a* 'woman'. The stem in (31c) includes only an initial and a final. Both are derivatives of intransitive verb stems; compare *atamê-wa* 'he smokes', *api-wa* 'he sits, is located'.

As we have already noted, initial components of verb stems typically also occur as bases of preverbs. Thus the root *peshikw-* 'physically straight, morally upright' occurs as an initial in (31a), but as the base of the preverb *peshikwi* in (32).

(32) Ke-peshikwi=châh=meko mani   wîtamô-nepwa...
     2-straight-so=EMPH   this.IN tell-1/22.IND
     'I have told you (pl.) this in an upright manner.' (Michelson 1925, 136.8–9)

Whether an initial occurs as the first component of a verb stem or as the base of a preverbal modifier depends on the material with which the initial is combined. While finals derived from stems are not uncommon, not every Meskwaki verb stem is paired with a final. When there is such a suffix, it is sometimes identical with the independent stem, as in the case of *api-* 'sit'. Often, however, the derivational suffix is partly or wholly distinct. The stem *wîseni-* 'eat', for example, is matched by the derivational suffix *-îseni-*. Thus we find *wîseni-wa* 'he eats', but *kîsh-îseni-wa* 'he has finished eating' (Goddard 1988, 62). The stem *nakamo-* 'sing' is matched by the final *-inâkê-*; thus *nakamo-wa* 'he sings', but *wêp-inâkê-wa* 'he starts to sing' (Goddard 1988, 62).

When no derivational suffix corresponds to a stem, the morphology of Meskwaki provides no way the stem can be directly combined with an initial such as *kîsh-* 'completed' or *wêp-* 'begin'. The combination of the initial and the stem is then formed instead by using a preverb based on the initial in question. So, for example, no derivational suffix corresponds to the stem *meno-* 'drink' (*meno-wa* 'he drinks'). This stem is instead modified by preverbs: *kîshi meno-wa* 'he has finished drinking' (Goddard 1988, 63).

For many combinations of a given initial with a given stem, we find only a derived stem or only the corresponding preverb-verb sequence. But in other cases both a derived stem and a preverb-verb combination are possible, although the alternative forms may differ in frequency. Thus both *kîshi wîseni-wa* 'he has finished eating' and *wêpi nakamo-wa* 'he starts to sing' are attested, but these forms are less common than *kîsh-îseni-wa* and *wêp-inâkê-wa* (Goddard 1988). Occasionally, however, formations of the two kinds appear essentially interchangeable.

Overall, we find that unitary verb stems are approximately (but only approximately) in complementary distribution with preverb-verb complexes: for any given meaning, we typically find either one form of expression or the other. This relationship between stems and preverb-verb combinations is reminiscent of the well-known phenomenon of *morphological blocking*, which Aronoff (1976, 43) has described as "the non-occurrence of one form due to the simple existence of another." In this case, the existence of a verb stem with a particular meaning frequently precludes the formation of a preverb-verb complex with the same meaning, even though the use of preverbal modifiers is otherwise fully productive.

It is typical of blocking relationships that they are sometimes partial, so that a given form may be subject to blocking only in some of its possible senses, and that they are subject to a variety of extralinguistic influences, such as word frequency (Bochner 1993, 5–7). The competition between unitary verbs and preverb-verb complexes that we find in Meskwaki appears to be of essentially this character, although the strength of the blocking effect seems to vary considerably from one predicate to another.

There would appear to be reasonable grounds, then, for attributing the choice between unitary verb forms and preverb-verb complexes in Meskwaki to morphological blocking, rather than to any formal principle of the grammar.[7] Note that this conclusion, if it can be sustained, provides support for the claim that preverb-verb complexes are lexical formations, despite their phrasal character. While it has sometimes been argued that syntactically formed expressions may be subject to blocking (Andrews 1990), most clearly established cases of this phenomenon involve lexical interactions.

Blocking probably also plays at least some role in a constraint that Goddard (1988, 69; 1990a, 41; 1990b, 479) has noted that governs the relative order of the initials *pem-* 'along' and *wêp-* 'begin' in preverb-verb complexes. For the most part, initials occur in preverb-verb complexes in an order that directly reflects their relative scope, as we see in the following examples (all from Jones 1911). In (33e), for example, we have *wêp-* 'begin', *pyêt-* 'hither', then *tetep-* 'in a circle'; and the resulting interpretation is 'begin to approach along a circle'.

(33) a. wêp-osê-wa
       'he begins to walk'
    b. pyêt-osê-wa
       'he comes walking'
    c. tetep-osê-wa
       'he walks round in a circle'
    d. wêpi pyêt-osê-wa
       'he begins to approach on the walk'
    e. wêpi pyêchi tetep-osê-wa
       'he begins to approach walking in a circle'

Thus when we combine *wêp-* 'begin' with stems consisting of *pem-* 'along, by' and the finals *-osê-* 'walk' and *-ipaho-* 'run', we expect to obtain the forms in (34). But we do not. Instead, we find the forms in (35).

(34) a. *wêpi pem-osê-wa
    b. *wêpi pem-ipaho-wa

(35) a. pemi wêp-osê-wa
       'he begins to walk along' (Goddard 1988, 69)
    b. pemi wêp-ipaho-wa
       'he begins to run along' (Goddard 1988, 69)

There is nothing ill-formed about the verbs themselves in (34): both *pem-osê-wa* 'he walks (along)' and *pem-ipaho-wa* 'he runs (along)' are common forms, attested for example by Jones (1911, 769). Nonetheless the forms in (34) are apparently either entirely impossible or strongly disfavored. Goddard (1988, 69) states explicitly that

(34a) does not occur; he is less explicit about (34b). Whatever the precise status of these examples, however, we may be confident that the contrast between (34) and (35) is linguistically significant, since the relevant formations are generally regular.

In Goddard's view, the facts summarized here show that "the syntactic concatenation of more than one word logically preced[es] the formation of stems" (1990b, 479). He further suggests that "this concatenation induces a morphologically governed adjustment in the order of elements involving stem decomposition and derivation" (1988, 69), a process that he calls "preverb bumping."

Once again, however, these conclusions follow only if we accept the hypothesis that the concatenation of preverbs with verbs is solely a matter of syntax. If preverb-verb combinations are lexically formed, then the items in (34) and (35) present no special problem. If the order in which *wêp-* and *pem-* occur must be lexically stipulated, this information can be stated in a lexical rule governing the form of the preverb-verb complexes in question (Ackerman and LeSourd 1994; Crysmann 1999).

In fact, however, it is not clear that such a rule is necessary. As Goddard (2000) has pointed out, the root *pem-* is actually semantically empty in one interpretation of the stem *pem-ôse-* 'walk'. In this case, and others like it, the meaning of the stem is really just that of the final alone. Note, however, that *wêp-* 'begin' is not semantically empty in *wêp-ôse-* 'begin to walk'. Moreover, speakers may be assumed to know this stem and thus to have established a lexical entry for it. Thus the existence of *wêp-osê-* 'begin to walk' should block the formation of *wêpi pem-ôse- in the same meaning, a correct result.

What about combinations involving both *wêp-* and *pem-* when the latter is *not* semantically empty, but instead has the meaning 'along, by'? In what order should we expect these two initials to appear when both are meaningful? At least in some cases that appear comparable, Meskwaki stations a component of the preverb-verb complex that serves to specify the spatial extent of an activity to the left of a component that specifies the inception of that activity. In (36), for example, the preverb *kîwi* 'around, about, in places' precedes the preverb *âpi* 'go and perform an act and then return', even though the logical order of these elements would appear to be the reverse: from the context of this sentence, it is clear that the referent of the subject goes out to beg in various places; there are not various places from which he goes out to beg.

(36) Êh=kîwi   âpi   natotâso-nichi wîh=wîseni-chi.
     AOR=in.places go.do.X.and.return beg-3′.CONJ   FUT=eat-3.CONJ
     'He (obv.) went out and begged for food in various places so that she could eat.' (Jones 1907, 220.8)

It seems possible, then, that the order of components that obtains in *pemi wêpo-sêwa* 'he begins to walk along' simply reflects a general principle that determines the semantic interpretation of preverb-verb complexes, rather than an idiosyncratic constraint that governs the relative order of the roots *wêp-* and *pem-*.[8] If this conclusion proves correct, we will not be able to appeal to the phenomenon of "preverb bumping" for evidence that bears on the status of preverb-verb complexes as lexically or syntactically derived forms.

14.8 Conclusions

In the preceding discussion, we have surveyed a series of arguments that have been advanced in support of the contention that the preverb-verb complexes of Meskwaki have a grammatical status comparable to that of simplex verb forms and should accordingly be regarded as analytically expressed predicates—that is, as lexically formed expressions consisting of more than one word.

Several of these lines of reasoning, as we have seen, are not persuasive. The inflectional properties of preverb-verb complexes do indeed parallel those of verbs in various respects, but it does not seem necessary to assign preverb-verb complexes a status comparable to that of words in order to accommodate these observations. It would appear sufficient to assign preverb-verb complexes and simplex verbs to the same phrasal category. The evidence that has been advanced to show that preverb-verb combinations may serve as bases for derivation likewise appears not to be compelling. Semantically based "bracketing paradoxes" would appear to be better analyzed in purely semantic terms. If so, then these cases do not, after all, require us to suppose that compound verb stems may be inputs to lexical operations. While nominalizations based on preverb-verb complexes do occur, the available evidence does not establish that these forms are the output of any productive category-changing rule. Thus these forms can simply be analyzed as lexically listed expressions.

The properties of valence-bearing roots provide less equivocal evidence, however, that suggests that preverb-verb complexes are indeed lexically formed. As we have seen, there are two classes of such roots. Some introduce oblique complements, while others introduce secondary objects. The valence-inducing properties of these roots, like the properties of other morphemes that serve as initial components of stems, are constant across the variety of formations in which they may occur. In particular, the argument-taking properties of preverb-verb complexes that include one of these morphemes parallel those of simplex verb stems that include the morpheme in question as an initial component. If only lexical processes can derive expressions that are associated with a unified argument structure, as generally assumed in lexicalist analyses, then preverb-verb complexes that include valence-bearing initials must be lexical formations in Meskwaki. This conclusion derives further support from the fact that the existence of a simplex verb stem with a particular meaning typically blocks the formation of a preverb-verb complex with the same meaning, or at least leads speakers to prefer the synthetic form to its analytically expressed counterpart. The existence of such blocking effects is predicted under an account in which preverb-verb complexes in general are lexical formations. I conclude, then, that there is indeed evidence that supports the analysis of preverb-verb combinations in Meskwaki as lexically formed but analytically expressed predicates.

Notes

1. Examples taken from texts are cited by page and line number: Michelson 1921, 64.8, indicates line 8 on p. 64 of Michelson 1921. Meskwaki forms are given in a practical orthography based on the writing system currently used in Oklahoma for the closely related Sauk language (Whittaker 1996). Long vowels are marked with a circumflex; "sh" represents /š/ and "ch" is /č/. Proclitics and enclitics are set off from their hosts by a double hyphen (=). The following abbreviations are used in glosses: 1 first person (prefix), first-person singular (suffix); 2 second person (prefix), second-person singular (suffix); 3 third person (prefix), third-person singular (suffix; unmarked: animate, proximate), 11 first-person plural exclusive; 12 first-person plural inclusive; 22 second-person plural; 33 third-person plural (unmarked: animate, proximate); 3' obviative (secondary) third-person singular; 1/2, etc. first-person singular subject with second-person singular object, etc.; ABS absentative; AN animate (grammatical gender); AOR aorist; CONJ conjunct indicative; EMPH emphatic particle; exc. exclusive; EXCLAM exclamatory particle; FUT future; IMP imperative mode; IN inanimate (grammatical gender); inc. inclusive; IND independent indicative mode; INTR intransitive; LOC locative; OBV, obv. obviative; NEG negative mode; PART participle; PL, pl. plural; POSS possessed; POT potential mode; PROHIB prohibitive mode; PROX proximate; RECIP reciprocal; REPORT reportative particle; SG, sg. singular; X unspecified subject. Singular grammatically animate referents are indicated in translations of Meskwaki examples with forms of the pronoun *he*, except in cases where such a translation would be inappropriate for the sense of the example or for its textual context. These referents are not necessarily either human or masculine.

2. A promising account of Meskwaki preverb-verb complexes in the HPSG framework is presented in Crysmann 1999.

3. I follow Goddard 1991 in analyzing these tense markers as proclitics. Dahlstrom (1996a) argues that they are better analyzed as affixes.

4. An oblique complement will be null, however, when it is subject to deletion as the relativized constituent in a relative clause. It should be noted as well that Rhodes (1998) suggests that null anaphora is routine in Ojibwa for antecedents of relative roots whose reference can be determined from context.

5. In Ojibwa, as in Meskwaki, oblique expressions such as locatives only appear with verbs that bear a valence for them, as noted by Rhodes (1998). Rhodes argues, however, that the antecedents of relative roots are grammatically distinct from other oblique complements. Only the antecedents of relative roots, for example, may be interpreted with definite pronominal reference in null anaphora.

6. The syntax of particles based on roots bearing a valence for a secondary object is different from that of particles based on relative roots. For instance, a preparticle derived from the root *kek-* 'with, having' is employed as a modifier of a second particle, which serves to discharge the

valence introduced by the root: *keki chîmân-e* 'including the canoe'; compare *chîmân-i* 'canoe'. (See Dahlstrom 1996b for an analysis of such expressions as prepositional phrases.) This property of the particle *keki* can nonetheless be seen as inherited from the underlying root, since *kek-* functions on its own in parallel formations: *kek-apenôh-e* 'including the children'; compare *apenôh-a* 'child'.

7. Following Dahlstrom 2000, Goddard (2002) suggests that a preverb and the corresponding initial should be regarded as alternative realizations of the same lexical item. Under the present proposal, however, the fact that the preverb typically makes the same contribution to a preverb-verb complex as the initial makes to a stem simply follows from the fact that the preverb is a derivative of the initial. Morphological blocking then accounts for the fact that speakers usually prefer to use a simplex stem, rather that a preverb-verb complex that would have the same meaning. Thus no special mechanism is needed to account for the related distributions of preverbs and initials.

8. The putative constraint requiring *pem-* to precede *wêp-* within the preverb-verb complex apparently cannot be completely general in any case. These components at least sometimes occur in the order that such a constraint would exclude: *êh=wêpi menwi **pem**-en-amowâchi* 'they began to take good care of it' (Michelson 1921, 66.4). (The stem of the verb *pem-en-* 'take care of' consists of *pem-* 'along' plus the common final *-en-* 'act on by hand'. Note, however, that the meaning of this stem is not compositional, so that *pem-* arguably does not have its usual meaning here.)

References

Ackerman, Farrell, and Phil LeSourd. 1994. Preverbs and complex predicates: Dimensions of wordhood. In V. Samiian and J. Nevis, eds., *Proceedings of the Twelfth Western Conference on Linguistics*, 1–16. Fresno: Department of Linguistics, California State University, Fresno.

Ackerman, Farrell, and Gert Webelhuth. 1998. A theory of predicates. Stanford, CA: CSLI.

Andrews, Avery. 1990. Unification and morphological blocking. *Natural Language and Linguistic Theory* 8:507–557.

Aronoff, Mark. 1976. *Word formation in generative grammar*. Cambridge, MA: MIT Press.

Baker, Mark C. 1988. *Incorporation: A theory of grammatical function changing*. Chicago: University of Chicago Press.

Beard, Robert. 1991. Decompositional composition: The semantics of scope ambiguities and "bracketing paradoxes." *Natural Language and Linguistic Theory* 9:195–229.

Bloomfield, Leonard. 1927. Notes on the Fox Language, sections IV–XI. *International Journal of American Linguistics* 4:181–219.

Bloomfield, Leonard. 1946. Algonquian. In C. Osgood, ed., *Linguistic Structures of Native America*, 85–129. Viking Fund Publications in Anthropology, no. 6. New York: Viking Fund.

Bochner, Harry. 1993. *Simplicity in generative grammar*. Berlin: Mouton de Gruyter.

Craig, Colette, and Ken Hale. 1988. Relational preverbs in some languages of the Americas: Typological and historical perspectives. *Language* 64:312–344.

Crysmann, Berthold. 1999. Morphosyntactic paradoxa in Fox: An analysis in linearisation-based morphology. In G. Bouma, E. Hinrichs, G.-J. Kruijff, and R. Oehrle, eds., *Constraints *and resources in natural language syntax and semantics: Studies in constraint-based lexicalism.* Stanford, CA: CSLI.

Dahlstrom, Amy. 1987. Discontinuous constituents in Fox. In Paul D. Kroeber and Robert E. Moore, eds., *Native American languages and grammatical typology*, 53–73. Bloomington: Indiana University Linguistics Club.

Dahlstrom, Amy. 1996a. Affixes vs. clitics in Fox. *Contemporary Linguistics* 2:47–57.

Dahlstrom, Amy. 1996b. Morphology and syntax of the Fox (Mesquakie) language. Ms., University of Chicago.

Dahlstrom, Amy. 2000. Morphosyntactic mismatches in Algonquian: Affixal predicates and discontinuous verbs. In A. Okrent and J. Boyle, eds., *The Proceedings from the Panels of the Chicago Linguistic Society's Thirty-Sixth Meeting*, 63–87. Chicago: Chicago Linguistic Society.

Goddard, Ives. 1987. Fox participles. In Paul D. Kroeber and Robert E. Moore, eds., *Native American languages and grammatical typology*, 105–118. Bloomington: Indiana University Linguistics Club.

Goddard, Ives. 1988. Post-transformational stem derivation in Fox. *Papers and Studies in Contrastive Linguistics* 22:59–72.

Goddard, Ives. 1990a. Paradigmatic relationships. In *BLS* 16: Special Supplementary Volume, 39–50. Berkeley: Berkeley Linguistics Society.

Goddard, Ives. 1990b. Primary and secondary stem derivation in Algonquian. *International Journal of American Linguistics* 56:449–483.

Goddard, Ives. 1990c. Some literary devices in the writings of Alfred Kiyana. In W. Cowan, ed., *Papers of the Twenty-First Algonquian Conference*, 159–171. Ottawa: Carleton University.

Goddard, Ives. 1991. Observations regarding Fox (Mesquakie) phonology. In W. Cowan, ed., *Papers of the Twenty-Second Algonquian Conference*, 157–181. Ottawa: Carleton University.

Goddard, Ives. 2000. Stem-internal ellipsis and meaning from context in Meskwaki (Fox). Paper delivered at the Annual Meeting of the Society for the Study of the Indigenous Languages of the Americas, Chicago.

Goddard, Ives. 2002. Post-syntactic stem derivation in Fox (Meskwaki). Paper presented at the Annual Meeting of the Society for the Study of the Indigenous Languages of the Americas, San Francisco. (Citations from handout.)

Jones, William. 1904. Some principles of Algonquian word-formation. *American Anthropologist* 6:369–411.

Jones, William. 1907. Fox texts. *American Ethnological Society Publications*, no. 1. Leiden: E. J. Brill for the American Ethnological Society.

Jones, William. 1911. Algonquian (Fox). In F. Boas, ed., *Handbook of American Indian languages*, part 1, 735–873. Bureau of American Ethnology Bulletin 40. Washington, DC: Government Printing Office.

Kroeber, Paul D., and Robert E. Moore, eds. 1987. *Native American languages and grammatical typology*. Bloomington: Indiana University Linguistics Club.

Michelson, Truman. 1917. Notes on Algonquian languages. *International Journal of American Linguistics* 1:50–57.

Michelson, Truman. 1921. *The owl sacred pack of the Fox Indians.* Bureau of American Ethnology Bulletin 72. Washington, DC: Government Printing Office.

Michelson, Truman. 1925. Accompanying papers. In *Bureau of American Ethnology Annual Report* 40, 21–658. Washington, DC: Government Printing Office.

Michelson, Truman. 1927. *Contributions to Fox ethnology.* Bureau of American Ethnology Bulletin 85. Washington, DC: Government Printing Office.

Michelson, Truman. 1929. *Observations on the Thunder Dance of the Bear Gens of the Fox Indians.* Bureau of American Ethnology Bulletin 89. Washington, DC: Government Printing Office.

Rhodes, Richard A. 1998. Clause structure, core arguments, and the Algonquian relative root construction. Ms., University of California, Berkeley.

Thomason, Lucy. 2005. Meskwaki prenouns. In H. C. Wolfart, ed., *Papers of the Thirty-Sixth Algonquian Conference*, 425–448. Winnipeg: University of Manitoba.

Whittaker, Gordon. 1996. *Conversational Sauk: A practical guide to the language of Black Hawk.* Stroud, OK: The Sac and Fox National Public Library.

15 Unpassives of Unaccusatives

Joan Maling

15.1 Introduction

The passive voice has figured prominently in syntactic theory from the very beginning of generative linguistics. In this chapter I will focus on the lexical restrictions on passive morphology known as "1AEX effects." In his influential 1978 paper on "Impersonal Passives and the Unaccusative Hypothesis," Perlmutter noted systematic restrictions on the set of intransitive verbs that can occur in the "impersonal passive" construction in languages like Dutch and German. An impersonal passive is a passive clause with no overt nominative argument with which the verb can agree.[1] Perlmutter illustrated this dichotomy with the following Dutch examples:

(1) a. Er wordt hier door de jonge lui veel gedanst.
    it was here by the young people much danced
    'Here there was much dancing by the young people.'
  b. Hier wordt (er) veel gewerkt.
    here was (it) much worked
    'Here people worked a lot.'
  c. *In dit weeshuis wordt er door de kinderen erg snel gegroied.
    in this orphanage was it by the children very fast grown
  d. *Er werd door de bloemen binnen een paar dagen verflenst.
    it is by the flowers in a few days wilted

Verbs like 'work' and 'dance' form impersonal passives; verbs like 'grow', 'wilt', and 'die' do not.

How can we account for this contrast? Perlmutter hypothesized that intransitive verbs divide in two classes, called unergatives and unaccusatives, which have different underlying representations. By hypothesis, unaccusative verbs differ from unergatives in that they have no underlying subject; in the terminology of Relational Grammar, they have no nominal argument that bears the 1-relation in the initial stratum. Perlmutter then showed how the Unaccusative Hypothesis could be used to account for the systematic syntactic differences between these two classes of verbs. The contrast with respect to impersonal passives was derived from the 1-Advancement Exclusiveness (1AEX) Law:

(2) *1-Advancement Exclusiveness (1AEX) Law*
There can be at most one advancement-to-1 per clause (Perlmutter 1978; Perlmutter and Postal 1984).

Since the derivation of both passives and unaccusatives involves the advancement of an underlying object, the passive of an unaccusative verb violates the 1AEX. The lexical restrictions on passive are thus often referred to as 1AEX effects.

15.2 Challenges to the Unaccusative Hypothesis

The Unaccusative Hypothesis proved to be one of the most influential contributions to linguistic theory, one that was adopted into other theoretical frameworks (see, e.g., Marantz 1984; Baker 1988, chap. 4;[2] Baker, Johnson, and Roberts 1989). The universality of the Unaccusative Hypothesis was challenged in the years that followed. Reports appeared in the literature of languages in which this restriction on passive morphology was claimed not to hold; in these languages, unaccusative verbs were claimed to form impersonal passives as productively as unergative intransitive verbs. These included Lithuanian (Timberlake 1982; Keenan and Timberlake 1985), Turkish (Knecht 1985; Özkaragöz 1986), and Finnish (Maling 1993, 2006; Kaiser and Vihman 2006).[3]

(3) a. Suomessa ollaan ystävällisiä.
    Finland-INE be-PASS friendly-PL.PAR
    'People are friendly in Finland.'
  b. Sodassa kadotaan usein jäljettömiin.
    war-INE disappear-PASS often traceless-PL.ILL
    'In a war people often disappear without a trace.'
  c. Ennen vanhaan kasvettiin hitaammin kuin nykyään.
    before old grow.up-PASS.PAST slowlier than nowadays
    'In the old days people grew up more slowly than nowadays.'
  d. Ennen Suomessa synnyttiin saunassa ja kuoltiin humalassa.
    before Finland-INE born-PASS.PAST sauna-INE and die-PASS.PAST drunk-INE
    'Before in Finland people were born in the sauna and died drunk.'

Although the relevant verbal suffix is often glossed as passive, other sources treat the marker as an (active) impersonal (Abondolo 1998, 171; Maling 1993; Shore 1988; Sulkala and Karjalainen 1992, 228; Tommola 1997; among others).[4]

Before turning to the syntactic evidence that bears on the choice between active and passive, observe that there are other lexical restrictions on impersonal passives that the Unaccusative Hypothesis does not explain. Consider the *-no/to* construction in Slavic (Maling 1993, 2006; Billings and Maling 1995; Maling and Sigurjónsdóttir 2002). Like Finnish, the Polish *-no/to* construction lacks 1AEX effects; clearly unaccusative verbs occur in this construction, as illustrated in (4).

(4) a. Rodzo**no** dzieci   w domu.
       bear-IMP children-ACC in home
       'Women gave birth at home.'
   b. Dawniej umeria**no** młodo.
       before   died-IMP young
       'In the old days people died young.'

In the literature on Polish, the *-no/to* suffix is sometimes glossed as passive, sometimes as impersonal. Unaccusative verbs occur with this affix only if the understood subject is [+human]. Siewierska (1988, 271) notes that such clauses have an "implied human subject"; Rothstein (1993, 713) remarks that "the unspecified subject...is understood to be human and indefinite."[5] Saloni (1986, 21) also states that the understood subject must be human and indefinite. However, "nonspecific" is a more accurate characterization than indefinite, since the construction may be used to describe situations in which the speaker knows the identity of the human agent, and in fact the doer may even be the speaker:

(5) Poda**no**   herbatę.
    serve-IMP tea-ACC
    'Tea is served.'

Since this sentence could be uttered by the person who is serving the tea, the construction does not obligatorily have a third-plural interpretation (as claimed, for example, by Dziwirek 1994, 179–182, esp. 226 n. 3–5).[6] The pragmatic constraint is that the doer of the action is not expressed, because speaker either does not know, is not intererested, or otherwise does not find it necessary to identify the agent (Billings and Maling 1995 n. 96).

There are telling minimal pairs involving the different Polish verbs meaning 'to give birth'. One verb is used for humans, another verb for animals; only the [+human] verb occurs in the *-no/to* construction, as illustrated by the contrast between (4a) and the unacceptable (6a), taken from Maling 1993.

(6) a. *Ocielo**no** się/okoco**no** się
       'There was given birth to a cow/cat.'
   b. *Szczeka**no** na gości.
       'There was barked at the guests.'
   c. *Zwiednię**to**.
       'There was wilted.'

According to my native-speaker consultants, sentences like those in (6) are not actually ungrammatical, but the subject is interpreted as human; needless to say, the intended interpretation is not polite.

Similarly in Finnish, the understood subject of verbs with so-called passive morphology, the suffix -*taan*, can only be interpreted as [+human].[7] As in Polish, Finnish has different verbs for humans versus animals.

(7) a. Katolilaisissa maissa   poi'itaan   hullun lailla
     Catholic-INE countries-INE give.birth-PASS crazy like
     'In Catholic countries they give birth like crazy (lit., like animals).'
   b. Hallituksessa   munitaan   taas
      government-INE lay.eggs-PASS again
      'In the government, someone laid an egg again.'

When the subject of the verb *muni* 'to lay eggs' is a human, it has the lexicalized meaning 'to make a bad mistake', and in this sense, it can occur with the so-called passive suffix -*taan*.

I suggest that the key to the apparent lack of 1AEX effects in Polish and Finnish is not unaccusativity, but rather the restriction to [+human] subjects. Note that one of Perlmutter's Dutch examples illustrating 1AEX effects, cited in (1d), is ungrammatical for independent reasons: the understood subject of the verb 'to wilt' is presumably inanimate. Controlling for this restriction, we might conclude that there are two basic types of languages: those in which impersonal passives of unaccusative verbs are grammatical, provided the underlying subject is [+human], and those in which unaccusative verbs cannot occur with passive morphology. The Germanic languages would belong to this second type, as illustrated here for Icelandic.

(8) a. *Í gamla daga var dáið ungt.
       in old   days was died young
       Intended: 'In the old days people died young.'
   b. *Það var átt börnin   heima.
       it was had the.children at.home
       Intended: 'Women gave birth at home.'

Contrast the ungrammaticality of these Icelandic examples with the grammaticality of the Polish and Finnish examples given above.

On this view, the variation between the two types of passives is unexplained, since it is not correlated with any other grammatical features of the languages. An alternative is to assume that this second type of passive should not be considered passive at all—that is, there is no suppression of the external argument. Rather it is an active construction with a thematic, albeit phonologically null, subject. In this analysis, these apparent passives are actually active-voice clauses, the functional equivalent of

Table 15.1
Syntactic properties of two "passive" constructions in Polish

Syntactic property	passive	-no/to
Agentive *by*-phrase	OK	*
Bound anaphors in object position	*	OK
Control of subject-oriented adjuncts	*	OK
Nonagentive ("unaccusative") verbs	*	OK

constructions with overt "impersonal" or "unspecified human" subject pronouns like French *on* or German *man*.[8]

15.3 Passive vs. Impersonal Constructions

15.3.1 The Polish *-no/to* Construction

There is considerable syntactic evidence in support of this conclusion (for detailed discussion, see Maling and Sigurjónsdóttir 2002; Blevins 2003; Kibort 2004; Maling 2006). Polish has two so-called passive constructions, a canonical passive and the *-no/to* construction.[9] Unlike the canonical passive, the *-no/to* construction has the syntactic properties of an active-voice construction rather than a passive one, as summarized in table 15.1.[10]

By hypothesis, the null subject of the Polish *-no/to* construction is a thematic subject, and as such, it can bind anaphors and control subject-oriented adjuncts, as illustrated in (9a,b); no agentive *by*-phrase is allowed, as illustrated in (9c). We have already seen that unaccusative verbs can occur with this so-called passive morphology. The relevant verbal morphology occurs with transitive, intransitive, ditransitive, and clausal-complement taking verbs. Since the [+human] restriction holds at S-structure, the derived subjects of passive and raising verbs can satisfy this semantic requirement, but verbs whose subjects are systematically nonhuman, including weather verbs and other predicates taking expletive subjects, are excluded. The construction has the same lexical restrictions as infinitival clauses with PRO-arb subjects (but because it has an obligatory past-tense interpretation, it has the same distribution as finite clauses); thus it can occur with raising verbs and copular verbs, as illustrated in (9d,e).

(9) a. Zamknię**to** się w fabryce.   Reflexives
       lock-IMP   self in factory
       'They locked themselves in the factory.'
    b. Pomaga**no** sobie wzajemnie.   Reciprocals
       helped-IMP REFL each.other
       'They helped each other.'

    c. Jana   obrabowano (*przez nich).   Agentive *by*-phrase
       John-ACC robbed-IMP   (*by   them)
    d. Zdawano   się   nas nie zauważać.   Raising verb
       seemed-IMP REFL us not notice-INF
       'They seemed not to be noticing us.'
    e. Przed wojną bywano w Grand Hotelu.   Copular verb
       before war be-IMP in Grand Hotel
       'Before the war people frequented the Grand Hotel.'

As noted above, the thematic object of a transitive verb with *-no/to* behaves morphologically and syntactically like an object and not a surface subject. In addition to the accusative case marking and the lack of subject-verb agreement, this argument obligatorily occurs in the GEN of negation, indicating that it remains inside the VP, unlike the derived subject of the canonical passive:

(10) a. Nie śpiewano piosenek.   *-no/to* construction
       NEG sing-IMP songs-GEN.F.PL
       'They didn't sing songs.'
    b. Nie były   śpiewane piosenki/*piosenek.   Canonical passive
       NEG be-PAST.F.PL sung-F.PL. songs-NOM/*GEN

Sobin (1985) and Babby (1989) both assume that *-no/to* clauses are "subjectless," but this assumption is demonstrably false (also noted by Siewierska 1988). Only subjects can control participial adjuncts in Polish (Dyła 1982; Dziwirek 1990, 84). The unspecified human subject of the *-no/to* construction can control a participial adjunct clause, whereas the agent of the true passive is not a possible controller:

(11) *Subject control*
    a. Wracając do domu śpiewano piosenkę.   *-no/to* construction
       returning to home sing-IMP song-ACC.F.SG
       'They sang a song returning home.'
    b. *Wracając do domu była   śpiewana   Canonical passive
       returning to home be-PAST.F.SG sung-F.SG.
       piosenka.
       songs-NOM.F.SG.
       'A song was sung returning home.'
    c. Jana   obrabowano po   pijanemu.   *-no/to* construction
       John-ACC rob-IMP   while drunk
       'While drunk, they robbed John.' [They were drunk.]
    d. Jan   został   obrabowany po pijanemu.   Canonical passive
       John-NOM became-3SG robbed-3SG.M while drunk
       'John was robbed while drunk.' [John was drunk.]

(12) *Reflexives*[11]
    a. Chwalo**no** swoją własną ojczyznę.   -*no/to* construction
       praised-IMP REFL-ACC.F.SG. own   motherland-ACC.F.SG
       'They praised their own motherland.'
    b. *Swoja własna ojczyzna   była   (przez nich)   Canonical passive
       REFL   own   discovery-NOM be-PAST (by them)
       chwalona.
       praised-F.SG
       'Self's own motherland was praised.'

In conclusion, the syntactic behavior of the Polish -*no/to* construction is the polar opposite of the canonical passive; it has all the syntactic properties expected of an active construction with a thematic subject.

15.3.2 The Irish Autonomous Form

The same properties hold of the special verbal morphology in Irish traditionally called the "autonomous" form (Stenson 1989; McCloskey, chapter 17, this volume; see also Anderson 1982 for Breton), a construction sometimes called passive. Baker (1988) cites data from Perlmutter and Postal 1984 showing that Welsh exhibits 1AEX effects, and concludes that this is true of Celtic generally. But in modern Irish, the so-called autonomous morphology occurs on clearly unaccusative verbs including the copular verb *tá* 'to be',[12] as long as the understood subject is human (or perhaps animate).

(13) a. Conas a   táthar   inniu.
       how   COMP are-PRES.AUT today
       'How are people today?'
    b. Beifear   ar an mhisean Dé Domhnaigh.
       be-FUT.AUT on the mission Sunday
       'People will be at the mission on Sunday.'
    c. Táthar   sásta   anseo.
       be-PRES.AUT satisfied here
       'People are satisfied here.'

As with the Finnish examples cited in (7), predicates that normally take inanimate subjects get interpreted "personally":

(14) a. Táthar   meirgeach anseo.
       be-PRES.AUT rusty   here
       'People are out of practice/*things are rusty here.'
    b. Táthar   caidheach fán   scioból seo.
       be-PRES.AUT dirty   around.the barn   this
       'People are dirty around this barn.'

Stenson (1989) argues that the autonomous form licenses an arbitrary PRO subject; no overt NP may appear in subject position, nor is an oblique agent phrase allowed. The verb form is unspecified for person or number but occurs in all three tenses: present, past, future. The invariant autonomous morpheme occurs with transitive, intransitive, ditransitive, and clausal-complement taking verbs. As noted above, it occurs with unaccusative verbs. Stenson states that the autonomous form does not exist for the raising verb *tosaigh* 'begin, start', but the example she gives to illustrate this restriction contains a weather verb (Stenson 1989, 390, ex. 14b). This is ungrammatical for independent reasons: weather verbs do not satisfy the [+human] requirement. In fact, autonomous forms do occur with the personal use of raising verbs, provided that the subject is [+human].[13] This is illustrated by the contrast in (15a,b):

(15) a. *Tosaíodh   ag báisteach. (Stenson 1989, ex. 14b)
        begin-PAST.AUT PRO graining
        'It began to rain.'
     b. Toisíodh   ar chleamhnas a shocrú.   Raising verb
        begin-PAST.AUT on match   arrange[-FIN]
        'People began to arrange a match.'

15.3.3 Reflexives versus Reciprocals

Stenson (1989, 384) claimed that reflexives and reciprocals are always bad when bound to the understood subject of a verb in the autonomous form. Recall that reflexive pronouns are perfectly fine in the Polish *-no/to* construction, so if both constructions involve *pro*-arb subjects, this restriction in Irish needs explanation. The autonomous-form examples with reflexives and bound pronouns are indeed ungrammatical, as illustrated in (16). However, reciprocals are grammatical,[14] as shown in (17).

(16) a. *Maraíodh   **iad féin**.
        kill-PAST.AUT them-REFL
        Intended: 'They killed themselves.'
     b. *Óltaí a sháith (a   sáith) ag na bainiseacha sa   tseanam.
        drank his fill (their fill) at the wedding.feasts in.the old.days
        [PAST.HABIT.AUT]
        Intended: 'In the old days people drank their fill at wedding feasts.'

(17) Labhradh   go dímhúinte   len- **a chéile** ag an chruinniú sin.
     speak-PAST.AUT ADV discourteously with each.other at that meeting DEMON
     'A lot of people spoke discourteously to one another at that meeting.'

There is a difference between reciprocals and other cases of bound pronouns. Why should this be so? Reflexives in Irish are constructed from the ordinary pronouns by adding to them the demonstrative particle *féin*. Since they are constructed from ordinary pronouns, they agree in the relevant features (person, number, and in the third singular, also gender) with their antecedent. Example (16b) illustrates another case of obligatory agreement between a (bound) pronoun and a subject antecedent where the binding is semantically vacuous in that there is no actual quantification in the interpretation of such examples. Examples (16a,b) are both sharply ungrammatical.

Reciprocals are different. The reciprocal has an invariant form, *a chéile*,[15] so there is no agreement difficulty for reciprocals as there is for reflexives and bound pronouns. A possible explanation for the observed contrast is that the autonomous form simply lacks the phi-feature specification needed to support the agreement required for reflexives.[16]

15.3.4 Agentive *by*-phrase

A possible problem for the analysis of the autonomouns form as an active impersonal is the fact that the construction may occur with an agentive *by*-phrase, as noted by Nerbonne (1982) and Stenson (1989). Stenson observes that the autonomous form "can be used in passive sentences, where the inflection marks an original object which has been moved into subject position of the verb **tá**."... Moreover, such sentences, despite the impersonal inflection, do allow an agent phrase, marked by the preposition **ag**" (pp. 392–393).

(18) a. Beifar   scanraithe ag taibhsí.
       be-FUT.AUT frightened by ghosts (Stenson 1989, 20a)
       'People will be frightened by ghosts.'
   b. Táthar   buailte againn. (Stenson 1989, 20b)
       be-PRES.AUT beaten by.us
       'They've been beaten by us.'

Note that the autonomous morphology appears on the auxiliary verb. I suggest that the Irish examples are not double passives, contra Nerbonne 1982, but are analogous to French *on*-sentences containing both an impersonal subject pronoun and an agentive *by*-phrase:

(19) On a   été   insulté par les étudiants.
      one has been insulted by the students
      'We were insulted by the students.'

The autonomous form licenses a PRO-arb subject; the perfective participle licenses the expression of the most prominent argument (of whatever type) of its base verb as an oblique PP. This suggestion requires further study, but whatever the details of the analysis, it seems clear that the *by*-phrases in the above examples are licensed not by the autonomous form of the verb but by the perfective participle (see McCloskey 2007 for discussion).

15.4 Double Passives in Turkish

With this suggestion in mind, let us turn to the so-called double passives, or passives of passives, in Turkish,[17] reported by Nerbonne (1982) and Özkaragöz (1986).

(20) a. Bu oda-da   döv-ül-ün-ür.
        this room-LOC beat-PASS-PASS-AOR
        'In this room, people were beaten.'
   b. Rusya-da   Sibirya-ya   gönder-il-in-ir.
        Russia-LOC Siberia-DAT send-PASS-PASS-AOR
        'In Russia, you get sent to Siberia.'

According to Özkaragöz (1986, 241–242), such double passives are relatively productive in Turkish, and they have the properties listed in (21).

(21) *Properties of Turkish double passives*
    a. Two passive suffixes attach to the verb stem.
    b. The tense must be aorist.
    c. The verb stem must be transitive, and the initial subject and object are both PRO (i.e., generic, unspecified).

However, as just suggested for the Irish autonomous form, such examples can be analyzed not as double passives, but rather as the combination of an (active) impersonal and a regular passive. The Turkish "double passive" in (20b) would then be analogous to the French example in (22), a single passive with an unspecified human subject:

(22) On est envoyé en Siberie.
     one is   sent   to Siberia
     'People are sent to Siberia.'

Özkaragöz (1986, 242 n. 6) notes that the preferred paraphrase for double passives has an overt "arbitrary reference" pronoun, *insan* 'one', as illustrated in (23b):

(23) a. Harp-te vur-ul-un-ur. (Özkaragöz 1986, 241, 25c)
       war-LOC shoot-PASS-PASS-AOR
       'People get shot in wartime.'
   b. Harp-te insan vur-ul-ur.
       war-LOC one   shoot-PASS-AOR
       'One gets shot in wartime.'

The Turkish passive morpheme seems to have two different, distinct functions: one function is to form a canonical passive, the other forms the active impersonal construction that we have seen in Polish, Irish, and Finnish. The restrictions on this morphology make it possible to tease apart the two distinct, homophonous morphemes.

(24) *Differences between personal and impersonal passives in Turkish*
  a. Only personal passives (i.e., of V_{trans}) allow a *by*-phrase.[18]
  b. Impersonal passives must be interpreted as [+human].[19]
  c. Passives of unaccusatives must be aorist (Sezer 1991, 64).

The morpheme that forms the canonical passive attaches to transitive verbs and unergative intransitives, and just as in Germanic, this construction exhibits 1AEX effects. The other morpheme forms an impersonal construction that requires an unspecified human subject (PRO-arb); as a syntactically active construction, it is not subject to the 1AEX.

The verb in this Turkish impersonal construction must be aorist—that is, the PRO-arb subject is licensed by [−AGR]. Since the impersonal "passive" of unaccusatives is noneventive,[20] it is incompatible with specific time adverbials such as 'last year/ yesterday', a restriction observed by Sezer (1991, 64), from whom examples (25)– (26) are taken:

(25) a. Dikkat   et, burada çok fena kay-ıl-ır.
         attention do, here   very badly skid-PASS-AOR
         'Be careful, one skids very badly here.'
     b. *Ay, dün   burada çok fena kay-ıl-dı.
         oh, yesterday here   very badly skid-PASS-PAST
         'Oh, yesterday it was skidded here very badly.'

Impersonal passives of unergative verbs, on the other hand, are not subject to such a restriction:

(26) Dün burada ne oldu?
     'What happened here yesterday?'
     a. oyna-n-di.
        'It was played.'
     b. çalış-ıl-di.
        'It was studied.'
     c. avlan-ıl-di.
        'It was hunted.'

Since passives are derived unaccusatives, the passive of a passive would violate the Unaccusative Hypothesis. But once the two distinct uses of the "passive" morphology are sorted out, we see that Turkish does not violate the 1AEX law. The "passive" morpheme can occur with any verb, including unaccusatives, as long as the subject can be interpreted as human.[21]

(27) a. Bu yetimhane-de   çabuk büyü-n-ür. (Baker 1988, 329)
        the orphanage-LOC fast   grow-PASS-AOR
        'They grow up quickly in this orphanage.'

b. Şu orman-da sIk sIk kaybol-un-ur.
   that forest-LOC often disappear-PASS-AOR
   'People often disappeared in that forest.'

Just as we have seen for Finnish, Irish, and Polish, such putative passives are better analyzed as impersonal actives with unspecified human subjects. The unaccusative verbs that can form "passives" are those that select human subjects, such as *grow* and *die*, but not *wilt*. Thus the occurrence of unaccusative verbs in this construction does not constitute violations of the 1AEX since the construction is not passive, but syntactically active.

This analysis of the so-called passive morpheme as homophonous leads to two further predictions. Double passives can contain at most one *by*-phrase, and the transitive verb stem must be a verb that selects a human object. That is, double passives should include verbs like *beat* and *send*, but not verbs like *read* and *write*. This prediction is borne out, as illustrated by the contrast in (28).

(28) a. *Rusya-da bazı kitap-lar gizlice oku-n-ul-ur.
        Russia-LOC some books-PL secretly read-PASS-PASS-AOR
     b. Rusya-da bazı kitap-lar gizlice oku-n-ur.
        Russia-LOC some books-PL secretly read-PASS-AOR
        'In Russia, certain books are read secretly.'

I have argued here for a dual analysis of the passive morpheme in Turkish. Özkaragöz (1986) pursues a unified analysis in which the passive morpheme has the unitary function of marking 2-to-1 advancement. She argues against the suggestion made by Knecht (1985) that intransitive Vs with unspecified human subjects may appear with passive affix, noting that it is not true that all such verbs can appear in the construction; in particular, she argues (p. 254) that Knecht's generalization cannot account for the ungrammaticality of examples like the following:

(29) a. *PRO git-ti.
        PRO go-PAST
        Intended: 'People went/left.'
     b. *PRO kapi-yi ac-ti.
        PRO door-ACC open-PAST
        Intended: 'People opened the door.'

But these examples are bad for independent reasons, namely they have the past-tense suffix rather than aorist, and hence their ungrammaticality cannot be taken to undermine Knecht's generalization.

In conclusion, whenever a transitive verb allows a human object, the corresponding passive can be impersonalized in languages like Turkish that contain both constructions. This treatment of Turkish reinforces the conclusions of Noonan (1994) and Blevins (2003), who independently argued for the same reanalysis of the putative "double passives."

15.5 Impersonal Passives of Unaccusatives in Dutch and German

There are exceptions to the 1AEX in Dutch and German that merit further investigation.[22] Nonagentive verbs including the verb *dø* 'die' do not passivize in Norwegian, as noted in a relatively recent Norwegian reference grammar (Faarlund, Lie, and Vannebo 1997, 840); the same seems to be true of the other Scandinavian languages. However, a Google search (April 2006) for *es wurde gestorben* 'it was died' got sixty-four hits, including the following example:

(30) Es wurde gestorben auf beiden Seiten.
   it was died on both sides
   'People died on both sides.'

Sixty-four hits is not a huge number, but it is sufficient to indicate that such examples cannot categorically be labeled ungrammatical in German. In *Grammatik der deutschen Sprache*, Zifonun, Hoffmann, and Strecker (1997) state that in general, one-place nonagentive predicates cannot passivize (p. 1805), but they go on to observe that in some contexts, a passive is possible for a one-place predicate with a nonagentive animate participant. In such cases, an agentive adjunct (*by*-phrase) is impossible, and a special effect is achieved, typically with a focus on general processes common to groups of individuals (p. 1806).[23] They give the following sentence to illustrate this (their example number (8)):

(31) Damals wurde in Deutschland rascher gelebt und viel gestorben.
   back.then was in Germany faster lived and much died.
   'Back then, life was faster in Germany and many more people died.'

Similarly, for at least some speakers, impersonal passives based on unaccusatives are quite acceptable in Dutch, provided they have human subjects:

(32) a. Er werd daar heel wat af-gevallen.
      it was there quite what off-fallen
      'People lost a lot of weight there.'
   b. Er werd daar aan de lopende band gestorven.
      it was there on the conveyor belt died
      'There was constant death/dying there.'

Adding the particle *af* 'off' or some adverbial modifier often helps (Marcel den Dikken, personal communication, May 4, 2006). These observations are consistent with the hypothesis that such sentences in Dutch and German should be analyzed not as impersonal "passives," but as impersonal actives, just like the Polish

-*no/to* construction. Further research is needed to explore the implications of this suggestion.

15.6 Conclusion

In both Polish and Irish, passive morphology has been reanalyzed as an invariant nonagreeing form that licenses an unspecified human (PRO$_{arb}$) subject. As the result of this reanalysis, a historically passive-voice construction has become a syntactically active construction with all the syntactic properties expected of a construction with a thematic subject. In Polish, both constructions coexist, but with distinct morphology; in Irish, only the autonomous form survives as a productive construction. It is dangerous to judge an affix by its name. A lot of things called passive in the literature turn out not to be passive in any useful sense; some so-called subjectless constructions turn out to have thematic null subjects. Identifying these apparent passives of unaccusative verbs as impersonal "unpassives" reveals the descriptive power of the Unaccusative Hypothesis.

Notes

I am grateful to the following people for native-speaker judgments and/or discussion of the theoretical issues: Loren A. Billings, Viviane Deprez, Marcel den Dikken, Robert Hornstein, Oleh S. Ilnytzkyj, Alexandra Isaievych, Ray Jackendoff, Zbigniew Kański, Jaklin Kornfilt, Murat Kural, Knud Lambrecht, Jim McCloskey, John Moore, Dónall Ó'Baoill, Silja Bára Ómarsdóttir, David Pesetsky, Engin Sezer, Halldór Ármann Sigurðsson, Sigríður Sigurjónsdóttir, Torgrim Solstad, Rex Sprouse, Beata Mirska Wang, and Annie Zaenen. The chapter has benefited from discussion at the University of California, Irvine, the University of Massachusetts at Amherst, the University of Helsinki, and the University of Iceland, where an early version was presented in colloquium talks in the spring of 1993. In the intervening years, a number of other scholars have independently arrived at similar conclusions about the analysis of these constructions; see especially Blevins 2003, Kibort 2004, and the references cited there. This research inspired the study of an ongoing syntactic change in Icelandic reported in Maling and Sigurjónsdóttir 2002. Last but not least, I am grateful to an anonymous reviewer for insightful comments and references to the literature, both recent and traditional.

1. The terminology "impersonal passive" is unfortunate, since as will be shown below, the understood subjects are necessarily human/personal; a better term would be indefinite, or autonomous (as used for Irish), or the Relational Grammar term "unspecified human subject" construction.

2. Ukrainian has no impersonal passives of (unergative) intransitive verbs (Sobin, personal communication; Goodall 1993), a fact that is inconsistent with the account proposed in Baker 1988.

3. The following abbreviations are used in the glosses: ACC = accusative, ADV = adverb, AOR = aorist, AUT = autonomous, COMP = complementizer, DAT = dative, DEMON = demonstrative, F = feminine, FIN = finite, FUT = future, GEN = genitive, HABIT = habitual, ILL =

illative, IMP = impersonal, INE = inessive, INF = infinitive, LOC = locative, M = masculine, NEG = negative, NOM = nominative, PAR = partitive, PASS = passive, PAST = past, PL = plural, PRES = present, PROG = progressive, REFL = reflexive, SG = singular.

4. Shore (1988) and Sulkala and Karjalainen (1992) call this form an "active indefinite," Abondolo (1998) refers to "impersonal inflection," while Tommola (1997) refers to the "ambipersonal." The terminology may differ, but these sources agree that the construction lacks the grammatical properties of a true passive.

5. I am indebted to an anonymous reviewer for these quotes. Although the understood subject is indeed generally understood as indefinite, this construction can be used to describe situations where there is a single human agent whose identity is known (Zbigniew Kański, personal communication).

6. In a footnote, Dzwirek (1994) does provide an example from scholarly writing with a first-singular agent.

7. An anonymous reviewer points out that the relevance of humanness rather than animacy is particularly clear in Estonian, as emphasized by Torn (2002).

8. Blevins (2003) defends the same analysis at some length.

9. An anonymous reviewer points out that Polish also has a reflexive impersonal construction, which is in many respects closer to the *-no/to* construction than the passive is. Rothstein (1993, 712) notes "the use of *sie* to express a generalized human subject (like the French *on* or the German *man*)," while de Bray (1980, 105) remarks that "a reflexive verb can be used impersonally, like the use of *one* in English, and can then govern an object."

10. As expected in a syntactically active clause, the thematic object in the *-no/to* construction is marked accusative. Interestingly, the cognate Ukrainian *-no/to* construction discussed by Sobin (1985) does have the syntactic properties of a passive, despite the accusative case marking on the thematic object. For detailed discussion, see Maling and Sigurjónsdóttir 2002; Maling 2006.

11. In Polish, unlike Russian and Ukrainian, only the derived subject and not the logical subject can antecede *swoj-*.

12. I am indebted to Jim McCloskey for the Irish examples not taken from other sources. McCloskey and Sells (1988) argue that *tá* is an unaccusative verb that selects a small clause complement.

13. But see McCloskey 2007, sec. 5, for examples where the autonomous argument is an inanimate cause.

14. Stenson (1989, 384) cites an ungrammatical example with a reciprocal. For discussion of this discrepancy see McCloskey, chapter 17, n. 3, this volume; 2007, 841. He attributes the variability in judgments to the fact that the reciprocal requires a *semantically* plural antecedent; since the null subject of the autonomous form has no syntactic number specification, two different interpretations are available, only one of which is compatible with the requirements of the reciprocal.

15. Historically *a chéile* means 'its fellow' or 'its mate' but it has been frozen in this invariant form for several centuries now (Jim McCloskey, personal communication).

16. This suggestion is due to Jim McCloskey.

17. The passive morpheme has three allomorphs: *-n* after vowels; *-In* after *l*; *-Il* otherwise.

18. See Kornfilt 1976, 438; 1991, 88. Kornfilt (1997, 326) observes that while agentive phrases do not generally occur in impersonal passives, "in official language, such constructions are sometimes found, especially when the verb has a non-specific direct object."

19. This is noted by Knecht (1985) and cited by Baker (1988, 479 n. 21), among others.

20. This noneventive restriction is language-specific; Turkish differs in this respect from both Irish and Polish.

21. Knecht (1985, 55–65) argues that the acceptability of the impersonal passive depends on the humanness of the agent, but in fact, it is not restricted to agents; what the construction requires is a human subject, regardless of theta role.

22. I am indebted to Torgrim Solstad for drawing my attention to this phenomenon.

23. "Allerdings ist in manchen Kontexten bei personalem [letztzubindendem Term] doch ein Eintakt-Passiv möglich; dabei ist jedoch K_prp ausgeschlossen, und es wird ein besonderer Effekt erreicht. Entweder wird auf allgemeine über individuelle Prozesse abgehoben (8)."

The second type mentioned includes imperative uses of 'to fall asleep.' I am indebted to Torgrim Solstad for this reference.

References

Abondolo, Daniel. 1998. Finnish. In D. Abondolo, ed., *The Uralic languages*, 149–183. London: Routledge.

Anderson, Stephen R. 1982. Where's morphology? *Linguistic Inquiry* 13:571–612.

Babby, Leonard. 1989. Subjectlessness, external subcategorization, and the projection principle. *Zbornik matice srpske za filologiju i lingvistiku* 32(2):7–40.

Baker, Mark. 1988. *Incorporation*. Chicago: University of Chicago Press.

Baker, Mark, Kyle Johnson, and Ian Roberts. 1989. Passive arguments raised. *Linguistic Inquiry* 20:219–251.

Barker, Chris, Jorge Hankamer, and John Moore. 1990. *Wa* and *Ga* in Turkish. In *Grammatical relations: A cross-theoretical perspective*, 21–43. Stanford, CA: CSLI.

Billings, Loren A., and Joan Maling. 1995. Accusative-assigning participial -no/-to constructions in Ukrainian, Polish, and neighboring languages: An annotated bibliography. *Journal of Slavic Linguistics* 3(1):177–217 (part 1: A–M); 3(2):396–430 (part 2: N–Z). www.indiana.edu/~slavconf/linguistics/noto.pdf.

Blevins, James P. 2003. Passives and impersonals. *Journal of Linguistics* 39:473–520.

de Bray, R. G. A. 1980. *Guide to the West Slavonic languages: Part 2*. Columbus, OH: Slavica.

Dyła, Stefan. 1982. Some further evidence against an impersonal passive analysis of Polish impersonal constructions. *Studia anglica posnaniensia: An international review of English studies* 15:123–128.

Dziwirek, Katarzyna. 1990. Two types of subject demotion contrasted: Evidence from Polish impersonals. *FLSM* 1:81–97.

Dziwirek, Katarzyna. 1994. Covert subjects. In K. Dziwirek, *Polish subjects*, 177–235. New York: Garland.

Faarlund, Jan Terje, Svein Lie, and Kjell Ivar Vannebo. 1997. *Norsk referansegrammatikk*. Oslo: Universitetsforlaget.

Goodall, Grant. 1993. On case and the passive morpheme. *Natural Language and Linguistic Theory* 11(1):31–44.

Kaiser, Elsi, and Virve-Anneli Vihman. 2006. Invisible arguments: Effects of demotion in Estonian and Finnish. In Benjamin Lyngfelt and Torgrim Solstad, eds., *Demoting the agent: Passive, middle and other voice-related phenomena*, 111–141. Linguistik Aktuell 96. Amsterdam: John Benjamins.

Keenan, Edward, and Alan Timberlake. 1985. Predicate formation rules in universal grammar. *WCCFL* 4:123–138.

Kibort, Anna. 2004. Passive and passive-like constructions in English and Polish: A contrastive study with particular reference to impersonal constructions. Doctoral dissertation, University of Cambridge.

Knecht, Laura. 1985. Subject and object in Turkish. Doctoral dissertation, MIT.

Kornfilt, Jaklin. 1976. The cycle against free rule application (evidence from Turkish). In J. Hankamer and J. Aissen, eds., *290r*: Harvard studies in syntax and semantics*, vol. 2, 359–444. Cambridge, MA: Department of Linguistics, Harvard University.

Kornfilt, Jaklin. 1991. Some current issues in Turkish syntax. In Hendrik E. Boeschoten and Ludoth Verhoeven, eds., *Turkish linguistics today*, 60–92. Leiden: E. J. Brill.

Kornfilt, Jaklin. 1997. *Turkish*. London: Routledge.

Lyngfelt, Benjamin, and Torgrim Solstad, eds. 2006. *Demoting the agent: Passive, middle and other voice-related phenomena*. Linguistik Aktuell 96. Amsterdam: John Benjamins.

Maling, Joan. 1993. Unpassives of unaccusatives. Colloquium talk presented at University of California Irvine, University of Massachusetts at Amherst, University of Helsinki, University of Iceland.

Maling, Joan. 2006. From passive to active: Syntactic change in progress in Icelandic. In Benjamin Lyngfelt and Torgrim Solstad, eds., *Demoting the agent: Passive, middle and other voice-related phenomena*, 197–223. Linguistik Aktuell 96. Amsterdam: John Benjamins.

Maling, Joan, and Sigríður Sigurjónsdóttir. 2002. The "new impersonal" construction in Icelandic. *Journal of Comparative Germanic Linguistics* 5:97–142.

Marantz, Alec. 1984. *On the nature of grammatical relations*. Cambridge, MA: MIT Press.

McCloskey, James. 2007. The grammar of autonomy in Irish. *Natural Language and Linguistic Theory* 25:825–857.

McCloskey, James, and Peter Sells. 1988. Control and A-chains in Modern Irish. *Natural Language and Linguistic Theory* 6:143–189.

Nerbonne, John A. 1982. Some passives not characterized by universal rules: Subjectless impersonal. In Brian D. Joseph, ed., *Grammatical relations and relational grammar*, 59–92. WPL 26. Columbus: Ohio State University.

Noonan, Michael. 1994. A tale of two passives in Irish. In B. Fox and P. J. Hopper, eds., *Voice: Form and function*, 279–311. Amsterdam: John Benjamins.

Özkaragöz, Inci Zühra. 1986. The relational structure of Turkish syntax. Unpublished doctoral dissertation, UCSD.

Perlmutter, David. 1978. Impersonal passives and the unaccusative hypothesis. *Proceedings of the Fourth Annual Meeting of the Berkeley Linguistics Society*, 157–189.

Perlmutter, David, and Paul Postal. 1984. The 1-advancement exclusiveness law. In D. Perlmutter and C. Rosen, eds., *Studies in relational grammar* 2, 81–125. Chicago: University of Chicago Press.

Rothstein, Robert A. 1993. Polish. In B. Comrie and G. Corbett, eds., *The Slavonic languages*, 686–758. London: Routledge.

Saloni, Zygmunt. 1986. Obligatory and optional arguments in the syntax of Polish verbs. *International Journal of Slavic Linguistics and Poetics* 3:17–25.

Sezer, Engin. 1991. Issues in Turkish syntax. Unpublished doctoral dissertation, Harvard University.

Shore, Susanna. 1988. On the so-called Finnish passive. *Word* 39:151–176.

Siewierska, Anna. 1988. The passive in Slavic. In M. Shibatani, ed., *Passive and voice*, 243–289. Amsterdam: John Benjamins.

Sobin, Nicholas. 1985. Case assignment in Ukrainian morphological passive constructions. *Linguistic Inquiry* 16:649–662.

Stenson, Nancy. 1989. Irish autonomous impersonals. *Natural Language and Linguistic Theory* 7:379–406.

Sulkala, Helena, and Merja Karjalainen. 1992. *Finnish*. London: Routledge.

Timberlake, Alan. 1982. The impersonal passive in Lithuanian. *Berkeley Linguistics Society* 8:508–523.

Tommola, Hannu. 1997. O supressive i ob ambipersonale. *Trudy po russkoj i slavjanskoj filologii. Lingvistika, Novaja serija, vyp. 1*, 173–187. Tartu: Tartu Ülikooli Kirjastus.

Torn, Reeli. 2002. The status of the passive in English and Estonian. In H. Hendriks, ed., *Working Papers in English and Applied Linguistics* 7, 81–106. Cambridge: Research Centre for English and Applied Linguistics.

Zifonun, Gisela, Ludger Hoffmann, and Bruno Strecker. 1997. *Grammatik der deutschen Sprache*. Vol. 3. Berlin: Mouton de Gruyter.

16 Semantic and Syntactic Subcategorization in Seri: Recipients and Addressees

Stephen A. Marlett

16.1 Introduction

A common goal of language description has been to relate semantic roles and syntactic relations in a given language. Some relationships are very common, such as Agent-Subject and Patient-Object. Different theories have had alternative ways of addressing these facts, although some hypotheses were shown to be too strong (see the Universal Alignment Hypothesis of Relational Grammar (Perlmutter and Postal 1984, 97–100) and the discussion in Rosen 1984, for example). But despite the problem areas here and there, no one wants to simply abandon all attempts to make some generalizations about the relationship between semantic roles and syntactic relations. Theories of language that are syntactocentric have included subcategorization frames focusing on syntactic relations that somehow must be linked with semantic roles (see the theta criterion (Chomsky 1981, 36), for instance).

In this chapter I present a range of facts relating to the semantic roles commonly referred to as Recipient and Addressee (plus a few others) in the Seri language.[1] These data have perplexed me for a number of years, and I have wondered how to understand them and how it is that a language learner can actually internalize them. I hope to show here that a few simple assumptions about default settings of linking or association between semantic arguments and syntactic arguments, together with a couple of verb-specific settings, take us a long way in the direction of something learnable. As I show below, I make use of Jackendoff's (2002) idea of "parallel architecture," in which neither syntactic relations nor semantic roles have priority; verb subcategorization requires both. The account also crucially depends on the notions of Chômeur and Indirect Object that were central to Relational Grammar.

It may be helpful to mention some typological facts about Seri before beginning. The language is typically SOV and pro-drop. It has no case marking on the nominals. Finite verbs agree in person with three nominals; infinitives agree in person with two nonsubject nominals and in number with the controlling subject. Verb morphology contains multiple indicators of transitivity of the clause, summarized in appendix 16.1; they are used in the argumentation that follows.

Table 16.1
Agreement morphology

	Set 3 Indirect object	Set 2 Direct object	Set 1 Subject
1 sg.	he-	him-	hp- (intransitive)
			h- (transitive)
1 pl.		hizi-	ha-
2 sg.	me-	ma-	m-
2 pl.		mazi-	ma-
3	co-	(no morphology)	(no morphology)
3:3		i-	
3:1		*he-	
3:2		*me-	

* These prefixes are portmanteaux that occur when third-person Indirect Object occurs with a first- or second-person Direct Object.

As table 16.1 shows, verb agreement morphology in Seri is organized into three sets of agreement prefixes. Set 1 is easily identified and labeled as being subject agreement. Sets 2 and 3 are a bit more problematic. In the vast majority of simple transitive clauses, the Patient or Undergoer or Theme is indicated by the morphology of Set 2, and therefore I refer to it as the direct-object agreement set. Set 3 is more interesting since the semantic roles are numerous and far more varied than expected (see Marlett 1990, 527–531). Most of these roles are not directly relevant to the presentation here, however, but they include Location, Instrument, Manner, and Reference as well as Recipient and Addressee. Just to have a simple label for this agreement set, I call it indirect-object agreement, although one must abandon the common prejudice of associating this rubric only with Recipient and Addressee.

The set of data that I consider here are the verb agreement patterns for approximately thirty-five verbs that conceptually take a Recipient or Addressee (or something similar—and all of these are prototypically human) and that are not causative verbs. These data are summarized in table 16.2. Causative verbs do not show any of the syntactic variation that we see below and so are of less interest.[2]

In the following sections, I look at the ways the two nonsubject arguments are encoded with these verbs. (Subjects are set aside for the sake of convenience since they do not contribute to the discussion of these verbs.) The nominal corresponding to the semantic Patient or Theme or Topic appears in one of three ways in Seri, depending primarily on the verb: as Direct Object, as Indirect Object, or as Chômeur (a term that I adopt from Relational Grammar and explain below). I argue that the *default* marking of such nominals is (to no one's surprise) as Direct Object. This default linking is indicated in (1) by a dotted line.

(1) Patient/Theme/Topic

Direct Object	Indirect Object	Chômeur
(13 verbs)	(10 verbs)	(2 verbs)

As shown in (2), the nominal corresponding to the semantic Recipient, Addressee, or Malefactive also appears in one of three ways, depending primarily on the verb: as Direct Object, as Indirect Object, or as Object of Postposition.[3] I do not claim that any of these is the default marking; therefore, no default linking is indicated.

(2) Recipient/Addressee/etc.

Direct Object	Indirect Object	Object of Postposition
(13 verbs)	(7 verbs)	(11 verbs)

If we look at both sets of semantic roles together (Patient/Theme/Topic and Recipient/Addressee/etc.), we see that there are actually four different grammatical relations to be accounted for: Direct Object, Indirect Object, Object of Postposition, and Chômeur. The difference between these relations is not based on just one isolated fact. A Direct Object determines direct-object agreement and also determines the transitivity of the verb for all of the morphology that is sensitive to transitivity (see appendix 16.1). This is the nominal that may also be the subject of a passive construction. An Indirect Object determines indirect-object agreement, does *not* determine the transitivity of the verb, and may *not* be the subject of a passive construction.[4] A Chômeur basically just sits there without any correlated morphology (case or agreement), although I have argued elsewhere (Marlett 1984, 234–236) that things are not quite that simple.[5] An Object of a Postposition is that and nothing else happens.

The main question I want to answer here is how the variety of combinations that appear in table 16.2 can be generated in simple fashion. What does one really need to memorize about each verb? To do this, I adopt the following position, which generally corresponds to that laid out in Jackendoff 2002: it is necessary to propose a parallel architecture for the verb's argument structure, and we therefore need to propose subcategorization frames for the semantic arguments as well as for the syntactic arguments of the verbs. I also appeal to the notion of Indirect Object as something distinct from Direct Object and Object of Postposition. The notion of Indirect Object is explicitly absent from the design of certain current and not-so-current frame-

Table 16.2
Agreement patterns for verbs that conceptually take a recipient or addressee

Groups		PP	Chômeur	Indirect	Direct	Subcategorization frames	
						Semantic	Syntactic
(1)	queque 'give (gift)', cocozj 'sell on credit'						[ ]
(2)	quique 'give (gift)', quitalhaa 'buy', czaxö 'discuss', quiisxö 'hide'				Item	Theme	[D.O.]
(3a)	quiiom 'petition for', quiso 'ask to borrow'	(Human)			Item	Theme (Addressee)	[D.O.]
(3b)	quimx 'say'	(Human$_{pl}$)			Item	Theme (Addressee$_{pl}$)	[D.O.]
(4a)	caaom 'petition'				Human	Addressee	[D.O.]
(4b)	hacx queesxö 'hide oneself (from)'				(Human)	(Maleficiary)	[(D.O.)]
(5)	queezi 'rent to'	Human				Recipient	[ ]
(6)	queeti 'fetch for'	Human$_{pl}$		Human$_{sg}$		Beneficiary	[I.O.$_{sg}$]
(7a)	(co)ccazit 'grab (from)', (co)ccooz 'rob ((from))'			(Human)	Item	Theme (Source/Maleficiary)	[(I.O.) D.O.]
(7b)	cöqueesxö 'hide from', cocqueetx 'return to'			Human	Item	Theme, Malef./Recipient	[I.O. D.O.]
(7c)	cöcaamx 'say/promise to'			Human$_{sg}$	Item	Theme, Addressee	[I.O.$_{sg}$ D.O.]
(7d)	(cö)quimjc 'take/bring (to)'	(Human$_{pl}$)		(Human$_{sg}$)	Item	Theme, Recipient	[(I.O.$_{sg}$) D.O.]

	Item	Human	Theme, Recipient_DO ✓	[D.O.]
(8) iique 'give (gift) to', quiye 'give (food) to'	Item		Theme, Recipient_DO ✓	[D.O.]
(9a) cöcocosot 'lend'	Item		Theme	[I.O.]
(9b) caaitom 'speak', quee 'say', comiit 'ask'	Item		(Theme)	[(I.O.)]
(10) cöcamiit 'ask'	Item	(Human_pl)	Theme_IO ✓, (Addressee_pl)	[I.O.]
(11a) cöquitalhaa 'sell (to)', cöcaasot 'lend (to)', cöcaatajquim 'insult', cöquinim 'splash (on)'†	Item	(Human_sg)	Theme_IO ✓, (Recip./Addr./Aff.)	[I.O. (D.O._sg)]
(11b) (cö)caaipot 'pay to', (co)czaxö 'discuss with', (cö)caazj 'sell on credit', (cö)quii 'tell'	(Item)	Human	(Theme_IO) ✓, Recip./Addr.	[(I.O.) D.O.]
(11c) (co)cmiiit 'ask (about)'	(Item)	Human_sg	(Theme_IO) ✓, Addressee	[(I.O.) D.O._sg]

† Other related verbs: cöcocotajquim ('insult') when the Addressee is plural, and cöqueenim ('splash') when the Affectee is plural. The Affectee is not optional for these verbs. The Affectee is not optional for these verbs.

works, but I do not believe an adequate description of these facts can be achieved without it.

16.2 The Description

16.2.1 Semantic Arguments

I begin by clarifying that I distinguish between the semantic/conceptual structure of a verb and some vaguer notion of spatial structure. As Jackendoff puts it (2002, 12), "One can think of spatial structure variously as an image of the scene that the sentence describes, a schema that must be compared against the world in order to verify the sentence ..., the physical (or non-propositional) model in which the truth conditions of semantic/conceptual structure are applied, or perhaps other construals." This is relevant for various verbs of speaking and giving in Seri.

Consider the verbs in group 1 in table 16.2. These verbs simply do not ever occur with a tautoclausal nominal that is Patient/Topic, nor do they occur with a nominal that is Recipient/Addressee. While one may obviously envision some person who is a Recipient and some thing that is a gift when these verbs are used, these nominals are not included in the Semantic Subcategorization frames of these verbs. Hence they do not occur in the Syntactic Subcategorization frame either. These verbs are simple intransitives. I state the relevant (unremarkable) assumption explicitly in (3).

(3) Some verbs have fewer semantic arguments (and hence fewer syntactic arguments) than conceptualization might suggest.

Part of what one has to memorize for each verb is the array of semantic arguments that it takes. This information is specified in the Semantic Subcategorization frame. As shown in the column labeled "Semantic" in table 16.2, the verb may or may not specify the presence of any role. The verbs in group 1 in table 16.2 subcategorize for no semantic arguments of the type Patient/Theme or Addressee/Recipient.

Another portion of what one has to memorize for each verb is the array of syntactic arguments that it takes. This information is specified in the Syntactic Subcategorization frame. As shown in the column labeled "Syntactic" in table 16.2, the verb may or may not specify the presence of a Direct Object or Indirect Object. In Jackendoff's system, this is separate from the Semantic subcategorization. It is noted by Jackendoff (2002, 150–151) that there is something special about the grammatical functions Subject, Direct Object, and Indirect Object (which are also the "Terms" of Relational Grammar, see Perlmutter 1983, x–xi). This specialness is an important part of the present analysis since I propose that syntactic subcategorization of verbs in Seri is limited to these functions. Two key assumptions for (nonsubject) subcategorization in Seri are the following:

Semantic and Syntactic Subcategorization in Seri

(4) Syntactic subcategorization frames in Seri refer only to Direct Objects and Indirect Objects.

(5) Syntactic subcategorization frames in Seri may contain only a Direct Object, only an Indirect Object, both, or neither.

16.2.2 Straightforward Linking of Semantic Arguments to Syntactic Arguments

The number of syntactic arguments is equal to or less than the number of semantic arguments (Jackendoff 2002, 139). A number of general principles account for the ways that the semantic arguments are linked to the syntactic arguments. I believe there are two major principles operating in Seri.

16.2.2.1 Patient/Theme as Direct Object First, as mentioned above, the default pattern is for a Patient/Theme to be linked to Direct Object; see (6) and the verbs in groups 2–3 in table 16.2, illustrated by examples (7)–(11) below.

(6) Default: Patient/Theme is linked to Direct Object.

In examples (7)–(9) the verbs carry the prefix *i-*, which is appropriate for a clause with a third-person subject and third-person direct object. There is no indirect-object agreement in any of the examples in (7)–(12); thus these clauses have no Indirect Object. In examples (10)–(11) the transitive allomorph of the first-person singular subject prefix is used. Example (12) has the transitive infinitival form of the verb. All these facts are consistent with the claim that these clauses contain a Direct Object and no Indirect Object or Addressee/Recipient (or similar nominal).[6]

(7) ¿I-trooqui quih i-t-eque?
    3P-vehicle the   3:3-Rl-give.gift
    'Did she/he give his/her car (as a gift)?' (quique 'give gift')

(8) ¿I-t-amx?
    3:3-Rl-say
    'Did she/he say it?' (quimx 'say')

(9) ¿Zixcam quih c-atxo   pac i-s-italhaa   haa-ya?
    fish   the SN-be.much some 3:3-Ir-buy/sell Aux-Int
    'Will she/he buy a lot of fish?' (quitalhaa 'buy')

(10) Ihyoomx. < h-yo-amx
     1sST-Dt-say
     'I said it.' (quimx 'say')

(11) Icaaitom ihmaa   mos zo h-yo-zaxö.
     word   another also a 1sST-Dt-discuss
     'I discussed another topic.' (czaxö 'discuss')

(12) Hasaj cap iha-talhaa   h-mii-mzo.
     basket the INFT-buy/sell 1sST-Px-want
     'I want to buy the basket.' (quitalhaa 'buy')

The ungrammatical sentences in (13) are all attempts to try to include mention of the person from whom the basket would be bought. None is successful because this verb simply does not subcategorize for one semantically.

(13) a. *Hasaj cap me-ihatalhaa hmiimzo.
              2IO-
     b. *Hasaj cap mi-ti ihatalhaa hmiimzo.
              2P-on
     c. *Hasaj cap ma-ihatalhaa hmiimzo.
              2sDO-
        'I want to buy the basket from you.' (quitalhaa 'buy')

To take a simple example here to illustrate how these facts are described, consider the verb *quique* 'give (gift)' (group 2 in table 16.2). This verb subcategorizes for one semantic argument (a Theme) and one syntactic argument (a Direct Object) other than subject. The principle in (6) permits a simple, unmarked association to take place between these.

16.2.2.2 Recipient/Addressee as Direct Object As for the second principle, it needs to be stated explicitly for Seri that Recipients/Addressees *may* be linked to Direct Object. In some languages such a linking is obligatory, in others permitted, and in others not permitted. The Seri version of this range of crosslinguistically attested possibilities is explained below. The statement in (14) is in itself unremarkable crosslinguistically.

(14) Recipient/Addressee/etc. may be linked to Direct Object or Indirect Object.

See group 4 in table 16.2 for examples of verbs where one sees an Addressee/etc. linked to Direct Object, as well as the sentences given in (15)–(19) below. Example (15) is ambiguous between an intransitive reading and a transitive reading, but examples (16)–(19) are unambiguously transitive and the person from whom the hiding or petitioning happens is the Direct Object. These clauses do not contain any evidence of the Indirect Object relation.

(15) ¿Me   hacx   qu-eesxö-ya?
     2PRO somewhere SN-hide.oneself-INT
     'Are you hiding?' [implied, 'yourself'] (intransitive reading)
     'Are you hiding?' [implied, 'yourself'] from him/her? (transitive reading)
     (queesxö 'hide self, hide self from')

(16) ¡Hacx   h-eesxö!
    somewhere Im-hide.oneself
    'Hide (yourself) from him/her!' (queesxö 'hide self, hide self from')

(17) ¿Hacx   ih-eesxö   in-t-amzo?
    somewhere InfT-hide.oneself 2sS-Rl-want
    'Do you want to hide (yourself) from him/her?' (queesxö 'hide self', 'hide self from')

In (18)–(19) the presence of direct-object agreement is indicative, of course, of the fact that the Addressee is Direct Object. (The allomorphy for first-person singular direct-object agreement is different in imperatives than in other forms.)

(18) ¡Hacx   ihp-∅-eesxö!
    somewhere 1sDO-Im-hide.oneself
    'Hide (yourself) from me!' (queesxö 'hide self, hide self from')

(19) Hin-y-aaom-oj.
    1sDO-Dt-petition-Pl
    'They were petitioning me.' (caaom 'petition')

The examples in (20) illustrate that alternative morphology (indirect-object agreement in (20a), postpositional marking in (20b)) is not possible with the verb *caaom* 'petition'. The examples in (21) illustrate that this verb does not subcategorize for a Patient/Theme.

(20) *He-yaaomoj. / *Hiti yaaomoj.
    1sIO   1P-on
    'They were petitioning me.' (caaom 'petition')

(21) *Siimet quih hin-yaaomoj. / he-yaaomoj. / hiti yaaomoj.
                 1sDO   1sIO   1P-on
    'They were petitioning me for bread.' (caaom 'petition')

16.2.2.3 Recipient/Addressee as Indirect Object Principles (6) and (14) straightforwardly account for the fact that when only a Patient/Theme occurs in Seri it is, in the vast majority of cases, a Direct Object. They also account for the fact that when only a Recipient/Addressee occurs it may be linked to whichever syntactic argument the verb subcategorizes for: either Direct Object or Indirect Object.

To take two simple examples here to illustrate, consider the verbs *caaom* 'petition' (group 4a in table 16.2) and *queeti* 'fetch for' (group 6 in table 16.2). The verb *caaom* 'petition' is derivationally related to another verb in table 16.2 (*quiiom*, group 3a); *caaom* subcategorizes only for one semantic argument (an Addressee) and one syntactic argument (a Direct Object). The principle in (14) permits a simple association to take place between these.

(22) Semantics: Addressee   caaom 'petition'
                        ⋮
    Syntax: Direct Object

Setting aside the detail of the singular/plural distinction until later, the verb *queeti* 'fetch for' subcategorizes for one semantic argument (a Beneficiary, or whatever one wishes to label this role) and one syntactic argument (an Indirect Object). The principle in (14) also permits a simple association to take place between these.

(23) Semantics: Beneficiary   queeti 'fetch for'
                        ⋮
    Syntax: Indirect Object

The following examples illustrate the above association. Notice in (24) the agreement with Indirect Object and the intransitive allomorphy of the subject agreement prefix. The examples in (25) are meant to illustrate that this verb does not subcategorize for a Patient/Theme.

(24) Me-hp-y-eeti.
     2IO-1sSI-DT-fetch
     'I fetched for you (sg.).' (queeti 'fetch for')

(25) *Ziix   zo me-hp-y-eeti.   / me-h-y-eeti.
     thing a   2IO-1sSI-DT-fetch   2IO-1sST-DT-fetch
     'I fetched something for you (sg.).' (queeti 'fetch for')

Various other verbs are more prototypical examples of Addressee/Recipients as Indirect Objects, but they subcategorize for two nonsubject nominals. Therefore they are discussed in the following sections.

16.2.3 Mediation between Principles

The principles in (6) and (14) need to be mediated in some way because when the verb has a Patient/Theme and also a Recipient/Addressee, we need to know how these link to the syntactic arguments. In some languages the Recipient/Addressee is preferentially the Direct Object. But that is not the case in Seri. In some way—such as by a ranking of these principles, or by another type of stipulation, or by a slight difference in the wording of them (my choice here)—we want to allow for the default pattern to be that when both occur, the Patient/Theme is the Direct Object. In this way, it appears, we are able to maintain the greatest amount of simplicity overall.

Thus principle (6) indicates the "default" association (Patient/Theme to Direct Object), while principle (14) gives two possibilities for Recipient/Addressees and uses the modal *may*. The verbs in group 7 in table 16.2 display this pattern, illustrated by examples (27–34) below. The dotted lines in the following illustration of the association between semantics and syntax indicate that the associations are by general principle.[7] Any other pattern would be a marked one (of which we see examples below).

(26) Semantics:　　　Recipient　　　　Theme　　　cocqueetx 'return to'

　　　Syntax:　　　Indirect Object　　Direct Object

In all of the examples immediately below, indirect-object agreement is present and relates to the semantic role that is not the Patient/Theme.[8] This pattern is not unusual crosslinguistically.

(27) Tom　　quih　he-i-yo-cazit.
　　　money　the　1IO-3:3-DT-grab
　　　'She/he grabbed the money away from me.' ((co)ccazit 'grab (from)')

(28) Tom　　quih　he-i-yo-cazitim.
　　　money　the　1IO-3:3-DT-grab/Impf
　　　'She/he grabbed the money away from us.' ((co)ccazit 'grab (from)')

(29) Tiix　　ziix　i-tac　　quih　haxz　cop　cö-i-m-cazit.
　　　that.one thing 3P-bone the　dog　the　3IO-3:3-Px-grab
　　　'She/he grabbed the bone away from the dog.' ((co)ccazit 'grab (from)')

(30) Eenim　hipcap　ah　he-i-m-cooz　　xo　mos　ih-m-exl.
　　　knife　this　Foc　1IO-3:3-Px-rob　but also 1sST-Px-take
　　　'She/he stole this knife from me, but I took it back.' ((co)ccooz 'rob (from)')

(31) ¡He-h-eesxö!
　　　1IO-IM-hide.from
　　　'Hide it from me/us!' (cöqueesxö 'hide from')

(32) Icaaspoj quih me-i-sc-m-eesxö　　　a-ha.
　　　pencil　the　2IO-3:3-IR-N-hide.from　AUX-DECL
　　　'She/he will not hide the pencil from you (sg./pl.).' (cöqueesxö 'hide from')

(33) Ih-y-aazi,　　¡hanzajipj qu-ii-pa　　hipcop ma-maz　　　co-h-queetx!
　　　1P-ON-carry pan　　SN-with-tail this　2P-grandmother 3IO-IM-return
　　　'Son, take this frying pan back to your grandmother.' (cocqueetx 'return to')

(34) Icaaspoj quih he i-∅-p-esxö　　　ih-mii-mzo.
　　　pencil　the　1IO-3P-AN-Pv-hide.from 1sST-Px-want
　　　'I want the pencil to be hidden from me.' (cöqueesxö 'hide from')

16.2.4 Linking Semantic Arguments to Syntactic Arguments When They Do Not Match in Number of Arguments

The number of syntactic arguments is independent of the number of semantic arguments (although never more than that number), and relatively independent of which particular semantic arguments occur. Two important consequences arise as a result of the mismatch of semantic subcategorization and syntactic subcategorization. The Recipient/Addressee might not be linked to any syntactic relation, or the Patient/Theme might not be linked to any syntactic relation. These consequences are elaborated in the following sections.

16.2.4.1 Recipient/Addressee That Cannot Be Linked
First, there may be a Recipient/Addressee that is not linkable to a syntactic relation. When this is the case, the Recipient/Addressee appears as the Object of a particular postposition (*iti* (literally 'on') for singular nominals, *ano* (literally 'in') for plural ones). The marking of a Recipient/Addressee in this way is a Seri-specific rule.

(35) An *unlinked* Recipient/Addressee/etc. is marked by the pospositions *iti* (for singular) and *ano* (for plural).[9]

One simple example is the verb *queezi* 'rent to' in group 5 in table 16.2. This verb (which literally means 'defeat (intransitive)') subcategorizes for a Recipient (the person to whom the item will be rented), but not for a tautoclausal Patient/Theme.

(36) Semantics: Recipient   *queezi* 'rent to'
     Syntax:

The verb is syntactically intransitive; the Recipient is marked according to rule (35).

(37) Haaco hyaa cop cmiique ihmaa   z ∅-ano p-iih ta   x,   i-ti   hp-s-eezi
     house mine the Seri   another a 3P-in Ir-be DS UT 3P-on 1sSI-Ir-rent.to
     a-ha.
     Aux-Decl
     'I am going to rent my house to someone.' (More literally, 'Another Seri person will be in my house, I will rent to him/her.')

Another example is the verb *quiiom* in group 3 in table 16.2.[10] It subcategorizes for only one syntactic argument, but two semantic arguments (the Addressee being optional). Illustrative sentences are given in (38–39).

(38) Siimet quih mi-ti   i-t-aaom, ...
     bread the 2P-on 3:3-Rl-petition
     'She/he was petitioning you (sg.) for bread, ...' (*quiiom* 'petition (y) for x')

(39) Ziix_cxatlc quih hi-n[11]   i-t-aaom, ...
     tortilla   the   1P-in/from   3:3-RL-petition
     'She/he was petitioning us for a tortilla, ...' (quiiom 'petition (y) for x')

The mechanics of the association of semantic roles and syntactic functions are illustrated in (40), where the default linking of Theme to Direct Object takes place but the optional Addressee is not linked to a syntactic relation (for lack of one in the subcategorization frame). This means that the Addressee is marked by rule (35).

(40) Semantics: (Addressee)   Theme   quiiom 'petition (y) for x'
                                     ⋮
     Syntax: Direct Object

One of the true idiosyncrasies of Seri is that some verbs mention the condition "singular" in the subcategorization frame, either for the Indirect Object or for the Direct Object (although in all cases it is the number of a Recipient/Addressee that is relevant). The verb *queeti* 'fetch for' (group 6, table 16.2), for example, only allows *singular* Indirect Objects, as illustrated in (24) above. This means that a plural Recipient/Beneficiary with this verb appears as object of a postposition, and the clause is intransitive (notice the intransitive allomorph of the subject agreement prefix in (41)).

(41) Comcaac tacoi ∅-ano hp-y-eeti.
     people   those 3P-in 1sSI-DT-fetch
     'I fetched for those people.' (queeti 'fetch for')

Examples (42) and (43) show that there is no way to configure this sentence in order to include mention of the item fetched and that it is ungrammatical to configure the plural Recipient/Beneficiary as an Indirect Object. The inclusion of the item fetched renders the sentence ungrammatical whether the verb is conjugated as an intransitive verb or as a transitive one, as the following examples illustrate.

(42) *Ziix zo comcaac tacoi ano hp-yeeti / h-yeeti.
     thing a   1sSI-   1sST-
     'I fetched something for those people.'

(43) *Comcaac tacoi ziix z ano hp-yeeti. / h-yeeti.
     'I fetched something for those people.'

The attempts are ungrammatical even if the verb is inflected for agreement with an indirect object.

(44) a. *Comcaac tacoi ziix zo co-h-yeeti. / co-hp-yeeti.
                              3IO-1sST-   3IO-1sST
     b. *Ziix zo comcaac tacoi co-h-yeeti. / co-hp-yeeti.
                              3IO-1sST-   3IO-1sSI-
        'I fetched something for those people.'

The lexical entry for this verb therefore looks something like the following, with the permitted default linking shown. The plural Beneficiary is marked with the postposition *ano* by rule (35).

(45) Semantics: Beneficiary   queeti 'fetch for'
                     ⋮
     Syntax: Indirect Object$_{sg}$

16.2.4.2 Patient/Theme That Cannot Be Linked   A second case of the mismatch of semantic and syntactic subcategorization is where a Patient/Theme is not linkable to a Direct Object function. When this is the case, the Patient/Theme is a Chômeur. This situation arises in only one case: when there is a marked subcategorization frame (indicated graphically by the icon ✗ in table 16.2) that essentially links the Recipient to the Direct Object (see group 8 in table 16.2), attested for only two verbs in Seri: *iique* 'give (gift)' and *quiye* 'give (food)' (both irregular conjugationally in different ways).[12] The syntactic subcategorization frame specifies only a Direct Object. The semantic subcategorization frame specifies a Theme and a Recipient, with the Recipient prelinked to the Direct Object, as indicated by the solid line in (46). This means that the Theme cannot be an Indirect Object (since none exists in the syntactic subcategorization); there is also no provision for it to be the object of a postposition. Thus it is a Chômeur; it has no marking (for lack of a specific rule in Seri), and it does not have one of the familiar grammatical functions (Direct Object, Indirect Object).

(46) Semantics: Recipient   Theme   quiye 'give (food) to'[13]
                     | iique 'give (gift) to'
     Syntax: Direct Object

The examples below illustrate the use of these verbs. Each has direct-object agreement with the Recipient; the clauses are also obviously transitive (see the allomorph of the first-person subject agreement prefix in (47)). The Theme *tom* 'money' is, I claim, a Chômeur.

(47) ¿Tom   quih ma-hi-t-e?
     money   the   2sDO-1sST-Rl-give.gift
     'Did I give you the money?' (iique 'give (gift) to')

(48) ¿Zixcam quih ma-t-ee?
     fish   the   2sDO-Rl-give.food
     'Did she/he give you fish?' (quiye 'give (food) to')

(49) Zixcam quih him-miy-e.
     fish   the   1sDO-Px-give.food
     'She/he gave me fish.' (quiye 'give (food) to')

In the following examples, the clauses are passive, the Recipient being the Subject. It is crucial to notice that each of these clauses is clearly intransitive (see appendix 16.1).[14]

(50) Tom   quih hp-yo-p-ehe.
money the 1sSI-DT-Pv-give.gift
'I was given the money.' (iique 'give (gift) to')

(51) ¿Zixcam quih hp-t-p-ee?
fish   the   1sSI-RL-Pv-give.food
'Was I given fish?' (quiye 'give (food) to')

(52) Zixcam quih ica-p-ehe   h-mii-mzo.
fish   the INFI-Pv-give.gift 1sST-Px-want
'I want to be given the fish.' (iique 'give (gift) to')

(53) Zixcam quih ica-p-ee   h-mii-mzo
fish   the INFI-Pv-give.food 1sST-Px-want
'I want to be given fish.' (quiye 'give (food) to')

16.2.5 Theme as Indirect Object

Perhaps the most surprising—and interesting—of the linkage patterns seen in table 16.2 is the one in which the Patient/Theme is an Indirect Object (see groups 9–11). The facts discussed here make it clear that this is not simply a matter of quirky case, in which the Patient/Theme simply looks like an Indirect Object. Instead, the Patient/Theme is indeed an Indirect Object.

16.2.5.1 Simple Matchup of Subcategorization Frames

The verb *cöcocosot* 'lend' in group 9a has only one semantic argument and only one syntactic argument, which are linked without special mention.[15] The Theme is an Indirect Object; the clause is intransitive.

(54) Semantics: Theme   cöcocosot 'lend'
⋮
     Syntax: Indirect Object

Note in example (55) the intransitive allomorph of the first-person singular subject agreement prefix and in (56) the lack of the 3:3 prefix *i-*. This evidence argues straightforwardly against a quirky-case analysis. It is also crucial to notice the third-person indirect-object agreement prefix *co-* in all three examples immediately below, agreeing with the Theme in these clauses.

(55) Hi-trooqui quij co-hp-yo-m-ocosot.
1P-car   the 3IO-1sSI-DT-N-lend
'I haven't lent my car.' (cöcocosot 'lend')

(56) ¿I-trooqui quij cö-t-ocosot?
   3P-car the 3IO-RL-lend
   'Did she/he lend his/her car?' (cöcocosot 'lend')

The verbs in group 9b in table 16.2 also illustrate this pattern, but they are less convincing, perhaps, because the Theme/Topic nominal is optional and actually quite uncommon; these verbs far more commonly occur without an Indirect Object. Some of the examples (but not all) seem analogous to the English phrases 'speak about (something)', 'ask about (something)', and so on.[16]

16.2.5.2 Prelinking of Patient/Theme with Indirect Object The verb *cöcamiiit* 'ask' in group 10 specifies that the Patient/Theme must be linked to Indirect Object.[17] This verb allows an optional plural Addressee. Since the syntactic subcategorization frame is already saturated with the Theme, however, the plural Addressee cannot be an Indirect Object; it must be marked by the postposition *ano*.

(57) Semantics: (Addressee$_{pl}$)   Theme   cöcamiiit 'ask'
                                            |
     Syntax: Indirect Object

The following examples display the evidence for the presence of an Indirect Object (the agreement prefixes agree with the Theme) and for the intransitivity of the clauses (lack of 3:3 prefix *i-* in (58) and intransitive first-person singular agreement allomorphy in (59)).

(58) ¿Cö-t-amiiit?
   3IO-RL-ask
   'Did she/he ask about him/her/it?' (cöcamiiit 'ask')

(59) Juan quih co-hp-y-amiiit.
        the 3IO-1sSI-DT-ask
   'I asked about John.' (cöcamiiit 'ask')

(60) ¿He-t-amiiit?
   1IO-RL-ask
   'Did she/he ask about me?' (cöcamiiit 'ask')

The following examples of this same verb are also demonstrably intransitive, but in these examples there is a plural Addressee. The plural Addressee is not able to link to any syntactic function, because the syntactic frame is saturated (see (57)).

(61) ¿Ziix zo mi-no cö-t-amiiit?
     thing a 2P-in 3IO-RL-ask
   'Did she/he ask you (pl.) something?' (cöcamiiit 'ask')

(62) ¿Ziix z ∅-ano cö-t-amiiit?
    thing a 3P-in 3IO-RL-ask
    'Did she/he ask them something?' (cöcamiiit 'ask')

Four verbs, including *cöquitalhaa* 'sell' and *cöcaasot* 'lend' in group 11a in table 16.2, specify a Theme and an *optional* Recipient, as well as an Indirect Object and an *optional* Direct Object. So there is a match in the number of arguments. However, the Theme is lexically prelinked to the Indirect Object, as with the verb *cöcamiiit* 'ask' just discussed. Another complication for these verbs: the Direct Object must be singular. So when the Recipient is singular, it is Direct Object, while the Patient/Theme is Indirect Object.

(63) Semantics: (Recipient)   Theme   cöquitalhaa 'sell'
                                                   cöcaasot 'lend'
     Syntax: (Direct Object_sg) Indirect Object

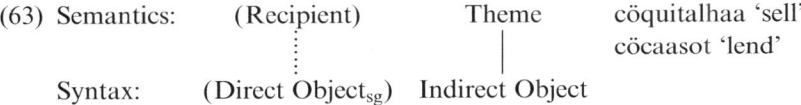

The following examples illustrate the use of these verbs. First, they may be used without any mentioned Recipient. The clauses are intransitive (the tests should now be familiar), and the Patient/Theme determines indirect-object agreement.

(64) Cö-t-m-italhaa   ho.
    3IO-RL-N-buy/sell DECL
    'She/he didn't sell it.' (cöquitalhaa 'sell')

(65) Zixcam hipcom co-hp-tc-m-italhaa   ho.
    fish   this   3IO-1sSI-RL-N-buy/sell DECL
    'I didn't sell this fish.' (cöquitalhaa 'sell')

(66) Hasaj cap cö-iqu-italhaa   h-mii-mzo.
    basket the 3IO-INFI-buy/sell 1sST-Px-want
    'I want to sell the basket.' (cöquitalhaa 'sell')

(67) Cmaax eenim ihyaa zo co-hp-sc-m-aasot   haa hi.
    now   knife mine a 3IO-1sSI-IR-N-lend AUX DECL
    'Now I won't lend my knife.' (cöcaasot 'lend')

A singular Recipient is Direct Object: it determines direct-object agreement and the clause is transitive by all tests.

(68) Co-h-y-italhaa.
    3IO-1sST-DT-buy/sell
    'I sold it to him/her.' (cöquitalhaa 'sell')

(69) Tiix   me-iha-talhaa   i-m-aa   ha.
    that.one 3IO+2DO-INFT-buy/sell SN+TR-N-know DECL
    'She/he can't sell it to you (sg.).' (cöquitalhaa 'sell')

(70) ¡He-h-aasot!
    3IO/1sDO-Im-lend
    'Lend me it!' (cöcaasot 'lend')

(71) Eenm haacni zo me-t-om-p-asot.[18]
    metal bow a 3IO+2DO-Rl-N-Pv-lend
    'You (sg.) weren't lent a rifle.' (cöcaasot 'lend')

A plural Recipient with these verbs cannot be Direct Object (because of the restriction in the syntactic subcategorization frame allowing only for *singular* Direct Objects); a plural Recipient therefore must be the object of a postposition. So the verb *cöquitalhaa* 'sell' with the meaning 'sell something to plural persons' is syntactically intransitive; the Patient/Theme is Indirect Object and the Recipient is object of a postposition.

(72) Eenm haaczoj quih coocj   quih hi-no   co-m-c-aasot.
    metal bows   the SN-two the 1P-in/from 3IO-Px-US-lend
    'One (unspecified) lent two rifles to us.' (cöcaasot 'lend')

(73) Mi-no cö-iqu-italhaa   h-mii-mzo.
    2P-in 3IO-Infl-buy/sell 1sST-Px-want
    'I want to sell it to you (pl.).' (cöquitalhaa 'sell')

(74) Hi-trooqui quih ∅-ano   co-hp-y-italhaa.
    1P-car   the 3P-in/from 3IO-1sSI-Dt-buy/sell
    'I sold them my car.' (cöquitalhaa 'sell')

(75) Hi-no   cö-y-italhaa.
    1P-in/from 3IO-Dt-buy/sell
    'She/he sold it to us.' (cöquitalhaa 'sell')

(76) Eenim zo hi-no cö-y-aasotim.[19]
    knife a 1P-in 3IO-Dt-lend/Impf
    'She/he lent a knife to us.' (cöcaasot 'lend')

The verbs in groups 11b and 11c in table 16.2 are similar to those in 11a except that the optional argument is the Theme/Patient/etc. When the Theme/Patient is present, it is an Indirect Object. Therefore these verbs also represent a marked arrangement.

(77) (cö)caaipot 'pay to', (cö)quii 'tell', (co)czaxö 'discuss with'
    Semantics: Recipient/Addressee   (Theme)

    Syntax: Direct Object   (Indirect Object)

The following examples illustrate verbs from groups 11b and 11c without a Theme mentioned. When there is no Theme (as in these examples), the clauses are simple transitives.

(78) Ox   i-mi-i.
     thus 3:3-Px-tell
     'Thus she/he told him/her/them.' ((cö)quii 'tell')

(79) Ox   hizi-mi-i.
     thus 1pDO-Px-tell
     'Thus she/he told us.' ((cö)quii 'tell')

(80) ¿Zó   ma-h-t-ai?
     how 2sDO-1sST-R<small>L</small>-tell
     'What (lit., how) did I tell you?' ((cö)quii 'tell')

(81) Tiix   ii-hax   ih-t-aai   ma, hin-y-aaipot.
     that.one 3P-with 1sST-R<small>L</small>-do DS 1sDO-D<small>T</small>-pay
     'I helped him and he paid me.' ((cö)caaipot 'pay to')

(82) ¿Mazi-t-cm-aaipotim?
     2pDO-R<small>L</small>-N-pay/Impf
     'Didn't she/he pay you (pl.)?' ((cö)caaipot 'pay to')

The following examples include the Theme, which is the Indirect Object; they illustrate the portmanteaux of table 16.1 and what elsewhere I have called Object Camouflage (Marlett 1981). That is, when a first- or second-person direct object co-occurs with a third-person indirect object, the morphology becomes a bit cloudy because the usual distinctions are blurred. Rather than two prefixes appearing on the verb, only one prefix appears.[20]

(83) Ziix   zo cö-i-yo-zaxö.
     thing a 3IO-3:3-D<small>T</small>-discuss
     'She/he discussed something with him/her/them.' ((co)czaxö 'discuss with')

(84) Taax me-h-n-zaxö.
     that 3IO:2DO-1sST-Px-discuss
     'I am discussing that with you (sg./pl.).' ((co)czaxö 'discuss with')

(85) Peez capxajö   me-h-s-aaipotim   haa hi.
     peso SN-three/Impf 3IO:2DO-1sST-pay/Impf A<small>UX</small> D<small>ECL</small>
     'I am going to pay three pesos to each one of you.' ((cö)caaipot 'pay to')

(86) ¿Ziix   zo he-t-miiit?
     thing a 3IO+1DO-R<small>L</small>-ask
     'Did she/he ask me (about) something?' ((co)cmiiit 'ask')

Table 16.3
Transitive-intransitive verb pairs

Basic		Derived	
(co)cmiiit (11c)	'ask (about)'	comiiit (9b)	'ask'
-miiit	Addressee is explicit Direct Object	-o-miiit	Addressee is implicit
quiisxö (2)	'hide'	hacx queesxö (4b)	'hide oneself (from)'
-isxö	Patient is explicit Direct Object	-Ablaut-isxö	Patient is implicit, although understood to be same as Agent
quiiom (3a)	'petition for'	caaom (4a)	'petition'
-âaom	Patient is explicit Direct Object	-aaom	Patient is implicit
(cö)caazj (11b)	'sell on credit'	cocozj (1)	'sell on credit'
-aazj	Recipient is explicit Direct Object	-oco-aazj	Recipient is implicit

16.3 Relationships between Verbs

It is clear that some verb roots appear in more than one place in table 16.2. A common pattern in Seri is for transitive verbs to have a "detransitivized" form when the Patient/Theme is not present (the "unspecified object" construction). The root *-tis* means 'point at' and is transitive and the Patient/Theme is referential; the stem *-otis* means 'point at' and no Patient/Theme is explicit. The prefix *o-* is easily segmentable as being the morpheme that either indicates "unspecified object" or that derives an intransitive verb that does not subcategorize for a Patient/Theme or Direct Object. When the verb root is vowel-initial, the morphological facts are a bit more complicated; I do not discuss them here except to say that the transitive root *-âaom* 'petition for' conjugates differently than the detransitivized verb *-aaom* 'petition'. The verbs in table 16.3 are related to each other in the way just mentioned.

A few other verbs have relationships between them that are idiosyncratic and not part of a more general pattern (see table 16.4). They are related by different morphology than what has been shown above. The prefix *a-* (allomorph *aa-* in stressed position) appears in the (presumably) derived forms; this prefix happens to be homophonous with the causative prefix. In the case of the verbs sharing the root *-amx*, the prefix functions something like an applicative prefix, permitting the syntactic frame to be expanded to include a *singular* Indirect Object.

In the case of the verbs sharing the root *-miiit*, the prefix functions something like an "antiapplicative" prefix, requiring the syntactic frame to be reduced by omitting

Table 16.4
Idiosyncratic verb pairs

Basic		Derived	
quimx (3b)	'say'	cöcaamx (7c)	'say', 'promise'
-amx	Addressee is *not* present as Indirect Object (is either implicit or is (pl.) object of Postposition)	-a-amx	Singular Addressee is explicit (Indirect Object)
(co)cmiiit (11c)	'ask (about)'	cöcamiiit (10)	'ask'
-miiit	Singular Addressee is explicit Direct Object	-a-miiit	Addressee is *not* present as Direct Object (is either implicit or is (pl.) object of Postposition)
quiisxö (2)	'hide'	cöqueesxö (7b)	'hide from'
(-isxö)	Person from whom the hiding is done is *not* explicit	(-Ablaut-isxö)	Person from whom the hiding is done is explicit

the *singular* Direct Object (which is the grammatical relation linked to Addressee in this marked verb).

These verbs are interesting to compare; they are the only ones that have been discovered in the language to have this kind of morphological relationship. One situation is almost the mirror image of the other (applicative in one case, antiapplicative in the other). In both situations the relevant nominal has the semantic role of Addressee, and indeed it is possible that the morphology is directly related to the presence or absence of a singular Addressee rather than to a grammatical relation.

The verb *cöqueesxö* 'hide from' (stem *-eesxö*) includes an explicit reference to the person from whom the hiding is done, unlike the verb *quiisxö* 'hide' (root *-isxö*).

Obviously the verbs *quitalhaa* 'buy' and *cöquitalhaa* 'sell' are related etymologically, but there is no difference in the shape of the stems. The difference in meaning is entirely dependent on the subcategorization frames in which they occur.

16.4 Conclusion

The semantic roles Addressee and Recipient in Seri are represented syntactically in three ways in active clauses: as Direct Object, as Indirect Object, and as Object of a Postposition. The semantic roles Patient and Theme are also represented in three ways: as Direct Object (most commonly), as Indirect Object, and as Chômeur. I presented an analysis of these facts in an attempt to discover what is marked and what is unmarked about the numerous configurations that are found. This analysis made

Table 16.5
Basis for subcategorization possibilities

Present semantically	Present syntactically
A None	1 None
B Patient / theme / etc.	2 Direct object
C Addressee / recipient / etc.	3 Indirect object
D Patient / theme and also addressee / recipient	4 Direct object and indirect object

Table 16.6
Logically possible subcategorization patterns attested in Seri

A1 attested by group 1
C1 attested by group 5 [Addressee/etc. is Object of P]
B2 attested by group 2
B3 attested by group 9
C2 attested by group 4
C3 attested by group 6 [Addressee/etc. is Object of P]
D2 attested by group 3 [Addressee/etc. is Object of P]; and by group 8 (marked) [Addressee/etc. is Chômeur] Markedness of group 8 is Recipient$_{DO}$
D3 attested by group 10 (marked) [Addressee/etc. is Object of P] Markedness of group 10 is Theme$_{IO}$
D4 attested by group 7 and by group 11 (marked) (The two groups have mirror-image arrangements of the link between semantic roles and grammatical relations.) Markedness of group 11 is Theme$_{IO}$

crucial use of Jackendoff's notion of parallel architecture, which permits a mismatch between the semantic and the syntactic subcategorization frames. The analysis also distinguished critically between all of the syntactic relations mentioned above: Object of Postposition is distinct from Indirect Object, and Direct Object is distinct from Chômeur and Indirect Object.

The analysis presented is built around the assumption that syntactic subcategorization in Seri can refer to Direct Object and Indirect Object, but not to Object of Postposition or Chômeur. When this assumption is connected with the possibility of a mismatch of the number of items in the semantic and syntactic subcategorization frames, the logical possibilities are limited to the sixteen derivable from table 16.5.

Some possibilities (namely, A2, A3, A4, B4, and C4) are ruled out by the principle mentioned in section 16.2.1, which requires that the number of syntactic arguments be equal to or less than the number of semantic arguments.

None of the constructions we have seen shows the verb subcategorized for a Patient/Theme without also having some syntactic relation in the syntactic subcategorization frame. B1 and D1 therefore do not exist. There is no antipassive construction in Seri that has an overt Patient/Theme expressed as a Chômeur; such a construction would be an example of B1. These logical possibilities must be explicitly ruled out in Seri in the absence of some general principle that would do this.

This still leaves us with nine logical possibilities, shown in table 16.6, and these are all attested in Seri. Two additional patterns are found because if two nominals are present semantically (box D of table 16.5), and if markedness plays a role (as it does), the number of logical possibilities is increased slightly.

APPENDIX 16.1: TESTS FOR TRANSITIVITY

The following tests are available for transitivity: (i) allomorphy of certain prefixes, (ii) relationship to passive, and (iii) the prefix *i-* (see table 16.1).

A16.1 Allomorphy

Some prefixes have suppletive allomorphy determined in whole or in part by the transitivity of the clause. Very simple examples are included here to illustrate these facts (see also Marlett 1981, 1984).

A16.1.1 First-Person Singular Subject Agreement

Two suppletive allomorphs for the first-person singular subject agreement prefix exist: *hp-* if the clause is intransitive and *h-* if the clause is transitive. (An epenthetic vowel *i* is inserted when a sonorant consonant—including a glottal stop—would not be syllabifiable. This vowel is different phonologically from the prefix *i-* discussed in section A16.3.)

Intransitive

(A1) Ihp-yo-m-afp.
1sSI-Dt-N-arrive
'I didn't arrive.'

(A3) Ihp-yo-m-p-azt.
1sSI-Dt-N-Pv-tattoo
'I wasn't tattooed.'

Transitive

(A2) Ih-yo-m-aho.
1sST-Dt-N-see
'I didn't see him/her/it.'

(A4) Ma-h-yo-m-aho.
2sDO-1sST-Dt-N-see
'I didn't see you (sg.).'

A16.1.2 First-Person Singular Emphatic Subject Agreement

Two suppletive allomorphs for the first-person emphatic subject agreement prefix exist: *ca-* if the clause is intransitive and *a-* if the clause is transitive. This prefix occurs in a different position in the word from the normal agreement affixes and substitutes for the normal first-person agreement.

Intransitive

(A5) Hatee s-om-caa-tax a-ha.
1EmPro Ir-N-1Em-go
Aux-Decl
'As for me, I won't go.'

(A7) Hatee s-ca-p-azt aha.
1EmPro Ir-1Em-Pv-tattoo
Aux-Decl
'As for me, I will be tattooed.'

Transitive

(A6) Hatee s-m-aa-hit a-ha.
1EmPro Ir-N-1Em-eat
Aux-Decl
'As for me, I won't eat it.'

A16.1.3 Infinitival Prefix

Two suppletive allomorphs for the infinitival prefix exist: *ica-* if the clause is intransitive and *iha-* (plus Ablaut) if the clause is transitive.

Intransitive

(A8) icaa-fp < ica-afp
InfI-arrive
'to arrive'

(A10) ica-p-azt
InfI-Pv-tattoo
'to be tattooed'

Transitive

(A9) ihaa-ho < iha-aho
InfT-see
'to see him/her/it'

(A11) ma-ihaa-ho
2sDO-InfT-see
'to see you (sg.)'

A16.1.4 Imperative

The imperative prefix has several suppletive allomorphs, the distribution of which is predictable based primarily on the phonological shape of the following morpheme, but also on certain other factors including the transitivity of the clause in limited situations. If the morpheme following the imperative prefix begins with a vowel other than *i*, *ii*, (short) *a*, or (short) *e*, transitivity is relevant. Intransitive forms take a zero prefix with ablauting effect; transitive forms take the prefix *h-*.

Intransitive

(A12) Stem: o-sanj
'carry (unspecified) on back'
Imperative: ∅-a-sanj

(A14) Root: oos 'sing'
Imperative: ∅-as

Transitive

(A13) Root: oocta 'look at'
Imperative: h-oocta

(A15) Root: aai 'make'
Imperative: h-aai

(A16) Root: aanpx 'go home'
Imperative: ∅-aanpx

A16.1.5 Nonfuture Action Nominalizer

The nonfuture action nominalizing prefix has several suppletive allomorphs, and the distribution of these allomorphs is also predictable based primarily on the phonological shape of the following morpheme. But if the morpheme following the imperative prefix begins with any vowel other than *a*, *e*, *i*, or *ii*, the transitivity of the clause is relevant. Intransitive forms take the prefix *y*- (plus ablaut), while transitive forms take the prefix *h*-. (Nominalizations are cited here in third person.)

Intransitive

(A17) Stem: o-sanj
'carry (unspecified) on back'
Nominalization: y-a-sanj[21]

(A19) Root: oos 'sing'
Nominalization: y-as

(A21) Root: aanpx 'go home'
Nominalization: y-aanpx

(A22) Root: eemej 'move slowly (intr.)'
Nominalization: y-eemej

Transitive

(A18) Root: oocta 'look at'
Nominalization: i-h-oocta

(A20) Root: aai 'make'
Nominalization: i-h-aai

(A23) Root: eetol 'push'
Nominalization: i-h-eetol

A16.2 Passive vs. Unspecified Subject

Transitive verbs may have passive counterparts; intransitive verbs in Seri do not. When one wishes to omit explicit reference to the Agent of a transitive verb, the passive form is used. When one wishes to do the same for an intransitive verb, the "unspecified subject" prefix is used on the verb. Therefore transitive verbs are straightforwardly distinguishable from intransitive verbs because this "unspecified subject" prefix cannot be used with transitive verbs. The forms below are all cited in the action nominalized form in third person.

Intransitive

(A24) icaafp < i-∅-ca-afp
3P-AN-US-arrive

(A26) icapanzx < i-∅-ca-panzx
3P-AN-US-run

Transitive

(A25) ihacazni < i-h-ah-cazni
3P-AN-Pv-bite

(A27) ipaho < i-∅-p-aho
3P-AN-Pv-see

A16.3 Details about *i*-

The prefix *i*- occurs on finite transitive verbs only when both the Subject and Direct Object are third person. Therefore it does not occur in (A28) because it is intransitive, nor in (A29) because the Direct Object is first person, nor in (A30) because the Subject is first person. But it does occur in (A31) because the conditions are met.

(A28)   Yoo-fp.
        Dt-arrive
        'She/he arrived.'

(A29)   Hin-yoo-ho.
        1sDO-Dt-see
        'She/he saw me.'

(A30)   Zo h-yoo-ho.
        one 1sST-Dt-arrive
        'I saw one.'

(A31)   I-yoo-ho.
        3:3-Dt-see
        'She/he saw it/her/him/them.'

This morpheme *i*- is not clearly phonetically perceptible when it follows the Indirect Object prefixes *he*- and *me*-, as in (A32), although there is subtle evidence that it is present phonologically. The evidence for its phonological presence is presented in Marlett 1984, 232–234.

(A32)   Hi-tis   he-i-yo-cazit.
        1P-harpoon.point   1sIO-3:3-Dt-take.away.forcibly
        'She/he/it took away my harpoon point.'

The prefix *i*- also occurs on finite verbs in one other situation that is not directly relevant here: impersonal passives of ditransitive verbs (Marlett 1984, 234–235). This situation does add a level of complexity to any generalization that refers simply to "third-person Subject and third-person Direct Object."

Notes

1. Seri is a language isolate spoken in northwestern Mexico. The data in this chapter have been collected over a period of more than fifty years by Edward W. Moser and Mary B. Moser and (more recently) by the author. Some of the data appeared in Marlett 1981, but that work did not sufficiently explore the present topic. Recent work on this topic for the Seri dictionary was supported in part by a grant from the National Science Foundation (BCS-0110676). I thank Xavier Moreno Herrera, René Montaño Herrera, Lorenzo Herrera Casanova, and Gen-

aro Herrera Astorga for their help in verifying and expanding the facts during the past few years. I also wish to express my deepest thanks to and admiration for David Perlmutter, whose life and work have been an inspiration to me and whose friendship I highly value.

2. Morphological causative verbs actually display two basic patterns (Marlett 1981, 191–192; 1990, 519–520). One pattern is used when the causative verb has the simple 'make happen' or 'let happen' meaning. The indirect object of the causative verb coreferences the transitive subject of the embedded verb. The other pattern is used when the verb has the meaning 'help happen (by participating in the action)'. In this assistive construction there is no indirect object in the clause; the subject of the embedded verb always appears as direct object of the causative verb.

3. The numbers may be misleading. Some verbs have one pattern for singular nominals and another for plural nominals, as shown below.

4. The facts therefore are not compatible with an analysis that might posit "quirky case." That is, it will not be productive to claim that the Patient/Theme nominals that determine Set 3 agreement Direct Objects that just irregularly determine Set 3 rather than Set 2 agreement. If that were true, the clauses should test positively for transitivity.

5. The notion of Chômeur in Relational Grammar is more interesting and coherent than is indicated here, and does not make sense really without the rest of the theory. The nominals that are described as Chômeurs in this chapter would have been informally referred to as Direct Object Chômeurs in Relational Grammar because they are Direct Objects at the level before which they are Chômeurs (see Perlmutter 1984, 32).

6. In the examples I use the Seri practical orthography. Abbreviations used are: 1 first person, 2 second person, 3 third person, 3:3 third-person subject and third-person direct object, AN Action/Oblique-oriented nominalizer, Aux auxiliary, Decl Declarative, DO direct object, DS different subject, Dt Distal, Em Emphatic, Foc Focus, Im Imperative, Impf Imperfective, InfI Infinitive (Intransitive), InfT Infinitive (Transitive), Int Interrogative, IO Indirect Object, Ir Irrealis, N Negative, ON Object Nominalizer, P Possessor, p / Pl plural, Pro Pronoun, Pv Passive, Px Proximal, Rl Realis, S subject, s / sg singular, SI Subject (Intransitive), SN subject nominalizer, ST Subject (Transitive), Tr Transitive Marker, US Unspecified Subject, UT Unspecified Time, ⚔ marked subcategorization frame. The citation form relating these data to the Seri dictionary (Moser and Marlett 2005) is included in the free-translation line.

7. The parentheses around the prefix *co-* in group 7 of table 16.2 and elsewhere indicate that these verbs optionally subcategorize for an Indirect Object that is Source/Maleficiary. The prefix *co-* is the third-person indirect-object agreement prefix (see table 16.1), which is included with these verbs in their citation forms. It is not a derivational prefix or anything resembling an applicative prefix. When the Indirect Object is present and is third person, the prefix *co-* occurs; when the Indirect Object is not present, the prefix does not occur; when the Indirect Object is first or second person, the appropriate prefixes occur in lieu of *co-*.

8. For those verbs that do not obligatorily subcategorize for a Recipient/Addressee/etc. nominal, additional examples can be provided easily that show the verb without that nominal. Such examples help to clarify the situation that is somewhat obscured by the portmanteau morphology indicated in table 16.1.

9. Postpositions in Seri are inflected for the person of the complement and typically appear in preverb position (often separated from their complement). The postposition *ano* is morphologically irregular in that it is the only one that does not use the typical prefix for third-person possessor. I indicate this in this chapter with a clumsy zero prefix for third-person possessor.

10. This verb is derivationally related to *caaom*. *Quiiom* is the transitive verb (root is *-âaom*, with a "weak" initial vowel that deletes following another vowel); *caaom* is the intransitive verb (root is *-aaom*, with a "strong" initial vowel that does not delete following another vowel). The relationship of these verbs is described briefly in section 16.3.

11. The postposition *ano* has the apocopated form *an* when it precedes a vowel.

12. The assistive construction mentioned in note 2 also arguably has a Chômeur when the embedded verb is transitive. The Direct Object of the morphological causative form corresponds to the Subject of the embedded verb. If the embedded verb is transitive, the Patient/Theme of that verb is not cross-referenced on the verb.

13. The food mentioned with this verb is nonspecific.

14. These facts were discussed in Marlett 1981, 288–298; 1984, 221–223; 1990, 523–524. It was noted that analogous clauses in English were labeled "transitive passives" in Hockett 1958, 205. The Seri facts clearly show that these passive clauses do not have a (surface) Direct Object.

15. Of course in some sense the pattern here is a "marked" pattern within the language and crosslinguistically because we usually expect a Theme to be linked to Direct Object.

16. The verb *caaitom* 'speak' sometimes occurs with a postpositional phrase headed by *iihax* 'with (someone)' (plural *iicot* 'with (some people)'). So the phrase *iihax cöcaaitom* means 'to talk with someone about something'.

17. This verb is obviously related to the verb in group 18. This verb pair and others are discussed in section 16.3.

18. An impersonal passive is required here. Impersonal passives occur if there is a plural direct object or if there is an indirect object in the clause, and if the other conditions for passive are met.

19. There are three ways to say this according to my consultants: (1) the form given in the text; (2) *Eenim zo hino he-yaasotim*, with the person of the Addressee actually appearing twice in the sentence; and (3) *Eenim z ano he-yaasotim*, where the person of the Addressee appears as Indirect Object and the postposition *ano* just sits there. This third option, which is preferred by some people, may represent a complication. The Addressee is Indirect Object; the Theme is not Direct Object (since the clause is intransitive). If the Theme is a Chômeur, what is the reason for *ano*? If the Theme is the complement of a postposition, this is the one situation where that option arises.

20. The details, though very interesting, are not relevant here. See Marlett 1990, 525–526; 1981, 38–39.

21. The *i* of the possessive prefix is lost phonetically before the *y* in forms like this.

References

Chomsky, Noam. 1981. *Lectures on government and binding*. Dordrecht: Foris.

Hockett, Charles F. 1958. *A course in modern linguistics*. New York: Macmillan.

Jackendoff, Ray. 2002. *Foundations of language: Brain, meaning, grammar, evolution*. New York: Oxford University Press.

Marlett, Stephen A. 1981. *The structure of Seri*. Doctoral dissertation. University of California, San Diego.

Marlett, Stephen A. 1984. Personal and impersonal passives in Seri. In David M. Perlmutter and Carol G. Rosen, eds. *Studies in Relational Grammar 2*, 217–239. Chicago: University of Chicago Press.

Marlett, Stephen A. 1990. Person and number inflection in Seri. *International Journal of American Linguistics* 56:503–541.

Moser, Mary B. and Stephen A. Marlett. 2005. *Comcáac quih yaza quih hant ihíip hac: Diccionario seri-español-inglés*. Hermosillo and Mexico City: Universidad de Sonora and Plaza y Valdés Editores.

Perlmutter, David M., ed. 1983. *Studies in relational grammar 1*. Chicago: University of Chicago Press.

Perlmutter, David M. 1984. The inadequacy of some monostratal theories of passive. In David M. Perlmutter and Carol G. Rosen, eds., *Studies in relational grammar 2*, 3–37. Chicago: University of Chicago Press.

Perlmutter, David M., and Paul M. Postal. 1984. The 1-advancement exclusiveness law. In David M. Perlmutter and Carol G. Rosen, eds., *Studies in relational grammar 2*, 81–125. Chicago: University of Chicago Press.

Perlmutter, David M., and Carol G. Rosen, eds. 1984. *Studies in relational grammar 2*. Chicago and London: University of Chicago Press.

Rosen, Carol G. 1984. The interface between semantic roles and initial grammatical relations. In David M. Perlmutter and Carol G. Rosen, eds., *Studies in relational grammar 2*, 38–77. Chicago: University of Chicago Press.

17 Impersonals in Irish and Beyond

James McCloskey

17.1 Introduction

There is in Irish a form of the finite verb known as the *briathar saor* or 'free (form of the) verb.' The English term usually used for this inflectional class is the 'autonomous' form, and that is the term I will use here. What I would like to do in this short chapter is to construct an understanding of the autonomous form, which is informed by, and will in turn contribute to, what we currently understand about impersonal constructions of various kinds. Doing that will require first clearing aside some alternative analytic possibilities.

Autonomous forms are derived by adding a distinctive suffix, one for each tense, to the verbal stem. From the verb *cuir* ('put, send, bury'), for example, five autonomous forms can be built:

cuir-tear   Present tense
cuir-eadh   Past tense
cuir-fear   Future tense
chuir-fí   Conditional mood
chuir-tí   Past habitual

These suffixes may attach to transitive verbs:[1]

(1) a. Tógadh   suas an corpán ar bharr na haille
 raise [**PAST-AUT**] up   the body   on top   the cliff [**GEN**]
 'The body was lifted to the top of the cliff.'
 b. scaoileadh   amach na líonta
 release [**PAST-AUT**] out   the nets
 'The nets were let out.'
 c. Cuirtear   i mboscaí iad
 put [**PRES-AUT**] in boxes   them
 'They are put in boxes.'

A broad array of intransitive verbs also accept autonomous inflection, as shown in (2), with the resultant forms often being difficult to render naturally in English.

(2) a. H-éirigheadh   cleachtuighthe le   daoine a bheith ag   teacht
       become [PAST-AUT] accustomed   with people be [-FIN] come [PROG]
       'One became accustomed to people coming.' DCA 81
    b. Do   chreidtí   insna seanscéalta sin   go léir fad ó shin
       [PAST] believe [PAST-HABIT-AUT] in-the old-stories DEMON all   long ago
       'People used to believe in all those old stories long ago.' CFC 32
    c. hItheadh,   hóladh,   ceoladh   agus ansin chuathas
       eat [PAST-AUT] drink [PAST-AUT] sing [PAST-AUT] and then go [PAST-AUT]
       a sheanchas
       storytelling [-FIN]
       'There was eating, drinking, singing, and then the storytelling began.' CCC 116
    d. Tostadh   seal   leis an iongantas
       be-silent [PAST-AUT] a-while with the surprise
       'People went silent for a time in surprise.' MD 19

17.2 Preliminaries

In terms of diachronic origin, such forms are passives, and their functional range in the contemporary language continues to be close to that of the agentless passive in English (that is how they are most naturally translated). For all that, the autonomous forms of the modern language are not passives—or not at least if by passive we mean a verbal form whose underlying object is rendered as a surface subject. The internal argument of an autonomous form derived from a transitive verb is indistinguishable in its behavior from any other direct object (see McCloskey 1979; Stenson 1981, 1989). At least three kinds of arguments establish this conclusion. First, the internal argument appears in the accusative rather than the nominative case:

(3) a. Cuirfear   é   sa   reilg   áitiúil.
       bury [FUT-AUT] him [ACC] in-the graveyard local
       'He will be buried in the local graveyard.'
    b. *Cuirfear   sé   sa   reilg   áitiúil.
       bury [FUT-AUT] he [NOM] in-the graveyard local
       'He will be buried in the local graveyard.'

Second, if the internal argument is a light pronominal, it may be postposed—an option permitted freely to direct objects but absolutely forbidden to subjects (Stenson 1981, 42–43; Chung and McCloskey 1987; Ó Siadhail 1989, 207–210; Duffield 1995, 66–81; Adger 1997; McCloskey 1999):

(4) a. Cuirfear   sa   reilg   áitiúil amárach   é
        bury [FUT-AUT] in-the graveyard local   tomorrow him [ACC]
        'He will be buried in the local graveyard tomorrow.'
   b. *Cuirfidh   é   sa   reilg   áitiúil siad
        bury [FUT] him in-the graveyard local   they
        'They will bury him in the local graveyard.'

Finally, the internal argument may be a resumptive pronoun—again an option permitted to direct objects but forbidden to subjects (see McCloskey 1990 and the references cited there).

(5) a. fear   gur   bualadh   le   camán   é
        man C-[PAST] strike [PAST-AUT] with hurley-stick him
        'a man that was struck with a hurley-stick' SAT 106
   b. *fear   gur   bhuail sé le   camán   mé
        man C-[PAST] struck he with hurley-stick me
        'a man that (he) struck me with a hurley-stick'

What these observations in sum indicate is that the autonomous inflection is not associated with promotion of a direct object to subject status.[2]

The puzzle of understanding the autonomous form, then, is the puzzle of understanding what becomes of the subject argument of the verb to which the inflection applies. Or to be more precise, what becomes of the most prominent of the verb's arguments? That in turn becomes a puzzle at the syntax-morphology interface. What is it about this set of inflectional endings that licenses silence where the most prominent of the verb's arguments ought to be?

To facilitate discussion, I will use the expression "autonomous argument" in what follows for the argument corresponding to this silence—the external argument of a transitive verb, the internal argument of an unaccusative (as in (2a)), the experiencer argument of a psych-predicate, and so on. If we adopt this nonce terminology, the analytic question becomes that of determining what the status of the autonomous argument might be, with the only sure starting point being that that argument has no phonological realization.

17.3 The Autonomous Argument

One possibility, of course, is that the autonomous argument is absent in a very fundamental sense—it is phonologically unrealized because autonomous forms of the verb have no external argument. On this view, there is nothing in the syntax to be realized where the external argument ought, so to speak, to be. This is in many ways an attractive analytic possibility. It requires us to believe that there is no general requirement of surface subjecthood in Irish (given the observations of (3)–(5)), but it has been argued on entirely independent grounds (see, for instance, McCloskey 1996, 2001) that no such requirement holds in the language. And it is tempting to understand the autonomous form in terms of event quantification (in the sense, say, of Parsons 1990 and much other work growing out of Davidson 1967) and the complete absence of the most prominent argument. That is, one could conclude that what the autonomous inflection does is license total elimination of the external (or most prominent) argument of a verb. One might then understand (6) in terms of a semantics like that in (7):

(6) Buaileadh   le   cloch é
    strike [PAST-AUT] with stone him
    'He was hit with a stone.'

(7) $\exists e$ [strike (e) ∧ **Theme** (e, pro) ∧ **Instr** (e, stone) ∧ **Past** (e)]

(7) claims that a striking event took place (in the past) whose Theme was the referent of the pronoun, and whose Instrument was a stone. No information is given about the striker, because the external argument of the verb, which would have provided such information, is simply absent (though commonsense reasoning about how the world works might lead a speaker or hearer to infer the existence, in the world, of an agent or a cause).

Attractive as this approach may seem, Nancy Stenson (1989, 384–393, drawing in part on earlier unpublished work by Dónal Ó Baoill) has developed a suite of decisive arguments that establish that it is incorrect. More specifically, Stenson's arguments establish that verbs to which the autonomous inflection has been added have the same number of arguments as their counterparts without the inflection, and that (in the case of transitive verbs in the autonomous form) the presence of an external argument is detectable in standard ways. The presence of such an argument is demonstrated, for instance, by its ability to act as a controller (as in (8a)), and by its ability to support subject-oriented adverbials (as in (8b)):

(8) a. Socraíodh   ar ionsaí a dhéanamh orthu.
       settle [PAST-AUT] on attack make [-FIN]   on-them
       'It was agreed to mount an attack on them.'
    b. Glacadh   go fonnmhar leis an ainmniúchán.
       take [PAST-AUT] eagerly   with the nomination
       'The nomination was eagerly accepted.'

Stenson also documents a systematic set of contrasts between the behavior of transitive verbs in the autonomous form and the behavior of unaccusative verbs (for which a semantics along the lines of (7) might well be appropriate). These arguments jointly establish very clearly that transitive verbs to which the autonomous inflection has been attached differ from unaccusative verbs exactly in their ability to license an external argument.

Such observations establish that in clauses built around autonomous forms of the verb, the autonomous argument is lexically present—available as a controller, as a subject for subject-oriented adverbs, and so on. It is a different question whether or not they also establish that that argument is syntactically realized. For it remains unclear whether phenomena such as those in (8) test for the presence of a structural subject as opposed to the presence of an argument—an argument that might remain implicit or syntactically unrealized. An English example like (9), for instance, will, on many accounts, involve a controller (the implicit agent) that has no syntactic realization.

(9) It was decided to go public.

To move forward at this point, we need a way to distinguish between, on the one hand, lexically present but syntactically unrealized arguments, and, on the other, arguments that are syntactically realized but phonologically unexpressed.

17.4 Syntactic Realization

A way to further probe the issue would be to ask if the silent subject of an autonomous form can bind reflexive or reciprocal pronouns, for it is widely accepted that such elements require syntactically realized antecedents:

(10) a. They arranged for each other to be on the committee.
    b. *They talked about it for days. It was finally arranged for each other to be on the committee.

Initial investigation of this territory might suggest that the autonomous argument has no syntactic realization. As Stenson (1989, 384) observes, reflexive pronouns may not have the autonomous argument as their antecedent:

(11) *Gortaíodh   é   féin
     hurt [PAST-AUT] him [REFL]
     'People hurt themselves.'

There is, however, an independent reason why examples such as (11) might be impossible. Reflexive pronouns are formed in Irish by adding the suffix *féin* to a personal pronoun. In (11), for example, *féin* is added to the third-person singular masculine pronoun *é*, to make the corresponding reflexive pronoun. When these composite pronouns enter into binding relations, the base pronoun must agree in person, number (and for third-person singular pronouns, also gender) with the binder. If there is a null argument in (11), that element might well lack the necessary person and number features that would allow it to bind the reflexive. It is hard to be sure, then, whether (11) is impossible because it contains no syntactic antecedent at all for the reflexive pronoun, or because the only available syntactic antecedent (the autonomous argument) lacks a crucial property.

No such issues arise for the reciprocal pronoun, which has a single invariant form (*a chéile*) no matter what form its binder takes:

(12) a. Chonaic muid a chéile
saw   we   each-other
'We saw each other.'
b. Chonaic sibh   a chéile.
saw   you [PL] each-other
'You saw each other.'
c. Chonaic siad a chéile.
saw   they each-other
'They saw each other.'

Among the kinds of arguments that may function as an antecedent to the reciprocal, if the conditions are right, is the autonomous argument, as shown in (13):[3]

(13) a. chuirtí   geall len- a chéile
put [PAST-HABIT-AUT] bet   with each-other
'People used to place bets with each other.' GSA 25
b. Tógadh   suas an corpán ar bharr na haille   ansan le   cabhair
raise [PAST-AUT] up   the body on top   the cliff [GEN] then with help
a chéile
each-other
'The body was raised to the top of the cliff then with each other's help.' FBF 136
c. Táthar   a' strócadh a chéile
be [PRES-AUT] tear [PROG] each-other
'People are tearing each other apart.' U 168
d. Théití   ag ithe   béile le   chéile
go [PAST-HABIT-AUT] eat [PROG] meal with each other
'People used to go for a meal with each other.' IA 351

From such observations, it seems reasonable to conclude that the reciprocals in (13) have syntactically realized antecedents and to conclude in turn that the autonomous argument contrasts in an important way with implicit agents in short passive constructions. If reciprocals require syntactically realized antecedents, the autonomous argument is syntactically realized. The contrast in this respect between (13b) (grammatical) and its English translation (ungrammatical) is particularly telling. This contrast turns on the inability of an implicit passive agent to bind a reciprocal (English) versus the ability of the autonomous argument to bind a reciprocal (Irish).

The autonomous argument can likewise serve as binder in certain other configurations of obligatory binding, as in (14):

(14) Fágadh   an campa ina   mbeirt   is   ina   mbeirt
     leave [PAST-AUT] the camp in-their two-people and in-their two-people
     'People left the camp in pairs.' LNT 94

We will return presently to the question of what makes (13) and (14) possible (as opposed to (11)). For now, though, we are brought by this route to the interim conclusion (following in the footsteps of Stenson 1989 and Bondaruk and Charzyńska-Wójcik 2003 for Irish and of Anderson 1982 for the corresponding construction in Breton) that the autonomous inflection involves no rearrangement of argument structure and no associated syntactic movement. Rather, that inflection, when attached to a finite verb, licenses the appearance of a silent argument with very particular semantic properties—close to those of elements usually called "arbitrary" or "impersonal." Viewed in this light (see Greene 1966, 52), the Irish autonomous inflection is close kin to the impersonal or arbitrary pronoun constructions commonly found in European languages (Italian *si*, French *on*, German *man*, Swedish *man*, Icelandic *maður*, Yiddish *me(n)*, and so on), as in the Italian and German examples of (15) (from D'Alessandro and Alexiadou 2003 and Malamud 2005 respectively):

(15) a. In quel ristorante si   mangiava   bene
        in that restaurant *Arb* eat [PAST-HABIT] well
        'People used to eat well in that restaurant.'
     b. Man   wäscht   die Hände vor   dem Essen
        Arb wash [PRES] the hands before the meal
        'One washes one's hands before meals.'

17.5 Parallels

To take this idea beyond the level of intuition, we can make use of the extensive and rich literature on the syntax, interpretation, and uses of impersonal constructions that has been developed over the past twenty years or more (see, among many others, Jaeggli 1986; Cinque 1988; Rizzi 1986; Authier 1989; Condoravdi 1989; Chierchia 1995; Kratzer 1997; Koenig 1999; Koenig and Mauner 2000; D'Alessandro and Alexiadou 2003; Egerland 2003; D'Alessandro 2004; Malamud 2005). If the autonomous argument in Irish really is a close relative of the impersonal pronouns of these European languages, we should be able to document detailed parallels in their interpretation, form, and use.

It is possible to distinguish three apparently distinct kinds of interpretation that are available to the autonomous argument. In the context of habitual aspects, the interpretation can be quasiuniversal or gnomic, as in (16):

(16) a. éinne   go bhfeicfí   breoiteacht farraige ag teacht   air,
       anyone C see [COND-AUT] sickness   sea   come [PROG] on-him
       déarfaí   leis   ...
       say [COND-AUT] with-him
       'anyone who you would see getting seasick, you would say to them...' CFC 130
   b. tugtar   'madadh uisce' (go minic) ar an dobharchú
       give [PRES-AUT] dog   water (often)   on the otter
       'The otter is often called a water dog.'
   c. Gaeilge a labhartar   anseo.
       Irish   C speak [PRES-AUT] here
       'It's Irish that people speak here.'

In the context of an episodic tense or aspect, however, the quantificational force is usually closer to that of an existential:

(17) a. léiríodh   drámaí leis   san Abbey
       produce [PAST-AUT] plays by-him in-the
       'Plays of his were produced at the Abbey.' IA 22
   b. Labhradh   go hiongantach, go buadhach, go feargach
       speak [PAST-AUT] wonderfully   victoriously   angrily
       'People spoke wonderfully, victoriously, angrily.' MD 151
   c. Tógadh   scoil úr bliain ina dhiaidh sin
       raise [PAST-AUT] school new year   after that
       'A new school was built a year later.'

Finally, the autonomous argument frequently has a pseudospecific use. By this, I mean that it can occur in a narrative in the course of which the reference of the autonomous argument has been clearly and unambiguously established before the autonomous form itself is used. In sentence (18a), for example, the reference of the autonomous argument is established in the preceding temporal clause. Sentence (18b), which is typical of a wide range of such uses, comes toward the end of a fairly long narrative in which it is established in an unambiguous, exhaustive, and specific way who the participants were in the events being described.

(18) a. Nuair a bhímis   ag dul   thairis siúd arís   chaití   clocha
       when C we-were go [PROG] by-this-guy again throw [PAST-HABIT-AUT] stones
       le ceann an tí
       at roof   the house
       'When we'd be going by this guy again, stones would be thrown at the roof of the house.' GSA 26

b. Bhí sé an-deireanach faoin am ar fágadh an Castle agus a
was it very-late by-the time C leave [PAST-AUT] the and C
ndeachthas abhaile
go [PAST-AUT] home
'It was very late by the time people left the Castle and went home.' IA 384

These interpretations parallel point for point the interpretations reported and widely discussed for impersonal pronouns. Such pronouns have a quasiuniversal or generic interpretation in the context of habitual aspect:

(19) a. Man spricht Englisch in Amerika.
Arb speak [PRES] English in America
'People in America speak English.' German, Malamud 2005
b. In Italia si beve molto vino.
In Italy *Arb* drink [PRES] much wine
'In Italy, everybody/people drink wine.' Italian, Chierchia 1995
c. Man måste arbeta till 65
Arb must work [-FIN] until 65
'People have to work until the age of 65.' Swedish, Egerland 2003

But their interpretation is existential in the context of an episodic tense:

(20) a. Man tanzte auf der Party
Arb dance [PAST] at the party
'People danced at the party.' German, Malamud 2005
b. In Italia ieri si è giocato male
In Italy yesterday *Arb* have [PRES] played badly
'In Italy yesterday people/they played badly.' Italian, Chierchia 1995
c. Man arbetade i två månader för att lösa problemet
Arb worked for two months to solve the problem
'People worked for two months to solve the problem.' Swedish, Egerland 2003

Arbitrary subjects also have a range of pseudospecific uses much like the Irish patterns of (18) (see especially Kratzer 1997 and Chierchia 1995).

An additional characteristic of arbitrary subjects that has been the focus of theoretical attention is the fact that they exhibit a very curious and very distinctive set of anaphoric properties. It is possible for an arbitrary pronoun to bind a reflexive or a reciprocal, as seen in the German example of (21):

(21) Man redete mit einander
Arb speak [PAST] with each other
'People talked to each other.' (Kratzer 1997)

or the Italian (22) (Cinque 1988):

(22) Si   era   parlato l'uno   con l'altro
     Arb be [PAST] spoken the-one with the-other
     'People talked to each other.'

And German (23) (Kratzer 1997) is possible (in contrast with (11)) because the reflexive pronoun in German is invariant *sich*—like the Irish reciprocal, but unlike the Irish reflexive:

(23) Man erkundigte   sich   nach mir
     Arb inquire [PAST] [REFL] after me
     'They/one inquired about me.'

It is also known that impersonal pronouns may enter into anaphoric relations with other arbitrary pronouns, as in (24) (Chierchia 1995, 109, (8b)):

(24) Ieri,   si è giocato male e   si è perso
     yesterday *Arb* is played badly and *Arb* is lost
     'Yesterday, people played badly and they/people lost.'

However, the pattern in (25), in which the arbitrary subject enters into a forward anaphoric relation with a personal pronoun, is firmly excluded. Italian (25) is from Chierchia 1995; French (26) and German (27) are from Koenig and Mauner 2000.

(25) *si$_j$ è detto che loro$_j$ hanno sbagliato
     Arb is said that they have erred
     'People$_j$ said that they$_j$ were wrong.'

(26) *On$_j$ a   assassiné la   présidente. Il$_j$ était du   Berry, paraît-il
     Arb has killed   the president   he was from-the Berry seems-it
     'Someone$_j$ murdered the (woman) president. He$_j$ comes from the Berry, it seems.'

(27) *Man$_j$ hat die Präsidentin erschossen. Er$_j$ kam aus   Bayern
     Arb has the president   shot   he came from Bavaria
     'Someone shot the (woman) president. He comes from Bavaria.'

The corresponding patterns in Irish are exactly parallel, as seen in (28):

(28) a. do   stadadh   agus scaoileadh   amach na líonta
        [PAST] stop [PAST-AUT] and release [PAST-AUT] out   the nets
        'One stopped and let out the nets.' LDS 73
     b. *Dúradh   go rabhadar   bocht.
        say [PAST-AUT] C be-[PAST]-[P3] poor
        'People$_j$ said that they$_j$ were poor.'

To express the intended meaning of (28b), one needs (29) instead:

(29) Dúradh   go rabhthas   bocht
     say [PAST-AUT] C be-[PAST-AUT] poor
     'People$_j$ said that they$_j$ were poor.'

These observations cumulatively indicate that the connection between the autonomous argument in Irish and the overt personal pronouns of Romance and Germanic go well beyond what could plausibly be attributed to happenstance.

17.6 Contrasts

There is also, however, one important respect in which the Irish autonomous argument goes its own way. Arbitrary pronouns in Germanic and Romance are subject to a sortal restriction that they are semantically plural (refer to groups) and refer only to humans. No such restriction holds of the autonomous argument in Irish. In the case of (30), the immediate linguistic context makes it clear that the intended referent of the autonomous argument is singular.

(30) Scríobhfad   chuig lucht   stiúrtha   Chonradh na   hÉireann
     write [FUT] [S$_1$] to people direct [GEN] League   the [GEN] Ireland [GEN]
     Scríobhadh   chuig Conradh na Gaeilge   i mBaile Átha Cliath.
     write [PAST-AUT] to   League   of Irish language in Dublin
     'I will write to those who run the Irish League. The Gaelic League in Dublin was written to.' CDC 64

Such observations indicate that there is no requirement of plurality. The examples in (31) indicate that the autonomous argument is further not restricted in its reference to human, or even animate, individuals. Inanimate causes appear routinely:

(31) a. níor   dóghadh   na nótaí
       NEG-PAST burn-[PAST-HABIT] the notes
       'The notes were not burned.' IAE 86
    b. Raiceáladh   ar chósta na   Síne   é   tráth
       wreck [PAST-AUT] on coast   the [GEN] China [GEN] him time
       'He was wrecked on the coast of China once.' IAE 105
    c. Nuair a dhearcaimid ar an méid   léinn,   litríochta, agus ceoil a
       when C we-look   on the quantity learning literature and music C
       tháinig as   áit   chomh beag leis, cuirtear   iontas orainn
       came   from place as   small as-it   put [PRES-AUT] wonder on-us
       'When we look at the quantity of learning, literature, and music that came from such a small place, we are amazed.' PNG 138

d. tháinig   lá   millteanach gaoithe   móire   agus rinneadh
   come [PAST] day terrible   wind [GEN] great [GEN] and make [PAST-AUT]
   smionagair den   choláiste adhmaid
   little-pieces of-the college wood [GEN]
   'There came a day of terrible storms and the wooden college was smashed
   to pieces.' PNG 139

What these observations cumulatively indicate is that there is no intrinsic requirement that arbitrary pronouns be subject to sortal restrictions on possible referents. This should hardly be a surprising conclusion, given the arbitrary character of such restrictions and given the historical origins of the lexical material out of which the Romance and Germanic pronouns have mostly been constructed (based on words that in origin mean 'human being' or 'man' or else, as in Italian, on reflexive pronouns). It would surely be a strange thing if arbitrary pronouns were universally subject to such strange and arbitrary restrictions.

Consider a final parallel. One of the threads that runs all through the literature on arbitrary pronouns is the intuition that such pronouns are similar to, or identical with, the "arbitrary" understanding of PRO—the silent subject of controlled infinitival clauses. It is striking, then, that examples such as that in (32) are possible in Irish.

(32) D'iarr sí   peann agus páipéar a thabhairt chuici. Tugadh
     asked she pen   and   paper   bring [-FIN] to-her bring [PAST-AUT]
     'She asked that pen and paper be brought to her. They were.' CDC 20

Example (32) illustrates an ellipsis construction in Irish that mimics point for point the properties of VP ellipsis in English. It has been standardly analyzed as ellipsis of the complement of one of the functional heads to which the finite verb raises (for detailed discussion see McCloskey 1991, Goldberg 2005, and the references cited there). A crucial property of this ellipsis, and one that is useful for our present purposes, is that (by contrast with English) the postverbal subject forms part of the elided material. Hence only the raised verb (along with any adverbial elements that attach high enough) survives to pronunciation.

The importance of (32) in the present context, however, lies in the fact that here the verb that has survived ellipsis (*tugadh*) is in the autonomous form. From that it follows, on our present assumptions, that the elided material contains an occurrence of the autonomous argument. The elided material, including the autonomous argument, must then meet the requirement of identity with an antecedent by which the ellipsis is licensed. The antecedent in (32) is a nonfinite clause whose subject is "arbitrary PRO." And it is arbitrary PRO that corresponds to the autonomous argument within the ellipsis site. From this in turn it follows that the autonomous argument must be similar enough in relevant respects to "arbitrary PRO" that it counts as being identical to it in whatever sense is necessary for the licensing of ellipsis.

Such observations provide support for the position of Stenson (1989), Anderson (1982), Harley (2002), and Bondaruk and Charzyńska-Wójcik (2003), all of whom identify the null subject of a verb in the autonomous form with the null subject of Control structures (i.e., with so-called PRO). If the autonomous argument just *is* arbitrary PRO, then obviously it will count as "similar enough" to arbitrary PRO to allow the kind of ellipsis exemplifed by (32).

I will return to the issues raised by these observations. For the moment, and in the larger frame, they serve as a final strand of confirmation for the general thesis that the autonomous argument of Irish shares the essential properties of the arbitrary pronoun subjects of Romance and Germanic.

17.7 Interim Summary

We have seen so far, then, that the autonomous inflectional ending on a finite verb licenses the appearance of a syntactically active but phonologically null element in the position of the most prominent of the verb's arguments. We have also seen that this element is close in its interpretive and anaphoric properties to the impersonal subject construction of Germanic and Romance languages. Being syntactically expressed, the null subject can bind anaphoric elements such as reciprocals. However, given the particularities of its interpretation (in particular, its failure to introduce a discourse marker, in the analysis of Koenig and Mauner 2000), it may not function as an antecedent for subsequent definite pronouns. Such arbitrary subjects we in turn take to be indefinites in the sense of dynamic semantics or Discourse Representation Theory ("ultraindefinites" or "a-indefinites" in the terminology of Koenig 1999 as well as Koenig and Mauner 2000). The autonomous argument in Irish differs from its European kin only in not being associated with sortal restrictions of any kind. This I take to be a welcome result, in that it removes from the domain of UG what would otherwise have been a very puzzling and implausible idiosyncrasy.

Finally, we have seen, in addition, that the element licensed in this position is either identical to PRO in one of its uses (the so-called arbitrary use), or else is similar enough in relevant respects to arbitrary PRO to make ellipsis of a containing constituent possible. This, in my view, is the most puzzling and most telling observation so far.

17.8 Licensing the Autonomous Argument

Given this much, the analytic task is to construct an understanding of the licensing of a null pronominal element (with interpretive properties similar to, or identical with, those of arbitrary PRO) by a set of verbal endings associated with finite tenses.

Framed in these terms, the task is simplified both by theoretical commitment and by knowledge of the larger patterns governing such licensing in the language.

The general syntactic configuration underlying agreement in Irish is that seen in (33):

(33)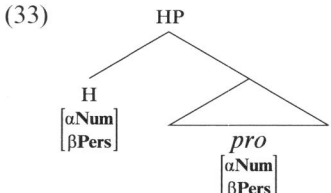

Here, the relation between H and *pro* is that of local command (i.e., *pro* is the most prominent nominal in the domain of H and is not contained within a phase that excludes H). H itself is a member of one of the four or so functional (closed-class) categories of the language that may bear person and number marking morphology. Specifically, H can be any of

- Finite Tense (giving rise to subject-verb agreement)
- D (giving rise to possessor agreement)
- *v* (giving rise to various species of object agreement)
- P (giving rise to agreement between a preposition and its object)

The first of these subcases is the one that is principally relevant to our present concerns. This is the case seen in (34) (in which Tense is the closed-class category that encodes finiteness and to which the verb raises in finite clauses).

(34)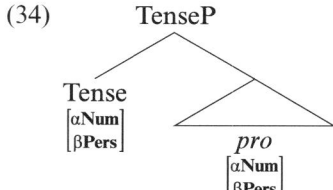

Schematic structures such as (34) surface in the form of examples like (35)

(35) a. Labhradar   *pro* leis na ceoltóirí
       speak-[PAST] -[P3] with the musicians
       'They spoke to the musicians.'
    b. Ní abraim   *pro* a dhath
       NEG say-[PRES] [S1]   anything
       'I don't say anything.'

in which the inflected verb occupies either the position of Tense or a position further to the left than Tense.

This overall view of the syntax of agreement represents a natural updating of McCloskey and Hale 1984 and is very much in harmony with current thinking about the generalized syntax of agreement relations. It is defended and amplified in McCloskey 2005. Since the autonomous argument is a null pronoun licensed only in the domain of a finite verb bearing the appropriate morphology, we are almost required to extend (34) to the current case, by assuming that features of person and number are not the only ones that can figure in the relationship of (34). Let us assume, more specifically, that the autonomous argument is a null pronominal that agrees with a finite Tense bearing the feature *Arb*. The null pronominal will in turn bear an occurrence of that same feature. The feature *Arb* is clearly uninterpretable on Tense, and equally clearly interpretable on *pro*, triggering, as it does, the interpretation in terms of a pure Heimian indefinite:

(36)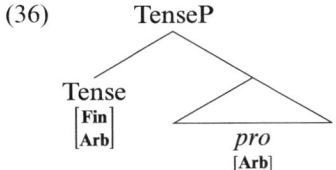

Routine as this proposal is (almost forced by current theoretical commitments), it brings with it some real analytic gains.

It allows us, in the first place, to understand why autonomous forms are restricted to "subject" position. This restriction is a reflection of the general requirement of locality on the syntax of the relation AGREE. Once the feature *Arb* appears on Tense, it is determined that there must be a null pronominal within its domain with respect to which it can act as a Probe (in the sense of Chomsky 2001). That null pronominal must, in addition, be the most prominent nominal in the domain of Tense; otherwise the crucial relationship of (36) will be blocked and the uninterpretable *Arb* feature on Tense will not be eliminated as required. The restriction to subjecthood thus follows from very basic design principles of language (as does the same requirement on agreement more generally).

In addition, we understand the requirement that the autonomous argument be null. Or at any rate we understand that requirement as being one facet of a larger pattern, since it is a general fact about this language that only null pronominals may participate in the agreement relation (see McCloskey and Hale 1984 and much subsequent work, especially Andrews 1990, Legate 1999, Ackema and Neeleman 2003, and McCloskey 2005).

The analysis, in addition, provides the right level of generalization to state the distribution of autonomous forms. That is, these patterns are available for all finite verbs—exactly the level of generality achieved by associating the crucial licensing feature with finite Tense.

We also understand the impossibility of (11), repeated here as (37):

(37) *Gortaíodh é féin
    hurt [PAST-AUT] him [REFL]
    'People hurt themselves.'

Since the complex reflexive formed by combining a personal pronoun with *féin* requires an antecedent with person and number features that match those of the pronoun—something that the autonomous argument lacks, given the analysis of (36)—we know why (37) fails.

We also understand the possibility of (13), represented here by (38):

(38) chuirtí geall len- a chéile
    put [PAST-HABIT-AUT] bet with each-other
    'People used to place bets with each other.' GSA 25

Since arbitrary pronouns in general are known to be able to bind reciprocals, and since the Irish reciprocal imposes no additional featural requirements on its antecedent, the well-formedness of (38) is understandable. What remains then is the more delicate empirical challenge of understanding the slightly marginal character of the phenomenon represented by (38) and by (13) (as reflected in Stenson's 1989 report of a judgment of ungrammaticality for a relevant example). For this, I think that we need to assume that the autonomous argument may be (but is not required to be) semantically plural. The task for a speaker asked to judge the well-formedness of (13), then, is first to determine (from whatever context is supplied or can be conjured up) whether or not the (variable of the) autonomous argument has singular or plural reference. If plural, the example will be judged well-formed; if singular, the example will be judged ill-formed. If this optionality has a syntactic correlate, we will assume that the autonomous argument bears a specification for number, as well as *Arb*. The crucially missing feature that makes (11) impossible must then be person. Compare Kratzer 1997 on German *man* and see Bondaruk and Charzyńska-Wójcik 2003 for the same proposal for Irish. This proposal will also, I think, make sense of the possibility of (14), which clearly involves agreement in number, but arguably not agreement in person.

Finally, these proposals allow us to make a link with a larger typological property of Irish. Like most verb-initial languages, Irish is a massively head-marking language, in the sense of Nichols 1986. That is, in grammatical relationships that link a head with a phrasal dependent (a probe with a goal in minimalist terms), the language marks the head (the probe) rather than the dependent (the goal). The contrast between Romance and Germanic on the one hand and Irish on the other now emerges as a contrast between languages that mark the licensing of the arbitrary pronoun on the licensed pronoun (Romance and Germanic languages) and those that mark it on the licensing head (Irish). Put another way, Irish emerges as the head-marking counterpart of the dependent-marking pattern found in other European languages, and this trait emerges as but one aspect of a much larger typological pattern.[4]

There is at least one large issue, however, that is left open in the partial analysis developed here. This issue emerges as a seeming contradiction at the heart of the proposal. On the one hand, it treats the autonomous argument as being licensed by the same kinds of mechanisms as license null personal pronouns in finite clauses (the mechanisms of *pro*-drop in the classic sense). On the other hand, it points to evidence that the autonomous argument is deeply similar to, or identical with, the null subject of arbitrary control infinitivals—the evidence of (27) in particular. Put differently, the discussion to date seems to identify the autonomous argument both with *pro* and with PRO, something that indeed was, in classic Government-Binding Theory, a contradiction.

There are in fact arguments in the literature (see Stenson 1989 as well as Bondaruk and Charzyńska-Wójcik 2003) that the identification of the autonomous argument with *pro* is misguided. These arguments rely on a certain set of diagnostics developed in McCloskey and Hale 1984 for the detection of null pronominals in Irish. Such pronominals can, in the first place, be coordinated with other nominals in left conjunct agreement contexts:

(39) d' fhanas-sa agus Mícheál i dteannta a chéile
[PAST] stay [S$_1$] and in company each other
'Mícheál and I stayed together.' P 171

Further, null pronominals can combine with many of the functional elements that definite pronouns in general combine with—demonstrative particles ((40a)), emphatic (focus) particles ((40b)), and so on:

(40) a. Bhíodar seo ar fad mór
be [PAST] [P$_3$] DEMON all great
'All of these (people) were great.' O 13
b. Bhíomar-na an-óg ag an am
be [PAST] [P$_1$] [EMPH] very-young at the time
'WE were very young at the time.'

None of these possibilities exist for the autonomous argument. Examples analogous to (40) but with autonomous inflection on the finite verb rather than a personal inflection are ruinously ungrammatical:

(41) *Caitheadh agus m' athair amach na líonta
throw [PAST-AUT] and my father out the nets
'People/they/one and my father threw out the nets.'

(42) a. *Bhíothas   seo   an-óg
       be [PAST-AUT] DEMON very-young
    b. *Bhíothas   -sa   an-óg
       be [PAST-AUT] [EMPH] very-young

Stenson 1989 and Bondaruk and Charzyńska-Wójcik 2003 take such facts to indicate that the silent argument I have called here the autonomous argument is not to be identified with null *pro*; they identify it, in turn, with PRO.

It is not clear to me, however, that these observations are very telling, since there are independent reasons why (41) and (42) would be expected to fail. For the coordinate examples in (41), note that it is utterly impossible to coordinate French *on*, German *man*, or Swedish *man* with any other nominal. If we identify the autonomous argument with an arbitrary null *pro*, then the explanation for the impossibility of (41) will be the same as for the corresponding examples with overt impersonal pronouns. Similarly, I think that it is plausible to believe that the semantics of the impersonal pronoun will be incompatible both with the demonstrative (which requires a definite DP to combine with; see McCloskey 2006) and with the emphatic particle, whose principal function is to produce a contrastively focused pronoun. I think that it is no accident that I could find no halfway plausible translation for the examples in (42).

It seems, then, that we can understand these impossibilities in the overall context of our proposals and maintain the connection (crucial here) with the licensing of null pronouns in the language in general.

And we are left with a real puzzle—the apparent contradiction between identifying the autonomous argument simultaneously with *pro* and with PRO. Whether the seeming contradiction is real, it seems to me, remains unclear. In a changed theoretical context, it is not obvious what the difference between *pro* and PRO might consist of, and the classic treatment of the limited distribution of PRO (that it can appear only in ungoverned positions) is not available. The correct characterization of the element called PRO is at present, as far as I know, an open theoretical issue. And insisting on the distinction between *pro* and PRO hardly seems to deepen understanding.

That being so, it appears reasonable to interpret facts like those considered here as revealing part of the truth about PRO. That truth I take to be something like this: among the very limited range of items that nonfinite Tense can license in its domain is a null pronominal whose interpretive properties mirror those of the autonomous argument in Irish and the arbitrary subject pronouns of Romance and Germanic. That is the fact that we need to understand.

17.9 Conclusion

Much work remains to be done on all of these matters. In particular, the quantificational, referential, and anaphoric properties of the autonomous argument need to be probed in a deeper and more serious way than has been possible here. In addition, the implications of these phenomena for the theory of Control and for the nature of the silent element called PRO remain to be properly thought through. But I hope to have shown that the proper typological context for those investigations is the context of arbitrary subject constructions generally. I also hope to have shown that a morphosyntactic analysis of the autonomous construction that grows very naturally (if not inevitably) out of current theoretical commitments achieves a reasonable level of descriptive success.

APPENDIX: SOURCES OF ATTESTED EXAMPLES

Many of the examples used in this chapter have been taken from published sources of one kind or another. When this is the case, it is indicated with a tag consisting of an abbreviation of the title of the publication followed by a page number. The title-abbreviations are explained here.

AII	*Allagar II*, Tomás Ó Criomhthain, ed. Pádraig Ua Maoileoin
AM	*An Mhiorbhailt*, trans. Niall Mac Suibhne
AT	*A Thig Ná Tit Orm*, Maidhc Dainín Ó Sé
CCC	*Cnuasach Céad Conlach*, Seán Bán Mac Meanman
CDC	*Castar na Daoine ar a Chéile, Scríbhinní Mháire 1*, Séamus Ó Grianna, ed. Nollaig Mac Congail
CFC	*Céad Fáilte go Cléire*, ed. Marion Gunn
DCA	*Dith-Chéille Almayer*, trans. Seosamh Mac Grianna
DII	*Desiderius a Dó*, Pádraig Ó Cíobháin
EMIT	*Eader Muir is Tír*, trans. Niall Ó Domhnaill
FBF	*Fiche Blian ag Fás*, Muiris Ó Súilleabháin
GSA	*An Giorria San Aer*, Ger Ó Cíobháin
I	*Ise*, trans. Niall Ó Domhnaill
IA	*Iomramh Aonair*, Liam Mac Con Iomaire
IAE	*In Aimsir Emmet*, trans. Colm Ó Gaora
LDS	*Lá Dár Saol*, Seán Ó Criomhthain
LG	*Le Gealaigh*, Pádraig Ó Cíobháin
LNT	*An Leacht Nár Tógadh*, Séamas Ó Conghaile
MD	*An Mairnéalach Dubh*, trans. Seosamh Mac Grianna
NCN	*Nár Chlos Ár Namhaid*, Ger Ó Cíobháin
O	*An t-Oileánach*, Tomás Ó Criomhthain
OT	*Ó Thuaidh*, Pádraig Ua Maoleoin
P	*Peig*, Peig Sayers, ed. Máire Ní Chinnéide
PMB	*Pádhraic Mháire Bhán*, Seán Ó Ruadháin

PNG   *Pobal na Gaeltachta*, ed. Gearóid Ó Tuathaigh, Liam Lillis Ó Laoire, and Seán Ua Súilleabháin
SAT   *Seanchas an Táilliúra*, Aindrias Ó Muimhneacháin
SS   *Scéalta Sealgaire*, trans. Maighréad Nic Mhaicín
SSOTC   *Sí-Scéalta ó Thír Chonaill*, ed. Seán Ó Heochaidh, Máire Ní Néill, and Séamas Ó Catháin
U   *Unaga*, trans. Eoghan Ó Neachtain
UMI   *Uaill-Mhian Iúdaigh*, trans. Tadhg Ó Rabhartaigh

Notes

Research for this chapter was completed while I was a visitor in the School of Celtic Studies of the Dublin Institute for Advanced Studies, and I am very grateful for the ideal working conditions that I enjoyed there. I am also grateful to Sandy Chung for many different kinds of help and to Line Mikkelsen for very helpful commentary and discussion. The chapter has also benefited a great deal from presentations and discussion at the University of Toronto (September 2005), at University College Dublin (November 2005), at MIT (December 2005), and at UCLA (April 2006). Comments and suggestions made by an anonymous reviewer and by John Moore were also extremely helpful in shaping the final version.

1. The following abbreviations are used in the glosses: ACC = accusative, *Arb* = arbitrary, AUT = autonomous, C = complementizer, COND = conditional, DEMON = demonstrative, EMPH = emphatic, -FIN = nonfinite, FUT = future, GEN = genitive, HABIT = habitual, NEG = negative, NOM = nominative, P1 = first-person plural, P3 = third-person plural, PL = plural, PRES = present, PROG = progressive, REFL = reflexive, s1 = first-person singular.

2. Overt agents with autonomous forms were common in earlier stages of the language but are not found in modern varieties, as shown in a very careful recent study by Ó Sé (2006).

3. Stenson (1989, 384) cites one example of the type in (13) as ungrammatical. However, such examples are easy to find in ordinary usage. Furthermore, a presentation of this material in November 2005 to an audience in Dublin that included native speakers and scholars of the language uncovered no doubts about the well-formedness of such examples as (13). For a suggestion about the kind of variability implied by Stenson's 1989 data, see McCloskey 2007 and below.

4. See McCloskey 2007 for further and more detailed arguments for the proposals developed here. As John Moore points out, the typological proposal made here depends on the assumption that the clitics found in this ue in Romance languages represent a kind of dependent marking rather than a kind of head marking. It is hardly obvious that this is a correct interpretation.

References

Ackema, Peter, and Ad Neeleman. 2003. Context-sensitive spell-out. *Natural Language and Linguistic Theory* 21:681–735.

Adger, David. 1997. VSO order and weak pronouns in Goidelic Celtic. *Canadian Journal of Linguistics* 42:9–29.

Anderson, Stephen. 1982. Where's morphology? *Linguistic Inquiry* 13:571–612.

Andrews, Avery. 1990. Unification and morphological blocking. *Natural Language and Linguistic Theory* 8:507–557.

Authier, J.-Marc P. 1989. Arbitary null objects and unselective binding. In O. Jaeggli and K. J Safir, eds., *The null subject parameter*, 45–67. Dordrecht: Kluwer.

Bondaruk, Anna, and Magdalena Charzyńska-Wójcik. 2003. Expletive *pro* in impersonal passives in Irish, Polish, and Old English. *Linguistische Berichte* 195:325–362.

Chierchia, Gennaro. 1995. The variability of impersonal subjects. In E. Bach, E. Jelinek, A. Kratzer, and B. Partee, eds., *Quantification in natural languages*, vol. 1, 107–143. Dordrecht: Kluwer.

Chomsky, Noam. 2001. Derivation by phase. In M. Kenstowicz, ed., *Ken Hale: A life in language*, 1–52. Cambridge, MA: MIT Press.

Chung, Sandra, and James McCloskey. 1987. Government, barriers, and small clauses in Modern Irish. *Linguistic Inquiry* 18:173–237.

Cinque, Guglielmo. 1988. On *Si* constructions and the theory of *Arb*. *Linguistic Inquiry* 19:521–581.

Condoravdi, Cleo. 1989. Indefinite and generic pronouns. In E. J. Fee and K. Hunt, eds., *Proceedings of the Eighth Annual West Coast Conference on Formal Linguistics*, 71–85. Stanford, CA: CSLI.

D'Alessandro, Roberta. 2004. Impersonal *si* constructions: Agreement and interpretation. Doctoral dissertation, University of Stuttgart.

D'Alessandro, Roberta, and Artemis Alexiadou. 2003. Inclusive and exclusive impersonal pronouns: A feature-geometrical analysis. Paper presented at the XXIV Incontro di Grammatica Generativa, Urbino, Italy, February 2003.

Davidson, Donald. 1967. The logical form of action sentences. In N. Rescher, ed., *The logic of decision and action*, 3–17. Pittsburgh: University of Pittsburgh Press.

Duffield, Nigel. 1995. *Particles and projections in Irish syntax*. Dordrecht: Kluwer.

Egerland, Verner. 2003. Impersonal pronouns in Scandinavian and Romance. *Working Papers in Scandinavian Syntax* 71:75–102.

Goldberg, Lotus. 2005. Verb-stranding vp ellipsis: A cross-linguistic study. Doctoral dissertation, McGill University, Montreal.

Greene, David. 1966. *The Irish language/an Ghaeilge*. Dublin: Published for the Cultural Relations Committee of Ireland at the Three Candles, Ltd.

Harley, Heidi. 2002. Irish, the EPP, and PRO. Ms. Tucson: University of Arizona.

Jaeggli, Osvaldo. 1986. On arbitrary plural pronominals. *Natural Language and Linguistic Theory* 4:43–76.

Koenig, Jean-Pierre. 1999. On a tué le président! The nature of passives and ultra-definites. In B. Fox, D. Jurafsky, and L. Michaelis, eds., *Cognition and function in language*, 256–272. Stanford, CA: CSLI.

Koenig, Jean-Pierre, and Gail Mauner. 2000. A-definites and the discourse status of implicit arguments. *Journal of Semantics* 16:207–236.

Kratzer, Angelika. 1997. German impersonal pronouns and logophoricity. Presented to *Sinn und Bedeutung*, Berlin 1997. Handout available at http://semanticsarchive.net.

Legate, Julie. 1999. The morphosyntax of Irish agreement. In K. Arregi, B. Bruening, C. Krause, and V. Lin, eds., *MITWPL 33: Papers on morphology and syntax, cycle one*, 219–240. Cambridge, MA: Department of Linguistics, MIT.

Malamud, Sophia A. 2005. (In)definiteness-driven typology of arbitrary items. In S. Manninen, K. Hietaam, E. Keiser, and V. Vihman, eds., *Passives and impersonals in European languages*. Amsterdam: John Benjamins.

McCloskey, James. 1979. *Transformational syntax and model theoretic semantics: A case-study in Modern Irish*. Dordrecht: Reidel.

McCloskey, James. 1990. Resumptive pronouns, Ā-binding, and levels of representation in Irish. In R. Hendrick, ed., *Syntax of the modern Celtic languages*, vol. 23 of *Syntax and Semantics*, 199–248. New York: Academic Press.

McCloskey, James. 1991. Clause structure, ellipsis and proper government in Irish. *Lingua* 85:259–302.

McCloskey, James. 1996. Subjects and subject-positions in Irish. In R. Borsley and I. Roberts, eds., *The syntax of the Celtic languages: A comparative perspective*, 241–283. Cambridge: Cambridge University Press.

McCloskey, James. 1999. On the right edge in Irish. *Syntax* 2:189–209.

McCloskey, James. 2001. The distribution of subject properties in Irish. In W. Davies and S. Dubinsky, eds., *Objects and other subjects: Grammatical functions, functional categories, and configurationality*, 1–39. Dordrecht: Kluwer.

McCloskey, James. 2005. Class materials from A Course on Irish Syntax, LSA Institute, Harvard and MIT. Summer 2005.

McCloskey, James. 2006. Irish nominal syntax 1: Demonstratives. University of California, Santa Cruz. http://ohlone.ucsc.edu/~jim/varia.html.

McCloskey, James. 2007. The grammar of autonomy in Irish. *Natural Language and Linguistic Theory* 25:825–857.

McCloskey, James, and Kenneth Hale. 1984. On the syntax of person-number marking in Modern Irish. *Natural Language and Linguistic Theory* 1:487–533.

Nichols, Johanna. 1986. Head-marking and dependent-marking grammar. *Language* 62:56–119.

Ó Sé, Diarmuid. 2006. Agent phrases with the autonomous verb in Modern Irish. *Ériu* 56:85–115.

Ó Siadhail, Mícheál. 1989. *Modern Irish: Grammatical structure and dialectal variation*. Cambridge: Cambridge University Press.

Parsons, Terence. 1990. *Events in the semantics of English: A study in subatomic semantics*. Cambridge. MA: MIT Press.

Rizzi, Luigi. 1986. Null objects in Italian and the theory of *pro*. *Linguistic Inquiry* 17:501–558.

Stenson, Nancy. 1981. *Studies in Irish syntax*. Tübingen: Max Niemeyer Verlag.

Stenson, Nancy. 1989. Irish autonomous impersonals. *Natural Language and Linguistic Theory* 7:379–406.

18   Does Spatial Make It Special? On the Grammar of Pointing Signs in American Sign Language

Richard P. Meier and Diane Lillo-Martin

18.1   Introduction

Pointing is a ubiquitous human communicative behavior. Pointing gestures are a fundamental part of the inventory of nonlinguistic gestures. They accompany spoken language and pick out referents from the physical environment in which a conversation is taking place. They appear early in child development: by their first birthday, children point communicatively. In signed languages, a variety of pointing signs indicate the referents of conversations; those referents can be physically present at the conversation or they can be tied to empty spatial loci that are established for purposes of anaphoric reference (Friedman 1975; Bellugi and Klima 1982). What are these pointing signs? They include deictic points—that is, signs translated as 'me', 'you', 'him', 'her', and so on—as well as certain verbs that are often said to "agree" with the spatial locations associated with the referents of their arguments; see figure 18.1. Although these verbs generally lack the extended index finger of the familiar pointing gesture, they nonetheless point out the location associated with a referent by orienting toward it or by moving toward it or away from it.

A crucial concern in work on the linguistics of signed languages has been an attempt to identify criteria by which we can determine the status of these pointing signs. Are they properly viewed as linguistic entities? Or are they gestures that have much the same status as the gestures that accompany spoken conversations? This was a problem in 1991 when David Perlmutter reviewed Oliver Sacks's (1990) *Seeing Voices* in the *New York Review of Books*. Sacks had taken the extensive use of space in pointing signs (notably the verb LOOK-AT) as an indication that sign languages were "new" and "miraculous"—radically different from spoken languages. Perlmutter brought the discussion back down to earth and asked for linguistic evidence bearing on the status of pointing signs. He noted that, on first exposure, one tends to see these pointing signs as being nonlinguistic gestures. After considering evidence from a group of pointing signs—specifically, ASL's system of pronouns—he

IX(I/me)

IX(you)

IX(Mary) 'she'
(present referent)

IX(right) 'she/he'
(non-present referent)

ASL Personal Pronouns

1-ASK-a 'I ask her'

a-ASK-b 'She asks him'

a-ASK-1 'She asks me'

An ASL Agreeing Verb

Figure 18.1
Examples of pointing signs in ASL

concluded that signed languages were much more like spoken languages than Sacks wanted to claim.

We too worried about the linguistic analysis of pointing signs in papers that we separately published in 1990 (Lillo-Martin and Klima 1990; Meier 1990). The status of these signs remains a problem even today. One issue concerns whether researchers have overattributed linguistic status to forms of pointing in signed languages; Liddell (1990, 1995, 2000) has argued that many pointing signs are at least in part gestural. Another issue has been whether pronominal points in ASL exhibit the range of person distinctions typical of spoken languages (Berenz 2002; Lillo-Martin and Klima 1990; McBurney 2002; Meier 1990).

In this chapter we return to the issue of the status of pointing signs. How do we determine whether they are linguistic or gestural? We take as our point of departure the set of criteria that Perlmutter proposed in 1991. Although his discussion was restricted to pronominal points, we will widen our focus to include those verbs that point. We will also propose additional criteria and will review some new evidence. We will conclude—as we did in 1990—that pointing signs are linguistic entities, although we will also acknowledge the close ties between these signs and nonlinguistic gestures.

18.2 Properties of Pronominal Systems

Perlmutter's review noted three properties of pronominal systems in spoken languages that seem—at first glance—not to be true of the pronominal pointing signs of ASL. Those properties are (1) the conventionality of pronominal lexical items, (2) the compositionality of pronouns at the phonological level, and (3) the types of morphosemantic distinctions marked by pronouns. Perlmutter argued that, despite the apparent surface differences between signed and spoken languages, pointing signs are indeed linguistic pronouns. In fact, he concluded that there is nothing linguistically special about pointing signs. As we have mentioned, this conclusion is not uniformly accepted. We begin by discussing Perlmutter's first two criteria for the linguistic status of pointing signs, and we add one of our own. Then we turn to Perlmutter's third criterion, which relates to issues that remain problematic.

18.2.1 Conventionality

Perlmutter noted that "in oral languages the relation between a word and its meaning is conventional and generally arbitrary" (p. 67). As his use of the adverb *generally* suggested, there are exceptions. Onomatopoetic words may not be fully arbitrary, but even they are fully conventional within their language; consequently American roosters greet the morning sun with *cockadoodle-doo* but early-rising Spanish roosters crow *kikiriki*. In contrast to the necessarily learned pairings of form and meaning that characterize spoken vocabularies, Perlmutter noted that "the pointing gestures that ASL uses as pronouns may seem to be not arbitrary but direct representations of the meaning; they seem understandable with no previous knowledge of the language" (p. 67). Indeed, the pointing signs used as singular pronouns in ASL are virtually identical in form to the pointing gestures that accompany spoken English.

Conventionality is not the exclusive province of linguistic systems; it is also true of important classes of gestures. For example, the "Hook-'em-Horns" handshape ( ) that George W. Bush produced when the University of Texas band paraded by his viewing stand at his second inauguration is a conventional part of the communicative behavior of everyone associated with the University of Texas at Austin, and is widely recognized even by rival Aggies fans. But in Norway, this gesture apparently has satanic associations and Norwegian viewers of the inaugural parade were shocked to see Bush produce it (Associated Press, January 21, 2005). The same gestural form has very different meanings in Texas and in Norway. How one points is also conventionalized: in their gesturing, the Cuna Indians of Panama favor lip pointing rather than pointing with an extended index finger (Sherzer 1972). The nascent signed language used by deaf individuals on Providence Island in the western Caribbean also uses extensive lip pointing (Washabaugh 1986).

Our question here is this: To what extent are the pointing signs of ASL conventional in form and meaning? Index-finger points in ASL and in nonlinguistic gesture look very similar; thus, the form of the sign ME may be identical to the nonlinguistic gesture by which a hearing speaker refers to himself or herself (see figure 18.1). The same goes for the signs usually translated as 'you' or 'he/him.' The form of these particular signs provides little evidence for the conventionalization of ASL pointing signs. But what about other pointing signs? We will run through some quick evidence suggesting that many ASL pointing signs are indeed conventional.

In his review, Perlmutter noted that possessive pronouns in ASL are conventional in form. These possessive pronouns point, but they do so with the open palm of a flat hand that has the fingers together (a B-handshape,). The palm is oriented to the signer if he or she is the possessor, to the addressee if that person is the possessor, and so on. Like their nonpossessive counterparts, these pronouns are pointing signs. However, the language's choice of a flat hand as a marker of possession is a learned pairing of form and meaning. Other signed languages have made different choices: in Italian Sign Language (LIS), possessive pronouns are distinguished not by their handshape, but by their movement—specifically, by a rotation of the forearm in the direction of the referent (Radutzky 1992).

We can similarly demonstrate that other ASL pronouns are conventional. ASL has a set of pronouns that incorporate number handshapes. The pronoun THREE-OF-US incorporates the handshape of the ASL number sign THREE (👌). Likewise, FOUR-OF-US incorporates the handshape of the sign FOUR (✋). These pronouns have a systematic, but conventional, association between their component parts and their respective meanings. Although the sign for THREE-OF-US has three extended fingers, it won't do to choose those fingers arbitrarily. The number handshapes used in these pronouns must be those conventionalized in ASL. The common gesture for 'three' used by hearing people in American culture, with the index, middle, and ring fingers extended (✋), is not part of ASL. Rather, the ASL form—used for the number sign THREE and incorporated into the pronoun THREE-OF-US—specifically requires a handshape with the thumb, index finger, and middle finger extended, and with the ring and little fingers closed to the palm.

Further evidence that ASL pronouns are conventional comes from the dual pronouns glossed as 'the two of us', 'the two of them', and 'the two of you'. These pronouns exhibit a back-and-forth movement between locations associated with their two referents. They also exhibit surprising idiosyncrasies in handshape. Given the facts of signs like THREE-OF-US, we would expect that TWO-OF-US and other dual pronouns would display the same handshape as the ASL number sign TWO (✌), specifically, the index and middle fingers extended and spread just as in the usual hearing gesture for 'two'. Instead, the dual pronouns have a K-handshape in which the thumb contacts the first segment of the middle finger. This pairing of form and meaning is conventional. In contrast to the ASL sign, the very similar sign TWO-OF-US in British Sign Language (BSL) does indeed show the extended index and middle fingers of the BSL (and ASL) number sign TWO (Cormier 2007).

As we mentioned earlier, there is also a class of verbs in ASL that have a pointing component. These verbs "point" to their subjects and objects by moving (generally) from a spatial locus associated with the subject, to one associated with the object (Fischer and Gough 1978; Meier 1982; Meir 2002; Padden [1983] 1988). We will discuss these verbs here because they make use of the same spatial locations as pronouns, and therefore similar questions can be raised about them.

Like pronouns such as ME, some verbs that point to the locations of their subjects and objects may seem as if they are "natural" gestures that directly represent their intended meanings and are thus not conventional. The verb GIVE is one such sign: this flat-O-hand sign (👌) has a handshape that looks much like the handshape that an individual would use in the action of giving a small object to another individual; see figure 18.2. The movement path of the verb starts at a location associated with the subject (the agent) and ends at a location associated with the indirect object (the recipient). Here the fact that the verb agrees with the location of subject and indirect

1-GIVE-a 'I give her'

Figure 18.2
The ASL sign GIVE

object—or, stated differently, the fact that the verb points to those locations—might seem an obvious consequence of mimetic enactment and therefore would seem not to be conventional.¹

However, other much less transparent verbs also participate in agreement. For example, the ASL sign TO-GIFT is an agreement verb. This verb uses an X handshape ( ). The unexpected handshape identifies this verb as being conventional—the sign does not represent its meaning directly, and we certainly would not expect all sign languages to have a verb of giving with this handshape.

The pointing signs that we have discussed thus far are conventional, but we have not demonstrated that the locations to which those signs point are conventionalized. We know of no evidence that the locations to which the signs glossed as 'you' or 'he' or 'she' point are conventional. However, there are other deictic signs that seem to have their origins in pointing but that no longer point clearly. Thus, signs that were once indexic seem now to be deindexicalized, perhaps as a consequence of becoming conventional. This is particularly true of certain plural pronouns. Frishberg (1975, 710) argues that the ASL sign WE was originally formed from "a series of separate thrusts, sometimes as many as five or six, first pointing at one's own chest, than at three or four other persons (real or imagined) and finally at the chest again." In this older form, the indexicality of the sign was clear. The modern sign WE, however, employs a simple index finger touch on the ipsilateral side of the chest, an arced movement, and a touch to the contralateral side of the chest; see figure 18.3. In the modern sign, indexicality is blurred.

Relatedly, Cormier (2007) has observed frequent deindexicalization of various first-person plural pronouns, both in ASL and in BSL. For example, ASL signs such as THREE-OF-US can indicate the approximate spatial location of the refer-

Figure 18.3
The modern ASL sign WE

ents included with the signer. Thus, if those other individuals are on the signer's left (i.e., the contralateral side to a right-handed signer's dominant hand), then the sign THREE-OF-US may also be articulated on the contralateral side. However, many of the first-person plural signs that Cormier elicited did not show the expected spatial location. Instead, many moved to the center of the chest or to the ipsilateral side (i.e., to the right side for a right-handed signer). If the referents were located on the signer's ipsilateral side, the first-person plural sign would often centralize, but would virtually never move to the signer's contralateral side. Cormier attributed this pattern of results to two factors: articulatory ease and/or the neutralization of number marking in favor of first-person marking at the center of the signer's chest.

Consistent with Perlmutter's discussion in 1991, we have demonstrated that crucial aspects of ASL pointing signs are conventional. The formational contrast between possessive and nonpossessive pronouns, the handshapes in number-incorporating pronouns, the form of agreeing verbs that point to locations associated with their subjects and objects, and the plural pronouns that have lost their indexic character are all the basis for an argument that the system of ASL pronouns and agreeing verbs is conventional. Looking across signed languages reveals further evidence. For example, Japanese and Taiwanese Sign Languages (Japan Sign Language Research Institute 1997; Smith and Ting 1979), as well as the Plains Indian Sign Language that was used by hearing groups as a lingua franca (Farnell 1995), all allow points to the nose as a first-person singular pronoun glossed as 'me.' Evidence such as this is convincing proof of the conventional status of specific signed pronouns. Yet, as we argued at the outset, the conventionalization of pointing signs is not a sufficient argument to demonstrate their linguistic status, inasmuch as many nonlinguistic gestures are also conventional. We turn now to the second criterion that Perlmutter suggested.

18.2.2 Compositionality

Perlmutter's review points out that "sentences, phrases, and words in oral languages are compositional: they consist of smaller units combined in different ways to convey different meanings" (p. 67). He argued that ASL pronouns are compositional, by being formed from "the same types of units of which all signs are composed: movement, handshape, and 'orientation'." In this, he was contending that ASL shows what other scholars have called duality of patterning (Hockett 1960). That is, meaningful linguistic symbols—spoken or signed—are built of meaningless units of form.

Nonlinguistic gestures can also be described in terms of their movement, handshape, and orientation. However, most researchers would agree that a phonological level of description is not required for gestures. That is, they can appropriately be considered unanalyzed wholes that lack internal structure. A gesturer can point with an index finger, an elbow, or a pen, among other possibilities, and still convey the same meaning. Hallmarks of a phonological system, exhibited by signs but not gestures, include a limited inventory of building blocks, as well as constraints on the combination of those building blocks. We will argue that ASL pronouns are compositional, although some may not be fully so.

Let's begin with the first-person pronoun ME; this sign is fully compositional. Like the nonpronominal signs CANDY and BORING, it has an index-finger handshape (). Its movement is a path movement to contact; such movements to contact also occur in KNOW (a movement to contact at the forehead) and in the sign MOTHER (a repeated movement to contact at the chin). The place of articulation of the sign ME is likewise one of the locations that may occur in nonpronominal signs; the signs HAPPY, FINE, and SORRY all exhibit this same location on the midline of the upper chest.

The handshapes used in ASL pronouns draw from the same inventory of handshapes used for nonpronominal signs. Just as the index () and B ()-handshapes are contrastive in the general vocabulary (e.g., the signs WEEK and NICE differ just in the handshape of the dominant hand—an index hand versus a B-hand, respectively), the contrast between an index handshape and B-handshape distinguishes nonpossessive from possessive pronouns. The contrast between a B-hand and an A-dot handshape (a fisted handshape with the thumb extended,) distinguishes a possessive from a reflexive pronoun. These handshapes are unexceptional in ASL. Many signs have either a B-hand (DEVELOP or MAJOR, as in a college major) or an A-dot handshape (NOT, HELP). In sum, the three handshapes we have been discussing—the index handshape, the B-hand, and the A-dot handshape—are contrastive within the system of ASL pronouns and in the ASL vocabulary generally.

However, non-first-person pronouns are problematic for the claim that ASL pronouns are fully compositional. Deictic pronouns glossed as 'you' or 'him' point to locations that are determined by the locations of their referents in the world. Anaphoric pronouns glossed as 'he' or 'she' point to locations that are established by the signer in the signing space (see Lillo-Martin and Klima 1990 for an analysis). As Liddell (2000) has observed, the set of locations to which these signs point are not listable in the phonology of ASL. Moreover, the locations to which these signs point are not contrastive in the general vocabulary of ASL; lexical signs are not distinguished by being articulated on the left versus the right, but a left-right contrast can make all the difference in determining the reference of a pointing sign.

In sum, consistent with Perlmutter's claim, some ASL pronouns are fully compositional phonologically, and others are at least partly so. But the locations indexed by non-first-person pronouns are particularly problematic for this criterion. To be fully compositional, non-first-person pronouns would need to be built of a finite inventory of sublexical units. To the best of our knowledge, these particular ASL pronouns do not meet this criterion.

18.2.3 Grammatically Constrained Distribution of Pronouns

Perlmutter did not mention this, but we think a further set of arguments for the grammatical status of pointing signs comes from their syntactic distribution. We will mention a few examples here, knowing that there are more to call on.

Pronouns adhere to the so-called binding conditions that constrain the interpretation of pronominal elements based on their syntactic positions. For example, in English the pronoun *he/him* can refer to *John* in the sentence *John thinks that he is intelligent*, but not in *He thinks that John is intelligent*, or in *John saw him*. Constraints similar in spirit, though different in detail, are found across the world's spoken languages. Observations about such coreference possibilities have been the focus of much work in linguistics, and there has been an extended debate concerning the proper characterization of such facts, and whether they are fundamentally syntactic or semantic.

Without going into any of this argumentation, it suffices to notice that ASL pronouns are likewise constrained (Lillo-Martin 1995; Sandler and Lillo-Martin 2006). If what we call pronouns in ASL were completely nonlinguistic, why would native signers consider it to be ungrammatical to use such a gesture with coreference in one syntactic configuration but not another? One explanation for the distribution of ASL pronouns might assume that pointing gestures in general are restricted in exactly the same way as spoken pronouns. However, they are not. The pointing gestures accompanying speech are not required to change form along with anaphoric versus reflexive pronouns (*he* versus *himself*). In fact, in certain contexts a pointing gesture helps a spoken pronoun get around the constraints on the interpretation of pronouns. For example, speaker A might ask, "Who does John support? Does John support Bill?" Speaker B can reply, while producing a pointing gesture toward John, "No, John supports HIM." The fact that ASL pronouns behave more like spoken-language pronouns than like the pointing gestures accompanying speech is more evidence of their linguistic status.

In many other ways, pronouns in ASL behave as grammatical elements, serving as verbal arguments and substituting for full noun phrases as in spoken languages. Padden ([1983] 1988) observed that pronouns can participate in a process she called "subject pronoun copy," by which a pronominal copy of the subject of a sentence appears in sentence-final position. This process can put a pronoun, but not a full noun phrase, in the sentence-final position. Such phenomena clearly indicate that ASL pronouns act as true pronouns, despite their surface similarity to spoken-language gestures.

Related arguments can be made about the pointing behavior of agreeing verbs. As verbs, these pointing signs are clearly grammatically constrained; their distribution is like that of other verbs. Furthermore, in many ways the pointing aspect of these verbs interacts with other aspects of grammar. For example, transitive verbs agree with their subject and direct object, while ditransitive verbs agree with their subject and indirect object. The class of verbs that takes agreement is definable by reference to argument structure (Meir 2002). Verbs with agreement participate in null-argument licensing (Lillo-Martin 1986). And the categorization of verbs as agreeing versus "plain" (i.e., as not showing agreement) relates to syntactic structure in several ways. Here we mention two. First, it has long been noted that ASL verbs marked with agreement show a greater flexibility of word order as compared with nonagreeing verbs (Fischer 1975). Second, verbs in Brazilian Sign Language that are marked with agreement show a different pattern with respect to the placement of negative signs as compared to verbs not marked with agreement (Quadros 1999). In that language, a sign for negation can appear in either the preverbal or the sentence-final position with agreeing verbs. With nonagreeing verbs, however, only the sentence-final position is available. How could such patterns be explained if verb agreement were not a syntactic phenomenon?

Finally, another aspect of pointing in verbs is relevant. In some sign languages, though not ASL, a "dummy" sign is used to indicate agreement, alongside an agreeing verb (in some cases) or a plain verb (in more cases). Such signs are sometimes referred to as auxiliary verbs (Smith 1990; Bos 1994; Quadros 1999) or as "Person Agreement Markers" (Rathmann 2000). Dummy signs can be used to point when a verb cannot, but only in very linguistically constrained ways. For example, only certain verbs may be used with the dummy sign, and its order with respect to the verb is constrained (in different ways in different languages).

All of these observations provide much more support for the claim that—despite appearances—signs that point have full linguistic status, parallel to their spoken-language equivalents.

18.2.4 Grammatical Distinctions Marked by Pronouns

Finally, Perlmutter observed that oral-language pronouns mark grammatical distinctions such as person, number, gender, and case, though pronominal systems vary as to which distinctions are made in which languages. As he summarized, some of these grammatical distinctions are also differentiated in ASL. For example, plurals are marked in ASL by adding an arc movement, although ASL is different from English (but not from certain other spoken languages) in that it marks dual as well as singular and plural (and as we noted above, it has number incorporation for several other forms). ASL also distinguishes inclusive and exclusive first-person plural forms, although these may exhibit subtle differences from their spoken-language counterparts (Cormier 2005).

The finding that pointing signs in ASL—and in at least some other sign languages—mark case by distinguishing possessives from nonpossessives is, as noted earlier, indisputable. The same goes for the observation that sign languages mark number in several ways (see Rathmann and Mathur 2002). However, there are complications that arise when we consider the grammatical distinctions marked by pointing signs as compared with spoken-language pronouns. The set of grammatical distinctions marked by pointing signs is not wholly identical to what we find in spoken languages. In contrast to the diversity of pronominal systems in spoken languages (McBurney 2002), sign languages do not seem to mark case other than possessive, although Irit Meir argues that an oblique case-marked pronoun has emerged in Israeli Sign Language (Meir 2003), and that ISL agreeing verbs mark dative case through the direction of facing (Meir 2002). More intriguingly, the "pointing" of verb agreement gives a clear priority to objects (and in particular, indirect objects) over subjects; manual marking of object agreement is obligatory, whereas subject agreement always seems optional (if the verb permits it at all). This last observation has yet to be fully explained.

Most problematic of all is the question of person marking. Perlmutter stated that "orientation of the hand indicates the first, second, or third person" (p. 67), but the system is not quite so straightforward. First person can be identified through the locus of the signer; pointing to one's own chest produces a first-person form. As Meier (1990) argued, the first-person plural forms WE and OUR have no ready morphological analysis by which they can be construed as consisting of a first-person pronoun and a plural marker, nor do these signs indexically indicate who besides the signer is being referred to. Therefore, these idiosyncratic forms constitute strong arguments for the grammatical marking of first person in ASL. Furthermore, the fact that the first-person singular form exhibits particular properties in so-called role-playing contexts also is an argument for the first-person grammatical distinction (Meier 1990; Lillo-Martin 1995).

However, the status of the distinction between second and third person is much more controversial, as we suggested earlier in this chapter. The movement path of a pointing sign translated into English as 'you' is determined by the addressee's location in space; moreover, the set of locations that may be indicated by a point to the addressee overlaps with the locations that may be indicated by a point that is directed to a nonaddressed participant in a conversation and that would be translated as 'him' or 'her'. This logic suggests that the articulatory cues that show us where a point points—that is, cues such as the precise movement direction, palm orientation, and spatial location—are not fixed linguistically and are instead determined by the location that a referent physically occupies (Meier 1990; Liddell 2000).

This leads to two ways in which sign-language pointing signs are different from spoken-language pronouns or verbs. First, there is a grammatical difference between first and non–first person, but not between second and third person. This analysis has been adopted not only for ASL (Meier 1990), but also for such other signed languages as Taiwanese (Smith 1990) and Danish (Engberg-Pedersen 1993). In contrast, the second- versus third-person distinction is a universal of the pronoun systems of spoken languages (Forchheimer 1953) that has just one apparent counterexample in Qawesqar, an Alacalufan language of Chile (Cysouw 2003). Consequently, the apparent absence of this distinction in sign languages is worthy of note.

Second, although only one non-first-person pronoun is lexically distinguished, the language is clearly capable of differentiating more than just a single non-first-person referent within a conversation. Signers can discuss multiple non-first-person referents by pointing to different locations in space, and because the signer maintains the association between a referent and a location, unambiguous interpretations result.

This latter property of sign languages may constitute one of the reasons for Sacks to claim in his book (following Poizner, Klima, and Bellugi 1987) that sign employs a spatial grammar. Perlmutter questioned this claim at length (p. 69), asking, "What is 'spatial grammar'?" As he showed, Sacks "provides no basis for the claim that sign language grammars are fundamentally different from those of oral languages."

In large part, we agree: the fundamental similarities between sign-language grammars and spoken-language grammars are impressive and important. However, we find the problem of non-first-person pointing signs to be, in fact, evidence of an equally important difference between signed and spoken languages. These signs appear to combine word and gesture within a single form. Non-first-person pointing signs can be compared to speakers simultaneously pointing at a real or imagined referent while they produce a spoken word. One can readily imagine such a situation, as when a speaker explains—clearly and unambiguously with the aid of gestures—that "I voted for her, not her." The sign-language pronouns themselves do both jobs at once. For this reason, researchers have analyzed the pronouns as making contact with the gestural system, in one way or another (Meier 2002a, 2002b; Lillo-Martin 2002; Rathmann and Mathur 2002; see also Liddell 2000).

18.3 Concluding Remarks

Perlmutter's review concluded that "although Sacks has performed a valuable service in introducing the general reader to the linguistic-cultural view of deafness, much of what he says about ASL is seriously flawed" (p. 72). Not only did Perlmutter discuss properties of ASL pronouns, but he also mentioned a range of other characteristics of ASL grammar, as well as a number of intriguing neurological studies of the basis in the brain for sign language. He took great issue with Sacks's hyperbole in interpreting these findings as evidence that signers—in Sacks's words—use "a new and extraordinarily sophisticated way of representing space." Perlmutter agreed with Sacks that "sign is indeed a miracle," but only insofar as speech is miraculous too.

We agree that what is most fascinating about sign language is what is also fascinating about language in general: the characteristics that we as humans must possess in virtue of the fact that we possess language. But as practicing sign linguists, we think that there is something special about sign language, something that the field of linguistics could not know if sign languages were not part of the data to be explained. Taking seriously both the similarities and the differences between signed and spoken languages will bring us farthest in our exploration of the nature of language. We thank David Perlmutter for his role in teaching us this.

Notes

We thank Bernice Hecker, Tracy Chen, and Hyun-Jong Hahm for discussions of issues raised in this chapter. Thanks also go to ASL sign models Doreen Simons-Marques and Brenda Scherz. Thomas Hanke provided the handshape drawings; the figures are copyright Diane Lillo-Martin. Finally we thank an anonymous reviewer for very helpful comments.

1. In its usage, the sign GIVE is not nearly as transparent as its form would suggest. For example, the sign can be used to refer to instances of giving objects of various shapes and sizes, such as apples, bottles, or cows. The handshape by which one would transfer a bottle to another person is not the handshape of the sign.

References

Bellugi, U., and E. S. Klima. 1982. From gesture to sign: Deixis in a visual-gestural language. In R. J. Jarvella and W. Klein, eds., *Speech, place, and action*, 297–313. Chichester: Wiley.

Berenz, N. 2002. Insights into person deixis. *Sign Language & Linguistics* 5:203–227.

Bos, H. 1994. An auxiliary in Sign Language of the Netherlands. In I. Ahlgren, B. Bergman, and M. Brennan, eds., *Perspectives on Sign Language Structure: Papers from the Fifth International Symposium on Sign Language Research*, 37–53. Durham: International Sign Linguistics Association, University of Durham.

Cormier, K. 2005. Exclusive pronouns in American Sign Language. In E. Filimonova, ed., *Clusivity: Typology and case studies of inclusive-exclusive distinction*, 241–268. Amsterdam: John Benjamins.

Cormier, K. 2007. Do all pronouns point? Indexicality of first person plural pronouns in BSL and ASL. In P. Perniss, R. Pfau, and M. Steinbach, eds., *Visible variation: Comparative studies on sign language structure*, 63–101. Berlin: Mouton de Gruyter.

Cysouw, M. A. 2003. *The paradigmatic structure of person marking*. Oxford: Oxford University Press.

Engberg-Pedersen, E. 1993. *Space in Danish Sign Language*. Hamburg: Signum.

Farnell, B. 1995. *Do you see what I mean? Plains Indian Sign Talk and the embodiment of action*. Austin: University of Texas Press.

Fischer, S. 1975. Influences on word order change in American Sign Language. In C. Li, ed., *Word order and word order change*, 1–25. Austin: University of Texas Press.

Fischer, S., and B. Gough. 1978. Verbs in American Sign Language. *Sign Language Studies* 7:17–48.

Forchheimer, P. 1953. *The category of person in language*. Berlin: Walter de Gruyter.

Friedman, L. 1975. Space and time reference in American Sign Language. *Language* 51:940–961.

Frishberg, N. 1975. Arbitrariness and iconicity: Historical change in American Sign Language. *Language* 51:696–719.

Hockett, C. 1960. The origin of speech. *Scientific American* 203:88–96.

Japan Sign Language Research Institute (Nihon syuwa kerkyuusho), ed. 1997. *Japanese Sign Language dictionary (Nihongo-syuwa diten)*. Tokyo: Japan Federation of the Deaf.

Liddell, S. K. 1990. Four functions of a locus: Reexamining the structure of space in ASL. In C. Lucas, ed., *Sign language research: Theoretical issues*, 176–198. Washington, DC: Gallaudet University Press.

Liddell, S. K. 1995. Real, surrogate, and token space: Grammatical consequences in ASL. In K. Emmorey and J. Reilly, eds., *Language, gesture, and space*, 19–41. Hillsdale, NJ: Erlbaum.

Liddell, S. K. 2000. Indicating verbs and pronouns: Pointing away from agreement. In K. Emmorey and H. Lane, eds., *The signs of language revisited: An anthology to honor Ursula Bellugi and Edward Klima*, 303–320. Mahwah, NJ: Erlbaum.

Lillo-Martin, D. 1986. Two kinds of null arguments in American Sign Language. *Natural Language and Linguistic Theory* 4:415–444.

Lillo-Martin, D. 1995. The point of view predicate in American Sign Language. In K. Emmorey and J. Reilly, eds., *Language, gesture, and space*, 155–170. Hillsdale, NJ: Erlbaum.

Lillo-Martin, D. 2002. Where are all the modality effects? In R. P. Meier, K. Cormier, and D. Quinto-Pozos, eds., *Modality and structure in signed language and spoken language*, 241–262. Cambridge: Cambridge University Press.

Lillo-Martin, D., and E. S. Klima. 1990. Pointing out differences: ASL pronouns in syntactic theory. In S. D. Fischer and P. Siple, eds., *Theoretical issues in sign language research, volume 1: Linguistics*, 191–210. Chicago: University of Chicago Press.

McBurney, S. 2002. Pronominal reference in signed and spoken language: Are grammatical categories modality-dependent? In R. P. Meier, K. Cormier, and D. Quinto-Pozos, eds., *Modality and structure in signed and spoken languages*, 329–369. Cambridge: Cambridge University Press.

Meier, R. P. 1982. Icons, analogues, and morphemes: The acquisition of verb agreement in ASL. Doctoral dissertation, University of California, San Diego.

Meier, R. P. 1990. Person deixis in American Sign Language. In S. D. Fischer and P. Siple, eds., *Theoretical issues in sign language research, volume 1: Linguistics*, 175–190. Chicago: University of Chicago Press.

Meier, R. P. 2002a. The acquisition of verb agreement: Pointing out arguments for the linguistic status of agreement in signed languages. In G. Morgan and B. Woll, eds., *Current developments in the study of signed language acquisition*, 115–141. Amsterdam: John Benjamins.

Meier, R. P. 2002b. Why different, why the same? Explaining effects and non-effects of modality upon linguistic structure in sign and speech. In R. P. Meier, K. Cormier, and D. Quinto-Pozos, eds., *Modality and structure in signed language and spoken language*, 1–25. Cambridge: Cambridge University Press.

Meir, I. 2002. A cross-modality perspective on verb agreement. *Natural Language and Linguistic Theory* 20:413–450.

Meir, I. 2003. Grammaticalization and modality: The emergence of a case marked pronoun in Israeli Sign Language. *Journal of Linguistics* 39:109–140.

Padden, C. A. [1983] 1988. *Interaction of morphology and syntax in American Sign Language*. New York: Garland. (Originally distributed as a doctoral dissertation, University of California, San Diego.)

Perlmutter, D. M. 1991. The language of the deaf. *New York Review of Books*, March 28, 65–72.

Poizner, H., E. S. Klima, and U. Bellugi. 1987. *What the hands reveal about the brain*. Cambridge, MA: MIT Press.

Quadros, R. M. de. 1999. Phrase structure of Brazilian Sign Language. Doctoral dissertation, Pontificia Universidade Católica do Rio Grande do Sul.

Radutzky, E. 1992. *Dizionario bilingue elementare della Lingua Italiani dei Segni*. Rome: Ediziona Kappa.

Rathmann, C. 2000. The optionality of agreement phrase: Evidence from signed languages. MA thesis, University of Texas at Austin.

Rathmann, C., and G. Mathur. 2002. Is verb agreement the same cross-modally? In R. P. Meier, K. Cormier, and D. Quinto-Pozos, eds., *Modality and structure in signed and spoken languages*, 370–404. Cambridge: Cambridge University Press.

Sacks, O. 1990. *Seeing voices: A journey into the world of the deaf.* Berkeley: University of California Press.

Sandler, W., and D. Lillo-Martin. 2006. *Sign language and linguistic universals.* Cambridge: Cambridge University Press.

Sherzer, J. 1972. Verbal and nonverbal deixis: The pointed lip gesture among the San Blas Cuna. *Language in Society* 2:117–131.

Smith, W. 1990. Evidence for auxiliaries in Taiwan Sign Language. In S. D. Fischer and P. Siple, eds., *Theoretical issues in sign language research, volume 1: Linguistics*, 211–228. Chicago: University of Chicago Press.

Smith, W., and L. F. Ting. 1979. *Shou neng sheng chyau* (Your hands can become a bridge). Vol. 1. Taipei: Deaf Sign Language Research Association of the Republic of China.

Washabaugh, W. 1986. *Five fingers for survival*. Ann Arbor, MI: Karoma.

19 Object-Controlled Restructuring in Spanish

John Moore

19.1 Introduction

A good deal of work in Romance syntax has concentrated on the analysis of restructuring or clause-reduction constructions (see Aissen and Perlmutter [1976] 1983[1] and Rizzi 1978, among others). These are constructions that involve infinitival complements but behave as single clauses in a number of respects—for example, they allow clitic climbing. That is, pronominal clitics that correspond to semantic arguments of the infinitive may attach to the main verb:

(1) Marta *lo* quiere comprar.
    'Marta wants to buy it.'

There have been numerous analyses of these constructions. One general approach emphasizes the modal or light-verb character of restructuring verbs (Napoli 1981; Myhill 1988; Rosen 1990; among others). Under this approach, verbs that participate as main verbs in restructuring constructions (trigger verbs) have an impoverished argument structure or semantic elaboration and can, therefore, behave in a modal-like fashion. A similar approach is presented in Roberts 1997, where he speculates that the core cases of restructuring might be assimilated with other auxiliaries by decomposing modal and aspectual restructuring triggers in an abstract D^0 or P^0 and an abstract copula *be* (see Kayne 1993). Under his approach, the embedded verb raises to check features of these restructuring auxiliaries. More recently, Cinque (2004) proposes that all cases of restructuring occur when the semantics of a restructuring predicate matches that of a functional head. This opens the possibility that the verb may occupy a functional head position, yielding a monoclausal structure. I will refer to this proposal as the functional trigger hypothesis.

This chapter examines a class of Spanish restructuring constructions that challenges this hypothesis. In particular, I discuss object-control restructuring constructions, such as those introduced by *permitir* 'permit':

(2) Marta no te lo permitió comprar.
'Marta didn't permit you to buy it.'

Other predicates that participate in these constructions include *ordenar* 'order' and *mandar* 'command'. Constructions like these are well known from the literature on Spanish restructuring (Luján 1980; Suñer 1980; Aissen and Perlmutter [1976] 1983; Bordelois 1988; González 1988; Moore 1996; among others), but have received relatively little attention in the general Romance literature.

Restructuring triggers such as these are problematic for the functional trigger hypothesis. Given their articulated semantics, and the fact that they select indirect-object controllers, they seem unlikely to be modal or light verbs, D^0/P^0+BE auxiliaries, or functional heads. Kayne (1989, 248) notes that this class of constructions is problematic for the head movement account he proposes for restructuring; therefore, he suggests that constructions like (2) may be "hidden instances of the causative construction." While he does not elaborate, his proposal opens a possible way to reconcile these constructions with the functional trigger hypothesis: true restructuring predicates are functional heads, while verbs such as *permitir* participate in whatever mechanism is used for causatives. Cinque (2004) argues that this is indeed the case, citing two similarities between *permitir* and causative constructions.[2]

This chapter argues against such a conflation. I point out systematic differences between the object-control restructuring and causative constructions that argue in favor of a matrix-clause controller in the case of *permitir* predicates, and the lack of such a controller in the case of causatives. These arguments against assimilating object-control restructuring with causative constructions raise doubt that the functional head analysis is the only route to Romance restructuring.

19.2 Reduced Constructions

Both restructuring and causative constructions belong to the class of reduced constructions (Moore 1996). Potential examples of these constructions are given in (3), where we see that they involve infinitival complements to verbs such as *querer* 'want', *acabar de* 'finish', *hacer* 'make', and *dejar de* 'stop'. Henceforth, verbs that participate in these constructions will be referred to as trigger verbs.

(3) a. Quiere [cantar una saeta].
    'She/he wants to sing a saeta.'
  b. Acabo de [comer].
    'I just finished eating.' ('I just ate.')
  c. Me hicieron [trabajar toda la noche].
    'They made me work all night.'
  d. Dejó de [fumar].
    'She/he stopped smoking.'

Since the influential works of Aissen and Perlmutter ([1976] 1983) on Spanish and Rizzi (1978) on Italian, it has been recognized that this class of trigger verbs participates in infinitival constructions that exhibit what one might characterize as monoclausal characteristics. That is, despite the superficial fact that the Spanish examples in (3) resemble biclausal, infinitival constructions, they allow clitics associated with the embedded verb to attach to the matrix verb (4a), they allow passivization across both the embedded and matrix verbs (4b), and they allow *tough*-movement over three clauses (4c). Given that clitic placement and passivization are local, clause-bounded phenomena, and *tough*-movement in Spanish is limited to adjacent clauses, the examples in (4) indicate that the trigger verbs and their infinitival complements exhibit a degree of cohesiveness that suggests that they may not be two full-fledged clauses.[3]

(4) a. *Clitic climbing* (Aissen and Perlmutter 1983, (15))
   Te_i los_j quiero [mostrar ec_j ec_i].
   'I want to show them to you.'
   b. *Long passive* (Aissen and Perlmutter 1983, (P33b))
   Las casas$_i$ fueron acabadas de [pintar e_i ayer].
   'The houses were finished to paint yesterday.'
   ('Someone finished painting the houses yesterday.')
   c. *Long* tough-*movement* (Aissen and Perlmutter 1983, (63))
   Estas galletas$_i$ son casi imposibles de [dejar de [comer ec_i]].
   'These cookies are almost impossible to stop eating.'

Both Aissen and Perlmutter and Rizzi show that these unexpected monoclausal properties turn up only when the matrix verb belongs to the class of trigger verbs. In other words, not all infinitival constructions exhibit monoclausal characteristics. Compare the examples in (4) with those in (5):

(5) a. *Luis *las$_i$* insistió en [comer ec_i].
   'Luis insisted on eating them.' (Aissen and Perlmutter 1983, (13a))
   b. **Estas sillas$_i$* fueron insistidas en [pintar e_i].
   'These chairs were insisted on to paint.'
   'Someone insisted on painting these chairs.'
   c. **Sinfonías como éasa$_i$* son fáciles de [soñar con [componer ec_i].
   'Symphonies like that one are easy to dream of composing.' (Aissen and Perlmutter 1983, (67))

Both Aissen and Perlmutter and Rizzi independently note that the class of trigger verbs varies from speaker to speaker, and conclude that membership in the class is a lexical property of the verbs in question.

Reduction triggers are often divided into two classes. One class contains causative verbs like *hacer* 'make' and *dejar* 'let', as well as the perception verbs; following RG terminology I refer to these as union triggers. The other class consists of restructuring verbs such as *querer* 'want', *poder* 'can', and *soler* 'tend'. These classes of reduction triggers are illustrated in (6).

(6) *Reduction triggers*
    a. *Union*   b. *Restructuring*
        hacer 'make'   *querer* 'want'
        dejar 'let'   *poder* 'can'
        ver 'see'   *soler* 'tend'

Union triggers might be distinguished from restructuring triggers by the fact that union triggers occur in reduced constructions where the matrix subject is distinct from the embedded subject, as illustrated in (7):

(7) a. *Pepe* se lo hizo comprar *a Curro*.
       '*Pepe* made *Curro* buy it.'
    b. *Marta* se la vio romper *al niño*.
       '*Marta* saw *the child* break it.'

The restructuring triggers in (6b) are either subject-control verbs (*querer*)[4] or raising-to-subject verbs (*poder* and *soler*). Thus, they only occur in constructions where the matrix subject is nondistinct from the embedded subject; furthermore, the embedded subject is never phonologically realized. This is illustrated in (8):[5]

(8) a. *José$_i$* lo quiere [*PRO$_i$* comprar].
       '*José$_i$* wants [*PRO$_i$* to buy it].'
    b. *Los niños$_i$* lo suelen [e_i romper].
       '*The children$_i$* tend [e_i to break it].'

In addition to the union and restructuring triggers considered so far, Spanish exhibits reduced-construction behavior with a class of (indirect) object-control predicates. Examples of these constructions are given in (9), where the possibility of clitic climbing indicates that these are indeed reduced constructions.

(9) a. Marta se *lo$_j$ permitió* [PRO$_i$ arreglar ec_j] al mecánico$_i$.
       'Marta allowed the mechanic$_i$ [PRO$_i$ to fix *it$_j$*].'
    b. Se *lo$_j$ mandaron* [PRO$_i$ construir ec_j] a la empresa nueva$_i$.
       'They commanded the new company$_i$ [PRO$_i$ to build *it$_j$*].'
    c. Se *la$_j$ ordenaron* [PRO$_i$ limpiar ec_j] *pro$_i$*.
       'They ordered them$_i$ [PRO$_i$ to clean *it$_j$*].'

The verbs in (9) are of interest because like union triggers, they occur with an overt NP that corresponds to the embedded subject but is distinct from the matrix subject. However, like some restructuring triggers, these are control verbs.

19.3 The Functional Trigger Hypothesis

As noted, the defining characteristic of reduced constructions is the greater degree of transparency between the matrix and embedded clauses. This property has motivated many researchers to analyze reduction triggers as undergoing some type of complex predicate formation. The implementation of such a process has differed in details—for example, predicate raising (Aissen 1979), clause union (Aissen and Perlmutter [1976] 1983; Gibson and Raposo 1986), parallel structures (Manzini 1983; Zubizarreta 1982, 1985; Goodall 1987), syntactic incorporation (Baker 1988), argument structure merger (Rosen 1990), and argument linking (Alsina 1992), among other approaches.

A slightly different approach is taken by Cinque (2004). Rather than treating restructuring predicates as verbal heads, he relegates them to the functional layer, proposing that they occupy one of his many proposed functional heads.[6] Under this functional trigger hypothesis, the monoclausal effects follow immediately, so that restructuring constructions are truly monoclausal.

This approach predicts that restructuring predicates will, like other modals, be nonthematic. Indeed, Cinque argues that putative subject-control triggers, such as *volere* 'want', lack external arguments. As mentioned in note 4, this is contested in Wurmbrand 2004 for the corresponding German predicates.

The focus here is on the companion prediction of Cinque's analysis—that restructuring predicates should lack internal theta roles. This explicitly predicts the lack of object-control restructuring. Cinque notes that such constructions appear to exist in Spanish but argues that they are not true instances of restructuring. Rather, following Kayne's suggestion, he argues that they are "hidden instances of the causative construction."[7] From a semantic perspective, this is not unreasonable, since *permitir* 'permit' is similar in meaning to the union trigger *dejar* 'allow'; the other object-control restructuring triggers, *ordenar* 'order' and *mandar* 'command', are semantically close to the causative *hacer* 'make'. However, a number of unusual syntactic properties are associated with the union constructions and, as demonstrated below, these properties are not shared by object-control restructuring constructions. Hence, in order to give substance to the claim that putative object-control restructuring is reducible to causative (union) constructions, one needs to show clearly parallel syntactic behavior.

19.4 Two Nonarguments for Conflation

Cinque discusses two syntactic similarities between union and *permitir* constructions.[8] Since the similar phenomena do not hold of other restructuring constructions, he takes them as evidence in favor of conflating union and *permitir* constructions and concludes, on the basis of these similarities, that "the conclusion that there exist object control 'restructuring' verbs finds no justification" (Cinque 2004, 145). In this section I propose an alternative account for one of these putative similarities; this alternative does not entail the conflation of Spanish causative and *permitir* constructions. Cinque's other data that show similarities between causative and *permitir* constructions cannot be replicated for Spanish. Hence, his second argument is moot with respect to the relevant Spanish constructions.

Cinque's first argument has to do with a restriction on animate clitic climbing. As noted in Bordelois 1974, Rivas 1977, Contreras 1979, Luján 1980, and Suñer 1980, among others, clitics with animate reference may not climb when the trigger is a union verb or from the *permitir* class:[9]

(10) a. Me hicieron educar*la*. (Luján 1980, (59))
 b. *?Me *la* hicieron educar. (Luján 1980, (59))
 'They made me educate her.'

(11) a. Me permitieron educar*la*. (Luján 1980, (59))
 b. *?Me *la* permitieron educar. (Luján 1980, (59))
 'They allowed me to educate her.'

As Cinque points out, other restructuring verbs lack this restriction:

(12) Lo quiero conocer.
 'I want to meet him.'

However, it is clear that this is not a restriction on union triggers and verbs of the *permitir* class. Rather, as Luján (1980) noted, it is a restriction on animate clitic climbing when the trigger verb already has an additional clitic. Since the embedded subject argument cliticizes to the union verb and *permitir* selects its own indirect object, these verbs both happen to have the additional clitics that are necessary to prevent animate clitic climbing. Other, non-object-control, restructuring verbs lack these extra clitics and, therefore, exhibit no animate clitic-climbing constraint.

Conclusive evidence that the restriction has to do with the additional matrix-clause clitic comes from union and *permitir* constructions where the matrix clitic is absent.[10] In the absence of a matrix clitic, even with union and *permitir* triggers, the animate clitic constraint disappears:

(13) a. Les sorbornó con 100 Euros y *la* hizo elegir.
 'He bribed them with 100 euros and got *her* selected.'
 b. Con el pago de 100 Euros, sí *la* permite elegir.
 'Paying 100 euros allows *her* to be selected.'

Hence, the shared restriction on animate clitic climbing is an accidental property of union and *permitir* verbs, because they both typically occur with independent matrix clitics. The data in (13) show that these verbs do not behave differently from other restructuring verbs, once these extra clitics are removed.

Cinque's second argument is based on a restriction against reflexive causees. Using the Italian verbs *fare* 'make' to represent union triggers and *insegnare* 'teach' to represent the *permitir* class, he notes that neither verb allows a reflexive or reciprocal clitic to correspond to the embedded subject:

(14) a. *Gianni e Mario si fecero imparare la procedura. (Cinque 2004, (51b))
 'Gianni and Mario had each other learn the procedure.'
 b. ?*Gianni e Mario si insegnarono imparare la procedura. (Cinque 2004, (52b))
 'Gianni and Mario taught each other the procedure.'

Cinque does not discuss the corresponding Spanish examples. In Spanish, *permitir* behaves differently from union verbs in this respect:

(15) a. *Jorge se hizo probrar los chapulines.[11]
 'Jorge made himself try the grasshoppers.'
 b. Jorge se permitió comer tres pasteles.
 'Jorge allowed himself to eat three pastries.'

(16) a. *?Jorge y Juan se hicieron probrar los chapulines (el uno al otro).
 'Jorge and Juan made each other try the grasshoppers.'
 b. Jorge y Juan se permitieron comer tres pasteles (el uno al otro).
 'Jorge and Juan allowed each other to eat three pastries.'

On the face of it, the Italian facts simply do not extend to Spanish. However, there is a possibility that needs to be dispensed with. The literature on Spanish reduced constructions generally holds that *hacer* must obligatorily participate in reduced constructions, while *permitir* verbs are compatible with both reduced and unreduced constructions. If this were true, then the grammaticality of (15b) and (16b) might be due to the possibility of an unreduced structure. Indeed, with positive evidence for reduction (e.g., clitic climbing), examples like (15b) become ungrammatical:

(17) *Jorge se los permitió comer.
 'Jorge allowed himself to eat them.'

However, this explanation of the Spanish facts does not extend to the Italian data in (14). In Italian, *fare* constructions are unambiguously reduced, while *insegnare* can occur in both reduced and unreduced constructions. Cinque provides the following examples that show optional clitic climbing with the latter predicate:

(18) a. Gli ho insegnato a far*lo* io. (Cinque 2004, (46a,b))
    b. Glie*l'*ho insegnato a fare io.
       'I taught him to do it.'

In addition, *insegnare* allows embedded sentential negation—a property that is a clear test for biclausality:

(19) Gli ho insegnato a *non* farlo io.
     'I taught him to not do it.'

Finally, in many varieties of Spanish, *hacer* may participate in both reduced and unreduced constructions. In Moore 1996, 124–135, I show that data have been used to argue for obligatory reduction—for example, the impossibility of embedded negation is not reproducible with speakers of Peninsular Spanish as well as many speakers of Latin American Spanish (see also Treviño 1992). Crucially, speakers for whom restructuring with *hacer* is optional have the judgments in (15) and (16). Hence, the contrast in Spanish and the lack of such a contrast in Italian must be orthogonal to whether the construction is reduced or not.

19.5 Against Conflation

Having established that the arguments for conflating union and *permitir* constructions do not hold for Spanish, I will argue in this section that the constructions crucially differ in that only verbs of the *permitir* class involve indirect-object control, while union verbs do not. Thus, the nonconflated hypothesis I propose assumes subcategorizations such as those given in (20):[12]

(20) *The nonconflated hypothesis*
     a. *hacer, dejar, ver,...*
        [__ VP]   no control
     b. *permitir, mandar, ordenar*
        [__ VP NP]   indirect-object control

Two basic differences between object-control restructuring and union constructions will be presented: differences in Case marking and the ability to participate in the *faire-par* construction.

In arguing for the nonconflated hypothesis in (20), I will be arguing against hypotheses under which causative and *permitir* constructions have the same analysis, as Kayne and Cinque suggest. Neither Kayne nor Cinque proposes an explicit account of these constructions, but Kayne (1989, 242) suggests that they involve VP complementation. Two possible hypotheses consistent with this suggestion are presented in (21):

(21) a. *Conflated hypothesis A*
 hacer, dejar, permitir, mandar, ordenar...
 [__ VP]   no control
 b. *Conflated hypothesis B*
 hacer, dejar, permitir, mandar, ordenar...
 [__ VP NP]   indirect-object control

I am not aware of the hypothesis in (21a) having been explicitly proposed, although Kayne's suggestion may have something along these lines in mind. An analysis similar to (21b) is proposed in Bordelois 1988.

19.5.1 Case Marking

The most obvious difference between the two constructions has to do with the Case marking of the argument that corresponds to the embedded subject. There has been an immense literature on this topic with respect to union constructions. One reason this area has attracted so much interest is that the causee/embedded subject of union constructions alternates between direct and indirect object, subject to various factors. First, there is an alternation based on the transitivity of the embedded predicate. As illustrated in (22), the subject of embedded intransitives can show up as direct objects, while embedded transitive subjects may be indirect objects:

(22) a. Esa película *lo* hizo llorar.   Intransitive base predicate
 'That movie made *him (DO)* cry.'
 b. Los propietarios *les* hicieron pagar el alquiler.   Transitive base predicate
 'The owners made *them (IO)* pay the rent.'

Although this is the pattern most often described for Spanish unions (e.g., Aissen and Perlmutter [1976] 1983; Rosen 1990; among many others), it is not inviolable. In certain semantically or pragmatically marked cases, the embedded subject may be Case-marked with the Case that is the opposite that one would expect based on the transitivity of the embedded predicate. This has been discussed for causative union triggers by Strozer 1976, Finnemann 1982, and Treviño 1992, among others. The essential pattern that emerges is as follows: if the embedded predicate is intransitive, and the causee argument is an indirect object instead of the expected direct object, then the causation is indirect; if the embedded predicate is transitive and the causee is a direct object instead of the expected indirect object, then the causation is direct. When the Case is as expected, based on transitivity, the causation is vague with respect to direct/indirect.

(23) a. *Le* hice correr.   Indirect causation
 'I had *him (IO)* run.' (Strozer 1976, (6.122a))

b. *Los* hico quemar las casas.   Direct causation
   'He made *them (DO)* burn down the houses.' (Strozer 1976, (6.122d))

A similar pattern is attested in some dialects of French (Authier and Reed 1991; Reed 1992). A detailed account of the interaction between the two Case-marking patterns in Spanish is presented in Ackerman and Moore 1999. This account, like most others, relies on complex-predicate formation. Under these accounts, the causee argument's Case varies depending on co-occurring arguments and the semantics of the complex predicate. Crucially, however, the causee does not receive inherent Case from the causative verb—this is expected under the analysis in (20a), because the verb does not directly select the causee argument.[13]

In contrast, verbs of the *permitir* class only take indirect objects. Hence, in the following examples, we see that a direct-object controller is impossible, regardless of the transitivity of the embedded predicate:

(24) a. Su abuelo no *le* permitio' jugar en el patio.
        'His grandfather didn't permit *him (IO)* to play in the patio.'
     b. *Su abuelo no *lo* permitio' jugar en el patio.

(25) a. Los propietarios *les* permitieron pagar el alquiler por domiciliación.
        'The owners permitted *them (IO)* to pay the rent through their bank accounts.'
     b. *Los propietarios *los* permitieron pagar el alquiler por domiciliación.

Since direct objects are systematically excluded in these constructions, there is no Case alternation—neither determined by transitivity, not by semantic/pragmatic factors. This is easily accounted for if verbs of the *permitir* class select indirect-object controllers.

The conflated hypotheses in (21) would have a difficult time accounting for these differences in Case marking. The noncontrol conflated hypothesis A in (21a) would have to ensure that the mechanisms that yield the Case alternations associated with union verbs do not do so when the verbs are of the *permitir* class. Conversely, the conflated hypothesis B in (21b) would have to explain why a consistent structural Case is not assigned in union constructions.

19.5.2 *Faire-Par* vs. *Faux-Faire-Par*

An advocate of the conflated hypothesis might argue that *permitir* and union constructions should be subject to the same analysis because the object-marked argument may be omitted in both constructions:

(26) a. Marta hizo [barrer la vereda].
        'Marta had the sidewalk swept.'

b. Marta permitió [barrer la vereda].
'Marta permitted the sidewalk to be swept.'

In fact, Bordelois (1988) uses such examples to argue that both union and *permitir* constructions select an optional controller—an account in line with conflated hypothesis B. Under conflated hypothesis A, one might seek to assimilate the example in (26b) with the well-known *faire-par* construction.

In his discussion of French causatives, Kayne (1975) distinguishes between two construction types: *faire*-infinitive constructions, in which the causee is overtly realized as an object, and *faire-par* constructions, in which the causee is either realized in an oblique *par*-phrase, or omitted altogether:

(27) a. Elle a fait visiter la ferme *à ses parents*.   *Faire*-infinitive
'She had her parents visit the farm.' (Kayne 1975, 204, (6c))
b. Elle fera manger cette pomme *par Jean*.   *Faire-par*
'She'll have that apple eaten by Jean.' (Kayne 1975, 234, (89a))
c. Elle fera manger cette pomme.   *Faire-par* (no *par*-phrase)
'She'll have that apple eaten.'

The examples of Spanish causative constructions considered so far have had overtly realized objects; hence, we have been dealing exclusively with *faire*-infinitive constructions. Spanish also has the counterpart to Kayne's *faire-par* construction; however, as illustrated in (28), the Spanish equivalent of these constructions is much better when the oblique *por*-phrase is omitted:

(28) a. ?Hicieron diseñar la casa *por los mejores arquitectos*.
'They had the house designed by the best architects.'
b. Hicieron diseñar la casa.
'They had the house designed.'

Whenever an argument is phonologically null, there are at least two possibilities regarding its syntactic status. It could be that there is no syntactic position corresponding to the embedded subject in (28b), or the argument could be phonologically null, yet syntactically present (as proposed in Rizzi 1986 for certain null objects).

In what follows, I argue that causative constructions are often structurally ambiguous between these two analyses. Hence, I distinguish two construction types: true *faire-par* constructions, in which the missing causee is a syntactically unexpressed oblique, and *faux-faire-par* constructions, where the causee is a phonologically silent object pronoun with arbitrary reference (pro_{ARB}) (see Guasti 1989 and Moore 1996 for discussions of *faux-faire-par*).

(29) a. *Faire-par* b. *Faux-faire-par*

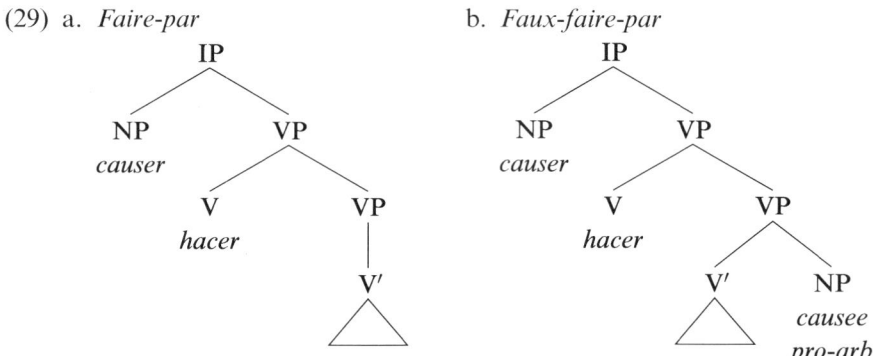

As is evident from these diagrams, the *faire-par* construction lacks a VP-internal subject position; this is consistent with an analysis whereby the external θ-role is suppressed. The *faux-faire-par* construction, on the other hand, has an embedded subject position, and is, therefore, a type of *faire*-infinitive construction, albeit one where the causee is phonologically silent.

Interestingly, object-control restructuring predicates do not participate in the *faire-par* construction. That is, I argue that *permitir* constructions like the one in (26b), which lack overt object-marked arguments, should be analyzed as a type of *faux-faire-par* construction:[14]

(30) *Faux-faire-par with object control*

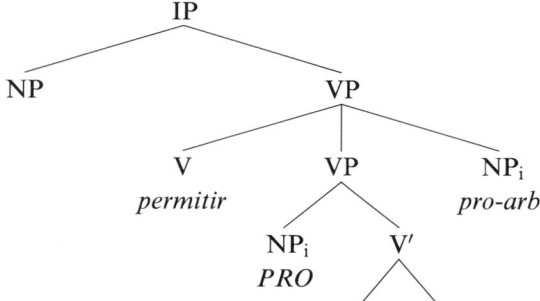

Thus, *permitir* constructions do not allow the type of structural ambiguity found with causative union constructions. I argue that this is a direct consequence of the non-conflated analysis. Hence, the differences that motivate this contrast between union and *permitir* constructions argue against conflation.

The first argument that *permitir* constructions do not participate in *faire-par* constructions comes from the impossibility of expressing the embedded subject as an oblique *por*-phrase. Although this is marginal in Spanish, even in union construc-

Object-Controlled Restructuring in Spanish

tions, the contrast is nevertheless robust. Thus, some speakers accept examples like (31a), but all speakers reject (31b):

(31) a. ?Hicieron diseñar la casa *por el mejor arcitecto*.
'They had the house designed by the best architect.'
b. *Permitieron diseñar la casa *por el mejor arcitecto*.
'They permitted the house to be designed by the best architect.'

There are a number of accounts of the oblique causee in *faire-par* constructions (see Kayne 1975; Aissen 1979; Zubizarreta 1985; Perlmutter 1986; Goodall 1987; Guast 1990; Legendre 1990; Rosen 1990; Postal 1992; Moore 1996; among others). In all of these accounts, the embedded subject is suppressed or demoted, yielding an oblique encoding. Under the nonconflated hypothesis, the suppression of the embedded subject of *permitir* would not affect the matrix controller; hence, under this account it is expected that object-control restructuring predicates should not participate in the *faire-par* construction. Under conflated hypothesis A, however, there is no matrix controller; hence, nothing should prevent both constructions from allowing *faire-par*.

Bordelois' (1988) version of conflated hypothesis B also makes the wrong predictions with respect to *faire-par*. Under this account, constructions without overt object-marked arguments would be analyzed as in (32):[15]

(32)

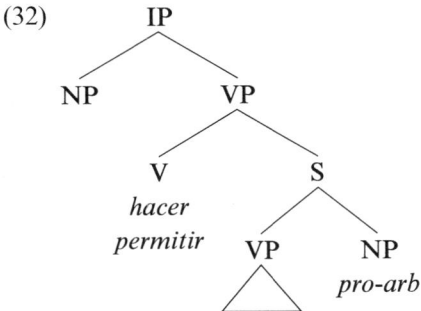

This structure results from omitting the optional controller argument, leaving the embedded clause with a *pro-arb* subject. However, given this analysis, it is unclear how the causee can be realized as an oblique, as in (31a). Presumably the external argument must be suppressed, as in the accounts mentioned above; however, if this were possible, then it is unclear what would allow this in the case of *hacer*, but not in the case of *permitir*.

A second argument for the distinction between union and *permitir* constructions with respect to *faire-par* constructions comes from the behavior of reflexives. In (33) we see that *faire-par* and *faire*-infinitive constructions contrast in reflexive binding options. In (33a) the matrix subject can reflexively bind an embedded object in a *faire-par* construction; (33b) shows that this kind of binding is impossible in the case of the *faire*-infinitive construction.[16]

(33) a. *Curro$_i$* se hizo [insultar *ec$_i$* (por sus compañeros)].   *Faire-par*
'*Curro* got *himself* insulted (by his friends).'
b. **Curro$_i$* se hizo [insultar *ec$_i$* a sus compañeros].   *Faire*-infinitive
'*Curro$_i$* made his friends insult *him$_i$*.' (Moore 1996, 148, (25))

These data provide motivation for the claim that *faire-par* constructions have no syntactic position that corresponds to the embedded subject. If the embedded clause had such a syntactic position in (33a), we would expect it to create an opaque domain and prevent anaphoric binding, as the embedded subject in the *faire*-infinitive construction in (33b) does. This provides evidence that the external argument of the embedded verb in a *faire-par* construction does not project. Thus, the possibility of anaphoric binding between the matrix subject and embedded object provides a positive diagnostic for the *faire-par* construction in cases where the causee is unexpressed.

Permitir constructions, on the other hand, do not permit this type of reflexive binding, neither when the controller is overt, as in (34a), nor when the controller is silent (34b):

(34) a. **Curro$_i$* se permite insultar *ec$_i$* a sus compañeros.
'*Curro$_i$* permits his friends to insult *him$_i$*.'
b. **Curro$_i$* se permite insultar *ec$_i$*.[17]
'*Curro$_i$* permits (people) to insult *him$_i$*.'

The ungrammaticality of (34b) can be accounted for if we assume that there is an embedded subject position that creates an opaque domain, and prevents anaphoric binding between the matrix subject and the embedded object.

The claim that *faux-faire-par* constructions are, in reality, *faire*-infinitive constructions makes a further prediction regarding anaphoric binding. Since these constructions do contain an embedded subject position, it should be possible for this phonologically silent subject to reflexively bind an embedded object. Since it is claimed that both causative and object-control restructuring constructions are compatible with the *faux-faire-par* construction, we should expect such binding with both verbs like *hacer* and *permitir*. From the examples in (35) we see that this prediction is borne out:[18]

(35) a. Nosotros, los accionistas, siempre hemos hecho peinarse con gomina para entrar en nuestro banco.
'We, the investors, have always made *people$_i$* comb *themselves$_i$* with gel before entering our bank.' (Moore 1996, 160, (49a))
b. En el Partido Popular permiten peinarse con gomina.
'In the Popular Party they allow *one$_i$* to comb *oneself$_i$* with gel.' (Moore 1996, 158, (42b))

It is precisely the fact that examples like (33a) and (35a) are grammatical that argues that causative constructions are compatible with both *faire-par* and *faux-faire-par* constructions. This contrasts with *permitir* constructions, which do not allow the former (see 34b) but do allow the latter (35b).

Finally, union and *permitir* constructions differ in their behavior with respect to passivization. It is well known that embedded objects may passivize in Italian causative constructions, both in Italian *faire*-infinitive and *faire-par* constructions:

(36) a. *Quei brani* furono fatti leggere a Giovanni.   Passivization out of
      'They had Giovanni read those passages.'   *faire*-infinitive
   b. *Quei brani* furono fatti leggere (da Giovanni).   Passivization out of
      'They had those passages read by Giovanni.'   *faire-par*
      (Zubizarreta 1985, (84b,a))

However, the facts in Spanish are less clear. Zubizarreta (1985) cites corresponding Spanish examples as ungrammatical, but also notes that there is a good deal of variation in this area. I have found speakers fairly willing to accept passivization of the embedded object of a Spanish *faire-par* construction (37a), but reluctant to accept the corresponding *faire*-infinitive examples (37b):

(37) a. ?*Este coche* fue hecho arreglar por mi hermano.[19]   Passivization out of
      'My brother had this car fixed.'   *faire-par*
   b. *?*El coche* fue hecho arreglar al mecánico.   Passivization out of
      'My brother had the mechanic fix that car.'   *faire*-infinitive

Unsurprisingly, *permitir* constructions pattern with (36b):

(38) *?*El coche* fue permitido arreglar al mecánico.
      'My brother permitted the mechanic to fix that car.'

Above I argued that *permitir* constructions are incompatible with the *faire-par* construction; I argued that cases where the controller is not realized overtly are *faux-faire-par* constructions. If this is true, we predict that even when the controller is unexpressed, passivization should be very marginal, as is the case for *faire*-infinitive constructions and for *permitir* constructions with overt object-marked arguments. We find this prediction borne out in examples like (39):

(39) *?*Estos vestidos* no fueron permitidos comprar.
      'It was not permitted that someone buy these dresses.'

Hence, we have provided evidence that there are systematic syntactic differences between causative/union *faire-par* constructions and *permitir* constructions with silent object-marked arguments. These differences follow from the nonconflated hypothesis; the external argument suppression associated with *faire-par* is impossible in conjunction with object-controlled restructuring because this external argument suppression does not affect the matrix controller. Such an explanation would not be available under either of the two conflated hypotheses.

19.6 Constituency Issues

Under the nonconflated hypothesis, the embedded VP of a *permitir* construction is claimed to be a maximal projection, independent of the object controller. In union constructions, on the other hand, the causee argument is part of the embedded VP. This suggests that syntactic phenomena that target maximal projections should be able to target the embedded VP of *permitir* constructions, stranding the object controller, but should not be able to target the VP, minus the cause, of union constructions. We see this prediction borne out in terms of sentential anaphor (40), clefting (41), and passivization of the embedded clause (42):[20]

(40) *Sentential anaphora*
    a. Mi padre no me permite/ordena/manda [salir por la noche]$_i$, pero mi madre sí me lo_i permite/ordena/manda.
       'My father doesn't permit/order/command me to go out at night, but my mother does permit/order/command that I do it.'
    b. *Mi padre no me hace/deja [salir por la noche]$_i$, pero mi madre si lo_i hace/deja.
       'My father doesn't make/let me to go out at night, but my mother does make/let me do it.'

(41) *Clefting*
    a. Lo que me permitió/ordenó/mandó fue [barrer la vereda].
       'What she/he permitted/ordered/commanded that I do was [sweep the sidewalk].'
    b. *Lo que me hizo/dejó fue [barrer la vereda].
       'What she/he made/allowed me to do was [sweep the sidewalk].'

(42) *Passivization*
    a. Me fue permitido/ordenado/mandado [salir por la noche].
       'It was permitted/ordered/commanded [that I go out at night].'
    b. *Me fue hecho/dejado [salir por la noche].
       'It was made/allowed [that I go out at night].'

However, there is a complication that renders this argument less compelling. Recall that in section 19.4 I noted that *permitir* constructions, and for many speakers, union constructions, could either be reduced or unreduced. Since the examples in (40)–(42) do not show positive evidence of clause reduction (e.g., clitic climbing), it is impossible to say whether these are reduced or unreduced. Furthermore, it turns out to be impossible to test for reduction (e.g., clitic climbing is impossible in these constructions for independent reasons). Thus, an advocate of the functional trigger hypothesis might maintain that the grammatical (a) examples in (40)–(42) are grammatical only when the construction is unreduced. It could be maintained that the separate constituency of the object controller and the embedded clause only obtains in unreduced *permitir* constructions; union constructions would have a single clausal argument in both reduced and unreduced alternatives. In (43) and (44) I present two hypotheses consistent with the data in (40)–(42):

(43) *Conflated hypothesis A'*
     hacer, dejar, permitir, mandar, ordenar
     [__ VP]   reduced
     hacer, dejar
     [__ CP]   unreduced
     permitir, mandar, ordenar
     [__ NP CP]   unreduced

(44) *Nonconflated hypothesis*
     hacer, dejar
     [__ {VP, CP}]   reduced, unreduced
     permitir, mandar, ordenar
     [__ NP {VP, CP}] reduced, unreduced

While the data in (40)–(42) do not bear on the choice between (43) and (44), (43) requires rather different selection properties for reduced and unreduced *permitir* constructions, while under (44), the difference is simply whether the constructions are reduced or not.

19.7 Conclusion

The arguments in section 19.5 pose a problem for the functional trigger hypothesis. This hypothesis must explain away putative cases of object-control restructuring; Cinque's proposal is to achieve this by conflating *permitir* constructions with union constructions. However, I have shown evidence that such conflation is untenable. Thus, *permitir* constructions are not "hidden incidents of the causative construction." Rather, they are object-control constructions that participate in the general phenomenon of restructuring. In particular, I have argued against two conflated hypotheses—one where neither causative nor *permitir* constructions are control structures (conflated hypothesis A, 21a) and the one where both involve object control (conflated hypothesis B, 21b). Since neither Cinque (2004) nor Kayne (1989) discusses the details of an analysis where *permitir* constructions are "hidden causatives," it is possible that neither of these conflated hypotheses are what they have in mind. For example, one might maintain that the nonconflated hypothesis in (20) is an instantiation of Kayne's suggestion—after all, under this approach, both union and *permitir* constructions involve VP-complementation. I cannot argue against this hypothetical position, except to note that it renders the functional trigger hypothesis unfalsifiable—any counterexample could be similarly assimilated with causatives in this manner. Therefore, while the route to restructuring phenomena might involve functional triggers, this cannot be the only route.

Notes

I wish to thank an anonymous reviewer for comments on this chapter, as well as the many Spanish speakers whose judgments have gone into this work over many years. Any errors are my responsibility. Finally, I thank David Perlmutter for, among other things, making this work possible in the first place.

1. Aissen and Perlmutter's work on clause reduction first appeared in the 1976 BLS proceedings. A revised and expanded version of this chapter was published as Aissen and Perlmutter 1983. References to examples from this work are from the 1983 paper.

2. Taking a different tack, Bordelois (1988) assimilates causative and object-control restructuring constructions by treating both as instances of object control.

3. There are a number of complicating factors. It is not the case that all infinitival constructions introduced by trigger verbs always exhibit all of the monoclausal phenomena in (4). While pretty much all of them allow clitic climbing, long passives are restricted to a subset of such constructions; this is probably for independent reasons. Thus, clitic climbing remains the best diagnostic for reduced constructions (*tough*-movement should also be a consistent diagnostic, except that it yields variable results, perhaps due to its independently marked nature).

4. Cinque (2004) argues that Italian triggers such as *volere* 'want' lack external arguments and are not control verbs. Wurmbrand (2004) argues that this class of verbs (i.e., putative subject-control restructuring verbs) do indeed take external arguments.

5. Rizzi (1978) discusses other differences between restructuring and union constructions, and argues that they should be subject to different analyses; Aissen and Perlmutter argue union and restructuring are instances of the same phenomenon, and that differences between them should follow from lexical differences between the trigger verbs in question. This difference in analysis may be a function of differences between Italian and Spanish. In particular, Rizzi points out two primary differences between union and restructuring based on auxiliary selection and embedded passivization; however, Spanish has no auxiliary selection, and the passivization facts are far from clear.

6. Based on functional morphology and adverb placement, Cinque (1999) proposes a highly articulated functional layer. This involves a few dozen functional heads that include several types of mood and aspect projections.

7. While Kayne (1989) does not propose a functional head account of restructuring, his head movement account of clitic-climbing also predicts the lack of object-control restructuring.

8. In the following sections, I refer to the putative object-control restructuring constructions as "*permitir* constructions" so as not to prejudice the discussion toward a particular analysis.

9. Examples (10b) and (11b) are cited as ungrammatical in Luján 1980, while Rivas 1977 describes them as 'non-preferred'; my consultants judged them to be marginal.

10. See section 19.5.2 for a discussion of these constructions.

11. Judgments vary with respect to reflexive causees. My consultants reject examples like (15a), while Torrego (1998) judges similar examples as marginal. Furthermore, Torrego cites cases like (i), which appear to be fine.

(i) El actor se hizo vomitar. (Torrego 1998, chap. 3, (51b))
'The actor made himself vomit.'

12. The lexical information given as subcategorization frames in (20) is for concreteness. The embedded event argument is given as a VP, following Strozer 1976, Zagona 1982, Pearce 1990, Rosen 1990, and Moore 1996, among others. This is the sense in which these are reduced constructions. Other analyses assume alternative realizations for this constituent; the analysis in (20) is not necessarily incompatible with such approaches. As mentioned in section 19.4, there is evidence that in addition to these subcategorizations, both causative and *permitir* verbs allow unreduced, full clausal complements.

13. I assume that the causee is the VP-internal subject of the VP-complement (or the equivalent in other approaches).

14. The diagrams in (29) and (30) show *faux-faire-par* constructions with VP-complements—that is, these are represented as reduced constructions. There is also evidence that there can be unreduced *faux-faire-par* constructions as well. See Moore 1996, 158–162, for discussion.

15. Bordelois analyzes the embedded clause of a reduced structure as an Infl-less S.

16. In these and subsequent examples *ec* is used to mark the embedded object position that is bound by a higher subject.

17. Example (34b) is marginally grammatical under a different reading. That is, it can, for some speakers, mean 'Curro permitted himself to insult people'.

18. While the data in (35) are clearly consistent with a *faux-faire-par* analyses, Legendre (1990) gives examples of French *faire-par* where the oblique causee is able to marginally antecede an embedded reflexive. Hence, the example in (35a) may marginally represent a true *faire-par* construction.

19. The *por*-phrase in (37a) does not correspond to the causee argument, rather the causer (matrix agent).

20. The sentential anaphora and passive data are discussed in Moore 1996 as evidence for a control analysis of *permitir* constructions. The contrast in passivization between object-control triggers and causative verbs is discussed in Torrego 1998, 110, where she argues for a noncor-flated account similar to the one proposed here.

References

Ackerman, Farrell, and John Moore. 1999. Syntagmatic and paradigmatic dimensions of causee encoding. *Linguistics and Philosophy* 22:1–44.

Aissen, Judith. 1979. *The syntax of causative constructions*. New York: Garland.

Aissen, Judith L., and David M. Perlmutter. 1976. Clause reduction in Spanish. In *Proceedings of the Second Annual Meeting of the Berkeley Linguistics Society*, 1–30. University of California, Berkeley. (Revised in 1983 in David M. Perlmutter, ed., *Studies in relational grammar 1*, 360–403. Chicago: University of Chicago Press.)

Alsina, Alex. 1992. On the argument structure of causatives. *Linguistic Inquiry* 23:517–555.

Authier, J. Marc, and Lisa Reed. 1991. Ergative predicates and dative cliticization in French causatives. *Linguistic Inquiry* 22:197–205.

Baker, Mark C. 1988. *Incorporation: A theory of grammatical function changing.* Chicago: University of Chicago Press.

Bordelois, Ivonne. 1974. The grammar of Spanish causative complements. Doctoral dissertation, MIT.

Bordelois, Ivonne. 1988. Causatives: From lexicon to syntax. *Natural Language and Linguistic Theory* 6:57–94.

Cinque, Guglielmo. 1999. *Adverbs and functional heads: A cross-linguistic perspective.* New York: Oxford University Press.

Cinque, Guglielmo. 2004. "Restructuring" and functional structure. In A. Belletti, ed., *Structures and beyond: The cartography of syntactic structures*, vol. 3, 132–191. New York: Oxford University Press.

Contreras, Heles. 1979. Clause reduction, the saturation constraint, and clitic promotion in Spanish. *Linguistic Analysis* 5:161–182.

Finnemann, David. 1982. Aspects of the Spanish causative construction. Doctoral dissertation, University of Minnesota.

Gibson, Jeanne, and Eduardo Raposo. 1986. Clause union, the stratal uniqueness law, and the chômeur relation. *Natural Language and Linguistic Theory* 4:295–331.

González, Nora. 1988. *Object and raising in Spanish.* New York: Garland.

Goodall, Grant. 1987. *Parallel structures in syntax: Coordination, causatives and restructuring.* Cambridge: Cambridge University Press.

Guasti, Maria Teresa. 1989. Romance infinitive complements of perception verbs. *MIT Working Papers* 11:31–45.

Guasti, Maria Teresa. 1990. The "faire-par" construction in Romance and Germanic. In A. L. Halperns, ed., *The Proceedings of the Ninth West Coast Conference on Formal Linguistics*, 205–218. Stanford: CSLI/SLA.

Kayne, Richard S. 1975. *French syntax.* Cambridge, MA: MIT Press.

Kayne, Richard S. 1989. Null subjects and clitic climbing. In O. Jaeggli and K. J. Safir, eds., *The null subject parameter*, 239–262. Dordrecht: Kluwer.

Kayne, Richard S. 1993. Towards a modular theory of auxiliary selection. *Studia Linguistica* 47:3–31.

Legendre, Géraldine. 1990. French causatives: Another look at *faire-par*. In K. Dziwirek, P. Farrell, and E. Mejías-Bikandi, eds., *Grammatical relations: A cross-theoretical perspective*, 247–262. Stanford: CSLI/SLA.

Luján, Marta. 1980. Clitic promotion and mood in Spanish verbal complements. *Linguistics* 18:381–484.

Manzini, Maria Rita. 1983. Restructuring and reanalysis. Doctoral dissertation, MIT.

Moore, John. 1996. *Reduced constructions in Spanish.* New York: Garland.

Myhill, John. 1988. The grammaticalization of auxiliaries: Spanish clitic climbing. *Berkeley Linguistics Society* 14:352–363.

Napoli, Donna Jo. 1981. Semantic interpretation vs. lexical governance: Clitic climbing in Italian. *Language* 57:841–887.

Pearce, Elizabeth. 1990. *Parameters in Old French syntax: Infinitival complements*. Dordrecht: Kluwer.

Perlmutter, David M. 1986. Some consequences of the unaccusative hypothesis for the theory of clause union. Talk delivered at the Sixteenth Meeting of the Northeastern Linguistic Society, MIT.

Postal, Paul M. 1992. Phantom successors and the French *faire-par* construction. In D. Brentari, G. N. Larson, and L. A. McLeod, eds., *The joy of grammar: A Festschrift in honor of James D. McCawley*, 289–321. Amsterdam: John Benjamins.

Reed, Lisa. 1992. On clitic case alternations in French causatives. In P. Hirschbühler and K. Koerner, eds., *Romance languages and modern linguistic theory: Papers from the 20th Linguistic Symposium on Romance Languages*, 205–224. Amsterdam: John Benjamins.

Rivas, Alberto. 1977. A theory of clitics. Doctoral dissertation, MIT.

Rizzi, Luigi. 1978. A restructuring rule in Italian syntax. In S. J. Keyser, ed., *Recent transformational studies in European languages*, 113–158. Cambridge, MA: MIT Press. (Revised from "Ristrutturazione," *Rivista di Grammatica Generativa* 1, 1976.)

Rizzi, Luigi. 1986. Null objects in Italian and the theory of *pro*. *Linguistic Inquiry* 17:501–557.

Roberts, Ian. 1997. Restructuring, head movement, and locality. *Linguistic Inquiry* 28:423–460.

Rosen, Sara Thomas. 1990. *Argument structure and complex predicates*. New York: Garland.

Strozer, Judith. 1976. Clitics in Spanish. Doctoral dissertation, University of California, Los Angeles.

Suñer, Margarita. 1980. Clitic promotion in Spanish revisited. In F. Neussel, ed., *Compemporary studies in Romance languages*, 300–330. Bloomington: Indiana University Linguistics Club.

Torrego, Esther. 1998. *The dependencies of objects*. Cambridge, MA: MIT Press.

Treviño, Esther. 1992. Subjects in Spanish causative constructions. In P. Hirschbühler and K. Koerner, eds., *Romance languages and modern linguistic theory*, 309–324. Amsterdam: John Benjamins.

Wurmbrand, Susi. 2004. Two types of restructuring—Lexical vs. functional. *Lingua* 114:991–1014.

Zagona, Karen T. 1982. Government and proper government of verbal projections. Doctoral dissertation, University of Washington.

Zubizarreta, Maria Luisa. 1982. On the relationship of the lexicon to syntax. Doctoral dissertation, MIT.

Zubizarreta, Maria Luisa. 1985. The relation between morphology and morphosyntax: The case of Romance causatives. *Linguistic Inquiry* 16:247–289.

20 Against All Expectations: Encoding Subjects and Objects in a New Language

Carol A. Padden, Irit Meir, Wendy Sandler, and Mark Aronoff

20.1 Introduction

All good linguistic fieldworkers bring to their task two sets of perfectly reasonable contradictory expectations. On the one hand, in true Boasian tradition, they have trained themselves to be open-minded and not to impose preconceptions on the data. On the other, in more modern Chomskyan fashion, they know that description cannot be done in the absence of a theory and that the more articulated their theory the deeper the questions they can ask. The sign languages of the world that have been well studied seem to resemble each other more closely than do spoken languages that are unrelated to one another. Elsewhere (Aronoff et al. 2004; Aronoff, Meir, and Sandler 2005) we have argued that the newness of individual sign languages and the visual medium through which they are transmitted together make unrelated sign languages more similar to one another than spoken languages are. This means that sign language researchers, on first encounter with a language, come equipped with fairly strong expectations.

The language that our group has been working on for the last several years was completely undescribed and unrecorded before we began our research. All that we knew when we first entered the Al-Sayyid Bedouin village was that a sign language was in use in the community (Scott et al. 1995). We knew that, although the language was only in its third generation, it was so widely used among both deaf and hearing members of the community that it was viewed simply as a second language of the Al-Sayyid village (Kisch 2004). We subsequently determined that it fully met the communicative needs of its users, was autochthonous, and was different in structure and lexicon from surrounding spoken and sign languages (Sandler et al. 2005).

Our previous work as a group on the morphological systems of other sign languages had dealt with verb agreement and classifier systems (Aronoff et al. 2003, 2005). These two types of morphological systems are both very similar across sign languages and very different in sign languages from their counterparts in spoken languages; in other words, they are morphological hallmarks of sign languages. We accordingly set out to focus on just these systems in Al-Sayyid Bedouin Sign Language (henceforth ABSL), expecting quite naively that ABSL, if it had any structure, would have these two systems. Very quickly, though, we learned that the language of the second generation of ABSL users, the group that we have studied most closely, has no verb agreement and very few classifiers, indeed almost no morphology (Aronoff et al. 2004).

Instead, we found robust structure in an area where we had not thought to look initially, because it was not an area where previous research had revealed properties that were especially characteristic of sign languages: word or constituent order within clauses. As reported previously (Sandler et al. 2005), ABSL has consistent word order, a fact that is of interest not simply because ABSL is a sign language, but also because it is a new language. In this chapter, we refine our earlier findings and respond to a suggestion that several colleagues have made about them: that the word-order regularities we observed may not be syntactic, but rather discourse-driven.[1] We also return to the question of the status of nominals in these structures, whether they are in fact subjects and objects or more appropriately labeled as semantic or discourse roles such as agent, patient, topic, background, or foreground.

We show first that the system of verbs in ABSL provides evidence for syntactic categories in the language, specifically the categories of subject and object. We then show that there are order effects at the discourse level, but that these can be quite neatly distinguished from the syntactically based order, so much so that the discourse effects actually provide additional evidence for our original syntactic claim.

20.2 Method

20.2.1 Subjects

We have identified three generations of signers. Deafness appeared in the community in the fifth generation after the community was founded. In that generation, there were four deaf siblings, all of whom are now deceased. Apart from reports that they did sign, and one very short videotape record of one of these individuals, information about their language is limited. We report here on nine signers of the second generation, eight deaf and one hearing, all currently in their thirties and forties, except one in her twenties. The third generation of signers, ranging from teenagers to young children, is not included here.

20.2.2 Data Elicitation and Analysis

All research was conducted in signers' homes in the village. For all elicitation tasks, the signer addressed another signing member of the community, to ensure that their language was produced in a communicative context to a competent user of ABSL. Signers provided spontaneous narratives in response to a request to recount a personal experience, and they described short videoclips created to elicit descriptions of single events portrayed by actors.[2] All responses to these tasks were videotaped and transcribed, and comprise our corpus.[3] The transcriptions consist of glosses for each individually identifiable sign production. The narratives were translated into Hebrew by a trilingual hearing signer and subsequently into English by the authors.

Signs were assigned to constituents according to both semantic and prosodic criteria. The utterances were divided into sentences based on signs for actions or events, each of which was classified as the predicate nucleus of a sentence. We classified other signs as noun arguments, adjectives, numerals, and negative markers, based on their meanings. Subjects (S), objects (O), and indirect objects (IO) were identified depending on their semantic roles in a clause and the standard mapping of these roles onto syntactic functions.

Constituency was further determined by careful observation of prosodic cues. Major breaks in the utterance were identified by shifts in the rhythm marked by a pause or lowering of the hands, together with a change in head or body position and facial expression. These same prosodic cues to major constituent breaks occur in Israeli Sign Language (henceforth ISL) (Nespor and Sandler 1999), and we have observed them in other sign languages as well. Examples of the way we applied these prosodic criteria in our analysis of ABSL are provided below.

Semantic criteria alone allowed us to provide an unambiguous syntactic parse for most sentences. But some could only be parsed correctly by attending to prosodic criteria and comparing them with the translation that our consultant provided independently. One signer, for example, describing his personal history, produced the following string: MONEY COLLECT BUILD WALLS DOORS. The first prosodic constituent is MONEY COLLECT. Like the majority of sentences in our data, it is unambiguous: semantics, prosodic criteria (described below), and the consultant's translation, 'I saved money,' confirm that it is an OV sentence. It is the sequence BUILD WALLS DOORS that fully illustrates our methodology. The semantics indicates that WALLS and DOORS are patients, related to the verb BUILD. In principle, then, this sequence could be an example of a VO string, contrary to the pattern we have found generally in the language. However, the prosodic analysis indicates otherwise, and that analysis was confirmed by the consultant's translation, as we now demonstrate.

In our analysis, we applied criteria for determining prosodic constituency developed in a study on ISL (Nespor and Sandler 1999), which depends on the observation that prosodic constituency, especially that of major constituents, is largely correlated with syntactic constituency in spoken languages (Nespor and Vogel 1986). In the Nespor and Sandler study on ISL, major prosodic breaks (intonational phrases) were systematically marked by a combination of manual and nonmanual phonetic cues. Three distinct manual cues were found to mark prosodic breaks:

holding the hands in place, pause and relaxation of the hands, or repeating the final sign in the constituent. Nonmanual cues at the intonational phrase boundary included both a clear change in head or body position, and a concomitant change in facial expression, the latter interpreted by the researchers as sign-language intonation (see also Wilbur 2002; Sandler and Lillo-Martin 2006; Dachkovsky and Sandler 2009). Eyeblink also correlates reliably with intonational phrase boundaries in ASL (Baker and Padden 1978; Wilbur 1994) and in ISL (Nespor and Sandler 1999). These breaks separate major prosodic/syntactic constituents, such as topics, extraposed elements, and nonrestrictive relative clauses, from the rest of the sentence, and they separate sentences from one another. Just as phrase-final lengthening and intonation excursions characterize intonational phrase (IP) boundaries across spoken languages generally, we proceeded on the assumption that the main cues associated with IP boundaries in other sign languages would help us in our analysis of ABSL as well.

The analysis of the string BUILD WALLS DOORS proceeds as follows (Sandler et al. 2005). In this string, the nominals are semantically related to the verb; they are patients. Syntactically, however, the nominals could be objects of the verb in the same sentence—that is, *I built walls, doors*... Or, alternatively, they could be in a separate fragment, conveying a list—*I built. Walls, doors*...,—on a par with *I began to eat/I ate. Chicken, pickles, corn*... Under the first interpretation, we have (S)VO order in a single syntactic unit. In the latter, we do not. Instead, the first sentence is just BUILD, and the last major prosodic constituent is the fragment WALLS, DOORS. Our prosodic criteria clearly selected the second structure. The break between BUILD and WALLS is characterized by holding the hands in position at the end of BUILD, and then moving the body first forward, then up, and enumerating the things being built, WALLS and DOORS. In addition to changes in manual rhythm, body posture and facial expression also changed at the boundary between BUILD and WALLS. The latter two are particularly reliable markers of intonational phrase boundaries in the ISL study. The facial articulation on BUILD was a contraction of the lower eyelid (Action Unit 7 in Ekman and Friesen's (1978) Facial Action Coding System). At the boundary between BUILD and WALLS, when the body posture changed by moving forward and up, the lower-eyelid contraction changed to neutral, and the eye gaze also shifted, making eye contact with the addressee. That is, manual and nonmanual prosodic cues indicated clearly that the words WALLS and DOORS were not in the same major constituent as BUILD, and the string is parsed as [V] [Noun, Noun]. Crucially, the prosodic analysis shows that it would be erroneous to parse this string as a [VO, O] sentence in which WALLS and DOORS are the objects of BUILD in the same clause. Our analysis, that the string represents a sentence consisting of a verb followed by a list fragment, was confirmed by our third criterion, translation. The spontaneous audiorecorded translation of the string by the consultant on the project was as follows: '*I saved some money. I started to build a house. Walls, doors...*'

We describe our analysis of this string in considerable detail because it is instructive due to the potential ambiguity and the atypical word order of one possible interpretation. However, the vast majority of sentences in our data that included objects were unambiguous, and straightforwardly (S)OV. We compile and discuss these findings in detail later, where we also further expand the relation between clause structure and prosody in our data.

20.3 Results

20.3.1 Verb Types in ASL and Other Sign Languages

To present our findings for ABSL, a brief discussion of verb types in American Sign Language (ASL) and other well-studied sign languages will be instructive. In ASL, verbs divide into three major classes: spatial, agreement, and plain (Padden 1988). The same general type of system is found in many sign languages described in detail to date (Sandler and Lillo-Martin 2006). Spatial verbs are those that incorporate fine distinctions of location and movement throughout the signing space—for example, DRIVE-TO and MOVE. In such signs, the movement begins at some location and ends at a different location, depicting the direction of motion of an entity.[4]

Verbs of the second category, agreement verbs, also involve path movement. But unlike spatial verbs, agreement verbs do not depict motion or location; instead they depict *transfer* from one entity to another (Meier, Cormier, and Quinto-Pozos 2002; Meir 1998, 2002). In ASL verbs like GIVE, SHOW, TELL, INFORM, AWARD, and SEND, the path movement is from the location of subject to object. In a subclass of verbs like BORROW, INVITE, COPY, and RECEIVE, the path movement is *opposite*, from object to subject. Because the subject is the recipient and not the instigator of the transfer, these verbs are termed "backward verbs." Meir's (1998, 2002) analysis describes the path movement of agreement verbs as from source to goal, capturing the direction of movement in both regular and backward verbs.

In agreement verbs, a locus on or near the region of the signer's chest marks first person. Any other locus around the body marks non–first person, including second and third person (Meier 1990). Second person is typically directly opposite first person, with third person occupying all other spaces. Importantly, agreement verbs do not mark location; thus a locus on or near the signer's body does not mean 'near where I am', but first person. There is no contrast between a locus slightly lower or slightly higher on the chest region where first person is marked. Likewise, there is no contrast in location slightly lower or slightly higher in the direction of non–first person. However, in spatial verbs, loci in the signing space are finely distinctive, where slight differences in locus may be used to encode a change in location. In agreement verbs, loci are categorical for person and number.

A third class of verbs, plain verbs, is so named because these verbs do not mark location, position, person, or number. Many of these verbs involve cognitive, emotive, or experiencer states, as in the ASL plain verbs THINK, LIKE, DRINK, CELEBRATE, and SUFFER. In these signs, differences in loci of the body and the signing space are only used for lexical contrast. We may treat plain verbs as a default category: a verb that does not fall into either of the other two categories, usually for semantic reasons, will be a plain verb.

The fact that many sign languages exhibit the same tripartite pattern suggests that this type of semantic organization may be general to sign languages because they have the potential for representing path, motion, and location (Meier, Cormier, and Quinto-Pozos 2002). Indeed, when we began to collect data on verbs in ABSL, we expected to see all three types of verbs represented in the language. However, ABSL did not conform to our expectations.

20.3.2 Verb Types in ABSL

To our surprise, instead of a tripartite division, we found a bipartite division in ABSL between verbs that depict motion and location and all other verbs. In other words, ABSL appears to have only the equivalent of two categories of verbs: spatial verbs and plain verbs. Verbs like GIVE and THROW, which semantically involve transfer from one entity to another and are typically agreement verbs in other sign languages, pattern like plain verbs in ABSL: they lack the fine locational distinctions seen in verb forms used to mark motion and location and they lack person marking as well. Instead, verbs that depict transfer from the subject to the object in ABSL involve movement from the center of the body outward, regardless of whether the subject is first person or non–first person. For example, in the sentence MAN APPLE GIVE ('The man gave an apple'), the signer notes the subject, MAN, then the object, APPLE, followed by GIVE in a short path movement extending outward from the body.

The form of "backward" verbs in ABSL, where the subject is not the source but the goal of the transfer—for example, CATCH—further supports the claim that the body marks subject but not first person in ABSL transfer verbs (and indeed generally in ABSL). In sentences with verbs like CATCH, the center movement is reversed and moves inward toward the body. This is true even when the subject is not first person, since the subject, represented by the body, is the semantic recipient. Most importantly, the system of verbs in ABSL provides evidence for the centrality of the notion subject in the language.

We now present an analysis of ABSL data to support our conclusion. ABSL signers were shown a set of 45 short videoclips that depict a range of transitive and

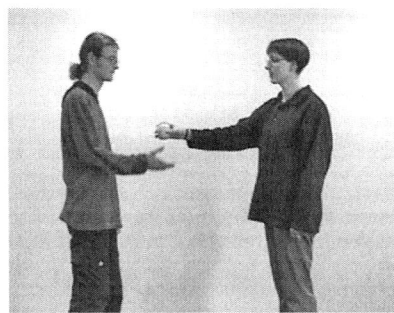

Figure 20.1
Woman gives ball to man

intransitive verbs across different semantic categories. From these we identified a subset of 11 as involving actions of transfer between 2 entities: GIVE, THROW, CATCH, TAKE, and FEED. We then analyzed a group of 9 signers' responses to these 11 elicitation clips, resulting in a total of 110 transfer forms produced by second-generation ABSL signers (which include repetitions and descriptions of single events with two clauses).[5]

Of the 110 transfer forms produced, 98 involved movement with respect to the body: center-out movement when the subject is the source (as in GIVE, THROW, and FEED), or center-in if the subject is the goal (as in the backward verbs TAKE and CATCH). There was little or no shifting of the movement to the side; instead the movement was either center-out or center-in. The center-out/in movement appeared despite the fact that the action clips showed the actors as transferring an object from one side of the screen to the other. Signers did not mimic the direction of motion in the action clip; instead they used movement along their own central plane. Figure 20.1 shows an action clip in which a woman gives a ball to a man. In her response, the signer indicates that the woman is to her right on the screen, and the man to her left, but her verb form did not make use of either of these locations; instead the movement of the verb GIVE was center-out. The signer's response is shown in figure 20.2.[6]

In a smaller number of responses (12 of 110), signers used a form with path movement not from the body, but from one side to the other. On closer analysis, we noticed that these involved holding or manipulating an object and moving it to another location. For example, five of these responses came from an action clip in which a man picks up a scarf lying on the floor and moves it in front of the woman, who then accepts the scarf (figure 20.3). This action is less like one of transfer than of picking up the scarf from its initial position on the floor and moving it to the woman's location. The scarf was not initially in the possession of the man, but on

STAND-right   STAND-left   GIVE

Figure 20.2
'He's standing here; she's standing there. She gave (the ball) to him.'

Figure 20.3
Man moves scarf to woman

the floor in front of him. We analyze these verb productions as spatial verbs, since they conform to those produced by the same signers in response to action clips in which an object is moving through space with no transfer involved (figure 20.4).

With respect to ABSL signers' use of center-out/in movement in verbs of transfer, we conclude that their verb forms do not mark person. That is, signers did not vary the direction of the verb form when the person of the subject and object of the clause varied. The data show that using direction-of-path movement to depict person agreement as well as spatial motion is not common to all sign languages. ABSL exploits location and movement only for one class of verbs, those denoting motion in space. Verbs that involve transfer from one entity to another behave like the default class of plain verbs.

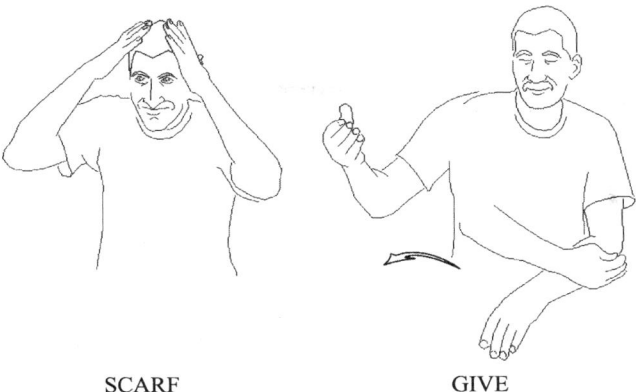

Figure 20.4
'There's a scarf; he handed (it) over (to her) (left to right).'

The generalization that unites ABSL plain verbs and verbs of transfer is that the body represents the subject argument. The body is the origin, the source and goal, and the location of the verb form itself. In all of these verbs, the body represents one particular argument participating in the event. It represents the agent in the verbs TALK and GIVE, patient in FALL-DOWN, experiencer in CRY, and recipient in CATCH and TAKE. In other words, the argument represented by the body can bear different thematic roles, depending on the particular verb. Instead of listing a variety of semantic roles that behave alike with respect to these verb forms, the notion of subject is general to all. Furthermore, the generalization expresses the fact that when there is both agent and patient in the clause as in PUSH, the body always represents the argument bearing the higher-ranking role, the subject. Nonspatial verbs in ABSL, then, can be characterized as a class of verbs for which the body represents subject (for a more comprehensive discussion, see Meir et al. 2007).

We conclude that ABSL has two types of verbs that are comparable to the spatial and plain types in other sign languages. We also conclude that ABSL lacks person as a morphological category. Using evidence from generational change and child language acquisition in sign languages, Meier (2002) has hypothesized that the direction of change is toward increased use of space for verb agreement. Whether ABSL will develop person as an additional category at some point in the future is an open question.

20.4 Word Order in ABSL

In previous work (Sandler et al. 2005), we showed that ABSL developed fixed SOV word order within the span of one generation. Our corpus consisted of data from eight signers of the second generation, seven deaf and one hearing. In the current study, we expanded our data, by videotaping more signers of that generation and by using additional elicitation material. The new material we created consists of thirty videoclips, each depicting a single event. There are six types of events, defined by the number and type of arguments involved: 1 inanimate argument, 1 human argument, 2 arguments (1 human and 1 inanimate), 2 human arguments, 3 arguments (2 human, 1 inanimate), and an event containing a spatial argument (location or path).[7]

Four signers of the second generation were videotaped describing the actions in this set of videoclips (three female and one male). The female signers are all sisters. Two are in their forties and have had only negligible exposure to spoken languages. The third is much younger (in her late twenties), had twelve years of school, has some knowledge of the spoken Arabic dialect used in the village, and reads and writes Hebrew. The male signer is in his late thirties, and, like the two older sisters, does not know Arabic or Hebrew.

20.4.1 Evidence for Clauses

One of the challenges in analyzing a new language is to provide evidence for clauses. We have previously offered an argument for constituency based on prosodic evidence. Underlying our claim that ABSL has SOV word order is the assumption that the language has clauses—that is, that the signing sequence can be divided into units that are syntactic in nature, rather than rooted in semantic roles or the exigencies of conversation. Let us illustrate this problem. A sequence of signs such as MAN GIRL THROW can be interpreted as a clause containing a subject, an (indirect) object, and a verb (SOV). We identify subjects as the arguments with the highest-ranking semantic role in the clause; objects are identified as the arguments with the lower-ranking semantic role; indirect objects are identified as the (nonagentive) recipient arguments in clauses denoting an event of transfer. Why not refer to semantic roles directly, especially in a new language with simple syntax?

In our data, we find that the highest-ranking semantic role will function as subject, regardless of what role that is, while the next-highest will function as object. Hence, word-order generalizations that are expressed in syntactic terms are lost when we use semantic terms directly. For example, in one-argument clauses in ABSL, the sole argument shows a uniform behavior with respect to word order—that is, it appears before the verb, irrespective of its semantic role. Subjects can be agents in FEED, TAP, PUSH, TEAR, RUN; patients in FALL, CRY, ROLL; recipients in CATCH, TAKE; or experiencers in SEE, BE-ANGRY. Similarly, the object can have one of several semantic roles: patients in TEAR, PUSH, PUT, DRAG; recipients in FEED, THROW(-TO); themes in LOOK-AT; or locatives in TAP. In addition, as shown above, the role of the body in the form of verbs in the language can only be captured by referring to the notion of "subject." As we have pointed out, the body in plain verbs does not represent first person, but rather the highest-ranking semantic role participating in the event—that is, the subject argument.

Alternatively, word order in ABSL might be interpreted as driven by discourse, introducing one argument, then another, and then signing the predicate that relates the two arguments. In the latter analysis, one might argue that the structure of the sequence is: Topic, Topic, Predicate. If that interpretation is correct, then the claim that the signs constitute one syntactic unit cannot be maintained.

What kind of evidence can be used to distinguish between the syntactic and discourse-based analyses? Semantic criteria are of no help; the fact that three signs are semantically related does not necessarily indicate that this relationship is syntactic. Markers of syntactic dependencies, such as case markers or agreement morphemes, have not been attested in the language so far; moreover, they are predicted not to occur in a new language, since the development of inflectional morphology takes time (Aronoff et al. 2004).

As we showed above for the sequence BUILD WALLS DOORS, one point of entry into the structure of the language and whether it is syntactically driven, is prosody. We use prosodic cues to determine whether or not a stretch of semantically related signs forms a clause: a stretch of signs is analyzed as a clause only if the signs form one major prosodic unit.[8] To illustrate our method further, consider two responses to a clip showing a woman giving a shirt to a man. One subject signed the following sequence:

GIRL INDEX
BOY
GIVE SHIRT GIVE

This stretch of discourse consists of three prosodic units, marked by major breaks in the signing, of the kind described earlier. For this reason, we do not regard the string as a single clause with S IO VOV order, but rather as three separate discourse units or clauses, more or less equivalent to: "There's a girl there, and there's a boy, and an action of giving a shirt occurs." Only the last prosodic unit, GIVE SHIRT GIVE, contains both a noun and a (repeated) verb. It is analyzed as VOV.

A second signer responded to the same clip as follows:

MAN STAND-HERE
WOMAN SHIRT GIVE
MAN TAKE

This sequence also comprises three prosodic units. The first unit consists of two signs, MAN and a handshape in neutral space, localizing the man ('A man standing here'). The second unit consists of three signs signed with no prosodic break between them, analyzed as one clause with SOV word order. The third unit consists of two signs and is analyzed as an SV sequence.

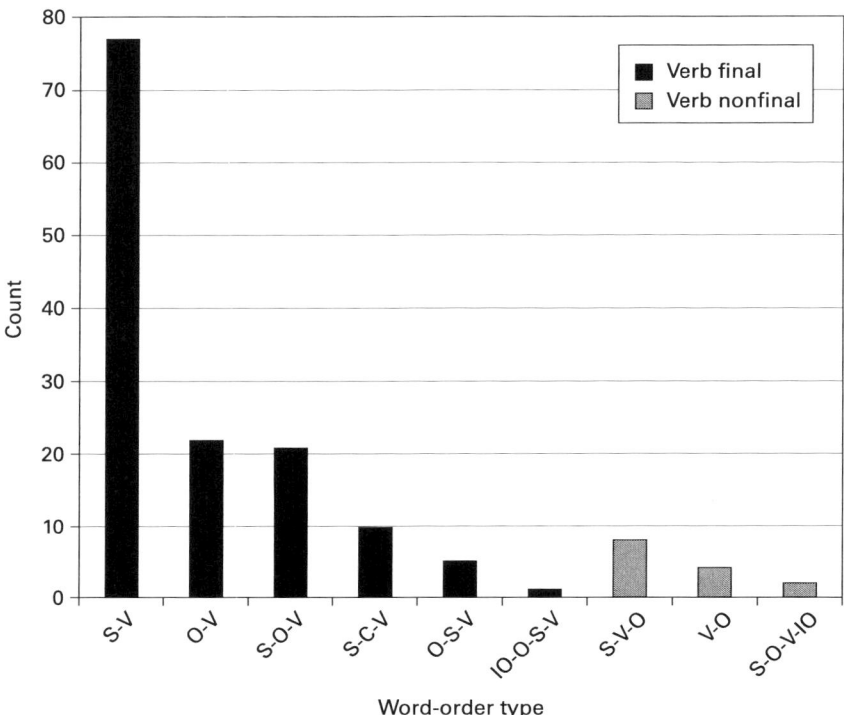

Figure 20.5
Frequency of clauses by word-order type

20.4.2 Results

The data were segmented into prosodic units by researchers of our team independently and by the whole team together. For word-order purposes, we included only those prosodic units that consist of at least two signs, where one is a noun and the other a verb. Out of 287 prosodic units, 150 units consisted of at least a noun sign and a verb sign, and consequently were regarded as clauses.[9] Figure 20.5 shows the count for each word-order type.[10] These results support our earlier findings: word order in second-generation signers is predominantly verb-final. Out of 150 clauses, 136 are verb-final. In transitive clauses, containing both an S and an O, we find that SOV is the predominant word order, supporting our earlier findings.

Seven of the eight SVO clauses were signed by the younger signer. As we discuss below, this signer has different word order than other second-generation signers, perhaps because she is influenced by some knowledge of the local Arabic dialect and Hebrew, whose basic word order is indeed SVO. As for the five OSV clauses, the addressee did not understand the signer for three of them, and the signer responded by reverting to standard SOV order.

Another observation about the syntactic structure of ABSL is the signers' tendency to prefer single-argument clauses. Eighteen of the 30 videoclips show events that involve two or more participants. Thus in principle we would have expected to get 72 two- or three-argument clauses in response to those clips. However, out of the 208 clauses describing the 18 transitive events, 98 contained one argument, and only 44 contained two or three arguments.[11] ABSL signers do not often use two-argument clauses, especially when both arguments are human. In such cases, they tend to break the event into two clauses, with two verb signs, each predicated of a different argument. Thus, an event in which a girl feeds a woman may be described as: WOMAN SIT; GIRL FEED. An event in which a man throws a ball to a girl can be rendered as: GIRL STAND; MAN BALL THROW; GIRL CATCH.[12] This tendency is characteristic of all signers, though there are certain differences among them, to which we turn now.

20.4.3 Differences among Signers

There are clear differences among the signers in terms of word order. The two older female signers as well as the male signer show clear preference for verb-final order: twenty-one sentences are SOV, four are OSV, and only one is SVO. The younger sister, on the other hand, shows a preference for SVO order: seven of her eleven transitive clauses are SVO.

As noted, this might very well be due to the fact that she has had more schooling, has been exposed to Signed Hebrew, and is literate in Hebrew. Further support for the effect of schooling on word order comes from observing the word order of the children of one of the second-generation signers: those children who have attended school for several years and have been exposed to Signed Hebrew or Signed Arabic use SVO order. By contrast, a younger child who has not yet attended school, as well as one of the hearing children, who were not exposed to signed Hebrew or signed Arabic, use SOV order.[13]

In other respects, the two older sisters differ from each other. One shows a clear preference for breaking an event into one-argument clauses. In her description of the eighteen transitive clips, she uses sixty-two clauses, of which 36 are one-argument clauses and ten are two-argument clauses—that is, only 16.1 percent of her clauses in this task are two-argument clauses. The other older sister, as well as the younger sister, use only thirty-five clauses to describe these same clips (that is, they are less repetitive), and the percent of the two-argument clauses is much higher (31.4 percent).

The clause structure of the single male signer in this study is much less clear. In many cases it is difficult to identify clauses at all. His signing is less fluid and has many prosodic units consisting of only one sign, many repetitions, and many cases of what seem to be false starts or afterthoughts. He seems to be constantly negotiating with the addressee to make sure that he got the point across. Additionally, many of his signs for actions are mimetic, involving the whole body. ABSL has lexical signs for LOOK, RUN, FALL, SLEEP, and STAND, which are used by the other signers, but this particular signer often uses mimetic depictions of these actions rather than the lexicalized signs. For example, to describe a clip in which a seated man stands up, this signer actually stood up from his chair. In those cases where clauses can be clearly identified, however, the predominant word order is SOV (eight clauses, versus three clauses of OSV).

20.4.4 Choice and Order of Arguments in Units Larger Than the Clause

In contrast with the consistency found in word order within a clause, discourse units larger than the clause exhibited considerable variation. As pointed out above, signers often use one-argument clauses, and when describing an event involving two or three arguments, they may break down the description into several one-argument clauses. Breaking an event into subevents in this way presents the signer with certain choices, such as which participant to introduce first, and which verb to use in order to describe the nonactive participant. Interestingly, though all signers use such sequences, the order in which the participants are introduced, and the particular way in which the event is broken down into clauses, vary greatly.

Consider, for example, the responses to a clip in which a man is showing a picture to a woman:

Signer 1: MAN SIT. WOMAN SIT. MAN PICTURE SHOW. WOMAN LOOK.
Signer 2: WOMAN LOOK. MAN PICTURE SHOW.
Signer 3: GIRL INDEX. BOY INDEX. SHOW-PICTURE. GIRL LOOK.
Signer 4: MAN WOMAN SIT. MAN PICTURE SHOW WOMAN.

Each signer employs a different order in introducing the participants and their actions. The first signer starts with the man sitting; the second begins with the woman looking; the third introduces the woman and then the man, followed by the event of showing the picture; and the fourth describes the man and the woman sitting, and then signs the picture-showing event.

Similarly, when describing a clip of a woman giving a shirt to a man, each signer described the event differently:

Signer 1: MAN TAKE. WOMAN GIVE.
Signer 2: MAN STAND. WOMAN SHIRT GIVE. MAN TAKE.
Signer 3: WOMAN ONE GIVE SHIRT. MAN TAKE.

The responses to some clips were more uniform. The events presented in these clips typically have one participant who is stationary, or passive, while the other participant is active. In such cases, there is a tendency in the data to introduce the stationary participant first, and then to describe the active participant and the action. For example, when describing a man tapping a girl on the shoulder, three signers located the girl (or child) first, and then described the man tapping:

Signer 1: CHILD THERE. MAN SHOULDER TAP-OTHER.
Signer 2: GIRL STAND-THERE. MAN TAP-OTHER SHOULDER TAP-OTHER.
Signer 3: GIRL STAND-THERE. MAN SHOULDER TAP-OTHER TAP-OTHER.

Similarly, when responding to a clip showing a woman taking a pair of scissors from a girl, all signers first described the girl holding the scissors, and then the woman approaching her and taking the scissors. Responding to a clip showing a girl feeding a woman, three of the four signers first described the woman sitting at the table, and then the girl feeding her.

It seems that the principle governing the order of introducing the participants in the above cases is that stationary participants, who constitute the background of the event, are introduced first. The principle could be stated as "background precedes foreground" (Talmy 1983). Notice, though, that this principle is cognitive in nature, not linguistic. Crucially, it contradicts the clause-internal word-order rule in ABSL, since the stationary object, which is mentioned first, is usually the patient argument, and hence the syntactic object. Thus, if an event is described in a sequence of clauses, signers often describe the patient (stationary argument) first; but if the same event is described by a single clause, then the active argument, the agent, is introduced first, typically yielding SOV order.

Returning at last to the question of whether the order of arguments is driven by discourse or syntax, we find two different patterns of order of participants once we identify clauses: clause-internal order is subject first, and is very consistent within and across signers, while the order of introducing the participants is governed by cognitive or pragmatic principles in sequences of clauses and is much more varied within and across signers.

These differences suggest strongly that ABSL has syntax, a structural level that cannot be derived from or motivated by principles from another domain. The particular SOV order of ABSL cannot be explained by resorting to cognitive principles such as "background first," nor can it be explained by discourse principles such as "topic first," because the subject argument is not always the topic in these descriptions. Our conclusion is that ABSL has developed syntax as an autonomous level of linguistic structure by the second generation of its existence.

Coppola and Newport (2005) also found evidence for the primacy of the notion of subject in a new linguistic system. Using a series of elicitation tasks given to three homesigners, they found that homesigners consistently signed the subject, but not the topic, in initial position before the verb within a clause. Both studies, then, Coppola and Newport's and the study presented here, demonstrate that the notion of subject captures important structural generalizations even in very young linguistic systems.

20.5 Conclusion

When we first encountered ABSL, we were excited to learn what this brand-new language might tell us about the emergent properties of sign languages, about which we already had fairly strong expectations. Instead, we found that ABSL reveals more about new languages, spoken as well as signed. Like other new languages, it has little if any morphology, a fact that is attributable to its newness (Aronoff et al. 2004; Aronoff, Meir, and Sandler 2005). It also has a robust, albeit simple, syntactic structure (Sandler et al. 2005). Certain aspects of this syntax have already been noted in connection with other new languages. For example, Givón (1979) remarks that pidgins, children's language, and informal language all show a preponderance of one-argument clauses. What we have now shown is that the rules governing this syntactic structure can be quite readily disentangled from, and indeed can run directly contrary to, more general cognitive and discourse-pragmatic factors, even in a brand-new language.

Notes

This research was supported by United States–Israel Binational Science Foundation grant 2000-372 ("A Beduin Sign Language of the Deaf and Hearing") and National Institutes of Health grant DC6473 ("Emergence of Grammar in a New Sign Language").

1. We thank Stephen Anderson, David Perlmutter, and Maria Polinsky, who each independently suggested to us that the order of nominals in ABSL could be governed by discourse principles.

2. Not all signers participated in both tasks.

3. We are grateful to the Language and Cognition Group at the Max Planck Institute for Psycholinguistics in Nijmegen, The Netherlands, for providing some of the videoclips used in our work.

4. We use the terms *movement* for the signifier and *motion* for the signified.

5. We appreciate Shannon Casey's assistance in transcribing signers' responses to these clips.

6. Illustrations are by Meir Etedgi of the Sign Language Research Lab at the University of Haifa.

7. Thanks to Ann Senghas for help in designing the new materials. We also thank the Sageev family for starring in our videoclips.

8. By "major prosodic unit," we refer to intonational phrases (IPs) or higher units, and exclude smaller prosodic breaks that more or less correspond to phrases rather than clauses.

9. The remaining 137 units consisted either of single noun or verb signs, or of sequences without verbs, such as noun + location or noun + description. A small number of elicitations were unclear and were excluded.

10. In the order type labeled "SCV," the C stands for a complement of the verb that is not the patient argument, such as an instrument ('feed with a spoon') or location ('tap somebody on the shoulder'). Such arguments, whose syntactic role is still unclear, pattern with the patient argument (the syntactic O) in that they precede the verb.

11. The remaining 66 clauses do not contain an N and a V sign, and are therefore irrelevant to the present discussion.

12. Senghas reports a similar structure in older signers of the new Nicaraguan Sign Language (Senghas et al. 1997).

13. The educational backgrounds of the deaf villagers, and the degree to which they are exposed to other languages, vary. Our field records include this information, which, though relevant, cannot be discussed in detail here, because of lack of space.

References

Aronoff, M., I. Meir, C. Padden, and W. Sandler. 2003. Classifier complexes and morphology in two sign languages. In K. Emmorey, ed., *Perspectives on classifier constructions in sign languages*, 53–86. Mahwah, NJ: Erlbaum.

Aronoff, M., I. Meir, C. Padden, and W. Sandler. 2004. Morphological universals and the sign language type. In G. Booj and J. van Marle, eds., *Yearbook of morphology 2004*, 19–39. Dordrecht: Kluwer.

Aronoff, M., I. Meir, and W. Sandler. 2005. The universal and the particular in sign language morphology. *Language* 81(2):301–344.

Baker, C., and C. Padden. 1978. Focusing on the nonmanual components of ASL. In P. Siple, ed., *Understanding language through sign language research (Perspectives in neurolinguistics and psycholinguistics)*, 27–57. New York: Academic Press.

Coppola, M., and E. Newport. 2005. Grammatical subjects in home sign: Abstract linguistic structure in adult primary gesture systems without linguistic input. *Proceedings of the National Academy of Sciences* 102(52):19249–19253.

Dachkovsky, S., and W. Sandler. 2009. Visual intonation in the prosody of a sign language. *Language and Speech* 52(2/3):287–314.

Ekman, P., and W. Friesen. 1978. *Facial action coding system*. Palo Alto, CA: Consulting Psychologists Press.

Givón, T. 1979. From discourse to syntax: Grammar as a processing strategy. In T. Givón, ed., *Discourse and syntax*. New York: Academic Press.

Kisch, S. 2004. Negotiating (genetic) deafness in a Bedouin community. In J. van Cleve, ed., *Genetics, disability, and deafness*, 148–173. Washington, DC: Gallaudet University Press.

Meier, R. 1990. Person deixis in American Sign Language. In S. Fischer and P. Siple, eds., *Theoretical issues in sign language research, Vol. 1: Linguistics*, 175–190. Chicago: University of Chicago Press.

Meier, R. 2002. The acquisition of verb agreement: Pointing out arguments for the linguistic status of agreement in sign languages. In G. Morgan and B. Woll, eds., *Directions in sign language acquisition*, 1–25. Philadelphia: John Benjamins.

Meier, R., K. Cormier, and D. Quinto-Pozos. 2002. *Modality and structure in signed and spoken languages*. Cambridge: Cambridge University Press.

Meir, I. 1998. *Thematic structure and verb agreement in Israeli Sign Language*. Unpublished dissertation, Hebrew University, Jerusalem.

Meir, I. 2002. A cross-modality perspective on verb agreement. *Natural Language and Linguistic Theory* 20(2):413–450.

Meir, I., C. Padden, M. Aronoff, and W. Sandler. 2007. Body as subject. *Journal of Linguistics* 43:531–563.

Nespor, M., and W. Sandler. 1999. Prosody in Israeli Sign Language. *Language and Speech* 42(2/3):143–176.

Nespor, M., and I. Vogel. 1986. *Prosodic phonology*. Dordrecht: Foris.

Padden, C. 1988. *Interaction of morphology and syntax in American Sign Language*. New York: Garland Press.

Sandler, W., and D. Lillo-Martin. 2006. *Sign language and linguistic universals*. Cambridge: Cambridge University Press.

Sandler, W., I. Meir, C. Padden, and M. Aronoff. 2005. The emergence of grammar: Systematic structure in a new language. *Proceedings of the National Academy of Sciences* 102(7):2661–2665.

Scott, D., R. Carmi, K. Eldebour, G. Duyk, E. Stone, and V. Sheffield. 1995. Nonsyndromic autosomal recessive deafness is linked to the DFNB1 locus in a large inbred Bedouin family from Israel. *American Journal of Human Genetics* 57:965–968.

Senghas, A., M. Coppola, E. Newport, and T. Supalla. 1997. Argument structure in Nicaraguan Sign Language: The emergence of grammatical devices. In E. Hughes and A. Greenhill, eds., *Proceedings of the Boston University Conference on Language Development 21*, 550–561. Boston: Cascadilla Press.

Talmy, L. 1983. How language structures space. In H. Pick and L. Acredolo, eds., *Spatial orientation: Theory, research, and application*, 225–282. New York: Plenum.

Wilbur, R. 1994. Eyeblinks and ASL phrase structure. *Sign Language Studies* 23(84):221–240.

Wilbur, R. 2000. Phonological and prosodic layering in American Sign Language. In H. Lane and K. Emmorey, eds., *The signs of language revisited*, 213–241. Hillsdale, NJ: Lawrence Erlbaum Associates.

21 Clitic Placement in Romance: A Phase-Theoretic Approach

Eduardo P. Raposo

21.1 Introduction

Some of the most contentious issues in Romance linguistics are why pronominal clitics move, where they move, and why they move where they move.[1] A complicating factor is that, even though the morphological properties of pronominal clitics seem to be constant across Romance (with minor phonological variations), the surface placement of clitics varies not only across clause types within a single language (as in Spanish finite versus infinitival clauses, with proclisis versus enclisis, respectively; cf. (1a,b)), but also across languages within a single clause type (as in Spanish versus French infinitival clauses, with enclisis versus proclisis, respectively; cf. (1b,c)).

(1) a. (nosotros) *los*   vemos con frecuencia (*...vemos los...)
       (we)   them see   often
       'We see them often.'
    b. para ver*los*,   viajamos   hasta Patagonia (*para los ver,...)
       for to-see-them, (we-)traveled until Patagonia
    c. pour *les* voir, nous avons voyagé jusqu'en Patagonie (*pour voir les,...)
       for   them to-see, we   have traveled until   Patagonia
       'In order to see them, we traveled to Patagonia.'

In addition, in a language like European Portuguese (henceforth EP), the same clause type can manifest either enclisis or proclisis. In finite matrix clauses, this depends on contextual factors. Thus, proclisis obtains in the presence of preverbal negation, of a particular set of preverbal adverbs, or of a moved *wh*-phrase (cf. (2a), where this pattern is illustrated with a *wh*-phrase), and enclisis elsewhere (cf. (2b)).[2]

(2) a. quando *os*   viste? (*...viste-os?)
       when   them (you-)saw?
       'When did you see them?'
    b. (nós) vemo-*los* com frequência (*os vemos...)
       '(We) see them often.'

In some clause types, however, dependence on contextual factors does not hold. This is the case, for example, in subordinate adverbial clauses introduced by "prepositional complementizers" such as *de* 'of' or *para* 'for', where both enclisis and proclisis are in free variation, as shown in (3).

(3) a. para vê-*los*, viajámos até à Patagónia
   b. para *os* ver, viajámos até à Patagónia
      'In order to see them, we traveled to Patagonia.'

In this chapter, I would like to present the outline of an analysis that explores the idea that this variable pattern of clitic placement in Romance can be reduced to a very general property of the PF interface that lexical items (including clitics) must satisfy, in interaction with independent syntactic properties of the different Romance languages. In particular, I will suggest that the notions of "enclisis" (likewise "enclitics") and "proclisis" (likewise "proclitics") are just descriptive terms that do not play any theoretical role in a principled account of the patterns of Romance clitic placement. This in turn opens up the possibility that these notions can be dispensed with more generally in linguistic theory.

The analysis developed here depends quite crucially on certain theoretical principles proposed recently by Chomsky within the Minimalist Program, in particular the idea that "narrow syntax" builds a derivation cyclically piece by piece, with each relevant unit processed in parallel both by the phonological and the semantic components (Chomsky 2001, 2004, 2008). In this view, each relevant syntactic unit (called a "phase") is transferred cyclically to the phonology and the semantics once it is processed by the rules of the narrow syntax. In this chapter, I will be exclusively concerned with the transfer to the phonological component (henceforth PF), called "Spell-Out." The analysis that I develop here builds on ideas of Raposo and Uriagereka 2005, but it differs from this work in the more prominent role given to Object Shift and in the way it exploits a particular set of assumptions about Spell-Out and the fate of traces in PF.

The chapter is organized as follows. In section 21.2, I propose that pronominal clitics are (minimal-maximal) determiners that must undergo a morphological operation of fusion that attaches them to a suitable host, and I give a characterization of the basic properties of this operation. In section 21.3, I discuss the phase-based theory of derivations and the form of Spell-Out. In section 21.4, I propose that, for motivated reasons, Object Shift always applies in the derivation of sentences with (complement) pronominal clitics, placing them at the edge of the vP phase. In section 21.5, I discuss clitic placement in infinitival clauses of Spanish and French. In the process, I introduce a few assumptions about trace deletion in PF and propose that the structure that serves as input to the operations of PF is itself the output of the application of "tree-pruning" operations to the structure provided by the narrow syntax. Crucially, fusion applies to the output of these tree-pruning rules, and this is what allows us to identify the domain where a clitic searches for its host as its minimal (c-command) domain, without any reference to directionality of fusion. In section 21.6, I discuss why verbal proclisis is the unmarked pattern of pronominal clitic placement in finite clauses of Romance (with the exception of EP). In section 21.7, I discuss clitic placement in finite root clauses of EP. In section 21.8, I discuss clitic placement in a particular type of adverbial infinitival clause of EP that I take to be representative of the general issues that arise with respect to clitic placement in infinitival clauses in this language. Finally, in section 21.9 I draw some conclusions.

Before continuing, I would like to mention that in no way is this an exhaustive study of clitic placement in Romance, especially when it comes to European Portuguese. My main goal here is to present some of the basic issues, motivate a few ideas that I think play a prominent role in this topic, and illustrate them with selected examples. A more complete analysis of the full set of structures with pronominal clitics using the theoretical assumptions and proposals of this chapter will have to await further study. Just to give an example, I will not discuss the phenomenon of clitic climbing. Also, for convenience, all my examples will contain only direct-object clitics. With certain additional assumptions about functional categories and Spell-Out, my analysis extends also to indirect-object clitics and prepositional clitics such as *y* 'there' and *en* 'from it/there', but I must leave those for future work.

21.2 On Romance Pronominal Clitics

Following Raposo and Uriagereka 2005, the analysis proposed here of the variable patterns of clitic placement in Romance does not rely on morphophonological differences in the pronominal systems of the particular languages, including such stipulated properties as "second-position clitic." I assume that pronominal clitics are underlying determiners heading a DP. For convenience, I will take them to be "minimal-maximal projections" in the sense of Chomsky 1995, merged in the same position as the corresponding arguments with a full DP structure (Postal 1969; Raposo 1973, 1999). In this respect, a more exact label for these items would be "determiner-clitic," rather than "pronominal-clitic."

Assuming the traditional characterization of "clitic" as a stressless, prosodically deficient lexical item, it follows that these elements will have to find an adequate (i.e., prosodically complete) host before they reach PF, in order to satisfy (4), which I take to be an interface condition of this level of representation (see also van der Leeuw 1997).

(4) At PF, every lexical item must be integrated within a prosodic word—that is, a unit with a single main stress.

Following Raposo and Uriagereka 2005, I will call "fusion" the operation by which a clitic (quite independently of its grammatical category) "leans on" or "attaches to" an adequate host in order to satisfy (4).[3] From a computational perspective, the simplest formulation of fusion is the one given in (5):

(5) *Fusion (a PF operation)*
 i. The clitic searches for a host within its minimal domain (i.e., within its c-command domain).
 ii. The host must be string-adjacent to the clitic.
 iii. The clitic leans on the side of the host that faces the clitic.

I assume that fusion is an operation of the early stages of the PF component, where "syntactic" structure is still preserved or, as I will propose below, adjusted in such a way as to reflect exclusively the presence of overt elements with phonological or morphological content. It is also important to note that fusion (an attachment operation) is not to be identified with clitic movement, a point also made in Otero 1996 and Raposo and Uriagereka 2005. In fact, the thrust of the analysis to be developed here (and to a large extent that of Raposo and Uriagereka 2005) is that clitics move in Romance precisely because they cannot undergo fusion in their base position (and also their derived position, in some cases).

The host of a clitic must be a phonologically overt word containing a single main stress (I will refer to such words as being "phonologically complete"). As an illustration, consider (7), where *las* 'the-fem-pl' fuses to *cartas* 'letters' (fusion is represented by "="):

(6) Juan escribió [$_{QP}$ todas [$_{DP}$ las=cartas]]
 J   wrote   all   the letters

In (6), both *todas* and *cartas* are adjacent to the determiner-clitic *las*, and both are phonologically complete; however, only *cartas* is in the search domain of the clitic (i.e., c-commanded by the clitic), so *las* fuses to *cartas*, not to *todas*. Structures with nominal ellipsis such as *me gustan los coches azules, pero prefiero los rojos* 'I like the blue cars but I prefer the red ones' will be accommodated with an analysis of ellipsis as PF-deletion (see Lasnik 1999), assuming that in the phonological component fusion is ordered after deletion (double strikeout indicates material deleted in PF):

(7) [$_{DP}$ los = rojos] from *los ~~coches~~ rojos*
     the-pl red-pl 'the red ones'

Summarizing, when a determiner-clitic projects nonvacuously (i.e., when it has an NP complement), it is always proclitic to its host, which will always be the first phonologically complete lexical item within the NP following the determiner (i.e., string-adjacent to the clitic).[4] This follows from configurational properties of projections, and the fact that in Romance heads precede their complements (a determiner precedes its NP complement).

21.3 On Phases and Spell-Out

Following Chomsky (2001, 2004, 2008), I assume that the (clausal) cyclic domains for the integrated application of the operations of narrow syntax, phonology, and semantics (the "strong" phases) are the categories CP and v*P (i.e., a transitive vP). The schematic form of a phase is given in (8a), and its two particular instantiations in the clausal domain in (8b,c) (in (8a), H is the head of the phase, α its spec, and β its complement):

(8) a. [$_{HP}$ α [H β]]
 b. [$_{CP}$ (spec) [C TP]]
 c. [$_{v*P}$ (spec) [v* VP]]

For reasons discussed in the works cited, Chomsky proposes that the complement β (TP and VP, respectively) is spelled-out at the stage HP (CP and v*P, respectively), but the "edge" of the phase, α H (i.e., (spec C) and (spec v*), respectively) are spelled-out at the stage of the next-highest phase ZP, except in root clauses. This particular form of Spell-Out is called by Chomsky "Spell-Out of sister."[5] Spell-Out of sister allows for an "escape hatch" for head and spec-raising, as well as for successive cyclic movement through the edge of a phase (the "Phase Impenetrability Condition," PIC). As will be seen, spell-Out of sister and PIC will be crucial as well for my account of Romance clitics.

Chomsky allows for a phase HP to be spelled-out in full when HP is a root clause. This is a somewhat unnatural exception. How does the derivation know, when it reaches stage HP, that HP is a root structure? Presumably the derivation would have to look at the numeration before Spell-Out and check whether it is empty in order to make a decision as to whether to spell-out just β or the complete structure.[6] I would like to propose that Spell-Out of the edge is always independent and separate from Spell-Out of the complement, even in root clauses. It seems to me that the computation is considerably simplified if this is the case. This means that once any HP (HP = a strong phase) is derived by the narrow syntax, we have the following operations: (i) β is spelled-out; (ii) the derivation goes back to the numeration, selects a new subarray corresponding to the next highest phase ZP, and expands HP by successive Merge until ZP is formed; and (iii) the complement of ZP is spelled-out. These operations are repeated as many times as necessary. If *at stage (ii)* (i.e., after spelling-out β) the numeration is empty, then Spell-Out of the edge α H of HP proceeds, but this now happens as an independent step subsequent to the Spell-Out of β.[7]

I will now introduce a slight modification to this picture. A considerable amount of work starting in the late 1980s (see, among other sources, Uriagereka 1995; Raposo and Uriagereka 1996; Rizzi 1997) has shown that the functional field traditionally covered by C must be exploded in a variety of different functional categories, perhaps ultimately dependent on C, as suggested in Chomsky 2008. Suppose that instead of (8b) we have (9), where the functional field of CP consists of two separate functional categories C–F:

(9) [$_{CP}$ (spec) [C [$_{FP}$ (spec) [F TP]]]]

I will assume that in a configuration like (9) only the highest CP category constitutes a strong phase, with a complex edge *(spec) C (spec) F*. In other words, FP is neither an independent (strong) phase nor is it ever sent independently to the phonology under spell-Out of sister, despite being a structural sister of C. Thus, at stage CP, Spell-Out of sister sends TP (rather than FP) to PF. Subsequently, if the numeration is empty (i.e., if CP is a root structure), the edge *(spec) C (spec) F* is spelled-out in full, independently of TP.[8]

Before I turn to the analysis of clitic placement, a final note is in order. With Chomsky (2004), I assume that the phonological component (at least its cyclical subpart) forgets about what has been transferred by Spell-Out at earlier phases. For example, when processing TP, the phonological component does not have access to VP and while processing the edge of CP in a root structure, the phonological component does not have access to TP.[9] As a way to capture this, I will assume that in the objects sent to PF such nodes are empty (for example, when TP is spelled-out, the PF object thus formed has an empty VP node and so forth). With this theoretical apparatus in place, we can now turn to cases of Romance determiner-clitic placement outside of DP.

21.4 The Generalized Role of OS in Clitic Placement

Consider the v*P stage of the derivation of *any* Romance sentence with a determiner-clitic when this is a minimal-maximal projection in the sense discussed above (i.e., when it is "pronominal"), whether the verb of that sentence is finite (such as (1a) and (2)) or infinitival (such as (1b,c) and (3)). For convenience, I illustrate with an example from Spanish containing the same verb and pronominal clitic as (1)–(3). The verb is given in infinitival form and written in capital letters, and I use the label "subj(ect)" to stand for the external argument, whether this is overt (such as *Juan*) or null, such as PRO in an infinitival clause or pro in a finite clause (henceforth, for convenience, I will use the label "vP" rather than "v*P" and I will boldface the copies that are pronounced at PF).

(10) [vP [DP **subj**] [v′ [v **VER-v**] [VP [v *t*(VER)] [DP **los**]]]]

The structure in (10) represents the sum of narrow-syntax operations that apply during the derivation of vP: V-to-v raising (leaving a trace indicated as *t(VER)*), and Merge of the external argument (subj) in spec,v. At this point, Spell-Out sends (11), the sister of v (VP), to the phonological component:

(11) [VP [v *t*(VER)] [DP **los**]]

Following Nunes 2004, I assume that traces are deleted in the phonological component (i.e., after Spell-Out), perhaps by the same operation that deletes overt material in nominal ellipsis (see the brief discussion of (7)). I also assume that deletion precedes fusion. Trace deletion (again represented by double strikeout) thus yields (12) from (11):[10]

(12) [VP [v *t*(VER)] [DP **los**]]

The result of this deletion is that the clitic *los* lacks a phonological host, fusion cannot apply, and the derivation crashes at PF ((4) is not satisfied).

Adapting ideas of Chomsky 2001, I will now assume that in order to allow the expression of sentences containing determiner clitics, which would otherwise always crash, Object Shift (henceforth OS) is allowed to apply at stage (10) of the derivation, crucially *before* VP is sent to PF by Spell-Out. Metaphoricaly speaking, rather than deliberately "commiting suicide," the derivation tries to converge in a different way before sending VP to Spell-Out. OS yields (13), where the clitic is now placed in a new window of opportunity, namely that of the next highest-phase CP:[11]

(13) [vP [DP **los**] [vP [DP **subj**] [v′ [v **VER-v**] [VP [v *t*(VER)] [DP *t*(los)]]]]]

At this stage, the VP of (13) is (innocuously) sent to PF by Spell-Out, where it trivially disappears, since it only consists of traces, which are deleted:

(14) [VP [v *t*(VER)] [DP *t*(los)]]

This amount of "displacement" of pronominal clitics (i.e., OS) is universal in (Romance) derivations involving them. It is important to note at this point that OS is *not* the operation responsible for either proclisis or enclisis of the pronouns. OS applies so that expressions containing clitics have a chance to converge at the CP phase, where the final configuration of proclisis or enclisis is decided by other factors (see the following sections). In other words, the differences between enclisis and proclisis are a function of distinct derivational histories within the CP phase. I turn to this issue now.

21.5 Infinitival Clauses in Spanish and French and Radical Trace Deletion

Pronominal clitics are obligatorily enclitic in infinitival clauses of Spanish, independently of contextual factors. Like (1b), (15) illustrates this point:

(15) a. me gustaría mucho ver*los* (*... *los* ver)
to-me would-like very-much to-see-them
'I would like very much to see them.'
b. ver*los* será un placer (**los* ver ...)
to-see-them will-be a pleasure
c. pedí para ver*los* (*... *los* ver)
(I-)asked for to-see-them
'I asked to see them.'

In Spanish, the position of negative and manner adverbials to the right of infinitival verbs (see (16)) suggests that there is v-to-T raising in infinitival clauses (for this type of argument, see Pollock 1989):

(16) a. para no *ver* *más* a María
in-order not to-see anymore to Mary
'in order not to see Mary anymore'
b. [*hacer bién* sus tareas], es la obligación de todo buen estudiante
'To do his work well is the obligation of every good student.'

Consider then the derivation of the infinitival clause *verlos* of the examples in (15), given in (17). (17a) illustrates the derivation of the lower vP, including OS of the clitic and Spell-Out of VP, indicated by a single strike; (17b) represents the derivation of CP, including raising of the external subject PRO to spec, TP and raising of *ver*-v to T:

(17) a. [$_{vP}$ [$_{DP}$ **los**] [$_{vP}$ [$_{DP}$ **PRO**] [$_{v'}$ [$_{v}$ **ver-v**] [$_{VP}$ [$_{V}$ *t*(ver)] [$_{DP}$ *t*(los)]]]]]
b. [$_{CP}$ C [$_{TP}$ [$_{DP}$ **PRO**] [$_{T'}$ [$_{T}$ [$_{v}$ **ver-v**]-T] [$_{vP}$ [$_{DP}$ **los**][$_{vP}$ [$_{DP}$ *t*(PRO)] [$_{v'}$ [$_{v}$ *t*(ver-v)] [$_{VP}$ [$_{V}$ *t*(ver)][$_{DP}$ *t*(los)]]]]]]]]

At this stage, Spell-Out of sister sends TP to the phonology. A few comments are appropriate at this point. First, recall that one of the properties of the "phase"-based model of derivations proposed in Chomsky 2001, 2004, 2008, is that the phonological component "forgets" about those phases that have been transferred previously by Spell-Out. In other words, material in such earlier phases is simply not visible to the phonological component at later stages. Thus, when TP is spelled-out, the contents of the lower VP node are not accessible anymore. I will assume that the PF object thus formed has an empty VP node. This is illustrated in the (simplified) tree (18):

(18)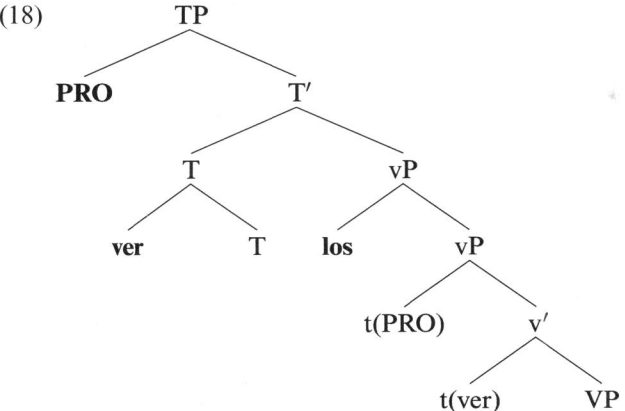

Second, I will assume a strong version of trace deletion at PF, whereby deletion wipes out not just the terminal string (under the copy theory) but also the structure exhaustively dominating it (call this "radical trace deletion"). This proposal makes sense, since the structure associated with traces obviously does not reach PF anymore than the copies themselves.[12] Radical trace deletion thus yields (19) from (18):

(19)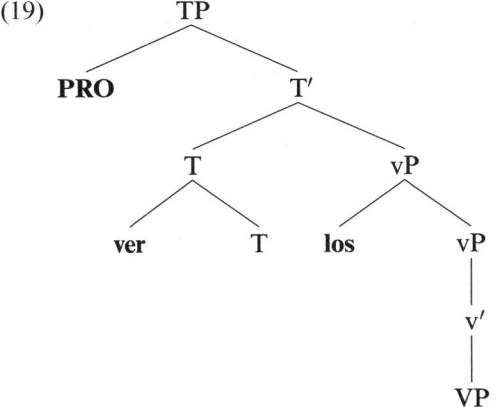

Suppose now that the following rules of "tree pruning" (see Ross 1969) are also at work at the initial stages of PF, after radical trace deletion:

(20) *Tree Pruning*
   i. Delete any empty node.
   ii. Delete any node that does not branch.

Tree pruning yields the PF structure (21) from (19):[13]

(21)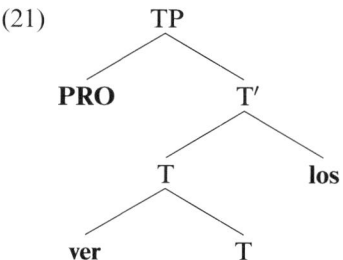

In (21), the clitic *los* is now a daughter of T'. Because of infinitival v-to-T raising in Spanish, the verb has risen past the clitic, and is in a configuration with the clitic such that the clitic c-commands it. Since the verb is an appropriate host for the clitic, the clitic fuses to it. Enclisis is just a by-product of the configuration.

Now consider French, which, contrary to Spanish, has infinitival proclitics rather than enclitics, as illustrated in (1c) as well as (22):

(22) a. j'aimerais bien *les* voir (*... voir *les*)
I would-like very-much them to-see
'I would like very much to see them.'
b. *les* voir sera un plaisir (*voir *les*...)
them to-see will-be a pleasure
c. j'ai demandé de *les* voir (*... voir *les*)
I have asked of them to-see
'I asked to see them.'

Pollock (1989) and Belletti (1990), among others, argue that infinitival verbs in French do not rise as high as finite verbs, contrary to other Romance languages like Spanish, Portuguese, and Italian. In particular, they appear to the right of negative adverbs such as *pas* or manner adverbs such as *bien*:

(23) a. pour ne *pas voir* Marie
'in order not to see Mary'
b. [*bien faire* ses devoirs], c'est l'obligation de tout bon étudiant
'To do his work well is the obligation of every good student.'

This suggests that nonfinite verbs in French make the usual short movement to v, but fail to rise further to T, thus remaining within vP. In light of this, consider the derivation of the infinitival clause *les voir* of the examples in (22), given in (24). (24a) illustrates the derivation of the lower vP, including OS of the clitic and Spell-Out of VP, indicated by a single strike; (24b) represents the derivation of CP, including raising of the external subject PRO to spec, TP:

(24) a. [vP [DP **les**] [vP [DP **PRO**] [v′ [v **voir-v**] [vP [v t(voire)] [DP t(les)]]]]]
    b. [CP C [TP [DP **PRO**] [T′ T [vP [DP **les**] [vP [DP t(PRO)] [v′ [v **voir-v**] [vP [v t(voire)] [DP t(les)]]]]]]]]

At this stage, Spell-Out of sister sends TP to PF. The combined effects of radical trace deletion and tree pruning (20) yield the PF structure (25):

(25)
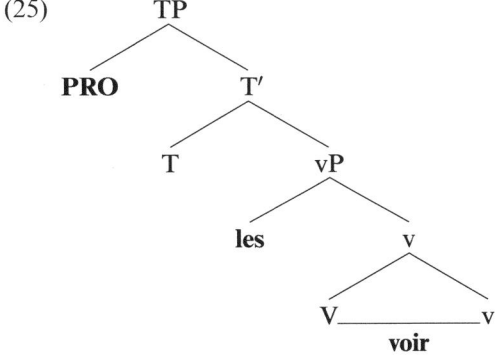

In (25), the clitic *les* is adjacent to *voir*, which belongs to its minimal search domain (i.e., *les* c-commands it). Since the verb is an appropriate host, the clitic fuses to it. Because there is no infinitival v-to-T raising in French, the clitic in its OS position is to the left of the verb, and ends up proclitic to it.

21.6 Finite Clauses in Spanish and French

With the exception of EP, which I leave aside until the next section, clitic pronouns are proclitic in Romance finite clauses, as illustrated in (1a) and in (26):

(26) a. (nosotros) *los* vemos con frecuencia (*... vemos*los*)
    b. nous *les* voyons souvent (*... voyons *les*)
       'We see them often.'

In both Spanish and French finite verbs raise to T, as shown by the position of manner adverbs (see Pollock 1989):

(27) a. Jean *voit souvent* Marie
    b. Juan *ve frecuentemente* a María
       'John often sees Mary.'

The derivation of finite clauses in both Spanish and French will thus resemble the derivation of infinitival clauses of Spanish, where the verb also raises to T. I illustrate such a derivation in (28) for the Spanish example (26a). As before, (28a) illustrates the derivation of vP (including OS and Spell-Out of VP), and (28b) the derivation of CP, including movement of the subject to spec, TP and raising of the finite verb to T (for convenience, I omit the adverbial):

(28) a. [vP [DP **los**] [vP [DP **nosotros**] [v′ [v **vemos-v**] [VP [V t(vemos)] [DP t(los)]]]]]
b. [CP C [TP [DP **nosotros**] [T′ [T [v **vemos-v**]-T] [vP [DP **los**] [vP [DP t(nosotros)] [v′ [v t(vemos-v) [VP [V t(vemos)][DP t(los)]]]]]]]

At this stage, Spell-Out of sister sends TP to PF. The combined effects of radical trace deletion and tree pruning yield the PF structure (29) (compare with (21)):

(29)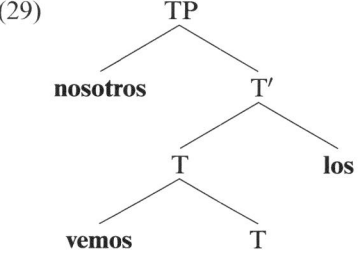

Just as in the case of Spanish inifinitival clauses, fusion should apply to (29), deriving the enclitic forms v*emoslos* and *voyons les*, for Spanish and French, respectively. This, however, is obviously an incorrect result. In other words, the analysis developed so far has the pronominal clitic at the wrong side of the finite verb in Spanish and French.

Noticing that clitics are rare with past participles in Romance (see Kayne 1991, 657–660), Raposo and Uriagereka (2005) suggest that there is a morphological filter that prevents pronominal clitics from fusing to the agreeing side of a finite verbal form. Pronominal clitics are basically the morphophonological realization of a bundle of agreement (Φ-)features. Fusing such a bundle to the agreeing side of a finite form creates a verb headed by two sets of Φ-features corresponding to two different arguments (the subject and a complement). Suppose that finite verbs must check their morphophonological (subject) Φ-features against the abstract, uninterpretable Φ-features of T (or some other functional category; see section 21.7), and that this checking takes place in the morphological subcomponent at the entrance of PF but after fusion has applied.[14] Adapting ideas from Uriagereka 1996, this checking process might be unable to overcome the ambiguity created by the presence of multiple sets of Φ-features. Fusing *los* to *vemos*-T in (29) yields *vemos*-T-*los* 'see-1pl-T-3pl', where the relevant segment of T (the one c-commanding the verb) is now adjacent to two different sets of Φ-features and presumably in a configuration where it can "see" both. It is plausible to speculate that this creates an "intolerable ambiguity" for T. Even though a precise formulation of the mechanism suggested here needs to be worked out, I will assume that it is in the right direction. Obviously, something will have to be said about the EP counterpart of Spanish *vemoslos*, which is perfectly grammatical (*vemo-los*). See section 21.7.

Recent proposals within the P&P theory, especially in the framework of Distributed Morphology, have suggested that movement processes motivated by the need to satisfy morphological or prosodical requirements are available within the PF component (see, among many others, Halpern 1992, Embick and Noyer 2001, and on the specific topic of Portuguese clitics, Barbosa 1996). This is exactly what I will propose here: the derivation of proclisis in (26) is the result of a local inversion rule motivated by the fact that the application of fusion directly to the output of OS in (29) creates an illegitimate morphological form, for the reasons discussed in the previous paragraph. This PF operation is schematically illustrated in (30):[15]

(30) [$_T$Verb-Φ-T]-clitic → clitic-[$_T$Verb-Φ-T]

Applied to (29), this rule yields (31), where I assume the clitic adjoins to T:

(31)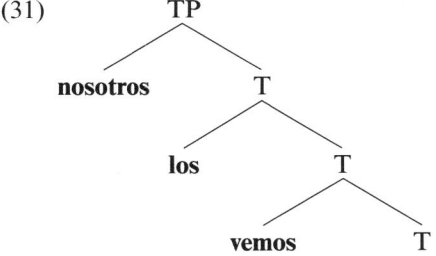

In (31), the clitic c-commands the segment of T containing the verb and fuses to it (or perhaps directly to the verb), yielding proclisis. Note that the clitic is now fused to the nonagreeing side of the verbal form. I conclude that this does not affect the checking procedure between T and the verb agreement features.[16]

In this analysis, (30) is the counterpart of the operation of "clitic placement" often discussed in the literature on Romance clitics. In this respect, the analysis proposed here and previous analyses both make the claim that proclisis in finite clauses of Romance languages is derived by overt movement. There are some differences, however. First, in my analysis, (30) is a PF operation, strictly local, applying under adjacency and motivated by morphological requirements, rather than an (unmotivated) syntactic movement having T as a somewhat arbitrary target, as in the analysis of Kayne 1991. Second, in the present analysis, clitics *do* move in the syntax, but this is now restricted to OS within the vP phase, for the reasons discussed in section 21.4.

21.7 Finite Root Clauses in EP

Although a complete discussion of the varied patterns of clitic placement in EP is not within the scope of this chapter, I will give a brief outline of the enclitic-proclitic complementary distribution in finite root clauses, and of the free variation between the two clitic positions in adverbial infinitival clauses. For a more detailed discussion, see Raposo 2000 as well as Raposo and Uriagereka 2005.

As mentioned in section 21.3 (see the references given there), a considerable amount of work initiated in the 1980s has converged on the idea that the CP field in Romance should be split in at least two different functional areas, CP and FP, with F standing for "focus." The proposed general structure of the clause is illustrated in (32):

(32) [$_{CP}$ ... C [$_{FP}$ ... F [$_{TP}$ ... T [$_{vP}$ ... v [$_{VP}$ ... V ...]]]]]

F may be endowed with a strong Focus feature responsible for the displacement of "focus phrases" (which Raposo and Uriagereka 1996 call "affective phrases") to spec, F in sentences such as (33):

(33) [MUITO WHISKEY]$_i$ deram eles ao capitão t_i
much whiskey gave they to-the captain!
'They gave TOO MUCH WHISKEY to the captain!'

Wh-phrases also target spec, F (see Rizzi 1997 for similar proposals). In addition, the preverbal negative morpheme *não* 'not' and the preverbal adverbs mentioned in the introduction (those that determine proclisis in finite clauses) are realized within the FP projection too, either in its spec or adjoined to F′.

Raposo and Uriagereka (1996) argue that F in EP has one important property that differentiates this language from its Romance kin, namely that F, rather than T, can be the functional "gate" for the uninterpretable subject Φ-features that are obligatory in finite clauses. In other words, in EP these features can be associated either to T or to F. Following the notation used in Raposo and Uriagereka 2005, I will represent F endowed with Φ-features as (lowercase) f, using F for the version without Φ-features (i.e., when these are associated to T). As Raposo and Uriagereka (1996) show, f licenses inflected infinitives in EP and attracts the verb, which raises all the way up to f (perhaps because its Φ-features trigger this movement). The verb, however, only raises up to T when F is present, such as in Spanish or French.

One interesting issue within a theory that accepts the existence of phonetically empty (functional) items is how these distribute among the morphological types *word*, *affix*, and *clitic*. I will make what seems to be the null hypothesis, and claim that phonologically empty (functional) heads distribute among these three types.[17] Raposo (2000) and Raposo and Uriagereka (2005) propose that f (i.e., F endowed with Φ-features) is a null clitic (rather than an affix). As such, it is subject to the operation of fusion (5).[18]

Now, in most Romance dialects, clitics that belong to the same clausal domain have an interesting property: they cluster within a single group. This is clearly illustrated in contexts of clitic climbing such as Spanish (34):

(34) a. quiere   darmelo
         (he)-wants to-give-to-me-it
     b. me   lo quiere   dar
         to-me it (he)-wants to-give
     c. *me quiere darlo
     d. *lo quiere darme

The two clitics *me* 'to-me' and *lo* 'it' must cluster together, either in the subordinate clause (34a) or in the matrix clause (34b), but they cannot be separated, each in a different clause (34c,d). I assume that in a clitic cluster, one clitic is adjoined to the other (*me* is adjoined to *lo* in (34a,b)).

In light of this, consider the derivation of (2b) in EP (*vemo-los com frequência.* '(we) see them often'), including the issue of why proclisis is impossible, as opposed to the Spanish (1a) *los vemos con frecuencia* or its French counterpart (26b). (35a) represents the vP phase and (35b) the structure up to the point where f is merged (again, I ignore the adverbial):

(35) a. [vP [DP **os**] [vP [DP **pro**] [v′ [v **vemos-v**] ~~[vP [v *t*(vemos)] [DP *t*(os)]]~~]]]
     b. [FP **f** [TP [DP **pro**] [T′ **vemos-v-T** [vP [DP **os**] [vP [DP *t*(pro)] [v′ [v *t*(vemos-v)]
         ~~[vP [v *t*(vemos)] [DP *t*(os)]]~~]]]]]]

Since (by hypothesis) f is a clitic, the determiner-clitic must now target f, in order to form a clitic cluster.[19] In addition, the finite verb also raises to f. Assuming that the verb moves through T, it raises to f before the clitic does, since T is closer to f than the clitic in its derived OS position. After Merge of C, we thus have the structure (35c):

(35) c. [CP C [FP [f **os**-[f **vemos-v-T-f**]] [TP [DP **pro**] [T′ t(vemos-v-T) [vP [DP t(os)]
         [vP [DP *t*(pro)] [v′ [v *t*(vemos-v)] ~~[vP [v *t*(vemos)] [DP *t*(os)]]~~]]]]]]]

Our proposal concerning Spell-Out when the CP field is exploded becomes relevant now (see section 21.3 and note 8). At stage (35c), TP is sent to PF by Spell-Out, with a vacuous result since it only consists of traces and the phonetically null *pro*. Subsequently, the remaining structure (the complex edge of C including f) is in turn sent to PF by Spell-Out. Crucially, by our assumptions, TP is simply an empty node, since its contents are not accessible anymore to this newly created PF object. This is illustrated in (36):

(36)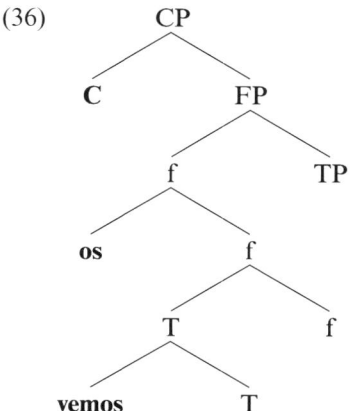

Tree pruning (20) of the empty TP node and subsequently of the resulting nonbranching FP node yields (37):

(37)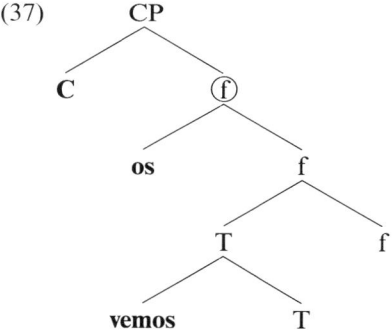

At this point we come to the licensing of clitics by fusion. Notice that in (37), it is not simply the pronominal clitic *os* that must be licensed by fusion, but rather the entire clitic cluster *os-f*. Assuming May's (1985) theory of adjunction, I take the clitic cluster to be the minimal segment of f that contains both the pronominal clitic and another segment of f (I circle this segment in (37) and the following examples). This segment of f searches for a host within its c-command domain. However, none exists: C is within its domain but is phonetically empty (thus not an appropriate host), and the finite verb (a potential host) is *contained* within the clitic cluster, therefore not in its search (c-command) domain. Notice, crucially, that even if spec, TP contained an overt subject rather than a null *pro*, such as the strong (nonclitic) pronoun *nós* 'we', this would still not be a host, since the Spell-Out domain where the clitic cluster is searching for a host cannot "see" (inside) TP. This derivation thus crashes at PF, since (4) is not satisfied.[20]

How do we derive enclisis then? I propose a solution in the same spirit as that proposed for Spanish/French proclisis in finite clauses. Derivation (35) has reached a dead end, and unless some adjustment is made, it will crash at PF. It then resorts to a minimal and local operation that can save it, namely a structural readjustment that "detaches" T from its position in (37) and readjoins it to the highest segment of f, thereby switching the order between the pronominal clitic and the verb as a side effect. This is illustrated in (38):[21]

(38)
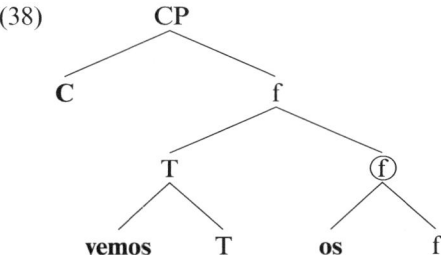

In (38), the (circled) segment exhaustively dominating the clitic cluster that needs to be licensed by fusion c-commands T containing the verb, and fuses with it. This derives *vemos os* '(we) see them', pronounced in EP as *vemo-los*.[22]

At this point, a legitimate question arises. Why is (finite) pronominal enclisis not disallowed in EP in the same way that it is in Spanish or French, especially given the reasons invoked in section 21.6 for the ungrammaticality of the latter? Notice that there is a crucial difference between structure (38) underlying the legitimate EP enclisis and structure (29) that would underlie the illegitimate enclisis in Spanish/French. In (29), we have a pronominal clitic fusing directly with a morphologically complex verb form, which includes a finite verb *and* the functional category (T) that checks the agreement features of the verb. In (38), however, the category that fuses with T (or directly with the verb) is the functional category that checks the agreement features of the verb itself—that is, f, which in turn *contains* the pronominal clitic buried within itself. This, I claim, makes all the difference between the legitimate Portuguese enclisis and the illegitimate Spanish/French version. Presumably, in (38) the relevant segment of f for feature checking (the one c-commanding T) cannot "see" the pronominal clitic, at least for checking purposes, leaving unhindered its checking relation with the verb. I leave for future work a complete elucidation of the checking mechanisms at work here.

Consider now the derivation of (2a) *quando os viste?* 'when did (you) see them?', with proclisis. The narrow syntax derivation of (2a) is similar to (35), with an important difference—that there is an overt *wh*-phrase in Spec, f:[23]

(39) [CP C [FP **quando** [f **os**-[f **viste-v-T-f**]] [TP [DP **pro**] [T' t(viste-v-T) [vP [DP t(os)]
     [vP [DP t(pro)] [v' [v t(viste-v)] [VP [V t(viste)] [DP t(os)] t(quando)]]]]]]]]

Consider now the PF object that results from Spell-Out of the edge of CP (subsequent to the independent Spell-Out of TP), given in (40):

(40)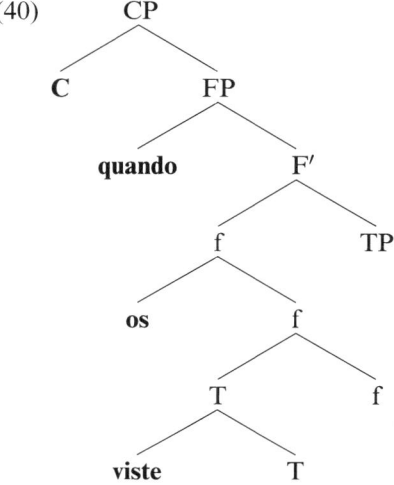

Tree pruning of the empty TP and of the resulting nonbranching F' node yields (41):

(41)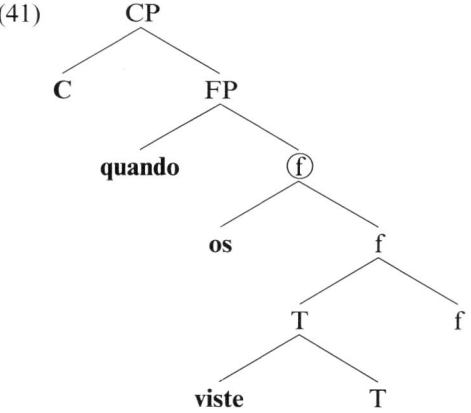

In (41), the (circled) segment of f exhaustively dominating the clitic cluster *os-f* has an adequate host within its search domain, namely the *wh*-word *quando* 'when' to its left, and it fuses with it. Note that fusion applied to (41) yields *enclisis* of the clitic cluster to the *wh*-word *quando*, rather than proclisis of *os* to the verb. Because the verb is contained within the clitic cluster, it is carried along with the pronominal clitic. As we see, recognition of clitic f and of the clitic cluster that it heads when there is an additional (pronominal) clitic in the structure thus leads to the conclusion that (41) is actually an *enclitic* configuration, despite appearances. More concretely, it is the clitic cluster headed by f that searches for a host, but since f is phonetically null, it looks like the relevant operation is triggered by the visible pronominal clitic, giving the impression of a (false) privileged relation between the verb and the pronoun. Carvalho (1989) was the first (to the best of my knowledge) to recognize that apparent proclitics in EP are in fact phonological enclitics to the word that precedes them, something that follows quite straightforwardly from the present account. Notice again that my analysis does not use such primitive notions of "enclisis" or "proclisis." The relevant principle is that clitics search for their host within their minimal (c-command) domain. Beyond this, whether a clitic is proclitic or enclitic is a by-product of the output of the narrow syntax, of the rules of tree pruning, and of last-resort PF rules of local inversion.

21.8 Clitic Placement in Infinitival Clauses of EP

I repeat paradigm (3) as (42), augmented with the version displaying agreement on the infinitive (the so-called inflected infinitive of Portuguese; see Raposo 1987):

(42) a. para vê-*los*,   viajámos   até à Patagónia
        for to-see-them, (we-)traveled to   Patagonia
    b. para *os*   ver,   viajámos   até à Patagónia
        for   them to-see, (we-)traveled to   Patagonia
    c. para *os* ver*mos*, viajámos até à Patagónia (*para ver*mo*-los, ...)
        'In order to see them, we traveled to Patagonia.'

One important issue in the study of infinitival structures is the featural composition of infinitives. Briefly, I propose that in EP there are three varieties of infinitives (rather than just two, as traditionally recognized), represented by each one of the examples of (42): an inflected infinitive (42c) and two varieties of noninflected (plain) infinitives, revealed by the different patterns of clitic placement. I further propose that both plain infinitives are specified for [person], but not for [number].[24] How are they distinguished? I would like to suggest that in (42a) the feature [person] is in T (call it the T-type infinitival), and in (42b) the feature [person] is in F—that is, f (call it the f-type infinitival). The T-type (42a) is the infinitival structure also found in Spanish and French. As we have seen, in languages where infinitival verbs rise to T, this determines enclisis. This is the case with EP; therefore we have enclisis.

The infinitival in (42b), on the other hand, is an f-type infinitival—that is, it has clitic f heading a clitic cluster and also attracting T containing the verb. Consider then the CP stage of the derivation of the adverbial clause of (42b), given in (43) (with Kayne 1984, I assume that items such as *para* 'for' are prepositional complementizers):

(43) [CP **para** [FP [f **os**-[f **ver-v-T-f**]] [TP [DP **PRO**] [T' t(ver-v-T) [vP [DP t(os)] [vP [DP t(PRO)] [v' [v t(ver-v)] [vP [v t(ver)][DP t(os)]]]]]]]]

At stage (43), first TP is sent to PF by Spell-Out, with vacuous effects. Subsequently, the edge of CP is spelled-out, yielding the following PF object:

(44)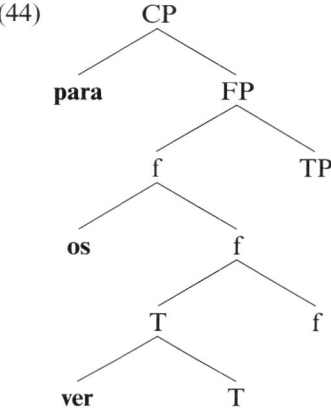

After tree pruning of TP and of the nonbranching FP, we derive (45):

(45)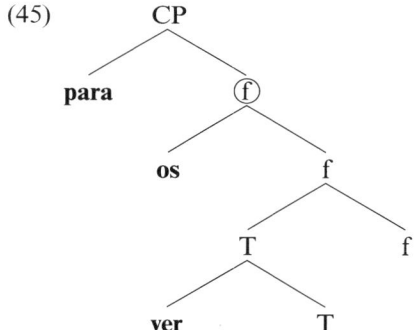

In (45), the clitic cluster exhaustively dominated by the circled f node has the complementizer *para* 'for' within its search domain and fuses with it. As in (41), we have enclisis of *os-f* to *para* rather than proclisis of *os* to *ver*.

Raposo and Uriagereka (1996) suggest that in inflected infinitives the agreement Φ-features are always in f rather than T. If this is correct, the derivation of (42c) proceeds just like the one for (42b), yielding proclisis. However, even if inflected infinitives have their features in T rather than in F, proclisis would still be the outcome, for the same reason that it is the outcome in finite clauses of Spanish/French (see section 21.6).

21.9 Conclusion

The basic idea of this chapter is that clitic *movement* must be distinguished from fusion, which "attaches" the clitic to an adequate adjacent host within its search (c-command) domain (see also Otero 1996; Raposo and Uriagereka 2005). Since, due to trace deletion, pronominal clitics are left without a host within the lower VP where they are initially merged, they must undergo Object Shift, which places them within the "window of opportunity" of the higher CP phase. It is then within the CP domain that clitics find their host. Once there, they will be subject to the vagaries of language-particular derivational histories. I have also shown that fusion is subject to morphological requirements that motivate a short displacement of the clitic, resulting in the generalized Romance pattern of proclisis to finite verbs. Moreover, I have demonstrated that the existence of f in EP creates another disturbance for clitics, resulting in the unusual (within Romance) pattern of enclisis in some finite root clauses. The crucial hypothesis here is that f is a clitic itself, thus attracting other pronominal clitics present in the derivation and forming a clitic cluster. I have also shown that we do not need primitive notions of "enclisis" and "proclisis" (i.e., statements on the directionality of attachment of clitics), at least for Romance. The relevant principle is that clitics search for their host within their minimal (c-command) domain. Beyond this, whether a clitic is proclitic or enclitic is a by-product of the output of the narrow syntax, of the rules of tree pruning, and of PF rules of local inversion that are motivated by morphological restrictions on fusion (as in Spanish/French finite proclisis) or by the need to locally adjust the structural position of the host (as in EP finite enclisis). If an analysis along the lines proposed here can be generalized to other clitics in other languages, we might perhaps be able to dispense with the notions of "enclitic" and "proclitic" altogether. Crucial to all this was the phase-based theory of derivations proposed by Chomsky within the Minimalist Program, and a radical idea of Spell-Out of sister where even in root structures the edge of the phase head is transferred to PF in a Spell-Out operation distinct from the one that transfers the complement of the phase head.

Notes

I would like to thank audiences at UCSB, at the Universidade Federal da Bahía, at the Universidade Federal de Maceió, at the Centro de Estudos da Universidade de Lisboa, at the 17th ABRALIN Institute (Universidade de Brasília), and at the workshop on the copy theory of movement on the PF side (University of Utrecht). Any errors are mine.

1. It is practically impossible to cite here all the many works that have been written about clitics in general, and Romance clitics in particular. Within generative grammar, Perlmutter 1971 and Kayne 1975 are the pioneering ones. See also Kayne 1991, Otero 1996, and Wanner

1991 and 1996 for important ideas (Otero 1996 also contains relevant historical background and a considerable number of references). My own previous work on this matter includes Raposo 2000 and Raposo and Uriagereka 2005.

2. When the verb ends in the consonants [r] or [ʃ] (written as -s), a following pronominal clitic keeps its onset [l-] and the preceding final consonant of the verb drops.

3. Not to be confused with the operation with the same name proposed by Halle and Marantz 1993, in the framework of Distributed Morphology. The operation I propose simply attaches a clitic to an immediately following or preceding host.

4. Fusion can also apply recursively, as in *do meu irmão*, literally 'of-the my brother' where both *o* and *d(e)* are clitics. First *o* fuses to *meu*, and subsequently *de* to *o=meu*. Fusion of *de* to *o=meu* involves further contraction of *de* with *o*, resulting in *do*. The final complex word *d=o=meu* satisfies (4).

5. Chomsky attributes the particular version of "Spell-Out of sister" to work by Jon Nissenbaum.

6. Alternatively, every time the numeration is accessed, it brings information on whether it is empty or not to the derivation, so that Spell-Out knows when to apply in full. This is rather akin to a nonlocal operation.

7. Spell-Out of the edge of simple (i.e., non-*wh*) clauses in languages such as English or Portuguese, which have null C, is trivially vacuous. If the edge of a root clause is not empty, the present proposal makes the strong claim that the phonological processing of TP is independent from the phonological processing of the edge of CP, and that (perhaps with the exception of postcyclical phonology) there should be no phonological interactions between the two domains. See section 21.8 for such a claim with respect to EP.

8. Assuming, with Chomsky 2001, 2004, that TP is a substantive rather than a functional category, and that phases are functionally headed XPs (with XP being a substantive category), Spell-Out could be formulated as in (i):

(i) *Spell-Out of substantive complement*
   a. At stage HP (HP = a strong phase) spell-out the maximal substantive phrase contained in HP.
   b. The remaining functional material is spelled-out at the level of the next-highest phase ZP.

For convenience I will continue to use the label "Spell-Out of sister," even though I mean a formulation of Spell-Out like (i).

9. This theoretical apparatus thus derives the PIC, at least in the phonological component.

10. I assume for convenience the copy theory of traces (Chomsky 1995; Nunes 2004), although nothing hinges on this.

11. Technically, OS is allowed by the presence of an EPP feature in v. In turn, an EPP feature is assigned to v "only if that has an effect on outcome" (in this case, PF outcome), "thus allowing (and requiring) OS" in the particular case of an object determiner-clitic. The two quotes in this note are from Chomsky 2001, 35 and 34, respectively. The logic of the argument in this section mirrors closely Chomsky's (2001) analysis of OS in Icelandic, with the crucial difference that it is driven by phonological-phonetic considerations, rather than semantic ones.

12. The structure associated with overt material, however, arguably makes it to PF once appropriately converted into prosodic structure. See Nespor and Vogel 1986 for discussion of

algorithms that perform this conversion. The rules of tree pruning that I propose below can be seen as part of this conversion.

13. Note that PF does not care about node labels, which are of significance only to the semantics.

14. For discussion of a model where morphology is at the entrance of PF, see among others, Embick and Noyer 2001. The checking discussed in the text is not to be confused with the checking of the (uninterpretable) Φ-features of T against the (interpretable) Φ-features of the subject. The checking system proposed here is closer to Chomsky 1995, chap. 3, where T was endowed with a dual set of verbal *and* NP/DP features, both of which had to be checked.

15. Embick and Noyer (2001), in particular, argue for the idea of postsyntactic readjustment operations modifying syntactic structures. As they note, operations of this type have been proposed by many authors (e.g., Halpern 1992; Barbosa 1996) in the domain of clitic placement for cases where the syntax does not provide a suitable host for the clitic.

16. In (31) the segment of T involved in this checking (the lowest segment, I assume) is not adjacent to the pronominal clitic. Pronominal proclitics to past participles are more common in Romance than assumed by Kayne 1991, for example in Brazilian Portuguese. This is what we would expect from the analysis in the text, since the clitic is fused to the nonagreeing side of the participle.

17. Although I have nothing to say about what factors determine what heads belong to what type.

18. Uriagereka 1995 speculates that f was overtly realized in Medieval Portuguese. Perhaps this f was a clitic that progressively weakened, losing its phonetic matrix but keeping the morphological property of a clitic.

19. A reviewer argues that since I have not explained what forces clitics to cluster, my analysis is speculative. To be honest, I do not know what forces clitics to cluster, but I also have never found a motivated account of this phenomenon in the literature on clitics. What is important in my analysis is that, for whatever reason, the phenomenon is real. Another issue is the status of f as a clitic. In my analysis, this is a hypothesis, good only insofar as it allows us to derive the facts of clitic placement in EP in a way as simple and motivated as possible.

20. We thus account for the ungrammaticality of *os vemos nós* 'them we see'. Note that a preverbal subject does not change this status: **nós os vemos* is equally ungrammatical. I assume that preverbal subjects in root clauses of EP are in a position between CP and FP, concretely in spec, TopP (see Rizzi 1997). It is easy to show that a phrase in this position cannot serve as host for the clitic cluster headed by f because it is not in the search (c-command) domain of f.

21. See note 15. In postulating a local inversion, my analysis is similar to that of Barbosa (1996), although its motivations and background are different from hers. Raposo and Uriagereka (2005) implement the same general idea in a different way: at stage (35b), the pronominal clitic adjoins to f *prior* to T containing the verb. However, if these movements belong to narrow syntax, this solution requires a global mechanism: in the narrow syntax, the derivation would have to anticipate a PF crash, thereby switching the order of raising between the pronoun and T. It is probably better to avoid global mechanisms of this type.

22. This pattern does not change with an overt subject; consider *vemo-los nós* and *nós vemo-los* 'we see them'. In the former, *nós* is in Spec, TP and therefore not visible to the clitic cluster; in

the latter, the subject is in Spec, TopP and therefore too far away to serve as a host. The switch yielding enclisis is therefore still required.

23. For convenience, I omit from (40) the successive cyclic movement of the *wh*-phrase *onde* 'where' through Spec, vP.

24. Since both plain infinitives license a PRO subject, within the "null Case" theory of Chomsky and Lasnik 1993, it follows that the [person] feature is sufficient (and also necessary) to license structural Case. Evidence for this is given in Raposo 2003. Under this view, overt verbal agreement is a reflex of the presence of both [person] and [number] features.

References

Barbosa, P. 1996. Clitic placement in European Portuguese and the position of subjects. In A. L. Halpern and A. M. Zwicky, eds., *Approaching second: Second position clitics and related phenomena*, 1–40. Stanford, CA: CSLI.

Belletti, A. 1990. *Generalized verb movement*. Turin: Rosenberg and Sellier.

Carvalho, J. 1989. Phonological conditions on Portuguese clitic placement: On syntactic evidence for stress and rythmical patterns. *Linguistics* 29:405–436.

Chomsky, N. 1995. *The Minimalist Program*. Cambridge, MA: MIT Press.

Chomsky, N. 2001. Derivation by phase. In M. Kenstowicz, ed., *Ken Hale: A life in language*, 1–52. Cambridge, MA: MIT Press.

Chomsky, N. 2004. Beyond explanatory adequacy. In A. Belletti, ed., *Structures and beyond: The cartography of syntactic structure*, vol. 3. Oxford: Oxford University Press.

Chomsky, N. 2008. On phases. In R. Freidin, C. P. Otero, and M. L. Zubizarreta, eds., *Foundational issues in linguistic theory*. Cambridge, MA: MIT Press.

Chomsky, N., and H. Lasnik. 1993. The theory of principles and parameters. In J. Jacobs, A. von Stechow, W. Sternefeld, and T. Venneman, eds., *An international handbook of contemporary research*. Berlin: Walter de Gruyter. (Reprinted in N. Chomsky, *The Minimalist Program*. Cambridge, MA: MIT Press, 1995.)

Embick, D., and R. Noyer. 2001. Movement operations after syntax. *Linguistic Inquiry* 32:555–595.

Halle, M., and A. Marantz. 1993. Distributed morphology and the pieces of inflection. In K. Hale and S. J. Keyser, eds., *The view from building 20: Essays in honor of Sylvain Bromberger*, 111–176. Cambridge, MA: MIT Press.

Halpern, A. 1992. Topics in the placement and morphology of clitics. Doctoral dissertation, Stanford University.

Kayne, R. 1975. *French syntax*. Cambridge, MA: MIT Press.

Kayne, R. 1984. *Connectedness and binary branching*. Dordrecht: Foris.

Kayne, R. 1991. Romance clitics, verb movement, and PRO. *Linguistic Inquiry* 22:647–686.

Lasnik, H. 1999. *Minimalist analyses*. Oxford: Blackwell.

Leeuw, F. van der 1997. *Clitics*. The Hague: Holland Academic Graphics.

May, R. 1985. *Logical form*. Cambridge, MA: MIT Press.

Nespor, M., and I. Vogel. 1986. *Prosodic phonology*. Dordrecht: Foris.

Nunes, J. 2004. *Linearization of chains and sideward movement*. Cambridge, MA: MIT Press.

Otero, C. 1996. Head movement, cliticization, precompilation and word insertion. In R. Freidin, ed., *Current issues in comparative grammar*. Dordrecht: Kluwer.

Perlmutter, D. 1971. *Deep and surface constraints in syntax*. New York: Holt, Rinehart and Winston.

Pollock, J.-Y. 1989. Verb movement, universal grammar and the structure of IP. *Linguistic Inquiry* 20:365–424.

Postal, P. 1969. On so-called "pronouns" in English. In D. A. Reibel and S. A. Schane, eds., *Modern studies in English: Readings in transformational grammar*, 201–224. Englewood Cliffs, NJ: Prentice Hall.

Raposo, E. 1973. Sobre a Forma *o* em Português. *Boletim de Filologia* 22:361–415.

Raposo, E. 1987. Case theory and Infl-to-Comp: The inflected infinitive in European Portuguese. *Linguistic Inquiry* 18:85–109.

Raposo, E. 1999. Some observations on the pronominal system of Portuguese. In Z. Borras and J. Sola, eds., *Catalan Working Papers in Linguistics* 6:59–93.

Raposo, E. 2000. Clitic positions and verb movement. In J. Costa, ed., *Portuguese syntax: New comparative studies*, 266–297. Oxford: Oxford University Press.

Raposo, E. 2003. Case theory and participle agreement in Romance. In I. Castro and I. Duarte, eds., *Razões e emoção: Miscelânea de estudos para Maria Helena Mateus*. Lisbon: Colibri.

Raposo, E., and J. Uriagereka. 1996. Indefinite SE. *Natural Language and Linguistic Theory* 14:749–810.

Raposo, E., and J. Uriagereka. 2005. Clitic placement in Western Iberian: A minimalist view. In R. Kayne and G. Cinque, eds., *Handbook of comparative grammar*, 639–697. Oxford: Oxford University Press.

Rizzi, L. 1997. The fine structure of the left periphery. In L. Haegeman, ed., *Elements of grammar: Handbook of generative syntax*, 281–337. Dordrecht: Kluwer.

Ross, J. R. 1969. A proposed rule of tree pruning. In D. A. Reibel and S. A. Schane, eds., *Modern studies in English: Readings in transformational grammar*, 288–299. Englewood Cliffs, NJ: Prentice Hall.

Uriagereka, J. 1995. An F position in Western Romance. In K. Kiss, ed., *Discourse configurational languages*. Oxford: Oxford University Press.

Uriagereka, J. 1996. Formal and substantive elegance in the Minimalist Program. In M. Bierwisch, H.-M. Gärtner, and C. Wilder, eds., *The role of economy principles in linguistic theory*. Berlin: Akademie-Verlag.

Wanner, D. 1991. The Tobler-Moussafia law in Old Spanish. In H. Campos and F. Martinez-Gil, eds., *Current Studies in Spanish Linguistics*. Washington, DC: Georgetown University Press.

Wanner, D. 1996. Second position clitics in Western Romance. In A. L. Halpern and A. M. Zwicky, eds., *Approaching second: Second position clitics and related phenomena*, 537–578. Stanford, CA: CSLI.

22 Missing Obliques: Some Anomalies in Ojibwe Syntax

Richard A. Rhodes

22.1 Introduction

Algonquian syntax is hard: it puts familiar kinds of syntactic patterns together in unfamiliar ways. For example, it marks disjoint reference (obviative) instead of coreference (reflexive). Obviatives appear in exactly the same class of structures in which reflexives appear crosslinguistically (Rhodes 1991a). Algonquian languages support Dryer's (1986) position that primary and secondary object configuration can be underived, contra Relational Grammar (henceforth RG) (Rhodes 1990). Algonquian languages have a surfeit of agent suppressing (or object highlighting) operations, a middle, two clearly distinct passive constructions, and, in some languages, a productive indefinite actor construction (Rhodes 1991b), alongside the type of inverse agreement system that reverses subjects and primary objects syntactically (Rhodes 1976; Perlmutter and Rhodes 1988; Zuñiga 2006). Finally, Algonquian syntax is hard because it brings us face to face with the syntax-morphology interface. One does not know a priori if the ungrammaticality of a test sentence is due to syntactic constraints or to morphological ones (Rhodes 1993b).

One of the ways to make Algonquian syntax more accessible is to use as a metalanguage those theoretical tools that highlight the most significant aspects of the syntactic patterns and background the rather substantial, but entirely derivative, morphological overhead. Since Algonquian languages are free word-order languages—that is, they use word order to signal discourse functions (Tomlin and Rhodes 1979)—and have very flat phrase structures, most of their syntax has to do with adjustments in grammatical relations. Since grammatical relations are reflected primarily in agreements and obviation rather than structure per se, the tools of RG serve well for describing Algonquian syntactic patterns. One can see this in contrast to an approach based on X-bar, which treats grammatical relations as derivative of structure and requires structures that would have to be disassembled to get the correct (lack of) surface phrasal groupings (e.g., Reinholtz 1999).[1] Thus in the following discussion I will use RG to highlight the syntactic patterns of Ojibwe, but will not be bound by strict adherence to the parts of the theory of RG that are problematic for Algonquian syntax, particularly the Universal Alignment Hypothesis and the Chômeur Law (Perlmutter and Postal 1983).

In this chapter I want to focus on an oddity of Algonquian syntax that has heretofore gone unnoticed. Algonquian languages are radically head marking, so much so that their lexicons and productive syntax are organized so as to largely avoid oblique nominals. In some Algonquian languages no more than a single oblique nominal per clause is permitted (outside of adjuncts marking setting). They have no verbs that license more than a single oblique, and even those are rarely used with an overt oblique. Furthermore, those oblique nominals that are present are syntactically ambiguous between being nominal and being adverbial. In the lexicon they have verbal morphemes that should, by their semantics, license oblique nominals but do not. Finally, the syntax of Algonquian languages conspires (in the sense of Kisseberth 1970) to avoid the creation of oblique nominals, either by suppression or by reranking of displaced nominals to a nonoblique grammatical relation. Involved in this conspiracy are all of the many rules reranking grammatical relations, and the half head-marked grammatical relation, the relative root complement just mentioned. In this chapter I will show how this conspiracy works in the Ottawa dialect of Ojibwe.

This chapter is divided into three sections. In the first I will show how the lexicon of Ojibwe is structured to avoid oblique nominals. In the second I will show how a new and unique grammatical relation, the relative root construction (Rhodes 2006), works to fill in much of the lexical gap created by the avoidance of truly oblique nominals. In the final section I will show how the various rules that rerank grammatical relations are organized to avoid creating oblique nominals.

22.2 The Missing Obliques of Ojibwe

At first blush, Ojibwe appears unremarkable with respect to nominals looking like obliques, as the following examples would suggest:[2]

(1) a. Nii-nokii **ngitgaanensing**. (Bl S15)
  ni-wii=anokii **ni-gitigaanens-ing**
  1SUBJ-FUT=work **1POSS-garden-LOC**
  'I will work **in my garden**.'
 b. Niidgemaagan nnanaamdabmi **biindig wiikwaaming**. (Bl S41)
  ni-wiidgemaagan ni-nanaamadabi-mi(n) **biindig wiikwaam-ing**
  1POSS-spouse 1SUBJ-sit.around-1PL **inside house-LOC**
  'My wife and I were sitting **in the house**.'

c. Gii-biinjse **dkibiing**. (Bl S67)
   gii=biinjise-w   **dakibi(w)-ing**
   PAST=fly.in-3SUBJ **spring-LOC**
   'It flew **into the spring**.'

d. **Wninjiing** bkitew. (Bl S796)
   o-ninji-ing   bakitew-i.
   3POSS$_i$-**hand-LOC** hit-IMPER.3OBJ$_i$.
   'Hit him **on his hand**.'

But a closer look reveals that the syntax of the sentences in (1) is not what it seems. To understand this we need to make a brief excursus into the syntax of obliques.

22.2.1 Two Kinds of Oblique Constructions

While much has been written, particularly in the literature of RG, about the typology of core clausal nominals, there is relatively little literature developing a typology of obliques. This is not surprising. They display little syntax aside from being the victims of rules that either assign them to core grammatical relations or simply move them from less marked to more marked places in clausal word order. The sole exception seems to be chômeurs in RG (Perlmutter and Postal 1977). When a change in the assignment of grammatical relations in a clause results in the loss of a grammatical relation by a nominal, then that nominal becomes a specific kind of oblique: one that is inert to all further syntactic operations, or in RG terms, a chômeur. Because not much syntax per se is associated with obliques, many of the arguments about obliques are based as much on semantic readings as on syntactic properties. This will be obvious in the first set of distinctions we need to make.

Oblique nominals play important roles in discourse structure. Grimes (1975) distinguishes seven types of information in (monologic) discourse: event, participant orientation, setting, explanation, evaluation, discourse irrealis, and performative information. This typology does not directly correlate with distinctions in form and so has not been incorporated into syntactic analysis. However, events are almost always in some kind of clausal form and explanations commonly are.

(2) He went to bed, because he was tired.
    Event   *Explanation*

But participant orientation, evaluation, and performative information can be signaled in a variety of formal ways: by morphological means or by modification of either parts of the clause or the whole clause, or even by lexical choice.[3] For our purposes, it will suffice to say that oblique nominal constructions are widely used to convey nonevent information, especially setting and evaluation information, as in the examples in (3).

(3) a. *Setting*
   i. Barry watched TV **in the living room**.
   ii. The moon rose **at 3 this morning**.
  b. *Evaluation*
   i. Arnold watched his ratings drop **with dismay**.
   ii. The car rounded the corner **at high speed**.

We need to distinguish between the kinds of oblique nominals exemplified in (3) and the kinds of oblique nominals like those in (4), in which the oblique nominal is directly connected to the semantics of the verb.

(4) a. Mark found the milk **in the refrigerator**.
  b. Janice moved the milk **from the refrigerator to the table**.
  c. Garry talked **to Maybelle about his heart problem**.

In (4a) the location is implicit in the finding. That is, one finds things in particular locations, so the existence of a location follows from our understanding of what it means to find something. Similarly, the notion of moving in (4b) entails that the moved object had an original location, it followed a path, and it ended up at a final location. And finally in (4c), talking entails interlocutors and topics. In such cases we say that the oblique nominals in question are licensed by the verb.

Oblique nominals licensed by verbs like those in (4) contrast with those in (3), in that all events take place in time and space, and reference to the specific time and place is therefore about the clause as a whole and does not properly belong to the verb. Similarly, speakers reporting events can give evaluative information about the event as a whole (3b). In standard X-bar based syntactic analyses, the obliques in (3) come from high in the phrase structure, while those in (4) are part of θ-role assignment in the VP. The claim I want to make about Ojibwe in particular and about Algonquian in general is that an extraordinary number of verbal morphemes that logically should entail the licensing of oblique nominals do not.

Looking through the lexicon of Ojibwe (or any Algonquian language for that matter), one runs across a number of morphemes like those in (5) that express a relationship between two objects or between a path and an object (in Langacker's (1987) terminology, between a trajector and a landmark).

(5) a. aazh- 'across'
   gii-**aazh**ge
   'He went across [a bridge, a river].'
   gii-**aazh**debzo
   'He drove across someone's path.'
   aazhoogam
   'across the lake'

b. baazhid- 'over [a barrier]'
gii-**baazhj**i-gwaashkni
'He jumped over [it].'
gii-**baazhd**agnaandam
'He hit a home run.'
wgii-**baazhd**ahaan
'He stepped over it.'
c. negw- 'under'
gii-**neg**oode
'He crawled under [it].'
gii-**negw**aabi
'He looked out from underneath.'
wgii-**neg**sidoon
'He placed it underneath.'
d. zhaabw-
wgii-**zhaabw**aabndaan
'He [could] see it through [it].'
gii-**zhaab**batoo
'He ran through [it].'
gii-**zhaabw**aakzo
'He was burned through.'

In most non-Algonquian languages such morphemes license, at least optionally, a syntactic realization of the landmark, generally as an oblique, but not in Ojibwe, as the examples in (6) show.

(6) a. aazh- 'across'
 *gii-**aazh**ge ziibi
 'He went across the river.'
 ??gii-**aazh**ge ziibing
 'He went across the river.'
 b. baazhid- 'over [a barrier]'
 *gii-**baazhj**i-gwaashkni mjigkan/mjigkaning
 'He jumped over the fence.'
 c. negw- 'under in an enclosed space'
 *wgii-**neg**sidoon naagan/naagning
 'He placed it underneath a dish.'
 d. zhaabw-
 *wgii-**zhaabw**aabndaan gboojgan/gboojganing
 'He [could] see it through the curtains.'

The landmarks associated with morphemes like those in (6) can only be expressed in one of three ways: with a derivational morpheme as in (7a), as the object of the verb as in (7b), or as a setting adverbial as in (7c). Most morphemes in this semantic class allow only one or two of these options. Some do not allow any. Furthermore, which of the options is available is determined not just by the trajector/landmark morpheme but by the full word form.

(7) a. aazh- 'across'
   aazhoogaam
   'across the lake'
   b. baazhid- 'over [a barrier]'
   wgii-**baazhd**ahaan
   'He stepped over it.'
   c. negw- 'down in(to) [an enclosed space], under'
   Mii dash gaa-zhichged aw gwiiwens gii-**neg**ooded <u>naami-nbaagan</u>.
   mii   dash CHANGE-gii=izhichige-d   aw   gwiiwens
   EMPH EMPH REL.CL=PAST=do-3SUBJ.C that boy
   gii=**negw**.oode-d   <u>anaami=nibaagan</u>
   PAST=crawl.**under**-3SUBJ.C <u>under=bed</u>
   'That's what the boy did, he crawled **down in** <u>under the bed</u>.'[4] (Bl T31.32)

The morphosyntax of this class of forms is more complex than I can fully address here. However, I do need to note that there are a few morphemes of this type that do license nominal obliques. The two most common trajector/landmark morphemes, *biind-* 'in' and *zaag(id)-* 'out', are in this class. It is the syntax of these morphemes that allows us to identify, by contrast, the fact that most trajector/landmark morphemes can only be associated with setting adverbials and not true obliques. Examples are given in (8).

(8) biind- 'in'
   a. gii-**biinj**se
      'He flew in.'
   b. Gii-**biinj**se dkibiing. (Bl S67)
      gii=biinjise-w   **dakibi(w)-ing**
      PAST=fly.in-3SUBJ **spring-LOC**
      'It flew **into** <u>the spring</u>.' (= [1c])

(9) zaag(id)- 'out'
   a. **zaagj**ibhiwewag
      'They run/ran out.'

b. Mii gii-gjibhiwewaad; **zaagj**ibhiwewag wiigwaamwaang, waakaahganing.
mii gii=gijibahiwe-waa-d; **zaagid**.ibahiwe-w-ag o-wiigwaam-iwaa-ing.
EMPH PAST=run.away-3PL-3SUBJ.C run.**out**-3SUBJ-3PL 3POSS-house-3PL-LOC
waakaahigan-ing.
fort-LOC
'They fled, running **out of** their house[s] and **out of** the fort.' (R2.1.188)

But even with such verbs, there is the option of treating the landmark as a setting adverbial rather than as an oblique nominal. For example, in (10) the locative phrase is an appositive phrase *maa mndoodoowgamgong*, lit. 'there, in/at/on the sweat lodge'.

(10) Mii dash gii-ziignamwaad, gaa-**biindge**yooded maa mndoodoowgamgong, iw mshkikwaaboo wii-wmbaabteg.
mii dash gii-ziiginam=owaa-d, CHANGE-gii=**biindige**-oode-d maa
EMPH EMPH PAST=pour-3PL-3SUBJ.C REL.CL-PAST=crawl.**in**-3SUBJ.C there
mandoodoowigamigw-ing iw mashkikwaaboo wii-ombaabiteg
sweatlodge-LOC that medicine FUT=steam.up-3INAN.SUBJ.C.
'Then, after he had crawled **into** the sweat lodge, they poured the medicine [onto the hot rocks] so it would turn to vapor.' (lit. '... when he had crawled **in** there at the sweat lodge...') (Bl T21.6)

There is much more to be said about the syntax of obiques in general, and about the nominal-adverbial cline that is so important to that syntax. For the purposes of this inquiry it is enough to observe that Ojibwe both avoids oblique nominals lexically and pushes even the oblique nominals that are there more into the syntax of adverbials than of nominals.

22.3 Relative Root Complements

Having just shown that nominal obliques are less common than one might expect, I turn to examine a construction that enables Ojibwe (and all of Algonquian for that matter) to cover the semantic space normally allocated to nominal obliques. There are a very large number of Ojibwe verbs containing morphemes that, in contrast with the limitations just discussed, do license an oblique in the clause. What is different with these morphemes, however, is that the syntax of this construction is unusual, if not typologically unique. In various ways the construction in question splits the difference between the syntax of core arguments and obliques. A full description of this syntax can be found in Rhodes 2006. In this chapter I will simply summarize the crucial points.

Ojibwe contains a small number of morphemes having, for the most part, preposition-like meanings, locative, goal, source, and extent. These are listed in (11).[5]

(11) akw-   'a certain length, so long'
    apiit-   'a certain extent, so much'
    daN-   'in a certain place' (short gloss: 'at')
    das(w)-   'a certain number, so many'
    iN-   'in a certain direction, in a certain way' (short gloss: 'to', 'like')
    ond-   'from a certain place, for a certain reason' (short gloss: 'from', 'because of')

Verbs containing these morphemes license an obligatory slot in the clause, as exemplified in (12). In (12) the licensing morpheme, the relative root, is in bold and its complement (henceforth RRC) is underlined.

(12) *Relative root complement construction*
   Niniing-sh go naa wgii-**n**aabmaan niwi mnidoon.
   aniniw$_k$-ing =sh   go   naa   o$_i$-gii=**in**$_k$-aabam-aa$_j$-an   niwi
   man$_k$-LOC EMPH EMPH EMPH 3ERG$_i$-PAST=**like**$_k$-see-AN.1OBJ$_j$-OBV this.OBV
   manidoo$_j$-an.
   spirit$_j$-OBV
   'He$_i$ saw the spirit$_j$ **in the form of** a man$_k$.' (2R.3.20)

From the fact that the sentence in (12) is transitive, we can see that the RRC is not a direct object. Further examination shows that the syntax of RRCs is distinct from the treatment of both primary objects with the more elaborate object agreements ((12a) illustrates agreement with an inanimate primary object and (12b) with an animate one) and secondary objects with only *n*-registration as agreement as in (13).[6]

(13) a. Ngii-gnd**aan** wiiyaas.
       ni-gii=gond-**am**$_i$-**n**$_i$ wiiyaas$_i$.
       1SUBJ-PAST=swallow-INAN.1OBJ$_i$-N$_i$ meat$_i$
       'I swallowed the meat.' (Bl S395)
    b. Piniin wdamw**aan**.
       apini$_i$-an   o(d)-amw-**aa**$_i$-an
       potato$_i$-OBV 3ERG-eat-AN.1OBJ$_i$-OBV
       'He is eating potatoes.' (Bl S329)

(14) a. Nbiish ngii-mnikwe**n**.
       nimbiish$_i$ ni-gii=minikwe-**n**$_i$.
       water$_i$ 1SUBJ-PAST=drink-N$_i$.
       'I drank some water.' (Bl S159)
    b. Miinwaa mtigoons wgii-nokaazo**n** gii-bshanzhehang...
       miinawaa mitigoons$_i$ o-gii=anokaazo-**n**$_i$ gii-bashanzheh=am-g
       and   stick$_i$ 3ERG-PAST=put.to.use-N$_i$ PAST=whip-INAN.1OBJ-3SUBJ.C
       'And she used a stick to whip it...' (Bl T20.16)

The syntax of relative root constructions is distinct from the syntax both of objects and of obliques. The following examples will illustrate this. As we have just seen, objects trigger agreements. RRCs do not; (15b) is ungrammatical.

(15) a. Gii-zhaa shpimsagong.
     gii=izhaa-(w)   ishpimisagw-ing
     PAST=go.to-3SUBJ upstairs-LOC
     'He went upstairs.' (Bl S54)
   b. *Wgii-zhaan shpimsag(ong).
     o-gii=izhaa-n   ishpimisagw(-ing)
     3ERG-PAST=go.to-N upstairs(-LOC)

In this way RRCs are like obliques. They also share with obliques the property that they cannot be made obviative. This assertion requires us to take a brief excursion into the syntax of obviation in general.

22.3.1 Obviation

The syntax and morphosyntax of obviation are quite complex. They have three basic parameters, morphological, syntactic, and functional. I will deal with these in reverse order.

At text level, obviation can be used to help track participant reference, but in Ojibwe, at least, this function has been largely grammaticalized away. I will have nothing more to say about that aspect here. At sentence and clause level, obviation is almost completely syntactic. Within clauses it is completely syntactic. There is a controller and a victim. The controller imposes on the victim the property of being obviative. The syntactic property of being obviative may or may not be overtly marked, depending on the morphosyntactic properties of the obviated nominal—only grammatical animates can be overtly marked for obviation. The general syntactic conditions on clausemate obviation are the following:[7]

(16) a. Only third-person animates may control obviation.
   b. Control of obviation follows the relational hierarchy.
   c. Only terms may be obviated.
   d. There is at most one term in a clause that is not obviated (i.e., obviation is obligatory).

The sentences in (17) show that obviation is only induced by third-person animates (16a) and that there is at most one nonobviative term (16d).[8]

(17) a. Nwaabmaa nini/*ninwan.
     ni-waabam-aa   aniniw / *aniniw-an
     1SUBJ-waabam-3AN.OBJ man / *man-OBV
     'I see the man (*obv).'

b. Gwaabmaa nini/*ninwan.
   gi-waabam-aa   aniniw / *aniniw-an
   2SUBJ-waabam-3AN.OBJ man / *man-OBV
   'You (sg.) see the man (*obv).'
c. Owaabmaan ninwan/*nini.
   o-waabam-aa-an   aniniw-an / *aniniw
   3ERG$_i$-waabam-3AN.OBJ$_j$-OBV$_j$ man$_j$-OBV$_j$ / *man$_j$
   'He sees the man (obv.)/*man (prox.).'

The following examples show that obviation follows the relational hierarchy (16b). The subject controls obviation of the primary object in (18), the subject controls obviation of the secondary object in (19), and the primary object controls obviation of a secondary object in (20).[9]

(18) Moozhwen wdayaawaan.
   moozhwe-**an** o(d)-ayaaw-aa-**an**
   scarf-**OBV**   3SUBJ-have-3AN.OBJ-**OBV**
   'He has a scarf.'

(19) a. Wgii-bwen**an** giigoony**an**.
      o-gii=abwe-n-**an**   giigoony-**an**
      3SUBJ-PAST=roast-N-**OBV** fish-**OBV**
      'He roasted the fish.'
   b. Giigoony**an** wgii-bwen**an**.
      giigoony-**an** o-gii=abwe-n-**an**
      fish-**OBV**   3SUBJ-PAST=roast-N-**OBV**
      'He roasted a fish.'

(20) a. Ngii-miinaag semaan giwi kiwenziinyag.
      ni-gii=miin-aa-**ag**   asemaa-**an** giwi akiwenziiny-**ag**
      1SUBJ-PAST=give-3AN.OBJ-PL tobacco-**OBV** those old.men-**PL**
      'I gave the old men tobacco.'
   b. Ngii-miinaag giwi kiwenziinyag semaan.
      ni-gii=miin-aa-**ag**   giwi akiwenziiny-**ag** asemaa-**an**
      1SUBJ-PAST=give-3AN.OBJ-PL those old.men-**PL**   tobacco-**OBV**
      'I gave the old men the tobacco.'

Finally, the sentences in (21) and (22) show that obviation cannot be triggered on nonterms (16c). Contrast (21), in which the subject controls obviation of the primary object, with (22), in which the subject does not control obviation of the locative, even though the locative and potential controller are clausemates in the appropriate relational configuration.

(21) Daabaanan wdayaawaan.
    odaabaan-**an** o(d)-ayaaw-aa-**an**
    car-**OBV**   3SUBJ-have-3AN.OBJ-**OBV**
    'He has a car.'

(22) a. Daabaan**ing** gii-boozi.
       odaabaan-**ing** gii=boozi-w
       car-**LOC**   PAST=get.in.vehicle-3SUBJ
       'He got in the car.'
    b. *Daabaan**ni**ng/Daabaan**an** gii-boozi.
       odaabaan-**ini**-ing / odaabaan-**an** gii=boozi-w
       car-**OBV-LOC** / car-**OBV**   PAST=get.in.vehicle-3SUBJ

This is the point of the excursus into the syntax of obviation: obliques are outside of the scope of obviation.

22.3.2 Obviation and Relative Root Complements

The test case to see if an RRC is obviatable is one in which the RRC is a grammatical animate like that in (12). Note that the form *niniing* 'man' there is locative and not obviative (which would be *ninwan* or possibly *ninwining*), showing that RRCs are not within the scope of obviation.

22.3.3 Relative Root Complement as a Grammatical Relation

RRCs, however, are like core arguments in several ways. First, they have null definite readings.

(23) Baamaa go ga-zhaami.
    baa(ni)maa go   (gi)-ga=**izh**aa-mi(n)
    afterward EMPH 2SUBJ-FUT=go.**to**-1PL
    'Afterward we'll *inc* go **there**.' (Bl S45)

In this they contrast with those few verbs that optionally license true nominal obliques like *boozid* 'embark'. In (24a) *boozid* licenses an oblique locative, but when there no explicit locative, as in (24b), there is nothing semantically or syntactically available in the clause.

(24) a. **Jiimaaning** ngii-boozmi miinwaa bezhig kwe, ...
       jiimaaning ni-gii=boozi-mi(n)   miinawaa bezhig kwe
       boat-LOC   1SUBJ-PAST=embark-1PL and   one   woman
       'She and I and another woman got into **a canoe**, ...' (Bl T5.2)
    b. Mii dash ge nii gii-boozyaan.
       mii dash ge nii(n) gii=boozi-yaan
       EMPH EMPH also I   PAST=embark-1SUBJ.C

'Then I, too, got on board.'[10] (Bl T8.9)
*'Then I, too, boarded **it**.'

That the vehicle implicit in the meaning of *boozid* is not syntactically available can also be shown by the fact that it is in an anaphoric island. Thus the sentence in (25) can only have the temporal reading and not the relative clause reading.[11]

(25) Gii-boozi, gaa-boozyaanh.
    gii=boozi-w   CHANGE-gii=boozi-yaanh
    PAST=embark-3SUBJ REL.CL-PAST=embark-1SUBJ.C
    'He got in the boat/car/train/plane after I had gotten in.'
    *'He got in the boat/car/train/plane that I got in.'

The second way that RRCs are like core arguments is that they can be the target of advancement. In relative clause formation all obliques, other than temporals, must be advanced to RRC to be the head of a relative clause, as in the locative head on (26b) and the instrumental head on (27b). Incidentally, this is prime facie evidence that RRC is a grammatical relation.

(26) a. Wii-mkadewag wiigwaaming.
       wii=makadeke-w-ag wiigiwaam-ing
       FUT=fast-3SUBJ-3PL   house-LOC
       'They will fast in the house.'
   b. ...[adv [rel.cl waa-dzhi-mkadekewaad] wiigwaaming]
       CHANGE-wii=**dazhi**=makadeke-waa-d wiigiwaam-ing
       REL.CL-FUT=**at**=fast-3PL-3SUBJ.C   house-LOC
       '... in the shelter where they would fast' (Bl T23.3)

(27) a. Wii-mno-yaawag iw zhoon'yaa.[12]
       wii=mino=ayaa-w-ag   iw   zhooniyaa
       FUT=good=be.(at)-3SUBJ-3PL that money
       'They will live comfortably with that money.'
   b. ...[NP iw zhoon'yaa [rel.cl waa-wnji-mno-yaawaad]]
       iw   zhooniyaa CHANGE-wii=**onji**=mino=ayaa-waa-d
       that money   REL.CL-FUT=**from**=good=be.(at)-3PL-3SUBJ.C
       '... the money with which they can live comfortably' (Bl T15.1)

Table 22.1 summarizes the basic facts relating to RRCs. These facts show that they are not obliques. While there is much more to the syntax of RRCs, this outline of the basic facts allows us to see that Ojibwe avoids nominal obliques by having a typologically rare grammatical relation that treats a large class of logically oblique nominals as being semi-head-marked. Seen in the larger perspective, this is a second way that Ojibwe—and all of Algonquian for that matter—avoids nominal obliques.

Table 22.1
Syntactic differences between RRC's and obliques

	Subj	1Obj	2Obj	RRC	Obl
Trigger verb agreement	+	+	+	−	−
Obviation possible	+	+	+	−	−
Understood definite reading	+	+	+	+	−
Target of advancement	+	+	+	+	−

22.4 Missing Chômeurs

The final, and most thorough, part of the conspiracy to avoid nominal obliques in Algonquian is the fact that no rule that reassigns grammatical relations has the side effect of requiring a nominal to be expressed as an oblique. It is one of the most significant insights of RG that rules reassigning grammatical relations can have the effect of creating a particular class of nominals, known in RG terminology as chômeurs, which are cast as oblique-marked nominals in many languages. Chômeurs arise just in case the nominal that holds a particular grammatical relation notionally has that relation reassigned to another nominal. For example, in a passive the notional subject is replaced as subject by the notional object. In RG terms, the notional subject of a passive is *overrun*. The fate of nominals that have been overrun is, in most languages, that they must either be deleted or that they appear as obliques. What is different about Algonquian languages in general, and Ojibwe in particular, is that overrun nominals never appear as obliques. Either they are deleted or they appear as objects—either primary or secondary objects, depending on the construction.

If there were only a few rules that reassign grammatical relations this would be unremarkable, but there are four types of rules that create subjects, three types that create primary objects, and several more that create secondary objects or RRCs. Only the rules reassigning subjecthood and primary objecthood ever result in overtly expressed overrun nominals. In the following sections I will review all rules that overrun nominals and show that none of them result in obliques. In RG terms, there are no nominal chômeurs in Ojibwe.[13]

In the following discussion I will use the logic and terminology of RG but will also use a number of grammatical relations that are not part of classical RG. The nontraditional grammatical relations I will use are as follows: 2 for primary object, 3 for secondary object, RRC for relational root complement, and INCORP for incorporated nominals. I have argued extensively for this treatment of objects in Rhodes 1990 and for the status of RRC in Rhodes 2006.

22.4.1 Overrun Objects as Terms: Advancements and Ascensions

The first set of rules that could potentially create chômeurs are those in constructions in which object arcs are overrun by either the advancement or ascension of another nominal to 2.

Certain obliques, namely benefactives and affectees, advance to 2. All such advancements are obligatory.[14] When the initial clause is transitive, there is an overrun relation. The sentence in (28) exemplifies such a case.

(28) Wgii-zhitmawaan e-gaachning wiigwaamens.
    o-gii=ozhit-amaw-aa-an   e=gaachin-ini-g
    3ERG-PAST=make-APPL-3AN.OBJ-OBV REL.CL=small-OBV-INAN.SUBJ
    wiigwaam-ens-∅[15]
    house-DIM-OBV
    'He made him a little hut.'

Crucially the relative clause, *e-gaachninig* 'that is small', modifying *wiigwaamens* 'hut', shows obviative agreement, guaranteeing that the latter is a term because, as I claimed above (16c), obliques are outside the scope of obviation. Thus, I posit that *wiigwaamens* 'hut' has retreated to the status of secondary object [3], as represented in the stratal diagram in (29). Crucially, the overrun 2 is reranked to 3, and is thus not a chômeur.

(29)
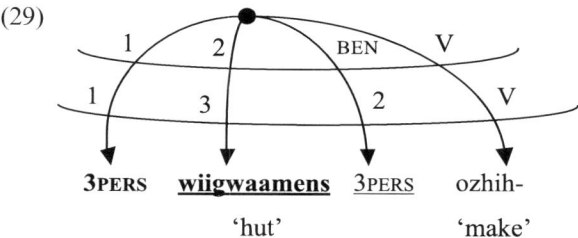

Similarly, another case of overrun of an object is seen in examples with possessor ascension in which the primary object is the host, as shown in (30):

(30) Ngii-bnaajtamwaa wjiimaan.
    Ni-gii=banaajit-amaw-aa   o-jiimaan
    1SUBJ-PAST=ruin-APPL-3AN.OBJ 3POSS-boat
    'I ruined his canoe.'

The animate object agreement on the verb in (30) shows that the possessor is the final 2.[16] However, arguing for the termhood of the possessee is more complex than with benefactive/affectee advancement. Since possessors govern obviation in their possessees, we need to be able to distinguish obviation induced by possession from term-governed obviation. Only third-person possessors induce obviation in their possessees, and therefore we turn to a clause with a first-person possessor to make the argument.[17]

(31) Mii dash gii-bnaajtamwid ndoodaabaanan.
mii   dash gii=banaajit-amaw-i-d   ni(nd)-odaabaan-**an**
EMPH EMPH PAST=see-APPL-1OBJ-3SUBJ 1POSS-car-**OBV**
'Then he ruined my car.'

Crucially *daabaan* 'car' is a victim of obviation, which guarantees that it is a term by the condition on victims of obviation that they be terms (16c). Thus, I posit that *daabaan* 'car' has retreated to the status of secondary object [3], as represented in the stratal diagram in (32).

(32)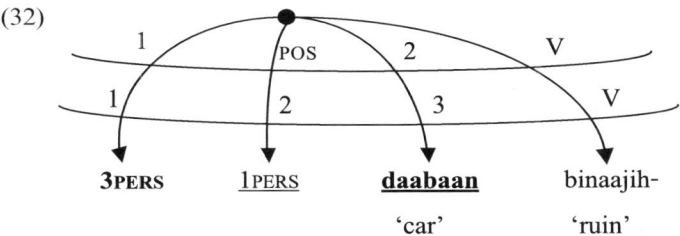

Again the overrun 2 is reranked to 3, and is thus not a chômeur. Possessor ascension does not produce nominal obliques.

22.4.2 Overrun 1s as Terms: The Inverse

In most languages, passives would be an obvious place to look for overrun 1s, but, in Ottawa, passives are obligatorily agentless and therefore produce no chômeurs (Rhodes 1991b). However, Algonquian languages do not disappoint: there is a typologically rare and hard-to-analyze construction, the inverse, which, under the analysis developed below, has an overrun 1 that surfaces as a term arc, specifically a 2.

Algonquian is famous for having verb forms in pairs in which the external agreement patterns are identical but an internal inflection signals which of the external agreement markers refer to the subject and which to the object. Examples of such verb pairs are given in (33), with inflections underlined and the direct and inverse markers in bold.

(33) *Direct inverse*

n̲waabm**aa**   n̲waabm**ig**   'I see him.'   'He sees me.'
n̲waabm**aa**g   n̲waabm**ig**oog   'I see them.'   'They see me.'
n̲waabm**aa**n̲aa   n̲waabm**ig**n̲aa   'We (ex.) see him.'   'He sees us (ex.).'
n̲waabm**aa**n̲aanig   n̲waabm**ig**n̲aanig   'We (ex.) see them.'   'They see us (ex.).'

The analysis of this construction has generated a large literature in several theories, including discussions of whether clause-level syntax is the proper domain for its analysis. (See Rhodes 1994 for arguments that it is.) In RG there are, however, only two discussions of the phenomenon, Rhodes 1976 and Perlmutter and Rhodes 1988. In both works evidence is presented that clauses containing inverse verb forms have a syntactic reversal of the initial grammatical relations, as sketched in (34).

(34)
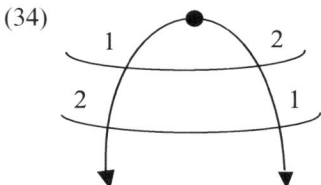

The synonymous sentences in (35) exemplify the construction. (35a) is the monostratal version, called direct in Algonquianist terminology. (35b) is the inverse version, with a structure like that in (34).

(35) a. Wnichiiwhaan aw kwe.
    o-nichiwih-**aa**-an   aw   akwew
    3SUBJ-yell.at-**3AN.OBJ**-OBV that woman
    'The woman yells at him.'
  b. Wnichiiwhigoon niw kwewan.
    o-nichiwih-**igo**-an   niw   akwew-an
    3SUBJ-yell.at-**INV**-OBV that.OBV woman-OBV
    'The woman yells at him.' (see Bloomfield 1958, ex. 603)

Because Rhodes 1976 was focused on accounting for the morphology and Perlmutter and Rhodes 1988 was never published, I will spend the rest of this section outlining the basic arguments for analyzing inverse clauses as containing their final 1s and 2s reversed from their initial alignment.

The general form of the argument is that initial 2s of inverse clauses share properties with 1s, whether the comparison 1s are underived as in monostratal clauses, both intransitive and transitive, or derived final 1s in multistratal clauses, such as passives. Conversely, initial 1s in inverse clauses share properties with 2s in monostratal transitive clauses.

22.4.2.1 Initial 2s of Inverses as 1s First let us consider the morphology. Inversion is found primarily in independent inflection.[18] In conjuncts it is limited to clauses containing two third persons. I will examine each case separately.

In independent monostratal clauses, first-person 1s are marked with the prefix *ni*-, as in (36).

(36) a. **n**giiwe
 'I'm going home.'
 b. **n**waabmaa
 'I see him.'

In passive clauses, initial 2s are final 1s. Again in both types of Ottawa passive clauses, initial first-person 2s are marked with *ni-*, as in (37).

(37) a. **n**waabmigoo
 'I'm seen.' (Passive I)
 b. **n**waabmigaaz
 'I'm seen.' (Passive II)

A parallel pattern obtains for second person. Second-person 1s are marked with the prefix *gi-*, shown in (38), as are the second-person subjects of passive, shown in (39).

(38) a. **g**giiwe
 'You (sg.) are going home.'
 b. **g**waabmaa
 'You (sg.) see him.'

(39) a. **g**waabmigoo
 'You (sg.) are seen.' (Passive I)
 b. **g**waabmigaaz
 'You (sg.) are seen.' (Passive II)

The first piece of evidence favoring an analysis of inverse clauses as containing reversed grammatical relations is given in (40). The initial 2s of inverse clauses are marked with *ni-* for first person and *gi-* for second person.

(40) a. **n**waabmig 'He sees me.'
 (cf. (36b), the corresponding direct)
 b. **g**waabmig 'He sees you (sg.).'
 (cf. (38b), the corresponding direct)

A parallel argument can be made from the marking of plurality. Monostratal transitive clauses mark the plurality of their 1s with *-naa(n)* for first person and *-waa* for second person, as shown in (41).

(41) a. **n**waabmaa**naa**
 'We (excl.) see him.' (cf. (36b), the corresponding singular)
 b. **g**waabmaa**naa**
 'We (incl.) see him.'
 c. **g**waabmaa**waa**
 'You (pl.) see him.' (cf. (38b), the corresponding singular)

Inverse clauses mark the plurality of their initial 2s with -*naa(n)* for first person and -*waa* for second person, as shown in (42).

(42) a. **n**waabmig**naa**
  'He sees us (excl.).' (cf. (40a), the corresponding singular)
 b. **g**waabmig**naa**
  'He sees us (excl.).'
 c. **g**waabmig**waa**
  'He sees you (pl.).' (cf. (40b), the corresponding singular)

Now let us turn to the syntactic evidence for the subjecthood of initial 2s. First, since control of obviation follows the relational hierarchy, the fact that initial 2s in inverse clauses control the obviation of other terms in the clause shows that they are 1s. An example is given in (43).

(43) Wwaabmigoon aw kiwenziinh niw shkinwen.
  o-waabam-igo-an aw akiwenziinh niw ashkiniwe-an
  3ERG-see-INV-OBV that old.man that.OBV young.man-OBV
  'The young man (obv.) sees the old man.'

Second, there is a constraint on obviation that a single clause cannot contain coreferential nominals in any syntactic configuration that requires each to control the obviation of the other. This situation only arises if one of the nominals is possessed by the other. In Rhodes 1993a the relevant constraint was formalized as in (44).

(44) *Possessor constraint*
  No sentence is good in which the syntax requires that a clausemate coreferent of a possessor must be obviated by its possessee.

Therefore, when a clause has the possessee of its object as an intitial 1, it must appear in a form in which the initial 2 outranks the initial 1.[19] An example is given in (45).

(45) Wwaabmigoon wgwisan aw kiiwenzii.
  o-waabam-igo-an o-gwis-an aw akiwenzii
  3SUBJ-see-INV-OBV 3SUBJ-son-OBV that old.man
  'The old man's son (obv.) sees him.'

Such clauses are always inverse; therefore inverse clauses must have the property that the initial 2 outranks the initial 1 in final structure. Since inverse clauses are simple transitives, the only possible analysis is that the initial 2 is final 1.

The third argument for the final 1-hood of the initial 2s of inverse clauses is also an argument from obviation. Only 1s control obviation into subordinate clauses. So there is a clear contrast between (46a) in which the subject is available as a controller of obviation and (46b) in which the object is not available for controlling obviation.

(46) a. Wgii-waabndaan maa ddibew mtigoonskaa(ni)g.
     o-gii=waaband-am-n   imaa dadibwe mitigoonsikaa-(ini)-g
     3ERG-PAST=see-INAN.OBJ-OBJ there on.shore there.are.bushes-(OBV)-INAN.SUBJ
     'He saw it by the shore where it (obv.) was bushy.'
   b. Ngii-waabmaa maa ddibew mtigoonskaa(*ni)g.
     ni-gii=waaband-am-n   imaa dadibwe
     1SUBJ-PAST=see-INAN.OBJ-OBJ there on.shore
     mitigoonsikaa-(*ini)-g
     there.are.bushes-(*OBV)-INAN.SUBJ
     'I saw him by the shore where it *(obv.) was bushy.'

In inverse clauses, it is the initial 2 that can control obviation, as in (47a), but if the initial 1 of an inverse clause is the potential controller, as in (47b), then obviation is not possible.

(47) a. Wgii-bzikaagon sin maa ddibew mtigoonskaa(ni)g.
     o-gii=bizikaw-igo-an   asin imaa dadibwe
     3ERG-PAST=hit-3AN.OBJ-OBV rock there on.shore
     mitigoonsikaa-(ini)-g
     there.are.bushes-(OBV)-INAN.SUBJ
     'The rock hit him by the shore where it (obv.) was bushy.'
   b. Ngii-bzikaag maa ddibew mtigoonskaa(*ni)g.
     ni-gii=bizikaw-igo   asin imaa dadibwe
     1SUBJ-PAST=hit-3AN.OBJ rock there on.shore
     mitigoonsikaa-(*ini)-g
     there.are.bushes-(*OBV)-INAN.SUBJ
     'He hit me by the shore where it *(obv.) was bushy.'

Again this array of facts supports the position that the initial 2 of inverse clauses is a final 1.

The last argument that the initial 2 of inverses is a final 1 is from subject to object raising. In Ottawa subject to object raising either raises a pronominal copy of the nominal or raises the nominal and leaves a pronominal copy of the raised argument in the launching clause. An example of the former sort is given in (48). In the upstairs clause of (48a), in which there is no raising, the verb shows inanimate object agreement with the complement clause, but in (48b) the verb of the upstairs clause agrees with the raised copy of the downstairs subject.

(48) a. Gaa wgii-gkendanziin nmanj ge-kidgwen aw noos.
     gaa o-gii=gikend-**am**-sii-n   namanj ge=ikido-g-wen
     not 3ERG-PAST=know-**INAN.OBJ**-NEG-OBV how   FUT=say.so-3SUBJ-DUBIT
     aw   n-oos
     that 1POSS-father

'She did know what my father would say.' (Bloomfield 1958, text 5, sentence 13)

b. Gaa wgii-gkenmaasiin nmanj ge-kidgwen aw noos.
gaa o-gii=gikenim-**aa**-sii-n namanj ge=ikido-**g**-wen
not 3ERG-PAST=know-**3AN.OBJ**-NEG-OBV how FUT=say.so-**3SUBJ**-DUBIT
aw n-oos
that 1POSS-father
'She did know what my father would say.'

Only subjects are available for raising, as exemplified in (49).

(49) a. Gaa wgii-gkenmaasiin nmanj gaa-waabmigwen aw noos.
gaa o-gii=gikenim-**aa**-sii-n namanj
not 3ERG-PAST=know-**3AN.OBJ**-NEG-OBV how
gaa=waabam-i-**g**-wen **aw n-oos**
PAST=see-1OBJ-**3SUBJ**-DUBIT **that 1POSS-father**
'She didn't know if my father had seen me.'

b. *Gaa ngii-gkenmigsiin nmanj gaa-waabmigwen aw noos.
gaa ni-gii=gikenim-**igo**-sii-n namanj gaa=waabam-i-**g**-wen
not 1SUBJ-PAST=know-**INV**-NEG-OBV how PAST=see-1OBJ-**3SUBJ**-DUBIT
aw n-oos
that 1POSS-father
'She didn't know if my father had seen me.'

In inverse clauses the initial 2 is available to raise as in (50), and therefore must be a final 1 in its clause.

(50) Gaa wgii-gkenmaasiin nmanj gaa-bzikaaggwen iw sin aw noos.
gaa o-gii=gikenim-**aa**-sii-n namanj gaa=bizikaw-igo-**g**-wen iw
not 3ERG-PAST=know-**3AN.OBJ**-NEG-OBV how PAST=see-INV-**3SUBJ**-DUBIT that
asin **aw n-oos**
rock **that 1POSS-father**
'She didn't know if my father had been hit by a rock.'

22.4.2.2 Initial 1s of Inverses as 2s The second part of the argument that inverses have reversed grammatical relations is that initial 1s of inverse clauses behave like 2s. There are fewer arguments for this, but they are reasonably strong. The first group of arguments is from morphology. The second is based on constraints on the distribution of non–third persons.

The first argument from morphology is that the agreement patterns of 2s in direct clauses parallel the agreement patterns of 1s in inverse clauses. In direct clauses there are two layers of object agreement: the inner layer that agrees in person and animacy as well as the outer layer that agrees in number, separated by several categories of morphemes, the most common of which is subject plural. The example in (51) shows the two layers. Object marking is in boldface. Subject marking is underlined.

(51) <u>n</u>waabm**aa**<u>naan</u>**ig**
<u>ni</u>-waabam-**aa**-<u>naan</u>-**ig**
<u>1SUBJ</u>-see-**3AN.OBJ**-<u>1PL</u>-**PL**
'We (excl.) see them.'

The parallels between the morphology marking the number of the initial 1s of direct clauses and the morphology marking the number of the initial 2s of inverse clauses are shown in the examples in (52), for verbs with initial animate 1s. In inverse clauses the marker of inversion appears in the same slot as the inner object marking, so the parallels are all with the outer, plural object marking. Again in (52) the outer layers of agreement suffixes are bold for final 2 agreement and underlined for final 1 argeement.

(52) a. *Singular final subjects*

    Direct   *Inverse*

  i. <u>n</u>waabmaa**g**   <u>n</u>waabmigoo**g**
    'I see them.'   'They see me.'
  ii. <u>g</u>waabmaa**g**   <u>g</u>waabmigoo**g**
    'You (sg.) see them.'   'They see you (sg.).'

b. *Plural final subjects*

  i. <u>n</u>waabmaa<u>naan</u>**ig**   <u>n</u>waabmig<u>naan</u>**ig**
    'We (excl.) see them.'   'They see us (excl.).'
  ii. <u>g</u>waabmaa<u>naan</u>**ig**   <u>g</u>waabmig<u>naan</u>**ig**
    'We (incl.) see them.'   'They see us (incl.).'
  iii. <u>g</u>waabmaa<u>waa</u>**g**   <u>g</u>waabmig<u>waa</u>**g**
    'You (pl.) see them.'   'They see you (pl.).'

The details are slightly different when the initial 1s are inanimate. Transitive verbs with inanimate 2s have a second object marker in the outer layer, which contains an *n*. This is what we have called *n*-registration, because it has other functions as well as object marking. An example is given in (53).

(53) a. **n**gii-bzik**aan**
ni-gii-bizik-**am-n(aa)**
1SUBJ-PAST-hit-**INAN.OBJ-N**
'I hit it.'
b. **n**gii-bzik**aanan**
ni-gii-bizik-**am-n(aa)-an**
1SUBJ-PAST-hit-**INAN.OBJ-N-INAN.PL**
'I hit them (inan.).'

N-registration also shows up in inverses with initial inanimate 1s. As shown in (54), the morphology of direct and inverse where inanimates are involved is more complex. The complexity is in the fact that the form of transitive stems is selected based on the animacy of the initial 2. Thus the stem in the examples in (53), *bizik-* 'hit', is selected for inanimate initial 2s, while the stem in the examples in (54), *bizikaw-* 'hit', is selected for animate initial 2s. Note that the inverse marker interacts morphophonemically with the final *aw* of the stem.

(54) a. ngii-bzik<u>aago</u>**n**
    ni-gii=bizikaw-<u>igo</u>-**n(aa)**
    1SUBJ-PAST=hit-<u>INV</u>-N
    'It hit me.'

 b. ngii-bzik<u>aag</u>**nan**
    ni-gii=bizikaw-<u>igo</u>-**n(aa)-an**
    1SUBJ-PAST=hit-<u>INV</u>-N-INAN.PL
    'They (inan.) hit me.'

Nevertheless the forms show complete parallels in the outer layers of agreement morphology, both with singulars and plurals, as the examples in (55) and (56) show. Final outer-layer object agreement markings are in boldface; final subject plural markings are underlined. Note that there is a quirk in that the first plural marker *-naa(n)* overwrites *-n* marking.

(55) *Singular final objects*
   a. *With singular final subjects*
        Direct   *Inverse*
      i. ngii-bzikaa**n**   ngii-bzikaago**on**
         'I hit it.'   'It hit me.'
      ii. ggii-bzikaa**n**   ggii-bzikaago**on**
         'You (sg.) hit it.'   'It hit you (sg.).'
   b. *With plural final subjects*
      i. ngii-bzikaa<u>naa</u>   ngii-bzikaag<u>naa</u>
         'We (excl.) hit it.'   'It hit us (excl.).'
      ii. ggii-bzikaa<u>naa</u> ggii-bzikaag<u>naa</u>
         'We (incl.) hit it.'   'It hit us (incl.).'
      iii. ggii-bzikaa**naa**<u>waa</u> ggii-bzikaag**naa**<u>waa</u>
         'You (pl.) hit it.'   'It hit you (pl.).'

(56) *Plural final objects*
   a. *With singular final subjects*
        Direct   *Inverse*
      i. ngii-bzikaa**nan**   ngii-bzikaagoo**nan**
         'I hit them (inan.).' 'They (inan.) hit me.'

ii. ggii-bzikaa**nan**   ggii-bzikaagoo**nan**
    'You (sg.) hit them (inan.).'   'They (inan.) hit you (sg.).'
b. *With plural final subjects*
    i. ngii-bzikaa<u>naan</u>**in**   ngii-bzikaa<u>naan</u>**in**
       'We (excl.) hit them (inan.).'   'They (inan.) hit us (excl.).'
    ii. ggii-bzikaa<u>naan</u>**in**   ggii-bzikaa<u>naan</u>**in**
        'We (incl.) hit them (inan.).' 'They (inan.) hit us (incl.).'
    iii. ggii-bzikaa**naa**<u>waa</u>**n**   ggii-bzikaag**naa**<u>waa</u>**n**
         'You (pl.) hit them (inan.).' 'They (inan.) hit you (pl.).'

The second set of arguments that initial 1s of inverses are final 2s comes from restrictions on the distribution of first and second persons. As argued in Rhodes 1990 and 2006, first and second persons can only be 1s or 2s. They are bad even as 3s, as (57) attests.

(57) a. Wgii-ggweji-daaweenan niw.
       o-gii=gagweji=adaawe-nan iniw
       3ERG-PAST=trying=sell-OBJ   that.OBV
       'He tried to sell her.'
   b. *Wgii-ggweji-daawee(nan) giin.
       o-gii=gagweji=adaawe-(nan) giin
       3ERG-PAST=trying=sell-(OBJ) you.SG
       'He tried to sell you.'
   c. *Wgii-ggweji-daawee(nan) niin.
       o-gii=gagweji=adaawe-(nan) niin
       3ERG-PAST=trying=sell-(OBJ) I/me
       'He tried to sell me.'

To express the meanings of (57b,c) one uses a specialized construction with a circumlocution in place of the pronoun, as in (58). In other syntactic contexts the possessive of *-iiyaw* 'body' refers to one's body, so this is a syntactic idiom.

(58) a. Wgii-ggweji-daaween giiyaw.
       o-gii=gagweji=adaawe-n(aa) g-iiyaw
       3ERG-PAST=trying=sell-OBJ   2POSS-body
       'He tried to sell you.'
   b. Wgii-ggweji-daaween niiyaw.
       o-gii=gagweji=adaawe-n(aa) n-iiyaw
       3ERG-PAST=trying=sell-OBJ   1POSS-body
       'He tried to sell me.'

The implication of this restriction on first and second persons is that the inverses of clauses containing only first and second persons must have their initial 1s as 2s. The forms are given in (59). The morphology associated with final 1s is underlined. The morphology associated with final 2s is given in bold.

(59) a. gwaabm<u>im</u>
gi-waabam-**i**-<u>mw</u>
2SUBJ-see-**1**OBJ-**2**PL
'You (pl.) see me.'
b. gwaabminim
gi-waabam-ini-<u>mw</u>
2SUBJ-see-INV-**2**PL
'I see you (pl.).'

For completeness I should point out that the morphology in relevant forms yields no particular evidence about the final 2s. But note that it is completely consistent with 2-to-1 advancement.

So in summary, I have shown in this section that both morphologically and syntactically there is evidence that the initial 2s of inverses are final 1s and initial 1s of inverses are final 2s—that is, the stratal diagram of inverse clauses is as in (34), repeated here as (60).

(60) (= [34])

This means that although the inverse involves overrunning a 1, no chômeur is created. In other words, from the point of view of the conspiracy, such constructions do not result in a nominal oblique.

22.4.3 Summary

In the previous sections I have examined a full range of rerankings, as summarized in (61).

(61) a. *Rerankings to 1*
passives, possessor ascension, and inversion
b. *Rerankings to 2*
advancements of certain obliques, possessor ascension, and advancement of relative root complements
c. *Rerankings to 3*
advancement of relative root complements
d. *Rerankings to RRC*
advancement of obliques in relative clause formation

Many of these rerankings have overrun preexisting grammatical relations, but I have shown that in no case does the construction contain an overtly expressed chômeur. Thus no rule adjusting grammatical relations in Ojibwe creates a nominal oblique.[26]

22.5 Conclusion

In this chapter I have shown that the syntax and lexicon of Ojibwe is structured in such a way as to both passively and actively avoid nominal obliques. Such an insight is only possible if one focuses on the manipulation of grammatical relations, as opposed to looking at syntax as the manipulation of structure. While there are things about Ojibwe syntax that present serious challenges to some of the positions taken by Relational Grammar, the general approach that underlies the theory is invaluable as a tool for unlocking the secrets of a syntax that is particularly foreign to that of better understood languages. For this, Algonquianists owe a debt of gratitude to the work of David Perlmutter and Paul Postal.

Notes

I wish to thank Donna Gerdts and Phil LeSourd for comments on this chapter. But a particular debt of gratitude is due to David Perlmutter, who pushed me with some of the hardest and most probing questions over a five-year period in the late 1980s. These drove me to ask deeper questions about analyses I had taken for granted for the first fifteen years of my work on Ojibwe. Rhodes 1990, 1991b, 1993a, and 1993b are all direct responses to questions raised as we worked on Perlmutter and Rhodes 1988. Much of the section of this chapter that deals with inverse clauses is an updated version of that latter paper, which was never completely finished because of the lack of knockdown arguments. David is responsible, in particular, for the form of the argument in that section. Any errors, both of omission and of commission, are the responsibility of the present author.

1. I have argued elsewhere (Kathol and Rhodes 2000), that an X-bar approach is, in principle, not workable for Ojibwe.

2. The abbreviations in the glosses are as follows: 1 first, 2 second, 3 third, AN animate, APPL applicative, BEN benefactive, C conjunct, DIM diminutive, DUBIT dubitative, EMPH emphatic, ERG ergative, FUT future tense, INAN inanimate, INCL inclusive, INV inverse, LOC locative, N *n*-registration, NEG negative, OBJ primary object, OBV obviative, PAST past tense, PERS person, PL plural, POSS possessor, REL.CL relative clause, SUBJ subject. CHANGE is a morpheme that is realized as an ablaut on the following morpheme. The vowels change in the following pattern:

i	e
a	e
o	we
ii	aa
e	aye
aa	ayaa
oo	waa

It has several distinct morphosyntactic functions.

3. Because this particular part of Grimes typology is tangential to the thrust of the chapter, I refer the reader to Grimes 1975 for examples.

4. With *nbaagan* or *nbaagning* the sentence would be bad.   *Naami-nbaagan* is not a nominal, but an adverb structurally equivalent to *aazhoogam* in (7a). Furthermore, *naami-* 'under [generally]' ≠ *negw-* 'down into under [in an enclosed space]'.

5. There are also a few relevantly monomorphemic verb roots that license relative root complements. See Rhodes 2006.

6. Paradigms comparing primary and secondary object agreements are given in (i).

(i) *Subject–primary object agreements (partial paradigm)*

bii- 'bring'	animate primary obj.	inanimate primary obj.
I ... him/it	*nbiinaa*	*nbiidoon*
you *sg* ... him/it	*gbiinaa*	*gbiidoon*
he ... s him/it	*wbiinaan*	*wbiidoon*
we *excl* ... him/it	*nbiinaanaa*	*nbiidoonaa*
we *incl* ... him/it	*gbiinaanaa*	*gbiidoonaa*
you *pl* ... him/it	*gbiinaawaa*	*gbiidoonaawaa*
they ... him/it	*wbiinaawaan*	*wbiidoonaawaa*
I ... them	*nbiinaag*	*nbiidoonan*
you *sg* ... them	*gbiinaag*	*gbiidoonan*
he ... s them	*wbiinaan*	*wbiidoonan*
we *excl* ... them	*nbiinaanaanig*	*nbiidoonaanin*
we *incl* ... them	*gbiinaanaanig*	*gbiidoonaanin*
you *pl* ... them	*gbiinaawaag*	*gbiidoonaawaan*
they ... them	*wbiinaawaan*	*wbiidoonaawaan*

Final secondary objects, animate or inanimate, are marked with a system that partially overlaps with the object marking system of primary inanimates. The main feature of this marking is that it involves a morpheme *-n(aa)-*. This *-n(aa)-* has other uses besides marking objecthood, and the conditions on its appearance are not simply those of agreement. Therefore we call it *n*-registration. At first approximation, the condition on the appearance of *-n(aa)-* is that it occurs on nonsubordinate verbs in clauses containing object arcs except if there is an arc that has a 2 on it and is headed by an animate in final structure.   The basic paradigm of *n*-registration is shown in (ii).

(ii) *Subject–secondary object agreements/n-registration*

miigwe- 'give away'	animate secondary obj.	inanimate secondary obj.
I ... him/it	*nmiigwenan*	*nmiigwen*
you *sg* ... him/it	*gmiigwenan*	*gmiigwen*
he ... s him/it	*wmiigwenan*	*wmiigwen*
we *excl* ... him/it	*nmiigwenaa*	*nmiigwenaa*
we *incl* ... him/it	*gmiigwenaa*	*gmiigwenaa*
you *pl* ... him/it	*gmiigwenaawaa*	*gmiigwenaawaa*
they ... him/it	*wmiigwenaawaa*	*wmiigwenaawaa*

I ... them	nmiigwe**nag**	nmiigwe**nan**
you *sg* ... them	gmiigwe**nag**	gmiigwe**nan**
he ... s them	wmiigwe**nan**	wmiigwe**nan**
we *excl* ... them	nmiigwe**naanig**	nmiigwe**naanin**
we *incl* ... them	gmiigwe**naanig**	gmiigwe**naanin**
you *pl* ... them	gmiigwe**naawaag**	gmiigwe**naawaan**
they ... them	wmiigwe**naawaag**	wmiigwe**naawaan**

7. There is a separate set of conditions on obviation controlled by possessors. The properties of obviation induced by clausemates and those induced by possessors are slightly different, but the syntax of possessor obviation isn't relevant to the present argument and is therefore beyond the scope of this chapter.

8. There is a general constraint in Ojibwe that only animates can be the subject of a transitive clause.

9. Note that word order is irrelevant to obviation. It only marks definiteness.

10. In Bloomfield's translation this sentence is rendered 'So then I, too, got on board the train.' But 'train' is only inferable.

11. By a quirk of syntax, one class of Ottawa temporal adjunct clauses largely overlaps in form with Ottawa relative clauses.

12. Not all Ottawa speakers like sentences like this. The bare instrumental construction is being replaced by clausal adjuncts.

13. Because the purpose of this chapter is to show that there are no nominal chômeurs, I will not discuss rerankings that do not overrun nominally headed arcs, either because there is no overrun arc at all or because the overrun arc is headed by a clause rather than a nominal. Clauses in Ojibwe are, at best, quasinominals. They trigger inanimate singular agreement, but otherwise have no clear nominal properties. The most obvious similarity is that, like, nominals, they can serve as RRCs, but adverbials can also do that.

14. It is also the case that commitatives appear as surface terms having obligatorily advanced, probably from RRC. However, the analysis is somewhat controversial and the source clauses are restricted to intransitives, so there is no overrun 2 and therefore no possible chômeur.

15. Inanimate nouns are never explicitly marked for obviation. It only can be seen in the agreements they trigger.

16. Possessor ascensions in Algonquian are all copy ascensions.

17. This example needs to be in conjunct inflection because the corresponding sentence in independent inflection triggers inversion, and that complicates the argument considerably.

18. Most Algonquian languages have two modes of inflection, one used primarily in independent clauses and one used in a wide variety of contexts, many of which are subordinate. They differ in the morphology marking person-number agreement. In the independent person agreement is largely prefixal with suffixal number and object agreement. In contrast, the subordinate person-number marking is entirely suffixal and most of the morphemes encode person and number as a portmanteau. A basic paradigm contrasting the two systems in an intransitive verb is given in (i).

(i) | *giiwe-* 'go home' | *indpendent inflection* | *conjunct inflection* |
|---|---|---|
| I | **n**giiwe | giiwe**yaanh** |
| you *sg* | **g**giiwe | giiwe**yan** |
| he | giiwe | giiwe**d** |
| we *excl* | **n**giiwe**mi** | giiwe**yaang** |
| we *incl* | **g**giiwe**mi** | giiwe**yang** |
| you *pl* | **g**giiwe**m** | giiwe**yeg** |
| they | giiwe**wag** | giiwe**waad** |

19. This class of sentences holds an important place in Algonquian linguistics. One learns early on that sentences with possessed nominal subjects must be in the inverse if the possessor is the object.

20. There is also one dummy insertion construction, the Antipassive, in Ottawa, in which the demoted object appears as a secondary object. Because this construction is archaic in Ottawa, and I do not have enough examples to be completely sure of the syntax, I exclude it from the discussion.

References

Bloomfield, L. 1958. *Eastern Ojibwa: Grammar, texts, and word list.* Ed. C. Hockett. Ann Arbor: University of Michigan Press.

Dryer, M. 1986. Primary and secondary objects, and antidative. *Language* 62:808–845.

Grimes, J. E. 1975. *The thread of discourse.* The Hague: Mouton.

Kathol, A., and R. A. Rhodes. 2000. Constituency and linearization of Ojibwe nominals. In M. Caldecott, S. Gessner, and E.-S. Kim, eds., *Proceedings of WSCLA 4: The Workshop on Structure and Constituency in Languages of the Americas.* Vancouver: University of British Columbia.

Kisseberth, C. 1970. On the functional unity of phonological rules. *Linguistic Inquiry* 1:291–306.

Langacker, R. 1987. *Foundations of cognitive grammar, vol. 1: Theoretical prerequisites.* Stanford, CA: Stanford University Press.

Perlmutter, D. M., and P. M. Postal. 1977. Towards a universal characterization of the passive. In K. Whistler, ed., *Proceedings of the Third Annual Meeting of the Berkeley Linguistics Society.* (Reprinted in D. M. Perlmutter, ed., *Studies in Relational Grammar 1*, 3–29. Chicago: University of Chicago Press, 1983.)

Perlmutter, D. M., and P. M. Postal. 1983. Some proposed laws of basic clause structure. In D. M. Perlmutter, ed., *Studies in relational grammar 1*, 81–128. Chicago: University of Chicago Press.

Perlmutter, D. M., and R. A. Rhodes. 1988. Syntactic-thematic alignments in Ojibwa. Paper presented at the LSA, New Orleans, December.

Reinholtz, C. 1999. On the characterization of discontinuous constituents: Evidence from Swampy Cree. *International Journal of American Linguistics* 65(2):201–227.

Rhodes, R. A. 1976. The morphosyntax of the Central Ojibwa verb. Doctoral dissertation, University of Michigan.

Rhodes, R. A. 1990. Ojibwa secondary objects. In K. Dziwirek, P. Farrell, and E. Mejías-Bikandi, eds., *Grammatical relations: A cross theoretical perspective*, 401–414. Stanford, CA: CSLI.

Rhodes, R. A. 1991a. Obviation, inversion, and topic rank in Ojibwa. In D. Costa, ed., *Proceedings of the Sixteenth Annual Meeting of the Berkeley Linguistics Society, Special Session on General Topics in American Indian Linguistics*, 101–115. Berkeley: Berkeley Linguistics Society.

Rhodes, R. A. 1991b. On the passive in Ojibwa. *Papers of the Twenty-Second Algonquian Conference*, 307–319. Ottawa: Carleton University.

Rhodes, R. A. 1993a. The possessor constraint. Paper presented at the 25th Algonquian Conference, Ottawa, October.

Rhodes, R. A. 1993b. Syntax vs. Morphology: A chicken and egg problem. In D. Peterson, ed., *Proceedings of the Nineteenth Annual Meeting of the Berkeley Linguistics Society, Special Session on Syntactic Issues in Native American Languages*, 139–147. Berkeley: Berkeley Linguistics Society.

Rhodes, R. A. 1994. Agency, inversion, and thematic alignment in Ojibwe. In S. Gahl, A. Dolbey, and C. Johnson, eds., *Proceedings of the Twentieth Annual Meeting of the Berkeley Linguistics Society*, 431–446. Berkeley: Berkeley Linguistics Society.

Rhodes, R. A. 2006. Clause structure, core arguments, and the Algonquian relative root construction. *The 1998 Belcourt Lecture*. Winnipeg: Voices of Rupert's Land.

Tomlin, R., and R. A. Rhodes. 1979. An introduction to information distribution in Ojibwa. *CLS* 15:307–320. (Also in D. Payne, *The pragmatics of word order flexibility*. Amsterdam: John Benjamins, 1993.)

Zuñiga, F. 2006. *Deixis and alignment: Inverse systems in indigenous languages of the Americas*. Amsterdam: John Benjamins.

23   Modeling the Mapping from "Conceptual Structure" to Syntax

Annie Zaenen

23.1   Introduction: General Characteristics of Mapping Theories

Several recent as well as some older grammatical theories try to ground subcategorization phenomena in a lexical-semantic or conceptual representation.[1] The aim of such endeavors is to make some or most of the subcategorization information itself "predictable" and to account for valency alternations. These lexical-semantic or conceptual representations can take different forms, from lists of semantic roles to more articulated representations of event structure. (For an overview of proposed schemata, the interested reader is referred to Levin and Rappaport 2005.) Even the more elaborate event structures, however, contain only a limited number of primitive elements and a limited amount of recursion and it is a firm tenet of this family of theories that only certain aspects of the meaning of words determine their syntactic behavior.[2] Syntactic theories also assume that the number of grammatical functions associated with the head of clause (typically the verb) is finite. This is true for theories where the mapping is to a VP-internal position but also in those like TAG grammars where the mapping would associate all the elementary lexical trees that a predicator subcategorizes for, encoding information not only about the behavior of the predicator and its arguments in what would correspond to deep structure position but to also all surface structure positions. Thus the interface theories propose to map the finite list of semantic roles to a finite list of syntactic ones. The power of such a system need not exceed that of finite-state grammars. The system could require more power if we would allow predicators to be built up through affixation to an arbitrary level of complexity. I discuss this problem in section 23.4.2. It might be that the question of the formal power needed for this mapping is never asked because the answer is obvious. Many approaches, however, use tools to describe the mapping that go typically beyond finite-state grammars. For example, in the systems developed by Baker 1988 and Marantz 1993, the mapping is embedded in GB-type grammar of which the mathematical properties are largely unknown. In what follows I will describe one mapping system, LMT, developed in LFG (section 23.2), apply it to some data from Bantu (section 23.3), and show how it can be modeled in the Xerox Finite State Calculus (section 23.4). Finally I discuss the extent to which this one system and the rather limited amount of data discussed here can be taken to be representative of lexicon-syntax interfaces in general.

23.2 Lexical Mapping Theory (LMT)

In LMT the semantic roles are represented as an ordered list. The most clearly identified roles are, in the order proposed:

(1) cause, agent, beneficiary, instrument, theme, location

They are mapped on four types of grammatical functions:

(2) subject (SUBJ), object (OBJ), object-theta (OBJθ), and oblique (OBL)

LFG syntax is surface syntax, so the grammatical functions are surface grammatical functions. The notions SUBJ and OBJ do not need further discussion at this point, because it is intuitively clear what is meant. The notion of oblique (OBL) used here is also the intuitive one. Oblique arguments come, of course, in various flavors: instrumentals, typically introduced by 'with' in English, and locatives, introduced by the various locative prepositions. The system that I describe below intends only to model the mapping from semantic roles to obliques in general. The realization as a specific kind of oblique is determined by the semantic role itself. OBJθ is a less immediately recognizable type. In general it is realized as a bare NP that is an immediate dependent of the verb but that does not exhibit normal object properties (see Levin 1988 for discussion).[3] A typical OBJθ is the second postverbal NP in a sentence like *John gave Mary the book*.

While early LFG took the grammatical functions as unanalyzed primitives, LMT decomposes each of the four functions above into a combination of two features: −/+r and −/+o. The r-feature specifies whether a role is mapped on a restricted or an unrestricted function. In LFG subject and object are unrestricted functions because they do not wear their thematic role on their sleeve: to know what the thematic role of a surface subject or object is, one has to look at the verb with which it occurs. Obliques indicate, through their preposition or case marking, which roles they play. While some ambiguity is allowed, the point is that the possibilities are restricted. The o-feature indicates whether a role can be realized as an object (thematic or direct) or not.

The mapping from semantic roles to syntactic functions in LMT is mediated through a level of *partial specifications* that associate semantic roles with at most one feature, and further *principles* that guide the specification of the other feature or lead to the nonrealization of the role.

The partial specifications form the following intermediate equivalence classes:

(3) Agents and causes are −o.
    Themes and beneficiaries are −r or +o.

The principles can be subdivided in two classes: *defaults* and *well-formedness constraints*. The defaults that have been proposed are the following:

(4) Add −r to the highest argument, if possible.
    Add +r to the others, if possible.
    Add −o and +o where possible.

It is not possible to add a feature when there is a conflicting value for the same feature (or the same value for the feature is already present).

The well-formedness constraints are

(5) Each verb has a subject (subject constraint).
    Each verb has only one subject (functional uniqueness constraint).
    Each verb has at most one object (functional uniqueness constraint).
    Each thematic role is mapped to at most one syntactic role.

Each of these constraints is controversial and in my modeling I will propose a different way of treating them from that proposed in the LFG literature up to now.

Apart from these general principles there is the effect of specific morphosyntactic operations to be reckoned with. I will depart from some previous LFG proposals in subdividing them in two classes: role-adding and role-suppression operations.[4] The main role-adding operations are *causativization* and *applied suffix addition*; the main role-suppression operations are *passive*, *reflexivization* (in certain languages), and *reciprocalization* (again in certain languages). The semantic difference between the two classes is that the suppression rules do not make anything semantically disappear; they merely organize the realization of a particular role, whereas the adding operations really add a role, so they change the semantics of the predicate.[5] The role-adding operations are taken to apply before the syntactic realization of the semantic roles is calculated. The suppression operations take place during the calculation. So a basic predicate can undergo the following chain of operations:

- Role addition
- Partial argument classification
- Grammatical role-suppression operations
- Defaults
- Well-formedness constraints

Let's illustrate this first with a simple case that does not involve argument addition or suppression; see (6).

(6) [John] ate [the apple]

Thematic roles	agent	theme
Partial spec	−o	−r
Defaults	−r	+o/−o
	SUBJ	
Well-formedness		OBJ

In a sentence like *John ate the apple*, John has the agent role and the apple is the theme. According to the partial specification principles given above, the agent is classified as −o and the theme as −r, following the intuition that agents are normally not realized as objects and themes tend to be realized as unrestricted functions. The defaults fill in a further feature for the agent, which is then completely realized as a subject, but they propose two possibilities for the theme. The selection of the −o possibility, however, would lead to a violation of a functional uniqueness well-formedness constraint, so the other option has to be chosen.

In the passive version, the system works as in (7).

(7) [John] ate [the apple]

Thematic roles	agent	theme
Partial spec	−o	−r
Passive	0	
Defaults		+o/−o
Well-formedness		SUBJ
Well-formedness		OBJ

Passive suppresses the expression of the agent function. For the rest the calculation proceeds as before, but now the subject well-formedness constraint kicks in and the theme is realized as a subject.

The exposition above summarized LMT as presented in the LFG literature between 1985 and the late 1990s. I propose one addition and one change to this setup. The addition is an explicit separation between *universal* partial specifications and *language- or construction-specific filters*. As we will see in what follows, across languages, it is not sufficient to propose that the theme is partially specified as −r; one also has to allow a specification as +o. Different languages allow a complete specification built on this partial specification. For example, in English, one can argue on the basis of sentences like *Mary gave Jane a book* that the partial specification of *a book* is +o (at least in the dialects that do not allow *A book was given Jane*) because a −r partial specification would allow the book to be mapped to subject. I propose to handle this type of variation with explicit filters, as will be illustrated in the next section. This is more a way of making explicit what is already part of LMT practice than a real change.

My second departure from previous statements of LMT is more substantial: I propose to treat the well-formedness constraints as violatable constraints, in the spirit of Optimality Theory. This will also be illustrated in the next section.

23.3 An Application: The Applied Suffix in Bantu

The effects of adding the applied suffix to a Bantu verb have been the subject of many studies on various linguistic theories. The bare-bones result of adding an applied suffix to a verb is that the valency of the verb changes. A direct argument is added: intransitive verbs become transitive and transitive verbs become bitransitive. A simple Chichewa example is the following.[6]

(8) a. Chitsiru chi-na-gul-a mphatso
7-fool 7s-PST-buy-FV 9-gift
'The fool bought the gift.'
b. Chitsiru chi-na-gul-ir-a atsikana mphatso
7-fool 7s-PST-buy-FV 2-girls 9-gift
'The fool bought the gift for the girls.'

One of the most fascinating aspects of the applied suffix is that in different contexts the semantic role that is added is different, and this difference in role corresponds to a difference in syntactic behavior. Languages differ in the semantic roles that can be added and in the syntactic behavior that the different role additions license. In what follows I will call the association of the set of semantic roles belonging to a given type of predicate with their syntactic realizations, a *construction family*. For example, the possible associations of the agent, theme, and beneficiary with their syntactic roles are a construction family; the associations of the agent, theme, and instrument are another. I will restrict my attention to transitive-bitransitive alternations. I rely mainly on Alsina 1993, 1996, Alsina and Mchombo 1993, Bresnan and Moshi 1993, and Zaenen 1984 for the basic generalizations, which can be summarized as follows:

• There are *asymmetrical* and *symmetrical* construction families.
• The asymmetrical construction families can be further subdivided into *alternating* and *nonalternating*.[7]

A construction family will be classified as *symmetrical* when two semantic roles can be realized as grammatical functions with object properties in the same sentence. It is *asymmetrical* otherwise.

A construction family will be classified as *alternating* when object properties can be associated with more than one semantic role, although this association cannot be made in the same sentence.

To give a schematic example: assume that both accusative case marking and noun incorporation are reflexes of objecthood in a given language. A symmetrical construction family in that language would allow sentences such as

(9) John book-gave Mary-accusative
    John Mary-gave book-accusative

In an asymmetrical construction family, one would not find both markings within the same sentence. In an alternating asymmetrical construction family we would find

(10) John gave Mary-accusative the book

and

(11) John gave book-accusative Mary

whereas in a nonalternating construction family one would find only one of these possibilities.

Previous literature treats languages and not construction families as symmetrical, and as alternating or nonalternating. But there is work that suggests the hypothesis that the facts can differ depending on the semantic roles involved. The existence of symmetrical languages was widely discussed as a result of Kimenyi's (1980) work on Kinyarwanda, because they violate at first blush the stratal uniqueness law of Relational Grammar and, of course, also the functional uniqueness constraint of LFG. The existence of alternating languages was first discussed by Zaenen (1984), who observed that Kikuyu differs from Kinyarwanda in that it does not allow the simultaneous realization of two arguments with object properties. Baker (1988) and Alsina and Mchombo (1993) discuss the alternations of Chichewa and observe that whether there are alternations or not depends not on the language as a whole but on the semantic role that the added argument plays—for example, locatives behave differently from benefactives.[8] Bresnan and Moshi (1993) contrast Chichewa and Kichaga and propose by and large the approach followed below.

Before proposing an account, however, I should describe what I call the objectlike properties of a grammatical function in more detail. Bantuists tend to agree on three main properties: immediate postverbal position, object marking on the verb, and realization as a subject in the passive. I illustrate these properties here with examples from Chichewa:

(12) Chitsiru chi-na-gul-*ir*-a   atsikina mphatso
     fool   7-PST-buy-APP-ASP girl   gift
     'The fool bought the girls a gift.'

(13) *Chitsiru chi-na-gul-*ir*-a mphatso atsikina
fool 7-PST-buy-APP-ASP gift girl
'The fool brought a gift the girls.'

In this language the word-order pattern indicates that only the grammatical function corresponding to the beneficiary is an object. This patterns with the result of the other object tests for Chichewa.⁹ Object marking is illustrated in the following example:

(14) Chitsiru chi-na-*wa*-gul-*ir*-a mphatso
fool 7-PST-2-buy-APP-ASP gift
'The fool bought them a gift.'

(15) *Chitsiru chi-na-*i*-gul-*ir*-a atsikana
fool 7-PST-9-buy-APP-ASP girl
'The fool bought the girls it.'

Here we see that the object marker can realize the role of a beneficiary but not that of a theme. I will take object marker as a reliable test for objecthood, although the function of the object marker, agreement, or pronoun can vary from language to language.

The third criterion, subjecthood in passive, is only an indirect indication of an objectlike characteristic in a surface theory like LFG. It is illustrated in the following pair of examples:

(16) Atsikana a-na-gul-*ir-idw*-a mphatso
girl 2-PST-buy-APP-PAS-ASP gift
'The girls were bought a gift.'

(17) *Mphatso i-na-gul-*ir-idw*-a atsikana
gift 9-PST-buy-APP-PAS-ASP girl
'The gift was bought the girls.'

As we have seen above, LFG does not derive passives from actives, but the partial feature specifications have to be compatible with the realization of the beneficiary as both a subject and an object in Chichewa, whereas the theme role in these sentences cannot be realized as either.

Before showing how the calculation proceeds, I look at the other possible cases. First I look at an alternating language, Kikuyu. The pattern we find there is the following:

(18) Moana ne-a-tuar-*e*-ire moarimo mahoa
child FOC-1-send-APP-IMP teacher flower
'The child sent the teacher flowers.'

(19) Moarimo ne-a-tuar-*e*-ir-*uo*   mahoa
    teacher 1-send-APP-IMP-PAS flower
    'The teacher was sent flowers.'

(20) Mahoa ne-ma-tuar-*e*-ir-*uo* moarimo
    flower 1-send-APP-IMP-PAS teacher
    'The flowers were sent the teacher.'

(21) Moana ne-a-*ma*-tuar-*e*-ire   moarimo
    child FOC-1-6-send-APP-IMP teacher
    'The child sent them (to) the teacher.'

(22) Moana ne-a-*mo*-tuar-*e*-ire   mahoa
    child FOC-1-1-send-APP-IMP flower
    'The child sent him/her the flowers.'

This pattern is rather different from Chichewa: in Kikuyu both the theme and the beneficiary can be realized as an object marker and both can be the subject of a passive. There are, however, constraints on the possible combinations of these realizations, as shown in the following examples:

(23) *Moarimo ne-a-*ma*-tuar-*e*-ir-*uo*
    teacher 1-send-APP-IMP-PAS
    'The teacher was sent them.'

(24) *Mahoa ne-ma-*mo*-tuar-*e*-ir-*uo*
    flower 1-send-APP-IMP-PAS
    'The flowers were sent him/her.'

In LFG terms, these examples show that when the beneficiary is realized as a subject, the theme cannot be realized as an object marker, and when the theme is realized as a subject, the beneficiary cannot be realized as an object marker.

This pattern contrasts in turn with what we find in Kichaga:

(25) N-a-i-lyi-*i*-a   mka kelya
    FOC-1-PRES-eat-APP-ASP wife food
    'He eats food for his wife.'

(26) Mka n-a-i-lyi-*i*-o   kelya
    wife FOC-1-pres-eat-APP-PAS food
    'The wife is eaten food (for).'

(27) Kelya k-i-lyi-*i*-o   mka
    food 7-PRES-eat-APP-PAS wife
    'The food is eaten (for) the wife.'

(28) N-a-i-*m*-lyi-*i*-a   kelya
    FOC-1-PRES-1-eat-APP-ASP food
    'He eats food (for) her.'

(29) N-a-i-*ki*-lyi-*i*-a   mka
    FOC-1-PRES-7-eat-APP-ASP wife
    'He eats it (for) the wife.'

(30) N-a-i-*ki*-lyi-*i*-*o*
    FOC-1-PRES-7-eat-APP-PAS
    'She is eaten it for.'

(31) K-i-*m*-lyi-*i*-*o*
    7-PRES-1-eat-APP-PAS
    'It is eaten for her.'

In Kichaga we can realize either the beneficiary or the theme as a subject or an object, but as the last pair of examples shows, we can also realize one as a subject and the other as an object marker in the same sentence.

The patterns illustrated above allow us to classify languages as symmetrical, asymmetrical, or alternating, but a further set of data shows that this is not the correct assumption. As discussed in Baker 1988 and Alsina and Mchombo 1993, not all cases of the applied suffix behave in the same way. Whereas the benefactive is nonalternating in Chichewa, the locative is alternating, as shown by the following examples:

(32) Alenje a-ku-luk-*ir*-a   pa-mchenga mikeka
    hunter 2-PRES-weave-APP-ASP 16-3-sand   mat
    'The hunters are weaving mats on the beach.'

(33) Alenje a-ku-*pa*-luk-*ir*-a   mikeka
    hunter 2-PRES-16-weave-APP-ASP mat
    'The hunters are weaving the mats (on) it.'

(34) Alenje a-ku-*i*-luk-*ir*-a   pa-mchenga
    hunter 2-PRES-4-weave-APP-ASP 16-3-sand
    'The hunters are weaving them (on) the beach.'

(35) Pa-mchenga pa-ku-luk-*ir-idwa*-a   mikeka
    beach   16-PRES-weave-APP-PAS-ASP mat
    'The beach is being woven mats on.'

(36) Mikeka i-ku-luk-*ir-idwa*-a   pa-mchenga
    mat   4-PRES-weave-APP-PAS-ASP 16-3-sand
    'The mats are being woven on the beach.'

A similar pattern can be found with the instrumental.[10]

Let's now describe how LMT accounts for this array of data. As said above, I will assume that the applied suffix adds one role to the valency of the predicate. More precisely, this role has to be lower than agent on the thematic hierarchy and cannot be the theme.[11] Universal principles of partial specification will assign a first set of features to the semantic roles, as shown in (37). A more specific filter will then reduce the possibilities. In Chichewa this filter will require that the beneficiary be marked −r and the theme +o.[12] The defaults and the well-formedness constraints then apply as discussed in the previous section.

(37)
Eat-for	agent	beneficary	theme
Partial spec	−o	−r/+o	+o/−r
Asymmetry filter	−o	−r	+o
Defaults	−r	+o/−o	+r
	SUBJ		OBJθ
Well-formedness		OBJ	

In the passive, the assignment will proceed as in (38).

(38)
Eat-for	agent	beneficiary	theme
Partial spec	−o	−r/+o	+o/−r
Asymmetry filter	−o	−r	+o
Passive	0		
Defaults		+o/−o	+r
			OBJθ
Well-formedness		SUBJ	

In an alternating construction family, the same partial specifications apply, but the filter here says only that a different feature assignment has to be selected for the beneficiary from that of the theme. So we get the solutions diagrammed in (39) and (40).

(39)
Eat-for	agent	beneficiary	theme
Partial spec	−o	−r/+o	+o/−r
Alternating filter		−r	+o
Defaults	−r	+o/−o	+r
	SUBJ		OBJθ
Well-formedness		OBJ	

(40) | **Eat-for** | agent | beneficiary | theme |
|---|---|---|---|
| Partial spec | −o | −r/+o | +o/−r |
| Alternating filter | | +o | −r |
| Defaults | −r | +r | +o/−o |
| | SUBJ | OBJθ | |
| Well-formedness | | | OBJ |

This leads in turn to two passives, as shown in (41) and (42).

(41) | **Eat-for** | agent | beneficiary | theme |
|---|---|---|---|
| Partial spec | −o | −r/+o | +o/−r |
| Alternating filter | | −r | +o |
| Passive | 0 | | |
| Defaults | | +o/−o | +r |
| | | | OBJθ |
| Well-formedness | | SUBJ | |

(42) | **Eat-for** | agent | beneficiary | theme |
|---|---|---|---|
| Partial spec | −o | −r/+o | +o/−r |
| Alternating filter | | +o | −r |
| Passive | 0 | | |
| Defaults | | +r | +o/−o |
| | | OBJθ | |
| Well-formedness | | | SUBJ |

In a symmetrical construction family, finally, the calculation for the active proceeds as in (43).

(43) | **Eat-for** | agent | beneficiary | theme |
|---|---|---|---|
| Partial spec | −o | −r/+o | +o/−r |
| Symmetry filter | | −r | −r |
| Defaults | −r | +o/−o | +o/−o |
| Well-formedness | SUBJ | *OBJ | OBJ |
| Or | *SUBJ | SUBJ | OBJ |

Here we see that there is no solution without violating a well-formedness constraint: we will have either more than one object or more than one subject.[13] I will assume that the well-formedness constraints can be violated and that it is worse to have two subjects than to have two objects. In the next section I discuss how to formalize these potential violations.

For completeness' sake, I give the calculation for the symmetrical passive in (44). It does not lead to any violations.

(44)
Eat-for	agent	beneficary	theme
Partial spec	$-o$	$-r/+o$	$+o/-r$
Symmetry filter		$-r$	$-r$
Passive	0		
Defaults		$-o/+o$	$+o/-o$
		SUBJ	OBJ
Well-formedness		OBJ	SUBJ

These diverse cases show that in LMT terms, "having objectlike properties" means to be classified as $-r$ after the partial specifications and the filters apply.[14]

The facts about the Chichewa locative will follow, if we assume that when the applied role is a location the alternating filter applies. The filters, then, are parameterized for language and for role assignment.

23.4 A Finite-State Model for LMT

LMT as illustrated above proposes the mapping from a finite number of semantic roles into a finite set of grammatical functions via a finite number of steps. It is immediately clear that such a system can be modeled by finite-state rules. I will first show how this can be done concretely and then discuss whether the overall characterization of LMT just given is realistic.

23.4.1 A Finite-State Model

The finite-state calculus that I will use has been developed at Xerox. It is based on finite-state transducers. Mathematically, a finite-state transducer encodes a regular relation, a mapping consisting of pairs of strings. To take a morphological example, a surface form like 'walked' and its lexical (underlying) form 'walk+pasttense' constitutes such a pair: the 'walk' part is mapped into itself and '+pasttense' is mapped into 'ed'.

(45) walk+pasttense—upper
      | |
      walk+ed—lower

The advantage of transducers is that they can be intersected and composed to model the interactions of various phenomena. In what follows I will use composition. The relation between the upper and the lower side of an individual transducer is indicated via finite-state rules that describe the relation (the "changes"). The relations used below are

(46) *'replace'*, written as →,
  negative restrictions: *'does not contain x'*, written as ~$[x] and
  positive restrictions, *'contains x'*, written as $[x].

These operators are well known from the morphological applications of the finite-state calculus (see, e.g., Beesley and Karttunen 2003). One less well-known operator I will use is 'lenient composition', as defined in Karttunen 1998 and 2006.[15]

The basic idea is the following: assume that R is a relation (a mapping that assigns to each input form a number of outputs) and C is a constraint that disallows some of the output forms. Lenient composition will eliminate all the output candidates that do not conform to C as long as there is at least one output that does conform. But when none of the output candidates meet the constraint, they are all redeemed. This way, every input will always have at least one output (see Karttunen 1998 and 2006 for examples in phonology).

Let's now see how we can use this apparatus to model the LMT fragment described above. Assuming that a basic verb is given in the basic lexicon with its semantic roles, the calculus I have described has six types of operations:

1. The addition of thematic roles caused by the presence of affixes
2. A partial grammatical specification of the roles that is universal
3. Filters that establish a typology of languages, as illustrated above
4. Role suppressions
5. Defaults
6. Well-formedness constraints

All this can be modeled rather neatly with finite-state transducers: the addition of roles by affixes and the partial specifications can be modeled by expressions containing the replace operator; the filters are instances of negative restrictions; defaults again involve replace operations. Given that no loss in the available information is allowed, only additions, the replace operations are in fact all of the type [ ]→ some feature. These five operations are then combined via composition. The last operation, the well-formedness constraints, are factored in via positive restrictions, but instead of using normal composition to combine them with the previous steps, we use lenient composition, which allows the constraints to be violated. The examples below illustrate the notation as applied to the domain under discussion:

(47) *Role addition, conditions by affixes*
e.g. [[[. .] → [Ben | Inst | Loc] | | $App Agent __]: in the presence of the applied suffix either the beneficiary, instrument, or location role is added to the valency structure

(48) *Universal partial specification: Replace expressions*
e.g. [[. .] → −o | | Agent __]: universally agents are specified as −o

(49) *Language-specific filters: Restrictions and prohibitions*
e.g. ∼$ [Ben +o]: in certain languages beneficiaries are never partially specified as +o

(50) *Role suppression*
e.g. [[−o] → 0 | | $Pas __]: in the presence of the passive morpheme, the −o argument is suppressed

(51) *Defaults: Replace expressions*
e.g. [[. .] → −r | | −o __]: the highest −o argument gets further specified as −r if there is not yet any further specification (0 counts as a specification)

(52) *Well-formedness constraints: Restrictions and prohibitions with lenient composition*
e.g. $[SUBJ]: each verb has a subject

As noted earlier, the first five types of constraints are composed together in the order given here. The filters will differ from language to language. The last type of constraint will be factored in with lenient composition so that it only has its effect if previous constraints have not made its application impossible.

23.4.2 Discussion

The use of lenient composition allows us to maintain the well-formedness conditions of LMT while avoiding their unwanted effect. As the illustration in section 23.2 shows, these conditions actually do quite a bit of work in the mapping from semantic roles to grammatical functions, but in some cases they backfire. The Bantu example with double objects is one plausible example of such misapplication, although there is some debate about its exact analysis. Another, to my mind, completely convincing example is the existence of German sentences like 'Mir ist kalt' or 'Ihm wird geholfen'. Only theory-internal reasons can lead anybody to postulate subjects in these sentences.[16] Under the proposal developed here, German would have an overall subject constraint, but lenient composition would allow its violations in these cases. A quick and incomplete summary of the different types of behavior of beneficiaries in Germanic based on Zaenen, Maling, and Thrainsson 1985 is given below:

(53) *Behavior of beneficiaries in Germanic*
- German has a filter that precludes the −r partial specification for beneficiaries and recipients; they will be marked +o or +r.
- After passivization, 'Ihm wird geholfen' has no subject.
- Icelandic is a symmetrical language, so 'Honum er hjalpad' has a subject.
- English has, for some speakers, alternating construction families; for other speakers it has the same constraints as Chichewa.

The advantage of lenient composition is, however, slightly tangential to the main topic of this chapter: the claim that the grammar of LMT is finite state. Because no complete mapping system is worked out, it might seem hazardous to extrapolate from such a small subset to a claim about the general power of the system. But as noted at the beginning of this section, if the input if finite, the output is finite, and the number of steps in between is finite, the system as a whole has to be finite.

Whether the input is in fact finite has been disputed. It is not obvious that a finite list of semantic roles can be given. In fact, another way of calculating the partial specifications has been proposed in Zaenen 1993, Alsina 1993, as well as Ackerman and Moore 2001a. Instead of unanalyzed semantic roles, these works propose adaptations of Dowty's (1991) protorole approach. But that approach also assumes a finite number of possibilities: protoroles are calculated on the basis of the number of agentlike or patientlike properties a given role has and the comparison between the number for the various candidates. This complicates the calculation but it does not make it infinite. Of course, other researchers will deny the possibility of having any kind of discrete semantic roles. Under those assumptions, however, the whole LMT approach falls apart and we are outside of the scope of this chapter.

The number of grammatical functions is also higher than what is discussed in this chapter, but again, it remains finite. As said in the introduction, in fact all OBL and OBJθ are subscripted by the semantic roles of their bearers. If we adopt the analysis of Kichaga sketched above, we will have to do the same with OBJθ. Again, this does not get us out of a finite domain.

The last component of the system are the mappings themselves. Here there would be a potential for infiniteness if an indefinite long sequence of valency-changing affixes could be added to any predicates. There are cases where the upper bound of such additions is not clear. For instance, in Finnish with certain verbs, one can have a seemingly indefinite number of causatives. It is not clear when the sequence becomes ungrammatical. But critically, after two, the meaning no longer changes. So these Finnish forms might be a problem for finite-state morphology, but they are not a problem for finite-state LMT.

LMT is only one among the many lexicon-syntax mapping proposals. Does what I claim here for it also hold for other ones? As long as they have the basic characteristics just stated, it will. In particular I think that my conclusions would hold for the proposals made in Baker 1988 and Marantz 1993. Marantz 1993, for example, postulates a mapping from a complex event structure with two events onto the specifier positions of various VPs. This is a quite limited mapping that empirically has the same properties as the LMT sketched above. But I leave it to proponents of these approaches to show this in detail, or to refute it. The conjecture is interesting, however, because these approaches embed the mapping in a wide syntactic context that obscures its finite-state character.

23.5 Conclusion

In this chapter I have proposed a finite-state model for LMT. While it is reasonably trivial to show that LMT is finite given the assumptions it makes about its input, its output, and its mapping devices, I think that the approach I have sketched shows that the modeling can be done straightforwardly and elegantly. Moreover, the use of lenient composition, as defined in the finite-state calculus, allows us to circumvent an empirical problem with the well-formedness constraints of LMT.

From a practical point of view, the result is interesting because it shows a way in which some of the valency alternations can be combined with a finite-state lexicon and morphology.

The proposal made above follows classical LFG practice in that it builds up the syntactic representation step by step, but it will not have escaped the attentive reader that the proposal made here also has an Optimality Theory flavor. And indeed I believe I can recast LMT in orthodox OT terms, eliminating possibilities from an initial set instead of building up the admissible forms. That, however, is another publication.

Notes

The formalizations used in this chapter are not the ones David Perlmutter would prefer, but I was inspired to look at these data and the issues raised by his teaching, of which I still have fond memories.

1. Relational Grammar and some versions of Government and Binding differ from the theories discussed here in including most of this mapping in the syntactic component proper.

2. Not that the truth of this is obvious. For a dissenting view see Taylor 1996.

3. In certain cases they can, however, be introduced by prepositions. See Alsina 1996 for discussion of the a-objects in Romance languages.

4. My proposal here is similar to the ones made in Sadler and Spencer 1998 as well as in Ackerman and Moore 2001b. See the latter for more references and more in-depth discussion.

5. This commits me to an argument-adding analysis of verbs like 'break' and the like.

6. The Chichewa examples are taken from Alsina and Mchombo 1993. The Kichaga examples are from Bresnan and Moshi 1993, and the Kikuyu examples from Masunaga 1983. The numbers associated with the nouns in the glosses indicate the noun class. The following abbreviations are used: APP applicative, ASP aspect, BEN beneficiary, FOC focus, FV final vowel, IMP imperfect, INST instrument, LOC locative, PAS passive, PRES present tense, PST past tense, S subject.

7. The terminology is due to Alsina 1996 but the generalization proposed here is slightly different from his.

8. I treat the various construction families here as independent. In fact, there is most likely an implicational hierarchy, in that when a language has a nonsymmetrical locative construction family, it will also have a nonsymmetrical benefactive construction family, but the available data do not allow one to argue conclusively for this.

9. The word-order test is not reliable as a test for objecthood across Bantu languages. Word order in Bantu, as in other language families, can be influenced by a host of different factors: semantic role but also discourse function, degree of animacy, and so on. In Chichewa, however, it seems to be a test for grammatical function.

10. There are also differences between the locative and the instrumental in Chichewa, as discussed in Alsina and Mchombo 1993. I ignore them in this summary.

11. Further language-specific restrictions apply but they have not been stated in enough detail to be taken into account here.

12. The exact formulation of this filter depends on further theoretical assumptions about the role of the thematic hierarchy. For instance, I could follow Alsina 1996 in proposing that the filter will choose −r for all roles above instrumental and +o for all lower ones. In this section, I will state it in a straightforward way, referring to the individual semantic roles rather than to the hierarchy. Below I will discuss whether this makes any difference to the points made in this chapter.

13. I follow here the assumptions of Alsina 1996 rather than those in Bresnan and Moshi 1993. For motivation see Alsina's paper.

14. This was, in fact, already proposed in Levin 1988.

15. Priority union was first introduced by Kaplan 1987 as an operation on feature structures, where failure of unification was precluded through the stipulation that in case of conflict one of the two feature structures "had priority."

16. Following Zaenen, Maling, and Thrainsson 1985, and the references cited there, I am assuming that the datives are not subjects in German.

References

Ackerman, Farrell, and John Moore. 2001a. Dowtyian proto-properties and lexical mapping theory. Talk presented at *LFG01*, CLSI Publications online, www.csli-publications.stanford.edu/LFG/1/lfg1.html.

Ackerman, Farrell, and John Moore. 2001b. *Protoproperties and argument encoding: A correspondence theory of argument selection.* Stanford, CA: CSLI.

Alsina, Alex. 1993. Predicate composition: A theory of syntactic function alternations. Dissertation, Stanford University.

Alsina, Alex. 1996. Passive types and the theory of object asymmetries. *Natural Language and Linguistic Theory* 14:673–723.

Alsina, Alex, and Sam Mchombo. 1993. Object asymmetries and the Chichewa applicative construction. In Sam Mchombo, ed., *Theoretical aspects of Bantu grammar*, 17–45. Stanford, CA: CSLI.

Baker, Mark. 1988. Theta role and the syntax of applicatives in Chichewa. *Natural Language and Linguistic Theory* 6:493–506.

Beesley, Ken, and Lauri Karttunen. 2003. *Finite state morphology*. Stanford, CA: CSLI.

Bresnan, Joan, and Lioba Moshi. 1993. Object asymmetries in comparative Bantu syntax. In Sam Mchombo, ed., *Theoretical aspects of Bantu grammar*, 47–91. Stanford, CA: CSLI.

Dowty, David. 1991. Thematic proto-roles and argument selection. *Language* 67:547–619.

Kaplan, Ronald. 1987. Three seductions of computational psycholinguistics. In P. Whitelock, M. M. Wood, H. L. Somers, R. Johnson, and P. Bennett, eds., *Linguistic theory and computer applications*, 149–188. London: Academic Press. (Reprinted in M. Dalrymple, R. M. Kaplan, J. T. Maxwell III, and A. Zaenen, eds., *Formal issues in lexical-functional grammar*. Stanford: CSLI, 1995.)

Karttunen, Lauri. 1998. The proper treatment of optimality theory in computational phonology. In L. Karttunen and K. Oflazer, eds., *FSMNL'98*, 1–12. Ankara, Turkey: Bilkent University.

Karttunen, Lauri. 2006. A finite-state approximation of optimality theory: The case of Finnish prosody. In T. Salakoski, F. Ginter, S. Pyysalo, and T. Pahikkala, eds., *Advances in natural language processing*, 4–15. Berlin: Springer.

Kimenyi, Alexandre. 1980. *A relational grammar of Kinyarwanda*. Berkeley: University of California Press.

Levin, Beth, and Malka Rappaport. 2005. *Argument realization*. Cambridge: Cambridge University Press.

Levin, Lorraine. 1988. *Operations on lexical forms: Unaccusative rules in Germanic languages*. New York: Garland.

Marantz, Alec. 1993. Implications of asymmetries in double object constructions. In Sam Mchombo, ed., *Theoretical aspects of Bantu grammar*, 113–150. Stanford, CA: CSLI.

Masunaga, Kiyoko. 1983. The applied suffix in Kikuyu. In J. Kaye, H. Koopman, D. Sportiche, and A. Dugas, eds., *Current approaches to African linguistics 2*, 283–295. Dordrecht: Foris.

Mchombo, Sam, ed. 1993. *Theoretical aspects of Bantu grammar*. Stanford, CA: CSLI.

Sadler, Louisa, and Andrew Spencer. 1998. Morphology and argument structure. In A. Spencer and A. Zwicky, eds., *The handbook of morphology*, 206–236. Oxford: Blackwell.

Taylor, J. R. 1996. On running and jogging. *Cognitive Linguistics* 7:21–34.

Zaenen, Annie. 1984. Double objects in Kikuyu? In C. Rosen and L. Zaring, eds., *Cornell Working Papers in Linguistics 5*, 199–206. Ithaca, NY: CLC Publications.

Zaenen, Annie. 1993. Unaccusativity in Dutch: An integrated approach. In J. Pustejovsky, ed., *Semantics and the lexicon*, 129–162. Dordrecht: Kluwer.

Zaenen, Annie, Joan Maling, and Hoskuldur Thrainsson. 1985. Case and grammatical functions: The Icelandic passive. *Natural Language and Linguistic Theory* 3:441–483.

Publications of David M. Perlmutter

1969a Evidence for deep structure constraints in syntax. In F. Kiefer, ed., *Studies in syntax and semantics*, 168–186. Dordrecht: Reidel.
1969b Les pronoms objets en espagnol: Un exemple de la nécessité de contraintes de surface en syntaxe [Object pronouns in Spanish: An example of the necessity of surface constraints in syntax]. *Langages* 14:81–133.
1970a On the article in English. In M. Bierwisch and K. Heidolph, eds., *Progress in linguistics*, 233–248. The Hague: Mouton.
1970b Surface structure constraints in syntax. *Linguistic Inquiry* 1:187–255.
1970c The two verbs "begin." In R. Jacobs and P. Rosenbaum, eds., *Readings in English transformational grammar*, 107–119. Waltham, MA: Blaisdell.
1970d (with J. R. Ross) A non-source for comparatives. *Linguistic Inquiry* 1:127–128.
1970e (with J. R. Ross) Relative clauses with split antecedents. *Linguistic Inquiry* 1:350.
1971 *Deep and surface structure constraints in syntax.* New York: Holt, Rinehart and Winston.
1972a Evidence for shadow pronouns in French relativization. In P. Peranteau et al., eds., *The Chicago which hunt: Papers from the Relative Clause Festival*, 73–105. Chicago: Chicago Linguistic Society.
1972b A note on semantic and syntactic number in English. *Linguistic Inquiry* 3:243–246.
1973a (with Janez Orešnik) Language-particular rules and explanation in syntax. In S. Anderson and P. Kiparsky, eds., *A Festschrift for Morris Halle*, 419–459. New York: Holt, Rinehart and Winston.
1973b (with Janez Orešnik) *Razlaganje sintaktičnih posebnosti* [The explanation of syntactic particularities]. Ljubljana: Institut "Jozef Stefan."
1974a Evidence for the cycle in Japanese. In *Descriptive and applied linguistics* 7, 25–48. Tokyo: International Christian University.

1974b On teaching syntactic argumentation. In F. Dinneen, ed., *Linguistics: Teaching and interdisciplinary relations.* Georgetown University Round Table on Languages and Linguistics (1974). Washington, DC: Georgetown University Press.

1974c (with Ferenc Kiefer, eds.) *Syntax und generative Grammatik* [Syntax and generative grammar]. 3 vols. Frankfurt: Athenaion Verlag.

1974d (with Janez Orešnik) Einzelsprachliche Regeln und Erklärung in der Syntax [Language-particular rules and explanation in syntax]. In F. Kiefer and D. M. Perlmutter, eds., *Syntax und generative Grammatik*, vol. 2, 161–230. Frankfurt: Athenaion Verlag.

1974e (with John R. Ross) Relativsätze mit gespalteten Vorgängern [Relative clauses with split antecedents]. In F. Kiefer and D. M. Perlmutter, eds., *Syntax und generative Grammatik*, vol. 3, 314–315. Frankfurt: Athenaion Verlag.

1975 Omezení v povrchové struktuře syntaxe [Constraints on surface structure in syntax]. In E. Hajičová et al., eds., *Studie z transformační gramátiky*, 134–194. Praha: Státní Pedagogické Nakladatelství.

1976a Evidence for subject downgrading in Portuguese. In J. Schmidt-Radefeldt, ed., *Readings in Portuguese linguistics.* Amsterdam: North Holland.

1976b (with Judith Aissen) Clause reduction in Spanish. In *Proceedings of the Second Annual Meeting of the Berkeley Linguistics Society*, 1–30. Berkeley.

1977 (with Paul Postal) Toward a universal characterization of passivization. In *Proceedings of the Third Annual Meeting of the Berkeley Linguistics Society.* Berkeley.

1978 Impersonal passives and the Unaccusative Hypothesis. *Proceedings of the Fourth Annual Meeting of the Berkeley Linguistics Society.* Berkeley.

1979a "Predicate": A grammatical relation. *Linguistic Notes from La Jolla* 6, 127–149. University of California, San Diego.

1979b Restrizioni di struttura superficiale in sintassi [Surface structure constraints in syntax]. In G. Graffi and L. Rizzi, eds., *La sintassi generativo-trasformazionale*, 167–230. Bologna: Società editrice il Mulino.

1979c Working 1s and inversion in Italian, Japanese, and Quechua. *Proceedings of the Fifth Annual Meeting of the Berkeley Linguistics Society.* Berkeley.

1979d (with Scott Soames) *Syntactic argumentation and the structure of English.* Berkeley: University of California Press.

1980 Relational grammar. In E. Moravcsik and J. Wirth, eds., *Syntax and semantics 13: Current approaches to syntax*, 195–229. New York: Academic Press.

1981 Functional grammar and relational grammar: Points of convergence and divergence. In T. Hoekstra, H. van der Hulst, and M. Moortgat, eds., *Perspectives on functional grammar*, 319–352. Dordrecht: Foris.

1982a Syntactic representation, syntactic levels, and the notion of subject. In P. Jacobson and G. Pullum, eds., *The nature of syntactic representation*, 283–340. Dordrecht: Reidel.

1982b (with Paul Postal) O formal'nom predstavlenii struktury predloženija [On the formal representation of sentence structure]. In A. E. Kibrik, ed., *Novoe v zarubežnoj lingvistike, 11: Sovremennye sintaksičeskie teorii v amerikanskoj lingvistike*, 76–82. Moscow: Izdatel'stvo Progress.

1982c (with Paul Postal) Zakon edinstvennosti prodviženija imennyx grupp v poziciju podležaščego [The law of the uniqueness of noun phrase promotion to subject position]. In A. E. Kibrik, ed., *Novoe v zarubežnoj lingvistike, 11: Sovremennye sintaksičeskie teorii v amerikanskoj lingvistike*, 83–110. Moscow: Izdatel'stvo Progress.

1983a Editor's afterword to the relational succession law. In D. Perlmutter, ed., *Studies in relational grammar 1*, 53–73. Chicago: University of Chicago Press.

1983b Personal vs. impersonal constructions. *Natural Language and Linguistic Theory* 1:141–200.

1983c (ed.) *Studies in relational grammar 1*. Chicago: University of Chicago Press.

1983d (with Judith Aissen) Clause reduction in Spanish. In D. Perlmutter, ed., *Studies in relational grammar 1*, 360–403. Chicago: University of Chicago Press.

1983e (with Paul Postal) The relational succession law. In D. Perlmutter, ed., *Studies in relational grammar 1*, 30–52, 73–80. Chicago: University of Chicago Press.

1983f (with Paul Postal) Some proposed laws of basic clause structure. In D. Perlmutter, ed., *Studies in relational grammar 1*, 81–128. Chicago: University of Chicago Press.

1983g (with Paul Postal) Toward a universal characterization of passivization. In D. Perlmutter, ed., *Studies in relational grammar 1*, 3–29. Chicago: University of Chicago Press.

1984a The inadequacy of some monostratal theories of passive. In D. Perlmutter and C. Rosen, eds., *Studies in relational grammar 2*, 3–37. Chicago: University of Chicago Press.

1984b Working 1s and inversion in Italian, Japanese, and Quechua. In D. Perlmutter and C. Rosen, eds., *Studies in relational grammar 2*, 292–330. Chicago: University of Chicago Press.

1984c (with Paul Postal) The 1-advancement exclusiveness law. In D. Perlmutter and C. Rosen, eds., *Studies in relational grammar 2*, 81–125. Chicago: University of Chicago Press.

1984d (with Paul Postal) Impersonal passives and some relational laws. In D. Perlmutter and C. Rosen, eds., *Studies in relational grammar 2*, 126–170. Chicago: University Chicago Press.

1984e (with Carol Rosen, eds.) *Studies in relational grammar 2*. Chicago: University of Chicago Press.

1984f (with Annie Zaenen) The indefinite extraposition construction in Dutch and German. In D. Perlmutter and C. Rosen, eds., *Studies in relational grammar 2*, 171–216. Chicago: University of Chicago Press.

1986 No nearer to the soul. *Natural Language and Linguistic Theory* 4:515–523.

1987 (with Carol Padden) American Sign Language and the architecture of phonological theory. *Natural Language and Linguistic Theory* 5:335–375.

1988a The split morphology hypothesis: Evidence from Yiddish. In M. Hammond and M. Noonan, eds., *Theoretical morphology*, 79–100. San Diego: Academic Press.

1988b Teaching syntactic argumentation. In R. Freidin, J. Kegl, and K. Miller, eds., *Linguistics in the undergraduate curriculum.* Princeton, NJ: Cognitive Science Laboratory, Princeton University.

1989 Multiattachment and the unaccusative hypothesis: The perfect auxiliary in Italian. *Probus: Journal of Latin and Romance Linguistics* 1:63–119.

1990a On the segmental representation of transitional and bidirectional movements in ASL phonology. In S. Fischer, ed., *Theoretical issues in sign language research* 1, 67–80. Chicago: University of Chicago Press.

1990b (with Barbara Allen, Donald Frantz, and Donna Gardiner) Possessor ascension and multistratal representation in Southern Tiwa. In P. Postal and B. Joseph, eds., *Studies in relational grammar 3*, 321–383. Chicago: University of Chicago Press.

1991a The language of the Deaf. *New York Review of Books*, March 28, 65–72.

1991b The role of the syllable in bimoraic foot systems: Evidence from Japanese. In C. Hunt, T. Perry, and V. Samiian, eds., *Proceedings of the Western Conference on Linguistics* 4, 251–260. California State University, Fresno.

1991c (with Patrick Farrell and Stephen Marlett) Notions of subjecthood and switch reference: Evidence from Seri. *Linguistic Inquiry* 22:431–456.

1992a Relational grammar and arc pair grammar. In W. Bright, ed., *The Oxford encyclopedia of linguistics* 3, 328–330. Oxford: Oxford University Press.

1992b Sign language phonology. In W. Bright, ed., *The Oxford encyclopedia of linguistics* 3, 438–439. Oxford: Oxford University Press.

1992c Sonority and syllable structure in American Sign Language. *Linguistic Inquiry* 23:407–442.

1993 Sonority and syllable structure in American Sign Language. In G. C. Coulter, ed., *Phonetics and phonology 3: Current issues in American Sign Language phonology*, 227–261. San Diego: Academic Press.

1995 Phonological quantity and multiple association. In J. Goldsmith, ed., *Handbook of phonological theory*, 309–317. Cambridge, MA: Blackwell.

1998 Interfaces: Explanation of allomorphy and the architecture of grammars. In S. G. Lapointe, D. K. Brentari, and P. M. Farrell, eds., *Morphology and its relation to syntax and phonology*, 302–338. Stanford, CA: CSLI Publications. (Distributed by Cambridge University Press.)

1999 (with John Moore) Case, agreement, and temporal particles in Russian infinitival clauses. *Journal of Slavic Linguistics* 7:219–246.

2000a A new way to distinguish raising from fronting in Russian. In S. Chung, J. McCloskey, and N. Sanders, eds., *Jorge Hankamer webfest.* http://ling.ucsc.edu/Jorge/perlmutter.html.

2000b (with John Moore) What does it take to be a dative subject? *Natural Language and Linguistic Theory* 18:373–416.
2001 *What is sign language? Frequently asked questions.* Brochure. Washington, DC: Linguistic Society of America.
2002 (with John Moore) Language-internal explanation: The distribution of Russian impersonals. *Language* 78:619–650.
2006 Some current claims about sign language phonetics, phonology, and experimental results. In L. Goldstein, D. H. Whalen, and C. T. Best, eds., *Laboratory phonology 8*, 315–338. Berlin: Mouton de Gruyter.
2007 In what ways can finite and nonfinite clauses differ? Evidence from Russian. In I. Nikolaeva, ed., *Finiteness: Theoretical and empirical foundations*, 250–304. Oxford: Oxford University Press.
2008 *Nobilior est vulgaris:* Dante's hypothesis and sign language poetry. In D. DeLuca, K. Lindgren, and D. J. Napoli, eds., *Signs and voices: Language, arts, and identity from Deaf to hearing*, 189–213. Washington, DC: Gallaudet University Press.

Author Index

Abondolo, D., 276
Abulaӡe, I., 214, 215
Ackema, P., 337
Ackerman, F., 250, 253, 259, 269, 370, 471
Adger, D., 91, 324
Aikhenvald, A., 1
Aissen, J., 3, 361, 362, 363, 365, 369, 373
Aldridge, E., 91
Alexiadou, A., 329
Alsina, A., 365, 461, 462, 465, 471
Anderson, S., 203, 281, 329, 335
Andrews, A., 268, 337
Aronoff, M., 250, 267, 383, 384, 393, 398
Authier, J-M., 329, 370
Avram, M., 42, 44, 45, 46, 47, 48, 49, 50, 56, 62, 63, 65

Babby, L., 19, 22, 23, 24, 26, 27, 31, 32, 280
Baerman, M., 44
Baker, C., 386
Baker, M., 173, 178, 179, 197, 238, 244, 249, 264, 276, 281, 365, 457, 462, 465, 472
Barbosa, P., 413
Battison, R., 83
Bauer, W., 91
Beard, R., 249, 257, 258
Beesley, K., 469
Belletti, A., 410
Bellugi, U., 345, 356
Berenz, N., 347
Berman, A., 222
Bever, T., 119
Billings, L., 277
Birdsall, J., 215

Bittner, M., 152, 154
Blevins, J., 203, 279, 287
Bloomfield, L., 247, 253, 259, 446
Blutner, R., 230, 236
Bochner, H., 250, 267
Boersma, P., 236
Bondaruk, A., 329, 335, 338, 339, 340
Bordelois, I., 362, 366, 369, 371, 373
Bos, H., 354
Bouchard, D., 237, 238
Bowden, J., 157
Brame, M., 112
Brentari, D., 84
Bresnan, J., 461, 462

Campbell, L., 203
Carvalho, J., 419
Charzyńska-Wójcik, M., 329, 335, 338, 339, 340
Chierchia, G., 24, 106, 329, 331, 332
Chitoran, I., 42
Chomsky, N., 123, 293, 337, 402, 403, 405, 406, 407, 408, 421
Chung, S., 93, 94, 97, 99, 102, 104, 105, 114, 115, 116, 198, 324
Cinque, G., 329, 332, 361, 362, 365, 366, 367, 368, 377
Cobeṭ, D., 50
Comrie, B., 153
Condoravdi, C., 329
Contreras, H., 366
Cooreman, A., 94, 96, 97, 103, 105, 106, 196
Coppola, M., 397, 398
Corbett, G., 44, 45, 46, 48, 49, 50, 51, 53

Cormier, K., 349, 350, 351, 355, 387, 388
Craig, C., 249, 263, 264
Č'relašvili, K., 211
Crysmann, B., 253, 259, 269
Culicover, P., 111
Cummins, S., 230, 238
Cysouw, M., 356
Czepluch, H., 165

Dahlstrom, A., 248, 251, 252, 253, 260, 262, 264
D'Alessandro, R., 329
Davidson, D., 326
Davies, W., 123, 124
de Hoop, H., 236
Delahunty, G., 112, 118, 123
Deseriev, J., 211
Diesing, M., 106
Dimitriu, C., 52, 63
Dixon, R. M. W., 152
Dowty, D., 242, 471
Dryer, M., 115, 117, 118, 119, 120, 155, 186, 427
Dubinsky, S., 123, 124
Duffield, N., 324
Dyla, S., 280
Dziwirek, K., 134, 138, 140, 142, 277, 280

Egerland, V., 329, 331
Ekman, P., 386
Embick, D., 413
Emonds, J., 112, 113, 114, 115, 117, 123
Engberg-Pedersen, E., 356
Erdmann, P., 118, 123

Faarlund, J., 287
Farkas, D., 45, 46, 49–51, 57, 60, 62–64
Farnell, B., 351
Farrell, P., 165, 166
Finnemann, D., 369
Fischer, S., 349, 354
Fodor, J., 119
Foley, W., 1, 152
Forchheimer, P., 356
Frantz, D., 173, 175
Fraser, N., 44
Frazier, L., 119

Friedman, L., 345
Friesen, W., 386
Frishberg, N., 350

Gagua, R., 211, 212
Galkina-Fedoruk, E., 27
Garrett, A., 203
Garrett, M., 119
Georgopoulos, C., 91
Gerdts, D., 184, 185, 188, 189, 190, 191, 194, 195
Gibson, E., 118, 121
Gibson, J., 365
Givón, T., 398
Goddard, I., 248, 249, 250, 253, 254, 255, 256, 258, 260, 261, 262, 265, 266, 267, 268, 269
Goldberg, A., 15
Goldberg, L., 334
Goldsmith, J., 84, 235
González, N., 362
Goodall, G., 365, 373
Gough, B., 349
Graur, A., 42, 44–50, 56, 62, 63
Greenberg, J., 91, 94
Greene, D., 329
Grimes, J., 429
Grimshaw, J., 236, 237
Grosu, A., 118, 119
Guasti, M., 371, 373
Guéron, J., 111

Haegeman, L., 111
Hale, K., 152, 154, 249, 263, 264, 337, 339
Hall, R., 45, 50, 51
Halpern, A., 413
Hankamer, J., 96, 98, 100
Harley, H., 335
Harris, A., 203, 205, 207, 208, 213
Harris, J., 53
Haviland, J., 14
Hawkins, J., 119
Hendriks, P., 236
Hériau, M., 230, 238, 241
Hinkson, M., 189
Hockett, C., 41, 352
Hoffmann, L., 287

Holisky, D., 210, 211, 212, 213, 214, 216
Hukari, T., 188, 191, 194, 195
Hulst, van der, H., 83, 84, 85, 86, 87

Iwakura, K.,112

Jackendoff, R., 81, 293, 295, 298, 299, 314
Jaeggli, O., 329
Johnson, D., 153
Johnson, K., 276
Johnson, R., 84
Jones, W., 247, 248, 252, 265, 266, 268, 269
Joseph, B., 223, 224

Kaiser, E., 276
Karjalainen, M., 276
Karmiloff-Smith, A., 61
Karttunen, L., 469
Kayne, R., 233, 361, 362, 365, 368, 369, 371, 373, 377, 378, 412, 413, 419
Keenan, E. L., 21, 153, 276
Kibort, A., 279
Kimenyi, A., 462
Kinkade, M., 189
Kisch, S., 383
Kisseberth, C., 428
Klima, E., 345, 347, 353, 356
Knecht, L., 276, 286
Koenig, J-P., 329, 332, 335
Koster, J., 111, 112, 113, 114, 115, 117, 118, 119, 121, 122, 123, 124
Kozinskij, I., 27
Kratzer, A., 329, 331, 332, 338
Kuroda, S., 24

Labelle, M., 229, 230, 231, 232, 238, 244
Ladusaw, W., 104, 198
Lambert, W., 53
Lambrecht, K., 239, 240, 241
Langacker, R., 429
La Polla, R., 154
Larson, R., 166
Lasnik, H., 111, 404
Laughlin, R., 10, 14
Lees, R., 123
Leeuw, F. van der, 403

Lefebvre, C., 1, 2
Legate, J., 337
Legendre, G., 230, 233, 236, 238, 241, 242, 244, 373
LeSourd, P., 253, 259, 269
Levelt, W., 41
Levin, B., 5, 214, 457
Levin, J., 116, 117
Levin, L., 458
Levine, R.,124
Lewandowska-Tomaszczyk, B., 134, 138, 140, 142
Liddell, S., 84, 347, 353, 356, 357
Lie, S., 287
Lillo-Martin, D., 80, 347, 353, 354, 356, 357, 386, 387
Luján, M., 362, 366

Mač'avariani, G., 214
McBurney, S., 347, 355
McCloskey, J., 27, 123, 124, 281, 283, 324, 325, 326, 334, 337, 339, 340
McIntyre, A., 2
Malamud, S., 329, 331
Maling, J., 276, 277, 279, 470
Mallinson, G., 42, 44, 46
Mandler, J., 61
Manzini, M., 365
Marandin, J-M., 238
Marantz, A., 237, 276, 457, 472
Marlett, S., 294, 295, 311
Massam, D., 116, 117
Mathur, G., 355, 357
Mauner, G., 329, 332, 335
May, R., 416
Mchombo, S., 461, 462, 465
Meier, R., 347, 349, 355, 356, 357, 387, 388, 391
Meir, I., 349, 354, 355, 383, 387, 391, 398
Mel'čuk, I., 25
Merchant, J., 101
Michelson, T., 247, 248, 251, 252, 253, 260, 263, 264, 265, 266
Mithun, M., 155, 190
Miyata, Y., 236
Moore, J., 20, 31, 157, 362, 368, 370, 371, 373, 374, 471

Moshi, L., 461, 462
Mostovaja, A., 137
Muravyova, I., 190
Myhill, J., 361

Nakajima, H., 193
Napoli, D., 361
Neeleman, A., 337
Nerbonne, J., 283, 284
Nespor, M., 84, 385, 386
Newport, E., 81, 397, 398
Nichols, J., 212, 338
Noonan, M., 286
Noyer, R., 413
Nuñes, J., 407

O'Baoill, D., 326
Oda, K., 91
Olson, M., 1
O'Siadhail, M., 324
Otero, C., 404, 421
Özkaragöz, I., 276, 284, 286

Padden, C., 84, 349, 354, 386, 387
Parsons, T., 326
Paul, I., 91, 101, 102
Perkowski, J., 57
Perlmutter, D., 19, 20, 31, 84, 134, 151, 157, 162, 163, 164, 183, 198, 229, 231, 238, 241, 244, 275, 278, 281, 293, 298, 345, 347, 348, 351, 352, 353, 355, 356, 357, 361, 362, 363, 365, 369, 373, 427, 428, 429, 442, 451
Petrucci, P., 46, 56
Pinker, S., 165
Pinkham, J., 96, 98
Poizner, H., 356
Pollock, J-Y., 238, 408, 410, 411
Postal, P., 112, 151, 165, 183, 231, 233, 238, 244, 281, 293, 373, 403, 428, 429, 451
Potsdam, E., 91, 101, 102
Prince, A., 230, 236

Quadros, R., 354
Quinlan, R., 55
Quinto-Pozos, D., 387, 388

Radford, A., 111, 114
Radutzky, E., 348
Ramchand, G., 91
Raposo, E., 365, 402, 403, 404, 406, 412, 414, 419, 420, 421
Rappaport Hovav, M., 214, 457
Rathmann, C., 354, 355, 357
Rayner, K., 119
Reed, L., 370
Reinholtz, C., 427
Rhodes, R., 427, 428, 433, 439, 441, 442, 444, 449
Rigault, A., 53
Rivas, A., 366
Rivière, N., 230, 238
Rizzi, L., 329, 361, 363, 371, 406, 414
Roberts, I., 276, 361
Rosen, C., 151, 241, 293
Rosen, S., 190, 361, 365, 369, 373
Rosenbaum, P., 111, 112, 114, 123
Rosetti, A., 42, 46
Ross, J., 409
Rothstein, R., 277
Rothstein, S., 20
Rude, N., 155
Ruwet, N., 231, 238

Sacks, O., 345, 347, 356, 357
Sadler, L., 64
Safir, K., 117
Saloni, Z., 277
Sanchez, J., 131
Sandler, W., 80, 84, 87, 88, 353, 383, 384, 385, 386, 387, 391, 398
Schiller, E., 1
Schmidt, K., 214
Scott, D., 383
Schrauf, R., 131
Seiter, W., 91
Šeljakin, M., 34
Senghas, A., 61
Sezer, E., 285
Sherzer, J., 348
Shore, S., 276
Siewierska, A., 165, 166, 277, 280
Sigurjónsdóttir, S., 277, 279
Slobin, D., 15

Smith, W., 351, 354, 356
Smolensky, P., 230, 236
Snyder, W., 61
Sobin, N., 280
Sorace, A., 244
Stenson, N., 281, 282, 283, 324, 326, 327, 329, 335, 338, 339, 340
Stowell, T., 111, 113, 114, 115, 123, 222
Strecker, B., 287
Strozer, J., 369, 370
Stump, G., 44
Sulkala, H., 276
Suñer, M., 362, 366
Supalla, T., 81
Suzman, S., 61

Talmy, L., 397
Tesar, B., 236
Thomason, L., 259
Thompson, S., 118, 119
Thrainsson, H., 470
Timberlake, A., 276
Ting, L., 351
Tomlin, R., 427
Tommola, H., 276
Treviño, E., 368, 369
Trofimov, V., 34
Tucker, G., 53

Ura, H., 154, 165
Uriagereka, J., 402, 403, 404, 406, 412, 414, 420, 421

Vannebo, K., 287
Van Valin, R., 152, 154, 156
Vasiliu, L., 42, 44–50, 56, 62, 65
Vihman, V-A., 276
Vikner, S., 236
Vrabie, E., 57, 64

Washabaugh, W., 348
Wasow, T., 119
Webelhuth, G., 250, 253
Wechsler, S., 64
Wierzbicka, A, 129, 130, 131, 133, 140, 142
Wilbur, R., 386
Williams, E., 20, 31, 222

Wilson, C., 236
Winkler, S., 11, 14
Wurmbrand, S., 365

Zaenen, A., 461, 462, 470, 471
Zaliznjak, A., 48
Zec, D., 64
Zifonun, G., 287
Zribi-Hertz, A., 231
Zubizarreta, M., 24, 365, 373, 375
Zuñiga, F., 427

Subject Index

1–Advancement Exclusiveness (1AEX) Law, 275–278, 281, 285–287
Acquisition of signed languages, 391
Agreement, 4, 5, 7, 9–13, 20, 22, 26, 27, 32, 34, 41–45, 48–52, 54, 57–65, 115, 116, 123, 124, 153, 154, 156, 161–163, 167, 173–175, 177–180, 184, 190, 191, 196, 210–212, 214, 254, 280, 283, 294–296, 299, 301–303, 305–309, 336–339, 350, 354, 355, 383, 384, 387–391, 393, 412, 413, 417, 419–420, 427, 434, 435, 439–441, 445–448, 463
Agreement verbs, 350, 387–388
Alacalufan, 356
Algonquian, 247, 248, 254, 427–429, 433, 438, 439, 441, 442, 451
Al-Sayyid Bedouin Sign Language (ABSL), 384–398
American Sign Language (ASL), 79–88, 345–357, 386–388
Animacy, 14, 34, 44, 46–48, 51, 53, 56, 61, 62, 64, 65, 80, 278, 281, 287, 333, 366, 367, 392, 434, 435, 437, 440, 445–448
Antipassive, 183–185, 194–198, 213, 315, 454
Arabic, 392, 394
Aramaic, 213
Argument structure, 19–21, 25–28, 31, 33, 35–36, 133, 175, 183, 196, 198, 226, 237, 249, 263, 266, 270, 295, 329, 354, 361, 365
Armenian, 210, 213
Austro-Asiatic languages, 2
Austronesian, 91, 92, 101, 108, 157

Autonomous constructions, 281–284, 288, 323–330, 333–335, 337–340
Azeri, 205, 210, 213

Bantu, 458, 461, 462, 470
Bats. *See* Batsbi
Batsbi, 204, 210–213, 217
Binding, 99, 283, 327, 329, 353, 373, 374
Brazilian Sign Language, 354
Breton, 281, 329
British Sign Language (BSL), 349, 350

Case, 4, 5, 7, 9, 10, 12, 13, 20–23, 26, 27, 33, 37, 43, 47, 48, 92, 93, 97, 98, 108, 111, 113–117, 122, 123, 133, 152–155, 157, 161, 173, 188, 190, 198, 203–217, 221, 223, 280, 293, 295, 307, 324, 355, 368–370, 393, 458, 462
Case marking, 43, 152, 154, 157, 188, 190, 203–205, 207–214, 216–217, 221, 280, 293, 368–370, 393, 458, 462
Caucasian, 204, 216
Causatives, 2, 3, 5, 6, 9, 13, 132, 133, 138, 142, 174, 183, 185, 188, 229, 231, 234, 294, 312, 362, 363, 365, 366, 368–372, 374, 375, 377, 378, 471
  serial, 1, 2, 13
Celtic, 281
Chamorro, 91–108, 115, 116
Chechen, 212
Chichewa, 461–466, 468, 471
Choctaw, 115
Chukchee, 190
Classical Latin. *See* Latin

Clitic climbing, 361, 363, 366, 367, 376, 403, 415
Clitics, 163, 211, 229, 230, 238–241, 361, 363, 364, 366, 367, 376, 401–408, 410–421
Common Kartvelian, 213
'Consider' sentences, 221–222, 224–225
Cultural differences, 129, 130

Dalmatian, 46
Danish Sign Language, 356
Depictives, 3, 7, 11–15
Doubling constructions, 184, 185, 188, 191, 194–198
Dutch, 275, 287
Dyirbal, 152

Emotion expressions, 129–142
Enclisis, 31, 174, 247, 401, 402, 407, 408, 410, 412, 414, 417–421
English, 5, 7, 8, 14, 20, 23, 24, 80, 81, 96, 98, 100, 101, 111–115, 117–125, 129–132, 137, 139–142, 157, 164–167, 222, 223, 229, 249, 257, 308, 324, 327, 328, 334, 348, 355, 385, 430, 458, 460, 471
  American, 141
English-based creoles, 2
Ergativity, 3, 4, 10, 116, 117, 152–155, 158, 184, 190, 191, 203, 205–217
European languages, 329, 335, 339
European Portuguese (EP). *See* Portuguese
Evolutionary linguistics, 203
Extraposition, 111–113, 118–120, 122, 386

Feature Geometry, 84–88
Finnish, 276, 278, 281, 284, 286, 471
Fon, 1, 2
Fox. *See* Meskwaki
French, 46, 101, 102, 229, 279, 283, 284, 329, 332, 340, 370, 371, 401, 402, 408, 410, 411, 412, 414, 415, 417, 419, 420, 421
French-based creoles, 2

Gender, 41, 42, 44–54, 56–65, 156, 196, 197, 211, 283, 327, 355
Georgian, 204, 210, 213–217
German, 25, 48, 132, 275, 279, 287, 329, 331, 332, 338, 340, 365, 470, 471

Germanic, 23, 278, 285, 287, 333, 334, 335, 340, 470, 471
Gesture, 345, 347–349, 351–354, 356, 357
Grammatical relations (GRs), 151–161, 163–165, 167–168, 221–222, 225–226
Greek, 213, 221

Haitian Creole, 2
Halkomelem, 183–198
Headless relative clauses, 91, 94–96, 98, 100–103, 105–108
Hebrew, 385, 392, 394, 395

Icelandic, 278, 329, 471
Ijo, 2
Impersonal constructions, 19–37, 230, 233–235, 237–241, 279, 285, 329
Impersonal passives, 25, 26, 33, 34, 275, 276, 278, 285, 287
Impersonal pronouns, 331, 332, 340
Inchoatives, 206, 229–234, 236–238, 241, 243–244
Incorporation, 173–175, 177–180, 190, 197, 204, 208, 214, 216, 249, 256, 263, 264, 266, 355, 365, 462
Indexicality, 121, 350, 355
Indo-European, 42, 210, 213
Ingush, 212
Innateness, 203, 217
Interrogatives, 91, 94–103, 105–108
Inuit, 152–154
Iranian languages, 213
Irish, 281, 282, 283, 284, 286, 288, 323–341
Israeli Sign Language (ISL), 84, 355, 385, 386
Italian, 46, 132, 157, 161–163, 363, 367, 368, 410
Italian Sign Language (LIS), 348

Japanese, 115
Japanese Sign Language, 351

Khmer, 1, 2
Kichaga, 462, 464, 465, 471
Kikuyu, 462, 463, 464
Kinyarwanda, 462

Subject Index

Latin, 41, 42, 46, 48, 54, 55
  Classical, 46
  Vulgar, 46
Latin American Spanish. *See* Spanish
Laz, 213
Lexical Functional Grammar (LFG), 458–460, 462–464, 472
Lexical Mapping Theory (LMT), 458, 460, 461, 466, 468, 470–472
Lezgian languages, 205
Lithuanian, 276

Malagasy, 91, 101, 102, 103
Maori, 91
Mayan languages, 2, 12
Meskwaki, 247–271
Mingrelian, 213
Mohawk, 190
Morphological blocking, 250, 267, 268, 271
Morphology, 12, 25, 41, 46, 79–88, 115, 129, 179, 184–186, 195–198, 213, 223, 244, 258, 266, 267, 275, 276, 278, 279, 281, 283, 288, 294, 295, 301, 311, 313, 325, 336, 337, 384, 393, 398, 413, 427, 442, 446–448, 450, 471, 472
Motivated Chômage Law, 183, 197, 198

Nakh-Daghestanian languages, 205, 210, 213
Nakh languages, 210
Native American languages, 263
Negative concord, 96, 103–105, 108
Nez Perce, 155
Niger-Congo languages, 2
Niuean, 116, 117
North-East Caucasian. *See* Nakh-Daghestanian languages
North-West Caucasian, 213
Norwegian, 287
Number, 41, 42, 44, 48, 50, 51, 60, 64, 68, 162, 173, 174, 196, 197, 251, 282, 283, 293, 305, 327, 336–338, 351, 355, 388, 419, 446, 447

Object control, 362, 366, 368–370, 372, 376, 377
Object shift (OS), 402, 406–408, 410–413, 415, 421

Oblique constructions, 428–433, 435, 437–441, 450, 451
Obviation, 427, 435–437, 439–441, 444, 445
Ojibwe, 428–451
Old Georgian, 214, 215, 216
Old Udi, 210
Optimality Theory (OT), 230, 235–237, 461, 472
Ottawa Ojibwe. *See* Ojibwe

Palauan, 91
Parallel architecture, 293, 295, 314
Passive, 14, 25, 26, 33–35, 156, 157, 162, 163, 165, 167, 223–225, 241, 275–281, 283–288, 295, 307, 324, 328, 363, 427, 439, 441–443, 450, 459, 460, 462–464, 466–468, 470
Peninsular Spanish. *See* Spanish
Persian, 115, 117
Person, 4, 9, 10, 121, 156, 162, 164, 173, 174, 178, 184, 190, 196, 197, 210–213, 248, 251–253, 255, 282, 283, 293, 294, 299, 301, 306–308, 311, 315, 327, 336–338, 350–356, 387, 388, 390, 391, 393, 419, 435, 440–444, 446, 449
Phase Impenetrability Condition (PIC), 405
Phases, 336, 402, 405–408, 413, 415, 421
Philippine languages, 91
Phonology, 41, 57, 79–88, 175, 247, 262, 278, 315, 325, 327, 335, 347, 352, 353, 364, 371, 372, 374, 401, 402, 405, 406, 408, 414, 419, 469
Plains Indian Sign Language, 351
Plain verbs, 354, 387, 388, 390–392
Pointing, 345–356
Polish, 129–142, 277, 278, 279, 280, 281, 282, 284, 286, 287, 288
Portuguese, 156, 161, 410, 413, 417, 419
  European (EP), 401, 403, 411, 413, 414, 415, 417, 419, 421
Prenouns, 247, 259
Preparticles, 247, 258
Pre-Udi, 205
Preverbs, 205, 247–254, 256–260, 262–271
PRO, 31, 282–285, 288, 334, 335, 339–341, 407, 408, 410

pro, 282, 293, 326, 336, 337, 339, 340, 371, 373, 407, 415, 416
Processing, 118, 119, 121, 122, 125, 406
Proclisis, 92, 157, 158, 160–162, 252, 253, 258, 265, 401–403, 405, 407, 410–411, 413–415, 417–421
Pronouns, 25, 92, 93, 99, 100, 105, 112, 113, 121, 154, 156, 158, 164, 165, 178–180, 211, 212, 223, 230, 233, 239, 240, 241, 247, 259, 260, 262, 279, 282–284, 325–329, 331–335, 337–340, 345–357, 371, 407, 411, 416, 449, 463
Prosody, 84, 118, 122, 385–387, 392–394, 396, 403, 404, 413
Proto-Nakh, 210
Proto-Nakh-Daghestanian, 210
Provençal, 46

Qawesqar, 356

Reciprocals, 156, 162, 163, 188, 198, 279, 282, 283, 327, 328, 331, 332, 335, 338, 367, 459
Reduced constructions, 362, 364, 365, 367, 368
Reflexive verbs, 129–134, 137–138, 140, 142
Reflexivization, 222–226, 327, 331, 332, 334, 338, 459
Relational Grammar (RG), 151, 153, 161, 163, 164, 167, 168, 183, 197, 221–223, 293, 295, 298, 363, 427–429, 439, 442, 451
Relative root complement constructions (RRC), 428, 433–435, 437–450
Restructuring, 255, 361, 362, 364–368, 372–375, 377, 378
Romance, 23, 41, 42, 46, 53, 62, 63, 64, 229, 333, 334, 335, 340, 361, 362, 401, 402, 403, 404, 405, 406, 407, 410, 411, 412, 413, 414, 415, 421
Romanian, 41–65
Russian, 19–37, 130, 132, 137, 213

Salish, 183, 188
Sama, 152
Saramaccan, 2
Scandinavian, 287
Secondary predication, 3, 7, 11–15

Seediq, 91
Semitic, 213
Sentential subjects, 111–125
Seri, 293–315
Serial causatives. *See* Causatives
Serial directional constructions, 1, 2, 5, 6, 13, 15
Serial verb constructions, 1, 2, 15
Signed languages, 345, 347, 348, 351, 354, 355, 356, 357, 383, 384, 388, 398
  Arabic, 395
  Hebrew, 395
Siouan, 264
Slavic, 129, 130, 142, 277
Sluicing, 96, 101–103
Southern Tiwa, 173
SOV order, 91, 94, 115, 117, 293, 391–397
Spanish, 14, 46, 62, 132, 361–378, 401, 402, 406, 408, 410, 411, 412, 413, 414, 415, 417, 419, 420, 421
  Latin American, 368
  Peninsular, 368
Spatial verbs, 387, 388, 390, 391
Specificity, 96, 105–108
Spell-Out, 402, 405–408, 410–412, 415, 416, 418, 420, 421
Sranan, 2
Stratal Uniqueness Law, 183, 197, 462
Subcategorization, 21, 168, 293, 295, 298–302, 304–308, 310, 312–314, 457
Subjecthood, 20–29, 31, 33–34, 37, 325, 337, 439, 444, 463
Suffixes, 3, 4, 14, 21, 22, 26, 28, 32, 34, 36, 79–88, 116, 159, 160, 173, 175, 184, 188–193, 195, 197, 205, 211, 212, 251, 253, 259, 262, 267, 276–278, 284, 286, 323, 327, 447, 459, 461, 465, 466, 470
Svan, 213
Swedish, 329, 331, 340

Taba, 157, 158, 159, 160, 161
Tagalog, 91
Taiwanese Sign Language, 351, 356
Teaching (of language), 131, 142
Telicity, 5, 6, 214, 215, 230–233, 235–238, 241–243
Thai, 2

Subject Index

Theta criterion, 293
Theta roles, 20–24, 27–29, 31, 34, 365
Tok Pisin, 1, 2
Tough movement, 166–167, 222, 363
Tree-Adjoining Grammar (TAG), 457
Tsova-Tush. *See* Batsbi
Turkic languages, 210, 213
Turkish, 25, 115, 117, 213, 276, 284, 285, 286
Tzotzil, 2–15

Udi, 204–210, 213, 217
Unaccusative Hypothesis, 230, 237, 275–277, 285, 288
Unaccusatives, 4, 8, 9, 15, 20, 21, 26–29, 161, 203–210, 212, 213, 216, 217, 229–231, 237–239, 241, 243–244, 275–279, 281, 282, 285–288, 325, 326
Underspecification, 49–52, 62, 85, 86, 88
Unergatives, 4, 9, 25–27, 193, 203–210, 212–217, 229, 230, 237–239, 242–244, 275, 276, 285
Uniformity of Theta Assignment Hypothesis (UTAH), 238, 244
Universal Alignment Hypothesis, 231, 238, 244, 293, 428

Vainakh languages, 210
Valence, 13, 15, 248, 249, 259, 261–266, 270, 457, 461, 466, 470–472
Verb-initial order, 3, 91, 92, 94, 108, 338
Verb stacking, 173
Verb stems, 173–180, 189, 249, 250, 252, 254, 256–259, 261, 264–267, 270, 284, 286
Vulgar Latin. *See* Latin

Weak hand spreading, 84–88
Weight (of constituent), 118–121, 123
Welsh, 281
Wh-movement, 91–96, 98–102, 105, 107, 108
Winnebago, 264

Xerox Finite State Calculus, 458, 468

Yaqui, 156, 164
Yiddish, 329
Yoruba, 2
Yuto-Aztecan, 156

Current Studies in Linguistics
Samuel Jay Keyser, general editor

1. *A Reader on the Sanskrit Grammarians*, J. F. Staal

2. *Semantic Interpretation in Generative Grammar*, Ray S. Jackendoff

3. *The Structure of the Japanese Language*, Susumu Kuno

4. *Speech Sounds and Features*, Gunnar Fant

5. *On Raising: One Rule of English Grammar and Its Theoretical Implications*, Paul M. Postal

6. *French Syntax: The Transformational Cycle*, Richard S. Kayne

7. *Panini as a Variationist*, Paul Kiparsky and S. D. Joshi, editors

8. *Semantics and Cognition*, Ray Jackendoff

9. *Modularity in Syntax: A Study of Japanese and English*, Ann Kathleen Farmer

10. *Phonology and Syntax: The Relation between Sound and Structure*, Elisabeth O. Selkirk

11. *The Grammatical Basis of Linguistic Performance: Language Use and Acquisition*, Robert C. Berwick and Amy S. Weinberg

12. *Introduction to the Theory of Grammar*, Henk van Riemsdijk and Edwin Williams

13. *Word and Sentence Prosody in Serbocroatian*, Isle Lehiste and Pavle Ivić

14. *The Representation of (In)definiteness*, Eric J. Reuland and Alice G. B. ter Meulen, editors

15. *An Essay on Stress*, Morris Halle and Jean-Roger Vergnaud

16. *Language and Problems of Knowledge: The Managua Lectures*, Noam Chomsky

17. *A Course in GB Syntax: Lectures on Binding and Empty Categories*, Howard Lasnik and Juan Uriagereka

18. *Semantic Structures*, Ray Jackendoff

19. *Events in the Semantics of English: A Study in Subatomic Semantics*, Terence Parsons

20. *Principles and Parameters in Comparative Grammar*, Robert Freidin, editor

21. *Foundations of Generative Syntax*, Robert Freidin

22. *Move α: Conditions on Its Application and Output*, Howard Lasnik and Mamoru Saito

23. *Plurals and Events*, Barry Schein

24. *The View from Building 20: Essays in Linguistics in Honor of Sylvain Bromberger*, Kenneth Hale and Samuel Jay Keyser, editors

25. *Grounded Phonology*, Diana Archangeli and Douglas Pulleyblank

26. *The Magic of a Common Language: Jakobson, Mathesius, Trubetzkoy, and the Prague Linguistic Circle*, Jindrich Toman

27. *Zero Syntax: Experiencers and Cascades*, David Pesetsky

28. *The Minimalist Program*, Noam Chomsky

29. *Three Investigations of Extraction*, Paul M. Postal

30. *Acoustic Phonetics*, Kenneth N. Stevens

31. *Principle B, VP Ellipsis, and Interpretation in Child Grammar*, Rosalind Thornton and Kenneth Wexler

32. *Working Minimalism*, Samuel David Epstein and Norbert Hornstein, editors

33. *Syntactic Structures Revisited: Contemporary Lectures on Classic Transformational Theory*, Howard Lasnik with Marcela Depiante and Arthur Stepanov

34. *Verbal Complexes*, Hilda Koopman and Anna Szabolsci

35. *Parasitic Gaps*, Peter W. Culicover and Paul M. Postal

36. *Ken Hale: A Life in Language*, Michael Kenstowicz, editor

37. *Flexibility Principles in Boolean Semantics: The Interpretation of Coordination, Plurality, and Scope in Natural Language*, Yoad Winter

38. *Phrase Structure Composition and Syntactic Dependencies*, Robert Frank

39. *Representation Theory*, Edwin Williams

40. *The Syntax of Time*, Jacqueline Guéron and Jacqueline Lecarme, editors

41. *Situations and Individuals*, Paul D. Elbourne

42. *Wh-movement: Moving On*, Lisa L.-S. Cheng and Norbert Corver, editors

43. *The Computational Nature of Language Learning and Evolution*, Partha Niyogi

44. *Standard Basque: A Progressive Grammar*, 2 volumes, Rudolf P. G. de Rijk

45. *Foundational Issues in Linguistic Theory: Essays in Honor of Jean-Roger Vergnaud*, Robert Freidin, Carlos P. Otero, and Maria Luisa Zubizarreta, editors

46. *The Boundaries of Babel: The Brain and the Enigma of Impossible Languages*, Andrea Moro

47. *The Nature of the Word: Studies in Honor of Paul Kiparsky*, Kristin Hanson and Sharon Inkelas, editors

48. *Contemporary Views on Architecture and Representations in Phonology*, Eric Raimy and Charles E. Cairns, editors

49. *Hypothesis A/Hypothesis B: Linguistic Explorations in Honor of David M. Perlmutter*, Donna B. Gerdts, John C. Moore, and Maria Polinsky, editors